Microprocessor Theory
and Applications with
68000/68020 and Pentium

Microprocessor Theory

and Applications with
68000/68020 and Pentium

M. RAFIQUZZAMAN, Ph.D.

Professor
California State Polytechnic University
Pomona, California
and
President
Rafi Systems, Inc.

WILEY

A JOHN WILEY & SONS, INC., PUBLICATION

Published by John Wiley & Sons, Inc., Hoboken, New Jersey.
Published simultaneously in Canada.

For general information on our other products and services or for technical support, please contact our
Customer Care Department within the United States at (800) 762-2974, outside the United States at (317) 572-
3993 or fax (317) 572-4002.

Wiley also publishes its books in a variety of electronic formats. Some content that appears in print may not be
available in electronic format. For information about Wiley products, visit our web site at www.wiley.com.

Library of Congress Cataloging-in-Publication Data:

Rafiquzzaman, Mohamed.
   Microprocessor theory and applications with 68000/68020 and Pentium / M.
Rafiquzzaman.
        p. cm.
   Includes bibliographical references and index.
   ISBN 978-0-470-38031-4 (cloth)
  1. Motorola 68000 series microprocessors. 2. Pentium (Microprocessor) I.
Title.
   QA76.8.M6895R34 2008
   004.165—dc22   2008011009

Printed in the United States of America.

10 9 8 7 6 5 4 3 2 1

To my wife, Kusum; my son, Tito; and my brother, Elan

CONTENTS

PREFACE

Microprocessors play an important role in the design of digital systems. They are found in a wide range of applications, such as process control and communication systems.

This book is written to present the fundamental concepts of assembly language programming and system design concepts associated with typical microprocessors, such as the Motorola 68000/68020 and Intel Pentium. The 68000 is a 16-bit microprocessor that continues to be popular. Since the 68000 uses linear memory and contains 32-bit general-purpose registers, it is an excellent educational tool for acquiring an understanding of both hardware and software aspects of typical microprocessors.

Conventional microprocessors such as the 68000 complete fetch, decode and execute cycles of an instruction in sequence. Typical 32-bit microprocessors such as the 68020 and Pentium use pipelining, in which instruction fetch and execute cycles are overlapped. This speeds up the instruction execution time of 32-bit microprocessors. Pipelining was used for many years in mainframe and minicomputer CPUs. In addition, other mainframe features, such as memory management and floating-point and cache memory, are implemented in 32-bit microprocessors. Hence, brief coverage of these topics is provided in the first part of the book.

The book is self-contained and includes a number of basic topics. A basic digital logic background is assumed. Characteristics and principles common to typical microprocessors are emphasized and basic microcomputer interfacing techniques are demonstrated via examples using the simplest possible devices, such as switches, LEDs, A/D converters, the hexadecimal keyboard, and seven-segment displays.

The book has evolved from classroom notes developed for three microprocessor courses taught at the Electrical and Computer Engineering Department, California State Poly University, Pomona for the last several years: ECE 343 (Microprocessor I), ECE 432 (Microprocessor II), and ECE 561 (Advanced Microprocessors).

The text is divided into 12 chapters. In Chapter 1, we provide a review of terminology, number systems, evolution of microprocessors, system design concepts and typical microprocessor applications.

Chapters 2 through 12 form the nucleus of the book. Chapter 2 covers typical microcomputer architectures for both 16-bit (conventional) and 32-bit microprocessors. The concepts of pipelining, superscalar processors and RISC vs. CISC are included.

Chapter 3 is focused on the memory organization of typical microprocessors. The basic concepts associated with main memory array design, including memory maps are also covered, as are memory management concepts and cache memory organization.

In Chapter 4, we describe microprocessor input/output techniques including programmed I/O, interrupt I/O, and direct memory access (DMA).

Chapter 5 contains programming concepts associated with a typical microprocessor. Topics include assembly language programming, typical addressing modes, and instruction sets.

The theory of assembly language programming and system design concepts covered in the early chapters is illustrated in Chapters 6 through 12 by means of a typical conventional 16-bit microprocessor such as the Motorola 68000 and typical 32-bit microprocessors such as the Motorola 68020 and Intel Pentium. Several examples of assembly language programming and I/O techniques associated with these microprocessors are included. These chapters also demonstrate how the software and hardware work together by interfacing simple I/O devices such as LEDs, a hexadecimal keyboard, and A/D converters. The concepts are described in a very simplified manner.

A CD containing a step-by-step procedure for installing and using a typical 68000/68020 assembler/debugger such as the ide68k21 and a Pentium assembler/debugger such as the MASM32 / OllyDebugger is provided. Note that these assemblers and debuggers are Windows-based and are very user friendly. Screen shots provided on the CD verify the correct operation of several assembly language programs for the 68000, 68020, and Pentium via simulations using test data.

The book can be used in a number of ways. Since the materials presented here are basic and do not require an advanced mathematical background, the book can easily be adopted as a text for two- semester courses in microprocessors taught at the undergraduate level in electrical/computer engineering and computer science departments.

The book will also be useful for graduate students and for practicing microprocessor system designers. Practitioners of microprocessor system design will find more simplified explanations, together with examples and comparison considerations, than are found in manufacturers' manuals.

I wish to extend my sincere appreciation to my students, Joseph Lee, Raffi Karkourian, Tony Lopez, Julius Ramos, David Ambasing, Kevin Asprer, William Cambell, Devine Jeyarajah, Huy Nguyen, Thuan Ho, Kenneth Kha, Darren Ly, Dat Nguy, and Sevada Isayan for reviewing the manuscript and making valuable comments, and to CJ Media of California for preparing the final version of the manuscript. I am indebted especially to my deceased parents, who were primarily responsible for my accomplishments.

Pomona, California   M. RAFIQUZZAMAN

CREDITS

The material cited here is used by permission of the sources listed below.

Copyright of Freescale Semiconductor, Inc. 2008, Used by Permission: Table 6.4, Table 7.1, Table 7.2, Table 7.3, Table 7.5, Tables 7.7 through 7.11, Tables 8.2 through 8.13, Tables 9.1 through 9.7, Tables 9.11 and 9.12, Table 10.21, Table 10.23, Figures 6.1 through 6.3, Figure 7.1, Figure 7.2, Figure 7.8, Figure 7.12, Figure 7.14, Figures 8.1 through 8.3, Figures 9.1 through 9.5, Figures 9.9(a) and 9.9(b), Figures 9.16 through 9.20, Appendix C, Appendix D. All mnemonics of Motorola microprocessors are courtesy of Freescale Semiconductor, Inc.

Copyright of Intel Corporation, Used by Permission: Table 10.5, Table 10.6, Tables 11.2 through 11.5, Table 11.7, Tables 12.1 through 12.8, Table 12.10, Table 12.12, Figure 2.9(b), Figure 10.1, Figure 10.2, Figure 10.5, Figures 11.1 through 11.4, Figures 12.1 through 12.6, Figure 12.12, Appendix F, Appendix H. All mnemonics of Intel microprocessors are courtesy of Intel Corporation. The 80386 microprocessor referred to in the text as the i386TM, the 80486 as the i486TM, and the Pentium as the PentiumTM, trademarks of Intel Corporation.

Microsoft: MASM32 software used by permission.

Oleh Yuschuk, The author of OllyDbg: OllyDbg software used by permission.

Peter J. Fondse, The author of Ide 68k: Ide 68k software used by permission.

1

INTRODUCTION TO MICROPROCESSORS

Digital systems are designed to store, process, and communicate information in digital form. They are found in a wide range of applications, including process control, communication systems, digital instruments, and consumer products. A digital computer, more commonly called simply a *computer*, is an example of a typical digital system.

A computer manipulates information in digital or more precisely, binary form. A *binary number* has only two discrete values: zero or one. Each discrete value is represented by the OFF and ON status of an electronic switch called a *transistor*. All computers understand only binary numbers. Any decimal number (base 10, with ten digits from 0 to 9) can be represented by a binary number (base 2, with digits 0 and 1).

The basic blocks of a computer are the central processing unit (CPU), the memory, and the input/output (I/O). The CPU of a computer is basically the same as the brain of a human being; so computer memory is conceptually similar to human memory. A question asked of a human being is analogous to entering a program into a computer using an input device such as a keyboard, and a person answering a question is similar in concept to outputting the program result to a computer output device such as a printer. The main difference is that human beings can think independently, whereas computers can only answer questions for which they are programmed. Computer *hardware* includes such components as memory, CPU, transistors, nuts, bolts, and so on. Programs can perform a specific task, such as addition, if the computer has an electronic circuit capable of adding two numbers. Programmers cannot change these electronic circuits but can perform tasks on them using instructions.

Computer *software* consists of a collection of programs that contain instructions and data for performing a specific task. All programs, written using any programming language (e.g., C++), must be translated into binary prior to execution by a computer because the computer understands only binary numbers. Therefore, a translator is necessary to convert such a program into binary and this is achieved using a translator program called a *compiler*. Programs in the binary form of 1's and 0's are then stored in the computer memory for execution. Also, as computers can only add, all operations, including subtraction, multiplication, and division, are performed by addition.

Due to advances in semiconductor technology, it is possible to fabricate a CPU on a single chip. The result is a *microprocessor*. Both metal-oxide semiconductor (MOS) and bipolar technologies are used in the fabrication process. The CPU can be placed on a single chip when MOS technology is used. However, several chips are required with bipolar technology. At present, HCMOS (high-speed complementary MOS) or BICMOS

1

(combination of bipolar and HCMOS) technology is normally used to fabricate a microprocessor on a single chip. Along with the microprocessor chip, appropriate memory and I/O chips can be used to design a *microcomputer*. The pins on each one of these chips can be connected to the proper lines on a system bus, which consists of address, data, and control lines. In the past, some manufacturers designed a complete microcomputer on a single chip with limited capabilities. Single-chip microcomputers were used in a wide range of industrial and home applications.

Microcontrollers evolved from single-chip microcomputers. Microcontrollers are typically used for dedicated applications such as automotive systems, home appliances, and home entertainment systems. Typical microcontrollers include a microcomputer, timers, and A/D (analog-to- digital) and D/A (digital to analog) converters, all on a single chip. Examples of typical microcontrollers are the Intel 8751 (8-bit)/8096 (16-bit), Motorola HC11 (8-bit)/HC16 (16-bit), and Microchip Technology's PIC (peripheral interface controller).

In this chapter we first define some basic terms associated with microprocessors. We then describe briefly the evolution of microprocessors and typical features of 32- and 64-bit microprocessors. Finally, microprocessor-based system design concepts and typical microprocessor applications are included.

1.1   Explanation of Terms

Before we go on, it is necessary to understand some basic terms.

- An *Address* is a pattern of 0's and 1's that represents a specific location in memory or a particular I/O device. Typical 8-bit microprocessors have 16 address lines, and, these 16 lines can produce 2^{16} unique 16-bit patterns from 0000000000000000 to 1111111111111111, representing 65,536 different address combinations.

- *Addressing mode* is the manner in which the microprocessor determines the operand (data) and destination addresses during execution of an instruction.

- An *Arithmetic-logic unit* (ALU) is a digital circuit that performs arithmetic and logic operations on two *n*-bit digital words. The value of *n* can be 4, 8, 16, 32, or 64. Typical operations performed by an ALU are addition, subtraction, ANDing, ORing, and comparison of two *n*-bit digital words. The size of the ALU defines the size of the microprocessor. For example, a 32-bit microprocessor contains a 32-bit ALU.

- *Bit* is an abbreviation for the term *binary digit*. A binary digit can have only two values, which are represented by the symbols 0 and 1, whereas a decimal digit can have 10 values, represented by the symbols 0 through 9. The bit values are easily implemented in electronic and magnetic media by two-state devices whose states portray either of the binary digits 0 and 1. Examples of such two-state devices are a transistor that is conducting or not conducting, a capacitor that is charged or discharged, and a magnetic material that is magnetized north to south or south to north.

- *Bit size* refers to the number of bits that can be processed simultaneously by the basic arithmetic circuits of a microprocessor. A number of bits taken as a group in this manner is called a *word*. For example, a 32-bit microprocessor can process a 32-bit word. An 8-bit word is referred to as a *byte*, and a 4-bit word is known as a *nibble*.

- A *bus* consists of a number of conductors (wires) organized to provide a means of communication among different elements in a microprocessor system. The conductors in a bus can be grouped in terms of their functions. A microprocessor normally has an address bus, a data bus, and a control bus. Address bits are sent to memory or to an external device on the *address bus*. Instructions from memory, and data to/from memory or external devices, normally travel on the *data bus*. Control signals for the other buses and among system elements are transmitted on the *control bus*. Buses are sometimes *bidirectional*; that is, information can be transmitted in either direction on the bus, but normally in only one direction at a time.

- *Cache* Memory   is a high-speed, directly accessible, relatively small, semiconductor read/write memory block used to store data/instructions that the microprocessor may need in the immediate future. It increases speed by reducing the number of external memory reads required by the microprocessor. Typical 32-bit microprocessors such as the Intel Pentium are provided with on-chip cache memory. Pentium II supports two levels of cache. These are L1 (Level 1 cache) and L2 (Level 2 cache) cache memories. The L1 cache (smaller in size) is contained inside the microprocessor while L2 cache (larger in size) is interfaced to the microprocessor. This two level cache enhances the performance of the microprocessor.

- A *Complex Instruction Set Computer* (CISC) contains a large instruction set. It is difficult to pipeline compared to RISC. Motorola 68020 is a CISC microprocessor.

- *Clock* is analogous to human heart beats. The microprocessor requires synchronization among its components, and this is provided by a *clock* or timing circuits.

- The *instruction set* of a microprocessor is a list of commands that the microprocessor is designed to execute. Typical instructions are ADD, SUBTRACT, and STORE. Individual instructions are coded as unique bit patterns which are recognized and executed by the microprocessor. If a microprocessor has 3 bits allocated to the representation of instructions, the microprocessor will recognize a maximum of 2^3, or eight, different instructions. The microprocessor will then have a maximum of eight instructions in its instruction set. It is obvious that some instructions will be more suitable than others to a particular application. For example, if a microprocessor is to be used in a calculating mode, instructions such as ADD, SUBTRACT, MULTIPLY, and DIVIDE would be desirable. In a control application, instructions inputting digitized signals to the processor and outputting digital control variables to external circuits are essential. The number of instructions necessary in an application will directly influence the amount of hardware in the chip set and the number and organization of the interconnecting bus lines.

- *Memory Management Unit (MMU)* allows programmers to write programs much larger than could fit in the main memory space available to the microprocessor. The programs are simply stored in a secondary device such as a hard disk and portions of the programs are swapped into the main memory as needed for execution by the microprocessor. The MMU is implemented as on-chip hardware in typical microprocessors such as the Pentium.

- A *microprocessor* is the CPU of a microcomputer contained on a single chip, and must be intefaced with peripheral support chips in order to function. In general, a CPU contains several *registers* (memory elements), an ALU, and a control unit. Note that the control unit translates instructions and performs the desired task. The number of peripheral devices depends on the particular application involved and may even vary within an application. As the microprocessor industry matures, more of these functions are being integrated onto chips, to reduce the system package count. In general, a *microcomputer* typically consists of a microprocessor (CPU) chip, input and output chips, and memory chips in which programs (instructions and data) are stored. Note that a *microcontroller*, on the other hand, is implemented on a single chip containing typically a CPU, memory, I/O, a timer, and A/D and D/A converter circuits.

- *Pipelining* is a technique that overlaps instruction fetch (instruction read) with execution. This allows a microprocessor's processing operation to be broken down into several steps (dictated by the number of pipeline levels or stages) so that the individual step outputs can be handled by the microprocessor in parallel. Pipelining is often used to fetch the microprocessor's next instruction while executing the current instruction, which speeds up the overall operation of the microprocessor considerably.

- *Random-access memory* (RAM) is a storage medium for groups of bits or words whose contents cannot only be read but can also be altered at specific addresses. A RAM normally provides *volatile storage*, which means that its contents are lost in case power is turned off. RAMs are fabricated on chips and have typical densities of 4096 bits to 1 megabit per chip. These bits can be organized in many ways: for example, as 4096-by-1-bit words or as 2048-by-8-bit words. RAMs are normally used for the storage of temporary data and intermediate results as well as programs that can be reloaded from a backup nonvolatile source. RAMs are capable of providing large storage capacity, in the megabit range.

- *Read-only memory* (ROM) is a storage medium for the groups of bits called *words*, and its contents cannot normally be altered once programmed. A typical ROM is fabricated on a chip and can store, for example, 2048 eight-bit words, which can be accessed individually by presenting to it one of 2048 addresses. This ROM is referred to as a 2K by 8-bit ROM. 10110111 is an example of an 8-bit word that might be stored in one location in this memory. A ROM is a *nonvolatile storage* device, which means that its contents are retained in case power is turned off. Because of this characteristic, ROMs are used to store programs (instructions and data) that must always be available to the microprocessor.

- A *register* can be considered as volatile storage for a number of bits. These bits may be entered into the register simultaneously (in parallel) or sequentially (serially) from right to left or from left to right, 1 bit at a time. An 8-bit register storing the bits 11110000 is represented as follows:

1	1	1	1	0	0	0	0

- *A reduced instruction set computer* (RISC) contains a simple instruction set. The RISC architecture maximizes speed by reducing clock cycles per instruction and makes it easier to implement pipelining. A Power PC is a RISC microprocessor.

- A *Superscalar* microprocessor is provided with more than one pipeline and can execute more than one instruction per clock cycle. The Pentium is a superscalar microprocessor.

1.2   Microprocessor Data Types

In this section we discuss data types used by typical microprocessors: unsigned and signed binary numbers, binary-coded decimal (BCD), ASCII (American Standard Code for Information Interchange), EBCDIC (extended binary coded decimal interchange code), and floating-point numbers.

1.2.1   Unsigned and Signed Binary Numbers

An *Unsigned binary number* has no arithmetic sign, therefore, are always positive. Typical examples are your age or a memory address, which are always positive numbers. An 8-bit unsigned binary integer represents all numbers from 00_{16} through $FF_{16} (0_{10}$ through $255_{10})$.

A *signed binary number*, on the other hand, includes both positive and negative numbers. It is represented in the microprocessor in two's-complement form. For example, the decimal number +15 is represented in 8-bit two's-complement form as 0000 1111 (binary) or 0F (hexadecimal). The decimal number -15 can be represented in 8-bit two's-complement form as 11110001 (binary) or F1 (hexadecimal). Also, the most significant bit (MSB) of a signed number represents the sign of the number. For example, bit 7 of an 8-bit number, bit 15 of a 16-bit number, and bit 31 of a 32-bit number represent the signs of the respective numbers. A "0" at the MSB represents a positive number; a "1" at the MSB represents a negative number. Note that the 8-bit binary number 11111111 is $255_{10}$when represented as an unsigned number. On the other hand, 11111111_2 is -1_{10} when represented as a signed number.

An error (indicated by overflow in a microprocessor) may occur while performing twos complement arithmetic. The microprocessor automatically sets an overflow bit to 1 if the result of an arithmetic operation is too big for the microprocessor's maximum word size; otherwise it is reset to 0. For signed arithmetic operations such as addition, the overflow, $V = C_f \oplus C_p$ where C_f is the final carry and C_p is the previous carry. This can be illustrated by the following examples.

Consider the following examples for 8-bit numbers. Let C_f be the final carry (carry out of the most significant bit or sign bit) and C_p be the previous carry (carry out of bit 6 or seventh bit). We will show by means of numerical examples that as long as C_f and C_p are the same, the result is always correct. If, however, C_f and C_p are different, the result is incorrect and sets the overflow bit to 1. Now, consider the following cases.

Case 1: C_f and C_p are the same.

$$
\begin{array}{ll}
0\ 0\ 0\ 0\ 0\ 1\ 1\ 0 & 06_{16} \\
\underline{0\ 0\ 0\ 1\ 0\ 1\ 0\ 0} & \underline{+14_{16}} \\
0\ \ 0\ 0\ 0\ 1\ 1\ 0\ 1\ 0 & 1A_{16}
\end{array}
$$

$C_f = 0$ $C_p = 0$

$$
\begin{array}{ll}
0\ 1\ 1\ 0\ 1\ 0\ 0\ 0 & 68_{16} \\
\underline{1\ 1\ 1\ 1\ 1\ 0\ 1\ 0} & \underline{-06_{16}} \\
1\ \ 0\ 1\ 1\ 0\ 0\ 0\ 1\ 0 & 62_{16}
\end{array}
$$

$C_f = 1$ $C_p = 1$

Therefore when C_f and C_p are either both 0 or both 1, a correct answer is obtained.

Case 2: C_f and C_p are different.

$$
\begin{array}{ll}
0\ 1\ 0\ 1\ 1\ 0\ 0\ 1 & 59_{16} \\
\underline{0\ 1\ 0\ 0\ 0\ 1\ 0\ 1} & \underline{+45_{16}} \\
0\ \ 1\ 0\ 0\ 1\ 1\ 1\ 1\ 0 & {}^{-}62_{16} \quad ?
\end{array}
$$

$C_f = 0$ $C_p = 1$

$C_f = 0$ and $C_p = 1$ give an incorrect answer because the result shows that the addition of two positive numbers is negative.

$$
\begin{array}{ll}
1\ 0\ 1\ 1\ 0\ 1\ 1\ 0 & {}^{-}4A_{16} \\
\underline{1\ 0\ 0\ 0\ 0\ 0\ 0\ 1} & \underline{{}^{-}7F_{16}} \\
1\ \ 0\ 0\ 1\ 1\ 0\ 1\ 1\ 1 & +37_{16} \quad ?
\end{array}
$$

$C_f = 1$ $C_p = 0$

$C_f = 1$ and $C_p = 0$ provide an incorrect answer because the result indicates that the addition of two negative numbers is positive. Hence, the overflow bit will be set to zero if the carries C_f and C_p are the same, that is, if both C_f and C_p are either 0 or 1. On the other hand, the overflow flag will be set to 1 if carries C_f and C_p are different. The relationship among C_f, C_p, and V can be summerized in a truth table as follows:

Inputs		Output
C_f	C_p	V
0	0	0
0	1	1
1	0	1
1	1	0

From the truth table, overflow, $V = \overline{C_f}\,C_p + C_f\,\overline{C_p} = C_f \oplus C_p$

Note that the symbol $\oplus$ represents exclusive-OR logic operation. Exclusive-OR means that when two inputs are the same (both one or both zero), the output is zero. On the other hand, if two inputs are different, the output is one. The overflow can be considered as an output while C_f and C_p are the two inputs. The answer is incorrect when the overflow bit is set to 1; the answer is correct if the overflow bit is 0.

Typical microprocessors have separate unsigned and signed multiplication and division instructions as follows: MULU (multiply two unsigned numbers), MULS (multiply two signed numbers), DIVU (divide two unsigned numbers), and DIVS (divide two signed numbers). It is important for the programmer to understand clearly how to use these instructions.

For example, suppose that it is desired to compute $X^2/255$. If X is a signed 8-bit number, the programmer should use the MULS instruction to compute $X * X$ which is always unsigned (the square of a number is always positive), and then use DIVU to compute $X^2/255$ (16-bit by 8-bit unsigned divide) since 255_{10} is positive. But if the programmer uses DIVS, both $X * X$ and 255_{10} (FF_{16}) will be interpreted as signed numbers. FF_{16} will be interpreted as -1^{10}, and the result will be wrong. On the other hand, if X is an unsigned number, the programmer needs to use MULU and DIVU to compute $X^2/255$.

1.2.2   ASCII and EBCDIC Codes

If it is to be very useful, a microprocessor must be capable of handling nonnumeric information. In other words, a microprocessor must be able to recognize codes that represent numbers, letters, and special characters. These codes are classified as alphanumeric or character codes. A complete and adequate set of necessary characters includes the following:

- 26 lowercase letters

- 26 uppercase letters

- 10 numerical digits (0–9)

- Approximately 25 special characters, which include +, /, #, %, and others.

This totals 87 characters. To represent 87 characters with some type of binary code would require at least 7 bits. With 7 bits there are $2^7 = 128$ possible binary numbers; 87 of these combinations of 0 and 1 bits serve as the code groups representing the 87 different characters.

The two most common alphanumerical codes are the American Standard Code for Information Interchange (ASCII) and the extended binary-coded-decimal interchange code (EBCDIC). ASCII is typically used with microprocessors; IBM uses EBCDIC code. Eight bits are used to represent characters, although 7 bits suffice, because the eighth bit is frequently used to test for errors and is referred to as a *parity bit*. It can be set to 1 or 0 so that the number of 1 bits in the byte is always odd or even.

Note that decimal digits 0 through 9 are represented by 30_{16} through 39_{16} in ASCII. On the other hand, these decimal digits are represented by $F0_{16}$ though $F9_{16}$ in EBCDIC.

A microcomputer program is usually written for code conversion when input/ output devices of different codes are connected to the microcomputer. For example, suppose that it is desired to enter the number 5 into a computer via an ASCII keyboard and to print this data on an EBCDIC printer. The ASCII keyboard will generate 35_{16} when the number 5 is pushed. The ASCII code 35_{16} for the decimal digit 5 enters the microcomputer and resides in the memory. To print the digit 5 on the EBCDIC printer, a program must be written that will convert the ASCII code 35_{16} for 5 to its EBCDIC code, $F5_{16}$. The output of this program is $F5_{16}$. This will be input to the EBCDIC printer. Because the printer understands only EBCDIC codes, it inputs the EBCDIC code $F5_{16}$ and prints the digit 5. Typical microprocessors such as the Intel Pentium include instructions to provide correct unpacked BCD after performing arithmetic operations in ASCII. The Pentium instruction, AAA (ASCII adjust for addition) is such an instruction.

1.2.3   Unpacked and Packed Binary-Coded-Decimal Numbers

The 10 decimal digits 0 through 9 can be represented by their corresponding 4-bit binary numbers. The digits coded in this fashion are called *binary-coded-decimal digits* in 8421 code, or BCD digits. Two unpacked BCD bytes are usually packed into a byte to form *packed BCD*. For example, two unpacked BCD bytes 02_{16} and 05_{16} can be combined as a packed BCD byte 25_{16}.

Let us consider entering data decimal 24 via an ASCII keyboard into a microcomputer. Two keys (2 and 4) will be pushed on the ASCII keyboard. This will generate 32 and 34 (32 and 34 are ASCII codes in hexadecimal for 2 and 4, respectively) inside the microcomputer. A program can be written to convert these ASCII codes into unpacked BCD 02_{16} and 04_{16}, and then to convert to packed BCD 24 or to binary inside the microcomputer to perform the desired operation. Unpacked BCD 02_{16} and 04_{16} can be converted into packed BCD 24 (00100100_2) by logically shifting 02_{16} four times to the left to obtain 20_{16}, then logically ORing with 04_{16}. On the other hand, to convert unpacked BCD 02_{16} and 04_{16} into binary, one needs to multiply 02_{16} by 10 and then add 04_{16} to obtain 00011000_2 (the binary equivalent of 24).

Typical 32-bit microprocessors such as the Motorola 68020 include PACK and UNPK instructions for converting an unpacked BCD number to its packed equivalent, and vice versa.

1.2.4   Floating-point Numbers

A number representation assuming a fixed location of the radix point is called *fixed-point representation*. The range of numbers that can be represented in fixed-point notation is severely limited. The following numbers are examples of fixed-point numbers:

$$0110.1100_2, \ 51.12_{10}, \ DE.2A_{16}$$

In typical scientific computations, the range of numbers is very large. Floating-point representation is used to handle such ranges. A *floating-point number* is represented as $N \times r^p$, where N is the mantissa or significand, r the base or radix of the number system, and p the exponent or power to which r is raised. Some examples of numbers in floating-point notation and their fixed-point decimal equivalents are:

Fixed-Point Number	Floating-Point Representation
0.0167_{10}	0.167×10^{-1}
1101.101_2	0.1101101×2^4
$BE.2A9_{16}$	$0.BE2A9 \times 16^2$

In converting from fixed-point to floating-point number representation, the resulting mantissas are normalized, that is, the digits of the fixed-point numbers are shifted so that the highest-order nonzero digit appears to the right of the decimal point and a 0 always appears to the left of the decimal point. This convention is normally adopted in floating-point number representation. Because all numbers will be assumed to be in normalized form, the binary point is not required to be represented in microprocessors.

Typical 32-bit microprocessors such as the Intel Pentium and the Motorola 68040 contain on-chip floating-point hardware. This means that these microprocessors can be programmed using instructions to perform operations such as addition, subtraction, multiplication, and division using floating-point numbers. The Motorola 68020 does not contain on-chip floating-point hardware but 68020 can be interfaced to a floating-point coprocessor chip to provide floating-point functions.

1.3 Evolution of the Microprocessor

The Intel Corporation is generally acknowledged as the company that introduced the first microprocessor successfully into the marketplace. Its first processor, the 4004, was introduced in 1971 and evolved from a development effort while making a calculator chip set. The 4004 microprocessor was the central component in the chip set, which was called the MCS-4. The other components in the set were a 4001 ROM, a 4002 RAM, and a 4003 shift register.

Shortly after the 4004 appeared in the commercial marketplace, three other general-purpose microprocessors were introduced: the Rockwell International 4-bit PPS-4, the Intel 8-bit 8008, and the National Semiconductor 16-bit IMP-16. Other companies, such as General Electric, RCA, and Viatron, also made contributions to the development of the microprocessor prior to 1971.

The microprocessors introduced between 1971 and 1972 were the first-generation systems designed using PMOS technology. In 1973, second-generation microprocessors such as the Motorola 6800 and the Intel 8080 (8-bit microprocessors) were introduced. The second-generation microprocessors were designed using NMOS technology. This technology resulted in a significant increase in instruction execution speed over PMOS and higher chip densities. Since then, microprocessors have been fabricated using a variety of technologies and designs. NMOS microprocessors such as the Intel 8085, the Zilog Z80, and the Motorola 6800/6809 were introduced based on second-generation microprocessors. A third generation HMOS microprocessor, introduced in 1978 is typically represented by the Intel 8086 and the Motorola 68000, which are 16-bit microprocessors.

During the 1980's, fourth-generation HCMOS and BICMOS (a combination of bipolar and HCMOS) 32-bit microprocessors evolved. Intel introduced the first commercial 32-bit microprocessor, the problematic Intel 432, which was eventually discontinued. Since 1985, more 32-bit microprocessors have been introduced. These include Motorola's 68020, 68030, 68040, 68060, PowerPC, Intel's 80386, 80486, the Intel Pentium family, Core Duo, and Core2 Duo microprocessors..

The performance offered by the 32-bit microprocessor is more comparable to that of superminicomputers such as Digital Equipment Corporation's VAX11/750 and VAX11/780. Intel and Motorola also introduced RISC microprocessors: the Intel 80960 and Motorola 88100/PowerPC, which had simplified instruction sets. Note that the purpose of RISC microprocessors is to maximize speed by reducing clock cycles per instruction. Almost all computations can be obtained from a simple instruction set. Note that, in order to enhance performance significantly, Intel Pentium Pro and other succeeding members of the Pentium family and Motorola 68060 are designed using a combination of RISC and CISC.

An overview of the Motorola 68XXX and PowerPC microprocessors will be provided next. Motorola's 32-bit microprocessors based on the 68000 (16-bit microprocessor) architecture include the MC68020, MC68030, MC68040, and MC68060. Table 1.1 compares the basic features of some of these microprocessors with the 68000.

MC68020 is Motorola's first 32-bit microprocessor. The design of the 68020 is based on the 68000. The 68020 can perform a normal read or write cycle in 3 clock cycles without wait states as compared to the 68000, which completes a read or write operation in 4 clock cycles without wait states. As far as the addressing modes are concerned, the 68020 includes new modes beyond those of the 68000. Some of these modes are scaled indexing, larger displacements, and memory indirection.

TABLE 1.1   Motorola 68000 vs. 68020/68030/68040

	68000	68020	68030	68040
Comparable Clock Speed	33MHz (4MHz min)*	33 MHz (8 MHz min.)*	33 MHz (8 MHz min.)*	33 MHz (8 MHz min.)*
Pins	64, 68	114	118	118
Address Bus	24-bit	32-bit	32-bit	32-bit
Addressing Modes	14	18	18	18
Maximum Memory	16 Megabytes	4 Gigabytes	4 Gigabytes	4 Gigabytes
Memory Management	NO	By interfacing the 68851 MMU chip	On-chip MMU	On-chip MMU
Cache (on chip)	NO	Instruction cache	Instruction and data cache	Instruction and data cache
Floating Point	NO	By interfacing 68881/68882 floating-point coprocessor chip	By interfacing 68881/68882 floating-point coprocessor chip	On-chip floating point hardware
Total Instructions	56	101	103	103 plus floating- point instructions
ALU size	One 16-bit ALU	Three 32-bit ALU's	Three 32-bit ALU's	Three 32-bit ALU's

*Higher clock speeds available

Furthermore, several new instructions are added to the 68020 instruction set, including the two new instructions are used to perform conversions between packed BCD and ASCII or EBCDIC digits. Note that a packed BCD is a byte containing two BCD digits.

68030 and 68040 are two enhanced versions of the 68020. The 68030 retains most of the 68020 features. It is a virtual memory microprocessor containing an on-chip MMU (memory management unit). The 68040 expands the 68030 on-chip memory management logic to two units: one for instruction fetch and one for data access. This speeds up the 68040's execution time by performing logical-to-physical-address translation in parallel. The on-chip floating-point capability of the 68040 provides it with both integer and floating-point arithmetic operations at a high speed. All 68000 programs written in assembly language in user mode will run on the 68020/68030 or 68040.

MC68060 is a superscalar (two instructions per cycle) 32-bit microprocessor. The 68060, like the Pentium Pro and the succeeding members of the Pentium family, is designed using a combination of RISC and CISC architectures to obtain high performance. For some reason, Motorola does not offer MC68050 microprocessor. The 68060 is fully compatible with the 68040 in the user mode. The 68060 can operate at 50- and 66-MHz clocks with performance much faster than the 68040. An striking feature of the 68060 is the power consumption control. The 68060 is designed using static HCMOS to reduce power during normal operation.

PowerPC family of microprocessors were jointly developed by Motorola, IBM, and Apple. The PowerPC family contains both 32- and 64-bit microprocessors. One of the noteworthy feature of the PowerPC is that it is the first top-of-the-line microprocessor to include an on-chip real-time clock (RTC). The RTC is common in single-chip microcomputers rather than microprocessors. The PowerPC is the first microprocessor to implement this on-chip feature, which makes it easier to satisfy the requirements of time-keeping for task switching and calendar date of modern multitasking operating systems. The PowerPC microprocessor supports both the Power Mac and standard PCs. The PowerPC family is designed using RISC architecture.

An overview of Intel's 80XXX, Pentium, and contemporary microprocessors will be provided in the following.

The original Pentium processor was introduced by Intel in 1993, and the name was changed from 80586 to Pentium because of copyright laws. The processor uses more than 3 million transistors and had an initial speed of 60 MHz. The speed has increased over the years to the latest speed of 233 MHz. Table 1.2 compares the basic features of the Intel 80386DX, 80386SX, 80486DX, 80486SX, 80486DX2, and Pentium. These are all 32-bit microprocessors. Note that the 80386SL (not listed in the table) is also a 32-bit microprocessor with a 16-but data bus like the 80386SX. The 80386SL can run at a speed of up to 25 MHz and has a direct addressing capability of 32 MB. The 80386SL provides virtual memory support along with on-chip memory management and protection. It can be interfaced to the 80387SX to provide floating-point support. The 80386SL includes an on-chip disk controller hardware.

The Pentium Pro was introduced in November 1995. The Pentium processor provides pipelined superscalar architecture. The Pentium processor's pipelined implementation uses five stages to extract high throughput and the Pentium Pro utilizes 12-stage, superpipelined implementation, trading less work per pipestage for more stages. The Pentium Pro processor reduced its pipe stage time by 33% compared with a Pentium processor, which means the Pentium Pro processor can have a 33% higher clock speed than a Pentium processor and still be equally easy to produce from a semiconductor manufacturing process. A 200-MHz Pentium Pro is always faster than a 200-MHz Pentium for 32-bit applications such as computer-aided design (CAD), 3-D graphics, and multimedia applications.

The Pentium processor's superscalar architecture, with its ability to execute two instructions per clock, was difficult to exceed without a new approach. The new approach used by the Pentium Pro processor removes the constraint of linear instruction sequencing between the traditional *fetch* and *execute* phases, and opens up a wide instruction pool. This approach allows the *execute* phase of the Pentium Pro processor to have much more visibility into the program's instruction stream so that better scheduling may take place. This allows instructions to be started in any order but always be completed in the original program order.

Microprocessor speeds have increased tremendously over the past several years, but the speed of the main memory devices has only increased by 60 percent. This increasing memory latency, relative to the microprocessor speed, is a fundamental problem that the Pentium Pro is designed to solve. The Pentium Pro processor *looks ahead* into its instruction pool at subsequent instructions and will do useful work rather than be stalled. The Pentium Pro executes instructions depending on their readiness to execute and not on their original program order. In summary, it is the unique combination of improved branch prediction, choosing the best order, and executing the instructions in the preferred order that enables the Pentium Pro processor to improve program execution over the Pentium

TABLE 1.2   **Intel 80386/80486/Pentium Microprocessors.**

Features	80386DX	80386SX	80486DX	80486SX	80486DX2	Pentium (original)
• Introduced	October 1985	June 1988	April 1989	April 1991	March 1992	March 1993
• Maximum Clock Speed (MHz)	40	33	50	25	100	233
• MIPS*	6	2.5	20	16.5	54	112
• Transistors	275,000	275,000	1.2 million	1.185 million	1.2 million	3.1 million
• On-chip cache memory	Support chips available	Support chips available	Yes	Yes	Yes	Yes
• Data bus	32-bit	16-bit	32-bit	32-bit	32-bit	64-bit
• Address bus	32-bit	24-bit	32-bit	32-bit	32-bit	32-bit
• Directly addressable memory	4 GB	16MB	4 GB	4 GB	4 GB	4 GB
• Pins	132	100	168	168	168	273
• Virtual memory	Yes	Yes	Yes	Yes	Yes	Yes
• On-chip memory management and protection	Yes	Yes	Yes	Yes	Yes	Yes
• Floating point unit	387DX	387SX	on chip	487SX	on chip	on chip

* MIPS means million of instructions per second that the microprocessor can execute. MIPS is typically used as a measure of performance of a microprocessor. Faster microprocessors have a higher MIPS value.

TABLE 1.3   **Pentium vs. Pentium Pro.**

Pentium	Pentium Pro
• First introduced March 1993	• Introduced November 1995
• 2 instructions per clock cycle	• 3 instructions per clock cycle
• Primary cache of 16K	• Primary cache of 16K
• Original clock speeds of 100, 120, 133, 150, 166, 200, and 233 MHz	• Original clock speeds 166, 180, 200 MHz
• More silicon is needed to produce the chip	• Tighter design reduces silicon needed and makes chip faster (shorter distances between transistors)
• Designed for operating systems written in 16-bit code	• Designed for operating systems written in 32-bit code.

processor. This unique combination is called *dynamic execution*.

The Pentium Pro does a great job running some operating systems such as Windows NT or Unix. The first release of Windows 95 contains a significant amount of 16-bit code in the graphics subsystem. This causes operations on the Pentium Pro to be serialized instead of taking advantage of the dynamic execution architecture. Nevertheless, the Pentium Pro is up to 30% faster than the fastest Pentium in 32-bit applications. Table 1.3 compares the basic features of the Pentium with the Pentium Pro.

The 32-bit Pentium II processor is Intel's next addition to the Pentium line of microprocessors, which originated form the widely cloned 80x86 line. It basically takes attributes of the Pentium Pro processor plus the capabilities of MMX technology to yield processor speeds of 333, 300, 266, and 233 MHz. The Pentium II processor uses 0.25 micron technology (this refers to the width of the circuit lines on the silicon) to allow increased core frequencies and reduce power consumption. The Pentium II processor took advantage of four technologies to achieve its performance ratings:

- Dual Independent Bus Architecture (DIB)

- Dynamic Execution

- Intel MMX Technology

- Single-Edge-Contact Cartridge

DIB was first implemented in the Pentium Pro processor to address bandwidth limitations. The DIB architecture consists of two independent buses, an L2 cache bus and a system bus, to offer three times the bandwidth performance of single bus architecture processors. The Pentium II processor can access data from both buses simultaneously to accelerate the flow of information within the system.

Dynamic execution was also first implemented in the Pentium Pro processor. It consists of three processing techniques to improve the efficiency of executing instructions. These techniques include multiple branch prediction, data flow analysis, and speculative execution. Multiple branch prediction uses an algorithm to determine the next instruction to be executed following a jump in the instruction flow. With data flow analysis, the processor determines the optimum sequence for processing a program after looking at software instructions to see if they are dependent on other instructions. Speculative execution increases the rate of execution by executing instructions ahead of the program counter that are likely to be needed.

MMX (**m**atrix **m**ath **ex**tensions) technology is Intel's greatest enhancement to its microprocessor architecture. MMX technology is intended for efficient multimedia and communications operations. To achieve this, 57 new instructions have been added to manipulate and process video, audio, and graphical data more efficiently. These instructions support single-instruction multiple-data (SIMD) techniques, which enable one instruction to perform the same function on multiple pieces of data. Programs written using the new instructions significantly enhance the capabilities of Pentium II.

The final feature in Intel's Pentium II processor is single-edge-contact (SEC) packaging. In this packaging arrangement, the core and L2 cache are fully enclosed in a plastic and metal cartridge. The components are surface mounted directly to a substrate inside the cartridge to enable high-frequency operation.

Intel Celeron processor utilizes Pentium II as core .The Celeron processor family includes: 333 MHz, 300A MHz, 300 MHz, and 266 MHz processors. The Celeron 266 MHz and 300 MHz processors do not contain any level 2 cache. But the Celeron 300A

MHz and 333 MHz processors incorporate an integrated L2 cache. All Celeron processors are based on Intel's 0.25 micron CMOS technology. The Celeron processor is designed for inexpensive or "Basic PC" desktop systems and can run Windows 98. The Celeron processor offers good floating-point (3D geometry calculations) and multimedia (both video and audio) performance.

The Pentium II Xeon processor contains large, fast caches to transfer data at super high speed through the processor core. The processor can run at either 400 MHz or 450 MHz. The Pentium II Xeon is designed for any mid-range or higher Intel-based server or workstation. The 450 MHz Pentium II Xeon can be used in workstations and servers.

The Pentium III operates at 450 MHz and 500 MHz. It is designed for desktop PCs. The Pentium III enhances the multimedia capabilities of the PC, including full screen video and graphics. Pentium III Xeon processors run at 500 MHz and 550 MHz. They are designed for mid-range and higher Internet-based servers and workstations. It is compatible with Pentium II Xeon processor-based platforms. Pentium III Xeon is also designed for demanding workstation applications such as 3-D visualization, digital content creation, and dynamic Internet content development. Pentium III-based systems can run applications on Microsoft Windows NT or UNIX-based environments. The Pentium III Xeon is available in a number of L2 cache versions such as 512-Kbytes, 1-Mbyte, or 2-Mbytes (500 MHz); 512 Kbytes (550 MHz) to satisfy a variety of Internet application requirements.

The Intel Pentium 4 is an enhanced Pentium III processor. It is currently available at 1.30, 1.40, 1.50, and 1.70 GHz. The chip's all-new internal design contains Intel NetBurstTM micro-architecture. This provides the Pentium 4 with hyper pipelined technology (which doubles the pipeline depth to 20 stages), a rapid execution engine (which pushes the processor's ALUs to twice the core frequency), and 400 MHz system bus. The Pentium 4 contains 144 new instructions. Furthermore, inclusion of an improved Advanced Dynamic Execution and an improved floating point pushes data efficiently through the pipeline. This enhances digital audio, digital video and 3D graphics. Along with other features such as streaming SIMD Extensions 2 (SSE2) that extends MMXTM technology, the Pentium 4 gives the advanced technology to get the most out of the Internet. Finally, the Pentium 4 offers high performance when networking multiple PCs, or when attaching Pentium 4 based PC to home consumer electronic systems and new peripherals.

Intel introduced the 32-bit Pentium M microprocessor in 2003. It was designed specifically for the mobile computing market. The Pentium M contains approximately 77 million transistors and originally ran at a speed of 1.3 to 1.6 GHz. In 2006, Intel introduced the 64-bit Core Duo microprocessor. The Core Duo is based on the Pentium M microarchitecture. The Core Duo contains approximately 151 million transistors. The original Core Duo ran at a speed of 1.66 to 2.33 GHz. The Core Duo is used primarily in servers.

Intel introduced the Core 2 Duo microprocessor in 2006, based on Core Duo microarchitecture. The Core 2 Duo contains approximately 291 million transistors and is used in desktop computers. The original Core 2 Duo ran at a speed of 1.86 to 2.93 GHz.

Note that Intel 4004 contained approximately 2300 transistors with a clock frequency of about 100 kHz. In contrast, contemporary microprocessors such as Intel Core Duo contain over 100 million transistors with a frequency of more than 2 GHz. These microprocessors are typically used in designing client and server systems for the Internet.

An overview of the latest microprocessors is provided in this section. Unfortunately, this may be old news within a few years. One can see, however, that both Intel and Motorola offer (and will continue to offer) high-quality microprocessors to satisfy demanding applications.

1.4 Typical Features of 32-bit and 64-bit Microprocessors

In this section we describe the basic aspects of typical 32- and 64-bit microprocessors. Topics include on-chip features such as pipelining, memory management, floating-point, and cache memory implemented in typical 32- and 64-bit microprocessors. The first 32-bit microprocessor, Intel's problematic iAPX432, was introduced in 1980. Soon afterward, the concept of *mainframe on a chip* or *micromainframe* was used to indicate the capabilities of these microprocessors and to distinguish them from previous 8- and 16-bit microprocessors.

The introduction of several 32-bit microprocessors revolutionized the microprocessor world. The performance of these 32-bit microprocessors is actually more comparable to that of superminicomputers such as Digital Equipment Corporation's VAX11/750 and VAX11/780. Designers of 32-bit microprocessors have implemented many powerful features of these mainframe computers to increase the capabilities of microprocessor chip sets: pipelining, on-chip cache memory, memory management, and floating-point arithmetic.

In pipelining, instruction fetch and execute cycles overlap. This method allows simultaneous preparation for execution of one or more instructions while another instruction is being executed. Pipelining was used for many years in mainframe and minicomputer CPUs to speed up the instruction execution time of these machines. The 32-bit microprocessors implement the pipelining concept and operate simultaneously on several 32-bit words, which may represent different instructions or part of a single instruction.

Although pipelining greatly increases the rate of execution of nonbranching code, pipelines must be emptied and refilled each time a branch or jump instruction appears in the code. This may slow down the processing rate for code with many branches or jumps. Thus, there is an optimum pipeline depth, which is strongly related to the instruction set, architecture, and gate density attainable on the processor chip.

With memory management, virtual memory techniques, traditionally a feature of mainframes, are also implemented as on-chip hardware on typical 32-bit microprocessors. This allows programmers to write programs much larger than those that could fit in the main memory space available to microprocessors; the programs are simply stored on a secondary device such as a hard disk, and portions of the program are swapped into main memory as needed.

Segmentation circuitry has been included in many 32-bit microprocessor chips. With this technique, blocks of code called *segments*, which correspond to modules of the program and have varying sizes set by the programmer or compiler, are swapped. For many applications, however, an alternative method borrowed from mainframes and superminis called *paging* is used. Basically, paging differs from segmentation in that pages are of equal size. *Demand paging*, in which the operating system swaps pages automatically as needed, can be used with all 32-bit microprocessors.

Floating-point arithmetic is yet another area in which the new chips mimick mainframes. With early microprocessors, floating-point arithmetic was implemented in software largely as a subroutine. When required, execution would jump to a piece of code that would handle the tasks. This method slows the execution rate considerably, however, so floating-point hardware such as fast bit-slice (registers and ALU on a chip) processors and, in some cases, special-purpose chips was developed. Other than the Intel 8087, these chips behaved more or less like peripherals. When floating-point arithmetic was required, the problems were sent to the floating-point processor and the CPU was freed to move on to other instructions while it waited for the results. The floating-point processor is implemented as on-chip hardware in typical 32-bit microprocessors, as in mainframe and minicomputer CPUs. Caching or memory-management schemes are utilized with all 32-bit microprocessors to minimize access time for most instructions.

A *cache*, used for years in minis and mainframes, is a relatively small, high-speed memory installed between a processor and its main memory. The theory behind a cache is that a significant portion of the CPU time spent running typical programs is tied up in executing loops; thus, chances are good that if an instruction to be executed is not the next sequential instruction, it will be one of some relatively small number of instructions clustering around a small region in the main memory, a concept known as *locality of reference*. Therefore, a high-speed memory large enough to contain most loops should greatly increase processing rates. Cache memory is included as on-chip hardware in typical 32-bit microprocessors such as the Pentium.

Typical 32-bit microprocessors such as Pentium and PowerPC chips are superscalar processors. This means that they can execute more than one instruction in one clock cycle. Also, some 32-bit microprocessors such as the PowerPC contain an on-chip real-time clock. This allows these processors to use modern multitasking operating systems that require timekeeping for task switching and for keeping the calendar date.

Typical 32-bit microprocessors implement a multiple-branch prediction feature. This allows these microprocessors to anticipate jumps of the instruction flow. Also, some 32-bit microprocessors determine an optimal sequence of instruction execution by looking at decoded instructions and determining whether to execute or hold them. Typical 32-bit microprocessors use a "look-ahead" approach to execute instructions. These 32-bit microprocessors maintain an instruction pool for a sequence of instructions and perform a useful task rather than executing the present instruction and going on to the next.

The 64-bit microprocessors such as Power PC 750 include all the features of 32-bit microprocessors. In addition, they contain multiple on-chip integer and floating-point units and a larger address and data buses. The 64-bit microprocessors can typically execute four instructions per clock cycle and can run at a clock speed of over 2 GHz. The original Pentium microprocessor is a CISC microprocessor. Pentium Pro and other succeeding members of the Pentium family are designed using a combination of mostly microprogramming (CISC) and some hardwired control (RISC) whereas the PowerPC is designed using hardwired control with almost no microcode. The PowerPC is a RISC microprocessorand therefore includes a simple instruction set. This instruction set includes register-to-register, load, and store instructions. All instructions involving arithmetic operations use registers; load and store instructions are utilized to access memory. Almost all computations can be obtained from these simple instructions. Finally, 64-bit microprocessors are ideal candidates for data-crunching machines and high-performance desktop systems and workstations.

1.5   Microprocessor-based System Design Concepts

A microprocessor-based system is typically designed using a *microcomputer development system* a tool that allows the designer to develop, debug, and integrate error-free application software in microprocessor systems. Development systems fall into one of two categories: systems supplied by the device manufacturer (nonuniversal systems) and systems built by after-market manufacturers (universal systems). The main difference between the two categories is in the range of microprocessors that a system will accommodate. *Nonuniversal systems* are supplied by the microprocessor manufacturer (e.g., Intel, Motorola) and are limited to use for the particular microprocessor manufactured by the supplier. In this manner, an Intel development system may not be used to develop a Motorola-based system. *Universal development systems* (e.g., Hewlett-Packard) can develop hardware and software for several microprocessors.

Within both categories of development systems, basically two types are available: single-user and networked systems. A *single-user system* consists of one development station that can be used by one user at a time. Single-user systems are low in cost and may be sufficient for small systems development. A *networked system* usually consists of a number of smart terminals capable of performing most development work and can be connected over data lines to a central microcomputer. The central microcomputer in a networked system usually is in charge of allocating disk storage space and will download some programs into the user's workstation microcomputer. A microcomputer development system is a combination of the hardware necessary for microprocessor design and software to control the hardware. The basic components of the hardware are a central processor, a terminal, a mass storage device (e.g., hard disk), and usually an in-circuit emulator (ICE).

In a single-user system, the central processor executes the operating system software, handles the input/output (I/O) facilities, executes the development programs (e.g., editor, assembler, linker), and allocates storage space for the programs being executed. In a large multiuser networked system the central processor may be responsible for the I/O facilities and execution of development programs. The terminal provides the interface between the user and the operating system or program under execution. The user enters commands or data via the keyboard, and the program under execution displays data to the user on the screen. Each program (whether system software or user program) is stored in an ordered format on disk. Each separate entry on the disk is called a *file*. The operating system software contains the routines necessary to interface between the user and the mass storage unit. When the user requests a file by a specific *file name*, the operating system finds the program stored on disk by the file name and loads it into main memory. Typical development systems contain *memory management* software that protects a user's files from unauthorized modification by another user. This is accomplished by means of a unique user identification code called *userid*. A user can only access files that have the user's unique code. The equipment listed here makes up a basic development system, but most systems have other devices, such as printers and EPROM programmers, attached. A printer is needed to provide the user with a hard copy record of the program under development.

After the application software has been developed and debugged completely, it needs to be stored permanently in the target hardware. The EPROM (erasable/programmable read-only memory) programmer takes the machine code and programs it into an EPROM. EPROMs are still widely used in typical system development..

Most development systems support one or more in-circuit emulators (ICEs). An ICE is a very useful tool for microprocessor hardware development. To use an ICE, the microprocessor chip is removed from the system under development (called the *target processor*) and the emulator is plugged into the microprocessor socket. Functionally and electrically, the ICE will act identically to the target processor with the exception that the ICE is under the control of development system software. In this manner the development system may exercise the hardware that is being designed and monitor all status information available about the operation of the target processor. Using an ICE, the processor register contents may be displayed on the screen and operation of the hardware observed in a single-stepping mode. In-circuit emulators can find hardware and software bugs quickly that might take many hours to locate using conventional hardware testing methods.

Typical programs provided for microprocessor development are the operating system, editor, assembler, linker, compiler, and debugger. The operating system is responsible for executing the user's commands. The operating system handles I/O functions, memory management, and loading of programs from mass storage into RAM for execution. The editor allows the user to enter the source code (either assembly language or some high-level language) into the development system.

Typical microprocessor development systems use a character-oriented editor, more commonly referred to as a *screen editor,* so called because the text is dynamically displayed on the screen and the display updates automatically any edits made by the user. The screen editor uses the pointer concept to point to characters that need editing. The pointer in a screen editor is called the *cursor*, and special commands allow the user to position the cursor at any location displayed on the screen. When the cursor is positioned, the user may insert characters, delete characters, or simply type over the existing characters.

Complete lines may be added or deleted using special editor commands. By placing the editor in the insert mode, any text typed will be inserted at the cursor position when the cursor is positioned between two existing lines. If the cursor is positioned on a line to be deleted, a single command will remove the entire line from the file. Screen editors implement the editor commands in different fashions. Some editors use dedicated keys to provide some cursor movements. The cursor keys are usually marked with arrows to show the direction of cursor movement. Some popular editors (such as the Hewlett-Packard HP 64XXX) use *soft keys* which are unmarked keys located on the keyboard directly below the bottom of the CRT screen. The mode of the editor decides what functions the keys are to perform. The function of each key is displayed on the screen directly above the appropriate key. The soft key approach is valuable because it allows the editor to reassign a key to a new function when necessary.

The source code generated on the editor is stored as ASCII or text characters and cannot be executed by a microprocessor. Before the code can be executed, it must be converted to a form accessible by the microprocessor. An *assembler* is the program used to translate the assembly language source code generated with an editor into object code (machine code), that can be executed by a microprocessor.

The output file from most development system assemblers is an *object file* usually a relocatable code that may be configured to execute at any address. The function of the linker is to convert the object file to an *absolute file*, which consists of the actual machine code at the correct address for execution. Absolute files thus created are used for debugging and for programming EPROMs.

Debugging a microprocessor-based system may be divided into two categories: software debugging and hardware debugging. Each debugging process is usually carried out separately because software debugging can be carried out on an out-of-circuit emulator without having the final system hardware. The usual software development tools provided with the development system are a single stepper and a breakpoint.

A *single stepper* simply allows the user to execute the program being debugged one instruction at a time. By examining the register and memory contents during each step, the debugger can detect such program faults as incorrect jumps, incorrect addressing, erroneous op-codes, and so on. A *breakpoint* allows the user to execute an entire section of a program being debugged. There are two types of breakpoints: hardware and software. A *hardware breakpoint* uses the hardware to monitor the system address bus and detect when the program is executing the desired breakpoint location. When the breakpoint is detected, the hardware uses the processor control lines to halt the processor for inspection or cause the processor to execute an interrupt to a breakpoint routine. Hardware breakpoints can be used to debug both ROM- and RAM-based programs. Software breakpoint routines may only operate on a system with the program in RAM because the breakpoint instruction must be inserted into the program that is to be executed.

Single-stepper and breakpoint methods complement each other. The user may insert a breakoint at the desired point and let the program execute up to that point. When the program stops at the breakpoint, the user may use a single-stepper to examine the program one instruction at a time. Thus, the user can pinpoint the error in a program.

There are two main hardware-debugging tools: the logic analyzer and the in-circuit emulator. *Logic analyzers* are commonly used to debug hardware faults in a system. The logic analyzer is the digital version of an oscilloscope because it allows the user to view logic levels in the hardware. *In-circuit emulators* can be used to debug and integrate software and hardware. Inexpensive PC-based workstations are used extensively as development systems.

The total development of a microprocessor-based system typically involves three phases: software design, hardware design, and program diagnostic design. A systems programmer will be assigned the task of writing the application software, a logic designer will be assigned the task of designing the hardware, and typically, both designers will be assigned the task of developing diagnostics to test the system. For small systems, one engineer may do all three phases, and on large systems several engineers may be assigned to each phase. Figure 1.1 shows a flowchart for the total development of a system. Notice that software and hardware development may occur in parallel to save time.

The first step in developing the software is to take the system specifications and write a flowchart to accomplish the tasks that will implement the specifications. The assembly language or high-level source code may now be written from the system flowchart. The complete source code is then assembled. The assembler is the object code and a program listing. The object code will be used later by the linker. The program listing may be sent to a disk file for use in debugging, or it may be directed to the printer.

The linker can now take the object code generated by the assembler and create the final absolute code that will be executed on the target system. The emulation phase will take the absolute code and load it into the development system RAM. From here, the program may be debugged using breakpoints or single stepping.

Working from the system specifications, a block diagram of the hardware must be developed. The logic diagram and schematics may now be drawn using the block diagram as a guide, and a prototype may now be constructed and tested for wiring errors. When the prototype has been constructed, it may be debugged for correct operation using standard electronic testing equipment such as oscilloscopes, meters, logic probes, and logic analyzers, all with test programs created for this purpose. After the prototype has been debugged electrically, the development system in-circuit emulator may be used to check it functionally. The ICE will verify the memory map, correct I/O operation, and so on. The next step in system development is to validate the complete system by running operational checks on the prototype with the finalized application software installed. The EPROMs are then programmed with the error-free programs.

1.6   Typical Microprocessor Applications

Microprocessors are extensively used in a wide variety of applications. A simple microprocessor application along with some typical applications are briefly described in the following.

1.6.1   A Simple Microprocessor Application

To put microprocessors into perspective, it is important to explore a simple application. For example, consider the microprocessor-based dedicated controller shown in Figure 1.2. Suppose that it is necessary to maintain the temperature of a furnace to a desired level to maintain the quality of a product. Assume that the designer has decided to control this temperature by adjusting the fuel. This can be accomplished using a microcomputer along with the interfacing components as follows. Temperature is an analog (continuous) signal. It can be measured by a temperature-sensing (measuring) device such as a thermocouple.

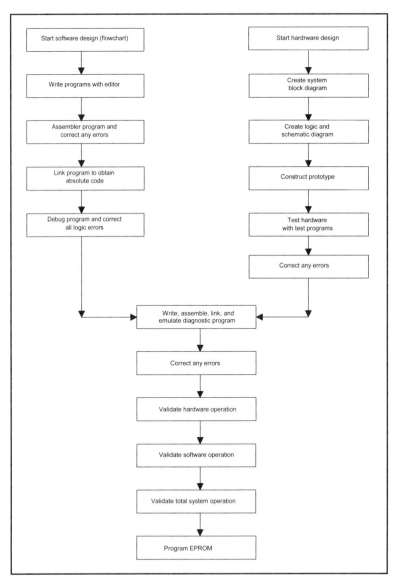

FIGURE 1.1   Microprocessor system development flowchart

The thermocouple provides the measurement in millivolts (mV) equivalent to the temperature. Since microcomputers only understand binary numbers (0's and 1's), each analog mV signal must be converted to a binary number using an analog-to-digital (A/D) converter chip.

First, the millivolt signal is amplified by a mV/V amplifier to make the signal compatible for A/D conversion. A microcomputer can be programmed to solve an equation with the furnace temperature as an input. This equation compares the temperature measured with the temperature desired which can be entered into the microcomputer using the keyboard. The output of this equation will provide the appropriate opening and closing of the fuel valve to maintain the appropriate temperature. Since this output is computed by the microcomputer, it is a binary number. This binary output must be converted into an analog current or voltage signal.

The D/A (digital-to-analog) converter chip inputs this binary number and converts it into an analog current (I). This signal is then input into the current/pneumatic (I/P) transducer for opening or closing the fuel input valve by air pressure to adjust the fuel to the furnace. The furnace temperature desired can thus be achieved. Note that a transducer converts one form of energy (analog electrical current in this case) to another form (air pressure in this example).

1.6.2   Examples of Typical Microprocessor Applications

Microprocessors are used in designing personal workstations. These workstations can provide certain sophisticated functions such as IC layout, 3D graphics, and stress analysis.

In many applications such as control of life-critical systems, control of nuclear waste, and unattended remote system operation, the reliability of the hardware is of utmost importance. The need for such reliable systems resulted in fault-tolerant systems. These systems use redundant microprocessors to provide reliable operation.

Real-time controllers such as flight-control systems for aircraft, flight simulators, and automobile engine control require high-performance microprocessors. For example, the flight simulators use multiple microprocessors to perform graphic manipulation, data gathering, and high-speed communications.

Microprocessors are widely used in robot control systems. In many cases, the microprocessor is used as the brain of the robot. In a typical application, the microprocessor will input the actual arm angle measurement from a sensor, compare it with the desired arm angle, and will then send outputs to a motor to position the arm. Mitsubishi manufactured the first 68020-based robot control system.

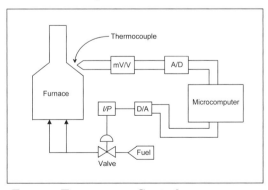

FIGURE 1.2   Furnace Temperature Control

Implementation of the on-chip floating-point unit (FPU) in 32-bit microprocessors such as the Pentium and 68040 makes it appropriate for wide areas of numeric applications:

- Typical FPU's can accept decimal operands and produce extra decimal results of up to several digits. This greatly simplifies accounting programming. Financial calculations that use power functions can take advantage of exponential and logarithmic functions.

- Many minicomputer and mainframe large simulation problems can be executed by the 32-bit microprocessors. These applications include complex electronic circuit simulations using SPICE and simulation of mechanical systems using finite element analysis.

- The FPU's implemented in typical 32-bit microprocessors can move and position machine control heads with accuracy in real time. Axis positioning can efficiently be performed by the hardware trigonometric support provided by the FPU. The 32-bit microprocessors can, therefore, be used for computer numerical control (CNC) machines. CNC machines are extensively used in manufacturing intraocular (cataract implant) lenses.

- The pipelined instruction feature of the 32-bit microprocessor makes it an ideal candidate for DSP (digital signal processing) and related applications for computing matrix multiplications and convolutions.

Embedded Control microprocessors, also called embedded controllers, are designed to manage specific tasks. Once programmed, the embedded controllers can manage the functions of a wide variety of electronic products. Since the microprocessors are embedded in the host system, their presence and operation are basically hidden from the host system. Typical embedded control applications include office automation products such as copiers, laser products, fax machines, and consumer electronics such as VCRs, microwave ovens. Applications such as laser printers require a high performance microprocessor with on-chip floating-point hardware. The RISC microprocessors are ideal for these types of applications. Note that the PC interfaced to the laser printer is the host.

RISC microprocessors such as the PowerPC are well suited for applications such as image processing, robotics, graphics, and instrumentation. The key features of the RISC microprocessors that make them ideal for these applications are their relatively low level of integration in the chip, and instruction pipeline architecture. These characteristics result in low power consumption, fast instruction execution, and fast recognition of interrupts.

Also, note that the Power PC contains an on-chip Real Time Clock (RTC). In the past, the on-chip RTC was common to single chip microcomputers, Power PC is the first top of the line microprocessor to implement the on-chip RTC. This facilitates implementation of multitasking operating systems which require time keeping for task switching as well as keeping the calendar date.

2

MICROCOMPUTER ARCHITECTURE

In this chapter we describe the fundamental material needed to understand the basic characteristics of microprocessors. It includes topics such as typical microcomputer architecture, timing signals and internal microprocessor organization. and status flags. The architectural features are then compared to the Intel Pentium. Finally, an overview of pipelining, superscalar microprocessors, RISC vs. CISC, and the branch prediction feature is included.

2.1   Basic Blocks of a Microcomputer

A microcomputer has three basic blocks: a central processing unit (CPU), a memory unit, and an input/output (I/O) unit. The CPU executes all the instructions and performs arithmetic and logic operations on data. The CPU of the microcomputer is called the *microprocessor* typically a single VLSI (very large scale integration) chip that contains all the registers and control unit, and arithmetic-logic circuits of the microcomputer.

A *memory unit* stores both data and instructions. The memory section typically contains ROM and RAM chips. The ROM can only be read and is nonvolatile; that is, it retains its contents when the power is turned off. A ROM is typically used to store instructions and data that do not change. For example, it might store a table of seven-segment codes for outputting data to a display external to the microcomputer for turning on a digit from 0 through 9.

One can read from and write into a RAM. The RAM is volatile; that is, it does not retain its contents when the power is turned off. A RAM is used to store programs and data that are temporary and might change during the course of executing a program. An *I/O unit* transfers data between the microcomputer and the external devices via I/O ports (registers). The transfer involves data, status, and control signals.

In a single-chip microcomputer, these three elements are on one chip, whereas in a single-chip microprocessor, separate chips are required for memory and I/O. Microcontrollers, which evolved from single-chip microcomputers, are typically used

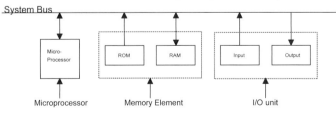

FIGURE 2.1   Basic blocks of a microcomputer.

for dedicated applications such as automotive systems, home appliances, and home entertainment systems. Typical microcontrollers therefore include on-chip timers and A/D (analog-to-digital) and D/A (digital-to-analog) converters. Two popular microcontrollers are Microchip Technology's 8-bit PIC (peripheral interface controller) microcontroller and Motorola's HC11 (8-bit). Figure 2.1 shows the basic blocks of a microcomputer. A system bus (comprised of several wires) connects these blocks.

2.2   Typical Microcomputer Architecture

In this section we describe the microcomputer architecture in more detail. The various microcomputers available today are basically the same in principle. The main variations are in the number of data and address bits and in the types of control signals they use.

To understand the basic principles of microcomputer architecture, it is necessary to investigate a typical microcomputer in detail. Once such a clear understanding is obtained, it will be easier to work with any specific microcomputer. Figure 2.2 illustrates a very simplified version of a typical microcomputer and shows the basic blocks of a microcomputer system. The various buses that connect these blocks are also shown. Although this figure looks very simple, it includes all the main elements of a typical microcomputer system.

2.2.1   System Bus
The microcomputer's system bus contains three buses, which carry all the address, data, and control information involved in program execution. These buses connect the microprocessor (CPU) to each of the ROM, RAM, and I/O chips so that information transfer between the microprocessor and any of the other elements can take place. In a microcomputer, typical information transfers are carried out with respect to the memory or I/O. When a memory or an I/O chip receives data from the microprocessor, it is called a *WRITE operation*, and data is written into a selected memory location or an I/O port (register). When a memory or an I/O chip sends data to the microprocessor, it is called a *READ operation*, and data is read from a selected memory location or an I/O port.

In the *address bus*, information transfer takes place in only one direction, from the microprocessor to the memory or I/O elements. This is therefore called a *unidirectional bus*. This bus is typically 20 to 32 bits long. The size of the address bus determines the total number of memory addresses available in which programs can be executed by the microprocessor. The address bus is specified by the total number of address pins on the microprocessor chip. This also determines the direct addressing capability or the size of the main memory of the microprocessor. The microprocessor can only execute programs

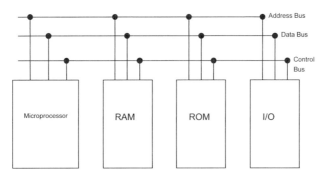

FIGURE 2.2   Simplified version of a typical microcomputer.

located in the main memory. For example, a microprocessor with 32 address pins can generate 2^{32} = 4,294,964,296 bytes [4 gigabytes(GB)] of different possible addresses (combinations of 1's and 0's) on the address bus. The microprocessor includes addresses from 0 to 4,294,964,295 (00000000_{16} through $FFFFFFFF_{16}$). A memory location can be represented by each of these addresses. For example, an 8-bit data item can be stored at address 00000200_{16}.

When a microprocessor such as the Pentium wants to transfer information between itself and a certain memory location, it generates the 32-bit address from an internal register on its 32 address pins, A_0–A_{31}, which then appears on the address bus. These 32 address bits are decoded to determine the desired memory location. The decoding process normally requires hardware (decoders) not shown in Figure 2.2.

In the *data bus*, data can flow in both directions, that is, to or from the microprocessor. This is therefore a bidirectional bus. The size of the data bus varies from one microprocessor to another. The Pentium contains a 64-bit data bus whereas the 68020 provides a 32-bit data bus.

The *control bus* consists of a number of signals that are used to synchronize operation of the individual microcomputer elements. The microprocessor sends some of these control signals to the other elements to indicate the type of operation being performed. Each microprocessor has a unique set of control signals. However, some control signals are common to most microprocessors. We describe some of these control signals later in this section.

2.2.2   Clock Signals

The system clock signals are contained in the control bus. These signals generate the appropriate clock periods during which instruction executions are carried out by the microprocessor. The clock signals vary from one microprocessor to another. Some microprocessors have an internal clock generator circuit to generate a clock signal. These microprocessors require an external crystal or an RC network to be connected at the appropriate microprocessor pins for setting the operating frequency. For example, the Intel 80186 (16-bit microprocessor) does not require an external clock generator circuit. However, most microprocessors do not have the internal clock generator circuit and require an external chip or circuit to generate the clock signal. Figure 2.3 shows a typical clock signal.

The number of cycles per second (hertz, abbreviated Hz) is referred to as the *clock frequency*. This number is defined as "Hertz" (abbreviated as Hz). The clock frequency of contemporary microprocessors is more than 2 GHz (2×10^9Hz). The clock defines the speed of the microprocessor. Note that, a clock cycle = $1/f$, where f is the clock frequency.

| One Clock
Cycle |

FIGURE 2.3   **Typical clock signal.**

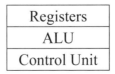

FIGURE 2.4   **Microprocessor chip with the main functional elements.**

The execution times of microprocessor instructions are provided in terms of the number of clock cycles. For example, the instruction for adding data in two registers inside the Pentium takes three clock cycles. This means that for a Pentium with a 100-MHz clock, the instruction ADD reg,reg will be executed in 30 ns [clock cycle = $1/(100 \times 10^6)$ = 10 ns]. On the other hand, for a 200-MHz Pentium, the instruction ADD reg,reg will be executed in 15 ns. This implies that the higher the clock frequency, the faster the microprocessor can execute the instructions.

2.3   Single-Chip Microprocessor

As mentioned earlier, the microprocessor is the CPU of the microcomputer. Therefore, the power of the microcomputer is determined by the capabilities of the microprocessor. Its clock frequency determines the speed of the microcomputer. The number of data and address pins on the microprocessor chip make up the microcomputer's word size and maximum memory size. The microcomputer's I/O and interfacing capabilities are determined by the control pins on the microprocessor chip.

The logic inside the microprocessor chip can be divided into three main areas: the register section, the control unit, and the arithmetic-logic unit (ALU). A microprocessor chip with these three sections is shown in Figure 2.4.

2.3.1   Register Section

The number, size, and types of registers vary from one microprocessor to another. However, the various registers in all microprocessors carry out similar operations. The register structures of microprocessors play a major role in designing microprocessor architectures. Also, the register structures for a specific microprocessor determine how convenient and easy it is to program the microprocessor. We first describe the most basic types of microprocessor registers, their functions, and how they are used. We then consider other common types of registers.

Basic Microprocessor Registers   There are four basic microprocessor registers: instruction register, program counter, memory address register, and accumulator.

- *Instruction register* (IR). The instruction register stores instructions. The contents of an instruction register are always decoded by the microprocessor as an instruction. After fetching an instruction code from memory, the microprocessor stores it in the instruction register. The instruction is decoded internally by the microprocessor, which then performs the operation required. The word size of the microprocessor determines the size of the instruction register. For example, a 32-bit microprocessor has a 32-bit instruction register.

- *Program Counter* (PC). The program counter contains the address of the instruction or operation code (op-code). The program counter normally contains the address of the next instruction to be executed. Note the following features of the program counter:

  1. Upon activating the microprocessor's RESET input, the address of the first instruction to be executed is loaded into the program counter.
  2. To execute an instruction, the microprocessor typically places the contents of the program counter on the address bus and reads ("fetches") the contents of this address (i.e., instruction) from memory. The program counter contents are incremented automatically by the microprocessor's internal logic. The microprocessor thus

executes a program sequentially, unless the program contains an instruction such as a JUMP instruction, which changes the sequence.

3. The size of the program counter is determined by the size of the address bus.

4. Many instructions, such as JUMP and conditional JUMP, change the contents of the program counter from its normal sequential address value. The program counter is loaded with the address specified in these instructions.

- *Memory Address Register* (MAR). The memory address register contains the address of data. The microprocessor uses the address, which is stored in the memory address register, as a direct pointer to memory. The contents of the address is the actual data that is being transferred.

- *General Purpose Register* (GPR). For an 8-bit microprocessor, the general-purpose register is called the *accumulator*. This is typically an 8-bit register. It stores the result after most ALU operations. These 8-bit microprocessors have instructions to shift or rotate the accumulator one bit to the right or left through the carry flag. The accumulator is typically used for inputting a byte into the accumulator from an external device or for outputting a byte to an external device from the accumulator. In 16- and 32-bit microprocessors the accumulator is replaced by a GPR. Typical 32-bit microprocessors such as the Pentium contain several GPRs. In these microprocessors, any GPR can be used as an accumulator.

Depending on the register section, the microprocessor can be classified either as an accumulator- or general-purpose register-based machine. In an accumulator-based microprocessor such as the Intel 8085 and Motorola 6809, the data is assumed to be held in a register called the accumulator. All arithmetic and logic operations are performed using this register as one of the data sources. The result of the operation is stored in the accumulator. Eight-bit microprocessors are usually accumulator based.

The general-purpose register-based microprocessor is usually popular with 16- and 32-bit microprocessors such as the Intel Pentium and the Motorola 68000/68020. The term *general-purpose* comes from the fact that these registers can hold data, memory addresses, or the results of arithmetic or logic operations. The number, size, and types of registers vary from one microprocessor to another.

Most registers are general-purpose, but some, such as the program counter (PC), are provided for dedicated functions. The PC normally contains the address of the next instruction to be executed. As mentioned before, upon activating the microprocessor chip's RESET input pin, the PC is normally initialized with the address of the first instruction. For example, the Pentium, upon hardware reset, reads the first instruction from the 32-bit hex address FFFFFFF0. To execute the instruction, the microprocessor normally places the PC contents on the address bus and reads (fetches) the first instruction from external memory. The program counter contents are then incremented automatically by the ALU. As mentioned earlier, the size of the PC varies from one microprocessor to another depending on the address size. For example, the 68000 has a 24-bit PC, whereas both the 68020 and the Pentium contain a 32-bit PC.

Other Microprocessor Registers   In the following we describe other microprocessor registers such as general-purpose registers, index register, status register and stack pointer register.

General-Purpose Register   Both 16-, and 32-bit microprocessors are register-oriented. They have a number of general-purpose registers for storing temporary data or for carrying out data transfers between various registers. The use of general-purpose registers speeds up the execution of a program because the microprocessor does not have to read data from external memory via the data bus if data is stored in one of its general-purpose registers. These registers are typically 16 to 32 bits. The number of general-purpose registers will vary from one microprocessor to another. Some of the typical functions performed by instructions associated with the general-purpose registers are given here. We will use [REG] to indicate the contents of the general-purpose register and [M] to indicate the contents of a memory location.

1.   Move [REG] to or from memory: [M] ← [REG] or [REG] ← [M].
2.   Move the contents of one register to another: [REG1] ← [REG2].
3.   Increment or decrement [REG] by 1: [REG] ← [REG] + 1 or [REG] ← [REG] - 1.
4.   Load 16-bit data into a register [REG] : [REG] ← 16-bit data.

Index Register   An *index register* is typically used as a counter in address modification for an instruction or for general storage functions. The index register is particularly useful with instructions that access tables or arrays of data. In this operation the index register is used to modify the address portion of the instruction. Thus, the appropriate data in a table can be accessed. This is called *indexed addressing*. This addressing mode is normally available to the programmers of microprocessors. The effective address for an instruction using the indexed addressing mode is determined by adding the address portion of the instruction to the contents of the index register. Index registers are typically 16 or 32 bits long. In a typical 16- or 32-bit microprocessor, general-purpose registers can be used as index registers.

Status Register   A *status register,* also known as a *processor status word register* or *condition code register*, contains individual bits, with each bit having special significance. The bits in the status register are called *flags*. The status of a specific microprocessor operation is indicated by each flag, which is set or reset by the microprocessor's internal logic to indicate the status of certain microprocessor operations such as arithmetic and logic operations. The status flags are also used in conditional JUMP instructions. We describe some of the common flags in the following.

A *carry flag* is used to reflect whether or not the result generated by an arithmetic operation is greater than the microprocessor's word size. As an example, the addition of two 32-bit numbers might produce a carry. The carry is generated out of the 32nd bit position, which results in setting the carry flag. However, the carry flag will be zero if no carry is generated from the addition. As mentioned before, in multibyte arithmetic, any carry out of the low-byte addition must be added to the high-byte addition to obtain the correct result. This can illustrated by the following 16-bit addition example:

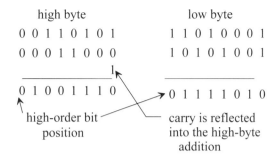

While performing BCD arithmetic with microprocessors, the carry out of the low nibble (4 bits) has a special significance. Because a BCD digit is represented by 4 bits, any carry out of the low 4 bits must be propagated into the high 4 bits for BCD arithmetic. This carry flag is known as an *auxiliary carry flag* and is set to 1 if the carry out of the low 4 bits is 1; otherwise, it is 0.

A *zero flag* is used to show whether the result of an operation is zero. It is set to 1 if the result is zero, and it is reset to 0 if the result is nonzero. A *parity flag* is set to 1 to indicate whether the result of the last operation contains either an even number of 1's (even parity) or an odd number of 1's (odd parity), depending on the microprocessor. The type of parity flag used (even or odd) is determined by the microprocessor's internal structure and is not selectable. A sign flag (sometimes called a negative flag) is used to indicate whether the result of the last operation is positive or negative. If the most significant bit of the last operation is 1, this flag is set to 1 to indicate that the result is negative. This flag is reset to 0 if the most significant bit of the result is zero: that is, if the result is positive.

As mentioned earlier, an *overflow flag* arises from representation of the sign flag by the most significant bit of a word in signed binary operation. The overflow flag is set to 1 if the result of an arithmetic operation is too big for the microprocessor's maximum word size, otherwise it is reset to 0. Let C_f be the final carry out of the most significant bit (sign bit) and C_p be the previous carry. It was shown in section 1.2.1 that the overflow flag is the exclusive- OR of the carries C_p and C_f.

$$\text{overflow} = C_p \oplus C_f$$

Stack Pointer Register   A *stack* consists of a number of RAM locations set aside for reading data from or writing data into these locations and is typically used by subroutines (a *subroutine* is a program that performs operations frequently needed by the main or calling program). The address of the stack is contained in a register called a *stack pointer*. Two instructions, PUSH and POP, are usually available with a stack. The *PUSH operation* is defined as writing to the top or bottom of the stack, whereas the *POP operation* means reading from the top or bottom of the stack. Some microprocessors access the stack from the top; others access via the bottom. When the stack is accessed from the bottom, the stack pointer is incremented after a PUSH and decremented after a POP operation. On the other hand, when the stack is accessed from the top, the stack pointer is decremented after a PUSH and incremented after a POP. Microprocessors typically use 16- or 32-bit registers for performing PUSH or POP operations. The incrementing or decrementing of a stack pointer depends on whether the operation is PUSH or POP and on whether the stack is accessed from the top or the bottom.

We now illustrate stack operations in more detail. We use 16-bit registers and 16-

bit addresses in Figures 2.5 through 2.8. All data (hex) are chosen arbitrarily. In Figure 2.5, the stack pointer is incremented by 2 (16-bit register) after the PUSH to contain the value 20CA. Now, consider the POP operation of Figure 2.6. The stack pointer is decremented by 2 after the POP. The contents of address 20CA are assumed to be empty conceptually after the POP operation. Next, consider the PUSH operation of Figure 2.7. The stack is accessed from the top. The stack pointer is decremented by 2 after a PUSH. Finally, consider the POP operation of Figure 2.8. The Stack pointer is incremented by 2 after the POP. The contents of address 20C6 are assumed to be empty conceptually after a POP operation.

Note that the stack is a LIFO (last in first out) memory. As mentioned earlier, a stack is   typically used during subroutine CALLs. The microprocessor automatically PUSHes the return address onto a stack after executing a subroutine CALL instruction in the main program. After executing a RETURN from a subroutine instruction (placed by the programmer as the last instruction of the subroutine), the microprocessor automatically POPs the return address from the stack (previously PUSHed) and then returns to the main program.

2.3.2   Control Unit

The main purpose of the control unit is to read and decode instructions from the program memory. To execute an instruction, the control unit steps through the appropriate blocks of the ALU based on the op-codes contained in the instruction register. The op-codes define the operations to be performed by the control unit to execute an instruction. The control unit interprets the contents of the instruction register and then responds to the instruction by generating a sequence of enable signals. These signals activate the appropriate ALU logic blocks to perform the required operation.

The control unit generates the *control signals*, which are output to the other microcomputer elements via the control bus. The control unit also takes appropriate actions in response to the control signals on the control bus provided by the other microcomputer elements. The control signals vary from one microprocessor to another. For each specific microprocessor, these signals are described in detail in the manufacturer's manual. It is impossible to describe all the control signals for various manufacturers. However, we cover some of the common ones in the following discussion.

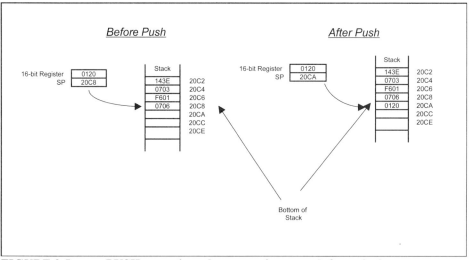

FIGURE 2.5   PUSH operation when accessing a stack from the bottom.

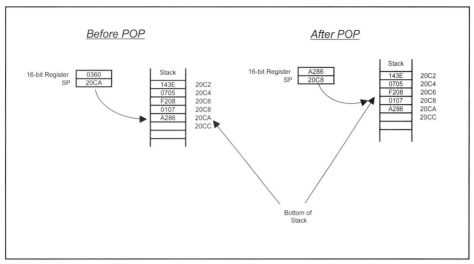

FIGURE 2.6   POP operation when accessing a stack from the bottom.

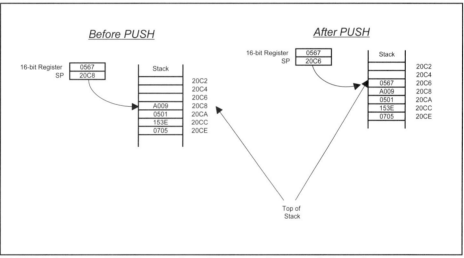

FIGURE 2.7   PUSH operation when accessing a stack from the top.

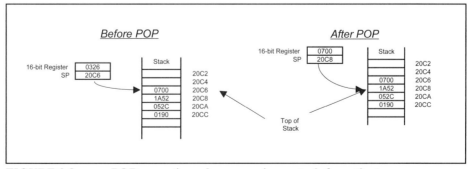

FIGURE 2.8   POP operation when accessing a stack from the top.

RESET.   This input is common to all microprocessors. When this input pin is driven HIGH or LOW (depending on the microprocessor), the program counter is loaded with a predefined address specified by the manufacturer. As mentioned before, in the Pentium, upon hardware reset, the program counter is loaded with $FFFFFFF0_{16}$. This means that the instruction stored at memory location $FFFFFFF0_{16}$ is executed first. In some other microprocessors, such as the Motorola 68000, the program counter is not loaded directly by activating the RESET input. In this case the program counter is loaded indirectly from two locations (such as 000004 and 000006) predefined by the manufacturer. This means that these two locations contain the address of the first instruction to be executed.

READ/WRITE ($R/\overline{W}$).   This output line is common to all microprocessors. The status of this line tells the other microcomputer elements whether the microprocessor is performing a READ or a WRITE operation. A HIGH signal on this line indicates a READ operation, and a LOW indicates a WRITE operation. Some microprocessors have separate READ and WRITE pins.

$\overline{READY}$,   This is an input to a microprocessor. Slow devices (memory and I/O) use this signal to gain extra time to transfer data to or receive data from a microprocessor. The $\overline{READY}$ signal is usually an active low signal; that is, LOW indicates that the microprocessor is ready. Therefore, when the microprocessor selects a slow device, the device places a LOW on the $\overline{READY}$ pin. The microprocessor responds by suspending all its internal operations and enters a WAIT state. When the device is ready to send or receive data, it removes the $\overline{READY}$ signal. The microprocessor comes out of the WAIT state and performs the appropriate operation.

Interrupt Request (INT or IRQ).   The external I/O devices can interrupt the microprocessor via this input pin on the microprocessor chip. When this signal is activated by the external devices, the microprocessor jumps to a special program called the *interrupt service routine*. This program is normally written by the user for performing tasks that the interrupting device wants the microprocessor to carry out. After completing this program, the microprocessor returns to the main program it was executing when the interrupt occurred.

2.3.3   Arithmetic-Logic Unit

The ALU performs all the data manipulations, such as arithmetic and logic operations, inside a microprocessor. The size of the ALU conforms to the word length of the microcomputer. This means that a 32-bit microprocessor will have a 32-bit ALU. Some of the typical functions performed by the ALU are:

1. Binary addition and logic operations
2. Finding the one's complement of data
3. Shifting or rotating the contents of a general-purpose register 1 bit to the left or right through a carry

2.3.4   Functional Representations of Simple and Typical Microprocessors

Figure 2.9(a) shows the functional block diagram of a simple microprocessor. Note that the data bus shown is internal to the microprocessor chip and should not be confused with the system bus. The system bus is external to the microprocessor and is used to connect all the necessary chips to form a microcomputer. The buffer register in Figure 2.9(a) stores

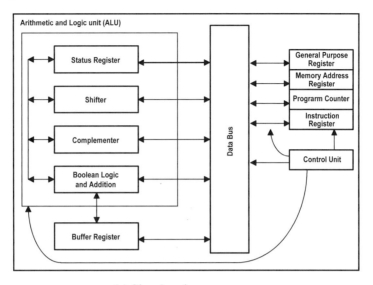

(a) Simple microprocessor

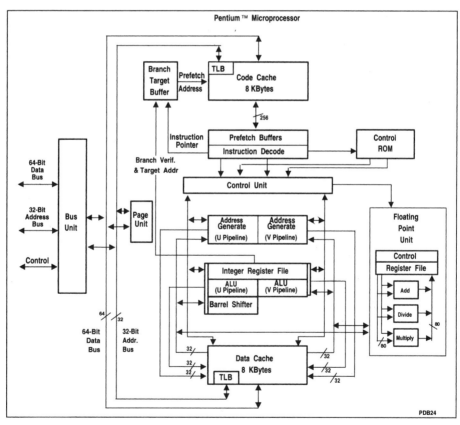

(b) Pentium Microprocessor

FIGURE 2.9   Microprocessor block diagrams.

any data read from memory for further processing by the ALU. All other blocks of Figure 2.9(a) have been discussed earlier. Note that the functional block diagram of a typical commercially available microprocessor such as the Pentium (discussed later) is more complex than the one shown in Figure 2.9(a). The simple microprocessor, although not practical, is presented here for illustrative purposes.

Figure 2.9(b) shows the block diagram of a realistic microprocessor, the Intel Pentium.

The figure shows that the Pentium contains two instruction pipelines: the U-pipe and the V-pipe. The U-pipe can execute all integer and floating-point instructions. The V-pipe can execute simple integer instructions and the FXCH floating-point instruction.

The instruction decode unit translates the prefetched instructions for the Pentium to execute the instruction. The control ROM contains a microprogrammed ROM that controls the sequence of operations that must be performed to implement the Pentium microprocessor architecture. The control ROM unit has direct control over both pipelines.

The Pentium contains two separate cache memories: code cache and data cache. The code cache, branch target buffer, and prefetch buffers are used to read instructions into the execution units of the Pentium. Instructions are fetched from the code cache or from the external bus. Branch addresses are stored in the branch target buffer. The integer register file contains all the Pentium's general-purpose registers, and the floating-point register file contains all the floating-point registers. The Pentium contains a barrel shifter for fast shift operation. The bus unit provides Pentium's 64-bit data bus, 32-bit address bus, and the control signals. This facilitates interfacing the Pentium to external memory and I/O chips.

2.3.5   Simplified Explanation of Control Unit design

The main purpose of the control unit is to translate or decode instructions and generate appropriate enable signals to accomplish the desired operation. Based on the contents of the instruction register, the control unit sends the data items selected to the appropriate processing hardware at the right time. The control unit drives the associated processing hardware by generating a set of signals that are synchronized with a master clock.

The control unit performs two basic operations: instruction interpretation and instruction sequencing. In the interpretation phase, the control unit reads (fetches) an instruction from the memory addressed by the contents of the program counter into the instruction register. The control unit inputs the contents of the instruction register. It recognizes the instruction type, obtains the necessary operands, and routes them to the appropriate functional units of the execution unit (registers and ALU). The control unit then issues the necessary signals to the execution unit to perform the desired operation and routes the results to the destination specified. In the sequencing phase, the control unit generates the address of the next instruction to be executed and loads it into the program counter.

There are two methods for designing a control unit: hardwired control and microprogrammed control. In the hardwired approach, synchronous sequential circuit design procedures are used in designing the control unit. Note that a control unit is a clocked sequential circuit. The name *hardwired control* evolved from the fact that the final circuit is built by physically connecting components such as gates and flip-flops. In the microprogrammed approach, on the other hand, all control functions are stored in a ROM inside the control unit. This memory is called the *control memory*. The words in this memory, called *control words*, specify the control functions to be performed by the control unit. The control words are fetched from the control memory and the bits are routed to appropriate functional units to enable various gates. An instruction is thus executed.

Design of control units using microprogramming (sometimes called *firmware* to distinguish it from hardwired control) is more expensive than using hardwired controls. To execute an instruction, the contents of the control memory in microprogrammed control must be read, which reduces the overall speed of the control unit. The most important advantage of microprogramming is its flexibility; alterations can be made simply by changing the microprogram in the control memory. A small change in the hardwired approach may lead to redesigning the entire system.

For simplicity, we illustrate the concepts of microprogramming using Figure 2.9(a). Let us consider incrementing the contents of the register by 1. This is basically an addition operation. The control unit will send an enable signal to execute the ALU adder logic. Incrementing the contents of a register consists of transferring the register contents to the ALU adder and then returning the result to the register. The complete incrementing process is accomplished via the five steps shown in Figures 2.10 through Figure 2.14. In all five steps, the control unit initiates execution of each microinstruction. Figure 2.10 shows the transfer of the register contents to the data bus. Figure 2.11 shows the transfer of the contents of the data bus to the adder in the ALU in order to add 1 to it. Figure 2.12 shows the activation of the adder logic. Figure 2.13 shows the transfer of the result from the adder to the data bus. Finally, Figure 2.14 shows the transfer of the data bus contents to the register.

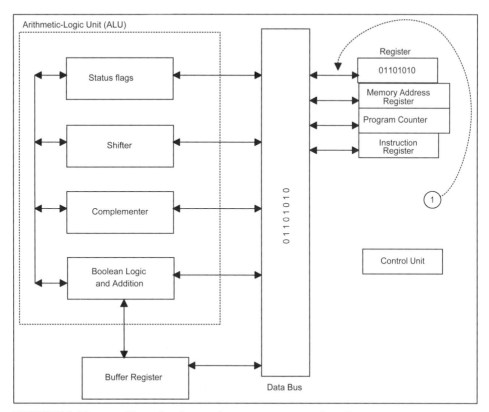

FIGURE 2.10   **Transferring register contents to a data bus.**

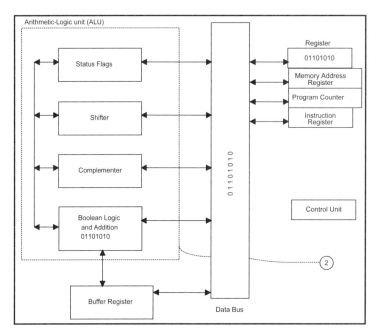

FIGURE 2.11　　**Transferring data bus contents to an ALU.**

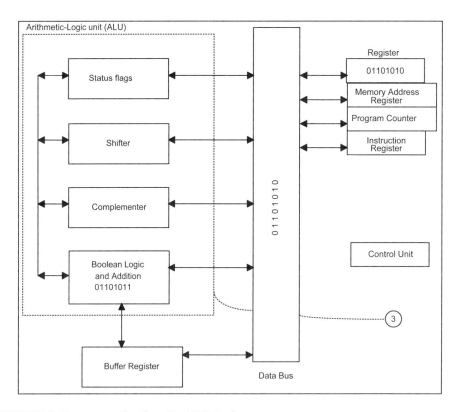

FIGURE 2.12　　**Activating the ALU logic.**

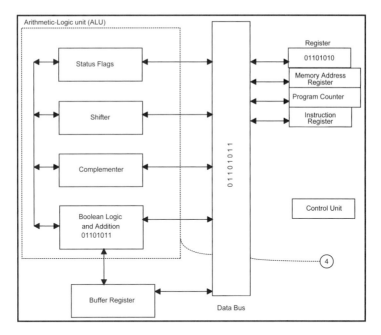

FIGURE 2.13   Transferring an ALU result to a data bus.

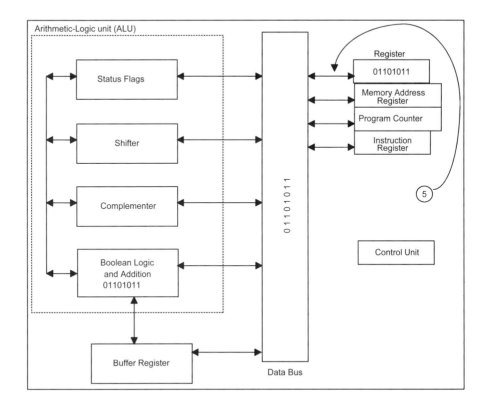

FIGURE 2.14   Transferring a data bus.

Microprogramming is typically used by a microprocessor designer to program the logic performed by the control unit. On the other hand, assembly language programming is a popular programming language used by a microprocessor user for programming a microprocessor to perform a desired function. A microprogram is stored in the control unit. An assembly language program is stored in the main memory. The assembly language program is called a *macroprogram*. A macroinstruction (or simply, an instruction) initiates execution of a complete microprogram.

2.4   Program Execution by Conventional Microprocessors

Conventional microprocessors include typical 8-bit microprocessors such as Intel 8085 and 16-bit microprocessors such as Motorola 68000. To execute a program, a conventional microprocessor repeats the following three steps for completing each instruction.

1. *Fetch*. The microprocessor fetches (instruction read) the instruction from the main memory (external to the microprocessor) into the instruction register.

2. *Decode*. The microprocessor decodes or translates the instruction using the control unit. The control unit inputs the contents of the instruction register, and then decodes (translates) the instruction to determine the instruction type.

3. *Execute*. The microprocessor executes the instruction using the control unit.   To accomplish the task, the control unit generates a number of enable signals required by the instruction.

For example, suppose that it is desired to add the contents of two registers, X and Y, and store the result in register Z. To accomplish this, a conventional microprocessor performs the following steps:

1. The microprocessor fetches the instruction into the instruction register.

2. The control unit (CU) decodes the contents of the instruction register.

3. The CU executes the instruction by generating enable signals for the register and ALU sections to perform the following:

a. The CU transfers the contents of registers X and Y from the Register section into the ALU.

b. The CU commands the ALU to ADD.

c. The CU transfers the result from the ALU into register Z of the register section.

2.5   Program Execution by typical 32-bit Microprocessors

As mentioned in Chapter 1, designers of 32-bit microprocessors such as the Pentium have implemented many powerful features of the mainframe computers in the same chip as the microprocessor. This enhances the capabilities of the 32-bit microprocessors. The on-chip hardware implemented in the 32-bit microprocessors include cache memory, memory management, pipelining, floating-point arithmetic, and branch prediction.

Cache memory is a high-speed read/wrte memory implemented as on-chip hardware in typical 32-bit microprocessors in order to increase processing rates. This topic is covered in more detail in Chapter 3.

Memory management allows programmers to write programs much larger than those that could fit in the main memory space available to the microprocessors; the programs are simply stored on a secondary device, such as a hard disk, and portions of the program are swapped into main memory as needed. This topic is covered in more detail in Chapter 3.

Other on-chip features such as pipelining, floating-point arithmetic, and branch prediction are discussed in the following.

2.5.1   Pipelining

As mentioned earlier, a conventional microprocessor such as the 68000 executes a program by completing one instruction at a time and then proceeds to the next. This means that the control unit would have to wait until the instruction is fetched from memory. Also, the ALU would have to wait until the required data are obtained. Since the speeds of 32-bit microprocessors are increasing at a more rapid rate than memory speeds, the control unit and ALU will be idle while the conventional microprocessor fetches each instruction and obtains the required data.

32-Bit microprocessors utilize the control unit and ALU efficiently by prefetching the next instruction(s) and the required data before the control unit and ALU require them. As mentioned earlier, conventional microprocessors such as the 68000 execute programs in sequence; 32-bit microprocessors such as the Pentium, on the other hand, implement the feature called pipelining to prefetch the next instruction while the control unit is busy decoding the current instruction. Hence, 32-bit microprocessors implement pipelining to increase system throughput. Pipelining was first implemented in Motorola's 68020. This was followed by Intel's pipelined implementation of the 80486. A brief overview of pipelining is provided in this section.

Basic Concepts   Assume that a task T is carried out by performing four activities: Al, A2, A3, and A4, in that order. Hardware Hi is designed to perform activity Ai. Hi is referred to as a segment, and it essentially contains combinational circuit elements. Consider the arrangement shown in Figure 2.15. In this configuration, a latch is placed between two segments so the result computed by one segment can serve as input to the following segment during the next clock period.

The execution of four tasks Tl, T2, T3, and T4 using the hardware of Figure 2.15 is described using the space-time chart shown in Figure 2.16.
Initially, task Tl is handled by segment 1. After the first clock, segment 2 is busy with Tl while segment 1 is busy with T2. Continuing in this manner, task Tl is completed at the end

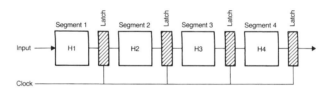

FIGURE 2.15   Four-segment pipeline.

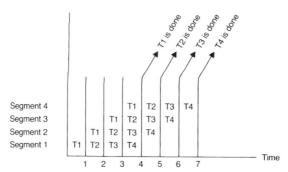

FIGURE 2.16   Overlapped execution of four tasks using a pipeline.

of the fourth clock. However, following this point, one task is shipped out per clock. This is the essence of the pipelining concept. A pipeline gains efficiency for the same reason as an assembly line does: Several activities are performed but not on the same material.

In 32-bit microprocessors, the pipeline concept is typically used for carrying out two tasks: arithmetic operations and instruction execution.

Arithmetic Pipelines   The pipeline concept is widely used in designing floating-point arithmetic units. Consider the process of adding two floating-point numbers $x = 0.9234 * 10^4$ and $y = 0.48 * 10^2$. First, notice that the exponents of x and y are unequal. Therefore, the smaller number should be modified so that its exponent is equal to the exponent of the greater number. For this example, modify y to $0.0048 * 10^4$. This modification step is known as *exponent alignment*. Here the decimal point of the significand 0.48 is shifted to the right to obtain the desired result. After exponent alignment, the significands 0.9234 and 0.0048 are added to obtain the final solution of $0.9282 * 10^4$.

As a second example, consider the operation $x - y$, where $x = 0.9234 * 10^4$ and $y = 0.9230 * 10^4$. In this case, no exponent alignment is necessary because the exponent of a equals the exponent of y. Therefore, the significand of y is subtracted from the significand of x to obtain $0.9234 - 0.9230 = 0.0004$. However, $0.0004 * 10^4$ cannot be the final answer because the significand, 0.0004, is not normalized. A floating-point number with base b is said to be normalized if the magnitude of its significand satisfies the following inequality: $\frac{1}{b} \leq |significand| < 1$.

In this example, since $b = 10$, a normalized floating-point number must satisfy the condition:

$$0.1 \leq |significand| < 1$$

(Note that normalized floating-point numbers are always considered because for each real-world number there exists one and only one floating-point representation. This uniqueness property allows processors to make correct decisions while performing compare operations).

The final answer is modified to $0.4 * 10^1$. In this modification step known as postnormalization, the significand is shifted to the left here to obtain the correct result.

In summary, addition or subtraction of two floating-point numbers calls for four activities:

1. Exponent comparison
2. Exponent alignment
3. Significand addition or subtraction
4. Postnormalization

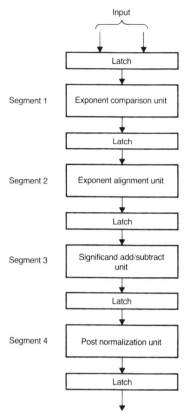

FIGURE 2.17   Pipelined floating-point add/subtract unit.

Based on this result, a four-segment floating-point adder/subtracter pipeline can be built, as shown in Figure 2.17. It is important to realize that each segment in this pipeline is composed primarily of combinational components such as multiplexers. The shifter used in this system is a barrel shifter. Note that a barrel shifter is a fast shift register that shifts data in one direction. 32-Bit microprocessors such as the Motorola 68040 (on-chip floating-point hardware) include a three-stage floating-point pipeline consisting of operand (data) conversion, execute, and result normalization.

Instruction Pipelines   32-Bit microprocessors such as the Motorola 68020 contain a three-stage instruction pipeline. Note that an instruction cycle typically involves the following activities:

1. Instruction fetch
2. Instruction decode
3. Operand fetch (Data Read)
4. Operation execution
5. Result routing.

This process can be carried out effectively by using the pipeline shown in Figure 2.18. As mentioned earlier, in such a pipelined scheme the first instruction requires five clocks to complete its execution. However, the remaining instructions are completed at a rate

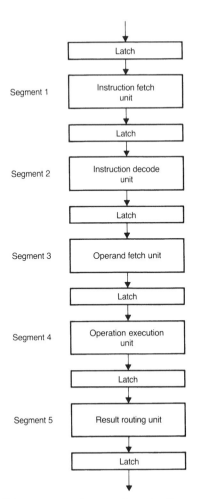

FIGURE 2.18   **Five-segment instruction pipeline.**

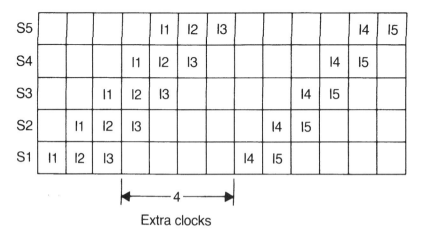

FIGURE 2.19   **Pipelined execution of a stream of five instructions that includes a branch instruction.**

of one per pipeline clock. Such a situation prevails as long as all the segments are busy.

In practice, the presence of branch instructions and conflicts in memory accesses poses a great problem to the efficient operation of an instruction pipeline. For example, consider the execution of a stream of five instructions: I1, I2, I3, I4, and I5, in which I3 is a conditional branch instruction. This stream is processed by the instruction pipeline (Figure 2.18) as depicted in Figure 2.19. When a conditional branch instruction is fetched, the next instruction cannot be fetched because the exact target is not known until the conditional branch instruction has been executed. The next fetch can occur once the branch is resolved. Four additional clocks are required, due to I3.

In 32-bit microprocessors, branch instructions are handled using a strategy called *target prefetch*. When a conditional branch instruction is recognized, the immediate successor of the branch instructions and the target of the branch are prefetched. The latter is saved in a register called a buffer until the branch is executed. If the branch condition is successful, one pipeline is still busy because the branch target is in the buffer.

Another approach to handling branch instructions is use of the delayed branch concept. In this case, the branch does not take place until after the following instruction. To illustrate this, consider the following assembly language instruction sequence (chosen arbitrarily):

Memory Address	Instruction		Comment
2000	LDA	X	; Load register A with contents of memory address X
2001	INC	Y	; Increment the contents of memory address Y by 1
2002	JMP	2050	; Jump to address 2050
2003	SUB	Z	; Subtract the contents of address Z from the contents
			; of register A, and store the result in A
	.		
	.		
	.		
2050	STA	W	; Store the contents of register A in memory address W

TABLE 2.1   Modified Sequence

Memory Address	Instruction	
2000	LDA	X
2001	INC	Y
2002	JMP	2051
2003	NOP	
2004	SUB	Z
-	-	
-	-	
2051	STA	W

TABLE 2.2   Pipelined Execution of a Hypothetical Instruction Sequence

Instruction Fetch	LDA X	INC Y	JMP 2051	NOP	STA W
Instruction Execute		LDA X	INC Y	JMP 2051	NOP

TABLE 2.3   Instruction Sequence with the Branch Instruction Reversed

Memory Address	Instruction	
2000	LDA	X
2001	JMP	2050
2002	INC	Y
2003	SUB	Z
-	-	
-	-	
2050	STA	W

TABLE 2.4   Execution of a Reversed Instruction Sequence

Instruction Fetch	LDA X	JMP 2050	INC Y	STA W
Instruction Execute		LDA X	JMP 2050	INC Y

Suppose that there is a NOP (no operation) instruction and that the branch instruction is changed to JMP 2051. The program semantics remain unchanged. This is shown in Table 2.1. This modified sequence will be executed by a two-segment pipeline, as shown in Table 2.2: instruction fetch and instruction execute. Because of the delayed branch concept, the pipeline still functions correctly without damage.

The efficiency of this pipeline can be improved further if the assembler produces a new sequence, as shown in Table 2.3. In this case, the assembler has reversed the instruction sequence. The JMP instruction is placed in location 2001, and the INC instruction is moved to memory location 2002. This reversed sequence is executed by the same two-segment pipeline, as shown in Table 2.4.

It is important to understand that due to the delayed branch rule, the INC Y instruction is fetched before execution of the JMP 2050 instruction; therefore, there is no change in the order of instruction execution. This implies that the program will still produce the same result. Since the NOP instruction was eliminated, the program is executed more efficiently. The concept of delayed branch is one of the key characteristics of RISC as it makes concurrency visible to a programmer.

2.5.2   Branch Prediction Feature

Typical 32-bit microprocessors implement a multiple-branch prediction feature. This allows these microprocessors to anticipate jumps of the instruction flow ahead of time. Also, some 32-bit microprocessors determine an optimal sequence of instruction execution by looking at decoded instructions and then determining whether to execute or hold the instructions. Typical 32-bit microprocessors use a "look ahead" approach to execute instructions. These 32-bit microprocessors maintain an instruction pool for a sequence of instructions and perform a useful task rather than executing the present instruction and then going on to the next.

The branch prediction feature of the Pentium speeds up execution of program loops. To accomplish this, the Pentium includes on-chip hardware called the *Branch Unit* (BU). The BU contains the branch execution unit (BEU) and the branch prediction unit (BPU). Whenever the Pentium encounters a conditional branch instruction, it sends it to the BU for execution. The BU evaluates the instruction's branch condition using the BEU and determines whether the branch should or should not be taken. Once the BU determines the branch condition, it calculates the starting address (Branch target) of the next block of code to be executed. The Pentium then starts fetching code at the new address.

The Pentium uses a technique called *speculative execution* using the BPU. Using this feature, the Pentium makes an educated guess at the Branch target before the branch's condition is actually evaluated. Instructions that are executed speculatively cannot write their results back to the registers until the branch condition is evaluated. If the BPU predicts the branch correctly, the results from the speculative instructions can be written just like regular instructions. If the Pentium predicts the branch target address incorrectly, it must flush the pipeline of the erroneous speculative instructions and associated results. After the pipeline flush, the Pentium obtains the correct Branch target address so that it can start executing the code at the correct position in the program.

2.6   Scalar and Superscalar Microprocessors

Scalar processors such as the 80486 can execute one instruction per cycle. The 80486 contains only one pipeline. Superscalar microprocessors, on the other hand, can execute more than one instruction per cycle. These microprocessors contain more than one pipeline. The Pentium, a superscalar microprocessor, contains two independent pipelines. This allows the Pentium to execute two instructions per cycle.

2.7   RISC vs. CISC

There are two types of microprocessor architectures: RISC and CISC. A RISC microprocessor such as the PowerPC emphasizes simplicity and efficiency. RISC designs start with a necessary and sufficient instruction set. The purpose of using RISC architecture is to maximize speed by reducing clock cycles per instruction. Almost all computations can be obtained from a few simple operations. The goal of RISC architecture is to maximize the effective speed of a design by performing infrequent operations in software and frequent functions in hardware, thus obtaining a net performance gain. The following list summarizes the typical features of a RISC microprocessor:

1. The RISC microprocessor is designed using hardwired control with little or no microcode. Note that variable-length instruction formats generally require microcode design. All RISC instructions have fixed formats, so microcode design is not necessary.
2. A RISC microprocessor executes most instructions in a single cycle.
3. The instruction set of a RISC microprocessor typically includes only register, load, and store instructions. All instructions involving arithmetic operations use registers, and load and store operations are utilized to access memory.
4. The instructions have a simple fixed format with few addressing modes.
5. A RISC microprocessor has several general-purpose registers.
6. A RISC microprocessor processes several instructions simultaneously and thus includes pipelining.

7. Software can take advantage of more concurrency. For example, jumps occur after execution of the instruction that follows. This allows fetching of the next instruction during execution of the current instruction.

RISC microprocessors are suitable for embedded applications. *Embedded microprocessors* or *controllers* are embedded in the host system. This means that the presence and operation of these controllers are basically hidden from the host system. Typical embedded control applications include office automation systems such as laser printers. Since a laser printer requires a high-performance microprocessor with on-chip floating-point hardware, RISC microprocessors such as PowerPC are ideal for these types of applications.

RISC microprocessors are well suited for applications such as image processing, robotics, graphics, and instrumentation. The key features of the RISC microprocessors that make them ideal for these applications are their relatively low level of integration in the chip and instruction pipeline architecture. These characteristics result in low power consumption, fast instruction execution, and fast recognition of interrupts. Typical 32- and 64-bit RISC microprocessors include PowerPC microprocessors.

CISC microprocessors, on the other hand, contain a large number of instructions and many addressing modes, while RISC microprocessors include a simple instruction set with a few addressing modes. Almost all computations can be obtained from a few simple operations. RISC basically supports a small set of commonly used instructions that are executed at a fast clock rate compared to CISC, which contains a large instruction set (some of which are rarely used) executed at a slower clock rate. To implement the fetch/execute cycle for supporting a large instruction set for CISC, the clock is typically slower.

In CISC, most instructions can access memory while RISC contains mostly load/store instructions. The complex instruction set of CISC requires a complex control unit, thus requiring microprogrammed implementation. RISC utilizes hardwired control which is faster. CISC is more difficult to pipeline; RISC provides more efficient pipelining. An advantage of CISC over RISC is that complex programs require fewer instructions in CISC with fewer fetch cycles, while RISC requires a large number of instructions to accomplish the same task with several fetch cycles. However, RISC can significantly improve its performance with a faster clock, more efficient pipelining, and compiler optimization.

PowerPC and Intel 80XXX utilize RISC and CISC architectures, respectively. Intel's original Pentium is a CISC microprocessor. Intel Pentium Pro and other succeeding members of the Pentium family and Motorola 68060 use a combination of RISC and CISC architectures for providing high performance. The Pentium Pro and other succeeding members of the Pentium family use RISC (hardwired control) to implement efficient pipelining for simple instructions. CISC (microprogrammed control) for complex instructions is utilized by the Pentium to provide upward compatibility with the Intel 8086/80X86 family.

Questions and Problems

2.1 What is the difference between a microprocessor and a single-chip micro-computer?

2.2 What is a microcontroller? Name one commercially available microcontroller.

2.3 What is the difference between:
   (a) A program counter and the memory address register?
   (b) An accumulator and an instruction register?
   (c) A general-purpose register-based microprocessor and an accumulator-based microprocessor. Name a commercially available microprocessor of each type.

2.4 Assuming signed numbers, find the sign, carry, zero, and overflow flags of:
   (a) $09_{16} + 17_{16}$
   (b) $A5_{16} - A5_{16}$
   (c) $71_{16} - A9_{16}$
   (d) $6E_{16} + 3A_{16}$
   (e) $7E_{16} + 7E_{16}$

2.5 What are PUSH and POP operations in the stack?

2.6 Suppose that a 16-bit microprocessor has a 16-bit stack pointer and uses a 16-bit register to access the stack from the top. Assume that initially the stack pointer and the 16-bit register contain $20C0_{16}$ and 0205_{16} respectively. After the PUSH operation:
   (a) What are the contents of the stack pointer?
   (b) What are the contents of memory locations $20BE_{16}$ and $20BF_{16}$?

2.7 Assuming the microprocessor architecture of Figure 2.9(a), write down a possible sequence of microinstructions for finding the one's complement of an 8-bit number. Assume that the number is already in the register.

2.8 What is pipelining?

2.9 Summarize the branch prediction feature of the Pentium.

2.10 What is the basic difference between program execution by a conventional microprocessor and a 32-bit microprocessor.

2.11 What is the difference between Scalar and Superscalar microprocessors? Name one example of each.

2.12 Discuss the basic features of RISC and CISC in terms of the Pentium Pro.

3

MICROPROCESSOR
MEMORY ORGANIZATION

In this chapter we describe concepts associated with memory organization in typical microprocessors. Topics include main memory array design, memory management, and cache memory concepts.

3.1   Introduction

A memory unit is an integral part of any microcomputer, and its primary purpose is to hold instructions and data. The major design goal of a memory unit is to allow it to operate at a speed close to that of a microprocessor. However, the cost of a memory unit is so prohibitive that it is practically not feasible to design a large memory unit with one technology that guarantees high speed. Therefore, to seek a trade-off between the cost and the operating speed, a memory system is usually designed with different technologies, such as solid state, magnetic, and optical. In a broad sense, a microcomputer memory system can be divided into three groups:
1. Microprocessor memory
2. Primary or main memory
3. Secondary memory

Microprocessor memory comprises to a set of microprocessor registers. These registers are used to hold temporary results when a computation is in progress. Also, there is no speed disparity between these registers and the microprocessor because they are fabricated using the same technology. However, the cost involved in this approach limits a microcomputer architect to include only a few registers in the microprocessor.

Main memory is the storage area in which all programs are executed. The microprocessor can directly access only those items that are stored in main memory. Therefore, all programs must be within the main memory prior to execution. CMOS technology is normally used in main memory design. The size of the main memory is usually much larger than processor memory, and its operating speed is slower than that of processor registers. Main memory normally includes ROMs and RAMs.

Electromechanical memory devices such as hard disks are used extensively as microcomputer's *secondary memory* and allow storage of large programs at low cost. The storage capacity of a typical hard disk ranges from 5 MB to several gigabytes. The rotational speed of the hard disk is typically 3600 rpm. These secondary memory devices access stored data serially. Hence, they are significantly slower than main memory. Hard disk is a popular secondary memory device. Programs are stored on disks in files. Secondary memory stores programs in excess of the main memory. Secondary memory is also referred

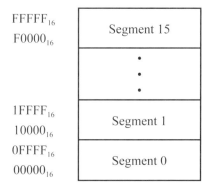

FIGURE 3.1   Main memory of the Pentium in the real mode.

to as *auxiliary or virtual memory*. The microcomputer cannot execute programs stored in the secondary memory directly, so to execute these programs the microcomputer must transfer them to its main memory by a program called the *operating system*.

Programs in hard disk memories are stored in tracks. A track is a concentric ring of programs stored on the surface of a disk. Each track is further subdivided into several sectors. Each sector typically stores 512 or 1024 bytes of information. The secondary memory typically uses magnetic media, except for optical memory, which stores programs on a plastic disk. CD (compact disc) memory and DVD (digital video disc) memory are examples of popular optical memory used with microcomputer systems. CD memory uses an infrared laser whereas DVD memory uses a red laser. Since a red laser has a shorter wavelength than an infrared laser, DVD memory provides a larger storage capacity than CD memory. Typical optical memories include CD-ROM, CD-RW, DVD-ROM, and DVD-RAM.

3.2   Main memory

The main or external memory (or simply, the memory) stores both instructions and data. For 8-bit microprocessors, the memory is divided into a number of 8-bit units called *memory words*. An 8-bit unit of data is termed a *byte*. Therefore, for an 8-bit microprocessor, *memory word* and *memory byte* mean the same thing. For 16-bit microprocessors, a word contains 2 bytes (16 bits). A memory word is identified in the memory by an address. For example, the Pentium microprocessor uses 32-bit addresses for accessing memory words. This provides a maximum of $2^{32} = 4,294,964,296 = 4$ GB of memory addresses, ranging from 00000000_{16} to $FFFFFFFF_{16}$ in hexadecimal.

An important characteristic of a memory is whether it is volatile or nonvolatile. The contents of a volatile memory are lost if the power is turned off. On the other hand, a nonvolatile memory retains its contents after power is switched off. ROM is a typical example of nonvolatile memory. RAM is a volatile memory unless backed up by batteries.

Some microprocessors, such as the Intel Pentium, divide the memory into segments. For example, Pentium in the real mode divides the 1-MB main memory into 16 segments (0 through 15). Each segment contains 64 kB of memory and is addressed by 16 bits. Figure 3.1 shows a typical main memory layout of the Pentium in real mode. In the figure, the high 4 bits of an address specify the segment number. As an example, consider address 10005_{16} of segment 1. The high 4 bits, 0001, of this address define the location

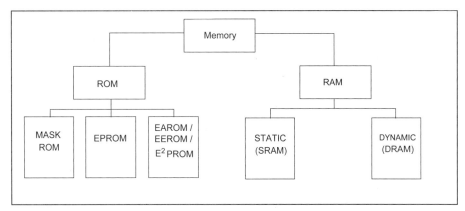

FIGURE 3.2   **Summary of available semiconductor memories for microprocessor systems.**

as in segment 1, and the low 16 bits, 0005_{16}, specify the particular address in segment 1. The 68000, on the other hand, uses linear or nonsegmented memory. For example, the 68000 uses 24 address pins to address $2^{24} = 16$ MB of memory directly with addresses from 000000_{16} to $FFFFFF_{16}$.

As mentioned before, memories can be categorized into two main types: read-only memory (ROM) and random-access memory (RAM). As shown in Figure 3.2, ROMs and RAMs are then divided into a number of subcategories, which are discussed next.

3.2.1   Read-Only Memory

ROMs can only be read, so is nonvolatile memory. CMOS technology is used to fabricate ROMs. ROMs are divided into two common types: mask ROM and erasable PROM (EPROM), such as 2732 and EAROM (electrically alterable ROM) [also called EEPROM or E^2PROM (electrically erasable PROM)] such as the 2864.

Mask ROMs are programmed by a masking operation performed on a chip during the manufacturing process. The contents of mask ROMs are permanent and cannot be changed by the user. EPROMs can be programmed, and their contents can also be altered by using special equipment, called an *EPROM programmer*. When designing a microcomputer for a particular application, permanent programs are stored in ROMs. Control memories used to microprogram the control unit are ROMs.

EPROMs can be reprogrammed and erased. The chip must be removed from the microcomputer system for programming. This memory is erased by exposing the chip to ultraviolet light via a lid or window on the chip. Typical erase times vary between 10 and 20 min. The EPROM can be programmed by inserting the chip into a socket of the EPROM programmer and providing proper addresses and voltage pulses at the appropriate pins of the chip.

EAROMs can be programmed without removing the memory from the ROM's sockets. These memories are also called *read-mostly memories* (RMMs), because they have much slower write times than read times. Therefore, these memories are usually suited for operations when mostly reading rather that writing will be performed. Another type of memory, called *Flash memory* (nonvolatile), invented in the mid-1980s by Toshiba, is designed using a combination of EPROM and E^2PROM technologies. Flash memory can be reprogrammed electrically while embedded on the board. One can change multiple bytes at a time. An example of flash memory is the Intel 28F020 (256K x 8-bit). Flash memory is typically used in cellular phones and digital cameras.

3.2.2   Random-Access Memory

There are two types of RAM: static RAM (SRAM), and dynamic RAM (DRAM). *Static RAM* stores data in flip-flops. Therefore, this memory does not need to be refreshed. RAMs are volatile unless backed up by battery. *Dynamic RAM* stores data in capacitors. That is, it can hold data for a few milliseconds. Hence, dynamic RAMs are refreshed typically by using external refresh circuitry. Dynamic RAMs (DRAMs) are used in applications requiring large memory. DRAMs have higher densities than static RAMs (SRAMs). Typical examples of DRAMs are the 4464 (64K × 4-bit), 44256 (256K × 4-bit), and 41000 (1M × 1-bit). DRAMs are inexpensive, occupy less space, and dissipate less power than SRAMs. Two enhanced versions of DRAM are EDO DRAM (extended data output DRAM) and SDRAM (synchronous DRAM).

The EDO DRAM provides fast access by allowing the DRAM controller to output the next address at the same time the current data is being read. An SDRAM contains multiple DRAMs (typically, four) internally. SDRAMs utilize the multiplexed addressing of conventional DRAMs. That is, like DRAMs, SDRAMs provide row and column addresses in two steps. However, the control signals and address inputs are sampled by the SDRAM at the leading edge of a common clock signal (133 MHz maximum). SDRAMs provide higher densities than conventional DRAMs by further reducing the need for support circuitry and faster speeds. The SDRAM has been used in PCs (personal computers).

3.2.3   READ and WRITE Timing Diagrams

To execute an instruction, the microprocessor reads or fetches the op-code via the data bus from a memory location in the ROM/RAM external to the microprocessor. It then places the op-code (instruction) in the instruction register. Finally, the microprocessor executes the instruction. Therefore, the execution of an instruction consists of two portions, instruction fetch and instruction execution. We consider the instruction fetch, memory READ, and memory WRITE timing diagrams in the following using a single clock signal. Figure 3.3 shows a typical instruction fetch timing diagram.

In Figure 3.3, to fetch an instruction, when the clock signal goes to HIGH, the microprocessor places the contents of the program counter on the address bus via address

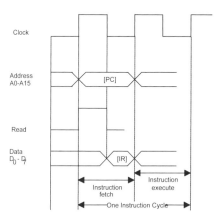

FIGURE 3.3   **Typical instruction fetch timing diagram for an 8-bit microprocessor.**

pins A_0–A_{15} on the chip. Note that since each of lines A_0–A_{15} can be either HIGH or LOW, both transitions are shown for the address in Figure 3.3. The instruction fetch is basically a memory READ operation. Therefore, the microprocessor raises the signal on the READ pin to HIGH. As soon as the clock goes to LOW, the logic external to the microprocessor gets the contents of the memory location addressed by A_0–A_{15} and places them on the data bus D_0–D_7. The microprocessor then takes the data and stores it in the instruction register so that it gets interpreted as an instruction. This is called *instruction fetch*. The microprocessor performs this sequence of operations for every instruction.

We now describe the READ and WRITE timing diagrams. A typical READ timing diagram is shown in Figure 3.4. Memory READ is basically loading the contents of a memory location of the main ROM/RAM into an internal register of the microprocessor. The address of the location is provided by the contents of the memory address register (MAR). Let us now explain the READ timing diagram of Figure 3.4.

1.   The microprocessor performs the instruction fetch cycle as before to READ the op-code.

2.   The microprocessor interprets the op-code as a memory READ operation.

3.   When the clock pin signal goes HIGH, the microprocessor places the contents of the memory address register on the address pins A_0–A_{15} of the chip.

4.   At the same time, the microprocessor raises the READ pin signal to HIGH.

5.   The logic external to the microprocessor gets the contents of the location in the main ROM/RAM addressed by the memory address register and places it on the data bus.

6.   Finally, the microprocessor gets this data from the data bus via pins D_0 – D_7 and stores it in an internal register.

Memory WRITE is basically storing the contents of an internal register of the microprocessor into a memory location of the main RAM. The contents of the memory address register provide the address of the location where data is to be stored. Figure 3.5 shows a typical WRITE timing diagram.

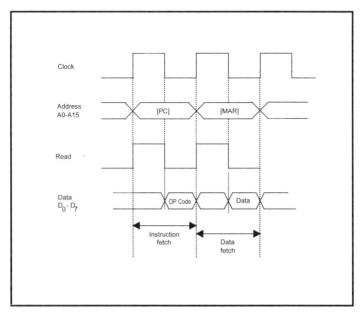

FIGURE 3.4   **Typical memory READ timing diagram.**

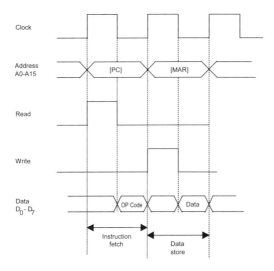

FIGURE 3.5   Typical memory WRITE timing diagram.

The microprocessor fetches the instruction code as before.

The microprocessor interprets the instruction code as a memory WRITE instruction and then proceeds to perform the DATA STORE cycle.

When the clock pin signal goes HIGH, the microprocessor places the contents of the memory address register on the address pins A_0–A_{15} of the chip.

At the same time, the microprocessor raises the WRITE pin signal to HIGH.

The microprocessor places data to be stored from the contents of an internal register onto data pins D_0–D_7.

The logic external to the microprocessor stores the data from the register into a RAM location addressed by the memory address register.

3.2.4   Main Memory Organization

As mentioned earlier, microcomputer main memory typically consists of ROMs/EPROMs and RAMs. Because RAMs can be both read from and written into, the logic required to implement RAMs is more complex than ROMs/EPROMs. A microcomputer system designer is normally interested in how the microcomputer memory is organized or, in other words, how to connect the ROMS/EPROMs and RAMs and then determine the memory map of the microcomputer. That is, the designer would be interested in finding out what memory locations are assigned to the ROMs/ EPROMs and RAMs. The designer can then implement the permanent programs in ROMs/ EPROMs and the temporary programs in RAMs. Note that RAMs are needed when subroutines and interrupts requiring a stack are desired in an application.

As mentioned before, DRAMs (dynamic RAMs) use MOS capacitors to store information and need to be refreshed. DRAMs are less inexpensive than SRAMs, provide larger bit densities and consume less power. DRAMs arc typically used when memory requirements are 16K words or larger. DRAM is addressed via row and column addressing. For example, 1-Mb (one megabit) DRAM requiring 20 address bits is addressed using 10 address lines and two control lines,$\overline{RAS}$ (row address strobe) and $\overline{CAS}$ (column address strobe). To provide a 20-bit address into the DRAM, a LOW is applied to $\overline{RAS}$ and 10 bits of the address are latched. The other 10 bits of the address are applied next and $\overline{CAS}$ is then held LOW.

The addressing capability of the DRAM can be increased by a factor of 4 by adding one more bit to the address line. This is because one additional address bit results into one additional row bit and one additional column bit. This is why DRAMs can be expanded to larger memory very rapidly with the inclusion of additional address bits. External logic is required to generate the $\overline{RAS}$ and $\overline{CAS}$ signals and to output the current address bits to the DRAM.

DRAM controller chips take care of the refreshing and timing requirements needed by DRAMs. DRAMs typically require a 4-ms refresh time. The DRAM controller performs its task independent of the microprocessor. The DRAM controller chip sends a wait signal to the microprocessor if the microprocessor tries to access memory during a refresh cycle.

Because of the large memory, the address lines should be buffered using the 74LS244 or 74HC244 (a unidirectional buffer), and data lines should be buffered using the 74LS245 or 74HC245 (a bidirectional buffer) to increase the drive capability. Also, typical multiplexers such as 74LS157 or 74HC157 can be used to multiplex the microprocessors address lines into separate row and column addresses.

3.2.5 Main Memory Array Design

We noticed earlier that the main memory of a microcomputer is fabricated using solid-state technology. In a typical microcomputer application, a designer has to implement the required capacity by interconnecting several memory chips. This concept is known as *memory array design*. We address this topic in this section and show how to interface a memory system with a typical microprocessor.

Now let us discuss how to design ROM/RAM arrays. In particular, our discussion is focused on the design of memory arrays for a hypothetical microcomputer. The pertinent signals of a typical microprocessor necessary for main memory interfacing are shown in Figure 3.6. There are 16 address lines, A_{15}-A_0, with A_0 being the least significant bit. This means that this microprocessor can address directly a maximum of 2_{16} = 65,536 or 64K bytes of memory locations.

The control line $M/\overline{IO}$ goes LOW if the microprocessor executes an I/O instruction; it is held HIGH if the microprocessor executes a memory instruction. Similarly, the microprocessor drives control line $R/\overline{W}$ HIGH for READ operation; it is held LOW for WRITE operation. Note that all 16 address lines and the two control lines ($M/\overline{IO}$, $R/\overline{W}$) described so far

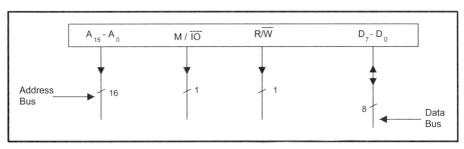

FIGURE 3.6 **Pertinent signals of a typical microprocessor required for main memory interfacing.**

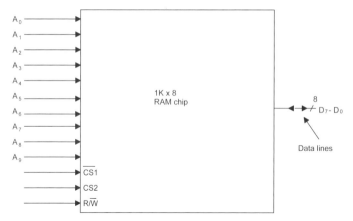

FIGURE 3.7   Typical 1K × 8 SRAM chip.

are unidirectional in nature; that is, information can always travel on these lines from the processor to external units. Eight bidirectional data lines, D_7-D_0 (with D_0 being the least significant bit) are also shown in Figure 3.6. These lines are used to allow data transfer from the processor to external units, and vice versa.

In a typical application, the total amount of main memory connected to a microprocessor consists of a combination of ROMs and RAMs. However, in the following we illustrate for simplicity how to design memory array using only SRAM chips.

The pin diagram of a typical 1K × 8 RAM chip is shown in Figure 3.7. In this chip there are 10 address lines , A_9-A_0, so one can read or write 1024 (2_{10} = 1024) different memory words. Also, in this chip there are eight bidirectional data lines, D_7-D_0 so that information can travel back and forth between the microprocessor and the memory unit. The three control lines $\overline{CS1}$, CS2, and R/$\overline{W}$ are used to control the SRAM unit according to the truth table shown in Table 3.1 from which it can be concluded that the RAM unit is enabled only when $\overline{CS1}$ = 0 and CS2 = 1. Under this condition, R/$\overline{W}$ = 0 and R/$\overline{W}$ = 1 imply write and read operations, respectively.

To connect a microprocessor to ROM/RAM chips, two address-decoding techniques are commonly used: linear decoding and full decoding. Let us discuss first how to interconnect a microprocessor with a 4K SRAM chip array comprised of the four 1K SRAM chips of Figure 3.7 using the linear decoding technique. Figure 3.8 uses linear decoding to accomplish this. In this approach, address lines A_9-A_0 of the microprocessor are connected to all SRAM chips. Similarly, the control lines M/$\overline{IO}$ and R/$\overline{W}$ of the microprocessor are connected to control lines CS2 and R/$\overline{W}$, respectively of each SRAM

TABLE 3.1   Truth Table for Controlling SRAM.

$\overline{CS1}$	CS2	R/$\overline{W}$	Function
0	1	0	Write Operation
0	1	1	Read Operation
1	X	X	The chip is not selected
X	0	X	The chip is not selected

X means Don't Care

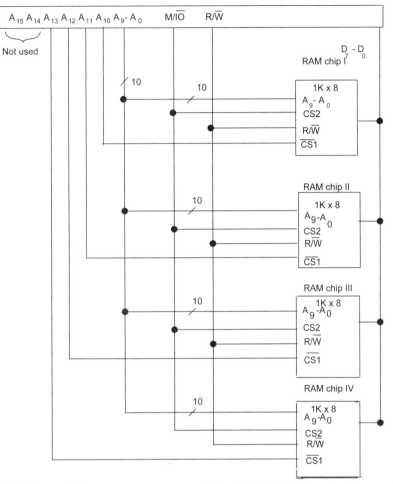

FIGURE 3.8   **Microprocessor connected to 4K SRAM using the linear select decoding technique.**

chip. The high-order address bits A_{10}-A_{13} act directly as chip selects. In particular, address lines A_{10} and A_{11} select SRAM chips I and II, respectively. Similarly, the address lines A_{12} and A_{13} select the SRAM chips III and IV, respectively. A_{15} and A_{14} are don't cares and are assumed to be zero. Table 3.2 describes how the addresses are distributed among the four 1K SRAM chips. The primary advantage this method, known as *linear select decoding*, is that it does not require decoding hardware. However, if two or more of lines A_{10}-A_{13} are low at the same time, more than one SRAM chip are selected, and this causes a bus conflict.

Because of this potential problem, the software must be written such that it never reads into or writes from any address in which more than one of bits A_{13}-A_{10} are low. Another disadvantage of this method is that it wastes a large amount of address space. For example, whenever the address value is B800 or 3800, SRAM chip I is selected. In other words, address 3800 is the mirror reflection of address B800 (this situation is also called *memory foldback*). This technique is therefore limited to a small system. The system of Figure 3.8 can be expanded up to a total capacity of 6K using A_{14} and A_{15} as chip selects for two more 1K SRAM chips.

TABLE 3.2   Address Map of the Memory Organization of Figure 3.8

Address Range (Hex)	SRAM Chip Number
3800-3BFF	I
3400-37FF	II
2C00-2FFF	III
1C00-1FFF	IV

To resolve problems with linear decoding, we use full decoded memory addressing. In this technique we use a decoder. The 4K memory system designed using this technique is shown in Figure 3.9. Note that the decoder in the figure is very similar to a practical decoder such as the 74LS138 with three chip enables. In Figure 3.9 the decoder output selects one of the four 1K SRAM chips, depending on the values of A_{12}, A_{11}, and A_{10} (Table 3.3).

Note that the decoder output will be enabled only when $\overline{E3} = \overline{E2} = 0$ and E1 = 1. Therefore, in the organization of Figure 3.9, when any one of the high-order bits A_{15}, A_{14}, or A_{13} is 1, the decoder will be disabled, and thus none of the SRAM chips will be selected. In this arrangement, the memory addresses are assigned as shown in Table 3.4.

This approach does not waste any address space since the unused decoder outputs (don't cares) can be used for memory expansion. For example, the 3-to-8 decoder of Figure 3.9 can select eight 1K SRAM chips. Also, this method does not generate any bus conflict. This is because the decoder output selected ensures enabling of one memory chip at a time.

Finally, FPGAs can now be used with 32-bit microprocessors such as the Intel Pentium and Motorola 68020 for performing the memory decode function.

3.3   Microprocessor on-chip memory management unit and cache

Typical 32-bit microprocessors such as the Pentium contain on-chip memory management unit hardware and on-chip cache memory. These topics are discussed next.

3.3.1   Memory Management Concepts

Due to the massive amount of information that must be saved in most systems, the mass storage device is often a disk. If each access is to a hard disk, system throughput will be reduced to unacceptable levels. An obvious solution is to use a large and fast locally accessed semiconductor memory. Unfortunately, the storage cost per bit for this solution is very high. A combination of both off-board disk (secondary memory) and on-board

TABLE 3.3 Decoding Guide.

A_{12}	A_{11}	A_{10}	SRAM Chip Number
0	0	0	I
0	0	1	II
0	1	0	III
0	1	1	IV

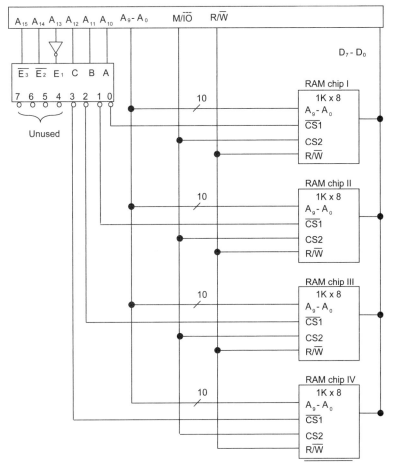

FIGURE 3.9 **Interconnecting a microprocessor with a 4K RAM using full decoded memory addressing.**

semiconductor main memory must be designed into a system. This requires a mechanism to manage the two-way flow of information between the primary (semiconductor) and secondary (disk) media. This mechanism must be able to transfer blocks of data efficiently, keep track of block usage, and replace them in a nonarbitrary way. The main memory system must therefore be able to dynamically allocate memory space.

An operating system must have resource protection from corruption or abuse by users. Users must be able to protect areas of code from each other while maintaining the

TABLE 3.4 **Address Map of the Memory Organization of Figure 3.9.**

Address Range (Hex)	RAM Chip Number
0000-03FF	I
0400-07FF	II
0800-0BFF	III
0C00-0FFF	IV

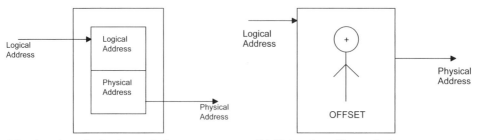

(a) using the substitution technique   (b) Using the offset technique

FIGURE 3.10   Address translation

ability to communicate and share other areas of code. All these requirements indicate the need for a device, located between the microprocessor and memory, to control accesses, perform address mappings, and act as an interface between the logical (programmer's memory) and   physical (microprocessor's directly addressable memory) address spaces. Because this device must manage the memory use configuration, it is appropriately called the *memory management unit* (MMU).

Typical 32-bit processors such as the Motorola 68030/68040 and the Intel Pentium include on-chip MMUs. An MMU reduces the burden of the memory management function of the operating system. The basic functions provided by an MMU are address translation and protection. It translates logical program addresses to physical memory address. Note that in assembly language programming, addresses are referred to by symbolic names. These addresses in a program are called *logical addresses* because they indicate the logical positions of instructions and data. The MMU translates these logical addresses to physical addresses provided by the memory chips. The MMU can perform address translation in one of two ways:

1.   By using the substitution technique [Figure 3.10(a)].
2.   By adding an offset to each logical address to obtain the corresponding physical address [Figure 3.10(b)].

Address translation using the substitution technique is faster than translation using the offset method. However, the offset method has the advantage of mapping a logical address to any physical address as determined by the offset value.

Memory is usually divided into small manageable units. The terms *page* and *segment* are frequently used to describe these units. Paging divides the memory into equal-sized pages; segmentation divides the memory into variable-sized segments. It is relatively easier to implement the address translation table if the logical and main memory spaces are divided into pages.

There are three ways to map logical addresses to physical addresses: paging, segmentation, and combined paging-segmentation. In a *paged system*, a user has access to a larger address space than physical memory provides. The virtual memory system is managed by both hardware and software. The hardware included in the memory management unit handles address translation. The memory management software in the operating system performs all functions, including page replacement policies to provide efficient memory utilization. The memory management software performs functions such as removal of the desired page from main memory to accommodate a new page, transferring a new page from secondary to main memory at the right instant in time, and placing the page at the right location in memory.

If the main memory is full during transfer from secondary to main memory, it is necessary to remove a page from main memory to accommodate the new page. Two popular page replacement policies are first in first out (FIFO) and least recently used (LRU). The FIFO policy removes the page from main memory that has been resident in memory longest. The FIFO replacement policy is easy to implement, but one of its main disadvantages is that heavily used pages are likely to be replaced. Note that heavily used pages are resident in main memory longest. This replacement policy is sometimes a poor choice. For example, in a time-shared system, several users normally share a copy of the text editor in order to type and correct programs. The FIFO policy on such a system might replace a heavily used editor page to make room for a new page. This editor page might be recalled to main memory immediately. FIFO would be a poor choice in this case. The LRU policy, on the other hand, replaces the page that has not been used for the longest amount of time.

In the *segmentation method*, an MMU utilizes the segment selector to obtain a descriptor from a table in memory containing several descriptors. A descriptor contains the physical base address for a segment, the segment's privilege level, and some control bits. When the MMU obtains a logical address from the microprocessor, it first determines whether the segment is already in physical memory. If it is, the MMU adds an offset component to the segment base component of the address obtained from the segment descriptor table to provide the physical address. The MMU then generates the physical address on the address bus for selecting the memory. On the other hand, if the MMU does not find the logical address in physical memory, it interrupts the microprocessor. The microprocessor executes a service routine to bring the desired program from a secondary memory such as disk to the physical memory. The MMU determines the physical address using the segment offset and descriptor as described earlier and then generates the physical address on the address bus for memory. A segment will usually consist of an integral number of pages, each, say, 256 bytes long. With different-sized segments being swapped in and out, areas of valuable primary memory can become unusable. Memory is unusable for segmentation when it is sandwiched between already allocated segments and if it is not large enough to hold the latest segment that needs to be loaded. This is called *external fragmentation* and is handled by MMUs using special techniques. An example of external fragmentation is shown in Figure 3.11. The advantages of segmented memory management are that few descriptors are required for large programs or data spaces and that internal fragmentation (discussed later) is minimized. The disadvantages include external fragmentation, the need for involved algorithms for placing data, possible restrictions on the starting address, and the need for longer data swap times to support virtual memory.

Address translation using descriptor tables offers a protection feature. A segment or a page can be protected from access by a program section of a lower privilege level. For example, the selector component of each logical address includes 1 or 2 bits indicating the

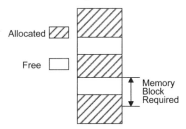

FIGURE 3.11 **Memory fragmentation (external).**

privilege level of the program requesting access to a segment. Each segment descriptor also includes 1 or 2 bits providing the privilege level of that segment. When an executing program tries to access a segment, the MMU can compare the selector privilege level with the descriptor privilege level. If the segment selector has the same or a higher privilege level, the MMU permits access. If the privilege level of the selector is lower than that of the descriptor, the MMU can interrupt the microprocessor, informing it of a privilege-level violation. Therefore, the indirect technique of generating a physical address provides a mechanism for protecting critical program sections in the operating system. Because paging divides the memory into equal-sized pages, it avoids the major problem of segmentation: external fragmentation. Because the pages are of the same size, when a new page is requested and an old one swapped out, the new one will always fit into the space vacated. However, a problem common to both techniques remains: internal fragmentation. Internal fragmentation is a condition where memory is unused but allocated due to memory block size implementation restrictions. This occurs when a module needs, say, 300 bytes and the page is 1 kB, as shown in Figure 3.12.

In the *paged-segmentation* method, each segment contains a number of pages. The logical address is divided into three components: segment, page, and word. The segment component defines a segment number, the page component defines the page within the segment, and the word component provides the particular word within the page. A page component of n bits can provide up to 2^n pages. A segment can be assigned with one or more pages up to maximum of 2^n pages; therefore, a segment size depends on the number of pages assigned to it.

A protection mechanism can be assigned to either a physical address or a logical address. Physical memory protection can be accomplished by using one or more protection bits with each block to define the access type permitted on the block. This means that each time a page is transferred from one block to another, the block protection bits must be updated. A more efficient approach is to provide a protection feature in logical address space by including protection bits in descriptors of the segment table in the MMU.

Virtual memory is the most fundamental concept implemented by a system that performs memory-management functions such as space allocation, program relocation, code sharing, and protection.The key idea behind this concept is to allow a user program to address more locations than those available in a physical memory. An address generated by a user program is called a *virtual address*. The set of virtual addresses constitutes the virtual address space. Similarly, the main memory of a microcomputer contains a fixed number of addressable locations, and a set of these locations forms the physical address space. The basic hardware for virtual memory is implemented in 32-bit microprocessors as an on-chip feature. These 32-bit processors support both cache and virtual memories. The

PAGES ≡ 1 K
IF 300 BYTES NEEDED, 1 K B is ALLOCATED

MEMORY UNUSED BUT ALLOCATED BECAUSE OF   1 K
IMPLEMENTATION RESTRICTIONS ON BLOCK SIZES   PAGE

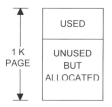

FIGURE 3.12   **Memory fragmentation (internal).**

virtual addresses are typically converted to physical addresses and then applied to cache.

3.3.2   Cache Memory Organization

The performance of a microprocessor system can be improved significantly by introducing a small, expensive, but fast memory between the microprocessor and main memory. The idea for *cache memory* was introduced in the IBM 360/85 computer. Later, the concept was implemented in minicomputers such as the PDP-11/70. With the advent of very large scale integration (VLSI) technology, the cache memory technique has been gaining acceptance in the microprocessor world. Studies have shown that typical programs spend most of their execution time in loops. This means that the addresses generated by a microprocessor have a tendency to cluster around a small region in the main memory, a phenomenon known as *locality of reference*. Typical 32-bit microprocessors can execute the same instructions in a loop from the on-chip cache rather than reading them repeatedly from the external main memory. Thus, the performance is greatly improved. For example, an on-chip cache memory is implemented in Intel's 32-bit microprocessor, the 80486/Pentium, and Motorola's 32-bit microprocessor, the 68030/68040. The 80386 does not have an on-chip cache, but external cache memory can be interfaced to it.

A block diagram representation of a microprocessor system that employs a cache memory is shown in Figure 3.13. Usually, a cache memory is very small in size and its access time is less than that of the main memory by a factor of 5. Typically, the access times of the cache and main memories are 100 and 500 ns, respectively. If a reference is found in the cache, we call it a *cache hit*, and the information pertaining to the microprocessor reference is transferred to the microprocessor from the cache. However, if the reference is not found in the cache, we call it a *cache miss*.

When there is a cache miss, the main memory is accessed by the microprocessor and the instructions and/or data are transferred to the microprocessor from the main memory. At the same time, a block containing the information needed by the microprocessor is transferred from the main memory to cache. The block normally contains 4 to 16 words, and this block is placed in the cache using standard replacement policies such as FIFO or LRU. This block transfer is done with the hope that all future references made by the microprocessor will be confined to the fast cache.

The relationship between the cache and main memory blocks is established using mapping techniques. Three widely used mapping techniques are direct mapping, fully associative mapping, and set-associative mapping. To explain these three mapping techniques, the memory organization of Figure 3.14 will be used. The main memory is capable of storing 4K words of 16 bits each. The cache memory, on the other hand, can store 256 words of 16 bits each. An identical copy of every word stored in cache exists in main memory. The microprocessor first accesses the cache. If there is a hit, the microprocessor accepts the 16-bit word from the cache. In case of a miss, the microprocessor reads the desired 16-bit word from the main memory, and this 16-bit word is then written to the cache. A cache memory may contain instructions only (Instruction cache) or data only (data cache) or both instructions and data (unified cache).

Direct mapping uses a RAM for the cache. The microprocessor's 12-bit address is divided into two fields, an index field and a tag field. Because the cache address is 8 bits wide ($2^8 = 256$), the low-order 8 bits of the microprocessor's address form the index field, and the remaining 4 bits constitute the tag field. This is illustrated in Figure 3.15.

In general, if the main memory address field is m bits wide and the cache memory address is n bits wide, the index field will then require n bits and the tag field will be $(m - n)$

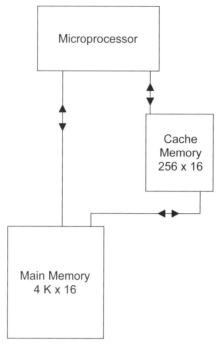

FIGURE 3.13   Memory organization of a microprocessor system that employs a cache memory.

bits wide. The *n*-bit address will access the cache. Each word in the cache will include the data word and its associated tag. When the microprocessor generates an address for main memory, the index field is used as the address to access the cache. The tag field of the main memory is compared with the tag field in the word read from cache. A hit occurs if the tags match. This means that the data word desired is in cache. A miss occurs if there is no match, and the required word is read from main memory. It is written in the cache along with the tag. One of the main drawbacks of direct mapping is that numerous misses may occur if two or more words with addresses that have the same index but different tags are accessed several times. This situation should be avoided or can be minimized by having such words far apart in the address lines.

Let us illustrate the concept of direct mapping for a data cache by means of the

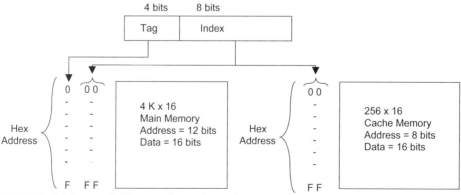

FIGURE 3.14   Addresses for main and cache memory.

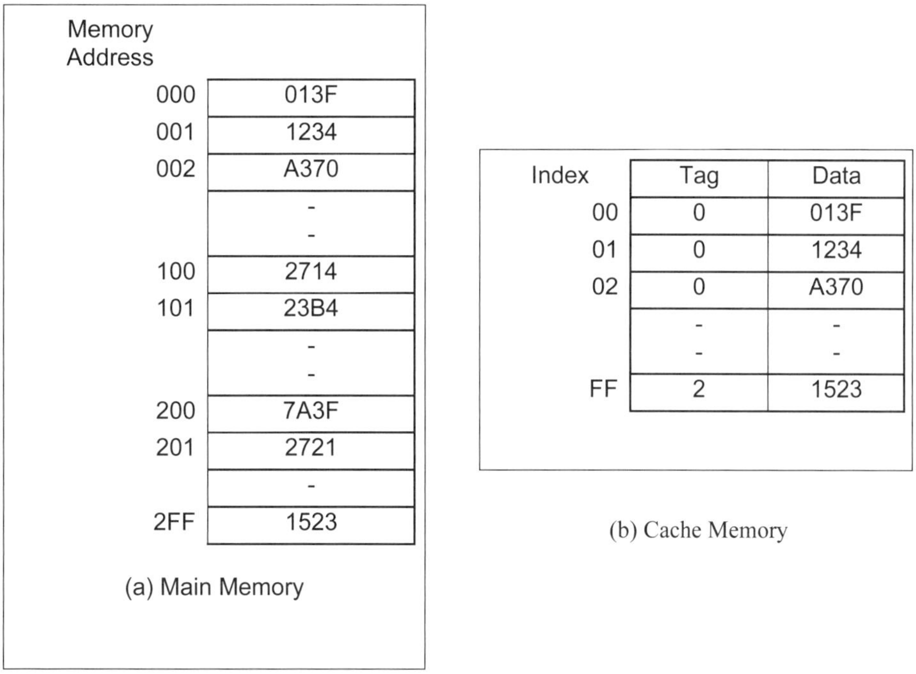

Memory
Address

Memory Address	
000	013F
001	1234
002	A370
	-
	-
100	2714
101	23B4
	-
	-
200	7A3F
201	2721
	-
2FF	1523

(a) Main Memory

Index	Tag	Data
00	0	013F
01	0	1234
02	0	A370
	-	-
	-	-
FF	2	1523

(b) Cache Memory

FIGURE 3.15   Direct mapping numerical example.

numerical example shown in Figure 3.15. All numbers are in hexadecimal. The content of index address 00 of cache is tag = 0 and data = 013F. Suppose that a microprocessor wants to access the memory address 100. The index address 00 is used to access the cache. Memory address tag 1 is compared with cache tag 0. This does not produce a match. Therefore, the main memory is accessed and the data 2714 is transferred into the microprocessor. The cache word at index address 00 is then replaced by a tag of 1 and data of 2714.

The fastest and most expensive cache memory known as *fully associative mapping* utilizes an associative memory. Each element in associative memory contains a main memory address and its content (data). When the microprocessor generates a main memory address, it is compared associatively (simultaneously) with all addresses in the associative memory. If there is a match, the corresponding data word is read from the associative cache memory and sent to the microprocessor. If a miss occurs, the main memory is accessed and the address and its corresponding data are written to the associative cache memory. If the cache is full, certain policies such as FIFO, are used as replacement algorithms for the cache. Associative cache is expensive but provides fast operation. The concept of associative cache is illustrated by means of a numerical example in Figure 3.16. Assume that all numbers are hexadecimal.

The associative memory stores both the memory address and its contents (data). The figure shows four words stored in the associative cache. Each word in the cache is a 12-bit address along with its 16-bit contents (data). When the microprocessor wants to access memory, the 12-bit address is placed in an address register and the associative cache memory is searched for a matching address. Suppose that the content of the microprocessor address register is 445. Because there is a match, the microprocessor reads the corresponding data 0FA1 into an internal data register.

Set-associative mapping is a combination of direct and associative mapping. Each

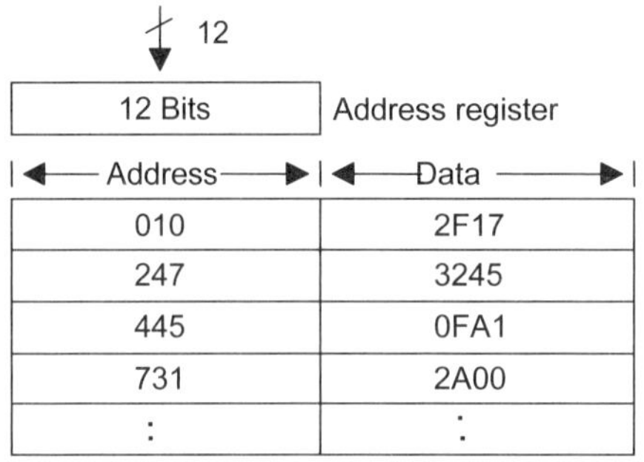

FIGURE 3.16   Numerical example of associative mapping.

cache word stores two or more main memory words using the same index address. Each main memory word consists of a tag and its data word. An index with two or more tags and data words forms a set.

When the microprocessor generates a memory request, the index of the main memory address is used as the cache address. The tag field of the main memory address is then compared associatively (simultaneously) with all tags stored under the index. If a match occurs, the desired dataword is read. If a match does not occur, the data word, along with its tag, is read from main memory and written into the cache. The hit ratio improves as the set size increases because more words with the same index but different tags can be stored in the cache.

The concept of set-associative mapping can be illustrated by the numerical example shown in Table 3.5. Assume that all numbers are hexadecimal. Each cache word can store two or more memory words under the same index address. Each data item is stored with its tag. The size of a set is defined by the number of tag and data items in a cache word. A set size of 2 is used in this example. Each index address contains two data words and their associated tags. Each tag includes 4 bits, and each data word contains 16 bits. Therefore, the word length $= 2 \times (4 + 16) = 40$ bits. An index address of 8 bits can represent 256 words. Hence, the size of the cache memory is 256×40. It can store 512 main memory words because each cache word includes two data words.

The hex numbers shown in Table 3.5 are obtained from the main memory contents shown in Figure 3.15. The words stored at addresses 000 and 200 of main memory in Figure 3.15 are stored in cache memory (shown in Table 3.5) at index address 00. Similarly, the words at addresses 101 and 201 are stored at index address 01. When the microprocessor wants to access a memory word, the index value of the address is used to access the cache. The tag field of the microprocessor address is then compared with both tags in the cache associatively (simultaneously) for a cache hit. If there is a match, appropriate data is read into the microprocessor. The hit ratio will improve as the set size increases because more words with the same index but different tags can be stored in the cache. However, this may increase the cost of comparison logic.

TABLE 3.5   Numerical Example of Set-Associative Mapping with a Set Size of 2

Index	Tag	Data	Tag	Data
00	0	013F	2	7A3F
01	1	23B4	2	2721

There are two ways of writing into cache: the write-back and write-through methods. In the *write-back method*, whenever the microprocessor writes something into a cache word, a "dirty" bit is assigned to the cache word. When a dirty word is to be replaced with a new word, the dirty word is first copied into the main memory before it is overwritten by the incoming new word. The advantage of this method is that it avoids unnecessary writing into main memory.

In the *write-through method*, whenever the microprocessor alters a cache address, the same alteration is made in the main memory copy of the altered cache address. This policy is easily implemented and ensures that the contents of the main memory are always valid. This feature is desirable in a multiprocesssor system, in which the main memory is shared by several processors. However, this approach may lead to several unnecessary writes to main memory.

One of the important aspects of cache memory organization is to devise a method that ensures proper utilization of the cache. Usually, the tag directory contains an extra bit for each entry, called a *valid bit*. When the power is turned on, the valid bit corresponding to each cache block entry of the tag directory is reset to zero. This is done to indicate that the cache block holds invalid data. When a block of data is transferred from the main memory to a cache block, the valid bit corresponding to this cache block is set to 1. In this arrangement, whenever the valid bit is zero, it implies that a new incoming block can overwrite the existing cache block. Thus, there is no need to copy the contents of the cache block being replaced into the main memory.

The growth in integrated circuit (IC) technology has allowed manufacturers to fabricate a cache on a microprocessor chip such as Motorola's 32-bit microprocessor, the 68020. The 68020 on-chip cache is a direct-mapped instruction cache. Only instructions are cached; data items are not.

Finally, microprocessors such as the Intel Pentium II support two levels of cache, L1 (level 1) and L2 (level 2) cache memories. The L1 cache (smaller in size) is contained inside the processor chip while the L2 cache (larger in size) is interfaced external to the microprocessor. The L1 cache normally provides separate instruction and data caches. The processor can access the L1 cache directly and the L2 cache normally supplies instructions and data to the L1 cache. The L2 cache is usually accessed by the microprocessor only if L1 misses occur. This two-level cache memory enhances microprocessor performance.

Questions and Problems

3.1   What is the basic difference between main memory and secondary memory?

3.2   A microprocessor has 24 address pins. What is the maximum size of the main memory?

3.3   Can the microprocessor execute programs directly in hard disk? Explain your answer.

3.4   What is the basic difference between: (a) EPROM and EEPROM? (b) SRAM and DRAM?

3.5   Given a memory with a 14-bit address and an 8-bit word size.
       (a)   How many bytes can be stored in this memory?
       (b)   If this memory were constructed from $1K \times 1$ RAMs, how many memory chips would be required?
       (c)   How many bits would be used for chip select?

3.6   What are the main differences between CD and DVD memories?

3.7   Draw a block diagram showing the address and data lines for the 2732, and 2764 EPROM chips.

3.8   (a)   How many address and data lines are required for a $1M \times 16$ memory chip?
       (b)   What is the size of a decoder with one chip enable ($\overline{CE}$) to obtain a $64K \times 32$ memory from $4K \times 8$ chips? Where are the inputs and outputs of the decoder connected?

3.9   A microprocessor with 24 address pins and eight data pins is connected to a $1K \times 8$ memory chip with one chip enable. How many unused address bits of the microprocessor are available for interfacing other $1K \times 8$ memory chips? What is the maximum directly addressable memory available with this microprocessor?

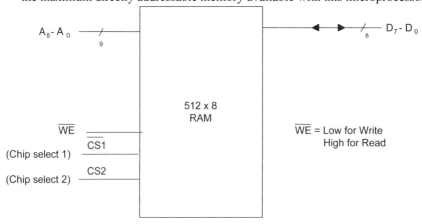

FIGURE P3.11

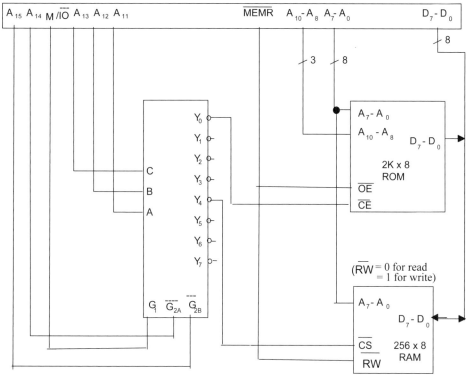

FIGURE P3.12

3.10 Name the methods used in main memory array design. What are the advantages and disadvantages of each?

3.11 The block diagram of a 512×8 RAM chip is shown in Figure P3.11. In this arrangement the memory chip is enabled only when $\overline{CS1} = L$ and $CS2 = H$. Design a $1K \times 8$ RAM system using this chip as the building block. Draw a neat logic diagram of your implementation. Assume that the microprocessor can directly address 64K with a $R/\overline{W}$ and eight data pins. Using linear decoding and don't-care conditions as 1's, determine the memory map in hexadecimal.

3.12 Consider the hardware schematic shown in Figure P3.12.

(a) Determine the address map of this system. *Note:* $\overline{MEMR} = 0$ for read, $\overline{MEMR} = 1$ for write, $M/\overline{IO} = 0$ for I/O and $M/\overline{IO} = 1$ for memory.

(b) Is there any possibility of bus conflict in this organization? Clearly justify your answer.

TABLE P3.13

Device	Size	Address Assignment (Hex)
EPROM chip	$1K \times 8$	8000–83FF
RAM chip 0	$1K \times 8$	9000–93FF
RAM chip 1	$1K \times 8$	C000–C3FF

TABLE P3.14

Device	Size	Address Assignment in hex
EPROM chip	1K × 8	7000–73FF
RAM chip 0	1K × 8	D000–D3FF
RAM chip 1	1K × 8	F000–F3FF

3.13 Interface a microprocessor with 16-bit address pins and 8-bit data pins and a R/$\overline{W}$ pin to a 1K × 8 EPROM chip and two 1K × 8 RAM chips such that the memory map shown in Table P3.13 is obtained:
Assume that both EPROM and RAM chips contain two enable pins: $\overline{CE}$ and $\overline{OE}$ for the EPROM and $\overline{CE}$ and $\overline{WE}$ for each RAM. Note that $\overline{WE}$ = 1 and $\overline{WE}$ = 0 indicate read and write operations for the RAM chip. Use a 74138 decoder.

3.14 Repeat Problem 3.13 to obtain the memory map shown in Table P3.14 using a 74138 decoder.

3.15 What is meant by foldback in linear decoding?

3.16 Comment on the importance of the following features in an operating system implementation:
(a)   Address translation
(b)   Protection

3.17 Explain briefly the differences between segmentation and paging.

3.18 What is the advantage of having a cache memory? Name a 32-bit microprocessor that does not contain an on-chip cache.

3.19 What basic functions are performed by a microprocessor's on-chip MMU?

3.20 Discuss briefly the various cache-mapping techniques.

3.21 A microprocessor has a main memory of 8K × 32 and a cache memory of 4K × 32. Using direct mapping, determine the sizes of the tag field, index field, and cach word of the cache.

3.22 A microprocessor has a main memory of 4K × 32. Using a cache memory address of 8 bits and set-associative mapping with a set size of 2, determine the size of the cache memory.

3.23 A microprocessor can address directly 1 MB of memory with a 16-bit word size. Determine the size of each cache memory word for associative mapping.

3.24 Under what conditions does the set-associative mapping method become one of the following?
(a)   Direct mapping
(b)   Fully associative mapping

4

MICROPROCESSOR INPUT/ OUTPUT

In this chapter we describe the basics of input/output (I/O) techniques utilized by typical microprocessors. Topics include programmed I/O, interrupt I/O, and DMA (direct memory access).

4.1   Introduction

The technique of data transfer between a microcomputer and an external device is called *input/output* (I/O). One communicates with a microcomputer via the I/O devices interfaced to it. The user can enter programs and data using the keyboard on a terminal and execute the programs to obtain results. Therefore, the I/O devices connected to a microcomputer provide an efficient means of communication between the microcomputer and the outside world. These I/O devices, commonly called *peripherals* and include keyboards, monitors (screens), printers, and hard disks.

The characteristics of I/O devices are normally different from those of a microcomputer. For example, the speed of operation of peripherals is usually slower than that of the microcomputer, and the word length of the microcomputer may be different from the data format of the peripheral devices. To make the characteristics of the I/O devices compatible with those of a microcomputer, interface hardware circuitry between the microcomputer and I/O devices is necessary. Interfaces provide all input and output transfers between the microcomputer and peripherals by using an I/O bus. An I/O bus carries three types of signals: device address, data, and command.

A microprocessor uses an I/O bus when it executes an I/O instruction. A typical I/O instruction has three fields. When the microprocessor executes an I/O instruction, the control unit decodes the op-code field and identifies it as an I/O instruction. The microprocessor then places the device address and command from respective fields of the I/O instruction on the I/O bus. The interfaces for various devices connected to the I/O bus decode this address, and an appropriate interface is selected. The identified interface decodes the command lines and determines the function to be performed. Typical functions include receiving data from an input device into the microprocessor or sending data to an output device from the microprocessor. In a typical microcomputer system, the user gets involved with two types of I/O devices: physical I/O and virtual I/O. When a microcomputer has no operating system, the user must work directly with physical I/O devices and perform detailed I/O design.

There are three ways of transferring data between a microcomputer and physical I/O devices: programmed I/O, interrupt I/O and direct memory access. Using *programmed I/O*, the microprocessor executes a program to perform all data transfers between

71

the microcomputer and the external device. The main characteristic of this type of I/O technique is that the external device carries out the functions dictated by the program inside the microcomputer memory. In other words, the microprocessor controls all transfers completely.

In *interrupt I/O*, an external device can force the microprocessor to stop executing the current program temporarily so that it can execute another program known as an *interrupt service routine*. This routine satisfies the needs of the external device. After completing this program, a   return from interrupt instruction can be executed at the end of the service routine to return control at the right place in the main program.

Direct memory access (DMA) is a type of I/O technique in which data can be transferred between microcomputer memory and an external device such as the hard disk, without microprocessor involvement. A special chip called the *DMA controller chip* is typically used with the microprocessor for transferring data using DMA.

In a microcomputer with an operating system, the user works with virtual I/O devices. The user does not have to be familiar with the characteristics of the physical I/O devices. Instead, the user performs data transfers between the microcomputer and the physical I/O devices indirectly by calling the I/O routines provided by the operating system using virtual I/O instructions.

Basically, an operating system serves as an interface between the user programs and actual hardware. The operating system facilitates the creation of many logical or virtual I/O devices and allows a user program to communicate directly with these logical devices. For example, a user program may write its output to a virtual printer. In reality, a virtual printer may refer to a block of disk space. When the user program terminates, the operating system may assign one of the available physical printers to this virtual printer and monitor the entire printing operation. This concept, known as spooling improves system throughput by isolating the fast processor from direct contact with a slow printing device. A user program is totally unaware of the logical-to-physical device-mapping process. There is no need to modify a user program if a logical device is assigned to some other available physical device. This approach offers greater flexibility over the conventional hardware-oriented techniques associated with physical I/O.

4.2   Simple I/O Devices

A simple input device such as a DIP switch can be connected to a microcomputer's I/O port as shown in Figure 4.1. The figure shows a switch circuit that can be used as a single bit input into an I/O port. When the DIP switch is open, V_{IN} is HIGH. When the switch is closed, V_{IN} is LOW. V_{IN} can be used as an input bit for performing laboratory experiments.

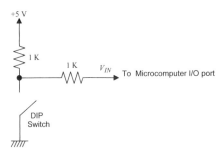

FIGURE 4.1   Typical switch for a microcomputer's input.

LEDs	Red	Yellow	Green
Current	10 mA	10 mA	20 mA
Voltage	1.7 V	2.2V	2.4V

TABLE 4.1   Current and Voltage Requirements of LEDs

Note that unlike TTL, a 1Kohm resistor is connected between the switch and the input of the MOS gate (port input). This provides protection against static discharge.

For performing simple I/O experiments using programmed I/O, light-emitting diodes (LEDs) and seven-segment displays can be used as output devices. An LED is typically driven by low voltage and low current, which makes it a very attractive device for use with microprocessors. Table 4.1 provides the current and voltage requirements for red, yellow, and green LEDs. Basically, an LED will be ON, generating light, when its cathode is sufficiently negative with respect to its anode. A microcomputer can therefore light an LED either by grounding the cathode (if the anode is tied to +5 V) or by applying +5 V to the anode (if the cathode is grounded) through an appropriate resistor value. A typical hardware interface between a microcomputer and an LED is depicted in Figure 4.2.

A microcomputer normally outputs 400 μA at a minimum voltage V_M = 2.4 volts for a HIGH. The red LED requires 10 mA at 1.7 volts. A buffer such as an inverter is required to turn the LED ON.

A HIGH at the microcomputer output will turn the LED ON. This will allow a path of current to flow from the +5 V source through R and the LED to the ground. The appropriate value of R needs to be calculated to satisfy the voltage and current requirements of the LED. The value of R can be calculated as follows:

$R= \frac{5-1.7}{10\,mA} = \frac{5-1.7}{10\,mA} = 330\ \Omega$

Therefore, the interface design is complete, and a value of R = 330 Ω is required. A seven-segment display can be used with programmed I/O to display, for example, decimal numbers from 0 to 9. The name *seven segment* is based on the fact that there are seven LEDs, one in each segment of the display. Figure 4.3 shows a typical seven-segment display. In the figure, each segment contains an LED. All decimal numbers from 0 through 9 can be displayed by turning the appropriate segment ON or OFF. For example, a zero can be displayed by turning the LED in segment *g* OFF and turning the other six LEDs in segments *a* through *f* ON. There are two types of seven-segment displays: common-cathode and common-anode. In a common-cathode arrangement, the microcomputer can send a HIGH to light a segment and a LOW to turn it off. In a common-anode configuration, on the other hand, the microcomputer sends a LOW to light a segment and a HIGH to turn it off.

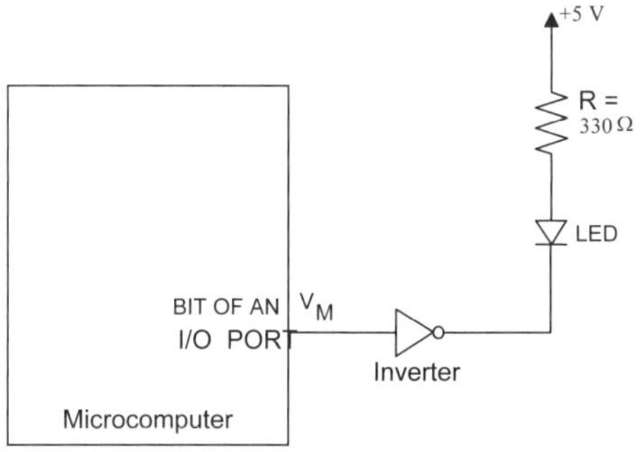

FIGURE 4.2   Microcomputer - LED interface via an inverter

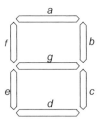

FIGURE 4.3   Seven-segment display.

Seven-segment displays can be interfaced to typical microprocessors using programmed I/O. BCD to seven-segment code converter chips such as 7447 or 7448 can be replaced by a look-up table. This table can be stored in a microcomputer's main memory. An assembly language program can be written to read the appropriate code for a BCD digit stored in this table. This data can be output to display the BCD digit on a seven-segment display connected to an I/O port of the microcomputer. Programs to accomplish this are written in 68000/68020 and Pentium assembly language later in the book.

4.3   Programmed I/O

A microcomputer communicates with an external device via one or more registers called *I/O ports* using programmed I/O. I/O ports are usually of two types. For one type, each bit in the port can be configured individually as either input or output. For the other type, all bits in the port can be set up as all parallel input or parallel output bits. Each port can be configured as an input or output port by another register called the *command* or *data-direction register*. The port contains the actual input or output data. The data-direction register is an output register and can be used to configure the bits in the port as inputs or outputs.

Each bit in the port can be set up as an input or output, normally by writing a 0 or a 1 in the corresponding bit of the data-direction register. As an example, if an 8-bit data-direction register contains 34H (34 Hex), the corresponding port is defined as shown in Figure 4.4. In this example, because 34H (0011 0100) is sent as an output into the data-direction register, bits 0, 1, 3, 6, and 7 of the port are set up as inputs, and bits 2, 4, and 5 of the port are defined as outputs. The microcomputer can then send output to external devices, such as LEDs, connected to bits 2, 4, and 5 through a proper interface. Similarly, the microcomputer can input the status of external devices, such as switches, through bits 0, 1, 3, 6, and 7. To input data from the input switches, the microcomputer inputs the complete byte, including the bits to which LEDs are connected. While receiving input data from an I/O port, however, the microcomputer places a value, probably 0, at the bits configured as outputs and the program must interpret them as "don't cares." At the same time, the microcomputer's outputs to bits configured as inputs are disabled.

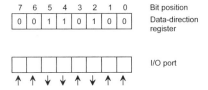

FIGURE 4.4   Bit configurable I/O port along with a data-direction register.

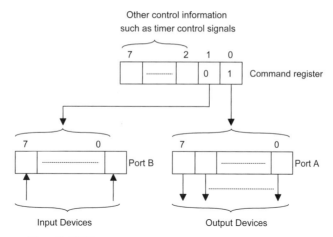

FIGURE 4.5   Parallel I/O ports.

For parallel I/O, there is only one data direction register for all ports. A particular bit in the data direction register configures all bits in the port as either inputs or outputs. Consider two I/O ports in an I/O chip along with one data direction register. Assume that a 0 or a 1 in a particular bit position defines all bits of port A or B as inputs or outputs respectively. An example is depicted in Figure 4.5. Some I/O ports are called *handshake* ports. Data transfer occurs via these ports through exchanging of control signals between the microcomputer and an external device.

I/O ports are addressed using either standard I/O or memory-mapped I/O techniques. *Standard I/O* or *port I/O* (called *isolated I/O* by Intel) uses an output pin such as the M/$\overline{\text{IO}}$ pin on the Intel Pentium microprocessor chip. The microprocessor outputs a HIGH on this pin to indicate to memory and the I/O chips that a memory operation is taking place. A LOW output from the microprocessor to this pin indicates an I/O operation. Execution of an IN or OUT instruction makes the M/$\overline{\text{IO}}$ LOW, whereas memory-oriented instructions, such as MOVE, drive the M/$\overline{\text{IO}}$ to HIGH.

In standard I/O, the microprocessor uses the M/$\overline{\text{IO}}$ pin to distinguish between I/O and memory. For typical microprocessors, an 8-bit address can be used for each I/O port. With an 8-bit I/O port address, these processors are capable of addressing 256 ports. In addition, 32-bit microprocessors can also use 16- or 32-bit I/O ports.

In memory-mapped I/O, the microprocessor does not use the M/$\overline{\text{IO}}$ control pin. Instead, the microprocessor uses an unused address pin to distinguish between memory and I/O. The microprocessor uses a portion of the memory addresses to represent I/O ports. The I/O ports are mapped as part of the microprocessor's main memory addresses which may not exist physically, but are used by the microprocessor's memory-oriented instructions, such as MOVE, to generate the necessary control signals to perform I/O. Motorola microprocessors such as the 68000 or 68020 do not have a control pin such as M/$\overline{\text{IO}}$ and use only memory-mapped I/O. Intel microprocessors can use both types.

When standard I/O is used, typical microprocessors such as the Pentium normally use an IN or OUT instruction with 8-bit ports as follows:

IN   AL, PORTA   ; Inputs 8-bit data from PORTA into the 8-bit register AL
OUT   PORTA,AL   ; Outputs the contents of the 8-bit register AL into PORTA

With memory-mapped I/O, the microprocessor normally uses an instruction(i.e., MOV as follows:

MOV   mem, reg   ; Inputs the contents of a register into a port called "mem"
                    ; mapped as a memory location
MOV   reg,mem   ; outputs the contents of a port called "mem" mapped as a
                    ; memory location into a register

4.4   Unconditional and Conditional Programmed I/O

There are typically two ways in which programmed I/O can be utilized: unconditional I/O and conditional I/O. The microprocessor can send data to an external device at any time using *unconditional I/O*. The external device must always be ready for data transfer. A typical example is that of a microprocessor outputting a 7-bit code through an I/O port to drive a seven-segment display connected to this port. In *conditional I/O*, the microprocessor outputs data to an external device via *handshaking*. This means that data transfer occurs via the exchange of control signals between the microprocessor and an external device. The

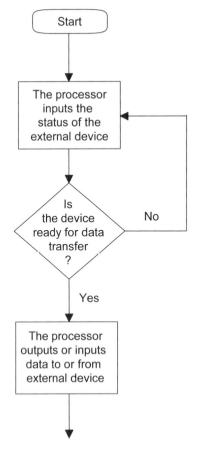

FIGURE 4.6   Flowchart for conditional programmed I/O.

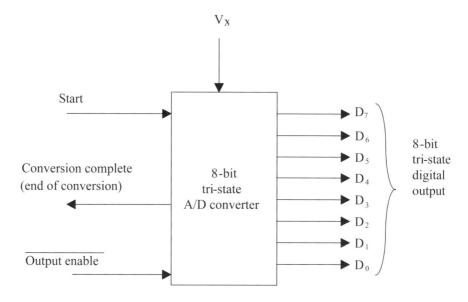

FIGURE 4.7   A/D converter.

microprocessor inputs the status of the external device to determine whether the device is ready for data transfer. Data transfer takes place when the device is ready. Figure 4.6 illustrates the concept of conditional programmed I/O.

The concept of conditional I/O will now be demonstrated by means of data transfer between a microprocessor and an analog-to-digital (A/D) converter. Consider, for example, the A/D converter shown in Figure 4.7, which transforms an analog voltage Vx into an 8-bit binary output at pins D_7-D_0. A pulse at the "start" pin initiates the conversion. This drives the "conversion complete" signal LOW. The signal stays LOW during the conversion process. The "conversion complete" signal goes HIGH as soon as the conversion ends. Because the A/D converter's output is tristated, a LOW on the Output enable transfers the converter's outputs. A HIGH on the Output enable drives the converter's outputs to a high-impedance state.

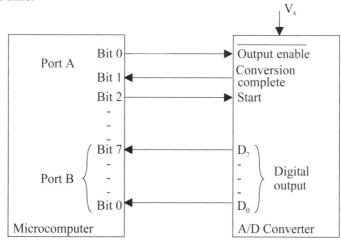

FIGURE 4.8   Interfacing an A/D converter to a microcomputer

The concept of conditional I/O can be demonstrated by interfacing an A/D converter to a typical microcomputer. Figure 4.8 shows such an interfacing example. The user writes a program to carry out the conversion process. When this program is executed, the microcomputer sends a pulse to the "start" pin of the converter via bit 2 of port A. The microcomputer then checks the "conversion complete" signal by inputting bit 1 of port A to determine if the conversion is completed.

If the "conversion complete" signal is HIGH (indicating the end of conversion), the microcomputer sends a LOW to the output enable pin of the A/D converter. The microcomputer then inputs the converter's D_0-D_7 outputs via port B. If the conversion is not completed, the microcomputer waits in a loop checking for the "conversion complete" signal to go HIGH.

4.5   Interrupt I/O

A disadvantage of conditional programmed I/O is that the microcomputer needs to check the status bit (a conversion complete signal of the A/D converter) by waiting in a loop. This type of I/O transfer is dependent on the speed of the external device. For a slow device, this waiting may slow down the microcomputer's ability to process other data. The interrupt I/O technique is efficient in this type of situation.

Interrupt I/O is a device-initiated I/O transfer. The external device is connected to a pin called the *interrupt* (INT) pin on the microprocessor chip. When the device needs an I/O transfer with the microcomputer, it activates the interrupt pin of the processor chip. The microcomputer usually completes the current instruction and saves the contents of the current program counter and the status register in the stack.

The microcomputer then loads an address automatically into the program counter to branch to a subroutine-like program called the *interrupt service routine*. This program is written by the user. The external device wants the microcomputer to execute this program to transfer data. The last instruction of the service routine is a RETURN, which is typically similar in concept to the RETURN instruction used at the end of a subroutine. The RETURN from interrupt instruction normally restores the program counter and the status register with the information saved in the stack before going to the service routine. Then the microcomputer continues executing the main program. An example of interrupt I/O is shown in Figure 4.9.

Assume that the microcomputer is 68000 based and is executing the following instruction sequence:

```
              ORG         $2000
              MOVE.B      #$81, DDRA      ;Configure bits 0 and 7
                                          ;of port A as outputs
              MOVE.B      #$00, DDRB      ;Configure port B as input
              MOVE.B      #$81, PORTA     ;Send a HIGH start pulse to A/D
                                          ;and a HIGH to output  enable
              MOVE.B      #$01, PORTA     ;Send a LOW to start and
                                          ; a HIGH to output enable
              CLR.W       D0              ;Clear 16-bit register D0 to 0
BEGIN         MOVE.W      D1, D2
              .
              .

              .
```

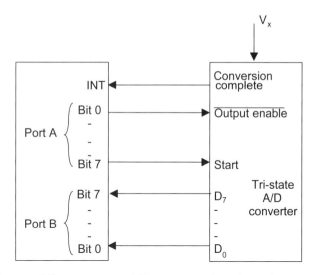

FIGURE 4.9   Microcomputer A/D converter interface via interrupt I/O.

The extensions .B and .W represent byte and word operations. Note that $ and # indicate hexadecimal number and immediate mode respectively. The preceding program is written arbitrarily.

The program logic can be explained using the 68000 instruction set. Ports DDRA and DDRB are assumed to be the data-direction registers for ports A and B, respectively. The first four MOVE instructions configure bits 0 and 7 of port A as outputs and port B as the input port, and then send a trailing "start" pulse (HIGH and then LOW) to the A/D converter along with a HIGH to the output enable. This HIGH output enable is required to disable the A/D's output.

The microcomputer continues with execution of the CLR.W D0 instruction. Suppose that the "conversion complete" signal becomes HIGH, indicating the end of conversion during execution of the CLR.W D0 instruction. This drives the INT signal to HIGH, interrupting the microcomputer. The microcomputer completes execution of the current instruction, CLR.W D0. It then saves the current contents of the program counter (address BEGIN) and status register automatically and executes a subroutine-like program called the service routine. This program is usually written by the user. The microprocessor manufacturer normally specifies the starting address of the *service routine*, or it may be provided by the user via external hardware. Assume that this address is $4000 and that the user writes a service routine to input the A/D converter's output as follows:

```
ORG         $4000
MOVE.B      #$00, PORTA    ;    Activate output enable
MOVE.B      PORTB, D1      ;    Input A/D
RTE                        ;    Return and restore PC and SR
```

In this service routine, the microcomputer inputs the A/D converter's output. The return instruction RTE, at the end of the service routine, pops the address BEGIN and the previous status register contents from the stack and loads the program counter and status register with them. The microcomputer executes the MOVE.W D1,D2 instruction at the address BEGIN and continues with the main program. The basic characteristics of interrupt I/O have been discussed so far. The main features of interrupt I/O provided with a typical microcomputer are discussed next.

4.5.1 Interrupt Types

There are typically three types of interrupts: external interrupts, traps or internal interrupts, and software interrupts. *External interrupts* are initiated through a microprocessor's interrupt pins by external devices such as A/D converters. External interrupts can be divided further into two types: maskable and nonmaskable. Nonmaskable interrupt cannot be enabled or disabled by instructions, whereas a microprocessor's instruction set contains instructions to enable or disable maskable interrupt. For example, the Intel Pentium can disable or enable maskable interrupt by executing instructions such as CLI (clear the interrupt flag in the status register to 0) or STI (set interrupt flag in the status register to 1) . The Pentium recognizes maskable interrupt after execution of the STI while ignoring it upon execution of the CLI. Note that the Pentium has an interrupt flag bit in the status register. A nonmaskable interrupt has a higher priority than a maskable interrupt. If maskable and nonmaskable interrupts are activated at the same time, the processor will service the nonmaskable interrupt first.

A nonmaskable interrupt is typically used as a power failure interrupt. Microprocessors normally use +5 V dc, which is transformed from 110 V ac. If the power falls below 90 V ac, the DC voltage of +5 V cannot be maintained. However, it will take a few milliseconds before the ac power drops below 90 V ac. In these few milliseconds, the power-failure-sensing circuitry can interrupt the processor. The interrupt service routine can be written to store critical data in nonvolatile memory such as battery-backed CMOS RAM, and the interrupted program can continue without any loss of data when the power returns.

Some microprocessors, such as the Pentium, are provided with a maskable handshake interrupt. This interrupt is usually implemented by using two pins: INTR and INTA. When the INTR pin is activated by an external device, the processor completes the current instruction, saves at least the current program counter onto the stack, and generates an interrupt acknowledge (INTA). In response to the INTA, the external device provides an 8-bit number using external hardware on the data bus of the microcomputer. This number is then read and used by the microcomputer to branch to the service routine desired.

Internal interrupts, or *traps*, are activated internally by exceptional conditions such as overflow, division by zero, or execution of an illegal op-code. Traps are handled in the same way as external interrupts. The user writes a service routine to take corrective measures and provide an indication to inform the user that an exceptional condition has occurred. Many microprocessors include software interrupts, or system calls. When one of these instructions is executed, the microprocessor is interrupted and serviced similarly to external or internal interrupts.

Software interrupt instructions are normally used to call the operating system. These instructions are shorter than subroutine calls, and no calling program is needed to know the operating system's address in memory. Software interrupt instructions allow the user to switch from user to supervisor mode. For some processors, a software interrupt is the only way to call the operating system, because a subroutine call to an address in the operating system is not allowed.

4.5.2 Interrupt Address Vector

The technique used to find the starting address of the service routine (commonly known as the *interrupt address vector*) varies from one processor to another. With some microprocessors, the manufacturers define the fixed starting address for each interrupt. Other manufacturers use an indirect approach by defining fixed locations where the interrupt address vector is stored.

4.5.3 Saving the Microprocessor Registers

When a microprocessor is interrupted, it normally saves the program counter (PC) and the status register (SR) onto the stack so that the microprocessor can return to the main program with the original values of PC and SR after executing the service routine. The user should know the specific registers the microprocessor saves prior to executing the service routine. This will allow the user to use the appropriate return instruction at the end of the service routine to restore the original conditions upon return to the main program.

4.5.4 Interrupt Priorities

A microprocessor is typically provided with one or more interrupt pins on the chip. Therefore, a special mechanism is necessary to handle interrupts from several devices that share one of these interrupt lines. There are two ways of servicing multiple interrupts: polled and daisy chain techniques.

Polled Interrupts   Polled interrupts are handled by software and therefore are slow in servicing the interrupts. The microprocessor responds to an interrupt by executing one general service routine for all devices. The priorities of devices are determined by the order in which the routine polls each device. The microprocessor checks the status of each device in the general service routine, starting with the highest-priority device, to service an interrupt. Once the microprocessor determines the source of the interrupt, it branches to the service routine for the device. Figure 4.10 shows a typical configuration of the polled-interrupt system.

In Figure 4.10, several external devices (device 1, device 2,..., device N) are connected to a single interrupt line of a microprocessor via an OR gate (not shown in the figure). When one or more devices activate the INT line HIGH, the microprocessor pushes the PC and SR onto the stack. It then branches to an address defined by the manufacturer of the microprocessor. The user can write a program at this address to poll each device, starting with the highest-priority device, to find the source of the interrupt. Suppose that the devices in Figure 4.10 are A/D converters. Each converter, along with the associated logic for polling, is shown in Figure 4.11.

Assume that in Figure 4.10 two A/D converters (devices 1 and 2) are provided with the "start" pulse by the microprocessor at nearly the same time. Suppose that the user assigns device 2 the higher priority. The user then sets up this priority mechanism in the general service routine. For example, when the "Conversion complete" signals from device 1 and/or 2 become HIGH, indicating the end of conversion, the processor is interrupted. In response, the microprocessor pushes the PC and SR onto the stack and loads the PC with the interrupt address vector defined by the manufacturer.

The general interrupt service routine written at this address determines the source of the interrupt as follows: A 1 is sent to PA1 for device 2 because this device has higher priority. If this device has generated an interrupt, the output (PB1) of the AND gate in Figure 4.11 becomes HIGH, indicating to the microprocessor that device 2 generated the interrupt. If the output of the AND gate is 0, the processor sends a HIGH to PA0 and checks the output (PB0) for HIGH. Once the source of the interrupt is determined, the microprocessor can be programmed to jump to the service routine for that device. The service routine enables the A/D converter and inputs the converter's outputs to the microprocessor.

Polled interrupts are slow, and for a large number of devices the time required to poll each device may exceed the time to service the device. In such a case, a faster mechanism, such as the daisy chain approach, can be used.

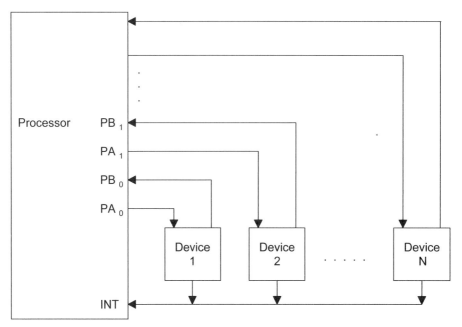

FIGURE 4.10   Polled interrupt.

Daisy Chain Interrupts   Devices are connected in daisy chain fashion, as shown in Figure 4.12, to set up priority systems. Suppose that one or more devices interrupt the processor. In response, the microprocessor pushes the PC and SR onto the stack and, generates an interrupt acknowledge ($\overline{INTA}$) signal to the highest-priority device (device 1 in this case). If this device has generated the interrupt, it will accept the $\overline{INTA}$; otherwise, it will pass the $\overline{INTA}$ onto the next device until the $\overline{INTA}$ is accepted.

Once accepted, the device provides a means for the processor to find the interrupt-address vector by using external hardware. Assume that the devices in Figure 4.12 are A/D converters. Figure 4.13 provides a schematic for each device and the associated logic.

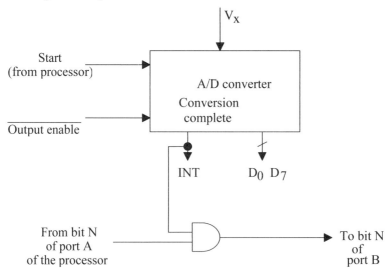

FIGURE 4.11   Device N and associated logic for polled interrupt.

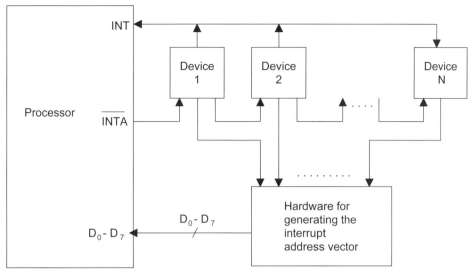

FIGURE 4.12   Daisy chain interrupt.

Suppose that the microprocessor in Figure 4.12 sends a pulse to start the conversions of the A/D converters of devices 1 and 2 at nearly the same time. When the "conversion complete" signal goes HIGH, the microprocessor is interrupted through the INT line. The microprocessor pushes the PC and SR. It then generates a LOW at the interrupt acknowledge ($\overline{INTA}$) for the highest-priority device. Device 1 has the highest priority; it is the first device in the daisy chain configuration to receive $\overline{INTA}$. If A/D converter 1 has generated the "conversion complete" HIGH, the output of the AND gate in Figure 4.13 becomes HIGH.

This signal can be used to enable external hardware to provide the interrupt address vector on the microprocessor's data lines. The microprocessor then branches to

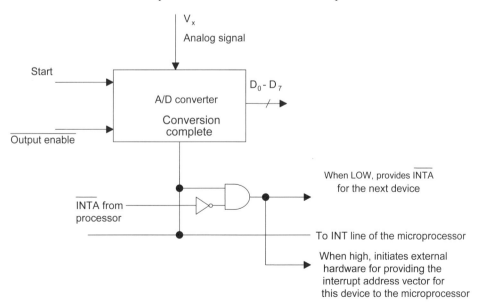

FIGURE 4.13   Each device and the associated logic in a daisy chain.

the service routine. This program enables the converter and inputs the A/D output to the microprocessor via port B. If A/D converter 1 does not generate the "conversion complete" HIGH, however, the output of the AND gate in Figure 4.13 becomes LOW (an input to device 2's logic) and the same sequence of operations takes place. In the daisy chain, each device has the same logic, with the exception of the last device, which must accept the INTA. Note that the outputs of all the devices are connected to the INT line via an OR gate (not shown in Figure 4.12).

4.6   Direct Memory Access (DMA)

Direct memory access (DMA) is a technique that transfers data between a microcomputer's memory and an I/O device without involving the microprocessor. DMA is widely used in transferring large blocks of data between a peripheral device such as a hard disk and the microcomputer's memory. The DMA technique uses a DMA controller chip for the data transfer operations. The DMA controller chip implements various components, such as a counter containing the length of data to be transferred in hardware in order to speed up data transfer. The main functions of a typical DMA controller are summarized as follows:

- The I/O devices request DMA operation via the DMA request line of the controller chip.

- The controller chip activates the microprocessor HOLD pin, requesting the microprocessor to release the bus.

- The microprocessor sends HLDA (hold acknowledge) back to the DMA controller, indicating that the bus is disabled. The DMA controller places the current value of its internal registers, such as the address register and counter, on the system bus and sends a DMA acknowledge to the peripheral device. The DMA controller completes the DMA transfer.

There are three basic types of DMA: block transfer, cycle stealing, and interleaved DMA. For *block transfer DMA*, the DMA controller chip takes over the bus from the microcomputer to transfer data between the microcomputer memory and the I/O device. The microprocessor has no access to the bus until the transfer is completed. During this time, the microprocessor can perform internal operations that do not need the bus. This method is popular with microprocessors. Using this technique, blocks of data can be transferred.

Data transfer between the microcomputer memory and an I/O device occurs on a word-by-word basis with cycle stealing. Typically, the microprocessor is generated by ANDing an INHIBIT signal with the system clock. The system clock has the same frequency as the microprocessor clock. The DMA controller controls the INHIBIT line. During normal operation, the INHIBIT line is HIGH, providing the microprocessor clock. When DMA operation is desired, the controller makes the INHIBIT line LOW for one clock cycle. The microprocessor is then stopped completely for one cycle. Data transfer between the memory and I/O takes place during this cycle. This method is called *cycle stealing* because the DMA controller takes away or steals a cycle without microprocessor recognition. Data transfer takes place over a period of time.

With *interleaved DMA*, the DMA controller chip takes over the system bus when the microprocessor is not using it. For example, the microprocessor does not use the bus while incrementing the program counter or performing an ALU operation. The DMA controller chip identifies these cycles and allows transfer of data between memory and the

I/O device. Data transfer for this method takes place over a period of time.

Because block transfer DMA is common with microprocessors, a brief description is provided. Figure 4.14 shows a typical diagram of block transfer DMA. In the figure, the I/O device requests DMA transfer via the DMA request line connected to the controller chip. The DMA controller chip then sends a HOLD signal to the microprocessor and waits for the HOLD acknowledge (HLDA) signal from the microprocessor. On receipt of the HLDA, the controller chip sends a DMA ACK signal to the I/O device. The controller takes over the bus and controls data transfer between RAM and the I/O device. On the completion of data transfer, the controller interrupts the microprocessor by the INT line and returns the bus to the microprocessor by disabling the HOLD and DMA ACK signals.

The DMA controller chip usually has at least three registers normally selected by the controller's register select (RS) line: an address register, a terminal count register, and a status register. Both the address and terminal counter registers are initialized by the microprocessor. The address register contains the starting address of the data to be transferred, and the terminal counter register contains the block to be transferred. The status register contains information such as completion of DMA transfer. Note that the DMA controller implements logic associated with data transfer in hardware to speed up the DMA operation.

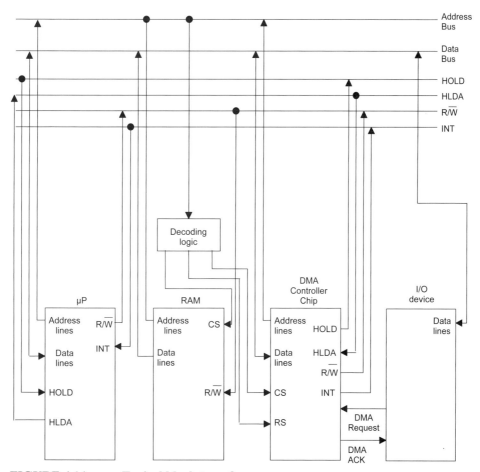

FIGURE 4.14   Typical block transfer.

4.7   Summary of I/O

Figure 4.15 summarizes various I/O techniques used with a typical microprocessor.

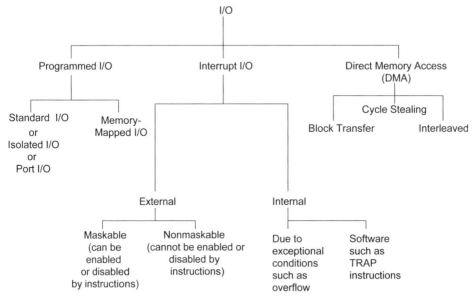

FIGURE 4.15   I/O structure of a typical microcomputer.

Questions and Problems

4.1 Define the three types of I/O. Identify each as either microprocessor-initiated or device-initiated.

4.2 What is the basic difference between standard I/O and memory-mapped I/O? Identify the programmed I/O technique (s) used by Intel and Motorola microprocessors.

4.3 What are programmed I/O and virtual I/O?

4.4 What is the difference between memory mapping in a microprocessor and memory-mapped I/O?

4.5 Discuss the basic difference between polled I/O and interrupt I/O.

4.6 What is the difference between subroutine and interrupt I/O?

4.7 What is an interrupt address vector?

4.8 Summarize the basic difference between maskable and nonmaskable interrupts. Describe how power failure interrupt is normally handled.

4.9 Why are polled interrupt and daisy chain interrupt used?

4.10 Discuss the basic difference between internal and external interrupts.

4.11 What are cycle stealing, block transfer, and interleaved DMA?

4.12 Summarize the typical functions performed by a DMA controller chip.

5

MICROPROCESSOR PROGRAMMING CONCEPTS

In this chapter we provide the fundamental concepts of microprocessor programming. Typical programming characteristics such as programming languages, basics of assembly language programming, instruction formats, instruction set architecture (ISA), microprocessor instruction sets, and addressing modes are discussed.

5.1   Microcomputer Programming Languages

Microprocessors are typically programmed using semi-English-language statements (assembly language). In addition to assembly languages, microcomputers use a more understandable human-oriented language called *high-level language*. No matter what type of language is used to write programs, microcomputers understand only binary numbers. Therefore, all programs must eventually be translated into their appropriate binary forms. The principal ways to accomplish this are discussed later.

Microprocessor programming languages can typically be divided into three main types: machine language, assembly language, and high-level language. A *machine language program* consists of either binary or hexadecimal op-codes. Programming a microcomputer with either one is relatively difficult, because one must deal only with numbers. The architecture and microprograms of a microprocessor determine all its instructions. These instructions are called the microprocessor's *instruction set*. Programs in *assembly* and *high-level languages* are represented by instructions that use English-language-type statements. The programmer finds it relatively more convenient to write programs in assembly or high-level language than in machine language. However, a translator must be used to convert such programs into binary machine language so that the microprocessor can execute the programs. This is shown in Figure 5.1.

An *assembler* translates a program written in assembly language into a machine language program. A *compiler* or *interpreter*, on the other hand, converts a high-level language program such as C or C++ into a machine language program. Assembly or high-level language programs are called *source codes*. Machine language programs are known as *object codes*. A *translator* converts source codes to object codes. Next, we discuss the three main types of programming language in more detail.

FIGURE 5.1   **Translating assembly or high-level language into binary machine language.**

89

5.2   Machine Language

A microprocessor has a unique set of machine language instructions defined by its manufacturer. No two microprocessors by two different manufacturers have the same machine language instruction set. For example, the Intel Pentium microprocessor uses the code $03C3_{16}$ for its addition instruction, whereas the Motorola 68020 uses the code 0640_{16}. Therefore, a machine language program for one microprocessor will not run on the microprocessor of a different manufacturer.

At the most elementary level, a microprocessor program can be written using its instruction set in binary machine language. As an example, the following program adds two numbers using the Intel Pentium machine language:

0110 0110 1011 1000 0000 0001 0000 0000
0110 0110 1011 1011 0000 0010 0000 0000
0110 0110 0000 0011 1100 0011
1111 0100

Obviously, the program is very difficult to understand unless the programmer remembers all the Pentium codes, which is impractical. Because one finds it very inconvenient to work with 1's and 0's, it is almost impossible to write an error-free program on the first try. Also, it is very tiring for a programmer to enter a machine language program written in binary into the microcomputer's RAM. For example, the programmer needs a number of binary switches to enter the binary program. This is definitely subject to error.

To increase the programmer's efficiency in writing a machine language program, hexadecimal numbers rather than binary numbers are used. The following is the same addition program in hexadecimal using the Intel Pentium instruction set:

66B80100

66BB0200

6603C3

F4

It is easier to detect an error in a hexadecimal program, because each byte contains only two hexadecimal digits. One would enter a hexadecimal program using a hexadecimal keyboard. A keyboard monitor program in ROM, usually offered by the manufacturer, provides interfacing of the hexadecimal keyboard with the microcomputer. This program converts each key actuation into binary machine language in order for the microprocessor to understand the program. However, programming in hexadecimal is not normally used.

5.3   Assembly Language

The next programming level is to use assembly language. Each line in an assembly language program includes four fields:
- Label field
- Instruction, mnemonic, or op-code field
- Operand field
- Comment field

As an example, a typical program for adding two 16-bit numbers written in Pentium assembly language is as follows:

Label	Mnemonic	Operand	Comment
START:	MOV	AX,1	Move 1 into AX
	MOV	BX,2	Move 2 into BX
	ADD	AX,BX	Add the contents of AX with BX
	JMP	START	Jump to the beginning of the program

Obviously, programming in assembly language is more convenient than programming in machine language, because each mnemonic gives an idea of the type of operation it is supposed to perform. Therefore, with assembly language, the programmer does not have to find the numerical op-codes from a table of the instruction set, and programming efficiency is improved significantly.

An assembly language program is translated into binary via a program called an *assembler*. The assembler program reads each assembly instruction of a program as ASCII characters and translates them into the respective binary op-codes. As an example, consider the HLT instruction for the Pentium. Its binary op-code is 11110100. An assembler would convert HLT into 11110100 as shown in Table 5.1.

An advantage of the assembler is address computation. Most programs use addresses within the program as data storage or as targets for jumps or calls. When programming in machine language, these addresses must be calculated by hand. The assembler solves this problem by allowing the programmer to assign a symbol to an address. The programmer may then reference that address elsewhere by using the symbol. The assembler computes the actual address for the programmer and fills it in automatically. One can obtain hands-on experience with a typical assembler for a microprocessor by downloading it from the Internet.

5.3.1 Types of Assemblers

Most assemblers use two passes to assemble a program. This means that they read the input program text twice. The first pass is used to compute the addresses of all labels in the program. To find the address of a label, it is necessary to know the total length of all the binary code preceding that label. Unfortunately, however, that address may be needed in that preceding code. Therefore, the first pass computes the addresses of all labels and stores them for the next pass, which generates the actual binary code. Various types of assemblers are available today:

* *One-Pass Assembler.* This assembler goes through an assembly language program once and translates it into a machine language program. This assembler has the problem of

TABLE 5.1   Conversion of HLT into Its Binary Op-Code

Assembly Code	Binary form of ASCII Codes as Seen by Assembler		Binary OP Code Created by Assembler
H	0100	1000	
L	0100	1100	1111 0100
T	0101	0100	

defining forward references. This means that a JUMP instruction using an address that appears later in the program must be defined by the programmer after the program is assembled.

- *Two-Pass Assembler.* This assembler scans an assembly language program twice. In the first pass, this assembler creates a symbol table. A symbol table consists of labels with addresses assigned to them. This way, labels can be used for JUMP statements and no address calculation has to be done by the user. On the second pass, the assembler translates the assembly language program into machine code. The two-pass assembler is more desirable and much easier to use.

- *Macroassembler.* This type of assembler translates a program written in macrolanguage into machine language. This assembler lets the programmer define all instruction sequences using macros. Note that by using macros, the programmer can assign a name to an instruction sequence that appears repeatedly in a program. The programmer can thus avoid writing an instruction sequence that is required many times in a program by using macros. The macroassembler replaces a macroname with the appropriate instruction sequence each time it encounters a macroname.

  It is interesting to see the difference between a subroutine and a macroprogram. A specific subroutine occurs once in a program. A subroutine is executed by CALLing it from a main program. The program execution jumps out of the main program and executes the subroutine. At the end of the subroutine, a RET instruction is used to resume program execution following the CALL SUBROUTINE instruction in the main program. A macro, on the other hand, does not cause the program execution to branch out of the main program. Each time a macro occurs, it is replaced by the appropriate instruction sequence in the main program. Typical advantages of using macros are shorter source programs and better program documentation. A typical disadvantage is that effects on registers and flags may not be obvious.

  Conditional macroassembly is very useful in determining whether or not an instruction sequence is to be included in the assembly, depending on a condition that is true or false. If two different programs are to be executed repeatedly based on a condition that can be either true or false, it is convenient to use conditional macros. Based on each condition, a particular program is assembled. Each condition and the appropriate program are typically included within IF and ENDIF pseudoinstructions.

- *Cross assembler.* This type of assembler is typically resident in a processor and assembles programs for another for which it is written. The cross assembler program is written in a high-level language so that it can run on different types of processors that understand the same high-level language.

- *Resident assembler.* This type of assembler assembles programs for a processor in which it is resident. The resident assembler may slow down operation of the processor on which it runs.

- *Meta-assembler.* This type of assembler can assemble programs for many different types of processors. The programmer usually defines the particular processor being used.

5.3.2   Assembler Delimiters

As mentioned before, each line of an assembly language program consists of four fields: label, mnemonic or op-code, operand, and comment. The assembler ignores the comment field but translates the other fields. The label field must start with an uppercase alphabetic character. The assembler must know where one field starts and another ends. Most assemblers allow the programmer to use a special symbol or delimiter to indicate the beginning or end of each field. Typical delimiters used are spaces, commas, semicolons, and colons:

- Spaces are used between fields.

- Commas (,) are used between addresses in an operand field.

- A semicolon (;) is used before a comment.

- A colon (:) or no delimiter is used after a label.

5.3.3   Specifying Numbers by Typical Assemblers

To handle numbers, most assemblers consider all numbers as decimal numbers unless specified otherwise. All assemblers will also specify other number systems, including hexadecimal numbers. The user must define the type of number system used in some way. This is generally done by using a letter before or after the number. For example, Intel uses the letter H after a number to represent it as a hex number, whereas Motorola uses a $ sign before the number to represent it as a hex number. As an example, 60 in hexadecimal is represented by an Intel assembler as 60H and by a Motorola assembler as $60.

Typical assemblers such as MASM32 require hexadecimal numbers to start with a digit (0 through 9). A 0 is typically used if the first digit of the hexadecimal number is a letter. This is done to distinguish between numbers and labels. For example, typical assemblers such as MASM32 will normally require the number F3H to be represented as 0F3H; otherwise, the assembler will generate an error. However, ide 68k assembler used in this book for assembling 68000 and 68020 assembly language programs does not require '0' to be used if the first digit of a hexadecimal number is a letter.

5.3.4   Assembler Directives or Pseudoinstructions

Assemblers use pseudoinstructions or directives to make the formatting of the edited text easier. Pseudoinstructions are not translated directly into machine language instructions. They equate labels to addresses, assign the program to certain areas of memory, or insert titles, page numbers, and so on. To use the assembler directives or pseudoinstructions, the programmer puts them in the op-code field, and if the pseudoinstructions require an address or data, the programmer places them in the label or data field. Typical pseudoinstructions are ORIGIN (ORG), EQUATE (EQU), DEFINE BYTE (DB), and DEFINE WORD (DW).

ORIGIN (ORG)   The directive ORG lets a programmer place programs anywhere in memory. Internally, the assembler maintains a program counter type of register called an *address counter*. This counter maintains the address of the next instruction or data to be processed.

An ORG directive is similar in concept to a JUMP instruction. Note that the JUMP instruction causes a processor to place a new address in the program counter. Similarly, the ORG pseudoinstruction causes the assembler to place a new value in the address counter.

Typical ORG statements are

        ORG 7000H
        HLT

The Pentium assembler will generate the following code for these statements:

    7000 F4

Most assemblers assign a value of zero to the starting address of a program if the programmer does not define this by means of an ORG.

Equate (EQU)   The directive EQU assigns a value in its operand field to an address in its label field. This allows the user to assign a numerical value to a symbolic name. The user can then use the symbolic name in the program instead of its numeric value. This reduces errors.

A typical example of EQU is START EQU 0200H, which assigns the value 0200 in hexadecimal to the label START. Typical assemblers such as the MASM32 require the EQU directive to use hexadecimal numbers to start with a digit. A 0 is typically used if the first digit of the hexadecimal number is a letter. This is done to distinguish between numbers and labels. For example, most assemblers will require the number A5H to be represented as 0A5H, as follows:

BEGIN EQU   0A5H

Another example is

               PORTA EQU   40H
                     MOV   AL,0FFH
                     OUT   PORTA,AL

In this example, the EQU gives PORTA the value 40 hex, and FF hex is the data to be written into register AL by MOV AL,FFH. OUT PORTA,AL then outputs this data FF hex to port 40, which has already been equated to PORTA.

Note that if a label in the operand field is equated to another label in the label field, the label in the operand field must have been defined previously. For example, the EQU statement

               BEGIN EQU   START

will generate an error unless START is defined previously with a numeric value.

Define Byte (DB)   The directive DB is generally used to set a memory location to a certain byte value. For example,

               START DB   45H

will store the data value 45 hex to the address START. With some assemblers, the DB pseudoinstruction can be used to generate a table of data as follows:

               ORG   7000H
            TABLE DB   20H,30H,40H,50H

In this case, 20 hex is the first data of the memory location 7000; 30 hex, 40 hex, and 50 hex occupy the next three memory locations. Therefore, the data in memory will look like this:

7000	20
7001	30
7002	40
7003	50

Define Word (DW)   The directive DW is typically used to assign a 16-bit value to two memory locations. For example,

          ORG   7000H
  START DW   4AC2H

will assign C2 to location 7000 and 4A to location 7001. It is assumed that the assembler will assign the low byte first (C2) and then the high byte (4A). With some assemblers, the DW directive can be used to generate a table of 16-bit data as follows:

                ORG   8000H
  POINTER   DW   5000H,6000H,7000H

In this case, the three 16-bit values 5000H, 6000H, and 7000H are assigned to memory locations starting at the address 8000H. That is, the array would look like this:

8000	00
8001	50
8002	00
8003	60
8004	00
8005	70

END   This directive indicates the end of the assembly language source program.

5.3.5   Assembly Language Instruction Formats

In this section, assembly language instruction formats available with typical microprocessors are discussed. Depending on the number of addresses specified, the following instruction formats can be used: three-address, two-address, one-address, zero-address. Because all instructions are stored in the main memory, instruction formats are designed in such a way that instructions take less space and have more processing capabilities. It should be emphasized that the microprocessor architecture has considerable influence on a specific instruction format. The following are some important technical points that have to be considered while designing an instruction format:

- The size of an instruction word is chosen such that it facilitates the specification of more operations by a designer. For example, with 4- and 8-bit op-code fields, we can specify 16 and 256 distinct operations, respectively.

- Instructions are used to manipulate various data elements, such as integers, floating-point numbers, and character strings. In particular, all programs written in a symbolic language such as C are stored internally as characters. Therefore, memory space will not be wasted if the word length of the machine is some integral multiple of the number of bits needed to represent a character. Because all characters are represented using typical 8-bit character codes such as ASCII or EBCDIC, it is desirable to have 8-, 16-, 32-, or 64-bit words for the word length.

• The size of the address field is chosen such that high resolution is guaranteed. Note that in any microprocessor, the ultimate resolution is a bit. Memory resolution is a function of the instruction length, and in particular, short instructions provide less resolution. For example, in a microcomputer with 32K 16-bit memory words, at least 19 bits are required to access each bit of the word. (This is because $2^{15} = 32K$ and $2^4 = 16$.)

The general form of a *three-address instruction* is

<op-code> Addr1,Addr2,Addr3

Some typical *three-address instructions* are

MUL	A,B,C	;	C <- A * B
ADD	A,B,C	;	C <- A + B
SUB	R1,R2,R3	;	R3 <- R1 - R2

In this specification, all alphabetic characters are assumed to represent memory addresses, and the string that begins with the letter R indicates a register. The third address of this type of instruction is usually referred to as the *destination address*. The result of an operation is always assumed to be saved in the destination address.

Typical programs can be written using three-address instructions. For example, consider the following sequence of three-address instructions:

MUL	A, B, R1	;	R1 <- A * B
MUL	C, D, R2	;	R2 <- C * D
MUL	E, F, R3	;	R3 <- E * F
ADD	R1,R2,R1	;	R1 <- R1 + R2
SUB	R1,R3,Z	;	Z <- R1 - R3

This sequence implements the statement Z = A * B + C * D - E * F. The three-address format, in addition to the other formats is normally used by typical 32-bit microprocessors such as the Intel Pentium and the Motorola 68000.

If we drop the third address from the three-address format, we obtain the two-address format, whose general form is

<op-code> Addr1,Addr2

Some typical *two-address instructions* are

MOV	A,R1	;	R1 <- A
ADD	C,R2	;	R2 <- R2 + C
SUB	R1,R2	;	R2 <- R2 - R1

In this format, the addresses Addr1 and Addr2 represent source and destination addresses, respectively. The following sequence of two-address instructions is equivalent to the program using three-address format presented earlier:

```
MOV   A,R1        ;        R1 <- A
MUL   B,R1        ;        R1 <- R1 * B
MOV   C,R2        ;        R2 <- C
MUL   D,R2        ;        R2 <- R2 * D
MOV   E,R3        ;        R3 <- E
MUL   F,R3        ;        R3 <- R3 * F
ADD   R2,R1       ;        R1 <- R1 + R2
SUB   R3,R1       ;        R1 <- R1 - R3
MOV   R1,Z        ;        Z <- R1
```

This format is predominant in typical general-purpose microprocessors such as the Pentium and 68000/68020. Typical 8-bit microprocessors such as the Intel 8085 and the Motorola 6809 are accumulator based. In these microprocessors, the accumulator register is assumed to be the destination for all arithmetic and logic operations. Also, this register always holds one of the source operands. Thus, we only need to specify one address in the instruction, and therefore, this idea reduces the instruction length. The one-address format is predominant in 8-bit microprocessors. Some typical *one-address instructions* are

```
LDA   B          ;        Acc <- B
ADD   C          ;        Acc <- Acc + C
MUL   D          ;        Acc <- Acc * D
STA   E          ;        E <- Acc
```

The following program illustrates how we can translate the C language statement, $z = (a * b) + (c * d) - (e * f)$; into a sequence of one-address instructions:

```
lda   e          ;        Acc <- e
mul   f          ;        Acc <- e * f
sta   t1         ;        t1 <- Acc
lda   c          ;        Acc <- c
mul   d          ;        Acc <- c * d
sta   t2         ;        t2 <- Acc
lda   a          ;        Acc <- a
mul   b          ;        Acc <- a * b
add   t2         ;        Acc <- Acc + t2
sub   t1         ;        Acc <- Acc - t1
sta   z          ;        Z <- Acc
```

In this program, t1 and t2 represent the addresses of memory locations used to store temporary results. Instructions that do not require any addresses are called *zero-address instructions*. All microprocessors include some zero-address instructions in the instruction set. Typical examples of zero-address instructions are CLC (clear carry) and NOP.

5.3.6   Instruction Set Architecture (ISA)

An instruction set architecture (ISA) defines the assembly instructions (instruction set) of a microprocessor. Each instruction specifies the operation to be performed and includes one or more operands. An assembly language program typically contains a number of assembly instructions. ISAs have been distinguished based on the number of operands that can be specified in each instruction. Typical examples include two- and three-operand instructions.

Earlier 8-bit microprocessors such as the Intel 8085 are accumulator-based machines. To add two numbers, these microprocessors used a dedicated register called the *accumulator* to hold one of the data to be added. A single-operand ADD instruction such as ADD B specifies the add operation to be performed between the contents of an 8-bit register B and the contents of the 8-bit accumulator. The 8-bit result is stored back in the accumulator. In these microprocessors, single-operand instructions are predominant.

Typical 32-bit microprocessors such as the Pentium assume that both operands to be added are stored in registers. For example, the Pentium instruction ADD BX,CX will add the 16-bit contents of register BX with the 16-bit contents of register CX. The 16-bit result will be stored in BX. Two-operand instructions are predominant in these microprocessors.

A particular microprocessor's hardware implementation of an ISA is normally called that microprocessor's *microarchitecture*. Since the 1990s, new microarchitectures have been implemented with existing ISAs. This is because the time and cost of developing assemblers/compilers and operating systems for a new ISA can be enormous. Microprocessors such as the Pentium have been designed basically with an existing ISA. Note that Intel's x86 hardware became more complex with each successive generation, whereas the ISA was mostly unchanged. Intel extended the original x86 ISA to include the floating-point instructions in the Pentium.

5.3.7   Typical Instruction Set

An instruction set of a specific microprocessor consists of all the instructions that it can execute. The capabilities of a microprocessor are determined to some extent by the types of instructions it is able to perform. Each microprocessor has a unique instruction set designed by its manufacturer to do a specific task. We discuss some of the instructions that are common to all microprocessors. We group together chunks of these instructions which have similar functions. These instructions typically include:

* *Arithmetic and Logic Instructions.* These operations perform actual data manipulations. The instructions typically include arithmetic/logic, increment/decrement, and rotate/shift operations. Typical arithmetic instructions include ADD, SUBTRACT, COMPARE, MULTIPLY, and DIVIDE. Note that the SUBTRACT instruction provides the result and also affects the status flags, whereas the COMPARE instruction performs subtraction without any result and affects the flags based on the result.

Typical microprocessors utilize common hardware to perform addition and subtraction operations for both unsigned and signed numbers. The instruction set for a microprocessor typically includes the same ADD and SUBTRACT instructions for both unsigned and signed numbers. The interpretations of unsigned and signed ADD and SUBTRACT operations are performed by the programmer. For example, consider adding two 8-bit numbers, A and B ($A = FF_{16}$ and $B = FF_{16}$) using the ADD instruction by a microprocessor as follows:

$$1111111 \leftarrow \text{Intermediate carries}$$
$$FF_{16} = 11111111$$
$$+ \quad FF_{16} = 11111111$$
$$\text{-------------------------}$$
$$\text{final carry} \rightarrow 111111110 = FE_{16}$$

When the addition above is interpreted by the programmer as an unsigned operation, the result will be A + B = FF_{16} + FF_{16} = 255_{10}+ 255_{10}= 510_{10} which is $FE_{16}$with a carry, as shown above. However, if the addition is interpreted as a signed operation, then A + B = FF_{16} + FF_{16} = (-1_{10}) + (-1_{10}) = -2_{10} which is FE as shown above, and the final carry must be discarded by the programmer. Similarly, the unsigned and signed subtraction can be interpreted by the programmer.

Typical 16- and 32-bit microprocessors include both unsigned and signed multiplication and division instructions. Several unsigned multiplication algorithms are available. Multiplication of two unsigned numbers can be accomplished via repeated addition. For example, to multiply 4_{10} by 3_{10}, the number 4_{10} can be added twice to itself to obtain the result, 12_{10}.

Division between unsigned numbers can be accomplished via repeated subtraction. For example, consider dividing 7_{10} by 3_{10} as follows:

Dividend	Divisor	Subtraction Result	Counter
7_{10}	3_{10}	7 − 3 = 4	1
		4 − 3 = 1	1 + 1 = 2

Quotient = counter value = 2

Remainder = subtraction result = 1

Here, 1 is added to a counter whenever the subtraction result is greater than the divisor. The result is obtained as soon as the subtraction result is smaller than the divisor.

Signed multiplication can be performed using various algorithms. A simple algorithm follows. Assume that *M* (multiplicand) and *Q* (multiplier) are in two's-complement form. For the first case, perform unsigned multiplication of the magnitudes without the sign bits. The sign bit of the product is determined as $M_n \oplus Q_n$, where M_n and Q_n are the most significant bits (sign bits) of the multiplicand (*M*) and the multiplier (*Q*), respectively. To perform signed multiplication, proceed as follows:

1. If $M_n = 1$, compute the twos complement of *M*.
2. If $Q_n = 1$, compute the twos complement of *Q*.
3. Multiply the *n* − 1 bits of the multiplier and the multiplicand using unsigned multiplication.
4. The sign of the result, $S_n = M_n \oplus Q_n$.
5. If $S_n = 1$, compute the two's-complement of the result obtained in step 3.

Next, consider a numerical example. Assume that *M* and *Q* are two's-complement numbers. Suppose that $M = 1100_2$ and $Q = 0111_2$. Because $M_n = 1$, take the two's-complement of $M = 0100_2$; because $Q_n = 0$, do not change *Q*. Multiply 0111_2 and 0100_2 using the unsigned multiplication method discussed before. The product is 00011100_2. The sign of the product $S_n = M_n \oplus Q_n = 1 \oplus 0 = 1$. Hence, take the two's-complement of the product 00011100_2 to obtain 11100100_2, which is the final answer: -28_{10}.

Unsigned division can be performed using repeated subtraction. However, the general equation for division can be used for signed division. Note that the general equation for division is *dividend = quotient * divisor + remainder*. For example, consider dividend = – 9, divisor = 2. Three possible solutions are shown below:

(a)   – 9 = – 4 * 2 – 1, Quotient = – 4, Remainder = – 1.
(b)   – 9 = – 5 * 2 + 1, Quotient = – 5, Remainder = +1.
(c)   – 9 = – 6 * 2 + 3, Quotient = – 6, Remainder = +3.

However, the correct answer is shown in (a), in which, the Quotient = – 4 and the remainder = – 1. Hence, for signed division, the sign of the remainder is the same as the sign of the dividend, unless the remainder is zero. Typical microprocessors such as the Pentium follow this convention.

Typical logic instructions perform traditional Boolean operations such as AND, OR, and EXclusive-OR. The AND instruction can be used to perform a masking operation. If the bit value in a particular bit position is desired in a word, the word can be logically ANDed with appropriate data to accomplish this. For example, the bit value at bit 2 of an 8-bit number 0100 1Y10 (where an unknown bit value of Y is to be determined) can be obtained as follows:

```
        0 1 0 0  1 Y 1 0  -- 8-bit number
AND     0 0 0  0 0 1 0  0 -- masking  data
        ---------------------
        0 0 0  0 0 Y 0 0  -- result
```

If the bit value Y at bit 2 is 1, the result is nonzero (flag Z = 0); otherwise, the result is zero (Flag Z = 1) . The Z flag can be tested using typical conditional JUMP instructions such as JZ (Jump if Z=1) or JNZ (Jump if Z = 0) to determine whether Y is 0 or 1. This is called a *masking operation*. The AND instruction can also be used to determine whether a binary number is ODD or EVEN by checking the least significant bit (LSB) of the number (LSB = 0 for even and LSB = 1 for odd). The OR instruction can typically be used to insert a 1 in a particular bit position of a binary number without changing the values of the other bits. For example, a 1 can be inserted using the OR instruction at bit 3 of the 8-bit binary number 0 1 1 1 0 0 1 1 without changing the values of the other bits:

```
        0 1 1 1 0 0 1 1 -- 8-bit  number
OR    0 0 0 0 1 0 0 0 -- data for inserting a 1 at  bit 3
        -------------------
        0 1 1 1 1 0 1 1 -- result
```

The Exclusive-OR instruction can be used to find the one's-complement of a binary number by XORing the number with all 1's as follows:

```
        0 1 0 1 1 1 0 0 - -  8-bit number
XOR  1 1 1 1 1 1 1 1 - -  data
        --------------------------
        1 0 1 0 0 0 1 1 -- Result ( Ones Complement  of the 8-bit number  0 1 0 1 1 1 0 0)
```

Next, the concept of logic and arithmetic shift and rotate operations is reviewed.

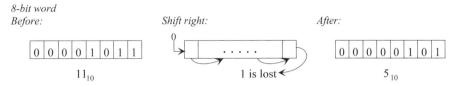

8-bit word
Before: Shift right: After:

| 0 | 0 | 0 | 0 | 1 | 0 | 1 | 1 | | 0 | 0 | 0 | 0 | 0 | 1 | 0 | 1 |

11_{10} 1 is lost 5_{10}

FIGURE 5.2   Logical right shift operation.

TABLE 5.2   Typical Logic/Arithmetic and Shift/ Rotate Operations

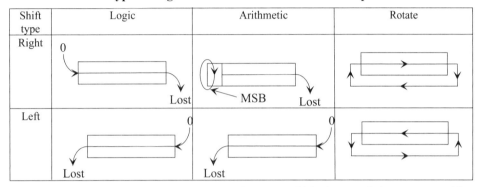

Shift type	Logic	Arithmetic	Rotate
Right	0 ... Lost	MSB ... Lost	
Left	0 ... Lost	0 ... Lost	

In a logical shift operation, a bit that is shifted out will be lost, and the vacant position will be filled with a 0. For example, if we have the number $(11)_{10}$, after a logical right shift operation, the register contents shown in Figure 5.2 will occur. Typical examples of logic/arithmetic and shift/rotate operations are given in Table 5.2.

It must be emphasized that a logical left or right shift of an unsigned number by n positions implies multiplication or division of the number by 2^n, respectively, provided that a 1 is not shifted out during the operation.

In the case of true arithmetic left or right shift operations, the sign bit of the number to be shifted must be retained. However, in computers, this is true for right shift and not for left shift operation. For example, if a register is shifted right arithmetically, the

Original	*After first shift*	*After second shift*
$0011_2 = (3)_{10}$	$0110_2 = (6)_{10}$	$1100_2 = (-4)$
	$3 \times 2 = 6$; correct	$6 \times 2 = 12$ not -4; incorrect

most significant bit (MSB) of the register is preserved, thus ensuring that the sign of the number will remain unchanged. This is illustrated in Figure 5.3.

There is no difference between arithmetic and logical left shift operations. If the

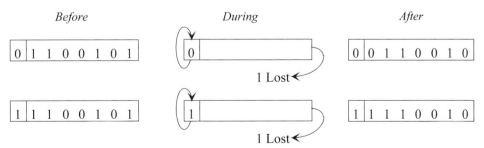

Before   During   After

| 0 | 1 | 1 | 0 | 0 | 1 | 0 | 1 | | 0 | | 0 | 0 | 1 | 1 | 0 | 0 | 1 | 0 |
                                1 Lost

| 1 | 1 | 1 | 0 | 0 | 1 | 0 | 1 | | 1 | | 1 | 1 | 1 | 1 | 0 | 0 | 1 | 0 |
                                1 Lost

FIGURE 5.3   True arithmetic right shift operation.

most significant bit changes from 0 to 1, or vice versa, in an arithmetic left shift, the result is incorrect and the microprocessor sets the overflow flag to 1. For example, if the original value of the register is $(3)_{10}$, the results of two successive arithmetic left shift operations are interpreted as follows:

• *Instructions for controlling microprocessor operations.* These instructions typically include those that set the reset specific flags and halt or stop the microprocessor.

• *Data movement instructions.* These instructions move data from a register to memory, and vice versa, between registers, and between a register and an I/O device.

• *Instructions using memory addresses.* An instruction in this category typically contains a memory address, which is used to read a data word from memory into a microprocessor register or for writing data from a register into a memory location. Many instructions under data processing and movement fall in this category.

• *Conditional and unconditional JUMP.* These instructions typically include one of the following:

1.   An unconditional JUMP, which always transfers the memory address specified in the instruction into the program counter.
2.   A conditional JUMP, which transfers the address portion of the instruction into the program counter based on the conditions set by one of the status flags in the flag register.

5.3.8   Typical Addressing Modes

One of the tasks performed by a microprocessor during execution of an instruction is the determination of the operand and destination addresses. The manner in which a microprocessor accomplishes this task is called the "addressing mode." Now, let us present the typical microprocessor addressing modes, relating them to the instruction sets of Motorola 68000.

An instruction is said to have "implied or inherent addressing mode" if it does not have any operand. For example, consider the following instruction: RTS, which means "return from a subroutine to the main program." The RTS instruction is a no-operand instruction. The program counter is implied in the instruction because although the program counter is not included in the RTS instruction, the return address is loaded in the program counter after its execution.

Whenever an instruction/operand contains data, it is called an "immediate mode" instruction. For example, consider the following 68000 instruction:

ADD   #15,D0 ;   D0 <- D0 + 15

In this instruction the # indicates to the assembler that it is an immediate mode instruction. This instruction adds 15 to the contents of register D0 and then stores the result in D0. An instruction is said to have a *register mode* if it contains a register as opposed to a memory address. This means that the operand values are held in the microprocessor registers. For example, consider the following 68000 instruction:

ADD   D1,D0   ; D0 <- D1 + D0

This ADD instruction is a two-operand instruction. Both operands (source and destination) have a register mode. The instruction adds the 16-bit contents of D0 to the 16-bit contents of D1 and stores the 16-bit result in D0.

An instruction is said to have an *absolute* or *direct addressing mode* if it contains a memory address in the operand field. For example, consider the 68000 instruction

ADD   3000, D2

This instruction adds the 16-bit contents of memory address 3000 to the 16-bit contents of D2 and stores the 16-bit result in D2. The source operand to this ADD instruction contains 3000 and is in the absolute or direct addressing mode.

When an instruction specifies a microprocessor register to hold the address, the resulting addressing mode is known as the *register indirect mode*. For example, consider the 68000 instruction

CLR (A0)

This instruction clears the 16-bit contents of a memory location whose address is in register A0 to zero. The instruction is in register indirect mode.

Conditional branch instructions are used to change the order of execution of a program based on the conditions set by the status flags. Some microprocessors use conditional branching using the absolute mode. The op-code verifies a condition set by a particular status flag. If the condition is satisfied, the program counter is changed to the value of the operand address (defined in the instruction). If the condition is not satisfied, the program counter is incremented, and the program is executed in its normal order.

Typical 16-bit microprocessors use conditional branch instructions. Some conditional branch instructions are 16 bits wide. The first byte is the op-code for checking a particular flag. The second byte is an 8-bit offset, which is added to the contents of the program counter if the condition is satisfied to determine the effective address. This offset is considered as a signed binary number with the most significant bit as the sign bit. It means that the offset can vary from -128_{10} to $+127_{10}$ (0 being positive). This is called the *relative mode*.

Consider the following 68000 example, which uses the branch not equal (BNE) instruction:

BNE 8

Suppose that the program counter contains 2000 (address of the next instruction to be executed) while executing this BNE instruction. Now, if $Z = 0$, the microprocessor will load $2000 + 8 = 2008$ into the program counter and program execution resumes at address 2008. On the other hand, if $Z = 1$, the microprocessor continues with the next instruction.

In the last example the program jumped forward, requiring a positive offset. An example for branching with negative offset is BNE -14

Suppose that the current program counter value = 2004_{16}

$$= 0010\ 0000 \quad 0000\ 0100$$

offset = two's complement of 14_{10} = $FFF2_{16}$ = $\boxed{1111\ 1111}$ $\ \ 1111\ 0010$

$$\nearrow 1\ \underbrace{0001\ 1111}\ /\ \underbrace{1111\ 0110}$$

ignore $\qquad 1 \quad F\ /\ F \quad 6_{16}$

reflect this 1 to the high byte
(sign extension)

Therefore, to branch backward to $1FF6_{16}$, the assembler uses an offset of F2 following the op-code for BNE.

An advantage of the relative mode is that the destination address is specified relative to the address of the instruction after the instruction. Since these conditional Jump instructions do not contain an absolute address, the program can be placed anywhere in memory, which can still be executed properly by the microprocessor. A program that can be placed anywhere in memory and can still run correctly is called a *relocatable program*. It is a good practice to write relocatable programs.

5.3.9   Subroutine Calls in Assembly Language

It is sometimes desirable to execute a common task many times in a program. Consider the case when the sum of squares of numbers is required several times in a program. One could write a sequence of instructions in the main program for carrying out the sum of squares every time it is required. This is all right for short programs. For long programs, however, it is convenient for the programmer to write a small program known as a *subroutine* for performing the sum of squares, and call this program each time it is needed in the main program. Therefore, a subroutine can be defined as a program carrying out a particular function that can be called by another program, known as the *main program*. The subroutine only needs to be placed once in memory starting at a particular memory location. Each time the main program requires this subroutine, it can branch to it, typically by using a jump to subroutine (JSR) instruction along with its starting address. The subroutine is then executed. At the end of the subroutine, a RETURN instruction takes control back to the main program.

The 68000 includes two subroutine call instructions. Typical examples include JSR 4000 and BSR 24. JSR 4000 is an instruction using the absolute mode. In response to the execution of JSR, the 68000 saves (pushes) the current program counter contents (address of the next instruction to be executed) onto the stack. The program counter is then loaded, with 4000 included in the JSR instruction. The starting address of the subroutine is 4000. The RTS (return from subroutine) at the end of the subroutine reads (pops) the return address saved into the stack before jumping to the subroutine into the program counter. The program execution thus resumes in the main program. BSR 24 is an instruction using relative mode. This instruction works in the same way as the JSR 4000 except that displacement 24 is added to the current program counter contents to jump to the subroutine.

The stack must always be balanced. This means that a PUSH instruction in a subroutine must be followed by a POP instruction before the RETURN from subroutine instruction so that the stack pointer points to the right return address saved onto the stack. This will ensure returning to the desired location in the main program after execution of the subroutine. If multiple registers are PUSHed in a subroutine, one must POP them in the reverse order before the subroutine RETURN instruction.

5.4   High-Level Language

As mentioned earlier, a programmer's efficiency increases significantly with assembly language compared to machine language. However, the programmer needs to be well acquainted with the microprocessor's architecture and its instruction set. Further, the programmer has to provide an op-code for each operation that the microprocessor has to carry out in order to execute a program. As an example, for adding two numbers, the programmer would instruct the microprocessor to load the first number into a register, add the second number to the register, and then store the result in memory. However, the programmer might find it tedious to write all the steps required for a large program. Also, to become a reasonably good assembly language programmer, one needs to have a lot of experience.

High-level language programs composed of English-language-type statements rectify all these deficiencies of machine and assembly language programming. The programmer does not need to be familiar with the internal microprocessor structure or its instruction set. Also, each statement in a high-level language corresponds to a number of assembly or machine language instructions. For example, consider the statement f = a + b;

written in a high-level language called C. This single statement adds the contents of a with b and stores the result in f. This is equivalent to a number of steps in machine or assembly language, as mentioned before. It should be pointed out that the letters a, b, and f do not refer to particular registers within the microprocessor. Rather, they are memory locations.

A number of high-level languages such as C and C++ are widely used at present. Typical microprocessors such as the Intel Pentium and the Motorola 68000/68020 can be programmed using these high-level languages. A high-level language is a problem-oriented language. The programmer does not have to know the details of the architecture of the microprocessor and its instruction set. Basically, the programmer follows the rules of the particular language being used to solve the problem at hand. A second advantage is that a program written in a particular high-level language can be executed by two different microcomputers, provided that they both understand that language. For example, a program written in C for a Pentium–based microcomputer will run on a 68020-based microcomputer because both microprocessors have a compiler to translate the C language into their particular machine language; minor modifications are required for I/O programs.

As mentioned before, like the assembly language program, a high-level language program requires a special program for converting the high-level statements into object codes. This program can be either an interpreter or a compiler. They are usually very large programs compared to assemblers. An interpreter reads each high-level statement such as F = A + B, and directs the microprocessor to perform the operations required to execute the statement. The interpreter converts each statement into machine language codes but does not convert the entire program into machine language codes prior to execution. Hence, it does not generate an object program. Therefore, an interpreter is a program that executes a set of machine language instructions in response to each high-level statement in order to carry out the function. A compiler converts each statement into a set of machine language instructions and also produces an object program that is stored in memory. This program must then be executed by the microprocessor to perform the required task in the high-level program.

In summary, an interpreter executes each statement as it proceeds, without generating an object code, whereas a compiler converts a high-level program into an object program that is stored in memory. This program is then executed.

5.5   Choosing a programming language

Compilers normally provide inefficient machine codes because of the general guidelines that must be followed for designing them. C/C++ is a high-level language that includes I/O instructions. However, the compiled codes generate many more lines of machine code than does an equivalent assembly language program. Therefore, the assembled program will take up less memory space and will execute much faster than the compiled C/C++. Although C/C++ language includes I/O instructions, applications involving I/O are normally written in assembly language. One of the main uses of assembly language is in writing programs for real-time applications. *Real time* indicates that the task required by the application must be completed before any other input to the program can occur that would change its operation. Typical programs involving non-real-time applications and extensive mathematical computations may be written in C/C++.

TABLE 5.3   Flowchart symbols

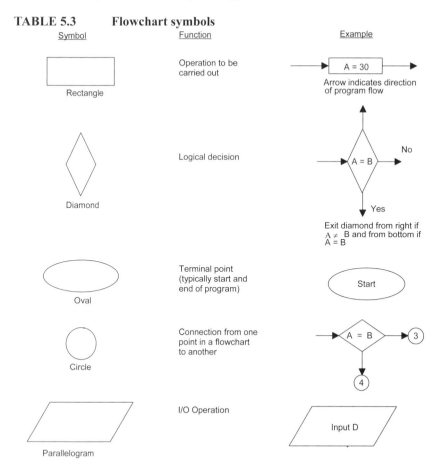

5.6   Flowcharts

Before writing an assembly language program for a specific operation, it is convenient to represent the program in a schematic form called a *flowchart*. A brief listing of the basic shapes used in a flowchart and their functions is given in Table 5.3.

Questions and Problems

5.1   What is the basic difference between assembly and high-level languages? Why
       would you choose one over the other?

5.2   Assume that two microprocessors, the Pentium and the 68020, have C compilers.
       Will a program written in C language run on both microprocessors?

5.3   Will a program written in Pentium assembly language run on a 68020?

5.4   Determine the contents of address 5004_{16} after assembling the following:
       (a)   ORG   5002H
                DB   00H, 05H, 07H, 00H, 03H
       (b)   ORG   5000H
                DW   0702H, 123FH, 7020H, 0000H

5.5   What is the difference between:
       (a)   A cross assembler and a resident assembler?
       (b)   A two-pass assembler and a meta-assembler?

5.6   Write a program equivalent to the C language assignment statement
       $$z = a + (b * c) + (d * e) - (f / g) - (h * i);$$
       Use only:
       (a)   Three-address instructions
       (b)   Two-address instructions

5.7   Assume that a microprocessor has only two registers, R1 and R2, and that only the
       following instruction is available:
                XOR   Ri,Rj   ; Rj <- Ri $\oplus$ Rj
                                ; i,j = 1,2
       Using this XOR instruction, find an instruction sequence to exchange the contents
       of registers R1 and R2.

5.8   Assume 2 two's-complement signed numbers, $M = 11111111^2$ and $Q = 11111100_2$.
       Perform signed multiplication using the algorithm described in Section 5.3.7.

5.9   Using the convention described in section 5.3.7, find the quotient and remainder
       of (-25)/3.

5.10   Find the logic operation and 8-bit data for clearing bits 2 and 4 of an 8-bit number,
       $7E_{16}$ to 0's without changing the other bits.

5.11   Find the logic operation and 8-bit data for setting bits 0 and 7 of an 8-bit
       number, $3A_{16}$ to 1's without changing the other bits.

5.12   Find the overflow bit after performing an arithmetic shift on $B6_{16}$ three times to
       the left.

5.13   Describe the meaning of each of the following addressing modes.

      (a)   Immediate   (b)   Absolute

      (c)   Register   (d)   Register indirect

      (e)   Relative   (f)   Implied

5.14   What are the advantages of subroutines?

5.15   Explain the use of a stack in implementing subroutine calls.

6

ASSEMBLY LANGUAGE PROGRAMMING WITH THE 68000

In this chapter we describe the fundamental concepts associated with assembly language programming using the Motorola 68000 microprocessor. Topics include 68000 registers, addressing modes, instruction sets, and assembly language programming.

6.1   Introduction

The 68000 is Motorola's first 16-bit microprocessor. Its address and data registers are all 32 bits wide, and its ALU is 16 bits wide. The 68000 requires a single 5-V supply. The processor can be operated from a maximum internal clock frequency of 25 MHz. The 68000 is available in several frequencies, including 4, 6, 8, 10, 12.5, 16.67, and 25 MHz. The 68000 does not have on-chip clock circuitry and therefore, requires an external crystal oscillator or clock generator/driver circuit.

The 68000 has several different versions, which include the 68008, 68010, and 68012. The 68000 and 68010 are packaged either in a 64-pin DIP (dual in-line package) with all pins assigned or in a 68-pin quad pack or PGA (pin grid array) with some unused pins. The 68000 is also packaged in 68-terminal chip carrier. The 68008 is packed in a 48-pin dual in-line package, whereas the 68012 is packed in an 84-pin grid array. The 68008 provides the basic 68000 capabilities with inexpensive packaging. It has an 8-bit data bus, which facilitates the interfacing of this chip to inexpensive 8-bit peripheral chips. The 68010 provides hardware-based virtual memory support and efficient looping instructions. Like the 68000, it has a 16-bit data bus and a 24-bit address bus. The 68012 includes all the 68010 features with a 31-bit address bus. The clock frequencies of the 68008, 68010, and 68012 are the same as those of the 68000. Table 6.1 summarizes basic differences among the 68000 family members:

TABLE 6.1   Basic Differences Among 68000 Family Members

	68000	68008	68010	68012
Data size (bits)	16	8	16	16
Address bus size (bits)	24	20	24	31
Virtual memory	No	No	Yes	Yes
Control registers	None	None	3	3
Directly addressable memory (bytes)	16 MB	1 MB	16 MB	2 GB

TABLE 6.2   68000 User and Supervisor Modes

	Supervisor Mode	User Mode
Enter mode by:	Recognition of a trap, reset, or interrupt	Clearing status bit S
System stack pointer	Supervisor stack pointer	User stack pointer
Other stack pointers	User stack pointer and registers A0-A6	Registers, A0-A6
Instructions available	All including: STOP RESET MOVE to/from SR ANDI to/from SR ORI to/from SR EORI to/from SR MOVE USP to (An) MOVE to USP RTE	All except those listed under supervisor mode
Function code pin FC2	1	0

To implement operating systems and protection features, the 68000 can be operated in two modes: *supervisor* and *user*. The supervisor mode is also called the *operating system mode*. In this mode, the 68000 can execute all instructions. The 68000 operates in one of these modes based on the S bit of the status register. When the S bit is 1, the 68000 operates in the supervisor mode; when the S bit is 0, the 68000 operates in the user mode.

Table 6.2 lists the basic differences between the 68000 user and supervisor modes. From the table, it can be seen that the 68000 executing a program in the supervisor mode can enter the user mode by modifying the S bit of the status register to 0 via an instruction. Instructions such as MOVE to SR, ANDI to SR, and EORI to SR can be used to accomplish this. On the other hand, the 68000 executing a program in the user mode can enter the supervisor mode only via recognition of a trap, reset, or interrupt. Note that upon hardware reset, the 68000 operates in the supervisor mode and can execute all instructions. An attempt to execute *privileged instructions* (instructions that can be executed only in the supervisor mode) in the user mode will automatically generate an internal interrupt (trap) by the 68000.

The logical level in the 68000 function code pin (FC2) indicates to the external devices whether the 68000 is currently operating in the user or the supervisor mode. The 68000 has three function code pins (FC2, FC1, and FC0), which indicate to the external devices whether the 68000 is accessing supervisor program/data or user program/data or performing an interrupt acknowledge cycle.

The 68000 can operate on five different data types: bits, 4-bit binary-coded-decimal (BCD) digits, bytes, 16-bit words, and 32-bit long words. The 68000 instruction set includes 56 basic instruction types. With 14 addressing modes, 56 instructions, and five data types, the 68000 contains over 1000 op-codes. The fastest instruction is one that copies the contents of one register into another register. It is executed in 500 ns at an 8-MHz clock rate. The slowest instruction is a 32-bit by 16-bit divide, which in executed in 21.25 μs at 8 MHz. The 68000 has no I/O instructions. Thus, the I/O is memory mapped. Hence, MOVE instructions between a register and a memory address are also used as I/O instructions. The

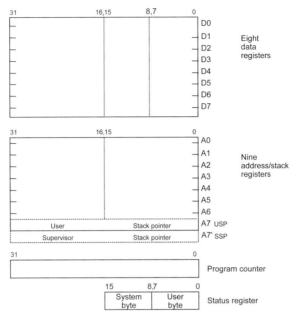

FIGURE 6.1   **68000 programming model.**

68000 is a general-purpose register-based microprocessor. Although the 68000 PC is 32 bits wide, only the low-order 24 bits are used. Because this is a byte-addressable machine, it follows that the 68000 microprocessor can directly address 16 MB of memory. Note that brackets [ ], are used in the examples throughout this chapter to indicate the contents of a 68000 register or a memory location.

6.2   68000 Registers

Figure 6.1 shows the 68000 registers. This microprocessor includes eight 32-bit data registers (D0–D7) and seven 32-bit address registers (A0–A6). Data registers normally hold data items such as 8-bit bytes, 16-bit words, and 32-bit long words. An address register usually holds the memory address of an operand; A0-A6 can be used as 16- or 32-bit. Because the 68000 uses 24-bit addresses, it discards the uppermost 8 bits (bits 24–31) while using the address registers to hold memory addresses. The 68000 uses A7 or A7' as the user or supervisor stack pointer (USP or SSP), respectively, depending on the mode of operation.

Note that the stack is basically read/write memory (RAM) addresses by the stack pointer. The stack is typically used during subroutine calls. For example, when the main program calls a subroutine using a 68000 instruction such as JSR (jump to subroutine). The 68000 automatically pushes the contents of the program counter (return address) onto the user or supervisor stack, depending on the S-bit. The RTS (return from subroutine) instruction, typically used at the end of the subroutine, pops the return address from the stack and transfers control to the proper place in the main program.

The 68000 status register consists of two bytes: a user byte and a system byte (Figure 6.2). The *user byte* includes typical condition codes such as C, V, N, Z, and X. The meaning of the C, V, N, and Z flags is obvious. Let us explain the meaning of the X bit. Note that the 68000 does not have any ADDC or SUBC instructions; rather, it has ADDX

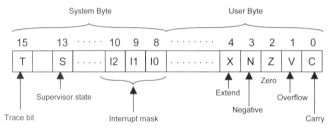

FIGURE 6.2   68000 status register.

and SUBX instructions. Because the flags C and X are usually affected in an identical manner, one can use ADDX or SUBX to reflect the carries or borrows in multiprecision arithmetic. The contents of the *system byte* include a 3-bit interrupt mask (I2, I1, I0), a supervisor flag (S), and a trace flag (T). When the supervisor flag is 1, then the system operates in the supervisor mode; otherwise, the user mode of operation is assumed. When the trace flag is set to 1, the processor generates a trap (internal interrupt) after executing each instruction. A debugging routine can be written at the interrupt address vector to display registers and/or memory after execution of each instruction, as this will provide a single-stepping facility. Note that the trace flag can be set to 1 in the supervisor mode by executing the instruction ORI# $8000, SR.

The interrupt mask bits (I2, I1, I0) provide the status of the 68000 interrupt pins $\overline{\text{IPL2}}, \overline{\text{IPL1}}$, and $\overline{\text{IPL0}}$. I2 I1 I0 = 000 indicates that all interrupts are enabled. I2 I1 I0 = 111 indicates that all maskable interrupts except the nonmaskable interrupt (Level 7) are disabled. The other combinations of I2, I1, and I0 provide the maskable interrupt levels. The signals on the $\overline{\text{IPL2}}, \overline{\text{IPL1}}$, and $\overline{\text{IPL0}}$ pins are inverted internally and then compared with I2, I1, and I0, respectively. The 68000 interrupts are covered in detail later in the chapter.

6.3   68000 Memory Addressing

The 68000 supports bytes (8 bits), words (16 bits), and long words (32 bits) as shown in Figure 6.3 . Byte addressing includes both odd and even addresses (0, 1, 2, 3, …), word addressing includes only even addresses in increments of 2 (0, 2, 4, …), and long word addressing contains even addresses in increments of 4 (0, 4, 8, …). As an example of the

	15	7	0	
Address = N	Byte 0	Byte 1	N + 1	
N + 2	Byte 2	Byte 3	N + 3	

(a) 68000 words stored in bytes (4 bytes)

	15		0	
Address = N	Word 0		N +1	
N + 2	Word 1		N + 3	
N + 4	Word 2		N + 5	

(b) 68000 word structure (3 words)

	15		0	
Address = N	Long word 0 (H)		N +1	
N + 2	Long word 0 (L)		N + 3	
N + 4	Long word 1 (H)		N + 5	
N + 6	Long word 1 (L)		N + 7	

(c) 68000 long word structure (2 long words)

FIGURE 6.3   68000 addressing structure (*N* is an even number).

TABLE 6.3   Conversion of RTS into Its Binary Op-Code

Assembly Code	Binary Form of ASCII Codes as Seen by the Assembler	Binary Op-Code Created by the 68000 Assembler
R	0101 0010	
T	0101 0100	0100 1110 0111 0101
S	0101 0011	

68000 addressing structure, consider MOVE.L D0,$506080. If prior to execution of the MOVE.L instruction, [D0] = $07F12481, then after this MOVE, [$506080] = $07, [$506081] = $F1, [$506082] = $24, [$506083] = $81, and [D0] = $07F12481 (unchanged).

Next, consider MOVE.W D0,$506080 with [D0] = $07F12481 prior to execution of the MOVE.L instruction. After execution of the instruction, [$506080] = $24, [$506081] = $81, and [D0] = $07F12481 (unchanged). Finally, consider MOVE.B D0,$506080 with [D0] = $07F12481 prior to execution of the MOVE.B instruction. After execution of the instruction, [$506080] = $81 and [D0] = $07F12481 (unchanged).

In the 68000, all instructions must be located at even addresses for byte, word, and long word instructions; otherwise, the 68000 generates an internal interrupt. The size of each 68000 instruction is even multiples of a byte. This means that once a programmer writes a program starting at an even address, all instructions are located at even addresses after assembling the program. For byte instructions, data can be located at even or odd addresses. On the other hand, data for a word and long word instruction must be located at even addresses; otherwise, the 68000 generates an internal interrupt.

Note that in 68000 for word and long word data, the low-order address stores the high-order byte of a number. This is called *big-endian byte ordering.* In contrast, the Pentium uses *little-endian byte ordering,* in which the Pentium assigns the low address to the low byte of a 16-bit register and the high address to the high byte of the 16-bit register for 16-bit transfers between the Pentium and main memory.

6.4   Assembly Language Programming with the 68000

The assembly language program is translated into binary via a program called an *assembler.* The assembler program reads each assembly instruction of a program as ASCII characters and translates them into the respective binary op-codes. For example, the 68000 assembler translates the RTS (Return from subroutine) instruction into its 16-bit binary op-code is 0100111001110101 (4E75 in hex), as depicted in Table 6.3.

An advantage of the assembler is address computation. Most programs use addresses within the program as data storage or as targets for jumps or calls. When programming in machine language, these addresses must be calculated by hand. The assembler solves this problem by allowing the programmer to assign a symbol to an address. The programmer may then reference that address elsewhere by using the symbol. The assembler computes the actual address for the programmer and fills it in automatically.

One can obtain hands-on experience with a typical assembler for a microprocessor by downloading it from the Internet. The ide68k21 assembler/debugger is used to assemble and debug all 68000 and 68020 assembly language programs in this book. It can be downloaded free of charge from the web site: http://home.hetnet.nl/~pj.fondse/ide68k/.

As mentioned in Chapter 5, each line in an assembly language program includes four fields:

1. Label field
2. Mnemonic or op-code field
3. Operand field
4. Comment field

The assembler ignores the comment field but translates the other fields. The label field must start with an uppercase alphabetic character.

The assembler must know where one field starts and another ends. Most assemblers allow the programmer to use a special symbol or delimiter to indicate the beginning or end of each field. Typical delimiters used are spaces, commas, semicolons, and colons:

- Spaces are used between fields.

- Commas (,) are used between addresses in an operand field.

- A semicolon (;) is used before a comment.

- A colon (:) or none is used after a label.

Note that the ide68k21 (68000/68020 assembler/debugger) used for developing programs in this book does not use a colon after a label.

To handle numbers, most assemblers, including the 68000, consider all numbers as decimal numbers unless specified otherwise. Most assemblers, including the 68000 assembler, will also allow other number systems, including hexadecimal. For example, with the 68000 assembler, the user can define a hexadecimal number by using a $ sign before the number. This means that $60 will imply that the number 60 is in hexadecimal. Typical assemblers such as the MASM32 require hexadecimal numbers to start with a digit (0 through 9). A 0 is typically used if the first digit of the hexadecimal number is a letter. This is done to distinguish between numbers and labels. For example, typical assemblers, such as the MASM32, will require the number F3H to be represented as 0F3H; otherwise, the assembler will generate an error. Note that the ide68k used in this book for assembling 68000 and 68020 assembly language programs does not require 0 to be used if the first digit of a hexadecimal number is a letter.

Assemblers use pseudoinstructions or directives to make the formatting of the edited text easier. These directives are not translated directly into machine language instructions. Typical assembler directives are discussed in the following.

ORIGIN (ORG)   The directive ORG lets the programmer place programs anywhere in memory. Typical ORG statements are

```
ORG          $7000
MOVE.W       D0,D1
```

Most assemblers assign a value of zero to the starting address of a program if the programmer does not define this by means of an ORG.

Equate (EQU)   The EQU assigns a value in its operand field to an address in its label field. This allows the user to assign a numerical value to a symbolic name. The user can then use the symbolic name in the program instead of its numerical value. A typical example of EQU is START EQU $0200, which assigns the value 0200 in hexadecimal to the label START. Typical assemblers, such as the ide68k21, require hexadecimal numbers to start with a digit when the EQU directive is used. A 0 is used if the first digit of the hexadecimal number is a letter; otherwise, an error will be generated by the assembler. This is done to distinguish between numbers and labels. For example, TEST   EQU $0A5 will assign A5 in hex to the label TEST.

Define Byte Constant (DC.B)   The directive DC.B is generally used to set a memory location to a certain byte value. For example,

```
          START             DC.B              $45
```

will store the data value 45 hex to the address START. The DC.B directive can be used to generate a table of data as follows:

```
                            ORG    $7000
          TABLE             DC.B    $20,$30,$40,$50
```

In this case, 20 hex is the first data of the memory location 7000; 30 hex, 40 hex, and 50 hex occupy the next three memory locations. Therefore, the data in memory will look like this:

```
          7000     20
          7001     30
          7002     40
          7003     50
```

Define Word Constant (DC.W)   The directive DC.W is typically used to assign a 16-bit value to two memory locations. For example,

```
                            ORG    $7000
          START             DC.W    $4AC2
```

will assign C2 to location 7001 and 4A to location 7000. It is assumed that the assembler will assign the high byte first (4A) and then the low byte (C2). The DC.W directive can be used to generate a table of 16-bit data as follows:

```
                            ORG    $8000
          POINTER           DW      $5000,$6000, $7000
```

In this case, the three 16-bit values $5000, $6000, and $7000 are assigned to memory locations starting at the address $8000. That is, the array would look like this:

```
          8000              50
          8001              00
          8002              60
          8003              00
          8004              70
          8005              00
```

Define Long Word Constant (DC.L)   Similar to DC.B and DC.W, the directive DC.L is typically used to assign a 32-bit value to four memory locations. The directive DC.W can be used to create a table in memory containing 32-bit data. As mentioned earlier, in order to develop 68000 assembly language programs in this book, ide68k21, containing the 68000/68020 assembler and simulator (debugger), is used. The ide68k21 software is window-based and is very userfriendly. These programs can be downloaded from the Internet free of charge. The zip files are provided in a CD. The CD also contains a tutorial showing step-by-step procedure for installing, assembling, and debugging a typical 68000 assembly language program using the ide68k21. Screen shots are provided on CD, verifying correct operation of all assembly language programs via simulations using test data.

A typical program for adding two 16-bit numbers written in 68000 assembly language is as follows:

Label Field	Mnemonic Field	Operand Field	Comment Field
	ORG	$2000	
	MOVE	#2,D0	; Move 2 into the low 16 bits of D0
	MOVE	#3,D1	; Move 3 into the low 16 bits of D1
	ADD	D0,D1	; Add D0 with D1,store result in D1
FINISH	JMP	FINISH	; Stop

Note that for a two-operand instruction such as ADD D0,D1, Motorola uses the first operand, D0, as the source operand and D1 as the destination operand. In contrast, for Pentium's MOV AX,BX instruction, Intel uses AX as the destination operand and BX as the source operand. Also, unlike Pentium Motorola, does not have a HALT instruction. Hence, an unconditional jump to the same address, such as FINISH   JMP FINISH, is used   to halt the program.

The assembly language program described above called a *source file*, contains all the instructions required to execute a program. The assembler converts the source file into an object file containing the binary codes or machine codes that the 68000 will understand. In typical assemblers, including the ide68k21, the source file must be stored with a file extension called .ASM. Suppose that the programmer stores the source file as SUM.ASM. To assemble the program, the source file SUM.ASM is presented as input to the assembler. The assembler typically generates two files: SUM.OBJ (object file) and SUM.LST (list file).

SUM.OBJ is an *object file*, a binary file containing the machine code and data that correspond to the assembly language program in the source file (SUM.ASM). The object file, which includes additional information about relocation and external references, is not normally ready for execution.

SUM.LST is a *list file* which shows how the assembler interprets the source file SUM.ASM. The list file may be displayed on the screen. The source file SUM.ASM is assembled using the ide68k21. The SUM.LST file is as follows:

```
2000                    1           ORG      $2000
2000    303C0002        2           MOVE     #2,D0
2004    323C0003        3           MOVE     #3,D1
2008    D240            4           ADD      D0,D1
200A    4EF8200A        5 FINISH    JMP      FINISH
```

Note that the assembled code shown on the left above is in hex. The first column gives the address values where the codes are stored. ORG $2000 generates the starting address, 002000 in hex. The machine code ($303C0002) for the first instruction, MOVE   #2,D0, is stored at the address $2000. Since this instruction takes 4 bytes, the machine code for the next instruction, MOVE #3,D1, starts at address $2004. Note that the comment fields in the SUM.ASM file are not translated by 68asmsim.

When a large program is being developed by a group of programmers, each programmer may write only a portion of the whole program. The individual program parts must be tested and assembled to ensure their proper operation. When all portions of the program are verified for correct operation, their object files must be combined into a single object program using a *Linker*, a program that checks each object file and finds certain characteristics, such as the size in bytes and its proper location in the single object program. The linker also resolves any problems with regard to cross-references to labels. A *library* of object files is typically used to reduce the size of the source file. The library files may contain frequently used subroutines and/or sections of codes. Rather than writing these codes repeatedly in the source file, a special pseudoinstruction is used to tell the assembler that the code must be inserted by the linker at linking time. When linking is completed, the final object file is called an *executable* (.EXE) *file*.

Finally, a program called a *Loader* can be used to load the .EXE file in memory for execution.

6.5   68000 Addressing Modes

The 14 addressing modes of the 68000 shown in Table 6.4 can be divided into six basic groups: register direct, address register indirect, absolute, program counter relative, immediate, and implied. As noted earlier, the 68000 has three types of instructions: no operand, single operand, and double operand. Single-operand instructions contain the effective address (EA) in the operand field. The EA for these instructions is calculated by the 68000 using the addressing mode used for this operand. In two-operand instructions, one of the operands usually contains the EA and the other operand is usually a register or memory location. The EA in these instructions is calculated by the 68000 based on the addressing mode used for the EA.

Some two-operand instructions have the EA in both operands. This means that the operands in these instructions use two addressing modes. Note that the 68000 address registers do not support byte-sized operands. Therefore, when an address register is used as a source operand, either the low-order word or the entire long word operand is used, depending on the operation size. When an address register is used as the destination operand, the entire register is affected, regardless of operation size. If the operation size is a word, an address register in the destination operand is sign-extended to 32 bits after the operation is performed. Data registers, on the other hand, support data operands of byte, word, or long word size.

To identify the operand size of an instruction, the following notation is placed after a 68000 mnemonic: .B for byte, .W or none (default) for word, and .L for long word: for example,

$$\text{ADD.B D0,D1} \quad ; \quad [D1]_{\text{low byte}} \leftarrow [D0]_{\text{low byte}} + [D1]_{\text{low byte}}$$
$$\text{ADD.W D0,D1} \quad ; \quad [D1]_{\text{low 16 bit}} \leftarrow [D0]_{\text{low 16 bit}} + [D1]_{\text{low 16 bit}}$$
$$\text{ADD.L D0,D1} \quad ; \quad [D1]_{\text{32 bits}} \leftarrow [D1]_{\text{32 bits}} + [D0]_{\text{32 bits}}$$

6.5.1   Register Direct Addressing

In the register direct mode, the eight data registers (D0–D7) or seven address registers (A0–A6) contain the data operand. For example, consider MOVE.W A0, D1. The source operand of this instruction is in addres register direct mode while the destination operand is in data register direct mode. Note that instructions with two operands have two addressing modes.

TABLE 6.4   68000 Addressing Modes.

Addressing Mode	Generation	Assembler Syntax
• Register direct addressing		
Data register direct	EA = Dn	Dn
Address register direct	EA = An	An
• Address register indirect addressing		
Register indirect	EA = (An)	(An)
Postincrement register indirect	EA = (An), An ¬ An + N	(An)+
Predecrement register indirect	An ¬ An - N, EA = (An)	-(An)
Register indirect with offset	EA = (An) + d$_{16}$	d(An)
Indexed register indirect with offset	EA = (An) + (Ri) + d$_8$	d(An, Ri)
• Absolute data addressing		
Absolute short	EA = (Next word)	xxxx
Absolute long	EA = (Next two words)	xxxxxxxx
• Program counter relative addressing		
Relative with offset	EA = (PC) + d$_{16}$	d
Relative with index and offset	EA = (PC) + (Ri) + d$_8$	d(Ri)
• Immediate data addressing		
Immediate	DATA = Next word(s)	#xxxx
Quick immediate	Inherent data	#xx
• Implied addressing		
Implied register	EA = SR, USP, SP, PC	

Notes:

EA	= effective address	USP	= user stack pointer
An	= address register	d$_8$	= 8-bit signed offset (displacement)
Dn	= data register	d$_{16}$	= 16-bit signed offset (displacement)
Ri	= address or data register used as index register	N	= 1 for byte, 2 for words, and 4 for long words
SR	= status register	( )	= contents of
PC	= program counter	←	= replaces
SP	= active system stack pointer		

6.5.2   Address Register Indirect Addressing

There are five different types of address register indirect mode. In this mode, an address register contains the effective address. The address must be even for word and long word operands; odd addresses are not allowed for .W and .L operands. However, for byte-sized operands, both even and odd addresses can be used.   Next, consider CLR.W(A1). If [A1.L] = $00003000; then after execution of CLR.W(A1), the 16-bit contents of the memory location addressed by $003000 (the low 24 bits of A0) is cleared to zero. This is depicted in Figure 6.4.

The postincrement address register indirect mode increments an address register by 1 for byte, 2 for word, and 4 for long word after it is used. For example, consider CLR.L (A0)+. If [A0] = $00005000, after execution of CLR.L (A0)+, the 32-bit contents of memory location addressed by $005000 (the low 24 bits of A0) is cleared to zero. This means that the 16-bit contents of each of the memory locations $005000 and $005002 is cleared to zero and [A0] = $00005000 + 4 = $00005004. This is shown in Figure 6.5.

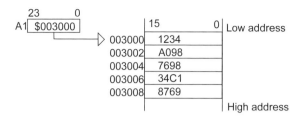

(a) Memory contents prior to execution of CLR.W (A1). All numbers in hex.

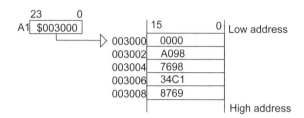

(b) Memory contents after execution of CLR.W (A1). All numbers in hex.

FIGURE 6.4   Illustration of the address register indirect mode

The postincrement mode is typically used with memory arrays stored from LOW to HIGH memory locations. For example, to clear 100 words starting at memory location $003000 and above, the following instruction sequence can be used:

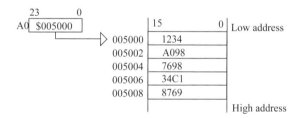

(a) Memory contents prior to execution of CLR.L (A0)+. All numbers in hex.
[A0] = $00005000.

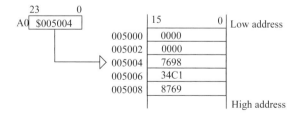

(b) Memory contents after execution of CLR.L (A0)+. All numbers in hex.
[A0] = $00005004.

FIGURE 6.5   Illustration of the postincrement address register indirect mode.

```
              MOVE.W    #100,D0          ; Load the length of data into D0
              MOVEA.L   #$00003000,A0    ; Load the starting address into A0
REPEAT        CLR.W     (A0)+            ; Clear a location pointed to
                                         ;by A0 and increment A0 by 2
              SUBQ.W    #1,D0            ;Decrement D0 by 1
              BNE       REPEAT           ;Branch to REPEAT if Z = 0
                .                        ;otherwise, go to next instruction
                .
                .
```

Although the instructions and addressing modes used in the program above are described in detail later, let us explain them briefly here. Note that # is used by Motorola to indicate the immediate mode. Hence, the first instruction, MOVE.W # 100, D0 loads 100 (the length of data to be cleared) into D0. MOVEA.L #$00003000,A0 loads $00003000 (initial pointer value) into A0.

CLR.W (A0)+ clears the 16-bit content of memory whose address is in the low 24 bits of A0. Note that CLR.W (A0)+ points automatically to the next location by incrementing A0 by 2 (for word) after clearing a 16-bit memory location to 0. Hence, A0 will contain $00003002 after clearing the first word. SUBQ.B #1,D0 decrements D0 by 1 and affects the zero flag. When D0 is decremented to 0, the ZF will be 1. BNE REPEAT will branch to label REPEAT if D0 is not zero (ZF = 0). When 100 words are cleared to 0, D0 will be 0 (ZF = 1), and the program will stop.

The predecrement address register indirect mode, on the other hand, decrements an address register by 1 for a byte, 2 for a word, and 4 for a long word before using a register. For example, consider CLR.W -(A0). If [A0] = $00005004, the content of A0 is first decremented by 2: that is, [A0] = $00005002. The content of memory location $005002 is then cleared to zero. This is depicted in Figure 6.6.

The predecrement mode is used with arrays stored from HIGH to LOW memory locations. For example, to clear 100 words starting at memory location 004000_{16} and below, the following instruction sequence can be used:

```
              MOVE.W    #100,D0          ;Load length of data into D0
              MOVEA.L   #$00004002,A0    ;Load starting address plus 2 into A0
REPEAT        CLR.W     -(A0)            ;Decrement A0 by 2 and clear memory
                                         ;location addressed by A0
              SUBQ.W    #1,D0            ;Decrement D0 by 1
              BNE       REPEAT           ;If Z = 0, branch to REPEAT
                .                        ;otherwise, go to next instruction
                .
                .
```

In this instruction sequence, CLR.W -(A0) first decrements A0 by 2 and then clears the location. Because the starting address is $004000, A0 must initially be loaded with $00004002. It should be pointed out that the predecrement and postincrement modes can be combined in a single instruction. A typical example is MOVE.W (A5)+,-(A3).

In two other address register indirect modes, offsets and indexes are included to an indirect address pointer. The *address register indirect with offset mode* determines the effective address by adding a 16-bit signed integer to the contents of an address register. For example, consider MOVE.W 4(A5),D3, in which the source operand is in the address register indirect with offset mode. If [A5] = $00002000 and [$002004] = $0014, then after

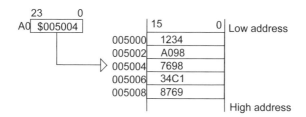

(a) Memory contents prior to execution of CLR.W -(A0). All numbers in hex. [A0] = $00005004.

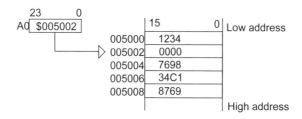

(b) Memory contents after execution of CLR.W-(A0). All numbers in hex. [A0] = $00005002.

FIGURE 6.6   Illustration of the predecrement address register indirect mode

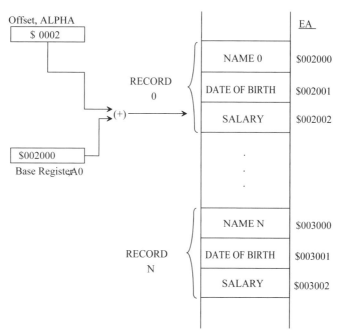

FIGURE 6.7   Accessing a fixed record stored in different places in memory using the address register indirect with offset mode.

execution of MOVE.W 4(A5),D3, register D3.W will contain $0014.

The address register indirect with offset mode can be used to access the elements in a table or a one-dimensional array when the size of each element is a byte. For example, consider an array of 50 bytes stored in memory starting at an address $3400. Note that the first element in the array is element 0 and the last element is element 49. Now, to access an element, say element 5 in the array, address register A5 can be initialized with address $3400, and the instruction MOVE.W 5(A5),D1 can be used to read element 5 into D1.B from the array.

The address register indirect with offset mode is useful when one wants to access the same record type among several occurrences in a data structure which may be stored at different places in memory. For example, consider Figure 6.7. In the figure, personal records of N employees are stored starting at an address $002000. Assume that each record type is 8 bits wide. For example, the element "salary" of the employee with NAME 0 can be loaded into an 8-bit register such as D0.B of the 68000 using the instruction MOVE.B ALPHA(A0),D0, where ALPHA is the 16-bit signed displacement $0002 and A0 contains the 24-bit starting address of RECORD 0. Now, to access the salary of RECORD N , the programmer simply changes the contents of A0 to $003000.

The *indexed register indirect with offset mode* determines the effective address by adding an 8-bit signed integer and the contents of a register (data or address register) to the contents of an address (base) register. The size of the index register can be a signed 16-bit integer or an unsigned 32-bit value. As an example, consider MOVE.W 6(A4,D3.W),D4 in which the source is in the indexed register indirect with offset mode. Note that in this instruction A4 is the base register and D3.W is the 16-bit index register (sign-extended to 32 bits). This register can be specified as 32 bits by using D3.L in the instruction, and 6 is the 8-bit offset that is sign-extended to 32 bits. If [A4] = $00003000, [D3.W] = $0200, and [$003206] = $0024, this MOVE instruction will load $0024 into the low 16 bits of register D4. The indexed register indirect with offset mode can also be used to access two-dimensional arrays such as matrices.

6.5.3   Absolute Addressing

In the absolute addressing mode, the effective address is part of the instruction. The 68000 has two modes: absolute short addressing, in which a 16-bit address is used (the address is sign-extended to 24 bits before use), and absolute long addressing, in which a 24-bit address is used. For example, consider an example of the absolute short mode such as MOVE.W $2000,D2. If prior to execution of this instruction, [$002000] = $0012 and [D2.W] – $0010, after execution of MOVE.W $2000,D2 , register D2.W will contain $0012, and [$002000] = $0012 (unchanged). The absolute short mode includes an address ADDR in the range $0 \leq$ ADDR $\leq$ $7FFF or $FF8000 $\leq$ ADDR $\leq$ $FFFFFF.

The absolute long addressing mode is used when the address size is more than 16 bits. For example, MOVE.W $240000,D5 loads the 16-bit contents of memory location $240000 into the low 16 bits of D5. Note that a single instruction may use both short and long absolute modes, depending on whether the source or destination address is less than, equal to, or greater than the 16-bit address. A typical example is MOVE.W $500002,$1000. Also, note that the absolute long mode must be used for a MOVE to or from address $008000. For example, MOVE.W $8000,D1 will move the 16-bit contents of location $FF8000 to the low 16 bits of D1, and MOVE.W $008000,D1 will transfer the 16-bit contents of address $008000 to D1.

6.5.4 Program Counter Relative Addressing

The 68000 has two program counter relative addressing modes: relative with offset and relative with index and offset. In the relative with offset mode, the effective address is obtained by adding the contents of the current PC with a signed 16-bit displacement providing the range -32768 to +32767 (0 being positive). Typical branch instructions such as BCC, BEQ, BRA, and BLE use the relative with offset mode.

Instructions using the relative with offset mode specify the operand as a signed 16-bit displacement relative to PC. An example is BCC START. This instruction means that if carry = 0, the PC is loaded with the current program counter contents plus the 16-bit signed value of START; otherwise, the next instruction is executed. This mode can also be used by some other instructions. For example, consider ADD $30(PC),D5, in which the source operand is in the relative with offset mode. Now suppose that the current PC contents is $002000, the content of $002030 is 0005, and the low 16 bits of D5 contain $0010. Then, after execution of this ADD instruction, D5 will contain $0015.

To illustrate the concept of relative branching, consider the following instruction sequence along with the machine code (all numbers in hex):

001000		1		ORG	$1000
001000	303C 0002	2	BACK	MOVE	#2,D0
001004	4EF8 1004	3	FINISH	JMP	FINISH
002000		4		ORG	$2000
002000	3401	5		MOVE	D1,D2
002002	6000 000A	6		BRA	DOWN
002006	3C3C 0005	7		MOVE	#5,D6
00200A	6000 EFF4	8		BRA	BACK
00200E	3206	9	DOWN	MOVE	D6,D1
002010	4EF8 2010	10	END	JMP	END

Note that all instructions, addresses, and data are chosen arbitrarily. The first branch instruction, BRA DOWN (line 6) at address $002002, has a machine code $6000000A. The instruction BRA (branch always) unconditionally branches to address DOWN, which has the relative addressing with offset mode. This means that DOWN is a positive number (the number of steps forward relative to the current program counter) indicating a forward branch. The machine code $6000000A means that the op-code for BRA is $60 and the relative displacement value is $000A (+10). This is a positive value indicating a forward branch. An additional $00 is included in the machine code to make it even multiples of a byte since all 68000 instructions must be at even addresses. Note that while executing BRA DOWN at address $002002, the 68000 points to address $002004 since the program counter is incremented by 2. This means that the program counter contains $002004. The offset $000A is added to address $002004 to find the target branch address where the program will jump unconditionally. The branch address can be calculated as follows:

$$\$002004 = 0000\ 0000\ \ 0010\ 0000\ 0000\ 0100$$
$$+\ \ \$000A = 0000\ 0000\ \ 0000\ 0000\ 0000\ 1010 \text{ (sign-extendedd to 24 bits)}$$
$$\overline{\hspace{6cm}}$$
$$0000\ 0000\ \ 0010\ \ 0000\ 0000\ 1110 = \$002000E$$

Hence, the instruction branches unconditionally to address $002000E. This can be verified in the instruction sequence above.

Next, consider the second branch instruction, BRA BACK (line 8). The machine code for this instruction at address $00200A is $6000 EFF4, where $60 is the op-code and $EFF4 is the signed 16-bit offset value. This offset is represented as a 16-bit two's-complement number. An additional $00 is included in the machine code to make it even multiples of a byte since all 68000 instructions must be at even addresses. Since $EFF4 is a negative number (-4108_{10}), this is a backward jump. Note that while executing BRA BACK at address $00200A, the 68000 points to address $00200C since the program counter is incremented by 2. This means that the program counter contains $00200C. The offset 4108 is subtracted from $00200A to find the address value where the program will jump unconditionally. The branch address is calculated as follows:

```
    $00200C  =  0000 0000  0010 0000 0000 1100
 +  $EFF4    =  1111 1111  1110 1111 1111 0100  (sign-extended to 24 bits)
    ----------------------------------------------------------------------
              ↗1 0000 0000  0001 0000 0000 0000 = $001000
       Ignore final carry
```

The branch address is $001000, which can be verified in the instruction sequence above. Also, in the instruction sequence, the JMP (unconditional jump) with absolute mode is used at lines 3 and 10. These two JMP instructions are used as halt since the 68000 does not have a HALT instruction in the user mode. Note that unconditionally jumping to the the same address is equivalent to HALT. The machine code for FINISH JMP FINISH (line 3) address $001004 is $4EF8 1004, where $4EF8 is the op-code, and $1004 is the jump address. Note that jump address $1004 is included with the instruction since JMP uses the absolute addressing mode. In contrast, BRA uses the relative with offset mode, so the machine code contains a signed offset relative to the program counter rather than an absolute address.

In the relative with index and offset mode, the effective address is obtained by adding the contents of the current PC, a signed 8-bit displacement (sign-extended to 32 bits), and the contents of an index register (address or data register). The index register can be 16 or 32 bits wide. For example, consider ADD.W 4(PC,D0.W),D2. If [D2] = $00000012, [PC] = $002000, [D0]low 16 bits = $0010, and [$002014] = $0002, then, after this ADD, [D2]low 16 bits = $0014. An advantage of the relative mode is that the destination address is specified relative to the address of the instruction after the instruction. Since 68000 instructions in the relative mode do not contain an absolute address, the program can be placed anywhere in memory and still be executed properly by the 68000. A program that can be placed anywhere in memory and can still run correctly is called a *relocatable* program. It is a good practice to write relocatable programs.

6.5.5   Immediate Data Addressing

Two immediate modes are available with the 68000: the immediate and quick immediate modes. In the *immediate mode*, the operand data is constant data, which is part of the instruction. For example, consider ADDI.W #$0005,D0. If [D0.W] = $0002, then after this ADDI instruction, [D0.W] = $0002 + $0005 = $0007. Note a # is used by Motorola to indicate the immediate mode. The *quick immediate mode* (ADD or SUBTRACT) allows one to increment or decrement a register or a memory location (.B, .W, .L) by a number from 0 to 7. For example, ADDQ.B #1,D0 increments the low 8-bit contents of D0 by 1. Note that the immediate data, 1, is inherent in the instruction. That is, data 0 to 7 is contained in the 3 bits of the instruction. Also, note that ADDQ.B #0,Dn is the same as the NOP instruction.

6.5.6 Implied Addressing

The instructions using the implied addressing mode do not require an operand, and registers such as PC, SP, or SR are referenced in these instructions. For example, RTS returns to the main program from a subroutine by placing the return address into a PC using the PC implicitly. It should be pointed out that in the 68000 the first operand of a two-operand instruction is the source and the second operand is the destination. Recall that in the case of the Pentium, the first operand is the destination and the second operand is the source.

6.6 68000 Instruction Set

The 68000 instruction set contains 56 basic instructions. Table 6.5 lists some of the instructions affecting the condition codes. Appendixes D and E provide the 68000 instruction execution times and the instruction set (alphabetical order), respectively.

TABLE 6.5   Some 68000 Instructions Affecting Conditional Codes

Instruction	X	N	Z	V	C
ABCD	✓	U	✓	U	–
ADD, ADDI, ADDQ, ADDX	✓	✓	✓	✓	✓
AND, ANDI	–	✓	✓	0	0
ASL, ASR	✓	✓	✓	✓	✓
BCHG, BCLR, BSET, BTST	–	–	✓	–	–
CHK	–	✓	U	U	U
CLR	–	0	1	0	0
CMP, CMPA, CMPI, CMPM	–	✓	✓	✓	✓
DIVS, DIVU	–	✓	✓	✓	0
EOR, EORI	–	✓	✓	0	0
EXT	–	✓	✓	0	0
LSL, LSR	✓	✓	✓	0	✓
MOVE (ea),(ea)	--	✓	✓	0	0
MOVE TO CCR	✓	✓	✓	✓	✓
MOVE TO SR	✓	✓	✓	✓	✓
MOVEQ	–	✓	✓	0	0
MULS, MULU	–	✓	✓	0	0
NBCD	✓	U	✓	U	✓
NEG, NEGX	✓	✓	✓	✓	✓
NOT	–	✓	✓	0	0

TABLE 6.5   **Cont.**

OR,ORI	–	✓	✓	0	0
ROL, ROR	–	✓	✓	0	✓
ROXL, ROXR	✓	✓	✓	0	✓
RTE, RTR	✓	✓	✓	✓	✓
SBCD	✓	U	✓	U	✓
STOP	✓	✓	✓	✓	✓
SUB, SUBI, SUBQ, SUBX	✓	✓	✓	✓	✓
SWAP	–	✓	✓	0	0
TAS	–	✓	✓	0	0
TST	–	✓	✓	0	0

✓ Affected, – Not Affected, U Undefined

Note: ADDA, B_{cc}, and RTS do not affect flags.

TABLE 6.6   **68000 Data Movement Instructions**

Instruction	Size	Comment
MOVE (EA), (EA)	B, W,L	(EA)s are calculated by the 68000 using the specific addressing mode used. (EA)s can be register or memory location. Therefore, data transfer can take place between registers, between a register and a memory location, and between different memory locations. Flags are affected. For byte-size operation, address register direct is not allowed. An is not allowed in the destination (EA). The source (EA) can be An for word or long word transfers.
MOVEA (EA), An	W, L	Content of the source is moved to the destination address register, An. Word size source operands are sign extended to 32 bits before the operation is done.
MOVEQ # data, Dn	L	This instruction moves the 8-bit data into the specified data register. The data is then sign-extended to 32 bits.
MOVEM reg list, (EA) or (EA), reg list	W, L	Specified registers are transferred to or from consecutive memory locations starting at the location specified by the effective address.

TABLE 6.6   Cont.

Instruction	Size	Comment
MOVEP Dn, d (Ay) or d (Ay), Dn	W, L	Two (W) or four (L) bytes of data are transferred between a data register and alternate bytes of memory, starting at the location specified and incrementing by 2. The high-order byte of data is transferred first, and the low-order byte is transferred last.This instruction has the address register indirect with displacement only mode.
EXG Rx,Ry	L	Exchange the contents of two registers. Rx or Ry can be any address or data register. No flags are affected.
SWAP Dn	W	Exchanges 16-bit halves of a data register.
LEA (EA), An	L	The effective address (EA) is calculated using the particular addressing mode used and then loaded into the address register. (EA) specifies the actual data to be loaded into An.
PEA (EA)	L	Computes an effective address and then pushes the 32-bit address onto the stack.
LINK An, #-displacement	Unsized	The current contents of the specified address register are pushed onto the stack. After the push, the address register is loaded from the updated SP. Finally, the 16-bit sign-extended displacement is added to the SP. A negative displacement is specified to allocate stack.
UNLK An	Unsized	An $\rightarrow$ SP; (SP) + $\rightarrow$ An

- (EA) in LEA (EA), An can use all addressing modes except Dn, An, (An) +, – (An), and immediate.

- Destination (EA) in MOVE (EA), (EA) can use all modes except An, relative, and immediate.

- Source (EA) in MOVE (EA), (EA) can use all modes.

- (EA) in MOVEA can use all modes.

- Destination (EA) in MOVEM reg list, (EA) can use all modes except An, (An)+, relative, and immediate.

- Source (EA) in MOVEM (EA), reg list can use all modes except Dn, An,– (An), and immediate.

- (EA) in PEA (EA) can use all modes except, An, (An)+, – (An), and immediate.

The 68000 instructions can be classified into eight groups as follows:
1.   Data movement instructions
2.   Arithmetic instructions
3.   Logic instructions
4.   Shift and rotate instructions
5.   Bit manipulation instructions
6.   Binary-coded decimal instructions
7.   Program control instructions
8.   System control instructions

6.6.1   Data Movement Instructions

These instructions allow data transfers from register to register, register to memory, memory to register, and memory to memory. In addition, there are special data movement instructions such as MOVEM (move multiple registers). Typically, byte, word, or long word data can be transferred. The 68000 data movement instructions are given in Table 6.6. Next, we explain the data movement instructions.

MOVE Instructions   The format for the basic MOVE instruction is MOVE.S (EA),(EA), where S = B, W, or L. (EA) can be a register or memory location, depending on the addressing mode used. Consider MOVE.B D3,D1, which uses the data register direct mode for both the source and the destination. If [D3.B] = $05 and [D1.B] = $01, then after execution of this MOVE instruction, [D1.B] = $05 and [D3.B] = $05 (unchanged).

There are several variations of the MOVE instruction. For example, MOVE.W CCR,(EA) moves the contents of the low-order byte of SR (16-bit status register) to the low-order byte of the destination operand; the upper byte of SR is considered to be zero. Note that CCR (condition code register) is the low byte of SR, containing the flags X, N, Z, V, and C. The source operand is a word. Similarly, MOVE.W (EA),CCR moves an 8-bit immediate number, or low-order 8-bit data, from a memory location or register into the condition code register; the upper byte is ignored. The source operand is a word. Data can also be transferred between (EA) and SR or USP (A7) using the following privileged instructions:

MOVE.W (EA),SR
MOVE.W SR,(EA)
MOVEA.L A7,An
MOVEA.L An,A7

MOVEA.W or.L (EA),An can be used to load an address into an address register. Word-size source operands are sign-extended to 32 bits. Note that (EA) is obtained by using an addressing mode. As an example, MOVEA.W #$2000,A5 moves the 16-bit word $2000 into the low 16 bits of A5 and then sign-extends $2000 to the 32-bit number $00002000. Note that sign extension means extending bit 15 of 2000_{16} from bit 16 through bit 31. As mentioned before, sign extension is required when an arithmetic operation between two signed binary numbers of different sizes is performed. The (EA) in MOVEA can use all addressing modes.

The MOVEQ.L #$d8, Dn instruction moves the immediate 8-bit data into the low byte of Dn. The 8-bit data is then sign-extended to 32 bits. This is a one-word instruction. For example, MOVEQ.L #$8F,D5 moves $FFFFFF8F into D5.

The MOVEM instruction can be used to push or pop multiple registers to or from

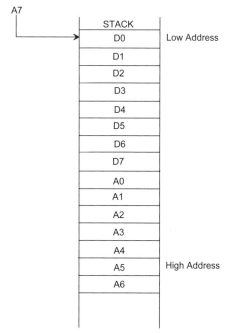

FIGURE 6.8 **Stack contents after execution of MOVEM.L D0-D7/A0-A6,-(A7)**

the user or supervisor stack. For example, MOVEM.L D0-D7/A0-A6,-(A7) saves the contents of all eight data registers and seven address registers in the user stack. Typical 68000 assemblers use the symbol '-' in D0-D7 and A0-A6 to indicate that registers D0 through D7 and registers A0 through A6 are included in the operation. Also, the MOVEM.L D0-D7/A0-A6,-(A7) instruction stores address registers in the order A6–A0 first, followed by data registers in the order D7–D0, regardless of the order in the register list. This is depicted in Figure 6.8.

MOVEM.L(A7)+,D0-D7/A0-A6 restores the contents of the registers in the order D0–D7, A0–A6, regardless of the order in the register list. Note that MOVEM.L(A7)+,D0-D7/A0-A6 will pop the register contents from the stack of Figure 6.8 in the correct order.

Next, consider the instruction MOVEM.L D5/D0/A0/A2/D7,-(A7). Note that the order is chosen arbitrarily. Typical 68000 assemblers use the symbol / to separate individual registers in the MOVEM.L D5/D0/A0/A2/D7,-(A7) instruction. The stack contents after execution of MOVEM.L D5/D0/A0/A2/D7,-(A7) are shown in Figure 6.9. Since A2 is the address register with the highest number in the list, A2 will be pushed first, then A0, followed by D7, D5, and D0. Note that no matter how the registers are ordered in the instruction, the order of pushing onto the stack is fixed (A6-A0 followed by D7-D0). The

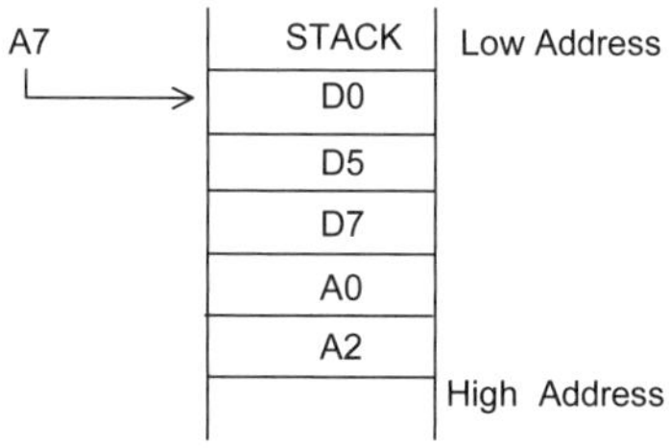

A7 ⟶ | STACK | Low Address
D0
D5
D7
A0
A2 | High Address

FIGURE 6.9 **Stack contents after execution of MOVEM.L D5/D0/A0/A2/D7,-(A7)**

order is also fixed for popping (D0-D7 followed by A0-A6). For example, MOVEM.L (A7)+,D5/D0/A0/A2/D7 will pop the register contents of the stack of Figure 6.9 in the correct order.

The MOVEM instruction can also be used to save a set of registers in memory. In addition to the preceding predecrement and postincrement modes for the effective address, the MOVEM instruction allows all the control modes. If the effective address is in one of the control modes, such as absolute short, the registers are transferred starting at the specified address and up through higher addresses. The order of transfer is from D0 to D7 and then from A0 to A6. For example, MOVEM.W A5/D1/D3/A1-A3,$2000 transfers the low 16-bit contents of D1, D3, A1, A2, A3, and A5 to locations $2000, $2002, $2004, $2006, $2008, and $200A, respectively.

To transfer data between the 68000 data registers and 6800 (8-bit) peripherals, the MOVEP instruction can be used. This instruction transfers 2 or 4 bytes of data between a data register and alternate byte locations in memory, starting at the location specified and incrementing by 2. Register indirect with displacement is the only addressing mode used with this instruction. If the address is even, all transfers are made on the high-order half of the data bus; if the address is odd, all transfers are made on the low-order half of the data bus. The high-order byte to/from the register is transferred first, and the low-order byte is transferred last. For example, consider MOVEP.L $0020(A2),D1. If [A2] = $00002000, [$002020$_{16}$] = 02, [002022_{16}$] = 05, [$002024$_{16}$] = 01, and [002026_{16}$] = 04, then after execution of this MOVEP instruction, D1 will contain 02050104$_{16}$.

EXG and SWAP Instructions   The EXG.L Rx, Ry instruction exchanges the 32-bit contents of Rx with that of Ry. The exchange is between two data registers, two address registers, or an address register and a data register. The EXG instruction exchanges only 32-bit long words. The data size (L) does not have to be specified after the EXG instruction because this instruction has only one data size (L) and it is assumed that the default is this single data size. No flags are affected. The SWAP.W Dn instruction, on the other hand, exchanges the low 16 bits of Dn with the high 16 bits of Dn. All condition codes are affected.

LEA and PEA Instructions   The LEA.L (EA),An instruction moves an effective address (EA) into the address register specified. The (EA) can be calculated based on the addressing mode of the source. For example, LEA $00256022,A5 moves $00256022 into A5. This instruction is equivalent to MOVEA.L #$00256022,A5. Note that $00256022 is contained in PC. It should be pointed out that the LEA instruction is very useful when address calculation is desired during program execution. The (EA) in LEA specifies the actual data to be loaded into An, whereas the (EA) in MOVEA specifies the address of actual data. For example, consider LEA $04(A5, D2.W),A3. If [A5] = 00002000$_{16}$ and [D2] = 0028$_{16}$, then the LEA instruction moves 0000202C16 into A3. On the other hand, MOVEA $04(A5, D2.W), A3 moves the contents of 00202C$_{16}$ into A3. Therefore, it is obvious that if address calculation is required, the instruction LEA is very useful.

The instruction PEA.L (EA) computes an effective address and then pushes it onto the supervisor stack (S = 1) or User stack (S = 0). This instruction can be used when the 16-bit address in absolute short mode is required to be pushed onto the stack. For example, consider PEA.L $9000 in the user mode. If [A7] = $00003006, then $9000 is sign-extended to 32 bits ($FFFF9000). The low-order 16 bits ($9000) are pushed at $003004, and the high-order 16 bits ($FFFF) are pushed at $003002.

LINK and UNLK Instructions   Before calling a subroutine, the main program quite often transfers the values of certain parameters to the subroutine. It is convenient to save these variables onto the stack before calling the subroutine. These variables can then be read from the stack and used by the subroutine for computations. The 68000 LINK and UNLK instructions are used for this purpose. In addition, the 68000 LINK instruction allows one to reserve temporary storage for the local variables of a subroutine. This storage can be accessed as needed by the subroutine and can be released using UNLK before returning to the main program. The LINK instruction is generally used at the beginning of a subroutine to allocate stack space for storing local variables and parameters for nested subroutine calls. The UNLK instruction is commonly used at the end of a subroutine before the RETURN instruction to release the local area and restore the stack pointer contents so that it points to the return address. The LINK An,# -displacement instruction causes the current contents of the specified An to be pushed onto the system stack (A7 or A7', depending on whether user or supervisor mode). The updated SP contents are then loaded into An. Finally, a sign-extended two's- complement displacement value is added to the SP. No flags are affected. For example, consider LINK A5,#-$100.

If [A5] = $00002100 and [A7] = $00004104, then after execution of the LINK instruction, the situation shown in Figure 6.10 occurs. This means that after the LINK instruction, [A5] = $00002100 is pushed onto the stack and the [updated A7] = $004100 is loaded into A5. A7 is then loaded with $004000, and therefore $100 locations are allocated to the subroutine at the beginning of which this particular LINK instruction can be used. Note that A5 cannot be used in the subroutine.

The UNLK instruction at the end of this subroutine before the RETURN instruction releases the 100_{16} locations and restores the contents of A5 and USP to those prior to using the LINK instruction. For example, UNLK A5 will load [A5] = $00004100 into USP and the two stack words $00002100 into A5. USP is then incremented by 4 to contain $00004104. This restores the contents of A5 and USP as they were prior to using the LINK instruction.

In this example, after execution of the LINK, addresses $0003FF and below can be used as the system stack. One hundred (hex) locations starting at $004000 and above can be reserved for storing the local variables of the subroutine. These variables can then be accessed with an address register such as A5 as a base pointer using the address register indirect with displacement mode. MOVE.W d(A5),D1 for read and MOVE.W D1,d(A5) for write are typical examples.

The use of LINK and UNLK can be illustrated by the following subroutine structure:

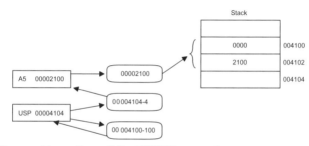

FIGURE 6.10   Execution of the LINK instruction.

SUBR	LINK A2, #-50	;	Allocate 50 bytes
	.		
	.		
	UNLK A2	;	Restore the original values
	RTS	;	Return to the subroutine

The LINK instruction is used in this case to allocate 50 bytes for local variables. At the end of the subroutine, UNLK A2 is used before RTS to restore the original values of the registers and the stack. RTS returns program execution in the main program.

EXAMPLE 6.1   Determine the effect of each of the following 68000 instructions:

- CLR D0

- MOVE.L D1,D0

- CLR.L (A0)+

- MOVE –(A0),D0

- MOVE 20(A0),D0

- MOVEQ.L #$D7,D0

- MOVE 21(A0, A1.L),D0

Assume the following initial configuration before each instruction is executed; also assume that all numbers are in hex:

$$[D0] = 22224444, \quad [D1] = 55556666$$
$$[A0] = 00002224, \quad [A1] = 00003333$$
$$[002220] = 8888, \quad [002222] = 7777$$
$$[002224] = 6666, \quad [002226] = 5555$$
$$[002238] = AAAA, [00556C] = FFFF$$

TABLE 6.7   Results for Example 6.1

Instruction	Effective Address	Net Effect (Hex)
CLR D0	Destination EA = D0	D0 = 22220000
MOVE.L D1,D0	Destination EA = D0	D0 = 55556666
CLR.L (A0)+	Destination EA = [A0]	[002224] = 0000
		[002226] = 0000
		A0 = 00002228
MOVE –(A0),D0	Source EA = [A0] – 2	A0 = 00002222
	Destination EA = D0	D0 = 22227777
MOVE 20(A0),D0	Source EA = [A0] + 20_{10}	D0 = 2222AAAA
	(or 14_{16}) = 002238	
	Destination EA = D0	
MOVEQ.L #$D7,D0	Source data = $D7_{16}$	D0 = FFFFFFD7
	Destination EA = D0	
MOVE 21(A0, A1.L),D0	Source EA = [A0] + [A1] + 21_{10}	D0 = 2222FFFF
	= 00556C	
	Destination EA = D0	

Solution   See Table 6.7

EXAMPLE 6.2   Find the affected   register(s) and/or memory locations for the following 68000 instruction sequence:

LEA.L	$00001000,A0
MOVEA .W	#$7002,A1
MOVE.L	#$12345678,D5
MOVE	D5,(A0)
SWAP.W	D5
MOVE	D5,-(A1)
MOVE	(A0)+,2(A1)

Solution

After execution of the instruction sequence above, (A0) = $00001002, (A1) = $00007002, (D5) = $56781234, ($007002) = $5678, and ($001000) = $5678.

Note that, LEA .L $00001000,A0 moves $00001000 directly into A0. MOVEA .W #$7002,A1 moves immediate 16-bit data into the low 16 bits of D5 and sign-extends to $00007002 in A1.

MOVE.L #$12345678,D5 moves $12345678 into D5. MOVE D5,(A0) moves $5678 into 16-bit memory location $001000. SWAP.W   D5   exchanges the low 16-bit ($5678) of D5 with the high 16-bit of D5 ($1234) so that (D5) = $56781234.

MOVE   D5,-(A1) decrements A1 by 2 so that A1 contains $007000, and then moves low 16 bit contents ($1234) into memory location $007000. MOVE (A0)+,2(A1) moves the 16-bit contents of memory addressed by A0 into the memory addressed by A1+2. Hence, $5678 is moved into memory location $007002; A0 is incremented by 2 to contain $00001002.

EXAMPLE 6.3   Write a 68000 assembly program at address $002000 to clear 100 consecutive bytes to zero from LOW to HIGH addresses starting at location $003000.

Solution

```
         ORG       $2000       ; #1 STARTING ADDRESS
         MOVEA .L #$3000,A0     ; #2 LOAD A0 WITH $3000
         MOVE.W   #99,D0        ; #3 MOVE 99 INTO  D0
LOOP     CLR.B     (A0)+        ; #4 CLEAR[$3000]+
         DBF.W     D0,LOOP      ; #5 DECREMENT AND
                                ;    BRANCH
FINISH   JMP       FINISH       ; #6 HALT
```

In order to explain the above program , line numbers are included with the comments. The instruction, DBF (Decrement and branch if false) is covered later in this chapter. Note that DBF.W Dn,LOOP decrements low 16 bits of the data register Dn by 1, and checks for Dn = -1. If Dn ≠ -1, then it branches to LOOP. If Dn = -1, then the next instruction is executed. That is, the loop is executed [Dn-1] times where Dn.W contains the loop count. Also, because DBF is a word instruction and considers D0's low 16-bit word as the loop count, one should be careful about initializing D0 using MOVEQ.L #d8,Dn since this instruction sign extends low byte of Dn to 32 bits.

In the above program, ORG $2000 at line #1 provides the starting address of the program. MOVEA.L #$3000,A0 instruction at line #2 loads A0 with $0000 3000 so that low 24 bits will be used as the starting address of the first byte in memory to be cleared to 0. MOVE.W #99,D0 at line #3 loads the loop count 99 into low 16 bits of D0. CLR.B (A0)+ at line #4 clears the byte pointed to by A0 (that is contents of $003000) to 0, and then increments A0 by 1 to point to $003001 (next location to be cleared). DBF.W D0,LOOP at line #5 decrements D0 by 1, checks if D0 = -1. Since D0 ≠ -1, branches to label LOOP. The LOOP is performed 100 times until D0 = -1.

Note that the 68000 has no HALT instruction.. Therefore, the unconditional jump to the same location such as FINISH JMP FINISH at line #6 is normally used at the end of the program to accomplish HALT.

EXAMPLE 6.4   Write a 68000 assembly language program at address $4000 to move a block of 16-bit data of length 100_{10} from the source block starting at location 002000_{16} to the destination block starting at location 003000_{16} from low to high addresses.

Solution

```
        ORG       $4000
        MOVEA.W   #$2000,A4    ;LOAD A4 WITH SOURCE ADDR
        MOVEA.W   #$3000,A5    ;LOAD A5 WITH DEST ADDR
        MOVE.W    #99,D0       ;LOAD D0 WITH COUNT -1=99
START   MOVE.W    (A4)+,(A5)+  ;MOVE SOURCE DATA TO DEST
        DBF.W     D0,START     ;BRANCH IF D0 IS NOT EQUAL TO -1
STAY    JMP       STAY         ;HALT
```

6.6.2   Arithmetic Instructions

Arithmetic instructions allow:

- 8-, 16-, or 32-bit additions and subtractions

- 16-bit by 16-bit multiplication (both signed and unsigned) and 32-bit by 16-bit division (both signed and unsigned)

- Compare, clear, and negate instructions

- Extended arithmetic instruction for performing multiprecision arithmetic

- A Test (TST) instruction for comparing the operand with zero

- A Test and set (TAS) instruction, which can be used for synchronization in a multiprocessor system

Typical microprocessors utilize common hardware to perform addition and subtraction operations for both unsigned and signed numbers. The instruction set of microprocessors typically include the same ADD and SUBTRACT instructions for both unsigned and signed numbers. The interpretations of unsigned and signed ADD and SUBTRACT operations are performed by the programmer. More detailed coverage is provided in Chapter 5.

Unsigned and signed multiplication and division operations can be performed using various algorithms. Typical 32-bit microprocessors such as the Pentium contain separate instructions for performing these multiplication and division operations.

These topics, along with some multiplication and division algorithms, are covered in chapter 5.

The 68000 arithmetic instructions are summarized in Table 6.8. Let us now explain the arithmetic instructions.

TABLE 6.8   68000 Arithmetic Instructions

Instruction	Size	Operation
Addition and Subtraction Instructions		
ADD (EA), (EA)	B, W, L	$[EA] + [EA] \rightarrow [EA]$
ADDI #Data, (EA)	B, W, L	$[EA] + \text{data} \rightarrow [EA]$
ADDQ #d_8, (EA)	B, W, L	$[EA] + d_8 \rightarrow [EA]$ d_8 can be an integer from 0 to 7
ADDA (EA), An	W, L	$An + [EA] \rightarrow An$
SUB (EA), (EA)	B, W, L	$[EA] - [EA] \rightarrow [EA]$
SUBI # data, (EA)	B, W, L	$[EA] - \text{data} \rightarrow [EA]$
SUBQ #d_8, (EA)	B, W, L	$[EA] - d_8 \rightarrow [EA]$ d_8 can be an integer from 0 to 7
SUBA (EA), An	W, L	$An - [EA] \rightarrow [An]$
Multiplication and Division Instructions		
MULS (EA), Dn	W	$[Dn]_{16} * [EA]_{16} \rightarrow [Dn]_{32}$ (signed multiplication)
MULU (EA), Dn	W	$[Dn_{16}] * [EA]_{16} \rightarrow [Dn]_{32}$ (unsigned multiplication)
DIVS (EA), Dn	W	$[Dn]_{32} / [EA]_{16} \rightarrow [Dn]_{32}$ (signed division, high word of Dn contains remainder and low word of Dn contains the quotient)
DIVU (EA), Dn	W	$[Dn]_{32} / [EA]_{16} \rightarrow [Dn]_{32}$ (unsigned division, remainder is in high word of Dn and quotient is in low word of Dn)
Compare, Clear, and Negate Instructions		
CMP (EA), Dn	B, W, L	$Dn - [EA] \rightarrow$ No result. Affects flags.
CMPA (EA), An	W, L	$An - [EA] \rightarrow$ No result. Affects flags.
CMPI # data, (EA)	B, W, L	$[EA] - \text{data} \rightarrow$ No result. Affects flags.
CMPM (Ay) +, (Ax)+	B, W, L	$(Ax)+ - (Ay)+ \rightarrow$ No result. Affects flags.
CLR (EA)	B,W,L	$0 \rightarrow [EA]$
NEG (EA)	B,W,L	$0 - [EA] \rightarrow [EA]$
Extended Arithmetic Instructions		
ADDX Dy,Dx	B, W, L	$Dx + Dy + X \rightarrow Dx$
ADDX $-$ (Ay), $-$ (Ax)	B, W, L	$- (AX) + - (Ay) + X \rightarrow (Ax)$

TABLE 6.8   Cont.

EXT Dn	W, L	If size is W, then sign extend low byte of Dn to 16 bits. If size is L, then sign extend low 16 bits of Dn to 32 bits.
NEGX (EA)	B, W, L	0 – [EA] – X → [EA]
SUBX Dy,Dx	B, W, L	Dx – Dy – X → Dx
SUBX – (Ay), – (Ax)	B, W, L	– (Ax) – – (Ay) – X → (Ax)

Test Instruction

TST (EA)	B, W, L	[EA] - 0 □ Flags are affected.

Test and Set Instruction

TAS (EA)	B	If [EA] = 0, then set Z = 1; else Z = 0, N = 1 and then always set bit 7 of [EA] to 1.

NOTE: If source (EA) in the ADDA or SUBA instruction is an address register, the operand length is WORD or LONG WORD.

(EA) in any instruction is calculated using the addressing mode used.

All instructions except ADDA and SUBA affect condition codes.

•   Source (EA) in the above ADD, ADDA, SUB, and SUBA can use all modes. Destination (EA) in the above ADD and SUB instructions can use all modes except An. relative, and immediate.

•   Destination (EA) in ADDI and SUBI can use all modes except An. relative, and immediate.

•   Destination (EA) in ADDQ and SUBQ can use all modes except relative and immediate.

•   (EA) in all multiplication and division instructions can use all modes except An.

•   Source (EA) in CMP and CMPA instructions can use all modes.

•   Destination (EA) in CMPI can use all modes except An, relative, and immediate.

•   (EA) in CLR and NEG can use all modes except An, relative, and immediate.

•   (EA) in NEGX can use all modes except An, relative and immediate.

•   (EA) in TST can use all modes except An, relative, and immediate.

•   (EA) in TAS can use all modes except An, relative, and immediate.

Addition and Subtraction Instructions   The 68000 addition and subtraction instructions are illustrated by means of numerical examples in the following.

•   Consider ADD.W $122000,D0. If [$122000] = $0012 and [D0] = $0002, then after execution of this ADD, the low 16 bits of D0.W will contain $0014. C = 0 (no Carry), X = 0 (same as C), V = 0 (no overflow since the previous carry and the final carry are the same), N = 0 (most significant bit of the result is 0), Z = 0 (nonzero result).

•   The ADDI instruction can be used to add immediate data to a register or memory location. The immediate data follows the instruction word. For example, consider ADDI.W #8,$100200. If [$100200] = $0002, then after execution of this ADDI, memory location $100200 will contain $000A. All condition codes are affected.

- ADDQ adds a number from 0 to 7 to a register or a memory location in the destination operand. This instruction occupies 16 bits, and the immediate data 0 to 7 is specified by 3 bits in the instruction word. For example, consider ADDQ.B #2, D1. If $[D1]_{lowbyte}$ = $20, then after execution of this ADDQ, the low byte of register D1 will contain $22.

- ADDA.L #4,A2 adds 4 to 32 bits of A2. For example, if prior to execution of this instruction, [A2] = $0A20 4000, then after execution of ADDA.L #4,A2, register A2.L will contain $0A20 4004. No condition codes are affected.

- All subtraction instructions subtract the source from the destination. For example, consider SUB.B $122200,D2. If [D2.L]= $23A50707 and [$122200] = $03, then, after execution of this SUB.B $122200,D2, register D2.L will contain $23A50704. The condition codes are affected as follows:

  Using two's-complement subtraction,   1111 111 $\leftarrow$ Intermediate Carries

                     [D2.B] = 0000 0111

        Add twos complement of $03 = 1111 1101

                  ----

                 final carry $\rightarrow$1 0000 0100

  The final carry is one's-complemented after subtraction to reflect the correct borrow. Hence, C = 0.

  Also, X = 0 (same as C), Z = 0 (nonzero Result), N = 0 (most significant bit of the result is zero), and V = Cf $\oplus$ Cp = 1 $\oplus$ 1 = 0.

- The SUBI instruction can be used to subtract immediate data from a register or memory location. For example, consider SUBI.B #9,D1. If prior to execution of this instruction, [D1.B] = $08, then after execution of SUBI.B #9,D1, the register will contain $FF or -1_{10}

- SUBQ subtracts a number from 0 to 7 from register or a memory location in the destination operand. This instruction occupies 16 bits, and the immediate data 0 to 7 is specified by 3 bits in the instruction word. For example, consider SUBQ.B #2,D1. If $[D1]_{low\ byte}$ = $05, then after execution of this SUBQ, the low byte of register D1 will contain $03.

- SUBA.L #4,A2 subtracts 4 to 32 bits of A2. No condition codes are affected. For example, if prior to execution of this instruction, [A2] = $0A204008, then after execution of SUBA.L #4,A2, register A2.L will contain $0A204004. No condition codes are affected.

Multiplication and Division Instructions   The 68000 instruction set includes both signed and unsigned multiplication of integer numbers. These instructions are explained using numerical examples in the following.

- MULS (EA),Dn multiplies two 16-bit signed numbers and provides a 32-bit result. For example, consider MULS #-2,D5. If [D5.W] = $0003, then after this MULS, D5 will contain the 32-bit result $FFFFFFFA, which is -6 in decimal.

- MULU (EA),Dn performs unsigned multiplication. Consider MULU (A0),D1. If [A0] = $00102000, [$102000] = $0300, and [D1.W] = $0200, then, after this MULU, D1 will contain the 32-bit result $00060000.

- Consider DIVS #2, D1. If [D1] = -5$_{10}$ = \$FFFFFFFB, then, after this DIVS, register D1 will contain

D1	FFFF	FFFE

16-bit   16-bit
remainder =   quotient =
−1$_{10}$ −2$_{10}$

Note that in the 68000, after DIVS, the sign of the remainder is always the same as the dividend unless the remainder is equal to zero. Therefore, in this example, because the dividend is negative (-5$_{10}$), the remainder is negative (-1$_{10}$). Also, division by zero causes an internal interrupt automatically. A service routine can be written by the user to indicate an error. N = 1 if the quotient is negative, and V = 1 if there is an overflow.

- DIVU is the same as the DIVS instruction except that the division is unsigned. For example, consider DIVU #4,D5. If [D5] = 14$_{10}$ = \$0000000E, then after this DIVU, register D5 will contain

D5	0002	0003

16-bit   16-bit
remainder   quotient

As with the DIVS instruction, division by zero using DIVU causes a trap (internal interrupt).

Compare, Clear, and Negate Instructions   The 68000 compare, clear, and negate instructions are illustrated by means of numerical examples in the following.

- The compare (CMP) instruction subtracts the source from the destination, providing no result of subtraction; all condition codes are affected based on the result. Note that the SUBTRACT instruction provides the result and also affects the condition codes. Consider CMP.B D3,D0. If prior to execution of the instruction, [D0.B] = \$40 and [D3.B] = \$30, then after execution of CMP.B D3,D0, the condition codes are as follows: C = 0, X = 0, Z = 0, N = 0, and V = 0. Suppose that it is desired to find the number of matches for an 8-bit number in a 68000 register such as D5.B in a data array (stored from low to high memory) of 50 bytes in memory pointed to by A0. The following instruction sequence with CMP.B (A0)+,D5 rather than SUB.B (A0)+,D5 can be used :

```
            CLR.B    D0         ; Clear D0.B to 0, D0.B to hold the number of
                                ; matches

            MOVE.B   #50,D1     ; Initialize the array count

START       CMP.B    (A0)+,D5   ; Compare the number to be matched in D5

            BNE.B    DECR       ; with a data byte in the array. If there is

            ADDQ.B   #1,D0      ; a match, Z=1 and increment D0.

DECR        SUBQ.B   #1,D1      ; Decrement D1 by 1 and go back to START if
```

      BNE.B   START   ; Z = 0. If Z = 1, go to the next instruction

                                 ; D0.B contains the number of matches

In the above, if SUB.B (A0)+,D5 were used instead of CMP.B (A0)+,D5, the number to be matched needed to be loaded after each subtraction because the contents of D5.B would have been lost after each SUB. Since we are only interested in the match rather than the result, CMP.B (A0)+,D5 instead of SUB.B (A0)+,D5 should be used in the above.

- The 68000 instruction set includes a memory-to-memory COMPARE instruction. For example, CMPM.W (A0)+,(A1)+. If [A0] = $00100000, [A1] = $00200000, [$100000] = $0005, and [$200000] = $0006, then after this CMPM instruction, N = 0, C = 0, X = 0, V = 0, Z = 0, [A0] = $00100002, and [A1] = $00200002.

- CLR.L D5 clears all 32 bits of D5 to zero.

- Consider NEG.W (A0). If [A0] = $00200000 and [$200000] = 5_{10}, then after this NEG instruction, the low 16 bits of location $200000 will contain $FFFB.

Extended Arithmetic Instructions   The 68000 extended arithmetic instructions are illustrated by means of numerical examples in the following.

- ADDX and SUBX instructions can be used in performing multiprecision arithmetic because there are no ADDC (add with carry) or SUBC (subtract with borrow) instructions. For example, to perform a 64-bit addition, the following two instructions can be used:

      ADD.L D0,D5   Add the low 32 bits of data and store in D5

      ADDX.L D1,D6   Add the high 32 bits of data along with any carry from
                                 the low 32-bit addition and store the result in D6

In the example above, D1D0 contains one 64-bit number and D6D5 contains the other 64-bit number. The 64-bit result is stored in D6D5. Note that the ADDX and SUBX instructions contain two operands. The addressing modes of these operands can be either both data register direct mode or both address register indirect with predecrement mode.

- SUBX.B D1,D2 subtracts the source byte (D1.B) plus the X-bit (the same as the carry flag) from the destination byte (D2.B); the result is stored in the destination byte, and no other bytes of the destination register are affected. All condition codes are affected. For example, if [D2.L] = $2AB10003, [D1.L] = $A2345602, and X = C = 1, then after SUBX.B D1,D2, the contents of D2.B = 03 - 02 - 1 = $00. [D2.L] = $2AB10000.

                                   1111 111 ← intermediate carries

using two's-complement subtraction, [D2.B]   =   0000 0011 (+3)

Add twos complement of 3 (D1.B plus Carry) = + 1111 1101 (-3)

                        ----

                  final carry → 1 0000 0000

The final carry is one's-complemented after subtraction to reflect the correct borrow. Hence, C = 0.

Also, X = 0 (same as C), Z = 1 (zero result), N = 0 (most significant bit of the result is zero), and V = $C_f \oplus C_p = 1 \oplus 1 = 0$.

- EXT.W Dn copies bit 7 of Dn to bits 8 through 15 of Dn. The upper 16 bits of Dn are not affected. Consider EXT.W D2. If [D2.L] = $421700F3, then after the EXT.W, [D2.L] = $4217FFF3. Note that sign extension is very useful when one wants to perform an arithmetic operation on two signed numbers of different lengths. For example. the 16-bit signed number $0020 can be added with the 8-bit signed number $E1 by sign-extending $E1 as follows:

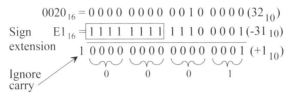

Another example of sign extension is that to multiply a signed 8-bit number by a signed 16-bit number, one must first sign-extend the signed 8-bit into a signed 16-bit number, and then the instruction MULS.W can be used for 16×16 signed multiplication. For unsigned multiplication of a 16-bit number by an 8-bit number, the 8-bit number must be zero-extended to 16 bits using a logical instruction such as AND before using the MUL instruction. For example, suppose that MULS.W D0,D1 will be used to multiply the low 8-bit contents of D0 by the low 16-bit contents of D1 and that prior to execution of this instruction, [D0.B] = $FF= -1 and [D1.W] = $0002 = +2. To perform this signed multiplication, the 8-bit contents of D0.B must be sign-extended to 16 bits using the EXT.W D0 instruction so that [D0.W] = $FFFF = -1. The multiplication instruction MULS.W D0,D1 can then be executed so that the 32-bit contents of D1 will contain the correct result, FFFFFFFEH (-2). Now, to perform unsigned multiplication, MUL.W D0,D1, with the same data, the low 8-bit contents of D0 must be zero-extended so that [D0.W] = $00FF (+255). This can be accomplished by using the logic AND instruction, which will be covered in the next section. Note that after execution of AND.W #$00FF,D0, the low 16 bits of register D0 will contain $00FF. The instruction MUL D0,D1 can then be executed so that 32 bits of D1 will contain the correct 32-bit product, 000001FEH (+510), since (D1.W) = 0002H.

- EXT.L Dn copies bit 15 of Dn to bits 16 through 31 of Dn. For example, if [D0.L] = $08A0A205, then after execution of EXT.L D0, the 32-bit contents of register D0 = $FFFF A205 since bit 15 (sign bit) of D0 is 1.

- The NEGX (EA) instruction subtracts destination operand (EA) and the X-bit from 0. The result is stored in the destination operand. All condition codes are affected. For example, consider NEG .L D2. If, prior to execution of this instruction, [D2.L] = 2, X = 0, then after execution of NEGX.L D1, the contents of the destination operand, D2 = 0 - 2 - 0 = -2 = $ FFFF FFFE.

Test Instruction   The 68000 test instruction is illustrated by means of numerical examples in the following.

- Consider TST.W (A0). If [A0] = 00300000_{16} and $[300000_{16}]$ = $FFFF_{16}$, then after TST.W (A0), the operation $FFFF_{16} - 0000_{16}$ is performed internally by the 68000, Z is cleared to 0, and N is set to 1. The V and C flags are always cleared to 0.

Test and Set Instruction   The 68000 test and set instruction is illustrated by means of numerical examples in the following.

- TAS.B (EA) is generally used to synchronize two processors in multiprocessor data

FIGURE 6.11   Two 68000s interfaced via shared RAM using the TAS instruction.

transfers. For example, consider two 68000-based microcomputers with shared RAM as shown in Figure 6.11.

Suppose that it is desired to transfer the low byte of D0 from processor 1 to the low byte of D2 in processor 2. A memory location, TRDATA, can be used to accomplish this. First, processor 1 can execute the TAS instruction to test the byte in the shared RAM with the address TEST for zero value. If it is, processor 1 can be programmed to move the low byte of D0 into location TRDATA in the shared RAM. Processor 2 can then execute an instruction sequence to move the contents of TRDATA from the shared RAM into the low byte of D2. The following instruction sequence will accomplish this:

Processor 1 Routine			Processor 2 Routine		
Proc_1	TAS.B	TEST	Proc_2	TAS.B	TEST
	BNE.B	Proc_1		BNE.B	Proc_2
	MOVE.B	D0,TRDATA		MOVE.B	TRDATA,D2
	CLR.B	TEST		CLR.B	TEST
	—			—	
	—			—	
	—			—	

Note that in these instruction sequences, TAS.B TEST checks the byte addressed by TEST for zero. If [TEST] = 0, then Z is set to 1; otherwise, Z = 0 and N = 1. After this, bit 7 of [TEST] is set to 1. Note that a zero value of [TEST] indicates that the shared RAM is free for use, and the Z bit indicates this after TAS is executed. In each instruction sequence, after a data transfer using the MOVE instruction, [TEST] is cleared to zero so that the shared RAM is free for use by the other processor. To avoid testing the TEST byte simultaneously by two processors, TAS is executed in a read-modify-write cycle. This means that once the operand is addressed by the 68000 executing TAS, the system bus is not available to the other 68000 until TAS is completed.

Arrays   The 68000 instructions and appropriate addressing modes to access one- and two-dimensional arrays are provided in the following.
* One-dimensional arrays (tables) can be accessed using the 68000 MOVE instruction with an appropriate addressing mode. For example, consider a table of five elements containing 5 bytes stored starting at the address $2000. The table is stored in memory such that $2000 points to element 0, $2001 points to element 1, and $2004 points to element 4. This is depicted in Figure 6.12(a).

An address register such as A0.L can be initialized with an element number to read the element from the table into an 8-bit data register such as D1.B. For example, if [A0.L] = 2, MOVE.B $2000(A0),D1 will load element 2 from address $2002 into D1.B. Note that if [A0.L] = 4, then MOVE.B $2000 (A0),D1 will transfer element 4 into

	7 Memory 0	Low Address
$2000	element 0	
$2001	element 1	
$2002	element 2	
$2003	element 3	
$2004	element 4	
		High Address

(a) 8-bit elements stored in memory

	31 Memory 0	Low Address
$4000	element 0	
$4004	element 1	
$4008	element 2	
$400C	element 3	
$4010	element 4	
		High Address

(b) 32-bit elements stored in memory

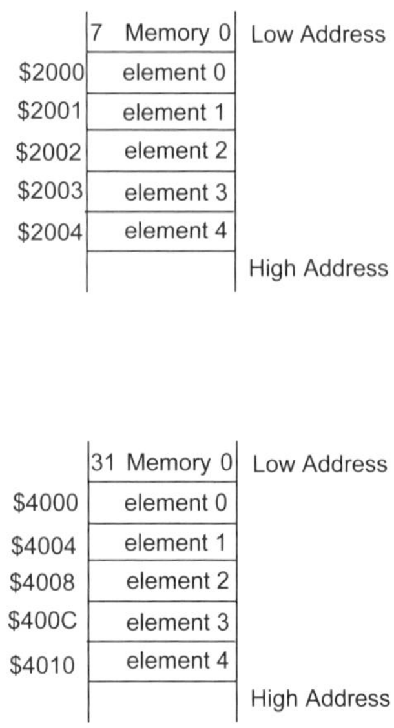

FIGURE 6.12   One-dimensional array stored in memory.

D1.B.

Suppose that an array of five elements containing 32-bit data words is stored starting at address $4000. This means that 4 bytes are needed to store each element. That is, $4000 through $4003 will contain element 0, while address $4010 through address 4013 will store element 4. Hence, address $4000 will contain element 0, address 4004 will contain element 1, address 4008 will contain element 2, and so on. This is shown in Figure 6.12 (b). Now, to move element 2 into D0.L, the following instruction sequence can be used:

```
LEA.L      $00004000,A0   ; Load the starting offset of the  array into A0.L
MOVE.L     #2, D1         ; Move element 2 into D1.L
LSL.L      #2,D1          ;Unsigned-multiply by 4 since a long word
MOVE.L     (A0,D1.L),D0   ; Load 32-bit value of element 2 into D0.L
```

The instruction, LSL.W #2,D1 in the above is covered in Section 6.6.3. LSL.W #2,D1 logically shifts the 32-bit contents of D1 twice to the left. This is the same as unsigned multiplication of a 32-bit number in D1 by 2^2 (or 4). This could have been accomplished using the MUL (unsigned multiplication) instruction. Since the execution time for MUL is much longer than for LSL, the instruction LSL is used for unsigned multiplication. In the instruction sequence above, the starting address ($4000) of the table is first loaded into a 32-bit address register such as A0. Element 2 is then transferred to an index register such as D1.L. Note that data register D1.L is used as an index register in the MOVE.L (A0,D1.L),D0 instruction. Register D1 is multiplied (unsigned multiplication since addresses are always positive) by 4 using the LSL.L instruction since each element is 4 bytes (32 bits). The value of element 2 is then loaded into a 32-bit register such as D0.L using MOVE (A0,D1.L),D0.

• Next, consider two-dimensional arrays or matrices. For example, assume a 2x3 matrix (two rows and three columns) as follows:

column 0	column 1	column 2
a [0,0]	a[0,1]	a[0,2]
a[1,0]	a[1,1]	a[1,2]

Since memory is one-dimensional, this matrix is stored in memory using column-major ordering.or row-major ordering .In column-major ordering, the elements are stored column by column, starting with the first column:

a[0,0]
a[1,0]
a[0,1]
a[1,1]
a[0,2]
a[1,2]

In row-major ordering, the elements are stored in memory row by row, starting with the first row:

a[0,0] --column 0 (start of array)
a[0,1]-- column 1
a[0,2]-- column 2
a[1,0]-- column 0
a[1,1]-- column 1
a[1,2]-- column 2

Since row-major ordering and subscripts start with 0 in the C language, the same convention will be used here. Assume that each element in the matrix is 16-bit wide. Hence, if the matrix is stored starting at address $2000, the matrix can be stored as row-major ordering:

$2000	a[0,0]
$2002	a[0,1]
$2004	a[0,2]
$2006	a[1,0]
$2008	a[1,1]
$200A	a[1,2]

In the C language, which uses row-major ordering and subscripts starting with zero, one can express displacement d of an element at row i and column j as $d = (i* t + j) * s$, where t is the total number of columns and s is the element size (1 for a byte, 2 for 16 bits, and 4 for 32 bits). Now, to find the displacement of an element such as a[1,2] with each element as 16 bits, the address can be determined as follows: Note that $i = 1, j = 2, t = 3$ (since this is a 2x3 matrix), and $s = 2$ (16-bit element). Hence, $d = (1*3 + 2)*2 = 10 = \$A$. Therefore, the address where element a[1,2] is stored = $2000 + \$A = \$200A$. This verifies the stored data. Now, to load element , a[1,2] into D0.W from the array, the following 68000 instruction sequence can be used:

```
         LEA.L      $00002000,A0   ; Low 16 bits of A0 to hold 16-bit address $2000
                                   ;with upper 16 bits as zero
         MOVE.W   #1,D2            ;Load i=1, row number into D2
         MUL.W    #3, D2           ; perform i*t, t = total columns =3
         ADDQ.L   #2,D2            ; compute i*t +j with  j = 2, store result in   D2.L
         LSL .L   #2,D2            ; unsigned multiply (i*t+j)*s  by 4, and store in D2.L
         MOVE.W   (A0 , D2.L),D0   ; Move 16-bit a[1,2] from address $200A into D0.W
```

EXAMPLE 6.5   Write a 68000 assembly language program that implements each of the following C language program segments:

(a)   if (x >= y)
               x = x + 10;
          else y = y – 12;
where x is the address of a 16-bit signed integer and y is the address of a 16-bit signed integer.

(b) sum = 0;
      for (i = 0; i <= 9; I = i + 1)
      sum = sum + a[i];
 where sum is the address of the 16-bit result of addition.

Solution

(a)   x   EQU   100
        y   EQU   200
                   LEA.L   x,A0   ;   Initialize A0
                   LEA.L   y,A1   ;   Initialize A1
                   MOVE.W   (A0),D0   ;   Move [x] into D0
                   CMP.W   (A1),D0   ;   Compare [x] with [y]
                   BGE.B   THPRT
                   SUBI.W   #12,(A1) ;   Execute else part
                   BRA.B   STAY
        THPRT   ADDI.W   #10,(A0) ;   Execute then part
        STAY   JMP   STAY   ;   Halt

(b)   Assume that register A0 holds the address of the first element of the array.

        SUM   EQU   300   ;   Initialize SUM to 300 for result
                   LEA.L   200,A0   ;   Point A0 to a[0]
                   CLR.W   D0   ;   Clear the sum to zero
                   MOVE.W   #9,D1   ;   Initialize D1 with loop limit
        LOOP   ADD.W   (A0)+,D0 ;   Perform the iterative summation
                   DBF.W   D1,LOOP
                   MOVE.W   D0,SUM   ;   Store 16-bit result in address SUM
        FINISH   JMP   FINISH   ;   Halt

Note that in the above, condition F in DBF is always false. Hence, the program exits from the LOOP when D1 = -1. Therefore, the addition process is performed 10 times.

EXAMPLE 6.6   Write a 68000 assembly language program to find $X^2/65535_{10}$ where X is a 16-bit signed number stored in D0.W. Store the 32-bit result (quotient and remainder) onto the user stack..

Solution

```
        MULS.W  D0,D0       ;  Compute X² and store in D0.L
        DIVU.W  #65535,D0   ;  Since X² and 655355 are both positive, use
        MOVE.L  D0,-(A7)    ;  unsigned division. Remainder in high word
FINISH  JMP     FINISH      ;  of D0 and quotient in low word of D0. Push
                            ;  D0.L to stack
```

EXAMPLE 6.7   What are the remainder, quotient, and register containing them after execution of the following 68000 instruction sequence?

```
        MOVE.W  #0FFFFH,D1
        DIVS.W  #2,D1
```

Solution

```
        MOVE.W  #0FFFFH,D1   ;    D1 = FFFFH = -1
        DIVS.W  #2,D1        ;    D1/2 = -1/2
```

High D1.W	Low D1.W
FFFFH	0000H

16-bit   16-bit
remainder =   quotient = 0
-1_{10}

EXAMPLE 6.8   Write a 68000 assembly language program at address $3000 to add two 64-bit numbers as follows:

```
  [D0.L] [D1.L]
+ [D2.L] [D3.L]
-----------------------
  [D2.L] [D3.L]
```

Solution

```
        ORG     $3000
        ADD.L   D1,D3        ; Add low 32 bits, store result in D3.L
        ADDX.L  D0,D2        ; Add with carry high 32 bits, store result
END     JMP     END          ; Halt
```

EXAMPLE 6.9   Write a 68000 assembly language program at address $2000 to add four 32-bit numbers stored in consecutive locations from low to high addresses starting at address $3000. Store the 32-bit result onto the user stack. Assume that no carry is generated, due to the addition of two consecutive 32-bit numbers and A7 is already initialized.

Solution

```
                ORG       $3000
                DC.L      1,2,3,4
                ORG       $2000
                MOVEQ.L   #3,D0       ;  Move 3  into D0
                MOVEA.L   #$3000,A0   ;  Initialize A0
                CLR.L     D1          ;  Clear sum to 0
START           ADD.L     (A0)+,D1    ;  Add
                DBF.W     D0,START    ;  perform loop
                MOVE.L    D1,-(A7)    ;  push result
FINISH          JMP       FINISH
```

EXAMPLE 6.10   Write a 68000 assembly language program at address $2000 to add ten 32-bit numbers stored in consecutive locations starting at address $3000. Initialize A6 to $00200504 and use the low 24 bits of A6 as the stack pointer to push the 32-bit result. Use only the ADDX instruction for adding two 32-bit numbers each time through the loop. Assume that no carry is generated, due to the addition of two consecutive 32-bit numbers; this will provide the 32-bit result. This example illustrates use of the 68000 ADDX instruction.

Solution

```
                ORG       $3000
                DC.L      2,3,7,5,1,9,6,4,6,1
START_ADR       EQU       $3000
                ORG       $2000
COUNT           EQU       9
                MOVEA.L   #START_ADR,A0   ;LOAD STARTING  ADDRESS IN A0
                MOVE.B    #COUNT,D0       ;USE D0 AS A COUNTER
                MOVEA.L   #$00200504,A6   ; USE A6 AS THE SP
                CLR.L     D1              ;CLEAR D1
                ADDI.B    #0,D6           ; CLEAR X BIT
AGAIN           MOVE.L    (A0)+,D3        ; MOVE A 32 BIT  NUMBER  IN D3
                ADDX.L    D3,D1           ;ADD NUMBERS  USING ADDX
                DBF.W     D0,AGAIN        ;REPEAT UNTIL  D0 = -1
                MOVE.L    D1,-(A6)        ;PUSH 32-BIT RESULT ONTO STACK
FINISH          JMP       FINISH
```

Note that ADDX adds the contents of two data registers or the contents of two memory locations using predecrement modes.

EXAMPLE 6.11 Write a 68000 assembly program at address $2000 to multiply an 8-bit signed number in the low byte of D1 by a 16-bit signed number in the high word of D5. Store the result in D3. Assume that the number is already stored in D1.B.

Solution

```
            ORG      $2000
            EXT.W    D1        ; SIGN EXTENDS LOW BYTE OF D1
            SWAP.W   D5        ; SWAP LOW WORD WITH HIGH WORD OF D5
            MULS.W   D1,D5     ; MULTIPLY D1 WITH D5, STORE RESULT
            MOVE.L   D5,D3     ; COPY RESULT IN D3
FINISH      JMP      FINISH
```

EXAMPLE 6.12 Write a 68000 assembly language program at address $2000 to compute $\sum_{i=1}^{N} X_i Y_i$, where the X_i's and Y_i's are signed 16-bit numbers and $N = 100$. Store the 32-bit result in D1. Assume that the starting addresses of the X_i's and Y_i's are 3000_{16} and 4000_{16} respectively.

Solution

```
P           EQU      $3000
Q           EQU      $4000
            ORG      $2000
            MOVE.W   #99,D0    ; MOVE 99 INTO DO
            LEA.L    P,A0      ; LOAD ADDRESS P INTO A0
            LEA.L    Q,A1      ; LOAD ADDRESS Q INTO A1
            CLR.L    D1        ; INITIALIZE D1 TO ZERO
LOOP        MOVE.W   (A0)+,D2  ; MOVE [X] TO D2
            MULS.W   (A1)+,D2  ; D2 <--[X]*[Y]
            ADD.L    D2,D1     ; D1 <-- SUM XiYi
            DBF.W    D0,LOOP   ; DECREMENT AND BRANCH
FINISH      JMP      FINISH    ; HALT
```

Note: To execute the program above, values for the Xi's and Yi's must be stored in memory using assembler directive DC.W.

EXAMPLE 6.13 Write a 68000 assembly language program to convert temperature from Fahrenheit to Celsius using the equation: $C = [(F - 32)/9] \times 5$; assume that the low byte of D0 contains the temperature in Fahrenheit. The temperature can be positive or negative. Store the result in D0.

Solution

```
            EXT.W    D0        ; SIGN EXTEND (F) LOW BYTE OF D0
            SUBI.W   #32,D0    ; PERFORM F-32
            MULS.W   #5,D0     ; PERFORM 5* (F-32)/9 AND STORE
            DIVS.W   #9,D0     ; REMAINDER IN HIGH WORD OF D0
FINISH      JMP      FINISH    ; AND QUOTIENT IN LOW WORD OF D0
```

EXAMPLE 6.14   Write a 68000 assembly program at address $1000 which is equivalent to the following C language segment:

sum = 0;

for (i = 0; i <= 9; i = i + 1)

sum = sum + x[i] * y[i];

Assume that the arrays, x[i] and y[i] contain unsigned 16-bit numbers already stored in memory starting at addresses $3000 and $4000 respectively. Store the 32-bit result at address $5000.

Solution

```
        ORG      $1000
x       EQU      $3000
y       EQU      $4000
sum     EQU      $5000
        MOVE.W   #9,D0        ;USE D0 AS A LOOP COUNTER
        LEA.L    x,A0         ;INITIALIZE A0 WITH x
        LEA.L    y,A1         ;INITIALIZE A1 WITH y
        LEA.L    sum,A2       ;INITIALIZE A2 WITH SUM
        CLR.L    D5           ;CLEAR SUM TO 0
LOOP    MOVE.W   (A0)+,D2     ;MOVE X[i] INTO D2
        MULU.W   (A1)+,D2     ;COMPUTE X[i] *y[i]
        ADD.L    D2,D5        ;UPDATE SUM
        DBF.W    D0,LOOP      ;REPEAT UNTIL D0=-1
        MOVE.L   D5,(A2)      ;STORE SUM IN MEMORY
FINISH  JMP      FINISH
```

EXAMPLE 6.15   Write a 68000 assembly language program at address $002000 to add all the elements in a table containing eight 16-bit numbers stored in memory in consecutive memory locations starting at the address $005000. Store the 16-bit result in D1.W.

Solution

```
        ORG      $005000
        DC.W     1,2,3,4
        DC.W     5,6,7,8
        ORG      $002000
        LEA.L    $00005000    ,A0; A0 = Starting address of the table
        MOVE.L   #0,D0        ; Move element number 0 into D0.L
        MOVE.L   D0,D3        ; Copy element number 0 into D3.L
        CLR.W    D1           ; Clear 16-bit sum in D1 to 0
        MOVE.W   #7,D2        ; Initialize D2.W with loop count
BACK    ADD      (A0,D0.L),D1 ; Add elements with sum in D1.W
        LSL.L    #1,D0        ; unsigned multiplication of element# by 2 forW
        ADDQ.L   #1,D3        ; Increment element number in D3.L by 1
        MOVE.L   D3,D0        ; Copy element number in D0.L
        DBF.W    D2,BACK      ; Decrement D2 and branch to BACK if D2 ≠ -1
END     JMP      END          ; Halt
```

EXAMPLE 6.16   Write a 68000 assembly language program at $1000 to find the trace (sum of the elements in the diagonal) of a 3x3 matrix containing 16-bit words. Store the 16-bit result in D0. Assume that the matrix is stored in row-major ordering starting at an offset $4000 as follows:

$4000   a[0,0]
$4002   a[0,1]
$4004   a[0,2]
$4006   a[1,0]
$4008   a[1,1]
$400A   a[1,2]
$400C   a[2,0]
$400E   a[2,1]
$4010   a[2,2]

Note that trace = a[0,0] + a[1,1] + a [2,2] and displacement, $d = (i *t +j) *s = i*t*s + j*s$ where i = row number, j = column number, t = total number of columns in the matrix, s = element size. In this example, $t = 3$ for 3x3 matrix, s=2 since each element is 16-bit. Hence, $d= 3*(2*i) + 2*j = 6 * i + 2 *j$. Hence, effective address where an element, aij will be stored = A0 + 6*i + 2*j where A0 = starting address of the array, i = row number, j = column number.

Solution

```
         ORG          $1000
         DC.W         $12, $56, $09    ;Data arbitrarily chosen
         DC.W          $78, $21,$89
         DC.W         $14, $21,$45
         ORG          $1000
         MOVE.L       #0,D1            ; Load column number 0 into D1
         MOVE.L       D1,D4            ; Copy D1 into D4
         MOVE.L       #0,D2            ; Load row number 0 into D2
         MOVE.L       D2,D6            ;Copy D2 into D6
         MOVE.W       #2,D7            ; initialize loop count
         CLR.W        D0               ; sum = 0
         LEA.L        $4000,A0         ; load starting address into A0
BACK     MULU.W       #6,D6            ; perform 6*i, result in D6.L
         ADDA.L       D6,A0            ; add A0 with 6*i
         ADD.W        (A0,D1.L),D0     ; sum diagonal elements in D0.W
         ADDQ.L       #1,D4            ; Increment column number by 1
         MOVE.L       D4,D1            ; save updated column# in D1.L
         LSL.L        #1,D1            ; Perform 2*j and save in D1.L
         ADDQ.L       #1,D2            ; Increment row number by 1
         MOVE.L       D2,D6            ; Copy updated row number into D6
         LEA.L        $4000,A0         ; re-initialize A0 to $4000 since [A0]was altered
         DBF.W        D7,BACK          ; Decrement D7.W by 1, branch if [D7.W] ≠ -1
FINISH   JMP          FINISH           ; Halt
```

TABLE 6.9   68000 Logic Instructions

Instruction	Size	Operation
AND (EA), (EA)	B, W, L	[EA] AND [EA] → [EA]; [EA] cannot be address register
ANDI # data, (EA)	B, W, L	[EA] AND # data → [EA]; ([A] cannot be address register
ANDI # data$_8$, CCR	B	[CCR] AND # data → [CCR]
ANDI # data$_{16}$, SR	W	[SR] AND# data → [SR]. Privileged Instruction.
EOR Dn, (EA)	B, W, L	[Dn] ⊕ [EA]→ [EA]; [EA] cannot be address register
EORI # data, (EA)	B, W, L	[EA] ⊕ # data → [EA]; [EA] cannot be address register
NOT (EA)	B, W, L	One's complement of [EA] → [EA];
OR (EA), (EA)	B, W, L	[EA] OR [EA] → [EA]; [EA] cannot be address register
ORI # data, (EA)	B, W, L	[EA] OR # data → [EA]; (EA) cannot be address register
ORI # data$_8$, CCR	B	[CCR] OR # data$_8$ → [CCR]
ORI # data$_{16}$, SR	W	[SR] OR # data → [SR], Privileged Instruction.

Source (EA) in AND and OR can use all modes except An.

*   Destination (EA) in AND or OR or EOR can use all modes except An, relative, and immediate.

*   Destination (EA) in ANDI, ORI, and EORI can use all modes except An, relative, and immediate.

*   (EA) in NOT can use all modes except An, relative, and immediate.

6.6.3   Logic Instructions

The 68000 logic instructions include logic OR, EOR, AND, and NOT, as shown in Table 6.9. We now explain the logic instructions.

*   Consider ANDI.B #$8F,D0. If prior to execution of this instruction, [D0.B] = $72, then after execution of AND.B #$8F,D0, the following result is obtained:

$$[D0.B] = \$72 = \quad 0111 \ 0010$$
$$AND \quad \$8F = \quad 1000 \ 1111$$
$$--------------$$
$$[D0.B] = 0000 \ 0010$$

Z = 0 (Result is nonzero) and N = 0 (most significant bit of the result is 0). C and V are always cleared to 0, and X is not affected after logic operation. The condition codes are similarly affected after execution of other logical instructions, such as OR, EOR, and NOT.

*   The AND instruction can be used to perform a masking operation. If the bit value in a particular bit position is desired in data (byte, word, or longword), the data can be logically ANDed with appropriate data to accomplish this. For example, the bit value at bit 2 of an 8-bit number 0100 1Y10 (where an unknown bit value of Y is to be determined) can be obtained as follows:

$$
\begin{array}{ll}
 & 0\ 1\ 0\ 0\ 1\ Y\ 1\ 0 \text{ -- 8-bit number} \\
\text{AND} & 0\ 0\ 0\ 0\ 0\ 1\ 0\ 0 \text{ -- Masking data} \\
 & \text{----------------------} \\
 & 0\ 0\ 0\ 0\ 0\ Y\ 0\ 0 \text{ -- Result}
\end{array}
$$

If the bit value Y at bit 2 is 1, the result is nonzero (flag $Z = 0$); otherwise, the result is zero ($Z=1$). The Z flag can be tested using typical conditional JUMP instructions such as BEQ (Branch if $Z = 1$) or BNE (Branch if $Z = 0$) to determine whether Y is 0 or 1. This is called a *masking operation*. The AND instruction can also be used to determine whether a binary number is ODD or EVEN by checking the least significant bit (LSB) of the number (LSB = 0 for even and LSB = 1 for odd).

*   Consider AND.W D1,D5. If [D1.W] = $0001 and [D5.W] = $FFFF, then after execution of this AND, the low 16 bits of both D1 and D5 will contain $0001.

*   Consider ANDI.B #$00,CCR. If [CCR] = $01, then after this ANDI, register CCR will contain $00.

*   Consider EORI.W #2,D5. If prior to execution of this instruction,[D5.W] = $2342, then after execution of EORI.W #2,D5, the low 16-bit contents of D5 will be 2340H. All condition codes are affected in the same manner as the AND instruction. The Exclusive-OR instruction can be used to find the one's-complement of a binary number by XORing the number with all 1's as follows:

$$
\begin{array}{ll}
 & 0\ 1\ 0\ 1\ 1\ 1\ 0\ 0 \text{ -- 8-bit number} \\
\text{XOR} & 1\ 1\ 1\ 1\ 1\ 1\ 1\ 1 \text{ -- data} \\
 & \text{--------------------------} \\
 & 1\ 0\ 1\ 0\ 0\ 0\ 1\ 1 \text{ -- result (one's-Complement of the 8-bit number } 0\ 1\ 0\ 1\ 1\ 1\ 0\ 0)
\end{array}
$$

*   Consider EOR.W D1,D2. If [D1.W] = $FFFF_{16}$ and [D2.W] = $FFFF, then after execution of this EOR, register D2.W will contain $0000, and D1 will remain unchanged at $FFFF.

*   Consider NOT.B D5. If [D5.B] = $02, then after execution of this NOT, the low byte of D5 will contain $FD.

*   Consider OR.B D2,D3. If prior to execution of this instruction, [D2.B] = $A2 and [D3.B] = $5D, then after exection of OR.B D2,D3, the content of D3.B is $FF. All flags are affected, similar to the case with the AND instruction. The OR instruction can typically be used to insert a 1 in a particular bit position of a binary number without changing the values of the other bits. For example, a 1 can be inserted using the OR instruction at bit 3 of the 8-bit binary number 0 1 1 1 0 0 1 1 without changing the values of the other bits as follows:

```
        0 1 1 1 0 0 1 1 -- 8-bit  number
OR      0 0 0 0 1 0 0 0 -- data for inserting a 1 at  bit 3
        -------------------
        0 1 1 1 1 0 1 1 -- result
```

- Consider ORI #$1002,SR. If [SR] = $111D, then after execution of this ORI, register SR will contain $111F. Note that this is a privileged instruction because the high byte of SR containing the control bits is changed and therefore can be executed only in the supervisor mode.

6.6.4   Shift and Rotate Instructions

The 68000 shift and rotate instructions are listed in Table 6.10. Let's look at them in detail.

- All the instructions in Table 6.10 affect N, Z, C, and X flags according to the result; V is cleared to zero for all shift and rotate instructions except for ASL.

- Note that in the 68000 there is no true arithmetic shift left instruction. In true arithmetic shifts, the sign bit of the number being shifted is retained. In the 68000, the instruction ASL does not retain the sign bit, whereas the instruction ASR retains the sign bit after performing the arithmetic shift operation.

- The basic concepts associated with shift and rotate instructions are covered in Chapter 5.

TABLE 6.10   68000 Shift and Rotate Instructions

Instruction	Size	Operation
ASL Dx,Dy	B, W, L	Shift [Dy] by the number of times to left specified in Dx; the low 6 bits of Dx specify the number of shifts from 0 to 63.
ASL # data,Dn	B, W, L	Same as ASL Dx, Dy, except that the number of shifts is specified by immediate data from 0 to 7.
ASL (EA)	B, W, L	(EA) is shifted 1 bit to left; the most significant bit of (EA) goes to x and c, and zero moves into the least significant bit.
ASR Dx,Dy	B, W, L	

TABLE 6.10   Cont.

		Arithmetically shift [Dy] to the right by retaining the sign bit; the low 6 bits of Dx specify the number of shifts from 0 to 63.
ASR # data,Dn	B, W, L	Same as above except the number of shifts is from 0 to 7.
ASR (EA)	B, W, L	Same as above except (EA) is shifted once to the right.
LSL Dx,Dy	B, W, L	
		Low 6 bits of Dx specify the number of shifts from 0 to 63.
LSL # data,Dn	B, W, L	Same as above except that the number of shifts is specified by immediate data from 0 to 7.
LSL (EA)	B, W, L	(EA) is shifted 1 bit to the left.
LSR Dx,Dy	B, W, L	
		Same as LSL Dx, Dy, except that the shift is to the right.
LSR # data,Dn	B, W, L	Same as above except that the shift is to the right by immediate data from 0 to 7.
LSR (EA)	B, W, L	Same as LSL (EA) except that the shift is once to the right.
ROL Dx Dy	B, W, L	
		Low 6 bits of Dx specify the number of times [Dy] to be rotated.
ROL # data,Dn	B, W, L	Same as above except that the immediate data specifies that [Dn] to be rotated from 0 to 7.
ROL (EA)	B, W, L	(EA) is rotated 1 bit to the left.

TABLE 6.10   **Cont.**

ROR Dx,Dy	B, W, L	

ROR # data,Dn	B, W, L	Same as above except that the rotate is to the right by immediate data from 0 to 7.
ROR (EA)	B, W, L	(EA) is rotated 1 bit to the right.
ROXL Dx,Dy	B, W, L	

Low 6 bits of Dx contain the number of rotates from 0 to 63.

ROXL # data,Dn	B, W, L	Same as above except that the immediate data specifies the number of rotates from 0 to 7.
ROXL (EA)	B, W, L	(EA) is rotated one bit to left.
ROXR Dx,Dy	B, W, L	

Low 6 bits of Dx contain the number of rotates from 0 to 63.

ROXR # data,Dn	B, W, L	Same as above except rotate is to the right by immediate data from 0 to 7.
ROXR (EA)	B, W, L	Same as above except rotate is once to the right.

Note: (EA) in ASL, ASR, LSL, LSR, ROL, ROR, ROXL, and ROXR can use all modes except Dn, An, relative, and immediate.

- Consider ASL.W D1,D5. If $[D1]_{low\ 16\ bits} = \$0002$ and $[D5]_{low\ 16\ bits} = \$9FF0$, then after this ASL instruction, $[D5]_{low\ 16\ bits} = \$7FC0$, C = 0, and X = 0. Note that the sign of the contents of D5 is changed from 1 to 0, and therefore, the overflow is set. The sign bit of D5 is changed after shifting [D5] twice. For ASL, the overflow flag is set to 1 if the sign bit changes during or after shifting. The contents of D5 are not updated after each shift. The ASL instruction can be used to multiply a signed number by 2^n by shifting the number n times to the left; the result is correct if V = 0 whereas the result is incorrect if V = 1. Since the execution time of the multiplication instruction is longer, multiplication by shifting may be more efficient when multiplication of a signed number by 2^n is desired. In communication systems, the number of samples is normally chosen by the designer as powers of 2. Hence, to multiply other parameters by the number of samples, multiplication using a shift instruction rather than a multiplication instruction can be used.This may be very useful in real-time systems.

- ASR retains the sign bit. For example, consider ASR.W #2, D1. If [D1.W] = $FFE2, then after this ASR, the low 16 bits of [D1] = $FFF8, C = 1, and X = 1. Note that the sign bit is retained. ASR can be used to divide a signed number by 2^n by shifting the number n times to the right as long as a 1 is not shifted out of the least significant bit.

- ASL (EA) or ASR (EA) shifts (EA) 1 bit left or right, respectively. For example, consider ASL.W (A0). If [A0] = $00002000 and [$002000] = $9001, then after execution of this ASL, [$002000] = $2002, X = 1, and C = 1. On the other hand, after ASR.W (A0), memory location $002000 will contain $C800, C = 1, and X = 1.

- The LSL and ASL instructions operate in the same way in the 68000 except that with the LSL, V is always cleared to 0. As mentioned earlier, V is set to 1 for ASL if the sign of the result is changed from the sign of the original value during or after shifting; otherwise, V is cleared to 0.

- LSL makes it possible to multiply an unsigned number by 2^n by shifting the number n times to the left; as long as a 1 is not shifted out of the most significant bit. Since the execution time of the multiplication instruction is longer, unsigned multiplication by LSL may be more efficient when multiplication of an unsigned number by 2^n is desired in applications such as communication systems.

- Consider LSR.W #3,D1. If [D1.W] = 8000_{16}, then after this LSR, [D1.W] = 1000_{16}, X = 0, and C = 0. LSR can be used to divide an unsigned number by 2^n by shifting the number n times to the right as long as a 1 is not shifted out of the least significant bit.

- ASR or LSR allows us to divide a signed or an unsigned number by 2^n by shifting the number n times to the left as long as a 1 is not shifted out of the most significant bit. Since the execution time of the division instruction is longer, signed division by ASR or unsigned division by LSR may be more efficient when multiplication of an unsigned number by 2^n is desired in applications such as communication systems.

- Consider ROL.B #2,D2. If [D2.B] = $B1 and C = 1, then, after this ROL, the low byte of [D2] = $C6 and C = 0. On the other hand, with [D2.B] = $B1 and C = 1, consider ROR.B #2,D2. After this ROR, low byte of register D2 will contain $6C and C = 0.

- Consider ROXL.W D2,D1. If [D2.W] = $0003, [D1.W] = $F201, C = 0, and X = 1 then after execution of this ROXL, [D1.W] = $900F, C = 1, and X = 1.

EXAMPLE 6.17   Write a 68000 assembly language program at address $3000 that will multiply a 32-bit unsigned number in D0.L by 4 to provide a 32-bit product , and then, perform the following operations on the contents of D0.L:
- Set bits 0 and 3 to 1 without changing other bits in D0.L.

- Clear bit 5 to zero without changing other bits in D0.L.

- One's-complement bit 7 without changing other bits in D0.L.

Use only logic and shift instructions. Do not use multiplication or any other instructions. Assume that the data is already in D0.L.

TABLE 6.11   Bit Manipulation Instructions

Instruction	Size	Operation
BCHG Dn, (EA) BCHG#data, (EA) }	B,L	A bit in (EA) specified by Dn or immediate data is tested: the 1's complement of the bit is reflected in both the *Z* flag and the specified bit position.
BCLR Dn, (EA) BCLR# data, (EA) }	B,L	A bit in (EA) specified by Dn or immediate data is tested and the 1's complement of the bit is reflected in the *Z* flag: the specified bit is cleared to zero.
BSET Dn, (EA) BSET# data, (EA) }	B,L	A bit in (EA) specified by Dn or immediate data is tested and the 1's complement of the bit is reflected in the *Z* flag: the specified bit is then set to one.
BTST Dn, (EA) BTST# data, (EA) }	B,L	A bit in (EA) specified by Dn or immediate data is tested. The 1's complement of the specified bit is reflected in the *Z* flag.

- (EA) in the above instructions can use all modes except An, PC relative, and immediate.

- If (EA) is memory location then data size is byte; if (EA) is Dn then data size is long word.

- If Dn is the destination, then the bit numbering is modulo 32 allowing bit manipulation on all bits in Dn. If a memory location is the destination, a byte is read from that location, the bit operation is performed using the bit number, modulo 8, and the byte is written back to the location.

- Only *Z*-flag is affected; N, V, C, and X are not affected.

Solution

```
        ORG     $3000
        LSL.L   #2,D0              ; Unsigned multiply D0 by 4
        ORI.L   #$00000009,D0      ; set bits 0 and 3 in D0.L to one
        ANDI.L  #$FFFFFFDF,D0      ; clear bit 5  in D0.L to zero
        EORI.L  #$00000080,D0      ; ones complement  bit 7 in D0
FINISH  JMP     FINISH            ; Stop
```

6.6.5   Bit Manipulation Instructions

The 68000 has four bit manipulation instructions, and these are listed in Table 6.11. Let's look at them in detail.

- In all of the instructions in Table 6.11, the one's-complement of the specified bit is reflected in the Z flag. The specified bit is ones complemented, cleared to 0, set to 1, or unchanged by BCHG, BCLR, BSET, or BTST, respectively. In all the instructions in Table 6.11, if (EA) is Dn, the length of Dn is 32 bits; otherwise, the length of the destination is one byte memory.

- Consider BCHG.B #2,$003000. If [$003000] = $05, then, after execution of this BCHG, Z = 0 and [$003000] = $01.

- Consider BCLR.L #3,D1. If [D1] = $F210E128, then after execution of this BCLR, register D1 will contain $F210E120 and Z = 0.

- Consider BSET.B #0,(A1). If [A1] = $00003000 and [$003000] = $00, then after execution of this BSET, memory location $003000 will contain $01 and Z = 1.

- Consider BTST.B #2,$002000. If [$002000] = $02, then after execution of this BTST, Z = 1, and [$002000] = $02; no other flags are affected.

EXAMPLE 6.18   Write a 68000 assembly language program that will   multiply a 16-bit unsigned number in D0 by 4 to provide a 32-bit product , and then perform the following operations on the contents of D0:
- Set bits 0 and 3 to 1 without changing other bits in D0.

- Clear bit 5 to zero without changing other bits in D0.

- Ones-complement bit 7 without changing other bits in D0.

Use only   shift and bit manipulation instructions. Do not use any multiplication or any other instructions. Assume that data is already stored in D0.

Solution

```
            LSL.L       #2,D0       ; Unsigned multiply D0 by 4
            BSET.L      #0,D0       ; set bit 0 in D0.L to one
            BSET.L      #3,D0       ; set bit 3 in D0.L to one
            BCLR.L      #5,D0       ; clear bit 5  in D0.L to zero
            BCHG.L      #7,D0       ; ones complement  bit 7 in D0
FINISH      JMP         FINISH      ; Halt
```

EXAMPLE 6.19   Write a 68000 assembly language program that will perform $5 \times X + 6 \times Y + [Y/8] \rightarrow [D1.L]$, where X is an unsigned 8-bit number stored in the lowest byte of D0 and Y is a 16-bit signed number stored in the upper 16 bits of D1. Neglect the remainder of $Y/8$.

Solution

```
            ANDI.W      #$00FF,D0    ;CONVERT X TO UNSIGNED 16-BIT
            MULU.W      #5,D0        ;COMPUTE UNSIGNED 5*X IN D0.L
            SWAP.W      D1           ;MOVE Y TO LOW 16 BITS IN D1
            MOVE.W      D1,D2        ;SAVE Y TO LOW 16 BITS OF D2
            MULS.W      #6,D1        ;COMPUTE SIGNED 6*Y IN D1.L
            ADD.L       D0,D1        ;ADD 5*X WITH 6*Y
            EXT.L       D2           ;SIGN EXTEND
            ASR.L       #3,D2        ;PERFORM Y/8;DISCARD REMAINDER
            ADD.L       D2,D1        ;PERFORM 5*X+6*Y +Y/8
FINISH      JMP         FINISH
```

6.6.6   Binary-Coded-Decimal Instructions

The 68000 instruction set contains three BCD instructions: ABCD for adding, SBCD for subtracting, and NBCD for negating. They operate on packed BCD byte(s) and provide a result containing one packed BCD byte. Note that packed BCD numbers are discussed in

TABLE 6.12   68000 Binary Coded Decimal Instructions

Instruction	Operand Size	Operation
ABCD Dy, Dx	B	$[Dx]10 + [Dy]10 + X \rightarrow [Dx]$
ABCD - (Ay), -(Ax)	B	$-(Ax)10 + -(Ay)10 + X \rightarrow (Ax)$
SBCD Dy, Dx	B	$[Dx]10 - [Dy]10 - X \rightarrow [Dx]$
SBCD - (Ay), - (Ax)	B	$-(Ax)10 - -(Ay)10 - X \rightarrow (Ax)$
NBCD (EA)	B	$0 - (EA)10 - X \rightarrow (EA)10$

- (EA) in NBCD can use all modes except An, relative, and immediate.

Chapter 1 (Section 1.2.3).

These instructions always include the extend (X) bit in the operation. They affect the condition codes as follows: $Z = 0$ if result is nonzero; $Z = 1$ otherwise, $C = 1$ if a carry (decimal) is generated; $C = 0$ otherwise; X is the same as C, N and V are undefined. The BCD instructions are listed in Table 6.12.

- Consider ABCD.B D1,D2. If [D1.B] = $25, [D2.B] = $15, and X = 0, then after execution of this ABCD instruction, [D2.B] = $40, C = X = 0, and Z = 0 as follows:

  [D1.B] = $25 = 00100101
  [D2.B] = $15 = 00010101

                00111010
                0110 Add 6 for correction since invalid BCD

          [D2.B] = 01000000 = $40, C = X = 0 since no carry, Z = 0 since result is nonzero

- Consider SBCD.B -(A2),-(A3). If [A2] = $00002004, [A3] = $00003003, [$002003] = $05, [$003002] = $06, and X = 1, then after execution of this SBCD instruction, [$003002] = $00, C = X = 0, and Z = 1.

- Consider NBCD.B (A1). If [A1] = [$00003000], [$003000] = $05, and C = X = 1, Z = 1, then after execution of this NBCD instruction, [$003000] = $FB = -6_{10} , C = X = 1 (borrow), Z = 0 (nonzero result).

EXAMPLE 6.20   Write a 68000 assembly language program at address $2000 to add two words, each containing two ASCII digits. The first word is stored in two consecutive locations (from LOW to HIGH), with the low byte pointed to by A0 at address 3000_{16}, and the second word is stored in two consecutive locations (from LOW to HIGH), with the low byte pointed to by A1 at 7000_{16}. Store the packed BCD result in D5.

Solution

```
          ORG        $2000
          MOVEQ.L    #1,D2          ;#1 INITIALIZE D2
          MOVEA.W    #$3000,A0      ;#2 INITIALIZE A0
          MOVEA.W    #$7000,A1      ;#3 INITIALIZE A1
START     ANDI.B     #$0F,(A0)+     ;#4 CONVERT IST # TO UNPAC.BCD
          ANDI.B     #$0F,(A1)+     ;#5 CONVERT 2ND # TO UNPAC.BCD
          DBF.W      D2,START       ;#6 DECREMENT AND BRANCH IF D2 ≠ -1
```

```
          MOVE.B    -(A0),D6      ;#7 GET HIGH UNPAC.BYTE OF IST#
          MOVE.B    -(A0),D7      ;#8 GET LOW UNPAC. BYTE OF IST#
          LSL.B     #4,D6         ;#9 SHIFT IST# HIGH BYTE 4 TIMES
          OR.B      D7,D6         ;#10 D6=PACKED BCD BYTE OF IST#
          MOVE.B    -(A1),D5      ;#11 GET HIGH UNPAC. BYTE OF 2ND#
          MOVE.B    -(A1),D4      ;#12 GET LOW UNPAC. BYTE OF 2ND#
          LSL.B     #4,D5         ;#13 SHIFT 2ND # HIGH BYTE 4 TIMES
          OR.B      D4,D5         ;#14 D5 HAS PACKED BCD BYTE OF 2ND#
          ADDI.B    #0,D0         ;#15 CLEAR X-BIT
          ABCD.B    D6,D5         ;#16 D5.B =PACKED BCD RESULT
FINISH    JMP       FINISH
```

Note: The above program will be explained in the following. Note that the # sign along with the line number is placed before each comment in order to explain the program. Assume that the ASCII data to be added are $3432 and $3231. The purpose of the program is to convert the first number, ASCII $3432 to unpacked BCD $0402 and then to packed BCD $42. Similarly, the second number, ASCII $3231 to unpacked BCD $0201, and then to packed BCD $21. Finally, the two packed BCD numbers are added using 68000's ABCD.B instruction.

Assume that [$3000] = $32, [$3001] = $34, [$7000] = $31, and [$7001] = $32. Line #1 initializes D2 with a loop count for converting the numbers from ASCII to unpacked BCD. Line #'s 2 and 3 initialize A0 and A1 with $00003000 and $00007000 respectively. Line #'s 4 through 6 convert the 4 bytes of ASCII codes into unpacked BCD. Line#'s 7 through 14 convert the unpacked BCD numbers into packed BCD bytes. This is done by logically shifting each high unpacked byte four times to the left, and then ORing with the low unpacked byte. For example, consider unpacked BCD $0402 for the ASCII $3432.

The instruction LSL.B #4,D6 at Line #9 will convert unpacked byte $04 to $40, and then OR.B D7,D6 at line #10 will provide packed $42, and store the result in D6.B. Similarly, line #'s 11 through 14 will convert the second unpacked BCD $0201 into packed BCD $21, and store it in D5.B. The instruction ADDI.B #0,D0 at Line# 15 clears the X-bit to 0. This is necessary since ABCD.B adds the packed BCD bytes along with the X-bit. ABCD.B D6, D5 at line # 16 will add the two packed BCD bytes, and store the result $63 (packed) in D5.B.

EXAMPLE 6.21   Write a 68000 assembly language program at address $2000 to subtract two 32-bit packed BCD numbers. BCD number 1 is stored at locations from $003000 through $003003, with the least significant byte at $003003 and the most significant byte at $003000. Similarly, BCD number 2 is stored at locations $004000 through $004003, with the least significant byte at $004003 and the most significant byte at $004000. BCD number 2 is to be subtracted from BCD number 1. Store the packed BCD result at addresses $005000 (the lowest byte of the result) through $005003 (the highest byte of the result). In the program, first initialize loop counter D7 to 4, source pointer A0 to $003000, source pointer A1 to $004000, and destination pointer A3 to $005000, and then write a program to accomplish the above using these initialized values.

Solution

```
            ORG         $003000
            DC.L        $99221133
            ORG         $004000
            DC.L        $33552211
            ORG          $2000
            MOVE.W      #4,D7          ;NUMBER OF BYTES TO BE SUBTRACTED
            MOVEA.W     #$3000,A0      ;STARTING ADDRESS FOR FIRST NUMBER
            MOVEA.W     #$4000,A1      ;STARTING ADDRESS FOR SECOND NUMBER
            ADDA.W      D7,A0          ;MOVE ADDRESS POINTERS TO THE END
            ADDA.W      D7,A1          ;OF EACH 32 BIT PACKED BCD NUMBER
            MOVEA.W     #$5000,A3      ;LOAD POINTER FOR DESTINATION ADDR
            SUBQ.W      #1,D7          ;SUBTRACT D7 by 1 for DBF
            ADDI.B      #0,D7          ;CLEAR X-BIT
LOOP        MOVE.B      -(A0),D0       ;GET A BYTE FROM FIRST NUMBER
            MOVE.B      -(A1),D1       ;GET A BYTE FROM SECOND NUMBER
            SBCD.B      D1,D0          ;BCD SUBTRACTION, RESULT IN D0
            MOVE.B      D0,(A3)+       ;STORE RESULT IN DESTINATION ADDR
            DBF         D7,LOOP        ;CONTINUE UNTIL COUNTER HAS EXPIRED
FINISH  JMP             FINISH
```

Note that SBCD subtracts the contents of two data registers or the contents of two memory locations using predecrement modes.

6.6.7   Program Control Instructions

Program control instructions include branches, jumps, and subroutine calls as listed in Table 6.13.

Consider Bcc *d*. There are 14 branch conditions. This means that the *cc* in Bcc can be replaced by 14 conditions providing 14 instructions: BCC, BCS, BEQ, BGE, BGT, BHI, BLE, BLS, BLT, BMI, BNE, BPL, BVC, and BVS. It should be mentioned that some of these instructions are applicable to both signed and unsigned numbers, some can only be used with signed numbers, and some are applicable to only unsigned numbers.

After signed arithmetic operations, instructions such as BEQ, BNE, BVS, BVC, BMI, and BPL can be used. On the other hand, after unsigned arithmetic operations, instructions such as BCC, BCS, BEQ, and BNE can be used. It should be pointed out that if V = 0, BPL and BGE have the same meaning. Similarly, if V = 0, BMI and BLT perform the same function.

TABLE 6.13   **68000 Program Control Instructions**

Instruction	Size	Operation
Bcc d	B,W	If condition code cc is true, then PC + d → PC. The PC value is current instruction location plus 2. d can be 8- or 16-bit signed displacement. If 8-bit displacement is used, then the instruction size is 16 bits with the 8-bit displacement as the low byte of the instruction word. If 16-bit displacement is used, then the instruction size is two words with 8-bit displacement field (low byte) in the instruction word as zero and the second word following the instruction word as the 16-bit displacement.
		There are 14 conditions such as BCC (Branch if Carry Clear), BEQ (Branch if result equal to zero, i.e., Z = 1), and BNE (Branch if not equal, i.e., Z = 0). Note that the PC contents will always be even since the instruction length is either one word or two words depending on the displacement widths.
BRA d	B,W	Branch always to PC + d where PC value is current instruction location plus 2. As with Bcc, d can be signed 8 or 16 bits. This is an unconditional branching instruction with relative mode. Note that the PC contents are even since the instruction is either one word or two words.
BSR d	B,W	PC → – [SP]
		PC + d → PC
		The address of the next instruction following PC is pushed onto the stack. PC is then loaded with PC + d. As before, d can be signed 8 or 16 bits. This is a subroutine call instruction using relative mode.
DBcc Dn, d	W	If *cc* is false, then Dn – 1 → Dn, and if Dn = – 1, then PC + 2 → PC
		If Dn ≠ – 1 , then PC + d → PC; else PC + 2 → PC.
JMP (EA)	unsized	[EA] → PC
		This is an unconditional jump instruction which uses control addressing mode.
JSR (EA)	unsized	PC → – [SP]
		[EA] → PC
		This is a subroutine call instruction which uses control addressing mode
RTR	unsized	[SP] + → CCR
		[SP] + → PC
		Return and restore condition codes
RTS	unsized	Return from subroutine
		[SP] + → PC

TABLE 6.13   Cont.

S*cc* (EA)	B	If *cc* is true, then the byte specified by [EA] is set to all ones; otherwise the byte is cleared to zero.

- (EA) in JMP and JSR can use all modes except Dn, An, (An) +, – (An), and immediate.

- (EA) in Scc can use all modes except An, relative, and immediate.

The conditional branch instruction can be used after typical arithmetic instructions such as subtraction to branch to a location if *cc* is true. For example, consider SUB.W D1,D2. Now if [D1] and [D2] are unsigned numbers, then

BCC *d* can be used if [D2] > [D1]
BCS *d* can be used if [D2] ≤ [D1]
BEQ *d* can be used if [D2] = [D1]
BNE *d* can be used if [D2] ≠ [D1]
BHI *d* can be used if [D2] < [D1]
BLS *d* can be used if [D2] ≤ [D1]

On the other hand, if [D1] and [D2] are signed numbers, then after SUB.W D1,D2, the following branch instruction can be used:

BEQ *d* can be used if [D2] = [D1]
BNE *d* can be used if [D2] ≠ [D1]
BLT *d* can be used if [D2] < [D1]
BLE *d* can be used if [D2] ≤ [D1]
BGT *d* can be used if [D2] > [D1]
BGE *d* can be used if [D2] ≥ [D1]

Now as a specific example, consider BEQ BEGIN. If current [PC] = $000200 and BEGIN = $20, then after execution of this BEQ, program execution starts at $000220 if Z = 1; if Z = 0, program execution continues at $000200. The instructions BRA and JMP are unconditional jump instructions. BRA uses the relative addressing mode, whereas JMP uses only the control addressing mode. For example, consider BRA.B START. If [PC] = $000200 and START = $40, then after execution of this BRA, program execution starts at $000240. Now consider JMP (A1) . If [A1] = $00000220, then after execution of this JMP, program execution starts at $000220.

- The instructions BSR and JSR are subroutine call instructions. BSR uses the relative mode, whereas JSR uses the control addressing mode. Consider the following program segment, assuming that the main program uses all registers and the subroutine stores the result in memory.

Main Program		Subroutine
—	SUB	MOVEM.L D0-D7/A0-A6, – (SP)
—		—
—		—
JSR SUB		—
START —		—
—		—
—		MOVEM.L (SP)+, D0–D7/A0–A6
		RTS

Main body of subroutine

Here the JSR SUB instruction calls the subroutine SUB. In response to JSR, the 68000 pushes the current PC contents called START onto the stack and loads the starting address SUB of the subroutine into PC. The first MOVEM in the SUB pushes all registers onto the stack, and after the subroutine is executed, the second MOVEM instruction pops all the registers back. Finally, RTS pops the address START from the stack into PC, and program control is returned to the main program. Note that BSR SUB could have been used instead of JSR SUB in the main program. In that case, the 68000 assembler would have considered the SUB with BSR as a displacement rather than as an address with the JSR instruction.

- DBcc Dn,d tests the condition codes and the value in a data register. DBcc first checks if cc (NE, EQ, GT, etc.) is satisfied. If cc is satisfied, the next instruction is executed. If cc is not satisfied, the specified data register is decremented by 1; if $[Dn] = -1$, then the next instruction is executed; on the other hand, if $Dn \neq -1$, then branch to PC + d is performed. For example, consider DBNE.W D5,BACK with $[D5] = 00003002_{16}$, BACK = -4, and $[PC] = 002006_{16}$. If Z = 1, then $[D5] = 00003001_{16}$. Because $[D5] \neq -1$, program execution starts at 002002_{16}. It should be pointed out that there is a false condition in the DBcc instruction and that this instruction is the DBF (some assemblers use DBRA for this). In this case, the condition is always false. This means that after execution of this instruction, Dn is decremented by 1 and if $[Dn] = -1$, the next instruction is executed. If $[Dn] \neq -1$, branch to PC + d.

- Consider SPL.B(A5). If $[A5] = 00200020_{16}$ and N = 0, then after execution of this SPL, memory location 200020_{16} will contain 11111111_2.

6.6.8   System Control Instructions

The 68000 system control instructions contain certain privileged instructions including RESET, RTE, STOP and instructions that use or modify SR. Note that the privileged instructions can be executed only in the supervisor mode. The system control instructions are listed in Table 6.14.

- (EA) in CHK can use all modes except An.

We now explain these instructions.

TABLE 6.14   68000 System Control Instructions

Instruction	Size	Operation
RESET	Unsized	If supervisor state, then assert reset line; else TRAP
RTE	Unsized	If supervisor state, then restore SR and PC; else TRAP
STOP # data	Unsized	If supervisor state, then load immediate data to SR and then STOP; else TRAP
ORI to SR MOVE USP ANDI to SR EORI to SR MOVE (EA) to SR		These instructions were discussed earlier

Trap and Check Instructions

Instruction	Size	Operation
TRAP # vector	Unsized	PC → - (SP) SR → - (SP) Vector address → PC
TRAPV	Unsized	TRAP if V = 1, if Dn < 0 or Dn > (EA), then TRAP;
CHK (EA), Dn	W	else, go to the next instruction.

Status Register

Instruction		Operation
ANDI to CCR EORI to CCR MOVE (EA) to/from CCR ORI to CCR MOVE SR to (EA)		(Explained earlier)

- When executed in the supervisor mode, the RESET instruction outputs a low signal on the reset pin of the 68000 to initialize the external peripheral chips. The 68000 reset pin is bidirectional. The 68000 can be reset by asserting the reset pin using hardware, whereas the peripheral chips can be reset using the software RESET instruction.

- MOVEA.L A7,An or MOVEA.L An,A7 can be used to save, restore, or change the contents of the A7 in the supervisor mode. A7 must be loaded in the supervisor mode because MOVE A7 is a privileged instruction. As an example, A7 can be initialized to $00005000 in the supervisor mode using   MOVEA.L #$00005000,A1

MOVE.L   A1,A7

- Consider TRAP #*n*. There are 16 TRAP instructions, with *n* ranging from 0 to 15. The hexadecimal vector address is calculated using the equation: hexadecimal vector address = $80 + 4 \times n$. The TRAP instruction first pushes the contents of the PC and then the SR onto the stack. The hexadecimal vector address is then loaded into PC. TRAP is basically a software interrupt. The TRAP instruction can be executed in the user mode to return control to the supervisor mode. This is useful in calling operating system routines from a user program. Thus, the TRAP instruction can be used for service calls to the operating system. For application programs running in the user mode, TRAP can be used to transfer control to a supervisor utility program. RTE at the end of the TRAP routine can be used to return to the application program by placing the saved SR from the stack, thus causing the 68000 to return to the user mode.

  There are other traps that occur due to certain arithmetic errors. For example, division by zero automatically traps to location 14_{16}. On the other hand, an overflow condition (i.e., if V = 1) will trap to address $00001C if the instruction TRAPV is executed.

- The CHK.W (EA),Dn instruction compares [Dn] with (EA). If $[Dn]_{low\ 16\ bits} < 0$ or if $[Dn]_{low\ 16\ bits} > (EA)$, a trap to location $000018 is generated. Also, N is set to 1 if $[Dn]_{low\ 16\ bits} < 0$, and N is reset to 0 if $[Dn]_{low\ 16\ bits} > (EA)$. (EA) is treated as a 16-bit two's-complement integer. Note that program execution continues if $[Dn]_{low\ 16\ bits}$ lies between 0 and (EA).

  Consider CHK.W (A5),D2. If $[D2]_{low\ 16\ bits} = \$0200$, [A5] = $00003000, and [$003000] = $0100, then after execution of this CHK, the 68000 will trap because [D2.W] = $0200 is greater than [$003000] = $0100. The purpose of the CHK instruction is to provide boundary checking by testing if the content of a data register is in the range from zero to an upper limit. The upper limit used in the instruction can be set equal to the length of the array. Then every time the array is accessed, the CHK instruction can be executed to make sure that the array bounds have not been violated.

  The CHK instruction is usually placed after computation of an index value to ensure that the index value is not violated. This permits a check of whether or not the address of an array being accessed is within array boundaries when the address register indirect with index mode is used to access an array element. For example, the following instruction sequence permits accessing of an array with base address in A2 and array length of 50_{10} bytes:

```
            —
            —
            —
CHK.W       #49,D2
MOVE.B      0(A2,D2.W),D3
            —
            —
```

Here, if the low 16 bits of D2 are less than 0 or greater than 49, the 68000 will trap to location $0018. It is assumed that D2 is computed prior to execution of the CHK instruction.

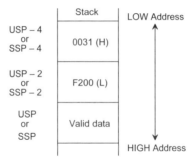

FIGURE 6.13   68000 system stack.

6.6.9   68000 Stack

The 68000 supports stacks with the address register indirect postincrement and predecrement addressing modes. In addition to two system stack pointers (A7 and A7'), all seven address registers (A0–A6) can be used as user stack pointers by using appropriate addressing modes. Subroutine calls, traps, and interrupts automatically use the system stack pointers: USP (A7) when S = 0 and SSP (A7') when S = 1. Subroutine calls push the PC onto the system stack; RTS pops the PC from the stack. Traps and interrupts push both PC and SR onto the system stack; RTE pops PC and SR from the stack.

The 68000 accesses the system stack from the top for operations such as subroutine calls or interrupts. This means that stack operations such as subroutine calls or interrupts access the system stack automatically from HIGH to LOW memory. Therefore, the system SP is decremented by 2 for a word or 4 for a long word after a push and incremented by 2 for a word or 4 for a long word after a pop. As an example, suppose that a 68000 CALL instruction (JSR or BSR) is executed when PC = $0031F200; then after execution of the subroutine call, the stack will push the PC as shown in Figure 6.13. Note that the 68000 SP always points to valid data.

In 68000, stacks can be created by using address register indirect with postincrement or predecrement modes. Typical 68000 memory instructions such as MOVE to/from can be used to access the stack. Also, by using one of the seven address registers (A0–A6) and system stack pointers (A7, A7'), stacks can be filled from either HIGH to LOW memory, or vice versa:

1.   Filling a stack from HIGH to LOW memory (the top of the stack) is implemented with predecrement mode for push and postincrement mode for pop.

2.   Filling a stack from LOW to HIGH (the bottom of the stack) memory is implemented with postincrement for push and predecrement for pop.

For example, the stack growing from HIGH to LOW memory addresses in which A7 is used as the stack pointer is shown in Figure 6.14.

To push the 16-bit contents 0504_{16} of memory location 305016_{16}, the instruction MOVE.W 3050_{16},-(A7) can be used as shown in Figure 6.15. The 16-bit data item 0504_{16} can be popped from the stack into the low 16 bits of D0 by using MOVE.W (A7)+,D0. Register A7 will contain 200504_{16} after the pop. Note that, in this case, the stack pointer A7 points to valid data. Next, consider the stack growing from LOW to HIGH memory addresses in which the user utilizes A6 as the stack pointer. This is depicted in Figure 6.16. To push the 16-bit contents 2070_{16} of the low 16 bits of D5, the instruction MOVE.W D5, (A6)+ can be used as shown in Figure 6.17. The 16-bit data item 2070_{16} can be popped from the stack into the 16-bit contents of memory location 417024_{16} by using MOVE.W

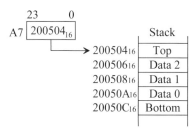

FIGURE 6.14 **68000 stack growing from HIGH to LOW memory.**

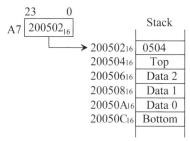

FIGURE 6.15 **PUSH operation for the 68000 stack growing from HIGH to LOW memory.**

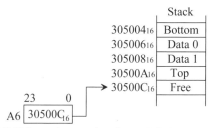

FIGURE 6.16 **68000 stack growing from LOW to HIGH memory.**

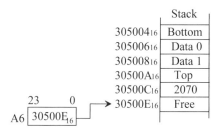

FIGURE 6.17 **PUSH operation for the 68000 stack growing from HIGH to LOW memory.**

–(A6), \$417024. Note that, in this case, the stack pointer A6 points to the free location above the valid data.

EXAMPLE 6.22 Write a 68000 subroutine to compute $Y = \sum_{i=1}^{N} X_i^2 / N$. Assume the X_i's are 16-bit signed integers and $N = 100$. The numbers are stored in consecutive locations. Assume A0 points to the X_i's and A7 is already initialized. Store 32-bit result in D1 (16-bit remainder in high word of D1 and 16-bit quotient in the low word of D1). Assume user mode. Also, write the main program at address $2000 that will initialize A0 to $005000, call the subroutine, and then stop.

Solution

Main Program

	ORG	$2000	
	MOVEA.W	#$5000,A0	;Initialize A0 to $005000
	JSR	SQR	;Call the subroutine
FINISH	JMP	FINISH	

Subroutine

SQR	MOVEM.L	D2/D3/A0,-(A7)	;SAVE REGISTERS
	CLR.L	D1	;CLEAR SUM
	MOVE.W	#99,D2	;INITIALIZE LOOP COUNT
BACK	MOVE.W	(A0)+,D3	;MOVE Xi's INTO D3
	MULS.W	D3,D3	;COMPUTE Xi**2 USING MULS
	ADD.L	D3,D1	;SINCE Xi**2 IS ALWAYS +VE
	DBF.W	D2,BACK	;COMPUTE
	DIVU.W	#100,D1	;SUM OF Xi**2/N USING DIVU
	MOVEM.L	(A7)+,D2/D3/A0	;RESTORE REGISTERS
	RTS		

Note: In this program, either DIVU or DIVS can be used for computing Xi**2/N if the most significant bits of both N and total sum are 0; however, DIVU must be used if the most significant bits of either or both are 1. Also, to execute the program above, values for *Xi* must be stored in memory using the assembler directive, DC.W.

6.7   68000 Delay Routine

Typical 68000 software delay loops can be written using MOVE and DBF instructions. For example, the following instruction sequence can be used for a delay loop of 2 ms:

	MOVE.W	#count,D0
DELAY	DBF.W	D0,DELAY

Note that DBF.W decrements D0.W by 1, and if D0.W $\neq$ -1, branches to DELAY; if D0.W = -1, the 68000 executes the next instruction. Since DBF.W checks for D0.W for -1, the value of "count" must be one less than the required loop count. The initial loop counter value of "count" can be calculated using the cycles (Appendix D) required to execute the following 68000 instructions:

MOVE.W #n,D0	(8 cycles)
DBF.W D0,DELAY	(10/14 cycles)

Note that the 68000 DBF.W instruction requires two different execution times. DBF.W requires 10 cycles when the 68000 branches if the content of D0.W is not equal to

-1 after autodecrementing D0.W by 1. However, the 68000 goes to the next instruction and does not branch when [D0.W] = -1 after autodecrementing D0.W by 1, and this requires 14 cycles. This means that the DELAY loop will require 10 cycles for "count" times, and the last iteration will take 14 cycles.

Assuming a 4-MHz 68000 clock, each cycle is 250 ns. For a 2 millisecond delay, total cycles $= \frac{2\,m\sec}{250\,n\sec} = 8000$. The loop will require 10 cycles for "count" times when D0.W $\neq$ -1 and the last iteration will take 14 cycles when no branch is taken (D0.W = -1). Thus, total cycles including the MOVE.W $= 8 + 10 \times ($count$) + 14 = 8000$. Hence, count $\cong 798_{10}$ $= 031E16$. Therefore, D0.W must be loaded with 798_{10} or $031E_{16}$.

Now, to obtain delay of two seconds, the above DELAY loop of 2 millisecond can be used with an external counter. Counter value $= \frac{2\,\sec}{2\,m\sec} = 1000$. The following instruction sequence will provide an approximate delay of two seconds:

```
            MOVE.W      #1000,D1    ;Initialize counter for 2 second delay
BACK        MOVE.W      #798,D0
DELAY       DBF.W       D0,DELAY    ;20msec delay
            SUBQ.W      #1,D1
            BNE.B       BACK
```

Next, the delay time provided by the in struction sequence above can be calculated. From Appendix D, the cycles required to execute the following 68000 instructions:
MOVE.W #n,D1 (8 cycles)

```
            SUBQ.W #n, D1           (4 cycles)
            BNE.B                   (10/8 cycles)
```

As before, assuming a 4-MHz 68000 clock, each cycle is 250 ns. The total time from the instruction sequence for a two-second delay = execution time for MOVE.W + 1000 * (2 msec delay) + 1000 * (execution time for SUBQ.W) + 999* (execution time for BNE.B for Z = 0 when D1 ! 0) + (execution time for BNE.B for Z = 1 when D1 = 0 for the last iteration) = 8 * 250ns + 1000 * 2msec + 1000 * 4 * 250ns + 999 * 10 * 250ns + 8 * 250ns $\cong$ 2.0035 seconds which is approximately 2 seconds discarding the execution times of MOVE.W, SUBQ.W, and BNE.B.

Questions and Problems

6.1   What are the basic differences between the 68000, 68008, 68010, and 68012?

6.2   What does a HIGH on the 68000 FC2 pin indicate?

6.3   (a)   If a 68000-based system operates in the user mode and an interrupt occurs, what will the 68000 mode be?

(b)   If a 68000-based system operates in the supervisor mode, how can the mode be changed to the user mode?

6.4   (a)   What is the purpose of 68000 trace and X flags?
       (b)   How can you set or reset these flags?

6.5   Indicate whether the following 68000 instructions are valid or not. Justify your answers.
       (a)   MOVE.B D0,(A1)
       (b)   MOVE.B D0,A1

6.6   How many addressing modes and instructions does the 68000 have?

6.7   What happens after execution of the following 68000 instruction?
       MOVE.L D0,$000013

6.8   What are 68000 privileged instructions?

6.9   Identify the following 68000 instructions as privileged or nonprivileged:
       (a)   MOVE (A2),SR
       (b)   MOVE CCR,(A5)
       (c)   MOVE.L A7,A2

6.10   (a)   Find the contents of locations $305020 and $305021 after execution of MOVE D5,$305020. Assume that [D5] = $6A2FA150 prior to execution of this 68000 MOVE instruction.
       (b)   If [A0] = $203040FF, [D0] = $40F12560, and [$3040FF] = $2070, what happens after execution of the 68000 instruction: MOVE (A0),D0?

6.11   Identify the addressing modes for each of the following 68000 instructions:
       (a)   CLR D0
       (b)   MOVE.L (A1)+,-(A5)
       (c)   MOVE $2000(A2),D1

6.12   Determine the contents of registers and memory locations affected by each of the following 68000 instructions:
       (a)   MOVE (A0)+,D1
       Assume the following data prior to execution of this MOVE:
       [A0] = $50105020   [$105021] = $51

[D1] = $70801F25   [$105022] = $52
[$105020] = $50   [$105023] = $7F
(b)   MOVEA D5,A2
Assume the following data prior to execution of this MOVEA:
        [D5] = $A725B600
        [A2] = $5030801F

6.13   Find the contents of register D0 after execution of the following 68000 instruction
        sequence:
                        EXT.W D0
                        EXT.L D0
        Assume that [D0] = $F215A700 prior to execution of the instruction sequence.

6.14   Write a 68000 assembly program to add a 16-bit number in the low word (bits
        0–15) of D1 with another 16-bit number in the high word (bits 16–31) of D1. Store
        the result in the high word of D1.

6.15   Write a 68000 assembly program to add the top two 16 bits of the stack. Store the
        16-bit result onto the stack. Assume the supervisor mode.

6.16   Write a 68000 assembly program to add two 48-bit data items in memory as shown
        in Figure P6.16. Store the result pointed to by A1. The operation is given by

                        $00 02 03 A1 07 20
                        $07 03 02 02 03 1A
                        $07 05 05 A3 0A 3A

        Assume that the data pointers and the data are already initialized.

6.17   Write a 68000 assembly language program to subtract two   64-bit numbers as
        follows:
                [D7.L][D6.L] - [D0.L][D1.L] → [D7.L][D1.L]

6.18   Write a 68000 assembly language program to subtract a 24-bit number (x) stored
        in low 24 bits of D0 from another 24-bit number (y) stored in consecutive memory

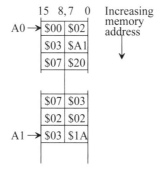

FIGURE P6.16

locations starting at $506080 (the highest byte at $506080 and the lowest byte at $506082). Store the result in low 24 bits of D7.

6.19   Write a 68000 assembly language program to perform $(X^2 + Y^2)$ where X is a signed 8-bit number stored in low 8 bits of D0 and Y is an unsigned 16-bit number stored in low 16 bits of D1. Save the 32-bit result onto the supervisor stack. Assume that the supervisor stack pointer is already initialized.

6.20   Write a 68000 assembly language program to multiply a 16-bit signed number stored in the high word of D1 by an 8-bit signed number stored in the lowest byte of D1. Store the result in D1.L.

6.21   Write a 68000 assembly program to multiply a 16-bit signed number in the low word of D0 by an 8-bit unsigned number in the highest byte (bits 31–24) of D0.

6.22   Find the contents of D1 after execution of DIVS.W #6,D1. Assume that [D1] = $FFFFFFF7 prior to execution of the 68000 instruction. Identify the quotient and remainder. Comment on the sign of the remainder.

6.23   Write a 68000 assembly program to divide a 16-bit signed number in the high word of D1 by an 8-bit signed number in the lowest byte of D1.

6.24   Write a 68000 assembly program to compute the following:

$$I = 6 \times J + K/M$$

where the locations $6000, $6002, and $6004 contain the 16-bit signed integers *J*, *K*, and *M*. Store the result into a long word starting at $6006. Discard the remainder of *K/M*.

6.25   Write a 68000 assembly program to compare two strings of 15 ASCII characters. The first string is stored starting at $502030. The second string is stored at location $302510. The ASCII character in location $502030 of string 1 will be compared with the ASCII character in location $302510 of string 2, [$502031] will be compared with [$302511], and so on. Each time there is a match, store $EEEE onto the stack; otherwise, store $0000 onto the stack. Assume the user mode.

6.26   Write a 68000 assembly language program to insert a '1' at bit 2 of D0.W without changing the other bits if D0.W contains a negative number. On the other hand, insert a '0' at bit 2 of D0.W without changing the other bits if D0.W contains a positive number.

6.27   Write a 68000 assembly program to divide a 9-bit unsigned number in the high 9 bits (bits 31–23) of D0 by 8_{10}. Do not use any division instruction. Store the result in D0. Neglect the remainder.

6.28   Write a 68000 assembly language program that will check whether the 16-bit signed number in D0.W is positive or negative. If the number is positive, the program will multiply the 16-bit unsigned number in D1.W by 16, and provide a 32-bit result; otherwise, the program will set the lowest byte D1.B to all 1's. Use only data movement, shift, bit manipulation, and program control instructions. Assume that the 16-bit numbers are already loaded intoD0.W and D1.W.

6.29   Write a subroutine in 68000 assembly language to compute

$$Z = \sum_{i=1}^{100} X_i$$

Assume that the X_i's are signed 8-bit and stored in consecutive locations starting at $504020. Assume that A0 points to the X_i's. Also, write the main program in 68000 assembly language to perform all initializations (A0 to $504020, A7 to $406020), call the subroutine, and then compute $Z/100$. Assume supervisor mode.

6.30   Write a subroutine in 68000 assembly language program to compute the trace of a 4 x 4 matrix containing 8-bit unsigned integers. Assume that each element is stored in memory as a 16-bit number with upper byte as zero in the row-major order form; that is, elements are stored in memory as row by row, and within a row, elements are stored as column by column. Note that the trace of a matrix is the sum of the elements of the leading diagonal.

6.31   Write a subroutine in 68000 assembly language to subtract two 32-bit packed BCD numbers. BCD number 1 is stored at a location from $500000 through $500003, with the least significant digit at $500003 and the most significant digit at $500000. BCD number 2 is stored at a location from $700000 through $700003, with the least significant digit at $700003 and the most significant digit at $700000. BCD number 2 is to be subtracted from BCD number 1. Store the result as packed BCD digits in D5.

6.32   Write a subroutine in 68000 assembly languauge to convert a three-digit unpacked BCD number to binary using unsigned multiplication by 10, and additions. The most significant digit is stored in a memory location starting at $3000, the next digit is stored at $3001, and so on. Store the binary result (N) in D3. Note that arithmetic operations for obtaining N will provide a binary result. Use the value of the three-digit BCD number,

$$N = N2 \times 10^2 + N1 \times 10^1 + N0$$

$$= ((10 \times N2) + N1) \times 10 + N0$$

6.33   Assume a 10-MHz 68000. Write a 68000 assembly language program to obtain a delay routine for one millisecond. Using this one-millisecond routine, write a 68000 assembly language program to provide a delay for 10 seconds.

7

68000
HARDWARE AND
INTERFACING

In this chapter we describe hardware aspects of the Motorola 68000. Topics include 68000 pins and signals, clock and reset circuits, timing diagrams, and memory and I/O interfacing techniques. Finally, the design of a 68000-based microcomputer is described along with memory and I/O maps.

7.1   68000 Pins And Signals

The 68000 is usually packaged in one of the following:
*   64-pin dual in-line package (DIP)

*   68-terminal chip carrier

*   68-pin quad pack

*   68-pin grid array (PGA)

Figure 7.1 shows the 68000 pin diagram for a DIP. For reliable operation, unused inputs should be connected to an appropriate signal level. Unused active LOW inputs should be connected to the Vcc. Unused active HIGH inputs should be connected to GROUND. Appendix C provides data sheets for the 68000 and support chips.

The 68000 is provided with two Vcc (+5 V) and two ground pins. Power is thus distributed to reduce noise problems at high frequencies. Also, to build a prototype to demonstrate that the paper design for the 68000-based microcomputer is correct, one must use either wire-wrap or solder for the actual construction. A breadboard should not be used, because at high frequencies (above 4 MHz), there will be noise problems due to stray capacitances. The 68000 consumes about 1.5 W of power.

D_0–D_{15} are the 16 data bus pins. All transfers to and from memory and I/O devices are conducted over the 8-bit (LOW or HIGH) or 16-bit data bus depending on the size of the device. A_1–A_{23} are the 23 address lines. A_0 is obtained by encoding the $\overline{UDS}$ (upper data strobe) and $\overline{LDS}$ (lower data strobe) lines.

The 68000 operates on a single-phase TTL-level clock at 4, 6, 8, 10, 12.5, 16.67, or 25 MHz. The clock signal must be generated externally and applied to the 68000 clock input line. An external crystal oscillator chip is required to generate the clock. Table 7.1 gives the clock timing specifications and Figure 7.2 shows the 68000 CLK wavform. The clock is at a TTL-compatible voltage. The clock timing specifications provide data for three different clock frequencies: 8, 10, and 12.5 MHz. The 68000 CLK input can be provided by an external crystal oscillator or by designing an external circuit.

FIGURE 7.1   **68000 pins and signals.**

TABLE 7.1   **68000 Clock Timing Specifications**

Characteristic	Symbol	8 MHz		10 MHz		12.5 MHz		Unit
		Min	Max	Min	Max	Min	Max	
Frequency of operation	f	4.0	8.0	4.0	10.0	4.0	12.5	MHz
Cycle time	t_{CVC}	125	250	100	250	80	250	ns
Clock pulse width	t_{CL}	55	125	45	125	35	125	ns
	t_{CH}	55	125	45	125	35	125	
Rise and fall times	t_{Cr}	—	10	—	10	—	5	ns
	t_{Cf}	—	10	—	10	—	5	

- The 68000 signals can be divided into five functional categories:
- Synchronous and asynchronous control lines
- System control lines
- Interrupt control lines

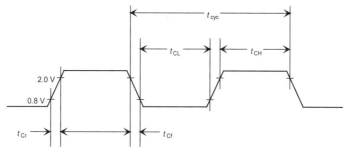

FIGURE 7.2 **68000 clock input timing diagram and AC electrical specifications.**

- DMA control lines
- Status lines

7.1.1 Synchronous and Asynchronous Control Lines

The 68000 bus control is asynchronous; that is, once a bus cycle is initiated, the external device must send a signal back to complete it. The 68000 also contains three synchronous control lines that facilitate interfacing to synchronous peripheral devices such as Motorola's inexpensive 6800 family.

In *synchronous operation* bus control is synchronized or clocked using a common system clock signal. In 6800 family peripherals, this common clock is the E clock signal, depending on the particular chip used. With synchronous control, all READ and WRITE operations must be synchronized with the common clock. However, this may create problems when interfacing with slow peripheral devices. This problem does not arise with asynchronous bus control.

Asynchronous operation is not dependent on a common clock signal. The 68000 utilizes the asynchronous control lines to transfer data between the 68000 and peripheral devices via handshaking. Using asynchronous operation, the 68000 can be interfaced to any peripheral chip regardless of the speed.

The 68000 has three control lines to transfer data over its bus in a synchronous manner: E (enable), $\overline{VPA}$ (valid peripheral address), and $\overline{VMA}$ (valid memory address). The E clock corresponds to the clock of the 6800. The E clock is output at a frequency that is one-tenth of the 68000 input clock. $\overline{VPA}$ is an input and tells the 68000 that a 6800 device is being addressed and therefore that data transfer must be synchronized with the E clock. $\overline{VMA}$ is the processor's response to $\overline{VPA}$ $\overline{VMA}$. is asserted when the memory address is valid. This also tells the external device that the next data transfer over the data bus will be synchronized with the E clock.

$\overline{VPA}$ can be generated by decoding the address pins and address strobe $(\overline{AS})$. Note that the 68000 asserts $\overline{AS}$ LOW when the address on the address bus is valid. $\overline{VMA}$ is typically used as the chip select of the 6800 peripheral. This ensures that the 6800 peripherals are selected and deselected at the correct time. The 6800 peripheral interfacing sequence is as follows:

1. The 68000 initiates a cycle by starting a normal read or write cycle.
2. The 6800 peripheral defines the 68000 cycle by asserting the 68000 $\overline{VPA}$ input. If $\overline{VPA}$ is asserted as soon as possible after assertion of $\overline{AS}$, then $\overline{VPA}$ will be recognized as being asserted after three cycles. If $\overline{VPA}$ is not asserted after

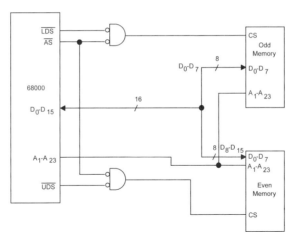

FIGURE 7.3   Interfacing of the 68000 to even and odd addresses.

three cycles, the 68000 inserts wait states until $\overline{\text{VPA}}$ is recognized by the 68000 as asserted. $\overline{\text{DTACK}}$ should not be asserted while $\overline{\text{VPA}}$ is asserted. The 6800 peripheral must remove $\overline{\text{VPA}}$ within one clock period after $\overline{\text{AS}}$ is negated.

3. The 68000 monitors enable (E) until it is LOW. The 68000 then synchronizes all READ and WRITE operations with the E clock. The $\overline{\text{VMA}}$ output pin is asserted LOW by the 68000.
4. The 6800 peripheral waits until E is active (HIGH) and then transfers the data.
5. The 68000 waits until E goes to LOW (on a read cycle, the data is latched as E goes to LOW internally). The 68000 then negates $\overline{\text{VMA}}$, $\overline{\text{AS}}$, $\overline{\text{UDS}}$, and $\overline{\text{LDS}}$. The 68000 thus terminates the cycle and starts the next cycle.

The 68000 utilizes five lines to control address and data transfers asynchronously: $\overline{\text{AS}}$ (address strobe), R/$\overline{\text{W}}$ (read/write), $\overline{\text{DTACK}}$ (data acknowledge), $\overline{\text{UDS}}$ (upper data strobe), and $\overline{\text{LDS}}$ (lower data strobe).

The 68000 outputs $\overline{\text{AS}}$ to notify the peripheral device when data is to be transferred. $\overline{\text{AS}}$ is active LOW when the 68000 provides a valid address on the address bus. The R/$\overline{\text{W}}$ output line indicates whether the 68000 is reading data from or writing data into a peripheral device. R/$\overline{\text{W}}$ is HIGH for read and LOW for write. $\overline{\text{DTACK}}$ is used to tell the 68000 that a transfer is to be performed. When the 68000 wants to transfer data asynchronously, it first activates the $\overline{\text{AS}}$ line and at the same time generates the required address on the address lines to select the peripheral device.

Because the $\overline{\text{AS}}$ line tells the peripheral chip when to transfer data, the $\overline{\text{AS}}$ line should be part of the address decoding scheme. After enabling $\overline{\text{AS}}$, the 68000 enters the wait state until it receives $\overline{\text{DTACK}}$ from the peripheral device selected. On receipt of $\overline{\text{DTACK}}$, the 68000 knows that the peripheral device is ready for data transfer. The 68000

TABLE 7.2   Definitions of $\overline{\text{UDS}}$ and $\overline{\text{LDS}}$

UDS	UDS	Data Transfer Occurs Via:	Address
1	0	D_0–D_7 pins for byte	Odd
0	1	D_8–D_{15} pins for byte	Even
0	0	D_0–D_{15} pins for word or long word	Even

then utilizes the R/$\overline{\text{W}}$ and data lines to transfer data. $\overline{\text{UDS}}$ and $\overline{\text{LDS}}$ are defined in Table 7.2.

A_0 is encoded from $\overline{\text{UDS}}$ and $\overline{\text{LDS}}$. When $\overline{\text{UDS}}$ is asserted, the contents of even addresses are transferred on the high-order eight lines of the data bus, D_8–D_{15}. The 68000 internally shifts this data to the low byte of the register specified. When $\overline{\text{LDS}}$ is asserted, the contents of odd addresses are transferred on the low-order eight lines of the data bus, D_0–D_7. During word and long word transfers, both $\overline{\text{UDS}}$ and $\overline{\text{LDS}}$ are asserted and information is transferred on all 16 data lines, D_0–D_{15} pins. Note that during byte memory transfers, A_0 corresponds to $\overline{\text{UDS}}$ for even addresses ($A_0 = 0$) and to $\overline{\text{LDS}}$ for odd addresses ($A_0 = 1$). The circuit in Figure 7.3 shows how even and odd addresses are interfaced to the 68000.

7.1.2   System Control Lines

The 68000 has three control lines, $\overline{\text{BERR}}$ (bus error), $\overline{\text{HALT}}$, and $\overline{\text{RESET}}$, which are used to control system-related functions. BERR is an input to the 68000 and is used to inform the processor that there is a problem with the instruction cycle currently being executed. With asynchronous operation, this problem may arise if the 68000 does not receive $\overline{\text{DTACK}}$ from a peripheral device. An external timer can be used to activate the BERR pin if the external device does not send $\overline{\text{DTACK}}$ within a certain period of time. On receipt of BERR, the 68000 does one of the following:

* Reruns the instruction cycle that caused the error

* Executes an error service routine

The troubled instruction cycle is rerun by the 68000 if it receives a $\overline{\text{HALT}}$ signal along with the $\overline{\text{BERR}}$ signal. On receipt of LOW on both the $\overline{\text{HALT}}$ and $\overline{\text{BERR}}$ pins, the 68000 completes the current instruction cycle and then goes into the high-impedance state. On removal of both $\overline{\text{HALT}}$ and $\overline{\text{BERR}}$ (i.e., when both $\overline{\text{HALT}}$ and $\overline{\text{BERR}}$ are HIGH), the 68000 reruns the troubled instruction cycle. The cycle can be rerun repeatedly if both $\overline{\text{BERR}}$ and $\overline{\text{HALT}}$ are enabled/disabled continually.

On the other hand, an error service routine is executed only if the $\overline{\text{BERR}}$ signal is received without $\overline{\text{HALT}}$. In this case, the 68000 will branch to a bus error vector address where the user can write a service routine. If two simultaneous bus errors are received via the $\overline{\text{BERR}}$ pin without $\overline{\text{HALT}}$, the 68000 goes into the halt state automatically until it is reset.

TABLE 7.3   Function Code Lines

FC2	FC1	FC0	Operation
0	0	0	Unassigned
0	0	1	User data
0	1	0	User program
0	1	1	Unassigned
1	0	0	Unassigned
1	0	1	Supervisor data
1	1	0	Supervisor program
1	1	1	Interrupt acknowledge

The $\overline{\text{HALT}}$ line can also be used by itself to perform single stepping or to provide DMA. When the $\overline{\text{HALT}}$ input is activated, the 68000 completes the current instruction and goes into a high-impedance state until $\overline{\text{HALT}}$ is returned to HIGH. By enabling/disabling the $\overline{\text{HALT}}$ line continually, single-stepping debugging can be accomplished. However, because most 68000 instructions consist of more than one clock cycle, single stepping using $\overline{\text{HALT}}$ is not normally used. Rather, the trace bit in the status register is used to single-step the complete instruction.

One can also use $\overline{\text{HALT}}$ to perform microprocessor-halt DMA. Because the 68000 has separate DMA control lines, DMA using the $\overline{\text{HALT}}$ line will not normally be used. The $\overline{\text{HALT}}$ pin can also be used as an output signal. The 68000 will assert the $\overline{\text{HALT}}$ pin LOW when it goes into a halt state as a result of a catastrophic failure. The double bus error (activation of $\overline{\text{BERR}}$ twice) is an example of this type of error. When this occurs, the 68000 goes into a high-impedance state until it is reset. The $\overline{\text{HALT}}$ line informs the peripheral devices of the catastrophic failure.

The $\overline{\text{RESET}}$ line of the 68000 is also bidirectional. To reset the 68000, the $\overline{\text{RESET}}$ and $\overline{\text{HALT}}$ pins must both be LOW for 10 clock cycles at the same time except initially when Vcc is applied to the 68000. In this case, an external reset must be applied for at least 100 ms. The 68000 executes a reset service routine automatically for loading the PC with the starting address of the program.

The 68000 $\overline{\text{RESET}}$ pin can also be used as an output line. A LOW can be sent to this output line by executing the RESET instruction in the supervisor mode in order to reset external devices connected to the 68000 $\overline{\text{RESET}}$ pin. Upon execution of the RESET instruction, the 68000 drives the $\overline{\text{RESET}}$ pin LOW for 124 clock periods and does not affect any data, address, or status registers. Therefore, the RESET instruction can be placed anywhere in the program whenever the external devices need to be reset.

Upon hardware reset, the 68000 sets S-bit in SR to 1 and then loads the supervisor stack pointer (A7') and the program counter (PC) from location $000000. In addition, the 68000 clears the trace bit in SR to 0 and sets bits I2 I1 I0 in SR to 111. No other registers are affected.

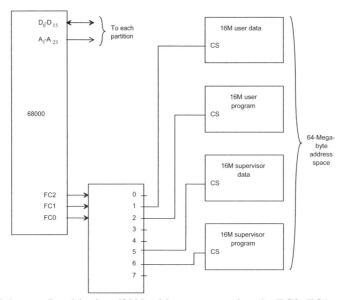

FIGURE 7.4   Partitioning 68000 address space using the FC2, FC1, and FC0 pins

7.1.3 ___ Interrupt Control Lines

$\overline{IPL0}$, $\overline{IPL1}$, and $\overline{IPL2}$ are the three interrupt control lines. These lines provide for seven interrupt priority levels ($\overline{IPL2}$, $\overline{IPL1}$, $\overline{IPL0}$ = 111 means no interrupt, and $\overline{IPL2}$, $\overline{IPL1}$, $\overline{IPL0}$ = 000 means nonmaskable interrupt with the highest priority). If there are no interrupts in the system, these three pins must be connected HIGH to disable the 68000's interrupts. The 68000 interrupts are discussed later in the chapter.

7.1.4 ___ DMA Control Lines

The $\overline{BR}$ (bus request), $\overline{BG}$ (bus grant), and $\overline{BGACK}$ (bus grant acknowledge) lines are used for DMA purposes. If the system does not use DMA, the $\overline{BR}$ and $\overline{BGACK}$ pins must be connected HIGH to disable the DMA function. The 68000 DMA is discussed later in the chapter.

7.1.5 ___ Status Lines

The 68000 has three output lines FC2, FC1, and FC0, called *function code pins*. These lines tell external devices whether user data/program or supervisor data/program is being addressed. These lines can be decoded to provide user or supervisor programs/data and interrupt acknowledge as shown in Table 7.3. The FC2, FC1, and FC0 pins can be used to partition memory into four functional areas: user data memory, user program memory, supervisor data memory, and supervisor program memory. Each memory partition can directly access up to 16 MB, and thus the 68000 can be made to directly address up to 64 MB of memory. This is shown in Figure 7.4.

Note that both supervisor and user memory are needed for multitasking or multiuser systems. However, one can design memory without using the FC2, FC1, FC0 pins in memory decoding logic for a single application or for systems requiring no operating systems. In that case, the 68000 will always operate in the supervisor mode. Upon hardware reset, the 68000 will operate in supervisor mode, and will continue to operate in that mode.

7.2 ___ 68000 Clock and Reset Signals

In this section we cover generation of the 68000 clock and reset signals in detail because the clock signal and the reset pins are two important signals of any microprocessor.

7.2.1 ___ 68000 Clock Signals

As mentioned earlier, the 68000 does not include an on-chip clock generation circuitry. This means that an external crystal oscillator chip is required to generate the clock. The 68000 CLK input can be provided by a crystal oscillator or by designing an external circuit. Figure 7.5 shows a simple oscillator to generate the 68000 CLK input.

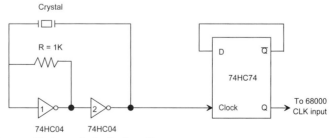

FIGURE 7.5   **External clock circuitry.**

This circuit uses two inverters connected in series. Inverter 1 is biased in its transition region by the resistor *R*. Inverter 1 inputs the crystal output (sinusoidal) to provide a logic pulse train at the output of inverter 1. Inverter 2 sharpens the wave and drives the crystal. For this circuit to work, HCMOS logic must be used for the inverters. Therefore, the 74HC04 inverter chip is used. The 74HC04 has high noise immunity and the ability to drive 10 LS-TTL loads. A coupling capacitor should be connected across the supply terminals to reduce the ringing effect during high-frequency switching of the HCMOS devices. Note that the ringing occurs when a circuit oscillates for a short time due to the presence of stray inductance and capacitance. In addition, the output of this oscillator is fed to the CLK input of a D flip-flop (74HC74) to reduce the ringing further. A clock signal of 50% duty cycle at a frequency of one-half the crystal frequency is generated. This means that this circuit with a 16-MHz crystal will generate an 8-MHz clock for the 68000.

7.2.2   68000 Reset Circuit

When designing a microprocessor's reset circuit, two types of reset must be considered: power-up and manual. These reset circuits must be designed using the parameters specified by the manufacturer. Therefore, a microprocessor must be reset when its Vcc pin is connected to power, called *power-up reset*. After some time during normal operation, the microprocessor can be reset by the designer upon activation of a manual switch such as a pushbutton. A reset circuit therefore needs to be designed following the timing parameters associated typically with the microprocessor's reset input pin specified by the manufacturer. The reset circuit, once designed, is typically connected to the microprocessor's reset pin.

Upon hardware reset, the 68000 sets the S-bit in SR to 1 and performs the following:

1.   The 68000 loads the 24-bit supervisor stack pointer (A7') from addresses $000000 through $000003 with the highest byte from address $000001 and the lowest byte from address $000003. Note that the contents of address $000000 are don't cares. The 68000 loads the 24-bit PC from addresses $000004 through $000007 with the highest byte from address $000005 and the lowest byte from address $000007. Note that the contents of address $000004 are don't cares. Typical 68000 assembler directives such as DC.L can be used for this purpose. For example, to load $200128 into supervisor SP and $3F1420 into PC, the following instruction sequence can be used:

    ORG $00000000
    DC.L $00200128
    DC.L $003F1420

2.   The 68000 clears the trace bit in SR to 0 and sets the interrupt mask bits I2 I1 I0 in SR to 111. No other registers are   affected.

To cause a power-up reset, Motorola specifies that both the $\overline{\text{RESET}}$ and $\overline{\text{HALT}}$ pins of the 68000 must be held LOW for at least 100 ms. This means that an external circuit needs to be designed that will generate a negative pulse with a width of at least 100 ms for both $\overline{\text{RESET}}$ and $\overline{\text{HALT}}$. The manual RESET requires that the $\overline{\text{RESET}}$ and $\overline{\text{HALT}}$ pins both be LOW for at least 10 cycles (1.25 microseconds for 8 MHz). In general, it is safer to assert $\overline{\text{RESET}}$ and $\overline{\text{HALT}}$ for much longer than the minimum requirements. Figure 7.6 shows a typical 68000 reset circuit that asserts $\overline{\text{RESET}}$ and $\overline{\text{HALT}}$ LOW for approximately 200 ms. The 555 timer is used in the circuit.

The reset circuit in the figure utilizes the 555 timer chip and provides for both power-up and manual resets by asserting the 68000 $\overline{\text{RESET}}$ and $\overline{\text{HALT}}$ pins for at least 200 ms. The computer designer does not have to know about the details of the 555 chip.

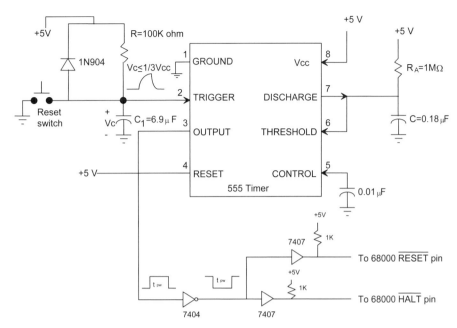

FIGURE 7.6   68000 RESET circuit.

Instead, the designer should know how to use the 555 chip to generate the 68000 RESET signal.

The 555 is a linear eight-pin chip. The TRIGGER pin is the input signal. When the voltage at the TRIGGER input pin is less than or equal to 1/3 V_{cc}, the OUTPUT pin is HIGH. The DISCHARGE and THRESHOLD pins are tied together to R_A and C. Note that the values of R_A and C determine the output pulse width. The CONTROL input pin controls the THRESHOLD input voltage. According to the manufacturer's data sheets, the control input should be connected to a 0.01-µF capacitor whose other lead should be grounded. Also, from the manufacturer's data sheets, the output pulse width $t_{pw} = 1.1\ R_A C$ seconds. The values of R_A and C can be chosen for stretching out the pulse width.

An RC circuit is connected at the 555 TRIGGER pin. A slow pulse obtained by charging and discharging the capacitor C_1 is applied at the 555 TRIGGER input pin. The 555 will generate a clean and fast pulse at the output. Capacitor C_1 is at zero voltage upon power-up. This is obviously lower than 1/3 V_{cc} with $V_{cc} = 5$ V. Thus, the 555 will generate a HIGH at the OUTPUT pin. The OUTPUT pin is connected through a 7404 inverter to provide a LOW at the 68000 $\overline{RESET}$ and $\overline{HALT}$ pins.

The 7404 output is buffered via two 7407s (noninverting buffers) to ensure adequate currents for the 68000 $\overline{RESET}$ and $\overline{HALT}$ pins. Note that the 7407 provides an open collector output. Therefore, a 1-Kohm pull-up is used for each 7407. Now, let us explain how the timing requirements for the 68000 RESET are satisfied.

As mentioned before, capacitor C_1 is initially at zero voltage upon power-up. C_1 then charges to V_{cc} after a definite time determined by the time constant, RC_1. The charging voltage across the capacitor is

$$Vc(t) = Vcc[1 - e^{-\frac{t}{RC_1}}]$$

$V_c(t)$ must be less than or equal to $V_{cc}/3$ volts (1.7 V). To be on the safe side, let us assume that $V_c = V_{cc}/4 = 5/4 = 1.25$ V.

$$\frac{Vc(t)}{Vcc(t)} = 1 - e^{-\frac{t}{RC_1}}$$

$$\text{Hence, } \frac{1}{4} = 1 - e^{-\frac{t}{RC_1}}$$

$$e^{-\frac{t}{RC_1}} = 0.75$$

$$-\frac{t}{RC_1} = \ln(0.75)$$

$$-\frac{t}{RC_1} = -0.29$$

$$\text{Therefore, } RC_1 = \frac{t}{0.29}$$

As mentioned earlier, it is desired to provide 200 ms (chosen arbitrarily; satisfying the minimum requirements specified by Motorola) reset time for both power-up and manual reset.

$$RC_1 = \frac{200 \text{ ms}}{0.29} = 689.65 \text{ ms}$$

$$\text{Hence, } RC_1 \cong 0.69 \text{ s}$$

If R is arbitrarily chosen as 100 KΩ, then $C_1 = 6.9$ μF.

The 555 output pulse width can be determined using the equation $t_{pw} = 1.1\, R_A\, C$. Since $t_{pw} = 200$ msec, hence $R_A\, C = 0.18$ seconds. If $R_A = 1$ MΩ (arbitrarily chosen) then $C = 0.18/10^6 = 0.18$ μF.

The reverse-biased diode (1N904) connected at the 555 TRIGGER input circuit is used to hold the capacitor (C_1 charged to 1.25 V) voltage at 1.25 V in case V_{cc} (obtained using a power supply from AC voltage) drops below 5 V to a level such that the capacitor C_1 may discharge through the 100-KΩ resistor. In such a situation, the diode will be forward biased, essentially shorting out the 100-Kohm resistor, thus maintaining the capacitor voltage at 1.25 V. In Figure 7.6, upon power-up, the capacitor C_1 charges to approximately 1.25 V. After some time, if the reset switch is depressed, the capacitor is short-circuited to ground. The capacitor therefore discharges to zero.

This logic 0 at the 555 TRIGGER input pin will provide 200 ms LOW at the 68000 $\overline{\text{RESET}}$ and $\overline{\text{HALT}}$ input pins. This will satisfy the minimum requirement of 10 clock cycles (1.25 microseconds for a 8-MHz clock) at the 68000 $\overline{\text{RESET}}$ and $\overline{\text{HALT}}$ pins for manual reset. The values of R and C_1 at the 555 TRIGGER input should be recalculated for other 68000 clock frequencies for manual reset. Note that the 68000 power-up reset time is fixed with a timing requirement of at least 100 ms, whereas the manual reset time depends on the 68000 clock frequency and must be at least 10 clock cycles.

Another way of generating the power-up and manual resets is by using a Schmitt trigger inverter such as the 7414 chip. Figure 7.7 shows a typical circuit.

Operation of the 68000 power-up and manual resets using the RC circuit in Figure 7.7 was described earlier. The purpose of the two 7414 Schmitt trigger inverters is primarily to shape up a slow pulse generated by the RC circuit to obtain a fast and clean negative

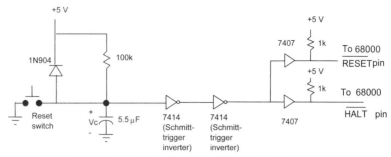

FIGURE 7.7 **68000 reset circuit using a Schmitt trigger.**

pulse. Two 7407 open-collector noninverting buffers are used to amplify currents for the 68000 RESET and HALT pins. Let us now determine the values of R and C.

When the input of the 7414 Schmitt trigger inverter is low (e.g., 0 V) , the output will be HIGH, typically at about 3.7 V. For input voltage from 0 to about 1.7 V, the output of the 7414 will be HIGH. Let us arbitrarily choose $V_c = 1.5$ V to provide a low at the input of the first 7414 in the figure. As before,

$$Vc = Vcc[1 - e^{-\frac{t}{RC}}]$$

$$\text{Hence, } 1 - e^{-\frac{t}{RC}} = \frac{1.5}{5}$$

$$e^{-\frac{t}{RC}} = 0.7$$

Let us design the reset circuit to provide 200 ms reset time. Therefore, $t = 200$ ms.

$$-\frac{0.2}{RC} = \ln(0.7)$$

$$-\frac{0.2}{RC} = -0.36$$

$$\text{Therefore, } RC = 0.55 \text{ seconds}$$

If R is chosen arbitrarily as 100 KΩ, then $C = 5.5$ μF.

7.3   68000 Read and Write Cycle Timing Diagrams

The 68000 uses a handshaking mechanism to transfer data between the processors and peripheral devices. This means that all these processors can transfer data asynchronously to and from peripherals of varying speeds. During the read cycle, the 68000 obtains data from a memory location or an I/O port. If the instruction specifies a word (such as MOVE.W $020504,D1) or a long word (such as MOVE.L $030808,D0), the 68000 reads both upper and lower bytes at the same time by asserting the $\overline{\text{UDS}}$ and $\overline{\text{LDS}}$ pins. When the instruction is for a byte operation, the 68000 utilizes an internal bit to find which byte to read and then outputs the data strobe required for that byte.

For byte operations, when the address is even ($A_0 = 0$), the 68000 asserts $\overline{\text{UDS}}$ and reads data via the D_8–D_{15} pins into the low byte of the data register specified. On the other hand, when the address is odd ($A_0 = 1$), the 68000 outputs a LOW on $\overline{\text{LDS}}$ and reads data via the D_0–D_7 pins to the low byte of the data register specified. For example, consider

MOVE.B $507144, D5. The 68000 outputs a LOW on $\overline{\text{UDS}}$ (because $A_0 = 0$) and a HIGH on $\overline{\text{LDS}}$. The memory chip's eight data lines must be connected to the 68000 D_8–D_{15} pins. The 68000 reads the data byte via the D_8–D_{15} pins into the low byte of D5. Note that for reading a byte from an odd address, the data lines of the memory chip must be connected to the 68000 D_0–D_7 pins. In this case, the 68000 outputs a LOW on $\overline{\text{LDS}}$ (because $A_0 = 1$) and a HIGH on $\overline{\text{UDS}}$, and then reads the data byte into the low byte of the data register.

Figure 7.8 shows the read/write timing diagrams. During S0, address and data signals are in the high-impedance state. At the start of S1, the 68000 outputs the address on

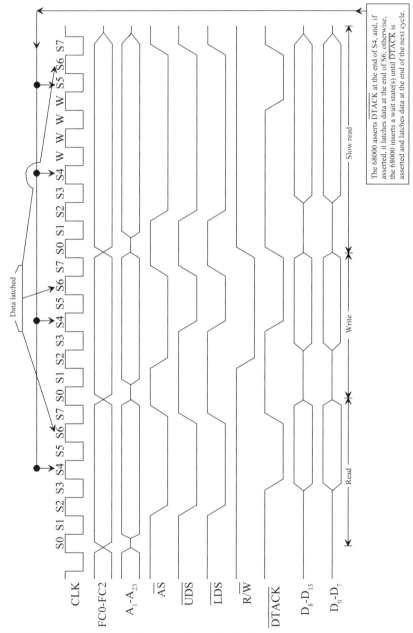

FIGURE 7.8   68000 read and write cycle timing diagrams

its address pins (A_1–A_{23}). During S0, the 68000 outputs FC2–FC0 signals. $\overline{AS}$ is asserted at the start of S2 to indicate a valid address on the bus. $\overline{AS}$ can be used at this point to latch the signals on the address pins. The 68000 asserts $\overline{UDS}$, $\overline{LDS}$, and R/$\overline{W}$ = 1 to indicate a READ operation. The 68000 now waits for the peripheral device to assert $\overline{DTACK}$. Upon placing data on the data bus, the peripheral device asserts $\overline{DTACK}$. The 68000 samples the $\overline{DTACK}$ signal at the end of S4. If $\overline{DTACK}$ is not asserted by the peripheral device, the processor automatically inserts a wait state(s) (W).

However, upon assertion of $\overline{DTACK}$, the 68000 negates the $\overline{AS}$, $\overline{UDS}$, and $\overline{LDS}$ signals and latches the data from the data bus into an internal register at the end of the next cycle. Once the peripheral device that has been selected senses that the 68000 has obtained data from the data bus (by recognizing the negation of $\overline{AS}$, $\overline{UDS}$, or $\overline{LDS}$), the peripheral device must negate $\overline{DTACK}$ immediately so that it does not interfere with the start of the next cycle. If $\overline{DTACK}$ is not asserted by the peripheral at the end of S4 (Figure 7.8, SLOW READ), the 68000 inserts wait states. The 68000 outputs valid addresses on the address pins and keeps asserting $\overline{AS}$, $\overline{UDS}$, and $\overline{LDS}$ until the peripheral asserts $\overline{DTACK}$. The 68000 always inserts an even number of wait states if $\overline{DTACK}$ is not asserted by the peripheral because all 68000 operations are performed using the clock with two states per clock cycle. Note in Figure 7.8 that the 68000 inserts four wait states or two cycles.

As an example of word read, consider that the 68000 is ready to execute the MOVE.W \$602122,D0 instruction. The 68000 performs as follows:

1. At the end of S0 the 68000 places the upper 23 bits of the address 602122_{16} on A_1–A_{23}.
2. At the end of S1, the 68000 asserts $\overline{AS}$, $\overline{UDS}$, and $\overline{LDS}$.
3. The 68000 continues to output a HIGH on the R/$\overline{W}$ pin from the beginning of the read cycle to indicate a READ operation.
4. At the end of S0, the 68000 places appropriate outputs on the FC2–FC0 pins to indicate either supervisor or user read.
5. If the peripheral asserts $\overline{DTACK}$ at the end of S4, the 68000 reads the contents of 602122_{16} and 602123_{16} via the D_8–D_{15} and D_0–D_7 pins, respectively, into the high and low bytes of D0.W at the end of S6. If the peripheral does not assert $\overline{DTACK}$ at the end of S4, the 68000 continues to insert wait states.

Figure 7.9 shows a simplified timing diagram illustrating the use of $\overline{DTACK}$ for interfacing external memory and I/O chips to the 68000. As mentioned before, the 68000 checks the $\overline{DTACK}$ input pin at the falling edge of S4 (three cycles), the external memory, or I/O in this case, drives the 68000 $\overline{DTACK}$ input LOW, and the 68000 waits for one cycle and latches data at the end of S6. However, if the 68000 does not find $\overline{DTACK}$ LOW at the falling edge of S4, it waits for one clock cycle and then again checks $\overline{DTACK}$ for LOW. If $\overline{DTACK}$ is LOW, the 68000 latches data after one cycle (the falling edge of S8). If the

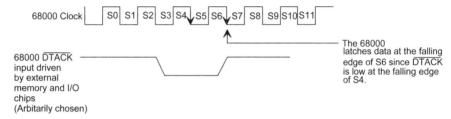

FIGURE 7.9 **68000 CLK and $\overline{DTACK}$ signals.**

68000 does not find $\overline{\text{DTACK}}$ LOW at the falling edge of S6, it checks for $\overline{\text{DTACK}}$ LOW at the falling edge of S8 and the process continues. Note that the minimum time to latch data is four cycles. This means that in the preceding example, if the 68000 clock frequency is 8 MHz, data will be latched after 500 ns because $\overline{\text{DTACK}}$ is asserted LOW at the end of S4 (375 ns). Note that $\overline{\text{DTACK}}$ can be asserted by $\overline{\text{AS}}$ if no wait states are required. This is because $\overline{\text{AS}}$ goes LOW after approximately two clock cycles.

7.4   68000 Memory Interface

One of the advantages of the 68000 is that it can easily be interfaced to memory chips with various speeds because it goes into a wait state if $\overline{\text{DTACK}}$ is not asserted (LOW) by the memory devices at the falling edge of S4. A simplified schematic showing an interface of a 68000 to two 2732s and two 6116s is given in Figure 7.10.

From the 2732 is a 4K × 8 EPROM and the 6116 is a 2K × 8 static RAM. For a 4-MHz clock, each cycle is 250 ns. Because the 68000 samples data at the falling edge of S4 (750 ns) and latches data at the falling edge of S6 (1000 ns), $\overline{\text{AS}}$ can be used to assert $\overline{\text{DTACK}}$

From the 68000 timing diagram of Figure 7.8, $\overline{\text{AS}}$ goes LOW after approximately two cycles (500 ns). The time delay between $\overline{\text{AS}}$ going LOW and the falling edge of S6 is 500 ns. Note that $\overline{\text{LDS}}$ and $\overline{\text{UDS}}$ must be used as chip selects as in Figure 7.10. They must not be connected to A_0 of the memory chips because in that case, half of the memory in each memory chip would be wasted. Note that $\overline{\text{LDS}}$ and $\overline{\text{UDS}}$ also go LOW after about two cycles (500 ns).

In Figure 7.10, a delay circuit for $\overline{\text{DTACK}}$ is not required because both 2732 and 6116 place data on the bus lines before the 68000 latches data. This is because the 68000 clock frequency is 4 MHz in this case. Thus, each clock cycle is 250 ns. The access times of the 2732 and 6116 are 200 ns and 120 ns, respectively. Because $\overline{\text{DTACK}}$ is sampled after three clock cycles (3 × 250 ns = 750 ns), both the 2732 and 6116 will have adequate time to place data on the bus for the 68000 to read.

For example, consider the even 2732 EPROM. $\overline{\text{UDS}}$ and $\overline{\text{AS}}$ are NORed and then NANDed with inverted A_{13} to select this chip. With the 200-ns access time of the 2732, data will be placed on the 68000 D_8–D_{15} pins after approximately 720 nanoseconds (500 ns for $\overline{\text{AS}}$ or $\overline{\text{UDS}}$ + 10 ns for the NOR gate + 10 ns for the NAND gate + 200 ns for the 2732). Therefore, no delay circuit for the 68000 $\overline{\text{DTACK}}$ is required because the 68000 latches data from the D_8–D_{15} pins after four cycles (1000 ns in this case). The timing parameters of the 68000-2732 with various 68000 frequencies are shown in Table 7.4.

Next, consider the odd 6116 static RAM (SRAM) with the 4-MHz 68000. Note that the 6116 signals $\overline{\text{W}}$ (write enable), $\overline{\text{G}}$ (output enable), and $\overline{\text{E}}$ (chip enable) are decoded as follows: When $\overline{\text{G}} = 0$ and $\overline{\text{E}}=0= 0$, then $\overline{\text{W}} = 1$ for read and $\overline{\text{W}} = 0$ for write. In this case, $\overline{\text{LDS}}$ and $\overline{\text{AS}}$ are NORed and NANDed with A_{13} to select this chip. With the 120-ns access time of the 6116 RAM, data will be placed on the 68000 D0–D7 pins after approximately 640 ns (500 ns for $\overline{\text{AS}}$ or $\overline{\text{LDS}}$ + 10 ns for the NOR gate + 10 ns for the NAND gate + 120 ns for the 6116). Because the 68000 latches data after four cycles (1000 ns in this case), no delay circuit for $\overline{\text{DTACK}}$ is required. The requirements for $\overline{\text{DTACK}}$ for the 68000/6116 for various 68000 clock frequencies can be determined similarly. In case a delay circuit for $\overline{\text{DTACK}}$ is required, a ring counter with D flip-flops can be used.

Let us now determine the memory maps. Figures 7.11(a) and 7.11 (b) show the 68000 interface to even 2732 and odd 6116 respectively. These figures are obtained from Figure 7.10. When $A_{13} = 0$, $\overline{\text{UDS}} = 0$, $\overline{\text{AS}} = 0$, and R/$\overline{\text{W}} = 1$, the even 2732 of Figure 7.11(a)

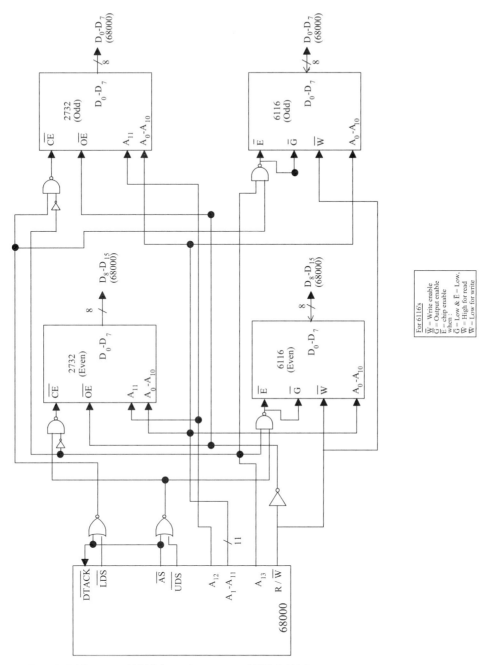

FIGURE 7.10   68000 interface to the 2732 / 6116.

will be selected by the 68000 to read data from the 68000's D_8–D_{15} pins.

When $A_{13} = 1$, $\overline{\text{LDS}} = 0$, $\overline{\text{AS}} = 0$, the odd 6116 of Figure 7.11(b) will be selected by the 68000 to read ($R/\overline{W} =1$) data from or write ($R/\overline{W} =0$) data to 68000 D_0–D_7 pins. For 2732, the 68000 address pins A_{23}–A_{14} are don't cares (assume 0's). For 6116, the 68000 address pins A_{23}–A_{14}, and pin A_{12} are don't cares (assume 0's).

The memory map for the even 2732 can be determined as follows:

TABLE 7.4   68000-2732 Timing Example

Case	68000 Frequency	Clock Cycle	Time before first $\overline{\text{DTACK}}$ is sampled	Comment
1	12.5 MHz	80 ns	3(80) = 240 ns	Not enough time for 2732 to place data on bus; needs delay circuit for $\overline{\text{DTACK}}$
2	16.67 MHz	60 ns	3(60) = 180 ns	Same as case 1
3	25 MHz	40 ns	3(40) = 120 ns	Same as case 1

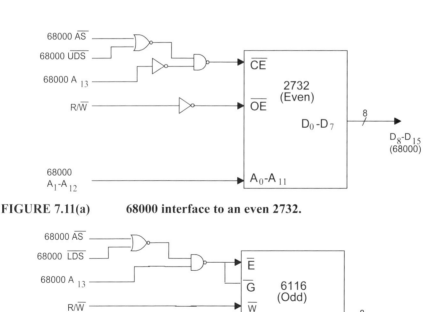

FIGURE 7.11(a)   68000 interface to an even 2732.

FIGURE 7.11(b)   68000 interface to an odd 6116.

- 2732 even

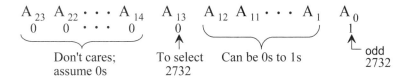

Address range: $000000, $000002, ... , $001FFE

Similarly, the memory for the odd 2732, even 6116, and odd 6116 can be determined as follows:

- 2732 odd

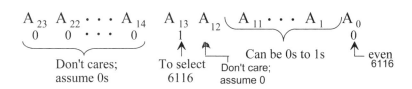

Address range: $000001, $000003, ... , $001FFF

- 6116 even

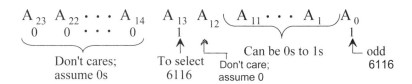

Address range: $002000, $002002, ... , $002FFE

- 6116 odd

Address range: $002001, $002003, ... , $002FFF

Static RAMs such as the 6116 are used for small memory system. Also, note that RAMs are needed when subroutines and interrupts requiring stack are desired in an application. Note that linear decoding is used in Figure 7.10. Since the 68000 uses memory-mapped I/O, an unused address pin must be used to distinguish between memory and I/O. If there is an I/O chip in Figure 7.10, an unused address pin such as A_{22} (arbitrarily chosen) must be used to distinguish between memory and I/O. $A_{22} = 0$ and $A_{22} = 1$ can respectively be used to select memory (2732 and 6116) and the I/O chip.

7.5   68000 I/O

In this section we cover I/O techniques associated with the Motorola 68000.

7.5.1   68000 Programmed I/O

As mentioned earlier, the 68000 uses memory-mapped I/O. Data transfer using I/O ports (programmed I/O) can be achieved in the 68000 in one of the following ways:

*   By interfacing the 68000 with an inexpensive slow 6800 I/O chip, such as the 6821

*   By interfacing the 68000 with its own family of I/O chips, such as the 68230

68000/6821 Interface   The Motorola 6821 is a 40-pin peripheral interface adapter (PIA) chip. It is provided with an 8-bit bidirectional data bus (D_0–D_7), two register select lines (RS0, RS1), read/write (R/$\overline{W}$) and reset ($\overline{RESET}$) lines, an enable line (E), two 8-bit I/O ports (PA0–PA7 and PB0–PB7), and other pins. Figure 7.12 shows the pin diagram of the 6821. There are six 6821 registers. These include two 8-bit ports (ports A and B), two data direction registers, and two control registers. Selection of these registers is controlled by the RS0 and RS1 inputs together with bit 2 of the control register. Table 7.5 shows how the registers are selected. In the table, bit 2 in each control register (CRA-2 and CRB-2) determines the selection of either an I/O port or the corresponding data direction register when the proper register select signals are applied to RS0 and RS1. A 1 in bit 2 in CRA or

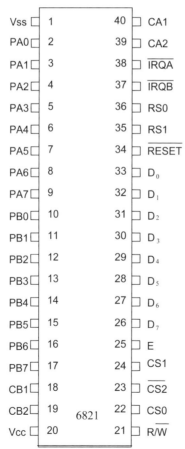

FIGURE 7.12   6821 pin diagram

TABLE 7.5   6821 Register Definition

		Control Register Bits 2		
RS1	RS0	CRA-2	CRB-2	Register Selected
0	0	1	X	I/O port A
0	0	0	X	Data direction register A
0	1	X	X	Control register A
1	0	X	1	I/O port B
1	0	X	0	Data direction register B
1	1	X	X	Control register B

X = don't care.

CRB allows access of I/O ports; a 0 in bit 2 of CRA or CRB selects the data direction registers.

Each I/O port bit can be configured to act as an input or output. This is accomplished by sending a 1 in the corresponding data direction register bit for those bits that are to be output and a 0 for those bits that are to be inputs. A LOW on the $\overline{RESET}$ pin clears all registers to 0. This has the effect of configuring PA0–PA7 and PB0–PB7 as inputs.

Three built-in signals in the 68000 provide an interface with the 6821: enable (E), valid memory address ($\overline{VMA}$), and valid peripheral address ($\overline{VPA}$). The enable signal (E) is an output from the 68000. It corresponds to the E signal of the 6821. This signal is the clock used by the 6821 to synchronize data transfer. The frequency of the E signal is one-tenth of the 68000 clock frequency. This allows one to interface the 68000 (which operates much faster than the 6821) with the 6821. The valid memory address ($\overline{VMA}$) signal is output by the 68000 to indicate to the 6800 peripherals that there is a valid address on the address bus. The valid peripheral address ($\overline{VPA}$) is an input to the 68000. This signal is used to indicate that the device addressed by the 68000 is a 6800 peripheral. This tells the 68000 to synchronize data transfer with the enable signal (E).

To configure and address a port, the following steps should be followed (seeTable 7.5):
1. Clear bit 2 of the control register of the port.
2. Move data to the data direction register of the port to configure the port as input(s) and/or output(s).
3. Set bit 2 of the control register of the port.

Let us now discuss how the 68000 instructions can be used to configure the 6821 ports. As an example, bit 7 of port A can be configured as an input, and bits 0–6 of port A can be configured as outputs using the following instruction sequence:

```
BCLR.B #2,CRA          ;        Address DDRA
MOVE.B #$7F,DDRA       ;        Configure port A
BSET.B #2,CRA          ;        Address port A
```

Once the ports are configured to the designer's specification, the 6821 can be used to transfer data from an input device to the 68000 or from the 68000 to an output device by using the MOVE.B instruction as follows:

```
MOVE.B (EA), Dn        ;        Transfer 8-bit data from an input port
                       ;        to the specified data register Dn
MOVE.B Dn, (EA)        ;        Transfer 8-bit data from the specified
                       ;        data register Dn to an output port
```

Figure 7.13(a) shows a block diagram of how two 6821s are interfaced to the 68000 to obtain four 8-bit I/O ports. Note that the least significant bit, A_0, of the 68000 address pin is internally encoded to generate two signals, the upper data strobe ($\overline{UDS}$) and lower data strobe ($\overline{LDS}$). For byte transfers, $\overline{UDS}$ is asserted if an even-numbered byte is being transferred, and $\overline{LDS}$ is asserted for an odd-numbered byte. In Figure 7.13(a), when $A_{22} = 1$ and $\overline{AS} = 0$, the OR gate output will be LOW. This OR gate output is used to assert $\overline{VPA}$. The inverted OR gate output, in turn, makes CS1 HIGH on both 6821s.

A LOW on $\overline{VPA}$ will tell the 68000 that the I/O device is 6800-type (6821 in this case) so that the 68000 can use the E clock. In response, the 68000 generates a LOW on $\overline{VMA}$. Inverted $\overline{VMA}$ will make CS0 on both 6821s HIGH. Execution of an input or output instruction with an even or odd port address will make $\overline{UDS}$ or $\overline{LDS}$ LOW. The 68000 will select the even or odd 6821 accordingly.

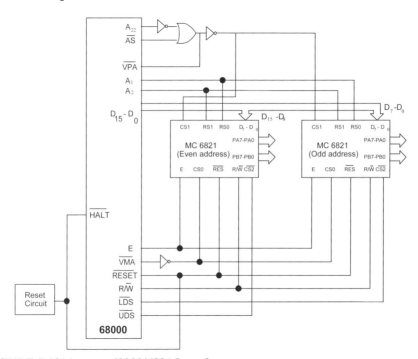

FIGURE 7.13(a)   **68000/6821 Interface.**

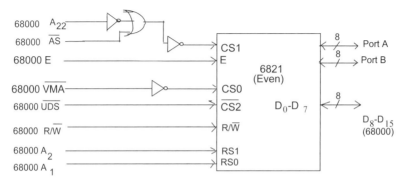

FIGURE 7.13(b)   **68000 interface to even 6821.**

TABLE 7.6 **I/O map**

	Port A or DDRA	CRA	Port B or DDRB	CRB
6821(even)	$400000	$400002	$400004	$400006
6821(odd)	$400001	$400003	$400005	$400007

Figure 7.13(b) is obtained from Figure 7.13(a). Figure 7.13(b) shows 68000-even 6821 interface along with pertinent connections. The addresses for Port A or DDRA for the even 6821 can be obtained as follows:

$$A_{23} \; A_{22} \; A_{21} \; A_{20} \; \cdots \; A_6 \; A_5 \; A_4 \; A_3 \; A_2 \; A_1 \; A_0$$
$$X \quad 1 \quad X \quad X \; \cdots \; X \quad X \quad X \quad X \quad \underline{0 \quad 0} \quad 0 = \$400000$$

Port A or DDRA — $\uparrow$ $\overline{UDS}$

Note that X's are don't cares, and are assumed 0's.

Since the 68000 uses memory-mapped I/O, an unused address pin such as A_{22} must be used to distinguish between memory and I/O. Note that A_{22} is chosen arbitrarily. Pin $A_{22} = 1$ is chosen to select I/O while Pin $A_{22} = 0$ will select memory. This will also ensure that the addresses for the ports and the reset vector are not the same.

Assuming that the don't care address lines A_{23} and A_{21}–A_3 are 0s, the addresses for port B or DDRB, and control registers (CRA and CRB) for the even 6821 ($A_0 = 0$) can

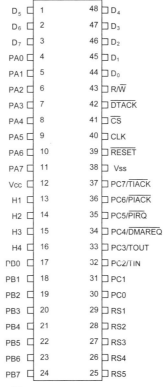

FIGURE 7.14 **68230 pin diagram**

be obtained ; similarly, the addresses for the ports or data direction registers, and control registers for the odd 6821 ($A_0 = 1$) can be determined. Table 7.6 shows the I/O map.

68000/68230 Interface   The 68230 is a 48-pin I/O chip designed for the 68000 family of microprocessors. The 68230 offers various functions such as, programmed I/O, an on-chip timer, and a DMA request pin for connection to a DMA controller. Figure 7.14 shows the 68230 pin diagram. The 68230 can be configured in two modes of operation: unidirectional and bidirectional. In the unidirectional mode, data direction registers configure the corresponding ports as inputs or outputs. This is the programmed I/O mode of operation.

Both 8- and 16-bit ports can be used. In the bidirectional mode, the 68230 provides data transfer between the 68000 and external devices via exchange of control signals (known as *handshaking*). In this section we cover only the programmed I/O feature of the 68230.

This 68230 ports can be configured in either unidirectional or bidirectional mode by using bits 7 and 6 of the port general control register, PGCR (R0), as shown in Table 7.7. The other bits of the PGCR are defined for handshaking.

Modes 0 and 2 configure ports A and B as unidirectional or bidirectional 8-bit ports. Modes 1 and 3, on the other hand, combine ports A and B to form a 16-bit unidirectional or bidirectional port. Ports configured as unidirectional 8-bit must be programmed further as submodes of operation using bits 7 and 6 of PACR (R6) and PBCR (R7) (see Table 7.8). Note that X means don't care. Nonlatched inputs are latched internally, but the values are not latched externally by the 68230 at the port. Bit I/O is used for programmed I/O.

The submodes define the ports as parallel input ports, parallel output ports, or bit-configurable I/O ports. In addition to these, the submodes further define the ports

TABLE 7.7   Port Configuration

PGCR Bits			
7	6	Mode	
0	0	0	(unidirectional 8-bit)
0	1	1	(unidirectional 16-bit)
1	0	2	(bidirectional 8-bit)
1	1	3	(bidirectional 16-bit)

TABLE 7.8 Submodes of Operation

Submode	Bit 7 of PACR or PBCR	Bit 6 of PACR or PBCR	Comment
00	0	0	Pin-definable double-buffered input or single-buffered output
01	0	1	Pin-definable double-buffered output or nonlatched input
1X	1	X	Bit I/O (pin-definable single-buffered output or nonlatched input)

TABLE 7.9 **Some 68230 Registers**

Register Select Bits					
RS5	RS4	RS3	RS2	RS1	Register Selected
0	0	0	0	0	PGCR, Port General Control Register (R0)
0	0	0	1	0	PADDR, Port A Data Direrction Register (R2)
0	0	0	1	1	PBDDR, Port B Data Direction Register (R3)
0	0	1	1	0	PACR, Port A Control Register (R6)
0	0	1	1	1	PBCR, Port B Control Register (R7)
0	1	0	0	0	PADR, Port A Data Register (R8)
0	1	0	0	1	PBDR, Port B Data Register (R9)

as latched input ports, interrupt-driven ports, DMA ports, and ports with various I/O handshake operations. Table 7.9 lists some of the 68230 registers. The registers required for programmed I/O are considered in the following discussion. Note that 68230 register select pins (RS5–RS1) are used to select the 68230 registers. Figure 7.15 illustrates how to obtain specific addresses for some of the 68230 I/O ports. For simplicity, port A and port B of the 68230 will be considered to illustrate the concept of 68000 programmed I/O with a typical 16-bit I/O chip.

The hardware schematic for the 68000/68230 interface is shown in Figure 7.15. Note that since the 68000 uses memory-mapped I/O, an unused address pin such as A_{23} must be used to distinguish between I/O and memory. In this case, A_{23} =1 is used to select I/O while A_{23} = 0 will select memory. Also, this will ensure that the port addresses are different from the 68000 reset vector addresses 000000_{16}–000007_{16}. The configuration in the figure will provide even port addresses because $\overline{UDS}$ is used to enable the 68230 $\overline{CS}$. The 68230 $\overline{DTACK}$ is an open-drain output. Hence, a pull-up resistor is required.

Note that A_{23} through A_6 are don't cares and are assumed to be 0's in the following. Hence, from the figure, addresses for registers PGCR (R0), PADDR (R2), PBDDR (R3), PACR (R6), PBCR (R7), PADR (R8), and PBDR (R9) can be obtained as shown below. For example, consider PGCR as follows:
Therefore, the address for PGCR is $800000. Similarly, the addresses for PADDR = $800004, for PBDDR = $800006, for PACR = $80000C, for PBCR = $80000E , for PADR = $800010, and for PBDR = $800012.

To configure a 68230 I/O port such as PADR or PBDR, the following steps should be followed:

• Clear bits 6 and 7 to 0 in PGCR.

• Set bit 7 to 1 in PACR (for PADR) or in PBCR (for PBDR)

• Move data to the data direction register of the port to configure the port as input(s) and/or output(s).

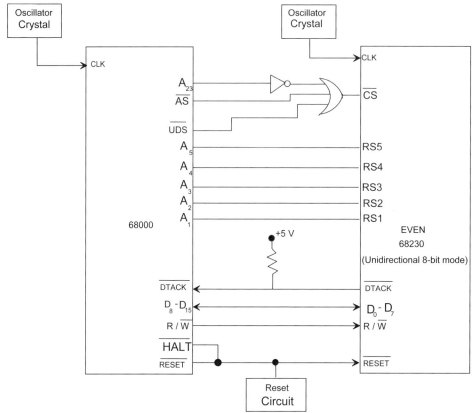

FIGURE 7.15   68000/68230 interface.

As an example, the following instruction sequence will select mode 0 and submode 1X and configure bits 0–5 of port A as outputs, bits 6 and 7 of port A as inputs, and port B as an input port:

```
PGCR    EQU     $800000
PADDR   EQU     $800004
PBDDR   EQU     $800006
PACR    EQU     $80000C
PBCR    EQU     $80000E
        ANDI.B  #$3F,PGCR     ;   Select mode 0
        BSET.B  #7,PACR       ;   Port A bit I/O submode
        BSET.B  #7,PBCR       ;   Port B bit I/O submode
        MOVE.B  #$3F,PADDR    ;   Configure port A bits 0-5 as
                              ;   outputs and bits 6 and 7 as inputs
        MOVE.B  #$00,PBDDR    ;   Configure port B as an input port
```

EXAMPLE 7.1   Draw a schematic showing connections between two 2732's (even and odd) and one 6821 (Odd) to a 4-MHz 68000 using relevant pins and signals. Determine memory and I/O maps. Use linear decoding. Assume no interrupts and no DMA. Comment on the unused input pins.

Solution

The schematic is shown in Figure 7.16. Since no interrupts and no DMA are used, connect $\overline{IPL2}$ through $\overline{IPL0}$ pins to HIGH, $\overline{BR}$ to HIGH and $\overline{BGACK}$ to HIGH. Also with a 4-MHz 68000, the 2732's, no delay circuit is needed for $\overline{DTACK}$. Hence, pin $\overline{AS}$ is used to assert $\overline{DTACK}$.

The memory map for the even 2732 can be determined as follows:

• 2732 even

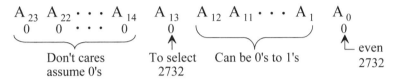

Address range: $000000, $000002, ... , $001FFE

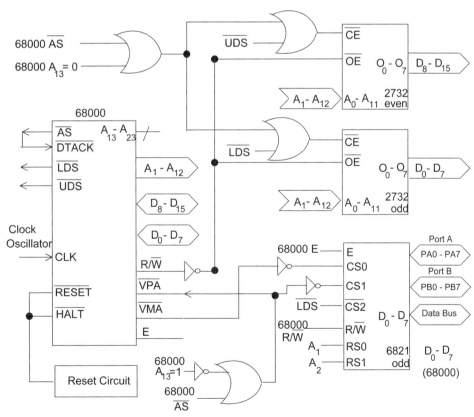

FIGURE 7.16   **Figure for Example 7.1**

Similarly, the memory for the odd 2732 can be determined as follows:

• 2732 odd

$$\underbrace{A_{23}\ A_{22}\ \cdots\ A_{14}}_{\substack{\text{Don't cares}\\ \text{assume 0's}}}\ \underset{\substack{\uparrow\\ \text{To select}\\ 2732}}{A_{13}}\ \underbrace{A_{12}\ A_{11}\ \cdots\ A_{1}}_{\text{Can be 0's to 1's}}\ \underset{\substack{\uparrow\\ \text{odd}\\ 2732}}{A_{0}}$$

(0   0 ··· 0)   (0)   1

Address range: \$000001, \$000003, … , \$001FFF

• 6821 odd

The addresses for Port A or DDRA for the even 6821 can be obtained as follows:

$$A_{23}\ A_{22}\ A_{21}\ A_{20}\cdots A_{13}\cdots A_{5}\ A_{4}\ A_{3}\ A_{2}\ A_{1}\ A_{0}$$

X   X   X   X……… 1……… X   X   X $\underset{\substack{\text{Port A}\\ \text{or}\\ \text{DDRA}}}{0\ \ \ \ 0}$ $\underset{\substack{\uparrow\\ \text{odd 6821}}}{1}$ = \$002001

Note that X's are don't cares, and are assumed 0's.

Since the 68000 uses memory-mapped I/O, an unused address pin such as A_{13} must be used to distinguish between memory and I/O. Note that A_{13} is arbitrarily chosen. Pin $A_{13} = 1$ is chosen to select I/O while Pin $A_{13} = 0$ will select memory.

Assuming that the don't care address lines A_{23} through A_{14} are 0's, the addresses for the other I/O ports, control registers, and data direction registers for the odd 6821 ($A_0 = 1$) can be obtained. The I/O map is provided below:

	Port A or DDRA	CRA	Port B or DDRB	CRB
6821(odd)	\$002001	\$002003	\$002005	\$002007

EXAMPLE 7.2   Write a 68000 assembly language program to drive an LED connected to bit 7 of Port A based on a switch input at bit 0 of Port A. If the switch is HIGH, turn the LED ON; otherwise turn the LED OFF. Assume a 68000/6821 microcomputer. Use port addresses of your choice.

Solution

```
       PORTA EQU       $001001
       DDRA  EQU       $001001
       CRA   EQU       $001003
             BCLR.B    #2,CRA         ;      address DDRA
             MOVE.B    #$80,DDRA      ;      Configure PORT A
             BSET.B    #2,CRA         ;      Address PORT A
       START MOVE.B    PORTA,D0       ;      Read switch
             ROR.B     #1,D0          ;      Rotate switch status
             MOVE.B    D0,PORTA       ;      Output to LED
             JMP       START          ;      Repeat
```

EXAMPLE 7.3   A 68000/68230-based microcomputer is required to drive an LED connected at bit 7 of port A based on two switch inputs connected at bits 6 and 7 of port B. If both switches are equal (either HIGH or LOW), turn the LED ON; otherwise turn it OFF. Assume that a HIGH will turn the LED ON and a LOW will turn it OFF. Write a 68000 assembly program to accomplish this.

Solution

```
PGCR    EQU     $800000
PACR    EQU     $80000C
PBCR    EQU     $80000E
PADDR   EQU     $800004
PBDDR   EQU     $800006
PADR    EQU     $800010
PBDR    EQU     $800012
        ANDI.B  #$3F,PGCR     ;   Select mode 0
        BSET.B  #7,PACR       ;   Port A bit I/O submode
        BSET.B  #7,PBCR       ;   Port B bit I/O submode
        MOVE.B  #$80,PADDR    ;   Configure port A bit 7 as output
        MOVE.B  #0,PBDDR      ;   Configure port B bits 6 and 7 as inputs
        MOVE.B  PBDR,D0       ;   Input port B
        ANDI.B  #$C0,D0       ;   Retain bits 6 and 7
        BEQ.B   LEDON         ;   If both switches LOW, turn LED ON
        CMPI.B  #$C0,D0       ;   If both switches HIGH, turn LED ON
        BEQ.B   LEDON
        MOVE.B  #$00,PADR     ;   Turn LED OFF
        JMP     FINISH
LEDON   MOVE.B  #$80,PADR     ;   Turn LED ON
FINISH  JMP     FINISH
```

7.5.2   68000 Interrupt System

The 68000 interrupt I/O can be divided into two types: external and internal interrupts.

External Interrupts   The 68000 provides seven levels of external interrupts, 1 through 7. The external hardware provides an interrupt level using the pins $\overline{IPL0}$, $\overline{IPL1}$, and $\overline{IPL2}$. Like other microprocessors, the 68000 checks for and accepts interrupts only between instructions. It compares the value of inverted $\overline{IPL0}$– $\overline{IPL2}$ with the current interrupt mask contained in bits 10, 9, and 8 of the status register.

   If the value of the inverted $\overline{IPL0}$– $\overline{IPL2}$ is greater than the value of the current interrupt mask, the 68000 acknowledges the interrupt and initiates interrupt processing. Otherwise, the 68000 continues with the current interrupt. Interrupt request level 0 ($\overline{IPL0}$– $\overline{IPL2}$ all HIGH) indicates that no interrupt service is requested. An inverted $\overline{IPL2}$, $\overline{IPL1}$, $\overline{IPL0}$ of 7 is always acknowledged. Therefore, interrupt level 7 is *nonmaskable*. Note that the interrupt level is indicated by the interrupt mask bits (inverted $\overline{IPL2}$, $\overline{IPL1}$, $\overline{IPL0}$).

   To ensure that an interrupt will be recognized, the following interrupting rules should be considered:

1.   The incoming interrupt request level must have a higher priority level than the mask level set in the interrupt mask bits (except for level 7, which is always recognized).
2.   The $\overline{IPL2}$–$\overline{IPL0}$ pins must be held at the interrupt request level until the 68000

acknowledges the interrupt by initiating an interrupt acknowledge ($\overline{\text{IACK}}$) bus cycle.

Interrupt level 7 is edge-triggered. On the other hand, interrupt levels 1–6 (maskable interrupts) are level sensitive. However, as soon as one of them is acknowledged, the processor updates its interrupt mask at the same level.

The 68000 does not have any EI (enable interrupt) or DI (disable interrupt) instructions. Instead, the level indicated by I2 I1 I0 in the SR disables all interrupts below or equal to this value and enables all interrupts above. For example, if I2 I1 I0 = 100, then interrupt levels 1–4 are disabled and 5–7 are enabled. Note that I2, I1, I0 = 000 enables all interrupts and I2, I1, I0 = 111 disables all interrupts except level 7 (nonmaskable).

Once the 68000 has decided to acknowledge an interrupt, it performs several steps:

1. Makes an internal copy of the current status register.
2. Updates the priority mask and address lines A_3–A_1 with the level of the interrupt recognized (inverted $\overline{\text{IPL}}$ pins) and then asserts $\overline{\text{AS}}$ to inform the external devices that A_1–A_3 has the interrupt level.
3. Enters the supervisor state by setting the S bit in SR to 1.
4. Clears the T bit in SR to inhibit tracing.
5. Pushes the program counter (PC) onto the supervisor stack.
6. Pushes the internal copy of the old SR onto the supervisor stack.
7. Runs an $\overline{\text{IACK}}$ bus cycle for vector number acquisition (to provide the address of the service routine).
8. Multiplies the 8-bit interrupt vector by 4. This points to the location that contains the starting address of the interrupt service routine.
9. Jumps to the interrupt service routine.
10. The last instruction of the service routine should be RTE, which restores the original status word and program counter by popping them from the supervisor stack.

External logic can respond to the interrupt acknowledge in one of three ways: by requesting automatic vectoring (autovector), by placing a vector number on the data bus (nonautovector), or by indicating that no device is responding (spurious interrupt).

Autovector (address vectors predefined by Motorola) If the hardware asserts $\overline{\text{VPA}}$ to terminate the $\overline{\text{IACK}}$ bus cycle, the 68000 directs itself automatically to the proper interrupt vector corresponding to the current interrupt level. No external hardware is inquired for providing the interrupt address vector. Table 7.10 shows the various interrupt vectors for autovector interrupts.

Nonautovector (user-definable address vectors via external hardware) The interrupting device uses external hardware to place a vector number on data lines D_0–D_7 and then

TABLE 7.10   Interrupt Vectors for Autovector Interrupts

	I2	I1	I0
Level 1 ← Interrupt vector $19 for	0	0	1
Level 2 ← Interrupt vector $1A for	0	1	0
Level 3 ← Interrupt vector $1B for	0	1	1
Level 4 ← Interrupt vector $1C for	1	0	0
Level 5 ← Interrupt vector $1D for	1	0	1
Level 6 ← Interrupt vector $1E for	1	1	0
Level 7 ← Interrupt vector $1F for	1	1	1

TABLE 7.11   68000 Interrupt Map

Vector Address		Vector Number
$60, $62	Spurious interrupt	$18
$64, $66	Autovector 1	$19
$68, $6A	Autovector 2	$1A
$6C, $6E	Autovector 3	$1B
$70, $72	Autovector 4	$1C
$74, $76	Autovector 5	$1D
$78, $7A	Autovector 6	$1E
$7C, $7E	Autovector 7	$1F
$80 to $BC	TRAP instructions	$20 to $2F
$C0 to $FC	Unassigned	$30 to $3F
$100 to $3FC	User interrupts (nonautovector)	$40 to $FF

performs a $\overline{\text{DTACK}}$ handshake to terminate the $\overline{\text{IACK}}$ bus cycle. The vector numbers allowed are $40 to $FF, but Motorola has not implemented protection on the first 64 entries, so that user interrupt may overlap at the discretion of the system designer.

Spurious Interrupt   Another way to terminate an interrupt acknowledge bus cycle is with the $\overline{\text{BERR}}$ (bus error) signal. Even though the interrupt control pins are synchronized to enhance noise immunity, it is possible that external system interrupt circuitry may initiate an $\overline{\text{IACK}}$ bus cycle as a result of noise. Because no device is requesting interrupt service, neither $\overline{\text{DTACK}}$ nor $\overline{\text{VPA}}$ will be asserted to signal the end of the nonexisting $\overline{\text{IACK}}$ bus cycle. When there is no response to an $\overline{\text{IACK}}$ bus cycle after a specified period of time (monitored by the user using an external timer), $\overline{\text{BERR}}$ can be asserted by an external timer. This indicates to the processor that it has recognized a spurious interrupt. The 68000 provides 18H as the vector to fetch the starting address of this exception-handling routine.

It should be pointed out that the spurious interrupt and bus error interrupt due to a troubled instruction cycle (when no $\overline{\text{DTACK}}$ is received by the 68000) have two different interrupt vectors. Spurious interrupt occurs when the $\overline{\text{BERR}}$ pin is asserted during interrupt processing.

Internal Interrupts   The internal interrupt is a software interrupt. This interrupt is generated when the 68000 executes a software interrupt instruction (TRAP) or by some undesirable events such as division by zero or execution of an illegal instruction.

68000 Interrupt Map   The 68000 uses an 8-bit vector n to obtain the interrupt address vector. The 68000 reads the long word located at memory $4*n$. This long word is the starting address of the service routine. Table 7.11 shows the interrupt map of the 68000. Vector addresses $00 through $2E (not shown in the figure) include vector addresses for reset, bus error, trace, divide by 0, and so on, and addresses $30 through $5C are unassigned. The RESET vector requires four words (addresses 0, 2, 4, and 6); the other vectors require only two words. After hardware reset, the 68000 loads the supervisor SP high and low words, respectively, from addresses 000000_{16} and 000002_{16}, and the PC high and low

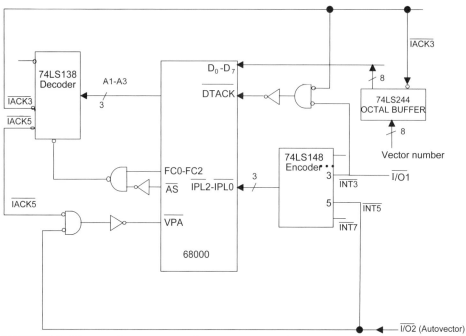

FIGURE 7.17   Autovector and nonautovector interrupts.

words, respectively, from 000004_{16} and 000006_{16}. The assembler directive DC (define constant) can be used to load the PC and supervisor SP. For example, the following will load A7' with $16F128 and PC with $781624:

```
ORG    $000000
DC.L   $0016F128
DC.L   $00781624
```

68000 Interrupt Address Vector   Suppose that the user decides to write a service routine starting at location $123456 using autovector 1. Because the autovector 1 address is $000064 and $000066, the numbers $0012 and $3456 must be stored in locations $000064 and $000066, respectively. This can be accomplished by using the assembler directive DC.L as follows:

```
ORG    $000064
DC.L   $00123456
```

Note that from Table 7.11, $n = \$19$ for autovector 1. Hence, the starting address of the service routine is obtained from the contents of the address $4 \times \$19 = \$000064$.

Example of Autovector and Nonautovector Interrupts   As an example to illustrate the concept of autovector and nonautovector interrupts, consider Figure 7.17. In this figure, I/O device 1 uses nonautovector and I/O device 2 uses autovector interrupts. The system is capable of handling interrupts from seven devices ($\overline{IPL2}$, $\overline{IPL1}$, $\overline{IPL0}$ = 111 means no interrupt) because an 8-to-3 priority encoder such as the 74LS148 is used.

The 74LS148 provides an inverted 3-bit output with input 7 as the highest priority and input 0 as the lowest priority. Hence, if all eight inputs of the 74LS148 are low simultaneously, the three-bit output will be 000 (inverted 111), indicating a LOW on input

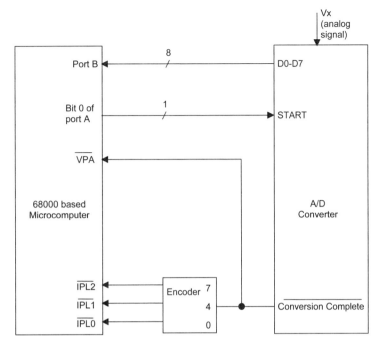

FIGURE 7.18 **Interfacing a typical 8-bit A/D converter to a a 68000-based microcomputer using autovector interrupt.**

7. In Figure 7.17, $\overline{\text{I/O1}}$ and $\overline{\text{I/O2}}$ from the interrupting devices are connected to inputs 3 and 5 of the 74LS148 encoder, respectively. This means that the device with $\overline{\text{I/O2}}$ as the interrupting signal will generate level 5 autovectored interrupt, while the device with $\overline{\text{I/O1}}$ as the interrupting signal will generate a nonautovectored interrupt.

Suppose that I/O device 2 drives $\overline{\text{I/O2}}$ LOW to activate line 5 of the 74LS148. This, in turn, will generate a LOW on input 5 of the 74LS148. This will provide 010 (inverted 101) on the $\overline{\text{IPL2}}$, $\overline{\text{IPL1}}$, and $\overline{\text{IPL0}}$ pins of the 68000, generating a level 5 autovectored interrupt. When the 68000 decides to acknowledge the interrupt, it drives FC0–FC2 HIGH. The interrupt level is reflected on A_1–A_3 when $\overline{\text{AS}}$ is activated by the 68000. The $\overline{\text{IACK5}}$ and $\overline{\text{I/O2}}$ signals are used to generate $\overline{\text{VPA}}$. Once $\overline{\text{VPA}}$ is asserted, the 68000 obtains the interrupt vector address using autovectoring.

In the case of $\overline{\text{I/O1}}$, line 3 of the priority encoder is activated to initiate a nonautovectored interrupt. By using appropriate logic, $\overline{\text{DTACK}}$ is asserted using $\overline{\text{IACK3}}$ and $\overline{\text{I/O1}}$. The vector number is placed on D_0–D_7 by enabling an octal buffer such as the 74LS244 using $\overline{\text{IACK3}}$. The 68000 inputs this vector number and multiplies it by 4 to obtain the interrupt address vector.

Interfacing a Typical A/D Converter to a 68000 Using Autovector and Nonautovector Interrupts Figure 7.18 shows the interfacing of a typical A/D converter to the 68000-based microcomputer using the autovector interrupt. In the figure, the A/D converter can be started by sending a START pulse. The signal can be connected to line 4 (for example) of the encoder.

Note that line 4 is 100_2 for $\overline{\text{IPL2}}$, $\overline{\text{IPL1}}$, $\overline{\text{IPL02}}$, which is a level 3 (inverted 100_2) interrupt. Conversion Complete can be used to assert $\overline{\text{VPA}}$, so that after acknowledgment of the interrupt, the 68000 will service the interrupt as a level 3 autovector interrupt. Note

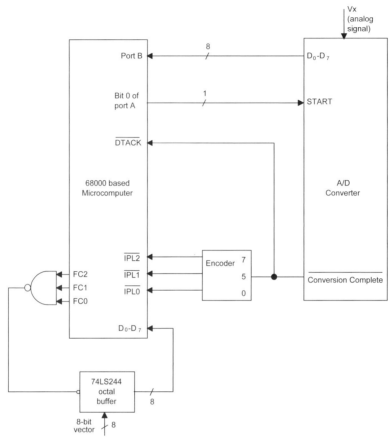

FIGURE 7.19   Interfacing of a typical 8-bit A/D converter to 68000-based microcomputer using nonautovector interrupt

that the encoder in Figure 7.18 is used for illustrative purposes. This encoder is not required for a single device such as the A/D converter in the example.

Figure 7.19 shows the interfacing of a typical A/D converter to the 68000-based microcomputer using the nonautovector interrupt. In the figure, the 68000 starts the A/D converter as before. Also, the Conversion Complete signal is used to interrupt the microcomputer using line 5 ($\overline{IPL2}$, $\overline{IPL1}$, $\overline{IPL02}$= 101, which is a level 2 interrupt) of the encoder. Conversion Complete can be used to assert $\overline{DTACK}$ so that, after acknowledgment of the interrupt, FC2, FC1, FC0 will become 111_2, which can be NANDed to enable an octal buffer such as the 74LS244 in order to transfer an 8-bit vector from the input of the buffer to the D_0–D_7 lines of the 68000. The 68000 can then multiply this vector by 4 to determine the interrupt address vector. As before, the encoder in Figure 7.19 is not required for the single A/D converter.

7.5.3   68000 DMA

Three DMA control lines are provided with the 68000: $\overline{BR}$ (bus request), $\overline{BG}$ (bus grant), and $\overline{BGACK}$ (bus grant acknowledge). The $\overline{BR}$ line is an input to the 68000. The external device activates this line to tell the 68000 to release the system bus. At least one clock period after receiving $\overline{BR}$, the 68000 will enable its $\overline{BG}$ output line to acknowledge the

DMA request. However, the 68000 will not relinquish the bus until it has completed the current instruction cycle. The external device must check the $\overline{AS}$ (address strobe) line to determine completion of the cycle by the 68000. When $\overline{AS}$ becomes HIGH, the 68000 will tristate its address and instruction data lines and will give up the bus to the external device. After taking over the bus, the external device must enable the $\overline{BGACK}$ line, which tells the 68000 and other devices connected to the bus that the bus is being used. The 68000 stays in a tristate condition until $\overline{BGACK}$ becomes HIGH.

7.6   68000 Exception Handling

A 16-bit microcomputer is usually capable of handling unusual or exceptional conditions. These conditions include situations such as execution of an illegal instruction or division by zero. In this section, the exception-handling capabilities of the 68000 are described.

The 68000 exceptions can be divided into three groups: 0, 1, and 2. Group 0 has the highest priority, and group 2 has the lowest priority. Within each group, there are additional priority levels. A list of 68000 exceptions together with individual priorities is as follows:

Group 0   Reset (the highest level in this group), address error (the next level), and bus error (the lowest level)

Group 1   Trace (the highest level), interrupt (the next level), illegal op-code (next level), and privilege violation (the lowest level)

Group 2   TRAP, TRAPV, CHK, and ZERO DIVIDE (no individual priorities assigned in group 2)

Exceptions from group 0 always override an active exception from group 1 or group 2.

Group 0 exception processing begins at the completion of the current bus cycle (two clock cycles). Note that the number of cycles required for a READ or WRITE operation is called a *bus cycle*. This means that if there is a group 0 interrupt during an instruction fetch, the 68000 will complete the instruction fetch and then service the interrupt. Group 1 exception processing begins at the completion of the current instruction. Group 2 exceptions are initiated through execution of an instruction. Therefore, there are no individual priority levels within group 2. Exception processing occurs when a group 2 interrupt is encountered, provided that there are no group 0 or group 1 interrupts.

When an exception occurs, the 68000 saves the contents of the program counter and status register onto the stack and then executes a new program whose address is provided by the exception vectors. Once this program is executed, the 68000 returns to the main program using the stored values of program counter and status register.

Exceptions can be of two types: internal or external. The internal exceptions are generated by situations such as division by zero, execution of illegal or unimplemented instructions, and address error. As mentioned before, internal interrupts are called *traps*. The external exceptions are generated by bus error, reset, or interrupt instructions. The basic concepts associated with interrupts, relating them to the 68000, have already been described. In this section we discuss the other exceptions.

In response to an exceptional condition, the processor executes a user-written program. In some microcomputers, one common program is provided for all exceptions. The beginning section of the program determines the cause of the exception and then branches to the appropriate routine. The 68000 utilizes a more general approach. Each exception can be handled by a separate program.

As mentioned earlier, the 68000 has two modes of operation: user state and supervisor state. The operating system runs in supervisor mode, and all other programs are executed in user mode. The supervisor state is therefore more privileged. Several privileged instructions, such as MOVE to SR can be executed only in supervisor mode. Any attempt to execute them in user mode causes a trap.

Next, we discuss how the 68000 handles exceptions caused by external resets, trap instructions, bus and address errors, tracing , execution of privileged instructions in user mode, and execution of illegal/unimplemented instructions:

- The reset exception is generated externally. In response to this exception, the 68000 automatically loads the initial starting address into the processor.

- The 68000 has a TRAP instruction, which always causes an exception. The operand for this instruction varies from 0 to 15. This means that there are 16 TRAP instructions. Each TRAP instruction has an exception vector. TRAP instructions are normally used to call subroutines in an operating system. Note that this automatically places the 68000 in supervisor state. TRAPs can also be used for inserting breakpoints in a program. Two other 68000 instructions cause traps if a particular condition is true: TRAPV and CHK. TRAPV generates an exception if the overflow flag is set. The TRAPV instruction can be inserted after every arithmetic operation in a program in order to cause a trap whenever there is the possibility of an overflow. A routine can be written at the vector address for the TRAPV to indicate to the user that an overflow has occurred. The CHK instruction is designed to ensure that access to an array in memory is within the range specified by the user. If there is a violation of this range, the 68000 generates an exception.

- A bus error occurs when the 68000 tries to access an address that does not belong to the devices connected to the bus. This error can be detected by asserting the $\overline{BERR}$ pin on the 68000 chip by an external timer when no $\overline{DTACK}$ is received from the device after a certain period of time. In response to this, the 68000 executes a user-written routine located at an address obtained from the exception vectors. An address error, on the other hand, occurs when the 68000 tries to read or write a word (16 bits) or long word (32 bits) in an odd address. This address error has a different exception vector from the bus error.

- The trace exception in the 68000 can be generated by setting the trace bit in the status register. In response to the trace exception, the 68000 causes an internal exception after execution of every instruction. The user can write a routine at the exception vectors for the trace instruction to display register and memory contents. The trace exception provides the 68000 with the single-stepping debugging feature.

- As mentioned earlier, the 68000 has privileged instructions, which must be executed in supervisor mode. An attempt to execute these instructions causes a privilege violation.

- Finally, the 68000 causes an exception when it tries to execute an illegal or unimplemented instruction.

7.7   68000/2732/6116/6821-Based Microcomputer

Figure 7.20 is a schematic of a 68000-based microcomputer with a 4K EPROM, a 4K static RAM, and four 8-bit I/O ports. Let us explain the various sections of the hardware schematic. Two 2732 and two 6116 chips are required to obtain the 4K EPROM and 4K RAM. The $\overline{LDS}$ and $\overline{UDS}$ pins are ORed with the memory select signal to enable the chip selects for the EPROMs and the RAMs. Address decoding is accomplished by using a 3 × 8 decoder (Full decoding). The decoder enables the memory or the I/O chips, depending on the status of address lines A_{12}–A_{14} and the $\overline{AS}$ line of the 68000. $\overline{AS}$ is used to enable the decoder. $\overline{I_0}$ selects the EPROMs, $\overline{I_1}$ selects the RAMs, and $\overline{I_2}$ selects the I/O ports.

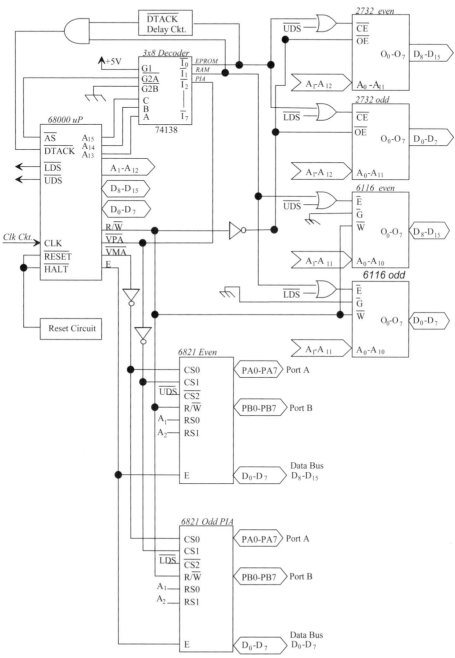

FIGURE 7.20   **68000-based microcomputer.**

When addressing memory chips, the $\overline{\text{DTACK}}$ input of the 68000 must be asserted for data acknowledge. The 68000 clock in the hardware schematic is 10 MHz. Therefore, each clock cycle is 100 ns. In Figure 7.20, $\overline{\text{AS}}$ is used to enable the 3×8 decoder. The outputs of the decoder are gated to assert 68000 $\overline{\text{DTACK}}$. This means that $\overline{\text{AS}}$ is used indirectly to assert $\overline{\text{DTACK}}$. From the 68000 read timing diagram, $\overline{\text{AS}}$ goes LOW after approximately two cycles (200 ns for the 10-MHz clock) from the beginning of the bus cycle. With no wait states, the 68000 samples $\overline{\text{DTACK}}$ at the falling edge of S4 (300 ns), and if $\overline{\text{DTACK}}$ is recognized, the 68000 latches data at the falling edge of S6 (400 ns). If $\overline{\text{DTACK}}$ is not recognized at the falling edge of S4, the 68000 inserts a one-cycle (100 ns in this case) wait state, samples $\overline{\text{DTACK}}$ at the end of S6, and, if $\overline{\text{DTACK}}$ is recognized, latches data at the end of S8 (500 ns), and the process continues. Because the access time of the 2732 is 200 ns, data will not be available at the output pins of the 2732s until after approximately 400 ns. To be on the safe side, $\overline{\text{DTACK}}$ recognition by the 68000 at the falling edge of S6 (400 ns) and latching of data at the falling edge of S8 (500 ns) will definitely satisfy the timing requirement. This means that the decoder output $\overline{I_0}$ for EPROM select should go to LOW at the end of S6. Therefore, a 200-ns delay (two cycles) for $\overline{\text{DTACK}}$ is assumed.

A delay circuit, as shown in Figure 7.21, is designed using two D flip-flops. EPPOM select activates the delay circuit. The input is then shifted right 2 bits to obtain a two-cycle wait state to allow sufficient time for data transfer. $\overline{\text{DTACK}}$ assertion and recognition are delayed by 2 cycles during data transfer with EPROMs. Figure 7.22 shows the timing diagram for the $\overline{\text{DTACK}}$ delay circuit. Note that DTACK goes LOW after about two cycles if asserted by $\overline{\text{AS}}$ providing an erronous result. Therefore, DTACK must be delayed.

When the EPROM is not selected by the decoder, the clear pin is asserted (the output of the inverter), so Q is forced LOW and $\overline{\text{Q}}$ is HIGH. Therefore, $\overline{\text{DTACK}}$ is not asserted. When the processor selects the EPROMs, the output of the inverter is HIGH, so the clear pin is not asserted. The D flip-flop will accept a high at the input, Q2 will be HIGH, and $\overline{\text{Q2}}$ will be LOW. Now that $\overline{\text{Q2}}$ is LOW, it can assert $\overline{\text{DTACK}}$. Q1 will provide one wait cycle, and $\overline{\text{Q2}}$ will provide two wait cycles. Because the 2732 EPROM has a 200-ns access time and the microprocessor is operating at 10 MHz (100-ns clock cycle), two wait cycles are inserted before asserting $\overline{\text{DTACK}}$ ($2 \times 100 = 200$ ns). Therefore, Q2 can be connected to the $\overline{\text{DTACK}}$ pin through an AND gate. No wait state is required for RAMs because the access time for the RAMs is only 120 nanoseconds.

Four 8-bit I/O ports are obtained by using two 6821 chips. When the I/O ports are

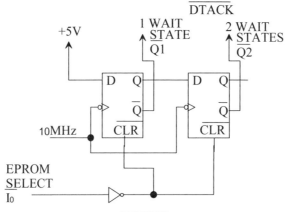

FIGURE 7.21   Delay circuit for $\overline{\text{DTACK}}$

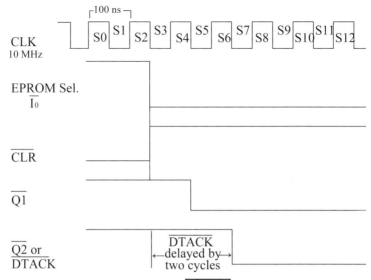

FIGURE 7.22 **Timing diagram for the $\overline{\text{DTACK}}$ delay circuit.**

selected, the $\overline{\text{VPA}}$ pin is asserted instead of $\overline{\text{DTACK}}$. This will acknowledge to the 68000 that it is addressing a 6800-type peripheral. In response, the 68000 will synchronize all data transfer with the E clock.

The memory and I/O maps for the schematic are as follows:

• *Memory maps* (all numbers in hex). A_{23} - A_{16} are don't cares and assumed to be 0s.

					$\overbrace{\text{LDS or } \overline{\text{UDS}}}$	
A_{23}–A_{16}	A_{15}	A_{14}	A_{13}	A_{12}–A_1	A_0	
0–0	0	0	0	0–0	0	EPROM(even) = 4K
				:		
0–0	0	0	0	1–1	0	\$000000, \$000002, \$000004, ... , \$001FFE
				:		
0–0	0	0	0	0–0	1	EPROM(odd) = 4K
				:		
0–0	0	0	0	1–1	1	\$000001, \$000003, \$000005, ... , \$001FFF
A_{23}–A_{10}	A_{15}	A_{14}	A_{13}	A_{11}–A_1	A_0	A_{12} is don't care for RAM (assume 0)
0–0	0	0	1	0–0	0	RAM(even) = 2K
				:		
0–0	0	0	1	1–1	0	\$002000, \$002002, ... , \$002FFE
				:		
0–0	0	0	1	0–0	1	RAM(odd) = 2K
				:		
0–0	0	0	1	1–1	1	\$002001, \$002003, ... , \$002FFF

Note that upon hardware reset, the 68000 loads the supervisor SP high and low words, respectively, from addresses $000000 and $000002 and the PC high and low words, respectively, from locations $000004 and $000006. The memory map contains these reset vector addresses in the even and odd 2732 chips.

- *Memory-mapped I/O* (all numbers in hex). A_{23}-A_{16} and A_{12}-A_3 are don't cares and assumed to be 0s.

					RS1	RS0	$\overline{UDS}$ or $\overline{LDS}$	
A_{23}–A_{16}	A_{15}	A_{14}	A_{13}	A_{12}–A_3	A_2	A_1	A_0	Register Selected (Address) — Even
0–0	0	1	0	0–0	0	0	0	Port A or DDRA = $004000
0–0	0	1	0	0–0	0	1	0	CRA = $004002
0–0	0	1	0	0–0	1	0	0	Port B or DDRB = $004004
0–0	0	1	0	0–0	1	1	0	CRB = $004006
								Register Selected (Address) — Odd
0–0	0	1	0	0–0	0	0	1	Port A or DDRA = $004001
0–0	0	1	0	0–0	0	1	1	CRA = $004003
0–0	0	1	0	0–0	1	0	1	Port B or DDRB = $004005
0–0	0	1	0	0–0	1	1	1	CRB = $004007

For both memory and I/O chips, $\overline{AS}$, $\overline{UDS}$, and $\overline{LDS}$ must be used in chip select logic. Note that:

1. For memory, both even and odd chips are required. However, for I/O chips, an odd-addressed I/O chip, an even-addressed I/O chip, or both can be used, depending on the number of ports required in an application. $\overline{UDS}$ and/or $\overline{LDS}$ must be used in I/O chip select logic, depending on the number of I/O chips used. The same chip select logic must be used for both the even and its corresponding odd memory chip.
2. $\overline{DTACK}$ must be connected to an external input (typically, a signal from the address decoding logic) to satisfy the timing requirements. In many instances, $\overline{AS}$ is connected directly to $\overline{DTACK}$.
3. The 68000 must be connected to ROMs, EPROMs, and E²PROMs such that the 68000 RESET vector address is included as part of the memory map.

7.8   Multiprocessing with the 68000 Using the TAS Instruction and the $\overline{AS}$ Signal

Earlier, the 68000 TAS instruction was discussed. The TAS instruction supports the software aspects of interfacing two or more 68000s via a shared RAM. When TAS is executed, the 68000 $\overline{AS}$ pin stays LOW. During both the read and write portions of the cycle, $\overline{AS}$ remains LOW and the cycle starts as the normal read cycle. However, in the normal read, $\overline{AS}$ going inactive indicates the end of the read. During execution of TAS, $\overline{AS}$ stays LOW throughout the cycle, so $\overline{AS}$ can be used in the design as a bus-locking circuit. Due to the bus locking, only one processor at a time can perform a TAS operation in a multiprocessor system. The

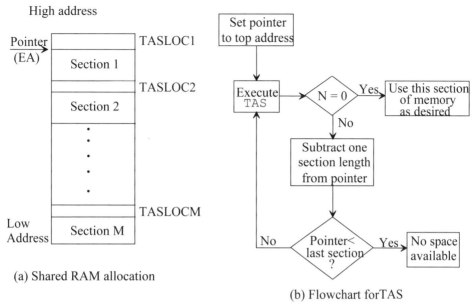

(a) Shared RAM allocation

(b) Flowchart forTAS

FIGURE 7.23   **Memory allocation using TAS.**

TAS instruction supports multiprocessor operations (globally shared resources) by checking a resource for availability and reserving or locking it for use by a single processor.

The TAS instruction can therefore be used to allocate free memory spaces. The shared RAM of the Figure 7.23(a) is divided into *M* sections. The first byte of each section will be pointed to by (EA) of the TAS (EA) instruction. The TAS instruction execution flowchart for allocating memory is shown in Figure 7.23(b). In Figure 7.23(a), (EA) first points to the first byte of section 1. The instruction TAS (EA) is then executed. The TAS instruction checks the most significant bit (N bit) in (EA). N = 0 indicates that section 1 is free; N = 1 indicates that section 1 is busy. If N = 0, section 1 will be allocated for use. If N = 1 (section 1 is busy), a program will be written to subtract one section

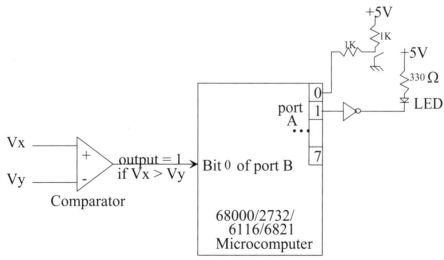

FIGURE 7.24   **Figure for Example 7.4**

length from (EA) to check the next section for availability. Also, (EA) must be checked with the value TASLOCM. If (EA) < TASLOCM, no space is available for allocation. However, if (EA) > TASLOCM, TAS is executed and the availability of that section is determined. In a multiprocessor environment, the TAS instruction provides software support for interfacing two or more 68000s via shared RAM. The $\overline{\text{AS}}$ signal can be used to provide the bus-locking mechanism.

EXAMPLE 7.4   Assume that the 68000/2732/6116/6821 microcomputer shown in Figure 7.24 is required to perform the following:

(a)   If Vx > Vy , turn the LED ON if the switch is open; otherwise, turn the LED OFF. Write a 68000 assembly language program starting at address $000300 to accomplish the above by inputting the comparator output via bit 0 of port B. Use port A address = $002000, port B address = $002004, CRA = $002002, and CRB = $002006. Assume that the LED is OFF initially.

(b)   Repeat part (a) using autovector level 7 and nonautovector (vector $40). Use port A (address $002000) for the LED and switch as above with CRA = $002002. Assume the supervisor mode. Write the main program and service routine in 68000 assembly language starting at addresses $000300 and $000A00, respectively. Also, initialize the supervisor stack pointer at $001200.

Solution

(a) *Using Programmed I/O.*   From Figure 7.24, the following 68000 assembly language program can be written:

```
            CRA     EQU     $002002
            CRB     EQU     $002006
            PORTA   EQU     $002000
            DDR     EQU     PORTA
            PORTB   EQU     $002004
            DDRB    EQU     PORTB
                    ORG     $000300
                    BCLR.B  #2,CRA      ;   Address DDRA
                    MOVE.B  #2,DDRA     ;   Configure PORTA
                    BSET.B  #2,CRA      ;   Address PORTA
                    BCLR.B  #2,CRB      ;   Address  DDRB
                    MOVE.B  #0,DDRB     ;   Configure PORTB
                    BSET.B  #2,CRB      ;   Address PORTB
    COMP            MOVE.B  PORTB,D0    ;   Input PORTB
                    LSR.B   #1,D0       ;   Check
                    BCC.B   COMP        ;   Comparator
                    MOVE.B  PORTA,D1    ;   Input switch
                    LSL.B   #1,D1       ;   Align LED data
                    MOVE.B  D1,PORTA    ;   Output to LED
    LED             JMP     LED
```

(b)   *Using Autovector Level 7 (nonmaskable interrupt).*   Figure 7.25 shows the pertinent connections for autovector level 7 interrupt.

Main program:

```
        CRA     EQU     $002002
        PORTA   EQU     $002000
        DDRA    EQU     PORTA
                ORG     $000300
                BCLR.B  #2,CRA      ;   Address DDRA
                MOVE.B  #2,DDRA     ;   Configure PORTA
                BSET.B  #2,CRA      ;   Address PORTA
        WAIT    JMP     WAIT        ;   Wait for interrupt
```

Service routine:

```
                ORG     $000A00
                MOVE.B  PORTA, D1   ;   Input switch
                LSL.B   #1, D1      ;   Align LED data
                MOVE.B  D1, PORTA   ;   Output to LED
        FINISH  JMP     FINISH      ;   Halt
```

Reset vector:

```
                ORG     0
                DC.L    $00001200
                DC.L    $00000300
```

Service routine vector:

```
                ORG     $00007C
                DC.L    $00000A00
```

Using nonautovectoring (vector $40). Figure 7.26 shows the pertinent connections for nonautovectoring interrupt.

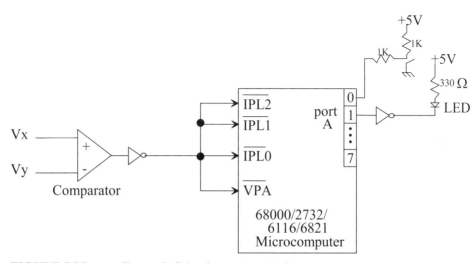

FIGURE 7.25   Example 7.4 using autovectoring

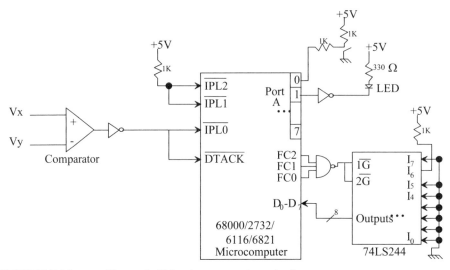

FIGURE 7.26   Example 7.4 using nonautovectoring

Main program:

CRA	EQU	$002002		
PORTA	EQU	$002000		
DDRA	EQU	PORTA		
	ORG	$000300		
	BCLR.B	#2,CRA	;	Address DDRA
	MOVE.B	#2,DDRA	;	Configure PORTA
	BSET.B	#2,CRA	;	Address PORTA
	ANDI.W	#$0F8FF,SR	;	Enable interrupts
WAIT	JMP	WAIT	;	Wait for interrupt

Service routine:

	ORG	$000A00		
	MOVE.B	PORTA,D1	;	Input switch
	LSL.B	#$01,D1	;	Align LED data
	MOVE.B	D1,PORTA	;	Output to LED
FINISH	JMP	FINISH	;	Halt

Reset vector:

	OR	0
	DC.L	$00001200
	DC.L	$00000300

Service routine vector:

	ORG	$000100
	DC.L	$00000A00

Questions and Problems

7.1 Find $\overline{\text{LDS}}$ and $\overline{\text{UDS}}$ after execution of the following 68000 instruction sequence:

MOVEA.L   #$0005A123,A2

MOVE.B   (A2),D0

7.2 Determine the status of $\overline{\text{AS}}$, FC2–FC0, $\overline{\text{LDS}}$, $\overline{\text{UDS}}$, and address lines immediately after execution of the following instruction sequence (before the 68000 tristates these lines to fetch the next instruction):

MOVE   #$2050,SR

MOVE.B   D0,$405060

Assume that the 68000 is in the supervisor mode prior to execution of the instructions.

7.3 Assume a 16.67-MHz 68000 in Figure P7.3. Also, assume that data is ready at the output pins of the memory chip at 300 ns. For the timing diagram of Figure P7.3, determine the time at which data will be read by the 68000.

7.4 Write 68000 instruction sequence so that upon hardware reset, the 68000 will initialize the supervisor stack pointer to 1000_{10} and the program counter to 2000_{10}.

7.5 Write a 68000 service routine at address $1000 for a hardware reset that will initialize all data registers to zero, address registers to $FFFFFFFF, supervisor SP to $502078, and user SP to $1F0524, and then jump to $7020F0.

7.6 Consider the following data prior to a 68000 hardware reset:

[D0] = $7F2A1620

[A1] = $6AB11057

[SR] = $001F

What are the contents of D0, A1, and SR after hardware reset?

7.7 Suppose that three switches are connected to bits 0–2 of port A and an LED to bit 6 of port B. If the number of HIGH switches is even, turn the LED ON; otherwise, turn the LED OFF. Write a 68000 assembly language program to accomplish this.

(a)   Assume a 68000-6821 system.

(b)   Assume a 68000-68230 system.

7.8 A 68000-68230 microcomputer-based microcomputer is required to drive the LEDs connected to bit 0 of ports A and B based on the input conditions set by

FIGURE P7. 3

switches connected to bit 1 of ports A and B. The I/O conditions are as follows:

- If the input at bit 1 of port A is HIGH and the input at bit 1 of port B is LOW, the LED at port A will be ON and the LED at port B will be OFF.

- If the input at bit 1 of port A is LOW and the input at bit 1 of port B is HIGH, the LED at port A will be OFF and the LED at port B will be ON.

- If the inputs of both ports A and B are the same (either both HIGH or both LOW), both LEDs of ports A and B will be ON.

Write a 68000 assembly language program to accomplish this.

7.9   A 68000-6821-based microcomputer is required to test a NAND gate. Figure P7.9 shows the I/O hardware needed to test the NAND gate. The microcomputer is to be programmed to generate the various logic conditions for the NAND inputs, input the NAND output, and turn the LED ON connected at bit 3 of port A if the NAND gate chip is found to be faulty. Otherwise, turn the LED ON connected at bit 4 of port A. Write 68000 assembly language program to accomplish this.

7.10   A 68000-68230-based microcomputer is required to add two 3-bit numbers stored in the lowest 3 bits of D0 and D1 and output the sum (not to exceed 9) to a common-cathode seven-segment display connected at port A as shown in Figure P7.10. Write 68000 assembly language program to accomplish this by using a look-up table.

7.11   A 68000-68230-based microcomputer is required to input a number from 0 to

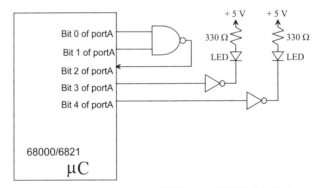

FIGURE P 7.9   (Assume that both LEDs are OFF initially.)

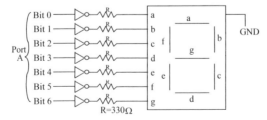

FIGURE P7.10

9 from an ASCII keyboard interfaced to it and output to an EBCDIC printer. Assume that the keyboard is connected to port A and the printer is connected to port B. Store the EBCDIC codes for 0 to 9 starting at an address $003030, and use this look-up table to write a 68000 assembly language program to accomplish the above.

7.12   Assume the pins and signal shown in Figure P7.12 for the 68000, 68230(odd), 2764(odd and even). Connect the chips and draw a neat schematic. Determine the memory map and I/O map (addresses for PGCR, PADDR, PBDDR, PACR, PBCR, PADR, PBDR). Assume a 16.67-MHz internal clock on the 68000.

7.13   Assume the 68000 stack and register values shown in Figure P7.13 before the occurrence of an interrupt. If an external device requests an interrupt by asserting the $\overline{IPL2}$, $\overline{IPL1}$, and $\overline{IPL0}$ pins with the value 000_2, determine the contents of A7' and SR during interrupt and after execution of RTE at the end of the service routine of the interrupt. Draw the memory layouts and show where A7' points to and the stack contents during and after interrupt. Assume that the stack is not used by the service routine.

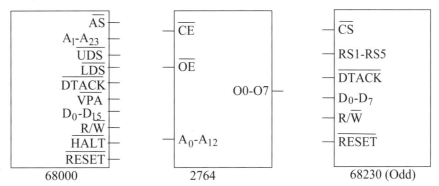

FIGURE P 7.12

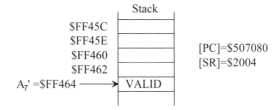

FIGURE P7.13

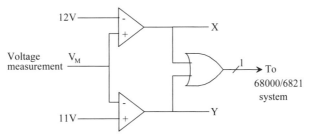

FIGURE P7.14

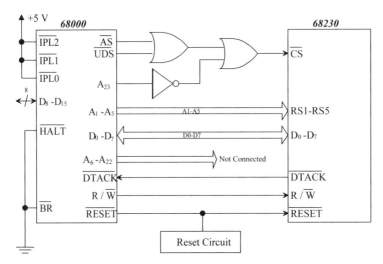

FIGURE P7.15

7.14   In Figure P7.14, if $V_M > 12$ V, turn an LED ON connected at bit 3 of port A. If $V_M <$ 11 V,   turn the LED OFF. Using ports, registers, and memory locations as needed and level 1 autovectored interrupt:

(a)   Draw a neat block diagram showing the 68000/6821 microcomputer and the connections to ports in the diagram in Figure P7.14.

(b)   Write the main program and the service routine in 68000 assembly language. The main program will initialize the ports and wait for an interrupt. The service routine will accomplish the task and stop.

7.15   Will the circuit in Figure P7.15 work? If so, determine the I/O port addresses for PGCR, PADR,   PADDR, PBDR, PBDDR, PACR, and PBCR. If not, comment briefly, modify the circuit, and determine the port addresses. Use only the pins and the signals shown. Assume all don't cares to be 0's.

7.16   Write a subroutine in 68000 assembly language using the TAS instruction to find, reserve, and lock a memory segment for the main program. The memory is divided   into three segments (0, 1, 2) of 16 bytes each. The first byte of each segment includes a flag byte to be used by the TAS instruction. In the subroutine, a maximum of three 16-byte memory segments must be checked for a free segment (flag byte $=$ 0). The TAS instruction should be used to find a free segment. The starting   address of the free segment (once found) must be stored in A0 and the low byte D0 must be cleared to zero to indicate a free segment, and the program control should return to the main program. If no free block is found, $FF must be stored in the low byte of D0 and the control should return to the main program.

8

ASSEMBLY LANGUAGE PROGRAMMING WITH THE 68020

In this chapter we describe the fundamental concepts associated with assembly language programming of the Motorola 68020 microprocessor. The 68020 contains new addressing modes and several new instructions beyond those of the 68000. To present the 68020 instruction set in a simplified manner, some of the 68020 advanced instructions are not covered. All 68000 assembly language programs can be executed by the 68020 without modifications. Note that a background in the 68000 software described in Chapter 6 is required before understanding the topics contained in this chapter.

8.1   Introduction

The 68020 was Motorola's first 32-bit microprocessor. The design of the 68020 is based on the 68000. The 68020 can perform a normal read or write cycle in three clock cycles without wait states as compared to the 68000, which completes a read or write operation in four clock cycles without wait states. As far as the addressing modes are concerned, the 68020 includes new modes beyond those of the 68000. Some of these modes are scaled indexing, larger displacements, and memory indirection. Furthermore, several new instructions are added to the 68020 instruction set, including the following:

- Bit field instructions are provided for manipulating a string of consecutive bits with a variable length from 1 to 32 bits.

- Two new instructions are used to perform conversions between packed BCD and ASCII or EBCDIC digits. Note that a packed BCD is a byte containing two BCD digits. This is covered in section 1.2 of Chapter 1.

- Enhanced 68000 array-range checking (CHK2) and compare (CMP2) instructions are included. CHK2 includes lower and upper bound checking; CMP2 compares a number with lower and upper values and affects flags accordingly.

- Four advanced instructions are included: CALLM, RTM, CAS, and CAS2. CALLM (CALL module) and RTM (return from module) support modular programming, and the two compare and swap instructions, CAS and CAS2, are provided to support multiprocessor systems. These instructions are not covered in this chapter.

The 68030 and 68040 are two enhanced versions of the 68020. The 68030 retains most of the 68020 features. It is a virtual memory microprocessor containing an on-chip memory management unit (MMU). The 68040 expands the 68030 on-chip memory management logic to two units: one for instruction fetch and one for data access. This speeds up the 68040's execution time by performing logical-to-physical-address translation in parallel. The on-chip floating-point capability of the 68040 provides it with both integer and floating-point arithmetic operations at high speed. All 68000 programs written in assembly language in user mode will run on the 68020, 68030 or 68040. The 68030 and 68040 support all 68020 instructions except CALLM and RTM. Let us now focus on the 68020 microprocessor in more detail.

8.2   68020 Functional Characteristics

The MC68020 is designed to execute all user object code written for the 68000. Like the 68000, it is manufactured using HCMOS technology. The 68020 consumes a maximum of 1.75 W. It contains 200,000 transistors on a 3/8-inch piece of silicon. The chip is packaged in a square (1.345-inch × 1.345-inch) pin grid array (PGA) and other packages. It contains 169 pins (114 pins used) arranged in a 13 × 13 matrix.

    The 68020 must be operated at a minimum frequency of 8 MHz. Like the 680000, it does not have any on-chip clock generation circuitry. The 68020 contains 18 addressing modes and 101 instructions. All addressing modes and instructions of the 68000 are included in the 68020. The 68020 supports coprocessors such as the 68881/68882 floating-point and 68851 MMU coprocessors. These and other functional characteristics of the 68020 are compared with the 68000 in Table 8.1.

TABLE 8.1   Functional Characteristics of 68000 vs. 68020

Characteristic	68000	68020
• Technology	HCMOS	HCMOS
• Number of pins	64, 68	169 (13 × 13 matrix; pins come out at bottom of chip; 114 pins currently used.)
• Control unit	Nanomemory (two-level memory)	Nanomemory (two-level memory)
• Clock frequency	8 MHz, 10 MHz, 12.5 MHz, 16.67 MHz, 20 MHz, 25 MHz, 33 MHz (4 MHz minimum requirement)	12.5 MHz, 16.67 MHz, 20 MHz, 25 MHz, 33 MHz (8 MHz minimum requirement)
• ALU	One 16-bit ALU	Three 32-bit ALUs
• Address bus size	24 bits with A_0 encoded from $\overline{UDS}$ and $\overline{LDS}$.	32 bits with no encoding of A_0 is required.

TABLE 8.1   Cont.

- Data bus size

	The 68000 can only be configured as 16-bit memory (two 8-bit chips) via D_0-D_7 for odd addresses and D_8-D_{15} for even addresses during byte transfers; for word and long word, uses D_0-D_{15}. The I/O can be configured as byte (one 8-bit I/O chip) or 16-bit (two 8-bit I/O chips).	The 68020 can be configured as 8-bit memory (a single 8-bit chip) via D_{31}-D_{24} pins or 16-bit memory (two 8-bit chips) via D_{31} - D_{16} pins or 32-bit memory (four 8-bit chips) via D_{31}-D_0 pins. I/O can be configured as 8-bit or 16-bit or 32-bit.
• Instructions and data access	Instructions must be at even addresses. Byte data can be accessed at either even or odd addresses while word and long word data must be at even addresses.	Instructions must be accessed at even addresses; data accesses can be at either even or odd addresses for .B, .W, .L.
• Instruction cache	None	128K 16-bit word cache. At start of an instruction fetch, the 68020 always outputs LOW on $\overline{ECS}$ (early cycle start) pin and accesses the cache. If instruction is found in the cache, the 68020 inhibits outputting LOW on $\overline{AS}$ pin; otherwise, the 68020 sends LOW on $\overline{AS}$ pin and reads instruction from main memory.
• Directly addressable memory	16 Megabytes	4 Gigabytes (4,294,964,296 bytes)
• Registers	8 32-bit data registers 7 32-bit address registers 2 32-bit SPs 1 32-bit PC (24 bits used) 1 16-bit SR	8 32-bit data registers 7 32-bit address registers 3 32-bit SPs 1 32-bit PC (all bits used) 1 16-bit SR 1 32-bit VBR (vector base register) 2 3-bit function code registers (SFC and DFC) 1 32-bit CAAR (cache address register) 1 CACR (cache control register)
• Barrel shifter	No	Yes. For fast-shift operations.
• Stack pointers	A7 (User SP), A7' (Supervisor SP)	A7 (User SP), A7'(interrupt SP), A7" (Master SP)

TABLE 8.1   Cont.

•	Status register	T, S, I2,I1, I0, X, N, Z, V, C	T0, T1, S, M, I2,I1, I0, X, N, Z, V, C
•	Coprocessor interface	Emulated in software; that is, by writing subroutines, coprocessor functions such as floating-point arithmetic can be obtained.	Can be directly interfaced to coprocessor chips, and coprocessor functions such as floating-point arithmetic can be obtained via 68020 instructions.
•	FC2, FC1, FC0 pins	FC2, FC1, FC0 = 111 means interrupt acknowledge.	FC2, FC1, FC0 = 111 means CPU space cycle; then by decoding A16-A19, one can obtain breakpoints, coprocessor functions, and interrupt acknowledge.

Some of the 68020 characteristics mentioned in Table 8.1 are deserving of further explanation.

- Three independent ALU's are provided for data manipulation and address calculations

- A 32-bit barrel shift register (occupies 7% of silicon) is included in the 68020 for very fast shift operations regardless of the shift count.

- The 68020 has three SP's. In the supervisor mode (when S = 1), two SP's can be accessed. These are A7'(when M = 0) and A7" (when M = 1). A7' (Interrupt SP) can be used to simplify and speed up task switching for operating systems.

- The vector base register (VBR) is used in interrupt vector computation. For example, in the 68000, the interrupt vector address is obtained by using VBR + 4 × 8-bit vector.

- The SFC (source function code) and DFC (destination function code) registers are 3 bits wide. These registers allow the supervisor to move data between address spaces. In supervisor mode, 3-bit addresses can be written into SFC or DFC using instructions such as MOVEC A2,SFC. The upper 29 bits of SFC are assumed to be zero. The MOVES.W (EA),Dn instruction, such as MOVES.W(A0),D0 can then be used to move a word to D0 from a location within the address space specified by SFC and [A0]. The 68020 outputs [SFC] to the FC2, FC1, and FC0 pins. By decoding these pins via an external decoder, the desired source memory location addressed by [A0] can be accessed.

- The new addressing modes in the 68020 include scaled indexing, 32-bit displacements, and memory indirection. The scaled index mode is an efficient way to index into an array when the element size is 2, 4, or 8 bytes. If the displacement contains the starting address of an array and the index register contains the subscript of the desired array element, the 68020 will automatically convert the subscript into an index by applying the scaling factor. To illustrate the concept of scaling, consider moving element 5 of an array containing 16-bit elements starting at an address $5000 into D1.W. Note that element 0 is the first element of the array stored at address $5000. Using the 68000, the following instruction sequence will accomplish this:

        MOVEA.W #$5000,A0   ; Move starting address into A0

```
        MOVE.W #5, D0            ; Move element number into D0.W
        LSL.W #1, D0            ; Multiply D0.W by 2 for Word
        MOVEA.W (A0, D0.W),D1;Move element 5 into D1.W
```
The scaled indexing mode can be used with the 68020 to perform the same as follows:
```
        MOVEA.W #$5000,A0         ; Move starting address into A0
        MOVE.W #5, D0            ; Move element number into D0.W
        MOVEA.W (A0, D0.W * 2),D1    ;Move element 5 into D1.W
```
Note that [D0] is scaled by 2. Scaling by 1, 2, 4, or 8 can be obtained.

- The new 68020 instructions include bit field instructions to better support compilers and certain hardware applications, such as graphics, 32-bit multiply and divide instructions, pack and unpack instructions for BCD, and coprocessor instructions. Bit field instructions can be used to input A/D converters and eliminate wasting main memory space when the A/D converter is not 32 bits wide. For example, if the A/D is 12 bits wide, the instruction BFEEXTU $22320000 {2:13},D0 will input bits 2-13 of memory location $22320000 into D0. Note that $22320000 is the memory-mapped port, where the 12-bit A/D is connected at bits 2–13. The next A/D can be connected at bits 14–25, and so on.

- FC2, FC1, FC0 = 111 indicates the CPU space cycle. The 68020 makes CPU space access for breakpoints, coprocessor operations, or interrupt acknowledge cycles. The CPU space classification is generated by the 68020 based on execution of breakpoint instructions or coprocessor instructions, or during an interrupt acknowledge cycle. The 68020 then decodes A_{16}–A_{19} to determine the type of CPU space. For example, FC2, FC1, FC0 = 111 and A_{19}, A_{18}, A_{17}, A_{16} = 0010 indicate coprocessor instructions.

- For performing floating-point operation, the 68000 user must write subroutines using the 68000 instruction set. The floating-point capability in the 68020 can be obtained by connecting a floating-point coprocessor chip such as the Motorola 68881. The 68020 has two coprocessor chips: the 68881 (floating point) and the 68851 (memory management). The 68020 can have up to eight coprocessor chips. When a coprocessor is connected to the 68020, the coprocessor instructions are added to the 68020 instruction set automatically, and this is transparent to the user. For example, when the 68881 floating-point coprocessor is added to the 68020, instructions such as FADD (floating-point add) are available to the user. The programmer can then execute the instruction FADD FD0,FD1. Note that registers FD0 and FD1 are in the 68881. When the 68020 encounters the FADD instruction, it writes a command in the command register in the 68881, indicating that the 68881 has to perform this operation. The 68881 then responds to this by writing in the 68881 response register. Note that all coprocessor registers are memory mapped. Hence, the 68020 can read the response register and obtain the result of the floating-point add from the appropriate locations .

8.3   68020 Registers

Figure 8.1 shows the 68020 user and supervisor programming models.

The user model has fifteen 32-bit general-purpose registers (D0–D7 and A0–A6), a 32-bit program counter (PC), and a condition code register (CCR) contained within the supervisor status register (SR). The supervisor model has two 32-bit supervisor stack pointers (ISP and MSP), a 16-bit status register (SR), a 32-bit vector base register (VBR), two 3-bit alternate function code registers (SFC and DFC), and two 32-bit cache-handling (address and control) registers (CAAR and CACR). The user stack pointer (USP) A7, interrupt stack pointer (ISP) A7', and master stack pointer (MSP) A7" are system stack pointers.

The status register, shown in Figure 8.2, consists of a user byte [condition code register (CCR)] and a system byte. The system byte contains control bits to indicate that the processor is in the trace mode (T1, T0), supervisor/user state (S), and master/interrupt state (M). The user byte consists of the following condition codes: carry (C), overflow (V), zero (Z), negative (N), and extend (X).

The bits in the 68020 user byte are set or reset in the same way as those of the 68000 user byte. Bits I2, I1, I0, and S have the same meaning as those of the 68000. In the 68020, two trace bits (T1, T0) are included, as opposed to one trace bit (T) in the 68000. These two bits allow the 68020 to trace on both normal instruction execution and jumps. The 68020 M-bit is not included in the 68000 status register.

The vector base register (VBR) is used to place the exception-processing vector table basically anywhere in memory. VBR supports multiple vector tables so that each process can manage independent exceptions properly. The 68020 distinguishes address spaces as supervisor/user and program/data. To support full access privileges in the supervisor mode, the alternate function code registers (SFC and DFC) allow the supervisor to access any address space by preloading the SFC/DFC registers appropriately. The cache registers (CACR and CAAR) allow software manipulation of the instruction code. The CACR provides control and status accesses to the instruction cache; the CAAR holds the address for those cache control functions that require an address.

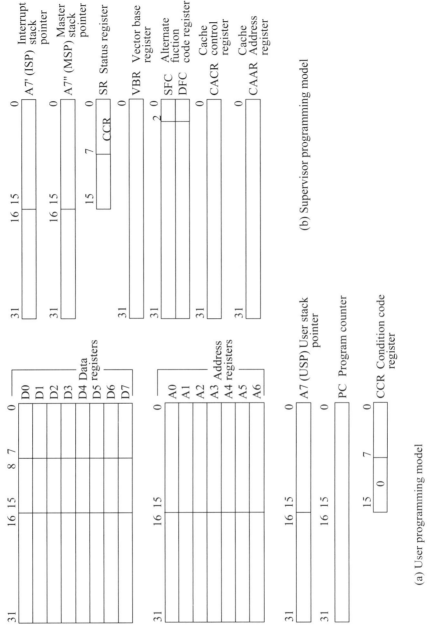

FIGURE 8.1   68020 programming models.

8.4   68020 Data Types, Organization, and CPU Space Cycle

As mentioned in Chapter 6, the 68000 supports data types of bits, BCD, bytes, 16-bit words, and 32-bit long words. In addition to these, four new data types are supported by the MC68020. These are variable-width bit field, packed BCD digits, 64-bit quad words, and variable-length operands. Data stored in memory is organized on a byte-addressable basis, where the lower addresses correspond to higher-order bytes. The 68020 does not

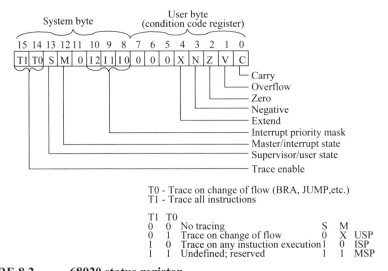

FIGURE 8.2   68020 status register.

require data to be aligned on even boundaries, but data that is not aligned is transferred less efficiently. Instruction words must be aligned on even byte boundaries. Figure 8.3 shows how data is organized in memory.

The function code pins FC2, FC1, and FC0 define the user/supervisor program and data in the same way as the 68000, except that FC2, FC1, FC0 = 111 for the 68020 defines a new cycle, the *CPU space cycle*. Note that for the 68000, FC2, FC1, FC0 = 111 indicates the interrupt acknowledge cycle. The CPU space cycle is not intended for general instruction execution, but is reserved for processor functions. Some of the processor functions are breakpoint acknowledge, interrupt acknowledge, and coprocessor communication. For example, the 68020 automatically sets FC2, FC1, FC0 to 111 during interrupt, and $A_{19}, A_{18}, A_{17}, A_{16}$ = 1111 during this CPU space cycle would indicate an interrupt acknowledge cycle.

8.5   68020 Addressing Modes

Table 8.2 lists the 68020's 18 addressing modes. Table 8.3 compares the addressing modes of the 68000 with those of the 68020. Because 68000 addressing modes were covered in detail in Chapter 6, the 68020 modes not available in the 68000 are provided in the following discussion.

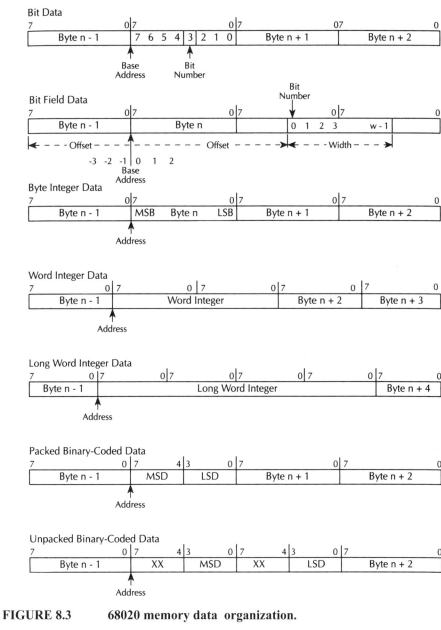

FIGURE 8.3 **68020 memory data organization.**

TABLE 8.2 **68020 Addressing Modes**

Mode	*Syntax*
• Register direct	
Data register direct	Dn
Address register direct	An
• Register indirect	

TABLE 8.2   Cont.

Mode	Syntax
Address register indirect (ARI)	(An)
Address register indirect with postincrement	(An)+
Address register indirect with predecrement	–(An)
Address register indirect with displacement	(d16, An)
• Register indirect with index	
Address register indirect with index (8-bit displacement)	(d8, An, Xn)
Address register indirect with index (base displacement)	**(bd, An, Xn)**
• Memory indirect	
Memory indirect, postindexed	([bd, An], Xn, od)
Memory indirect, preindexed	([bd, An, Xn], od)
• Program counter indirect with displacement	(d16,PC)
• Program counter indirect with index	
PC indirect with index (8-bit displacement)	(d8, PC, Xn)
PC indirect with index (base displacement)	(bd, PC, Xn)
• Program counter memory indirect	
PC memory indirect, postindexed	([bd, PC], Xn, od)
PC memory indirect, preindexed	([bd, PC, Xn], od)
• Absolute	
Absolute short	(xxx).W
Absolute long	(xxx).L
• Immediate	#data

Notes:

Dn = data register, D0 -D7

An = address register, A0-A6

d8, = 2's complement or sign-extended displacement; added as part
d16   of effective address calculation; size is 8 (d8) or 16 (d16) bits;
       when omitted, assemblers use a value of 0

Xn = address or data register used as an index register; form is
       Xn.size * scale, where size is .W or .L (indicates index register
       size) and scale is 1, 2, 4, or 8 (index register is multiplied by
       scale); use of size and/or scale is optional

bd = 2's complement base displacement; when present, size can be
       16 or 32 bits

TABLE 8.2 **Cont.**

Mode	Syntax
od =	outer displacement, added as part of effective address calculation after any memory indirection; use is optional with a size of 16 or 32 bits
PC =	program counter
<data> =	immediate value of 8, 16, or 32 bits
( ) =	effective address
[ ] =	use as indirect address to long word address
ARI =	Address Register Indirect

TABLE 8.3 **Addressing Modes for, 68000 vs. 68020**

Addressing Modes Available	Syntax	68,000	68020
Data register direct	Dn	Yes	Yes
Address register direct	An	Yes	Yes
Address register indirect (ARI)	(An)	Yes	Yes
ARI with postincrement	(An)+	Yes	Yes
ARI with predecrement	–(An)	Yes	Yes
ARI with displacement (16-bit disp)	(d, An)	Yes	Yes
ARI with index (8-bit disp)	(d, An, Xn)	Yes*	Yes*
ARI with index (base disp; 0, 16, 32)	(bd, An, Xn)	No	Yes
Memory indirect (postindexed)	([bd, An], Xn, od)	No	Yes
Memory indirect (preindexed)	([bd, An, Xn], od)	No	Yes
PC indirect with disp. (16-bit)	(d, PC)	Yes	Yes
PC indirect with index (8-bit disp)	(d, PC, Xn)	Yes*	Yes*
PC indirect with index (base disp)	(bd, PC, Xn)	No	Yes
PC memory indirect (postindexed)	([bd, PC], Xn, od)	No	Yes
PC memory indirect (preindexed)	([bd, PC, Xn], od)	No	Yes
Absolute short	(xxxx).W	Yes	Yes
Absolute long	(xxxxxxxx).L	Yes	Yes
Immediate	#<data>	Yes	Yes
*68000 has no scaling capability; 68020 can scale Xn by 1,2,4,or 8.			

8.5.1   Address Register Indirect (ARI) with Index and 8-Bit Displacement

- Assembler syntax: (d8, An, Xn.size * scale)

- EA = (An) + (Xn.size * scale) + d8

- Xn can be W or L.

If the index register (A*n* or D*n*) is 16 bits, it is sign-extended to 32 bits and multiplied by 1, 2, 4, or 8 to be used in EA calculations. An example is MOVE.W (0, A2, D2.W * 2),D1. Suppose that [A2] = $50000000, [D2.W] = $1000, and [$50002000] = $1571; then after the execution of this MOVE, [D1]$_{\text{low 16 bits}}$ = $1571 because EA = $5000000 + $1000 * 2 + 0 = $50002000.

8.5.2   ARI with Index (Base Displacement, bd: Value 0 or 16 Bits or 32 Bits)

•   Assembler syntax: (bd, A*n*, X*n*.size * scale).

•   EA = (A*n*) + (X*n*.size * scale) + bd.

•   Base displacement, bd, has a value 0 when present or can be 16 or 32 bits.

Figure 8.4 shows the use of ARI with the index X*n*, and base displacement bd, for accessing tables or arrays. An example is MOVE.W ($5000, A2, D1.W * 4), D5. If [A2] = $30000000, [D1.W] = $0200, and [$30005800] = $0174, then after execution of this MOVE, [D5]$_{\text{low 16 bits}}$ = $0174 because EA = $5000 + $30000000 + $0200 * 4 = $30005800.

8.5.3   Memory Indirect

The memory indirect mode is distinguished from the address register indirect mode by the use of square brackets in the assembler notation. The concept of memory indirect mode is depicted in Figure 8.5. Here, register A5 points to the effective address $20000501. Because CLR ([A5]) is a 16-bit clear instruction, 2 bytes in locations $20000501 and $20000502 are cleared to 0.

The memory indirect mode can be indexed with scaling and displacements. There are two types of memory indirect mode with scaled indexing and displacements: postindexed memory indirect mode and preindexed memory indirect mode.

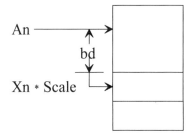

FIGURE 8.4   **ARI with index and base displacement.**

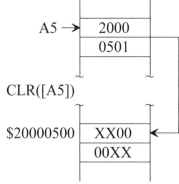

FIGURE 8.5   **Memory indirect.**

For postindexed memory indirect mode, an indirect memory address is first calculated using the base register (An) and base displacement (bd). This address is used for an indirect memory access of a long word followed by adding a scaled indexed operand and an optional outer displacement (od) to generate the effective address. Note that bd and od can be zero, 16 bits, or 32 bits. In postindexed memory indirect mode, indexing occurs after memory indirection.

- Assembler syntax: ([bd, A*n*], X*n*.size * scale, od)

- EA = ([bd + A*n*]) + (X*n*.size * scale + od)

An example is MOVE.W ([$0004, A1], D1.W * 2, 2), D2. If [A1] = $20000000, [$2000004] = $00003000, [D1.W] = $0002, and [$00003006] = $1A40, then after execution of this MOVE, intermediate pointer = (4 + $20000000) = $20000004, [$2000004], which is $00003000 used as a pointer. Therefore, EA = $00003000 + $00000004 + 2 = $00003006. Hence, $[D2]_{low\ 16\ bits}$ = $1A40.

For the memory indirect preindexed mode, the scaled index operand is added to the base register (An) and base displacement (bd). This result is then used as an indirect address into the data space. The 32-bit value at this address is read and an optional outer displacement (od) is added to generate the effective address. The indexing therefore occurs before indirection.

- Assembler syntax: ([bd, A*n*, X*n*.size * scale], od)

- EA = (bd, A*n* + X*n*.size * scale) + od

As an example of the preindexed mode, consider several I/O devices in a system. The addresses of these devices can be held in a table pointed to by An, bd, and Xn. The actual programs for these devices can be stored in memory pointed to by the respective device addresses plus od.

The memory indirect preindexed mode will now be illustrated by a numerical example. Consider

MOVE.W ([$0002, A1,D0.W*2], 2), D1

If [A1] = $20000000, [D0.W] = $0004, [$2000000A] = $00121502, and [$00121504] = $F124, then after execution of this MOVE, intermediate pointer = $20000000 + $0002 + $0004*2 = $2000000A. Therefore, [$2000000A], which is $00121502, is used as a memory pointer. Hence, $[D1]_{low\ 16\ bits}$ = $F124.

8.5.4   Memory Indirect with PC

In this mode, PC (the program counter), rather than an address register, is used to form the address. The effective address calculation is similar to memory indirect using address register. The various types of memory index with mode are described below.

PC Indirect with Index (8-Bit Displacement)   The effective address is obtained by adding PC contents, the sign-extended displacement, and the scaled indexed (sign-extended to 32 bits if it is 16 bits before calculation) register.
- Assembler syntax: (d8,Xn.size *scale), EA = [PC] + [Xn.size * scale] + d8
For example, consider MOVE.W D2,(2,PC,D1.W*2). If [PC] = $40000020, [D1.W] = $0020, and [D2.W] = $20A2, then after this MOVE, EA = 2 + $40000020 + $0020 *2 = $40000062. Hence, [$40000062] = $20A2.

PC Indirect with Index (Base Displacement, bd)   The address of the operand is obtained by adding the PC contents, the scaled index register contents, and the base displacement.

- Assembler syntax: (bd,PC,Xn.size*scale), EA = [PC] + [Xn.size*scale] + bd, Xn and bd are sign-extended to 32 bits if either or both are 16 bits.

As an example, consider MOVE.W (4,PC,D1.W*2),D2. If [PC] = $20000004, [D1.W] = $0020, [$20000048] = $2560, then after this MOVE, [D2.W] = $2560.

PC Indirect (Postindexed)   An intermediate memory pointer in program space is calculated by adding PC (used as a base register), and bd (base displacement). The 32-bit contents of this address are used in the EA calculation. EA is obtained by adding the 32-bit contents with a scaled index register and od (outer displacement). Note that bd, od, and index register are sign-extended to 32 bits before being used in the calculation if one (or more) of them is 16 bits before EA calculation.

- Assembler syntax: ([bd,PC],Xn.size*scale,od), EA = ([bd + PC] + Xn.size * scale + od)

As an example, consider MOVE.W ([2,PC],D1.W*4,0),D1. If [PC] = $30000000, [D1.W] = $0010, [$300 0002] = $20400050, and [$20400090] = $A240, then after this MOVE, [D1.W] = $A240.

PC Indirect (Preindexed)   The scaled index register is added to the PC and bd. The sum is then used as an indirect address into the program space. The 32-bit value at this address is added to od to find EA.

- Assembler syntax: ([bd,PC,Xn.size*scale],od), EA = (bd + PC +Xn.size * scale) + od where od, bd, and the index register contents are sign-extended to 32 bits if one (or more) of them is 16 bits before EA calculation.

As an example, consider MOVE.W ([4,PC,D1.W*2],4),D5. If [PC] = $50000000, [D1.W] = $0010, [$50000024] = $20507000, and [$20507004] = $0708, then after this MOVE, [D5.W] = $0708.

EXAMPLE 8.1   The 68000 instruction sequence:

```
MOVEA.L 8(A7),A0
MOVE.W (A0),D3
```

is used by a subroutine to access a parameter whose address has been passed into A0 and then moves the parameter to D3. Find the equivalent 68020 instruction.

Solution

```
MOVE.W ([8,A7]),D3
```

EXAMPLE 8.2   Write a 68020 assembly language program that will be used to convert an ASCII code for a specific BCD number stored in register D0.B into its equivalent EBCDIC code in D0.B. Assume that the ASCII codes for the 10 BCD numbers (0 through 9) are stored in a look-up table starting at an address $00002030. Also, assume that an address $00001000 is passed into register A0 by a subroutine, and address $00001000 contains $00002000. Using A0 as the pointer, and along with the data above to access the table, write a 68020 assembly language program to accomplish the above.

Solution

```
        ORG       $00002030              ;EBCDIC codes for the BCD numbers
        DC.B      $F0,$F1,$F2,$F3,$F4,$F5
        DC.B      $F6,$F7,$F8,$F9
        ORG       $00001000              ;$00002000 stored at address
                                         ;$00001000
        DC.L      $00002000
        MOVE.W    #$35,D0                ;Move ASCII $35 into D0.W
        LEA.L     $00001000,A0           ;Load $00001000 into A0 to be used
                                         ;as pointer in memory indirect mode
        MOVE.B    ([A0],D0.W),D0         ; Load EBCDIC equivalent $F5 of the
                                         ;ASCII $35 into D0.B
FINISH  JMP       FINISH                 ;Halt
```

The 68020 program above illustrates the concept of memory indirect addressing mode. First, the EBCDIC codes for the 10 BCD numbers (0 through 9) are stored starting at memory location $00002030 using the assembler directive DC.B. Next, the address $00002000 is stored in address $0000100 using the DC.L directive. MOVE.W #$35,D0 moves $0035 (ASCII for 5) into the low 16 bits of D0. Note that BCD 5 is chosen arbitrarily. A word instruction MOVE.W is used because the IDE assembler for the 68020 allows word or long word for the index register. Hence, $35 is moved into D0.W using the MOVE.W #$35,D0 instruction. The correct operation of the program above is verified using the debugger. After single stepping through the program, D0.W contains $F3.

EXAMPLE 8.3 Write a 68020 assembly language program at address $00002000 to add all the elements in a table containing eight 16-bit numbers stored in memory in consecutive memory locations starting at an address $00005000. Store the 16-bit result in D1.W.

Solution

```
        ORG       $00005000
        DC.W      1,2,3,4
        DC.W      5,6,7,8
        ORG       $00002000
        LEA.L     $00005000,A0     ; A0 = Starting address of the table
        MOVE.L    #0,D0            ; Move element number 0 into D0.L
        CLR.W     D1               ; Clear 16-bit sum in D1 to 0
        MOVE.W    #7,D2            ; Initialize D2.W with loop count
BACK    ADD       (A0,D0.L*2),D1   ; Add elements with sum in D1.W
        ADDQ.L    #1,D0            ; Increment element number in D0.L by 1
        DBF.W     D2,BACK          ; Decrement D2 and branch to BACK if D2
END     JMP       END              ; Halt
```

EXAMPLE 8.4 Write a 68020 assembly language program at $00001000 to find the trace (sum of the elements in the diagonal) of a 3x3 matrix containing 16-bit words. Store the 16-bit result in D0. Assume that the matrix is stored in row-major ordering starting at an address $00002000 as follows:

$00002000	a[0,0]
$00002002	a[0,1]
$00002004	a[0,2]
$00002006	a[1,0]
$00002008	a[1,1]
$0000200A	a[1,2]
$0000200C	a[2,0]
$0000200E	a[2,1]
$00002010	a[2,2]

Note that trace = a[0,0] + a[1,1] + a [2,2] and displacement, $d = (i *t +j) *s = i*t*s + j*s$ where i = row number, j = column number, t = total number of columns in the matrix, s = element size. In this example, t = 3 for 3x3 matrix, s=2 since each element is 16-bit. Hence, $d = 3*(2*i) + 2*j = 6 * i + 2 *j$. Hence, effective address where each element a_{ij} will be stored = A0 + 6*i + 2*j where A0 = starting address of the array, i = row number, and j = column number.

Solution

```
          ORG      $00002000
          DC.W     1,2,3
          DC.W     4,5,6
          DC.W     7,8,9
          ORG      $00001000
          MOVE.L   #0,D1              ; Load column number 0 into D1
          MOVE.L   D1,D4              ; Copy D1 into D4
          MOVE.L   #0,D2              ; Load row number 0 into D2
          MOVE.L   D2,D6              ; copy D2 into D6
          MOVE.W   #2,D7              ; initialize loop count
          CLR.W    D0                 ; sum = 0
          LEA.L    $00002000,A0       ; load starting address into A0
BACK      MULU.W   #6,D6              ; perform 6*i, result in D6.L
          ADDA.L   D6,A0              ; add A0 with 6*i
          ADD.W    (A0,D1.L*2),D0     ; sum diagonal elements in D0.W
          ADDQ.L   #1,D1              ; Increment column number by 1 in D1.L
          ADDQ.L   #1,D2              ; Increment row number by 1
          MOVE.L   D2,D6              ; Copy updated row number into D6
          LEA.L    $2000,A0           ; re-initialize A0 to $2000 since [A0]was altered
          DBF.W    D7,BACK            ; Decrement D7.W by 1, branch if [D7.W]
FINISH    JMP      FINISH             ; Halt
```

TABLE 8.4   68020 New Instructions

Instruction	Description
BFCHG	Bit field change
BFCLR	Bit field clear
BFEXTS	Bit field signed extract
BFEXTU	Bit field unsigned extract
BFFFO	Bit field find first one set
BFINS	Bit field insert
BFSET	Bit field set
BFTST	Bit field test
CALLM	Call module
CAS	Compare and swap
CAS2	Compare and swap (two operands)
CHK2	Check register against upper and lower bounds
CMP2	Compare register against upper and lower bounds
cpBcc	Coprocessor branch on coprocessor condition
cpDBcc	Coprocessor test condition, decrement, and branch
cpGEN	Coprocessor general function
cpRESTORE	Coprocessor restore internal state
cpSAVE	Coprocessor save internal state
cpSETcc	Coprocessor set according to coprocessor condition
cpTRAPcc	Coprocessor trap on coprocessor condition
PACK	Pack BCD
RTM	Return from module
UNPK	Unpack BCD

8.6   68020 Instructions

The 68020 instruction set includes all 68000 instructions plus some new ones. Appendix E lists some of the 68020 instructions that will also run on the 68000. Some of the 68020 instructions are enhanced 68000 instructions. Over 20 new instructions are added to provide new functionality. A list of these instructions is given in Table 8.4. In succeeding sections we discuss the 68020 instructions listed next:

• 68020 new privileged move instructions

• RTD instruction

• CHK/CHK2 and CMP/CMP2 instructions

• TRAP*cc* instructions

• Bit field instructions

• PACK and UNPK instructions

- Multiplication and division instructions
- 68000 enhanced instructions

8.6.1   68020 New Privileged Move Instructions

The 68020 new privileged move instructions can be executed by the 68020 in the supervisor mode. These instructions are listed in Table 8.5. Note that Rc includes VBR, SFC, DFC, MSP, ISP, USP, CACR, and CAAR. Rn can be either an address or a data register. The operand size (.L) indicates that the MOVEC operations are always long words. Notice that only register-to-register operations are allowed. A control register (Rc) can be copied to an address or a data register (Rn), or vice versa. When the 3-bit SFC or DFC register is copied into Rn, all 32 bits of the register are overwritten and the upper 29 bits are "0."

The MOVES (move to alternate space) instruction allows the operating system to access any address space defined by the function codes. It is typically used when an operating system running in the supervisor mode must pass a pointer or value to a previously defined user program or data space. The operand size (.S) indicates that the MOVES instruction can be byte (.B), word (.W), or long word (.L). The MOVES instruction allows register-to-memory or memory-to-register operations. When a memory to register move occurs, this instruction causes the contents of the source function code register to be placed on the external function hardware pins. For a register-to-memory move, the processor places the destination function code register on the function code pins. The MOVES instruction can be used to move information from one space to another.

EXAMPLE 8.5   Find the contents of address $70000023 and the function code pins FC2, FC1, and FC0 after execution of MOVES.B D5,(A5). Assume the following data prior to execution of this MOVES instruction: [SFC] = 001_2, [DFC] = 101_2 , [A5] = $70000023, [D5] = $718F2A05, [$70000020] = $01, [$70000021] = $F1, [$70000022] = $A2, [$70000023] = $2A

Solution

After execution of this MOVES instruction, FC2 FC1 FC0 = 101_2 and [$70000023] = $05.

8.6.2   Return and Delocate Instruction

The return and delocate (RTD) instruction is useful when a subroutine has the responsibility to remove parameters off the stack that were pushed onto the stack by the calling routine. Note that the calling routine's JSR (jump to subroutine) or BSR (branch to subroutine) instructions do not automatically push parameters onto the stack prior to the call as do the

TABLE 8.5   68020 New privileged MOVE instructions

Instruction	Operand Size	Operation	Notation
MOVE	16	SR → destination	MOVE SR, (EA)
MOVEC	32	Rc → Rn	MOVEC.L Rc, Rn
		Rn → Rc	MOVEC.L Rn, Rc
MOVES	8, 16, 32	Rn → destination using DFC	MOVES.S Rn, (EA)
		Source using SFC → Rn	MOVES.S (EA),Rn

CALLM instructions. Rather, the pushed parameters must be placed there using the MOVE instruction. The format of the RTD instruction is as follows:

Instruction	Operand Size	Operation	Notation
RTD	Unsized	$(SP) \to PC, SP + 4 + d \to SP$	RTD # <disp>

As an example, consider RTD #8, which at the end of a subroutine deallocates 8 bytes of unwanted parameters off the stack, by adding 8 to the stack pointer and returns to the main program. The size of the displacement is 16 bits.

8.6.3   CHK/CHK2 and CMP/CMP2 Instructions

The 68020 check instruction (CHK) compares a 32-bit two's-complement integer value residing in a data register (Dn) against a lower bound (LB) value of zero and against an upper bound (UB) value of the programmer's choice. The upper bound value is located at the effective address (EA) specified in the instruction format. The CHK instruction has the following format: CHK.S (EA),Dn where the operand size (.S) designates word (.W) or long word (.L). If the data register value is less than zero (Dn < 0) or if the data register is greater than the upper bound (Dn > UB), the processor traps through exception vector 6 (offset $18) in the exception vector table. Of course, the operating system or the programmer must define a check service handler routine at this vector address. The condition codes after execution of the CHK are affected as follows: If Dn < 0, then N = 1; if Dn > UB (upper bound), then N = 0. If $0 \leq Dn \leq UB$ then N is undefined. X is unaffected and all other flags are undefined and program execution continues with the next instruction.

The CHK instruction can be used to maintain array subscripts because all subscripts can be checked against an upper bound (i.e., UB = array size - 1). If the subscript compared is within the array bounds (i.e., $0 \leq$ subscript value $\leq$ UB value), the subscript is valid and the program continues normal instruction execution. If the subscript value is out of array limits (i.e., 0 > subscript value or subscript value > UB value), the processor traps through the CHK exception.

The purpose of the CHK instruction is to provide boundary checking by testing if the content of a data register is in the range from zero to an upper limit. The upper limit used in the instruction can be set equal to the length of the array. Then, every time the array is accessed, the CHK instruction can be executed to make sure that the array bounds have not been violated. The CHK instruction is usually placed after the computation of an index value to ensure that the index value is not violated. This permits a check of whether or not the address of an array being accessed is within array boundaries when address register indirect with index mode is used to access an array element. For example, the following instruction sequence permits accessing of an array with base address in A0 and an array

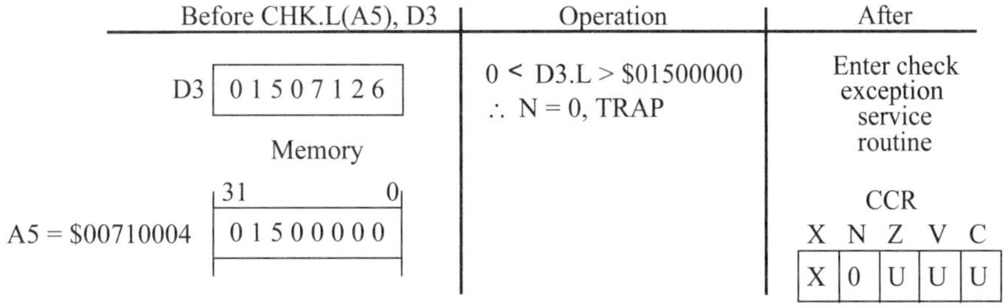

FIGURE 8.6   Illustration of the CHK.L (A5),D3 instruction using numerical data

length of 100 bytes:

.

.

.

CHK.W #99,D0

MOVE.B (A0,D0.W),D1

.

.

.

Here, if the low 16 bits of D0 are less than 0 or greater than 99, the 68020 will trap to location $0018. It is assumed that the value of the index register D2.W is computed prior to execution of the CHK instruction.

EXAMPLE 8.6   Determine the effects of the execution of CHK.L (A5),D3, where A5 represents a memory pointer to the array's upper bound value. Register D3 contains the subscript value to be checked against the array bounds. Assume the following data prior to execution of this CHK instruction:

$$[D3] = \$01507126$$
$$[A5] = \$00710004$$
$$[\$00710004] = \$01500000$$

Solution

The long word array subscript value $01507126 contained in data register D3 is compared against the long word UB value $01500000 pointed to by address register A5. Because the value $01507126 contained in D3 exceeds the UB value $01500000 pointed to by A5, the N bit is cleared. (X is unaffected and the remaining CCR bits are undefined.) This out-of-bounds condition causes the program to trap to a check exception service routine. This is depicted in Figure 8.6.

The operation of the CHK instruction is as follows:

Instruction	Operand Size	Operation	Notation
CHK	16, 32	If Dn < 0 or Dn > source, then TRAP	CHK (EA), Dn

The 68020 CMP.S (EA), Dn instruction subtracts (EA) from Dn and affects the condition codes without any result. The operand size designator (.S) is either byte (.B) or word (.W) or long word (.L).

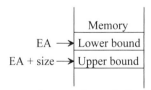

FIGURE 8.7   Lower and upper bounds for CHK2/CMP2

The CHK2 and the CMP2 instructions have similar formats:

CHK2.S (EA), Rn

and

CMP2.S (EA), Rn

They compare a value contained in a data or address register (designated by Rn) against two bounds chosen by the programmer. The size of the data to be compared (.S) may be specified as byte (.B), word (.W), or long word (.L). As shown in Figure 8.7, the lower bound (LB) value must be located in memory at the effective address (EA) specified in the instruction, and the upper bound (UB) value must follow immediately at the next-higher memory address. That is, UB addr = LB addr + size, where size = B (+1), W (+2), or L (+4).

If the register compared is a data register (i.e., Rn = Dn) and the operand size (.S) is a byte or word, only the appropriate low-order part of the data register is checked. If the register compared is an address register (i.e., Rn = An) and the operand size (.S) is a byte or word, the bound operands are sign-extended to 32 bits and the extended operands are compared against the full 32 bits of the address register. After execution of CHK2 and CMP2, the condition codes are affected as follows:

Carry	=	1	if the contents of Dn are out of bounds
	=	0	otherwise
Z	=	1	if the contents of Dn are equal to either bound
	=	0	otherwise

When an upper bound equals the lower bound, the valid range for comparison becomes a single value. The only difference between the CHK2 and CMP2 instructions is that for comparisons determined to be out of bounds, CHK2 causes exception processing

Before CMP2.W(A2), D1	Operation	After
	Signed comparison	CCR
D1 │ 5 0 0 0 0 2 0 0 │		X N Z V C
	-$5000 < D1.W <+ $5000	│X│ ? │0│ ? │0│
Memory	∴ C = 0	
│15 0│	-$5000 ≠ D1.W≠ + $5000	X is not
A2 = $00007000 │ B 0 0 0 │	∴ Z = 0	affected
A2+2 = $00007002 │ 5 0 0 0 │		N and V
		are undefined

FIGURE 8.8   **Register and memory contents for Example 8.7.**

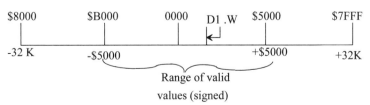

FIGURE 8.9   **Range of valid values for D1.W for Example 8.7.**

utilizing the same exception vector as the CHK instructions, whereas the CMP2 instruction execution affects only the condition codes.

In both instructions, the compare is performed for either signed or unsigned bounds. The 68020 evaluates the relationship between the two bounds automatically to determine which type of comparison to employ. If the programmer wishes to have the bounds evaluated as signed values, the arithmetically smaller value should be the lower bound. If the bounds are to be evaluated as unsigned values, the programmer should make the logically smaller value the lower bound.

The following CMP2 and CHK2 instruction examples are identical in that they both utilize the same registers, comparison data, and bound values. The difference lies in how the upper and lower bounds are arranged.

EXAMPLE 8.7   Determine the effects of execution of CMP2.W (A2),D1. Assume the following data prior to execution of this CMP2 instruction:
[D1] = $50000200, [A2] = $00007000, [$00007000] = $B000, and [$00007002] = $5000.

Solution

Figure 8.8 shows register and memory contents before and after execution of CMP2.W(A2),D1. In this example, the word value $B000 contained in memory (as pointed to by address register A2) is the lower bound and the word value $5000 immediately following $B000 is the upper bound. Because the lower bound is the arithmetically smaller value, the programmer is indicating to the 68020 to interpret the bounds as signed numbers. The twos complement value $B000 is equivalent to an actual value of –$5000. Therefore, the instruction evaluates the word contained in data register D1 ($0200) to determine whether it is greater than or equal to the upper bound, +$5000, or less than or equal to the lower bound, -$5000. Because the compared value $0200 is within bounds, the carry bit (C) is cleared to 0. Also, because $0200 is not equal to either bound, the zero bit (Z) is cleared. Figure 8.9 shows the range of valid values that D1 could contain.

A typical application for the CMP2 instruction would be to read in a number

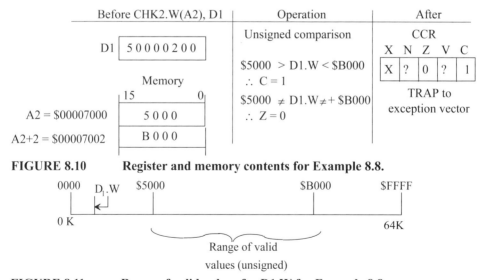

FIGURE 8.10   **Register and memory contents for Example 8.8.**

FIGURE 8.11   **Range of valid values for D1.W for Example 8.8.**

of user entries and verify that each entry is valid by comparing it against the valid range bounds. In the preceding CMP2 example, the user-entered value would be in register D1, and register A2 would point to a range for that value. The CMP2 instruction would verify whether the entry is in range by clearing the CCR carry bit if it is in bounds and setting the carry bit if it is out of bounds.

EXAMPLE 8.8   Determine the effects of execution of CHK2.W (A2),D1. Assume the following data prior to execution of this CHK2 instruction: [D1] = $50000200, [A2] = $00007000,

$$[\$00007000] = \$5000, \text{ and } [\$00007002] = \$B000.$$

Solution

Figure 8.10 shows register and memory contents before and after execution of CHK2.W(A2),D1. This time, the value $5000 located in memory is the lower bound and the value $B000 is the upper bound. Figure 8.11 shows the range of valid values that D1 could contain. Now, because the lower bound contains the logically smaller value, the programmer is indicating to the 68020 to interpret the bounds as unsigned numbers, representing only a magnitude.

Therefore, the instruction evaluates the word contained in register D1 ($0200) to determine whether it is greater than or equal to the lower bound, $5000, or less than or equal to the upper bound, $B000. Because the value being compared, $0200 is less than $5000, the carry bit is set to indicate an out-of-bounds condition and the program traps to the CHK/CHK2 exception vector service routine. Also, because $0200 is not equal to either bound, the zero bit (Z) is cleared. The figure above shows the range of valid values that D1 could contain.

A typical application for the CHK2 instruction would be to cause a trap exception to occur if a certain subscript value is not within the bounds of some defined array. Using the CHK2 example format just given, if we define an array of 100 elements with subscripts ranging from 0 through 99_{10}, and if the two words located at (A2) and (A2 + 2) contain 50 and 99, respectively, and if register D1 contains 100_{10}, execution of the CHK2instruction would cause a trap through the CHK/CHK2 exception vector. The operation of the CMP2 and CHK2 instructions are summarized in Table 8.6.

8.6.4   Trap-on-Condition Instructions

The new trap condition, TRAP*cc* instruction shown in Table 8.7 allows a conditional trap exception on any of the condition codes shown in Table 8.8. These are the same conditions that are allowed for the set-on-condition (S*cc*) and the branch-on-condition

TABLE 8.6   **CMP2 and CHK2 Instructions**

Instruction	Operand Size	Operation	Notation
CMP2	8,16, 32	Compare R*n* < source – lower bound or R*n* > source – upper bound and set CCR	CMP2 (EA), R*n*
CHK2	8, 16, 32	If R*n* < source – lower bound or R*n* > source – upper bound, then TRAP	CHK2 (EA), R*n*

(B*cc*) instructions. The TRAP*cc* instruction evaluates the test condition selected based on the state of the condition code flags, and if the test is true, the 68020 initiates exception processing by trapping through the same exception vector as the TRAPV instruction (vector 7, offset $1C, VBR = VBR + offset). The trap-on-condition instruction format is

$$\text{TRAP}cc \text{ or } \text{TRAP}cc.S \text{ \#<data>}$$

where the operand size (.S) designates word (.W) or long word (.L).

If either a word or a long word operand is specified, a one- or two-word immediate operand is placed following the instruction word. The immediate operand(s) consists of argument parameters that are passed to the trap handler to further define requests or services that it should perform. If *cc* is false, the 68020 does not interpret the immediate operand(s) but instead, adjusts the program counter to the beginning of the following instruction. The exception handler can access this immediate data as an offset to the stacked PC. The stacked PC is the next instruction to be executed.

TABLE 8.7   TRAPcc Instruction

Instruction	Operand Size	Operation	Notation
TRAP*cc*	None	If *cc*, then TRAP	TRAP*cc*
	16	Same	TRAP*cc*.W #<data>
	32	Same	TRAP*cc*.L #<data>

TABLE 8.8   Conditions for TRAPcc

Code	Description	Result
CC	Carry clear	$\overline{C}$
CS	Carry set	C
EQ	Equal	Z
F	Never true	0
GE	Greater or equal	$N \cdot V + \overline{N} \cdot \overline{V}$
GT	Greater than	$N \cdot V \cdot \overline{Z} + \overline{N} \cdot \overline{V} \cdot \overline{Z}$
HI	High	$\overline{C} \cdot \overline{Z}$
LE	Less or equal	$Z + N \cdot \overline{V} + \overline{N} \cdot V$
LS	Low or same	$C + Z$
LT	Less than	$N \cdot \overline{V} + \overline{N} \cdot V$
MI	Minus	N
NE	Not equal	$\overline{Z}$
PL	Plus	N
T	Always true	1
VC	Overflow clear	$\overline{V}$
VS	Overflow set	V

8.6.5   Bit Field Instructions

The bit field instructions, which allow operations to clear, set, ones-complement, input, insert, and test one or more bits in a string of bits (bit field), are listed in Table 8.9. Note that the condition codes are affected according to the value in the field before execution of the instruction. All bit field instructions affect the N and Z bits as shown for BFTST. That is, for all instructions, $Z = 1$ if all bits in a field prior to execution of the instruction are zero; $Z = 0$ otherwise. $N = 1$ if the most significant bit of the field prior to execution of the instruction is 1; $N = 0$ otherwise. C and V are always cleared. X is always unaffected. Next, consider BFFFO. The offset of the first bit set 1 in a bit field is placed in Dn; if no set bit is found, Dn contains the offset plus the field width. Immediate offset is from 0 to 31, whereas offset in Dn can be specified from -2^{31} to $2^{31} - 1$. All instructions are unsized.

The bit field instructions are useful for graphics or digital image processing, and for managing disk storage. Because of the large amount of data in graphics or image processing, data storage requirements can by reduced by packing data fields together where the bit field instructions provide an efficient access to data. Also, the BFFFO instruction can be used to find the first unused page in a virtual memory system. Hence, the BFFFO instruction is useful in managing disk storage.

As an example, consider BFCLR $5002{4:12}. Assume the memory contents of Figure 8.12 prior to execution of BFCLR $5002{4:12}. Bit 7 of the base address $5002 has the offset value 0. Therefore, bit 3 of $5002 has the offset value 4. Bit 0 of location

TABLE 8.9   68020 Bit Field Instructions

Instruction	Operand Size	Operation	Notation
BFTST	1-32	Field MSB $\rightarrow$ N, $Z = 1$ if all bits in field are zero; $Z = 0$ otherwise	BFTST (EA) {offset:width}
BFCLR	1-32	0's $\rightarrow$ Field	BFCLR (EA) {offset:width}
BFSET	1-32	1's $\rightarrow$ Field	BFSET (EA) {offset:width}
BFCHG	1-32	$\overline{\text{Field}}$ $\rightarrow$ Field	BFCHG (EA) {offset:width}
BFEXTS	1-32	Field $\rightarrow$ Dn; sign-extended	BFEXTS (EA) {offset:width}, Dn
BFEXTU	1-32	Field $\rightarrow$ Dn; Zero-extended	BFEXTU (EA) {offset:width}, Dn
BFINS	1-32	Dn $\rightarrow$ field	BFINS Dn, (EA) {offset:width}
BFFFO	1-32	Scan for first bit-set in field	BFFFO (EA) {offset:width}, Dn

```
                                      7 6 5 4 3 2 1 0  ← Bit number
                      $5001         1 0 1 0 0 0 0 1
                      $5002         1 0 0 1 1 1 0 0
             (Base address)→
                      $5003         0 1 1 1 0 0 0 1
                      $5004         0 0 0 1 0 0 1 0
```

FIGURE 8.12   Memory contents prior to execution of BFCLR $5002{4:12}.

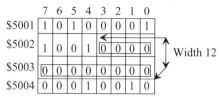

FIGURE 8.13   Memory contents after execution of BFCLR $5002{4:12}.

$5001 has the offset value -1, bit 1 of $5001 has the offset value -2, and so on. The example BFCLR instruction just given clears 12 bits starting with bit 3 of $5002. Therefore, bits 0–3 of location $5002 and bits 0–7 of location $5003 are cleared to 0. The memory contents after execution of BFCLR $5002{4:12} are shown in Figure 8.13.

The use of bit field instructions may result in memory savings. For example, assume that an input device such as a 12-bit A/D converter is interfaced via a 16-bit port of an 68020-based microcomputer. Now, suppose that 1 million pieces of data are to be collected from this port. Each 12 bits can be transferred to a 16-bit memory location, or bit field instructions can be used.

*   Using a 16-bit location for each 12 bits:

    memory requirements = 2 x 1 million
    = 2 million bytes

*   Using bit fields:

    12 bits = 1.5 bytes

    memory requirements = 1.5 x 1 million
    = 1.5 million bytes

    savings = 2 million bytes - 1.5 million bytes
    = 500,000 bytes

EXAMPLE 8.9   Determine the effect of each of the following bit field instructions:

(a)   BFCHG $5004{D5:D6}
(b)   BFEXIU $5004{2:4},D5
(c)   BFINS D4,(A0){D5:D6}
(d)   BFFFO $5004{D6:4},D5

Assume the data shown in Figure 8.14 prior to execution of each of the given

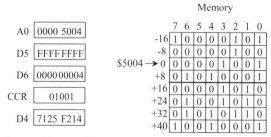

FIGURE 8.14   Data prior to execution of each instruction in Example 8.9.

instructions. Register contents are given in hex, CCR and memory contents in binary, and offset to the left of memory in decimal.

Solution

(a)   BFCHG $5004 {D5:D6}
Offset = - 1, width = 4

(b)   BFEXTU $5004 {2:4},D5
Offset = 2, width = 4

```
              X N Z V C
        CCR  0 0 0 0 0

        D5  0 0 0 0 0 0 0 2
```

(c)   BFINS D4,(A0) {D5:D6}
Offset = - 1, width = 4

```
              Memory                    X N Z V C
                    0            CCR  0 0 1 0 0
        $5004  1 0 0
```

(d)   BFFFO $5004 {D6:4},D5
Offset = 4, width = 4

```
              X N Z V C
        CCR  0 1 0 0 0

        D5  0 0 0 0 0 0 0 4
```
(Hex)

8.6.6   PACK and UNPK Instructions

The details of the PACK and UNPK instructions are listed in Table 8.10. Both instructions have three operands and are unsized. They do not affect the condition codes. The PACK

TABLE 8.10   68020 PACK and UNPK Instructions

Instruction	Operand Size	Operation	Notation
PACK	16 → 8	Unpacked source + #data → packed destination	PACK –(An), –(An), #<data>
			PACK Dn, Dn,#<data>
UNPK	8 → 16	Packed source → unpacked source	UNPK –(An), –(An), #<data>
		unpacked source + #data → unpacked destination	UNPK Dn, Dn,#<data>

instruction converts two unpacked BCD digits to two packed BCD digits:

```
              15   12 11   8 7    4 3    0
Unpacked BCD: |0 0 0 0|BCD0|0 0 0 0|BCD1|

              7       4 3      0
Packed BCD:   | BCD0  |  BCD1 |
```

     The UNPK instruction reverses the process and converts two packed BCD digits to two unpacked BCD digits. Immediate data can be added to convert numbers from one code to another. That is, these instructions can be used to translate codes such as ASCII or EBCDIC to a BCD, and vice versa.

     The PACK and UNPK instructions are useful when I/O devices such as an ASCII keyboard and an ASCII printer are interfaced to an MC68020-based microcomputer. Data can be entered into the microcomputer via the keyboard in ASCII codes. The PACK instruction can be used with appropriate adjustments to convert these ASCII codes into packed BCD. Arithmetic operations can be performed inside the microcomputer, and the result will be in packed BCD. The UNPK instruction can be used similarly with appropriate adjustments to convert packed BCD to ASCII codes for outputting to the ASCII printer.

EXAMPLE 8.10   Determine the effect of execution of each of the following PACK and UNPK instructions:

(a)   PACK D0,D5,#$0000
(b)   PACK-(A1),-(A4),#$0000
(c)   UNPK D4,D6,#$3030
(d)   UNPK-(A3),-(A2),#$3030

Assume the data shown in Figure 8.15 prior to execution of each of the instructions above.

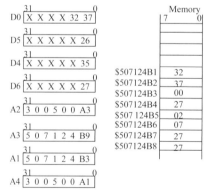

FIGURE 8.15   **Data prior to execution of each of the instructions of Example 8.7**

Solution

(a)   PACK D0,D5,#$0000

$$[D0] = 32 \quad 37$$
low
word
$$+\ 00 \quad 00$$
$$\overline{32 \quad 37}$$
$$[D5] = \quad 27$$

Note that ASCII code for 2 is $32 and for 7 is $37. Hence, this pack instruction converts ASCII code to packed BCD.

(b)   PACK -(A1),-(A4),$0000

$$[\$5071\ 24B2] = 37 \qquad 3237$$
$$[\$5071\ 24B1] = 32 \qquad \underline{0000}$$
$$\overline{3237}$$
$$\therefore [3005\ 00A0] = 27 \text{ packed BCD}$$

Hence, this pack instruction with the specified data converts two ASCII digits to their equivalent packed BCD form.

(c)   UNPK D4,D6,#$3030

$$[D4] = XXXXXX \ 35$$
$$03 \ 05$$
$$+\ 30 \ 30$$
$$\overline{33 \ 35}$$
$$\therefore [D6] = XXXX \ 33 \ 35$$
$$[D4] = XXXXXX \ 35$$

Therefore, this UNPK instruction with the assumed data converts from packed BCD in D4 to ASCII code in D6; the contents of D4 are not changed.

(d)   UNPK -(A3),-(A2),#$3030

$$[\$5071\ 24B8] = 27$$
$$\boxed{02 \ 07}$$
$$30 \ 30$$
$$\overline{32 \ 37}$$
$$\therefore [\$300500A2] = 37$$
$$[\$300500A1] = 32$$

This UNPK instruction with the assumed data converts two packed BCD digits to their equivalent ASCII digits.

EXAMPLE 8.11   Write a 68020 assembly language program at address $2000 to add two words, each containing two ASCII digits. The first word is stored in D0.W and the second word is stored in D1.W. Store the packed BCD result in D4.W.

Solution

```
            ORG      $2000
            MOVE.W   #$3536,D0    ;Move two ASCII digits to low word of D0
            MOVE.W   #$3235,D1    ;Move two ASCII digits to low word of D1
            PACK     D0,D3,#$0000 ;Convert D0.W into packed BCD byte in D3.B
            PACK     D1,D4,#$0000 ;Convert D1.W into packed BCD byte  in D4.B
            ADDI.B   #0,D0        ;Clear X-bit since ABCD instruction includes x-bit
            ABCD.B   D3,D4        ;Packed BCD addition. D4.B contains result
FINISH   JMP        FINISH
```

Comparing this problem with Example 6.20, it can be concluded that since the 68000 does not have a PACK instruction to convert from ASCII to packed BCD, many more instructions are needed for the conversion.

In the program above,   MOVE.W   #$3536,D0 loads two ASCII digits $35 (ASCII for 5) and $36 (ASCII for 6) into the low word of D0. The instruction MOVE.W #$3235,D1 loads two other ASCII digits, $32 (ASCII for 2) and $35 (ASCII for 5), into the low word of D1. PACK   D0,D3,#$0000 converts ASCII $3536 in D0.W into a packed BCD byte $56 in D3.B. Similarly, PACK D1,D4,#$0000 converts ASCII $3235 in D1.W into a packed BCD byte $25 in D4.B. Since ABCD.B D3,D4 adds the packed BCD bytes in D3.B and D4.B along with the X-bit, the X-bit is cleared to 0 before using the ABCD instruction. ABCD.B D3,D4 performs the BCD addition as follows:

```
[D3.B] = $56 = 0101 0110
[D4.B] = $25 = 0010 0101
                 -------------------
                    0111 1011
                        0110 --Add 6 for BCD correction
                 ---------------------
                    1000  0001 = $81 = [D4.B]
```
The result above is verified using the IDE68K debugger.

8.6.7   Multiplication and Division Instructions

Table 8.11 shows the   68020 shows the 68020   signed and unsigned multiplication instructions. In the table, (EA) can use all modes except An. The condition codes N, Z, and V are affected; C is always cleared to 0, and X is unaffected for both MULS and MULU. For signed multiplication, overflow (V = 1) can occur only for 32 × 32 multiplication, producing a 32-bit result if the high-order 32 bits of the 64-bit product are not the sign extension of the low-order 32 bits. In the case of unsigned multiplication, overflow (V = 1) can occur for 32 × 32 multiplication, producing a 32-bit result if the high-order 32 bits of the 64-bit product are not zero.

Both MULS and MULU have a word form and a long word form. For the word form (16 × 16), the multiplier and multiplicand are both 16 bits and the result is 32 bits. The result is saved in the destination data register. For the long word form (32 × 32), the multiplier and multiplicand are both 32 bits and the result is either 32 or 64 bits. When the result is 32 bits for a 32-bit × 32-bit operation, the low-order 32 bits of the 64-bit product are provided.

TABLE 8.11   68020 Signed and Unsigned Multiplication Instructions

Instruction	Operand Size	Operation
MULS.W (EA), D*n* *or* MULU	$16 \times 16 \rightarrow 32$	$(EA)_{16} * (Dn)_{16} \rightarrow (Dn)_{32}$
MULS.L (EA), D*n* *or* MULU	$32 \times 32 \rightarrow 32$	(EA) * D*n* $\rightarrow$ D*n* D*n* holds 32 bits of the result after multiplication. Upper 32 bits of the result are discarded.
MULS.L (EA),D*h*:D*n* *or* MULU	$32 \times 32 \rightarrow 64$	(EA) * D*n* $\rightarrow$ D*h*:D*n* (EA) holds 32-bit multiplier before multiplication D*h* holds high 32 bits of product after multiplication. D*n* holds 32-bit multiplicand before multiplication and low 32 bits of product after multiplication.

Table 8.12 shows the 68020 signed and unsigned division instructions , in which the source is the divisor, the destination is the dividend.

In the table, (EA) can use all modes except A*n*. The condition codes for either signed or unsigned division are affected as follows: N = 1 if the quotient is negative; N = 0 otherwise. N is undefined for overflow or divide by zero. Z = 1 if the quotient is zero; Z = 0 otherwise. Z is undefined for overflow or divide by zero. V = 1 for division overflow; V = 0 otherwise. X is unaffected. Division by zero causes a trap. If overflow is detected before completion of the instruction, V is set to 1, but the operands are unaffected.

Both signed and unsigned division instructions have a word form and three long word forms. For the word form, the destination operand is 32 bits and the source operand is 16 bits. The 32-bit result in D*n* contains the 16-bit quotient in the low word and the 16-bit remainder in the high word. The sign of the remainder is the same as the sign of the dividend.

For the instruction

DIVS.L (EA), D*q*

or

DIVU

both destination and source operands are 32 bits. The result in D*q* contains the 32-bit quotient and the remainder is discarded.

For the instruction

DIVS.L (EA), D*r*:D*q*

or

DIVU

the destination is 64 bits contained in any two data registers and the source is 32 bits. The 32-bit register D*r* (D0–D7) contains the 32-bit remainder and the 32-bit register D*q* (D0–D7) contains the 32-bit quotient.

TABLE 8.12   **68020 Signed and Unsigned Division Instructions**

Instruction	Operation
DIVS.W (EA), Dn *or* DIVU	$32/16 \rightarrow 16r{:}16q$
DIVS.L (EA), Dq *or* DIVU	$32/32 \rightarrow 32q$ No remainder is provided.
DIVS.L (EA),Dr:Dq *or* DIVU	$64/32 \rightarrow 32r{:}32q$
DIVSL.L (EA),Dr:Dq *or* DIVUL	Dr/(EA) $\rightarrow 32r{:}32q$ Dr contains 32-bit dividend

For the instruction

DIVSL.L (EA), Dr:Dq

or

DIVUL

the 32-bit register Dr (D0–D7) contains the 32-bit dividend and the source is also 32 bits. After division, Dr contains the 32-bit remainder and Dq contains the 32-bit quotient.

EXAMPLE 8.12   Determine the effect of execution of each of the following multiplication and division instructions.
(a)   MULU.L #2,D5 if [D5] = $FFFFFFFF
(b)   MULS.L #2,D5 if [D5] = $FFFFFFFF
(c)   MULU.L #2,D5:D2 if [D5] = $2ABC1800 and [D2] = $FFFFFFFF
(d)   DIVS.L #2,D5 if [D5] = $FFFFFFFC
(e)   DIVS.L #2,D2:D0 if [D2] = $FFFFFFFF and [D0] = $FFFFFFFC
(f)   DIVSL.L #2,D6:D1 if [D1] = $00041234 and [D6] = $FFFFFFFD

Solution

(a)   MULU.L #2,D5 if [D5] = $FFFFFFFF

Therefore, [D5] = $FFFFFFFE, N = 0 since the most significant bit of the result is 0, Z = 0 because the result is nonzero, V = 1 because the high 32 bits of the 64-bit product are not zero, C = 0 (always), and X is not affected.

(b)   MULS.L #2,D5 if [D5] = $FFFFFFFF

$$\begin{array}{r}
\text{\$FFFFFFFF} \quad (-1) \\
* \;\text{\$00000002} \quad (+2) \\
\hline
\text{\$FFFFFFFF} \quad \underbrace{\text{\$FFFFFFFE}}_{\text{Result in D5}} \quad (-2)
\end{array}$$

Therefore, [D5] = $FFFFFFFE, X is unaffected, C = 0, N = 1, V = 0, and Z = 0.

(c)   MULU.L #2,D5:D2 if [D5] = $2ABC1800 and D2 = $FFFFFFFF

$$\begin{array}{r}
\text{\$FFFFFFFF} \\
* \;\text{\$00000002} \\
\hline
\underbrace{\text{00000001}}_{\text{D5}} \quad \underbrace{\text{FFFFFFFE}}_{\text{D2}}
\end{array}$$

Here N = 0, Z = 0, V = 0, C = 0, and X is not affected.

(d)   DIVS.L #2,D5 if [D5] = $FFFFFFFC

[D5] = $FFFFFFFE, X is unaffected, N = 1, Z = 0, V = 0, and C = 0 (always).

(e)   DIVS.L #2,D2:D0 if [D2] = $FFFFFFFF and [D0] = $FFFFFFFC

$$\overset{-2}{\overbrace{}}\qquad\overset{0}{\overbrace{}}$$
$$q = \text{FFFF FFFE}, \; r = \text{0000 0000}$$
$$\underbrace{\text{0000 0002}}_{2} \;\big|\; \underbrace{\text{FFFF FFFF FFFF FFFC}}_{-4}$$

[D2] = $00000000 = remainder, [D0] = $FFFFFFFE = quotient, X is unaffected, Z = 0, N = 1, V = 0, and C = 0 (always).

(f)   DIVSL.L #2,D6:D1 if [D1] = $00041234 and [D6] = $FFFFFFFD

$$\overset{-1}{\overbrace{}}\qquad\overset{-1}{\overbrace{}}$$
$$q = \text{FFFFFFFF}, \; r = \text{FFFFFFFF}$$
$$\text{0000 0002} \;\big|\; \underbrace{\text{FFFFFFFD}}_{-3}$$

[D6] = $FFFFFFFF = remainder, [D1] = $FFFFFFFF = quotient, X is unaffected, N = 1, Z = 0, V = 0, and C = 0 (always).

EXAMPLE 8.13   Write a program in 68020 assembly language to multiply a 32-bit signed number in D2 by a 32-bit signed number in D3 by storing the multiplication result in the following manner:

TABLE 8.13   68000 Enhanced instructions

Instruction	Operand Size	Operation
BRA *label*	8, 16, 32	PC + d → PC
Bcc *label*	8, 16, 32	If *cc* is true, then PC + d → PC; else next instruction
BSR *label*	8, 16, 32	PC → –(SP); PC + d → PC
CMPI.S #data, (EA)	8, 16, 32	Destination – #data → CCR is affected
TST.S (EA)	8, 16, 32	Destination – 0 → CCR is affected
LINK.S An, -d	16, 32	An → –(SP); SP → An; SP + d → SP
EXTB.L Dn	32	Sign-extend byte to long word

(a) Store the 32-bit result in D2. Assume that the numbers are already in registers prior to multiplication.
(b) Store the high 32 bits of the result in D3 and the low 32 bits of the result in D2. Assume that the numbers are already in registers prior to multiplication.

Solution

(a)

	MULS.L	D3,D2
FINISH	JMP	FINISH

(b)

	MULS.L	D3,D3:D2
FINISH	JMP	FINISH

8.6.8   68000 Enhanced Instructions

Table 8.13 lists the 68000 enhanced instructions. In the table, S can be B, W, or L. In addition to 8- and 16-bit signed displacements for BRA, B*cc*, and BSR like the 68000, the 68020 allows signed 32-bit displacements. LINK is unsized in the 68000. (EA) in CMPI and TST supports all 68000 modes plus PC relative. An example is CMPI.W #$2000,(START, PC). In addition to EXT.W D*n* and EXT.L D*n,* like the 68000, the 68020 provides an EXTB.L instruction.

8.6.9   68020 Subroutines

Like the 68000, the instructions, BSR and JSR are subroutine call instructions in the 68020. BSR uses the relative addressing mode, whereas JSR uses the absolute addressing mode. As mentioned in Chapter 6, the 68000 uses 16- and 24-bit addresses with the JSR instruction. In addition to these addresses, the 68020 JSR instruction can use 32-bit address. Also, as mentioned in Chapter 6, the 68000 BSR uses 8- and 16-bit displacements. The 68020 can use 32-bit displacement in addition to 8-, and 16-bit displacements.

In order to illustrate the concept of subroutine CALL and RETURN instructions, consider the following program segment assuming that the main program uses all registers and that the subroutine stores the result in memory:

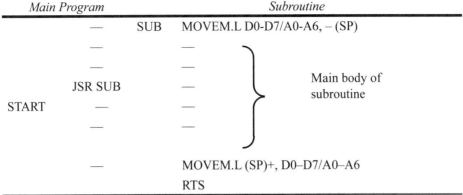

Here, the JSR SUB instruction calls the subroutine SUB. In response to JSR, the 68020 pushes the current PC contents called START onto the stack and loads the starting address SUB of the subroutine into PC. The first MOVEM in the SUB pushes all registers onto the stack, and after the subroutine is executed, the second MOVEM instruction pops all the registers back. Finally, RTS pops the address START from the stack into PC, and program control is returned to the main program. Note that BSR SUB could have been used instead of JSR SUB in the main program. In that case, the 68020 assembler would have considered the SUB with BSR as a displacement rather than as an address with the JSR instruction.

EXAMPLE 8.14   Write a subroutine in 68020 assembly language to implement the C language assignment statement: p = p + q; where the addresses p and q hold two 16-digit (64-bit) packed BCD numbers (N1 and N2). The main program will initialize addresses p and q to $3000 and $4000, respectively. Address $3007 will hold the lowest byte of N1 with the highest byte at address $3000, and address $4007 will contain the lowest byte of N2 with the highest byte at address $4000. Also, write the main program at address $2000, which will perform all initializations including address p (pointer A0 to $3000), address q (pointer A1 to $4000), loop count (D1 to 7), and then call the subroutine at $8000 and stop. The subroutine will accomplish the task with the initialized values of A0, A1, and D1 in the main program. Use ABCD.B for BCD addition with the predecrement mode. Assume the supervisor mode. Note that the 68020 supervisor stack pointer is initialized upon hardware reset.

Solution

```
            ORG      $2000
            MOVEA.W  #$3000,A0      ; LOAD A0.L WITH $00003000
            MOVEA.W  #$4000,A1      ; LOAD A1.L WITH $00004000
            MOVE.W   #7,D1          ; INITIALIZE COUNTER WITH 7
            JSR      BCDADD         ; CALL SUBROUTINE
STAY        JMP      STAY
            ORG      $8000
BCDADD LEA.L       1(A0,D1.W),A0    ;UPDATE A0
            LEA.L    1(A1,D1.W),A1    ;AND A1
            ADDI.B   #0,D0          ;X-BIT =0
ALOOP   ABCD.B      -(A1),-(A0)     ;ADD
            DBF.W    D1,ALOOP
            RTS
```

Questions and Problems

8.1   Name three new 68020 instructions that are not provided with the 68000.

8.2   Find the contents of the affected registers and memory locations after execution of the 68020 instruction MOVE ($1000,A5,D3.W*4),D1. Assume the following data prior to execution of this MOVE: [A5] = $0000F210, [$ 00014218] = $4567, [D3] = $00001002, [$ 0001421A] = $2345, and [D1] = $F125012A.

8.3   Assume the 68020 memory configuration shown in Figure P8.3.

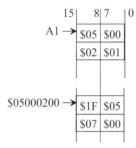

FIGURE P8.3

Find the contents of the affected memory locations after execution of MOVE.W #$1234,([A1]).

8.4   Find the 68020 compare instruction with the appropriate addressing mode to replace the following 68000 instruction sequence:
          ASL.L #1,D5
          CMP.L 0 (A0,D5.L),D0

8.5   Find the contents of D1, D2, A4, and CCR and the memory locations after execution of each of the following 68020 instructions:
                   (a) BFSET $5000 {D1:10}
                   (b) BFINS D2, (A4) {D1:D4}
       Assume the data given in Figure P8.5 prior to execution of each of these instructions.

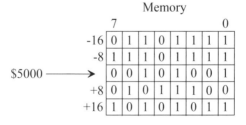

[D1] = $00000004, [D4] = $00000004
[D2] = $12345678, [A4] = $00005000

FIGURE P8.5

8.6 Identify the following 68020 instructions as valid or invalid. Justify your answers.
(a) DIVS A0,D1
(b) CHK.B D0,(A0)
(c) MOVE.L D0,(A0)
Assume that [A0] = $1025671A prior to execution of the MOVE.

8.7 Determine the values of the Z and C flags after execution of each of the following 68020 instructions:
(a) CHK2.W (A5),D3
(b) CMP2.L $2001,A5
Assume the data shown in Figure P8.7 prior to execution of each of these instructions:

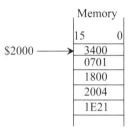

Memory

15   0
3400
0701
1800
2004
1E21

$2000 →

[D3] = $02001740, [A5] = $0002004

FIGURE P8.7

8.8 Write a 68020 assembly language program to move two columns of 100 32-bit numbers from A (i) to B (i). In other words, move A(0) to B(0), A(1) to B(1), and so on from LOW to HIGH memory addresses. Assume A0 and A1 point to A (*i*) to B (*i*) respectively.

8.9 Write a 68020 assembly program to add two 64-bit numbers in D1D0 with another 64-bit number in D2D3. Store the result in D1D0.

8.10 Write a 68020 assembly language program at address $5000 to convert a word consisting of two ASCII digits stored in the upper 16 bits of D0 into a packed BCD byte. Store the packed BCD result in the lowest byte of D1.

8.11 Write a program in 68020 assembly language to convert 10 packed BCD bytes (20 BCD digits), stored in memory starting at address $00002000 and above, to their ASCII equivalents and store the result in memory locations starting at $FFFF8000.

8.12 Write a 68020 assembly program to multiply a 32-bit signed number in D5 by another 16-bit signed number in D1. Store the 64-bit result in D5D1.

8.13 Write a program in 68020 assembly language to multiply a signed byte by a 32-bit signed number to obtain a 64-bit result. Assume that the numbers are pointed to by the addresses that are passed on to the user stack by a subroutine pointed to by (A7 + 6) and (A7 + 8). Store the 64-bit result in D2:D1.

8.14   Write a program in 68020 assembly language to find the first one in a bit field which is greater than or equal to 16 bits and less than or equal to 512 bits. Assume that the number of bits to be checked is divisible by 16. If no 1's are found, store zero in D3; otherwise, store the offset of the first set bit in D3, and then stop. Assume that A2 contains the starting address of the array, and D2 contains the number of bits in the array.

8.15   Write a 68020 assembly language program that will convert a BCD number in D0.B to a seven-segment code in D2.B using a lookup table containing the seven-segment codes of the BCD numbers. Use common-cathode display. Assume that the table is stored in memory starting at an address $00004000.

8.16   Write a subroutine in 68020 assembly language to compute $Y = \sum_{i=1}^{50} \dfrac{Xi^2}{50}$

Assume the X_1's are signed 32-bit numbers and the array starts at $500000F1. Store 32-bit quotient in D1, and 32-bit remainder in D2. Neglect overflow.

8.17   Write a subroutine in 68020 assembly language at address $00002000 that can be called by a main program at address $00003000. The subroutine will compute the 16-bit sum
$$\Sigma a_{kk}^2$$
where a_{kk} are diagonal elements of a 3x3 matrix, and k = 0 to 2. Assume that each element in the matrix is signed 16-bit. Store the result in D0.W. The main program will initialize A7 to $00000800, obtain the three diagonal elements from memory stored starting at address $0000 1000 in row-major order, call the subroutine, and then stop.

8.18   Write a subroutine in 68020 assembly language at address $00003000 that can be called by a main program at address $00006000. Assume supervisor mode. The subroutine will compute the 32-bit sum
$$Y = \Sigma X_i^2 \text{ where } i = 1 \text{ to } 256.$$

Assume the X_1's are signed 32-bit numbers and the array starts at $50000021. Also, write the main program that will initialize A7 to $0030 4000, A1 to $50000021, initialize loop count, clear SUM to 0, call the subroutine, perform other operations as necessary, divide Y by 256 (discard remainder), store 32-bit result in D1, and then stop. Do not use any divide instructions.

8.19   It is desired to convert a four-digit unpacked BCD number to binary using the following equation: binary value, V of the four-digit BCD number,
$$V = \quad N_3 * 1000 + N_2 * 100 + N_1 * 10 + N_0$$
where N_3 is the most significant digit and N_0 is the least significant digit. Write a subroutine in 68020 assembly language at address $30708000 that will compute 10* N where N is an unsigned 8-bit number in D0.B. The most significant digit is stored in a memory location starting at address $00004000, and the least

significant is stored at address $00004003. Write the main program at address $10000000 that will call the subroutine , and compute V via multiplications by 10 and additions as follows:

$$V = (((N_3 *10) * 10) * 10) +((N_2 *10) * 10) +(N_1 * 10) + N_0.$$

The main program will first initialize A0 to $00004000, A7 to $00002000, SUM in D1.W to 0,obtain each digit from memory, call the subroutine as many times as needed, store the 16-bit result in D1.W, and then stop. Assume supervisor mode.

9

68020 HARDWARE AND INTERFACING

In this chapter we describe the fundamental concepts associated with hardware aspects of the Motorola 68020 microprocessor. Significant modifications have been made to the 68020 bus structure beyond those of the 68000. One of these enhancements is *dynamic bus sizing*. Hence, this feature along with 68020 system design concepts are included. Topics covered in this chapter include 68020 pins and signals, dynamic bus sizing, and system design concepts. Finally, design concepts associated with a 68020-based voltmeter and a 68020-based microcomputer interface to a hexadecimal keyboard and a seven-segment display are covered. These topics are described in a simplified manner. Note that a background in the 68000 software and hardware described in Chapters 6 and 7 is required to understand the topics contained in this chapter.

9.1   Introduction

In this section we describe hardware aspects of the 68020. Topics include 68020 pins and signals, aligned and misaligned transfers, dynamic bus sizing, and timing diagrams. Numerous changes have been made to the 68020 bus structure. Note that the 68020 does not support 6800-type I/O devices. As mentioned in Chapter 7, the 68000 supports both 6800-type I/O devices such as 6821 and 16-bit devices such as 68230. Also, the 68020 can complete read or write bus cycles in three clock cycles without wait states. This is due to enhancements made in the 68020 bus control logic. The 68000, on the other hand, requires four cycles to complete read or write cycles without wait states.

9.1.1   68020 Pins and Signals

The 68020 is arranged in a 13×13 matrix array (114 pins defined) and fabricated in a pin grid array (PGA) or other packages, such as an RC suffix package. Both the 32-bit address (A_0–A_{31}) and data (D_0–D_{31}) pins of the 68020 are nonmultiplexed. The 68020 transfers data with an 8-bit device via D_{31}–D_{24}, with a 16-bit device via D_{31}–D_{16}, and with a 32-bit device via D_{31}–D_0. Figure 9.1 shows the 68020 functional signal group. For reliable operation, unused inputs should be connected to an appropriate signal level. Unused active LOW inputs should be connected to Vcc. Unused active HIGH inputs should be connected to GROUND.

Table 9.1 lists these signals along with a description of each. Ten Vcc (+5 V) and 13 ground pins are used to distribute power in order to reduce noise. As stated above, unused inputs should not be kept floating. Unused active LOW inputs should be connected to Vcc. Unused active HIGH inputs should be connected to GROUND. Like the 68000, the three function code signals FC2, FC1, and FC0 identify the processor state (supervisor or user) and the address space of the bus cycle currently being

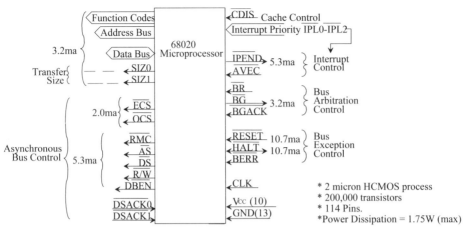

FIGURE 9.1   68020 functional signal groups.

TABLE 9.1   Hardware Signal Index

Signal Name	Mnemonic	Function
Address bus	A_0-A_{31}	32-bit address bus used to address any of 4,294,967,296 bytes.
Data bus	D_0-D_{31}	32-bit data bus used to transfer 8, 16, 24, or 32 bits of data per bus cycle.
Function codes	FC0-FC2	3-bit function code used to identify the address space of each bus cycle.
Size	SIZ0/SIZ1	Indicates the number of bytes remaining to be transferred for this cycle; these signals, together with A0 and A1, define the active sections of the data bus.
Read-modify-write cycle	$\overline{RMC}$	Provides an indicator that the current bus cycle is part of an indivisible read-modify-write operation.
External cycle start	$\overline{ECS}$	Provides an indication that a bus cycle is beginning.
Operand cycle start	$\overline{OCS}$	Identical operation to that of $\overline{ECS}$ except that $\overline{OCS}$ is asserted only during the first bus cycle of an operand transfer.
Address strobe	$\overline{AS}$	Indicates that a valid address is on the bus.
Data strobe	$\overline{DS}$	Indicates that valid data is to be placed on the data bus by an external device or has been placed on the data bus by the MC68020.
Read/write	R/$\overline{W}$	Defines the bus transfer as a 68020 read or write.
Data buffer enable	$\overline{DBEN}$	Provides an enable signal for external data buffers.
Data transfer and size acknowledge	$\overline{DSACK1}$/ $\overline{DSACK1}$	Bus response signals that indicate the requested data. transfer operation are completed; in addition, these two lines indicate the use of the external bus port on a cycle-by-cycle basis.

TABLE 9.1   Cont.

Cache disable	$\overline{\text{CDIS}}$	Dynamically disables the on-chip cache.
Interrupt priority level	IPL0-IPL2	Provides an encoded interrupt level to the processor.
Autovector	$\overline{\text{AVEC}}$	Requests an autovector during an interrupt acknowledge cycle.
Interrupt pending	$\overline{\text{IPEND}}$	Indicates that an interrupt is pending.
Bus request	$\overline{\text{BR}}$	Indicates that an external device requires bus mastership.
Bus grant	$\overline{\text{BG}}$	Indicates that an external device may assume bus mastership.
Bus grant acknowledge	$\overline{\text{BGACK}}$	Indicates that an external device has assumed bus control.
Reset	$\overline{\text{RESET}}$	System reset.
Halt	$\overline{\text{HALT}}$	Indicates that the processor should suspend bus activity.
Bus error	$\overline{\text{BERR}}$	Indicates that an illegal bus operation is being attempted.
Clock	CLK	Clock input to the processor.
Power supply	VCC	+5 volt ± 5% power supply.
Ground	GND	Ground connection.

TABLE 9.2   68020 Function Code Signals

FC2	FC1	FC0	Cycle Type
0	0	0	Undefined, reserved
0	0	1	User data space
0	1	0	User program space
0	1	1	Undefined, reserved
1	0	0	Undefined, reserved
1	0	1	Supervisor data space
1	1	0	Supervisor program space
1	1	1	CPU space

executed except that the 68020 defines the CPU space cycle as shown in Table 9.2. Note that in the 68000, FC2, FC1, FC0 = 111 indicates the interrupt acknowledge cycle. In the 68020, it indicates the CPU space cycle. In this cycle, by decoding address lines A_{19}–A_{16}, the 68020 can perform various types of functions, such as coprocessor communication, breakpoint acknowledge, interrupt acknowledge, and module operations, as depicted in Table 9.3.

Note that A_{19}, A_{18}, A_{17}, A_{16} = 0011_2 to 1110_2 is reserved by Motorola. In the coprocessor communication CPU space cycle, the 68020 determines the coprocessor type by decoding A_{15}–A_{13} as shown in Table 9.4.

TABLE 9.3   Decoding of A_{19}–A_{16} Pins During a CPU Space Cycle

A_{19}	A_{18}	A_{17}	A_{16}	Function performed
0	0	0	0	Breakpoint acknowledge
1	0	0	1	Module operations
0	0	1	0	Coprocessor communication
1	1	1	1	Interrupt acknowledge

TABLE 9.4   Coprocessor Communication During a CPU Space Cycle

A_{15}	A_{14}	A_{13}	Coprocessor Type
0	0	0	68851 paged memory management unit
0	0	1	68881 floating-point coprocessor

Let us explain some of the other 68020 pins. The $\overline{ECS}$ (external cycle start) pin is a 68020 output pin. The 68020 asserts this pin during the first one-half clock of every bus cycle to provide the earliest indication of the start of a bus cycle. The use of $\overline{ECS}$ must be validated later with $\overline{AS}$, because the 68020 may start an instruction fetch cycle and then abort it if the instruction is found in the cache. In the case of a cache hit, the 68020 does not assert $\overline{AS}$, but provides A_{31}–A_0, SIZ1, SIZ0, and FC2–FC0 outputs.

The 68020 $\overline{AVEC}$ input is activated by an external device to service an autovector interrupt. The $\overline{AVEC}$ on the 68020 provides the same function as the $\overline{VPA}$ on the 68000 during autovector interrupt. The functions of other signals, such as $\overline{AS}$, R/$\overline{W}$, $\overline{IPL2}$ - $\overline{IPL0}$, $\overline{BR}$, $\overline{BG}$, and $\overline{BGACK}$, are similar to those of the 68000.

The 68020 system control pins are functionally similar to those of the 68000. However, there are some minor differences. For example, for hardware reset, the $\overline{RESET}$ and $\overline{HALT}$ pins need not be asserted simultaneously. Therefore, unlike the 68000, the $\overline{RESET}$ and $\overline{HALT}$ pins are not required to be tied together in the 68020 system .

The $\overline{RESET}$ and $\overline{HALT}$ pins are bidirectional and open drain (external pull-up resistances are required), and their functions are independent. When asserted by an external circuit for a minimum of 520 clock periods, the $\overline{RESET}$ pin resets the entire system, including the 68020. Upon hardware reset, the 68020 completes any active bus cycle in an orderly manner and then performs the following:

- Reads the 32-bit content of address $00000000 and loads it into the ISP (the contents of $00000000 are loaded to the most significant byte of the ISP, and so on).

- Reads the 32-bit contents of address $00000004 into the PC (contents of $00000004 to the most significant byte of the PC, and so on).

- Sets the I2 I1 I0 bits of the SR to 1 1 1, sets the S bit in the SR to 1, and clears the T1, T0, and M bits in the SR.

- Clears the VBR to $00000000.

- Clears the cache enable bit in the CACR.

- No other registers are affected by hardware reset.

     When the RESET instruction is executed, the 68020 asserts the $\overline{RESET}$ pin LOW for 512 clock cycles, and the processor resets all the external devices connected to the

TABLE 9.5   Decoding of SIZ0 and SIZ1 Pins

SIZ1	SIZ0	Number of Bytes Remaining to be Transferred
0	1	Byte
1	0	Word
1	1	3 bytes
0	0	Long words

TABLE 9.6   Device Size Definition by $\overline{\text{DSACK0}}$ and $\overline{\text{DSACK1}}$ Pins

$\overline{\text{DSACK1}}$	$\overline{\text{DSACK0}}$	Device Size
0	0	32-bit device
0	1	16-bit device
1	0	8-bit device
1	1	Data not ready; insert wait states

$\overline{\text{RESET}}$ pin. Software reset does not affect any internal register.

In asynchronous operation, the 68020 typically uses bus signals such as $\overline{\text{AS}}$, $\overline{\text{DS}}$, $\overline{\text{DSACK1}}$, and $\overline{\text{DSACK0}}$ to control data transfer. Using asynchronous operation, $\overline{\text{AS}}$ starts the bus cycle and $\overline{\text{DS}}$ is used as a condition of valid data on a write cycle. Decoding SIZ1, SIZ0, A_1, and A_0 provides enable signals, which indicate the portion of the data bus that is used in data transfer. The memory or I/O chip then responds by placing the requested data on the correct portion of the data bus for a read cycle or latching the data on a write cycle and asserting $\overline{\text{DSACK1}}$ and $\overline{\text{DSACK0}}$, corresponding to the memory or I/O port size (8-, 16-, or 32-bit), to terminate the bus cycle.

SIZ0 and SIZ1 pins indicate the number of bytes remaining to be transferred for a cycle; these signals, together with A_0 and A_1, define the active sections of the data bus. The decoding of SIZ0 and SIZ1 and the $\overline{\text{DSACK0}}$ and $\overline{\text{DSACK1}}$ pins are shown in Tables 9.5 and 9.6, respectively.

EXAMPLE 9.1   Determine the contents of PC, SR, MSP, and ISP after a 68020 hardware reset. Assume a 32-bit memory with the following data prior to the reset: [$00000000] = $50001234, [$00000004] = $72152614, [MSP] = $27140124, [ISP] = $61711420, [PC] = $35261271, and [SR] = $0301.

Solution

After hardware reset, the following are the memory and register contents: [$00000000] = $50001234, [$00000004] = $72152614, [MSP] = $27140124, [ISP] = $50001234, [PC] = $72152614, and [SR] = $2701. Note that [SR] = $2701 = 00100111000000012. Compared with Figure 8.2, T1T0 = 00, S = 1, M = 0, and I2, I1, I0 = 111; other bits are not affected.

9.1.2   68020 Dynamic Bus Sizing

The 68020 offers a feature called *dynamic bus sizing*, which enables designers to use 8-, 16-, and 32-bit memory and I/O devices without sacrificing system performance. The SIZ0, SIZ1, $\overline{\text{DSACK0}}$, and $\overline{\text{DSACK1}}$ pins are used to implement the 68020 dynamic bus sizing.

During each bus cycle, the external device indicates its width via $\overline{\text{DSACK0}}$ and $\overline{\text{DSACK1}}$. The $\overline{\text{DSACK0}}$ and $\overline{\text{DSACK1}}$ pins are used to indicate completion of the cycle. At the start of a bus cycle, the 68020 always transfers data to lines D_0–D_{31}, taking into consideration that the memory or I/O device may be 8, 16, or 32 bits wide. After the first bus cycle, the 68020 knows the device size by checking the $\overline{\text{DSACK0}}$ and $\overline{\text{DSACK1}}$ pins and generates additional bus cycles if needed to complete the transfer.

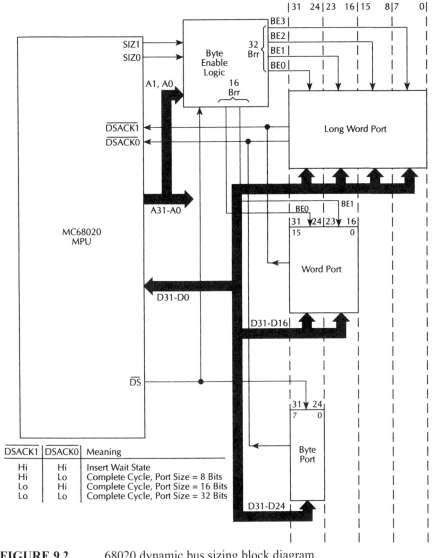

$\overline{\text{DSACK1}}$	$\overline{\text{DSACK0}}$	Meaning
Hi	Hi	Insert Wait State
Hi	Lo	Complete Cycle, Port Size = 8 Bits
Lo	Hi	Complete Cycle, Port Size = 16 Bits
Lo	Lo	Complete Cycle, Port Size = 32 Bits

FIGURE 9.2   68020 dynamic bus sizing block diagram.

Next, consider an example of dynamic bus sizing. The 4 bytes of a 32-bit data can be defined as follows:

31	23	15	7	0
OP0	OP1	OP2	OP3	

If this data is held in a data register Dn and is to be written to a memory or I/O location, the address lines A_1 and A_0 define the byte position of data. For a 32-bit device, $A_1A_0 = 00$ (addresses 0, 4, 8, …), $A_1A_0 = 01$ (addresses 1, 5, 9, …), $A_1A_0 = 10$ (addresses 2, 6, 10, …), and $A_1A_0 = 11$ (addresses 3, 7, 11, …) will store OP0, OP1, OP2, and OP3, respectively. This data is written via the 68020 D_{31}–D_0 pins. However, if the device is 16-bit, data is always transferred as follows:

- All even-addressed bytes via pins D_{31}–D_{24}

- All odd-addressed bytes via pins D_{23}–D_{16}

Finally, for an 8-bit device, both even- and odd-addressed bytes are transferred via pins D_{31}–D_{24}. The 68020 always starts transferring data with the most significant byte first.

Figure 9.2 is a functional block diagram for 68020 interfaces to 8-, 16-, and 32-bit memory and I/O devices. Note that 8-bit devices perform data transfer with the 68020 via D_{31}–D_{24} pins, 16-bit devices via D_{31}–D_{16}, and 32-bit devices via D_{31}–D_0 pins. Aligned long word transfers to 8-, 16-, and 32-bit devices are shown in Figure 9.3. For a 32-bit device, an address starting with $A_1A_0 = 00$ indicates a long word aligned transfer. The 68020 instruction, MOVE.L D1,$50001234 is an example of an aligned long word transfer since $A_1A_0 = 00$. 68020 byte addressing is summarized in Figure 9.4. Figure 9.4 shows how four bytes of a 32-bit longword are transferred between the 68020 and a 32-bit device, 16-bit device, or an 8-bit device.

Figure 9.5 shows misaligned long word transfers to 8-, 16-, and 32-bit devices. The 68020 instruction MOVE.L D1,$50001235 is an example of a misaligned long word transfer since $A_1A_0 = 01$.

As an example of dynamic bus sizing, consider MOVE.L D1,$20107420. This is a long word aligned transfer. In the first bus cycle, the 68020 does not know the size of the device and hence outputs all combinations of data on pins D31–D0, taking into consideration that the device may be 8, 16, or 32 bits wide. Assume that the content of D1 is $02A10512 (OP0 = $02, OP1 = $A1, OP2 = $05, and OP3 = $12). In the first bus cycle, the 68020 sends SIZ1 SIZ0 = 00, indicating a 32-bit transfer, and then outputs data on its D31–D0 pins as follows:

D_{31}:D_{24}	D_{23}:D_{16}	D_{15}:D_8	D_7:D_0
$02	$A1	$05	$12

If the device is 8-bit, it will take data $02 from pins D_{31}–D_{24} in the first cycle and will then assert $\overline{DSACK1}$ and $\overline{DSACK0}$ as 10, indicating an 8-bit device. The 68020 then transfers the remaining 24 bits ($A1 first, $05 next, and $12 last) via pins D_{31}–D_{24} in three consecutive cycles, with a total of four cycles being necessary to complete the transfer.

However, if the device is 16-bit, in the first cycle the device will take the 16-bit data $02A1 via pins D_{31}–D_{16} and will then assert $\overline{DSACK1}$ and $\overline{DSACK0}$ as 01, indicating a 16-bit

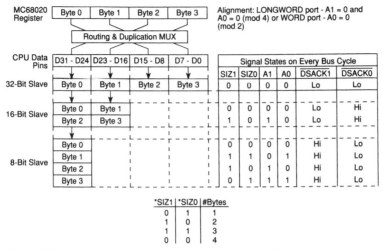

FIGURE 9.3   Aligned long word transfer.

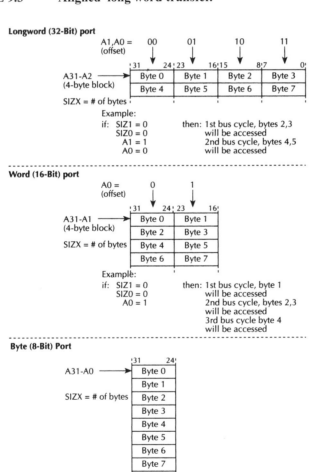

FIGURE 9.4   MC68020 byte addressing.

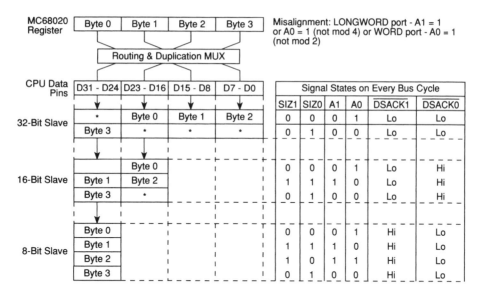

* These bytes must not be overwritten. Therefore, individual data strobes must be generated by external hardware either at the phone or at the 68020.

FIGURE 9.5   **Misaligned long word transfer.**

device. The 68020 then transfers the remaining 16 bits ($0512) via pins D_{31}–D_{16} in the next cycle, requiring a total of two cycles for the transfer.

Finally, if the device is 32-bit, the device receives all 32-bit data $02A10512 via pins D_{31}–D_0 and asserts $\overline{DSACK1}\ \overline{DSACK0}$ = 00 to indicate completion of the transfer. Aligned data transfers for various devices are shown in Figure 9.6.

Next, consider a misaligned transfer such as MOVE.W D1,$02010741 with [D1] = $20F107A4. The 68020 outputs $0707A4XX on its D_{31}-D_0 pins in its first cycle, where the XX are don't cares. Data transfers to various devices are summarized in Figure 9.7.

8-bit device:

		31.......		0 ←—Bit number

Register D1 | 02 | A1 | 05 | 12 |

68020 pins	D_{31}	D_{24}	SIZ1	SIZ0	A_1	A_0	$\overline{DSACK1}$	$\overline{DSACK0}$
First cycle	02		0	0	0	0	1	0
Second cycle	A1		1	1	0	1	1	0
Third cycle	05		1	0	1	0	1	0
Fourth cycle	12		0	1	1	1	1	0

16-bit device:

68020 pins	D_{31} D_{24}	D_{23} D_{16}	SIZ1	SIZ0	A_1	A_0	$\overline{DSACK1}$	$\overline{DSACK0}$
First cycle	02	A1	0	0	0	0	0	1
Second cycle	05	12	1	0	1	0	0	1

32-bit device:

68020 pins	D_{31} ... D_0	SIZ1	SIZ0	A_1	A_0	$\overline{DSACK1}$	$\overline{DSACK0}$
First cycle	02 A1 05 12	0	0	0	0	0	0

FIGURE 9.6   **Aligned data transfers.**

8-bit device:

		31	23	15	7	0	←—Bit number
Register	D1	20	F1	07	A4		

68020 pins	D_{31} D_{24}	SIZ1	SIZ0	A_1	A_0	$\overline{DSACK1}$	$\overline{DSACK0}$
First cycle	07	1	0	0	1	1	0
Second cycle	A4	0	1	1	0	1	0

16-bit device:

68020 pins	D_{31} D_{24}	D_{23} D_{16}	SIZ1	SIZ0	A_1	A_0	$\overline{DSACK1}$	$\overline{DSACK0}$
First cycle		07	1	0	0	1	0	1
Second cycle	A4		0	1	1	0	0	1

32-bit device:

68020 pins	D_{31} D_{24}	D_{23} D_{16}	D_{15} D_8	D_7 D_0	SIZ1	SIZ0	A_1	A_0	$\overline{DSACK1}$	$\overline{DSACK0}$
First cycle		07	A4		1	0	0	1	0	0

FIGURE 9.7   Misaligned data transfers.

(a)   32-bit memory: Note the misaligned transfer for 32-bit memory since $A_1A_0= 11$ for the starting address \$20002053.

68020 pins	D_{31} D_{24}	D_{23} D_{16}	D_{15} D_8	D_7 D_0	SIZ1	SIZ0	A_1	A_0	$\overline{DSACK1}$	$\overline{DSACK0}$
First cycle				50	0	0	1	1	0	0
Second cycle	12	61	24		1	1	0	0	0	0

(b)   16-bit memory

68020 pins	D_{31} D_{24}	D_{23} D_{16}	SIZ1	SIZ0	A_1	A_0	$\overline{DSACK1}$	$\overline{DSACK0}$
First cycle		50	0	0	1	1	0	1
Second cycle	12	61	1	1	0	0	0	1
Third cycle	24		0	1	1	0	0	1

(c)   8-bit memory

68020 pins	D_{31} D_{24}	SIZ1	SIZ0	A_1	A_0	$\overline{DSACK1}$	$\overline{DSACK0}$
First cycle	50	0	0	1	1	1	0
Second cycle	12	1	1	0	0	1	0
Third cycle	61	1	0	0	1	1	0
Fourth cycle	24	0	1	1	0	1	0

FIGURE 9.8   Solution for Example 9.2.

EXAMPLE 9.2   Determine the number of bus cycles, the bytes written to memory (in hex), and signal levels of A_1, A_0, $\overline{DSACK1}$, $\overline{DSACK0}$, SIZ1, and SIZ0 pins that would occur when the instruction MOVE.L   D1,(A0) with [D1] = \$50126124 and [A0] = \$20002053 is executed by the MC68020. Assume:

(a)   32-bit memory
(b)   16-bit memory
(c)   8-bit memory

Solution See Figure 9.8.

9.1.3 68020 Timing Diagrams

Figure 9.9 (a) and (b) show typical 68020 read and write timing diagrams (general form). The read and write cycle parameter specifications are provided in Table 9.7.

Note that in Figure 9.9, signals such as SIZ1, SIZ0, $\overline{\text{DSACK1}}$, $\overline{\text{DSACK0}}$, D_0- D_{31}, A_1, and A_0 which distinguish data transfers between 8-, 16-, and 32-bit devices, are kept in general form. A simplified explanation of the read and write timing diagrams of Figures 9.9 (a) and (b) are provided in the following.

Consider the read timing diagram of Figure 9.9(a). In response to executing a

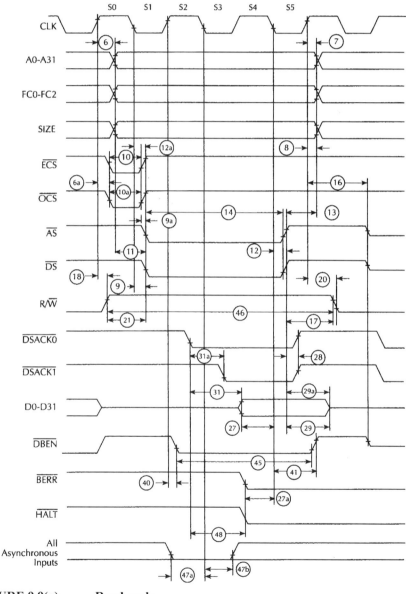

FIGURE 9.9(a) **Read cycle**

read instruction such as MOVE.L $50207080,D0 (address chosen arbitrarily), the 68020 places the 32-bit address on the A_{31}- A_0 pins during S0, outputs LOW on $\overline{AS}$ and $\overline{DS}$ during S1, and places a HIGH on the $R/\overline{W}$ pin during S0, indicating a read operation. The 68020 then samples $\overline{DSACK1}$ and $\overline{DSACK0}$ at the falling edge of S2 (two cycles). The pins $\overline{DSACK1}$ and $\overline{DSACK0}$ are asserted as 00 (32-bit memory) by the external memory using parameter 31a of Table 9.7. Hence, no wait state(s) are required. Assuming that the data is placed on the 68020's D_{31} - D_0 pins, the 68020 reads data approximately at the falling edge of S4 (three cycles). Note that all other relevant 68020 signals required during the read operation shown in Figure 9.9(a) satisfy the timing parameters according to the

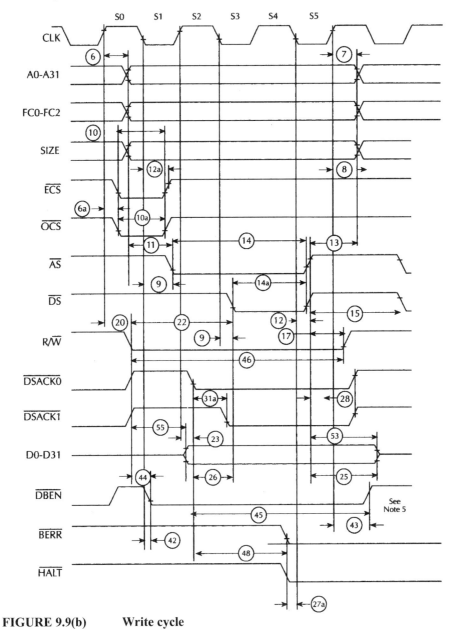

FIGURE 9.9(b)   Write cycle

TABLE 9.7   **Read and Write Cycle Specifications**

Num.	Characteristic	12.5 MHz		16.67 MHz		20 MHz		25 MHz		Unit
		Min	Max	Min	Max	Min	Max	Min	Max	
6	Clock High to Address/FC/Size/$\overline{RMC}$ Valid	0	40	0	30	0	25	0	25	ns
6A	Clock High to $\overline{ECS}$, $\overline{OCS}$ asserted	0	30	0	20	0	15	0	15	ns
7	Clock High to Address/Data/FC/$\overline{RMC}$/Size High Impedance	0	80	0	60	0	50	0	40	ns
8	Clock High to Address/FC/Size/$\overline{RMC}$ Invalid	0	–	0	–	0	–	0	–	ns
9	Clock Low to $\overline{AS}$, $\overline{DS}$ Asserted	3	40	3	30	3	25	3	20	ns
9A[1]	$\overline{AS}$ to $\overline{DS}$ Assertion (Read) (Skew)	-20	20	-15	15	-10	10	-10	10	ns
10	$\overline{ECS}$ Width Asserted	25	–	20	–	15	–	10	–	ns
10A	$\overline{OCS}$ Width Asserted	25	–	20	–	15	–	10	–	ns
10B[7]	$\overline{ECS}$, $\overline{OCS}$ Width Negated	20	–	15	–	10	–	5	–	ns
11[6]	Address/FC/Size/$\overline{RMC}$ Valid to $\overline{AS}$ Asserted (and $\overline{DS}$ Asserted, Read)	20	–	15	–	10	–	5	–	ns
12	Clock Low to $\overline{AS}$, $\overline{DS}$ Negated	0	40	0	30	0	25	0	20	ns
12A	Clock Low to $\overline{ECS}$, $\overline{OCS}$ Negated	0	40	0	30	0	25	0	20	ns
13	AS, DS Negated to Addess/FC/Size/$\overline{RMC}$ Invalid	20	–	15	–	10	–	5	–	ns
14	$\overline{AS}$ (and $\overline{DS}$ Read) Width Asserted	120	–	100	–	85	–	65	–	ns
14A	$\overline{DS}$ Width Asserted, Write	50	–	40	–	38	–	30	–	ns
15	$\overline{AS}$, $\overline{DS}$ Width Negated	50	–	40	–	38	–	30	–	ns
15A[8]	$\overline{DS}$ Negated to $\overline{AS}$ Assertedd	45	–	35	–	30	–	25	–	ns
16	Clock High to $\overline{AS}/\overline{DS}/R/W/\overline{DBEN}$ High Impedance	–	80	–	60	–	50	–	40	ns
17[6]	$\overline{AS}$, $\overline{DS}$ Negated to R/W High	20	–	15	–	10	–	5	–	ns
18	Clock High to R/W High	0	40	0	30	0	25	0	20	ns
20	Clock High to R/W Low	0	40	0	30	0	25	0	20	ns
21[6]	R/W High to $\overline{AS}$ Asserted	20	–	–	–	–	–	–	–	ns
22[6]	R/W Low to $\overline{DS}$ Asserted (Write)	90	–	–	–	–	–	–	–	ns
23	Clock High to Data Out Valid	–	–	–	–	–	–	–	–	ns
25[6]	$\overline{AS}$, $\overline{DS}$ Negated to Data Out Invalid	20	–	15	–	10	–	5	–	ns
25A[9]	$\overline{DS}$ Negated to $\overline{DBEN}$ Negated (Write)	20	–	15	–	10	–	5	–	ns
26[6]	Date out Valid to $\overline{DS}$ Asserted (Write)	20	–	15	–	10	–	5	–	ns
27	Data-In Invalid to Clock Low (Data Setup)	10	–	5	–	5	–	5	–	ns
27A	Late $\overline{BERR}/\overline{HALD}$ Asserted to Clock Low Setup Time	25	–	20	–	15	–	10	–	ns
28	$\overline{AS}$, $\overline{DS}$ Negated to DSACKx/BERR/HALT/AVEC Negated	0	110	0	80	0	65	0	50	ns
29	$\overline{DS}$ Negated to Data-In Invalid (Date-In Hold Time)	0	–	0	–	0	–	0	–	ns
29A	$\overline{DS}$ Negated to Data-In (High Impedance)	–	80	–	60	–	50	–	40	ns
31[2]	DSACKx Asserted to Data-In Invalid	–	60	–	50	–	43	–	32	ns
31A[3]	DSACKx Asserted to $\overline{DSACKx}$ Valid ($\overline{DSACK}$ Asserted Skew)	–	20	–	15	–	10	–	10	ns

specifications of Table 9.7.

Next, consider the write timing diagram of Figure 9.9(b). In response to executing a write instruction such as MOVE.L D0,$50708000 (address arbitrarily chosen), the 68020 outputs the 32-bit address on the A_{31}- A_0 pins during S0, outputs LOW on $\overline{AS}$ during S2, and places a LOW on the R/$\overline{W}$ pin during S0, indicating a write operation. The 68020 then samples $\overline{DSACK1}$ and $\overline{DSACK0}$ at the falling edge of S2 (two cycles). The pins $\overline{DSACK1}$ and $\overline{DSACK0}$ are asserted as 00 (32-bit memory) by the external memory using parameter 31a of Table 9.7. The 68020 places data on its D_{31} - D_0 pins during S2, and then asserts $\overline{DS}$ LOW using parameter 26 of Table 9.7. The external memory then writes the data into the addressed memory location. Note that all other relevant 68020 signals required during the write operation shown in Figure 9.9 (b) satisfy the timing parameters according to the specifications of Table 9.7.

TABLE 9.7   cont.

Num.	Characteristic		12.5 MHz		16.67 MHz		20 MHz		25 MHz		Unit
			Min	Max	Min	Max	Min	Max	Min	Max	
32	RESET Input Transition Time		–	1.5	–	1.5	–	1.5	–	1.5	Chks
33	Clock Low to BG Asserted		0	40	0	30	0	25	0	20	ns
34	Clock Low to BG Negated		0	40	0	30	0	25	0	20	ns
35	BR Asserted to BG Asserted (RMC Not Asserted)		1.5	3.5	1.5	3.5	1.5	3.5	1.5	3.5	Chks
37	BGACK Asserted to BG Negated		1.5	3.5	1.5	3.5	1.5	3.5	1.5	3.5	Chks
37A	BGACK Asserted to BR Negated		0	1.5	0	1.5	0	1.5	0	1.5	Chks
39	BG Width Negated		120	–	90	–	75	–	60	–	ns
39A	BG Width Asserted		120	–	90	–	75	–	60	–	ns
40	Clock High to DBEN Asserted (Read)		0	40	0	30	0	25	0	20	ns
41	Clock High to DBEN Negated (Read)		0	40	0	30	0	25	0	20	ns
42	Clock Low to DBEN Asserted (Write)		0	40	0	30	0	25	0	20	ns
43	Clock Low to DBEN Netgated (Write)		0	40	0	30	0	25	0	20	ns
44[6]	R/W Low to DBEN Asserted (Write)		20	–	15	–	10	–	5	–	ns
45[6]	DBEN Width Asserted	Read	80	–	60	–	50	–	40	–	ns
		Write	160		120		100		80		
46	R/W Width Asserted (Write and Read)			–		–		–		–	ns
47A	Asynchronous Input Setup Time		180	–	150	–	125	–	100	–	ns
47B	Asynchronous Input Hold Time		10	–	5	–	5	–	5	–	ns
48[4]	DSACKs Asserted to BERR/HALT Asserted		–	35	–	30	–	25	–	20	ns
53	Date Out Hold from Clock High		0	–	0	–	0	–	0	–	ns
55	R/W Asserted to Data Bus Inpedance Changes		40	–	30	–	25	–	20	–	ns
56	RESET Pulse Width (Reset Instruction)		512	–	512	–	512	–	512	–	Chks
57	BERR Negated to HALT Negated (Rerun)		0	–	0	–	0	–	0	–	ns
58[10]	BGACK Negated to Bus Driven		1	–	1	–	1	–	1	–	Chks
59[10]	BG Negated to Bus Driven		1	–	1	–	1	–	1	–	Chks

Notes:
1. This number can be reduced to 5 nanoseconds if strobes have equal loads.
2. If the asynchronous setup time (#47) requirements are satisfied, the DSACKx low to data setup time (#31) and DSACKx low to BERR low setup time (#48) can be ignored. The data must only satisfy the data-in to clock low setup time (#27) for the following clock cycle. BERR must only satisfy the late BERR low to clock low setup time (#27A) for the following clock cycle.
3. This parameter specifies the maximum allowable skew between DSACK0 to DSACK1 asserted or DSACK1 to DSACK0 asserted, specification #47 must be met by DSACK0 to DSACK1.
4. In absence of DSACKx, BERR is an asynchronous input using the asynchronous input setup time (#47).
5. DBEN may stay asserted on consecutive write cycles.
6. Actual value depends on the clock input waveform.
7. This is a new specification that indicates the minimum high time for ECS and OCS in the event of an internal cache hit followed immediately by a cache miss or operand cycle.
8. This is a new specification that guarantees operation with the MC68881, which specifies a minimum time for DS negated to AS asserted (specification #13A). Without this specification, incorrect interpretation of specifications #9A and #15 would indicated that the MC68020 does not meet the MC68881 requirements.
9. This is a new specification that allows a system designer to guarantee data hold times on the output side of data buffers that have output enable signals generated with DBEN.
10. These are new specifications that allow system designers to guarantee that an alternate bus master has stopped driving the bus when the MC68020 regains control of the bus after an arbitration sequence.

9.2   68020 System Design

This section contains 68020 interfacing to 27C256 EPROM, LH62256C/CH SRAM, and 68230 I/O chips. Memory and I/O maps are also determined. As mentioned before, the 68020 uses only asynchronous bus cycles in which $\overline{DS}$, $\overline{DSACK1}$, and $\overline{DSACK0}$ pins are used as handshaking signals   for data transfers. Also, for 16-bit or 32-bit memory or I/O

TABLE 9.8   Decoding Guide

68000 Address Pins		Chip Selected
A_{17}	A_{18}	
0	0	27C256
0	1	2256C/CH
1	N.C	68230

Note: N.C. Not Connected (A_{18} is not connected to 68230)

chips, the correct byte enable must be produced to ensure that appropriate memory or I/O chip(s) is enabled.

Note that both supervisor and user memory are needed for multitasking or multiuser systems. However, one can design memory without using the FC2, FC1, and FC0 pins in memory decoding logic for a single application or for systems requiring no operating systems. In that case, the 68000 will always operate in the supervisor mode. Upon hardware reset, the 68020 will operate in the supervisor mode and will continue to operate in that mode.

9.2.1 Memory Decode Logic for Memory and I/O

In the following, an 8-MHz 68020 is used. The system will contain four 27C256s (32K × 8 HCMOS EPROM with 120-ns access time) and four LH2256C/CHs (32K x 8 CMOS SRAM with 70 ns speed). Because EPROM or SRAM is 32 kB wide, the 68020 address lines A_2–A_{16} are used to address the EPROMs or SRAMs. The 68020 SIZ1, SIZ0, A_1, A_0, DSACK1, and DSACK0 pins are utilized for selecting the memory chips.

Since the 68000 uses memory-mapped I/O, an unused address pin must be used to distinguish between memory and I/O. To keep things simple, only one 68230 is used in this design. The 68020 A_{17} pin will be used to select memory or I/O. $A_{17} = 0$ will select the memory chips and $A_{17} = 1$ will select the I/O chip. The 68020 A_{18}, on the other hand, will be used to select EPROM or SRAM. $A_{18} = 0$ will select 27C256, whereas $A_{18} = 1$ will select 2256C/CH. Pins A_{17} and A_{18} are chosen arbitrarily. The memory and I/O decoding is listed in Table 9.8.

To manipulate memory configuration, 32-bit data bus control byte enable logic is incorporated to generate byte enable signals ($\overline{DBBE1}$, $\overline{DBBE2}$, $\overline{DBBE3}$, and $\overline{DBBE4}$). These byte enables are generated by using 68020's SIZ1, SIZ0, A_1, A_0, and $\overline{DS}$ pins, as shown

TABLE 9.9   Memory Enables for 32-Bit Memory

SIZ1	SIZ0	A_1	A_0	DBBE11	DBBE22	DBBE33	DBBE44
0	1	0	0	1	0	0	0
		0	1	0	1	0	0
		1	0	0	0	1	0
		1	1	0	0	0	1
1	0	0	0	1	1	0	0
		0	1	0	1	1	0
		1	0	0	0	1	1
		1	1	0	0	0	1
1	1	0	0	1	1	1	0
		0	1	0	1	1	1
		1	0	0	0	1	1
		1	1	0	0	0	1
0	0	0	0	1	1	1	1
		0	1	0	1	1	1
		1	0	0	0	1	1
		1	1	0	0	0	1

in the individual logic diagrams of the byte enable logic. An FPGA can be programmed to implement this logic.

Table 9.9 shows the memory enables for the 32-bit memory. Figure 9.10 shows the K-maps for the enable logic. A logic diagram can be drawn for generating the memory byte enable signals $\overline{DBBE1}$, $\overline{DBBE2}$, $\overline{DBBE3}$, and $\overline{DBBE4}$.

9.2.2   68020-27C256 Interface

The 68020 system with 32-bit EPROM consists of four 27C256s, each connected to its associated portion of the system data bus ($D_{31}-D_{24}$, $D_{23}-D_{16}$, $D_{15}-D_8$, and D_7-D_0). 68020 pins A_2 through A_{16} are connected to A_0 through A_{14} of each 27C256. For example, 68020 A_2 is connected to A_0 of 27C256s, 68020 A_3 to A_1 of the 27C256s, and so on. A schematic of the 68020–27C256 interface is shown in Figure 9.11. Linear decoding is used for selecting memory banks to enable the appropriate memory chips. Figure 9.12 obtained from Figure 9.11 shows the 68020 interface to EPROM #1. The 27C256 memory map can be determined from Figure 9.12 as follows:

EPROM #1

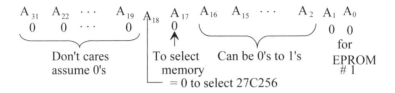

Note that the A_0 pin of EPROM # 1 is connected to the 68020 A_2 pin, A1 pin of EPROM # 1 is connected to the 68020 A_3 pin, and so on. Hence the address range for EPROM #1: $\$00000000$, $\$00000004$, … , $\$0001FFFC$ and the 27C256 memory map:

EPROM #1 $\$00000000$, $\$00000004$, …, $\$0001FFFC$
EPROM #2 $\$00000001$, $\$00000005$, …, $\$0001FFFD$
EPROM #3 $\$00000002$, $\$00000006$, …, $\$0001FFFE$
EPROM #4 $\$00000003$, $\$00000007$, …, $\$0001FFFF$

$\overline{DSACK1}$ and $\overline{DSACK0}$ are generated by ANDing the $\overline{DBBE1}$, $\overline{DBBE2}$, $\overline{DBBE3}$, and $\overline{DBBE4}$ outputs of the byte enable logic circuit. When one or more EPROM chips are selected, the appropriate enables ($\overline{DBBE1}$– $\overline{DBBE4}$) will be low, thus asserting $\overline{DSACK1}$ = 0 and $\overline{DSACK0}$ = 0. This will tell the 68020 that the memory is 32 bits wide. Data from the selected memory chip(s) will be placed on the appropriate data pins of the 68020.

Let us discuss the timing requirements of the 68020-27C256 system. In response to execution of a READ instruction such as MOVE.L $\$00001234$,D0, the 68020 checks $\overline{DSACK1}$ and $\overline{DSACK0}$ for LOW at the falling edge of S2 (two cycles). From the 68020 timing diagram (in the Motorola manual), $\overline{AS}$, $\overline{DS}$, and all other output signals used in memory decoding go to LOW at the end of approximately one clock cycle. For an 8-MHz 68020 clock, each cycle is 125 ns. From byte enable logic diagrams, a maximum of four gate delays (40 ns) are required. Therefore, the EPROM(s) selected will be enabled after 165 ns (125 ns + 40 ns). With a 90-ns access time for the 27C256, the EPROM(s) will place data on the output lines after approximately 255 ns (165 ns + 90 ns). With an 8-MHz 68020

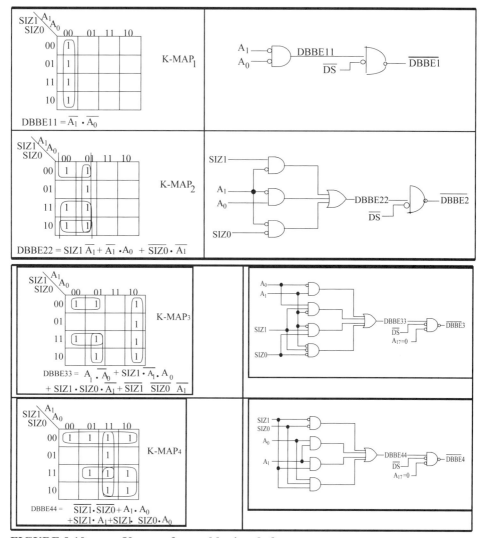

FIGURE 9.10 **K-maps for enable signals for memory.**

clock, $\overline{\text{DSACK1}}$ and $\overline{\text{DSACK0}}$ will be checked for LOW (32-bit memory) after two cycles (250 ns), and if LOW, the 68020 will latch data after three cycles (375 ns). Hence, no delay circuit is required for $\overline{\text{DSACK1}}$ and $\overline{\text{DSACK0}}$. In case a delay circuit is required for the 68020 with a higher clock frequency, a ring counter can be used.

9.2.3 68020- 2256C/CH (SRAM) Interface

The Sharp LH2256C/CH is a 32K x 8 CMOS SRAM. The 2256C/CH READ and WRITE operations are decoded shown in Table 9.10. The 68020 system with 32-bit SRAM consists of four 2256C/CHs, each connected to its associated portion of the system data bus (D_{31}–D_{24}, D_{23}–D_{16}, D_{15}–D_8, and D_7–D_0). 68020 pins A_2 through A_{16} are connected to A_0 through A_{14} of each 2256C/CH. For example, 68020 A_2 is connected to A_0 of the 2256C/CHs , 68020 A_3 to A_1 of the 2256C/CHs, and so on. A schematic of the 68020–2256C/CH interface is shown in Figure 9.13.

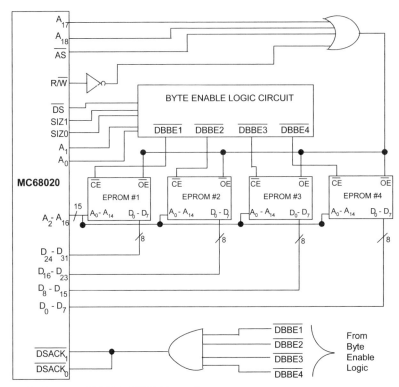

FIGURE 9.11   68020-27C256 interface.

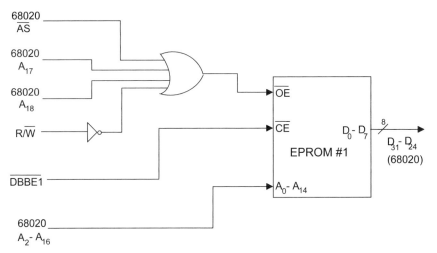

FIGURE 9. 12   68020 interface to EPROM #1.

TABLE 9.10   Decoding Guide

$\overline{CS}$	$\overline{OE}$	$\overline{WE}$	Operation performed
L	L	H	READ
L	X	L	WRITE

Note: X means don't care.

Linear decoding is used for selecting memory banks to enable the appropriate memory chips. Figure 9.14 obtained from Figure 9.13 shows the 68020 interface to SRAM #1. The SRAM #1 memory map can be determined from Figure 9.14 as follows:

SRAM #1

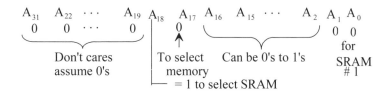

Note that the A_0 pin of SRAM # 1 is connected to the 68020's A_2 pin, the A_1 pin of SRAM # 1 is connected to the 68020's A_3 pin, and so on. Hence, the address range for SRAM #1: \$00040000, \$00040004, ... , \$0005FFFC.

Hence, the 62256C memory map:

$$
\begin{array}{ll}
\text{SRAM \#1} & \$00040000, \$00040004, \ldots, \$0005FFFC \\
\text{SRAM \#2} & \$00040001, \$00040005, \ldots, \$0005FFFD \\
\text{SRAM\#3} & \$00040002, \$00040006, \ldots, \$0005FFFE \\
\text{SRAM \#4} & \$00040003, \$00040007, \ldots, \$0005FFFF
\end{array}
$$

As with EPROMs, $\overline{\text{DSACK1}}$ and $\overline{\text{DSACK0}}$ are generated by ANDing the $\overline{\text{DBBE1}}$, $\overline{\text{DBBE2}}$, $\overline{\text{DBBE3}}$, and $\overline{\text{DBBE4}}$ outputs of the byte enable logic circuit. When one or more SRAM chips are selected, the appropriate enables ($\overline{\text{DBBE1}}$–$\overline{\text{DBBE4}}$) will be low, thus asserting $\overline{\text{DSACK1}} = 0$ and $\overline{\text{DSACK0}} = 0$. This will tell the 68020 that the memory is 32 bits wide. Data from the memory chip(s) selected will be placed on the appropriate data pins of the 68020. Also, it can be shown that no delay circuits for $\overline{\text{DSACK1}}$ and $\overline{\text{DSACK0}}$ are required since the 2256C/CH has read and write times of 70 ns each.

9.2.4   68020 Programmed I/O

The 68020 I/O-handling features are very similar to those of the 68000. This means that the 68020 uses memory-mapped I/O, and the 68230 I/O chip can be used for programmed I/O. In the hardware schematic for the 68020-68230 interface shown in Figure 9.15, A_{17} is chosen to be HIGH to select the 68230 chip so that the port addresses are different from the 68020 reset vector addresses $00000000_{16} - 00000006_{16}$. The 68230 $\overline{\text{DTACK}}$ is an open-drain output. Hence, a pull-up resistor is required. $\overline{\text{DTACK}}$ is used to assert $\overline{\text{DSACK1}}$ $\overline{\text{DSACK0}} = 10$ for indicating 8-bit I/O. Table 9.11 shows some of the 68230 register definitions.

Let us now determine the I/O map. Note that A_{31} through A_{18} ,and A_{16} through A_5 are don't cares and are assumed to be 0's in the following. Also, $A_{17}= 1$ for I/O. Hence, from the figure, addresses for registers PGCR (R0), PADDR (R2), PBDDR (R3), PACR (R6), PBCR (R7), PADR (R8), and PBDR (R9) can be obtained as shown below. For example, consider PGCR as follows:

$$
\begin{array}{ccccccccccc}
A_{31} & \cdots & A_{21} & \cdots & A_{17} & \cdots & A_5 & A_4 & A_3 & A_2 & A_1 & A_0 \\
0 & 0 & 0 & 1 & & 0 & 0 & 0 & 0 & 0 & 0
\end{array} = \$00020000
$$

RS5 - RS1

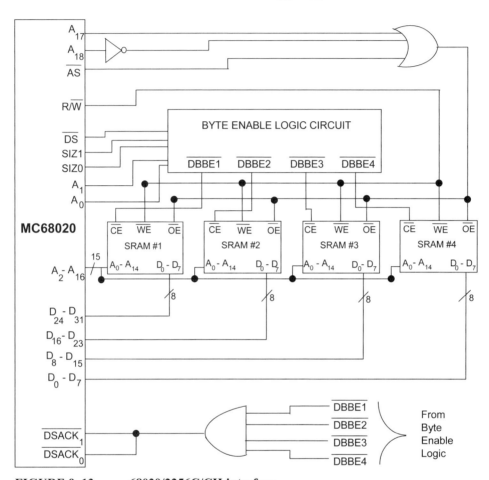

FIGURE 9. 13   68020/2256C/CH interface.

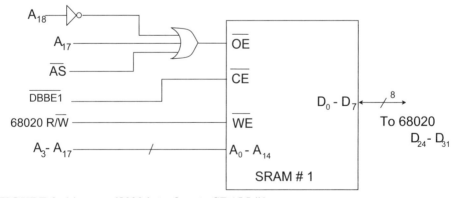

FIGURE 9. 14   68020 interface to SRAM #1.

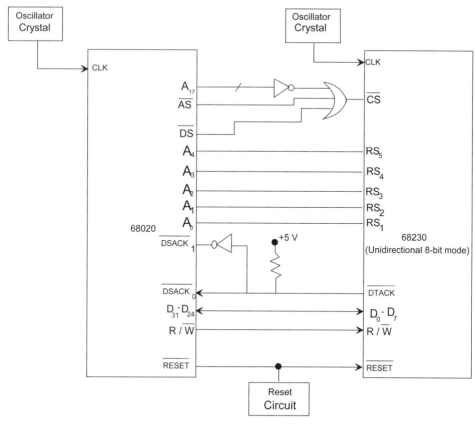

FIGURE 9.15   **68020/68230 interface.**

Therefore, address for PGCR = $00020000. Similarly, address for PADDR = $00020002, address for PBDDR = $00020003, address for PACR = $00020006, address for PBCR = $00020007 address for PADR   = $00020008,   address for PBDR = $00020009.

As an example, the following instruction sequence will select mode 0, submode 1X, and configure bits 0–5 of Port A as outputs, bits 6 and 7 of Port A as inputs, and port B as an input port:

TABLE 9.11   **Some 68230 Registers**

Register Select Bits					Register Selected
RS5	RS4	RS3	RS2	RS1	
0	0	0	0	0	PGCR, port general control register (R0)
0	0	0	1	0	PADDR, port A data direrction register (R2)
0	0	0	1	1	PBDDR, port B data direction register (R3)
0	0	1	1	0	PACR, port A control register (R6)
0	0	1	1	1	PBCR, port B control register (R7)
0	1	0	0	0	PADR, port A data register (R8)
0	1	0	0	1	PBDR, port B data register (R9)

```
PGCR      EQU               $00020000
PADDR     EQU               $00020002
PBDDR     EQU               $00020003
PACR      EQU               $00020006
PBCR      EQU               $00020007
ANDI.B    #$3F,PGCR     ;   Select mode 0
BSET.B    #7,PACR       ;   Port A bit I/O submode
BSET.B    #7,PBCR       ;   Port B bit I/O submode
MOVE.B    #$3F,PADDR    ;   Configure port A bits 0-5 as
                        ;   outputs and bits 6 and 7 as inputs
MOVE.B    #$00,PBDDR    ;   Configure port B as an input port
```

9.3   68020 Exception processing

The 68020 exceptions are functionally similar to those of the 68000 with some minor variations. The 68020 exceptions can be generated by external or internal causes. Externally generated exceptions include interrupts, bus errors, reset, and coprocessor-detected errors. Internally generated exceptions are caused by certain instructions, address errors, tracing, and breakpoints. Instructions that may cause internal exceptions as part of their instruction execution are CHK, CHK2, CALLM, RTM, RTE, DIV, and all variations of the TRAP instructions. In addition, illegal instructions, privilege violations, and coprocessor violations cause exceptions. Table 9.12 lists the priority and characteristics of all 68020 exceptions.

The 68020 exception processing is similar to the 68000 with some minor variations. In the 68020, exception processing occurs in four steps and varies according to the cause of the exception. The four steps are summarized below:

1.   An internal copy is made of the SR, and the S-bit set is to 1 for exception processing. This means that the 68020 enters the supervisor state and tracing is disabled.

2.   The vector number of the exception vector is determined from either the exception-requesting peripheral (nonautovector) or internally upon assertion of the $\overline{\text{AVEC}}$ (autovector) input. Note that in the 68000, $\overline{\text{VPA}}$ is asserted for autovectoring. The VBR register points to the base of the 1-kB exception vector table, which contains 256 exception vectors. The 68020 uses exception vectors as memory pointers to fetch the starting address of service routines that handle the various exceptions.

3.   The processor saves PC and SR onto the supervisor stack. For coprocessor exceptions, additional internal state information is saved on the stack as well.

4.   The final step is the same for all exceptions. The exception vector is determined by multiplying the vector number by 4, and adding it to the contents of the VBR to determine the memory address of the exception vector. The PC (and ISP for reset exception) is loaded with the exception vector. The instruction located at the address given in the exception vector is fetched and the exception-handling routine is thus executed.

Exception processing saves certain information on the top of the supervisor stack. This information is called the *exception stack frame.*

The 68020 provides six different stack frames. The sizes of these frames vary from four words to 46 words depending on the exception. For example, the normal four-word stack frame is generated by exceptions such as interrupts and privilege violations. A six-word stack frame is generated by instruction-related exceptions such as CHK/CHK2 and zero divide.

The 68020 utilizes the concept of two supervisor stacks pointed to by MSP and

ISP. The M-bit (when S = 1) determines the active supervisor stack pointer. The 68020 accesses MSP when S = 1, M = 0. The MSP can be used for program traps and other exceptions, while the ISP can be used for interrupts. The use of two supervisor stacks allows isolation of user processes or tasks and asynchronous supervisor I/O tasks.

The 68020 $\overline{IPL2}$, $\overline{IPL1}$, $\overline{IPL0}$, $\overline{AVEC}$, and $\overline{IPEND}$ pins are used as the 68020 hardware interrupt control signals (Figure 9.16). Like the 68000, the 68020 supports seven levels of prioritized interrupts encoded by using the $\overline{IPL2}$, $\overline{IPL1}$, and $\overline{IPL0}$ pins.

In Figure 9.16, when interrupting priority levels 1 through 6 are requested, the 68020 compares the interrupt level (inverted interrupt pins) to the interrupt mask to determine whether the interrupt should be processed. An interrupt recognized as valid does not force immediate exception processing; a valid interrupt causes $\overline{IPEND}$ to be asserted, signaling to external devices that the 68020 has an interrupt pending. The deskew logic in Figure 9.17 continuously samples the $\overline{IPL2}$, $\overline{IPL1}$, and $\overline{IPL0}$ pins on every falling edge of the clock , but deskews or latches an interrupt request when it remains at the same level for two consecutive falling edges of the input clock. Figure 9.17 gives an example of the 68020 interrupt deskewing logic.

Whenever the 68020 reaches an instruction execution boundary, it checks for a pending interrupt. If it finds one, the 68020 begins an exception processing and executes an interrupt acknowledge cycle with FC2, FC1, FC0 = 111, and $A_{19},A_{18},A_{17},A_{16}$ = 1111. The 68020 basic hardware interrupt sequence is shown in Figure 9.18.

Figure 9.19 shows the interrupt acknowledge flowchart. Before the interrupt acknowledge cycle is completed, the 68020 must receive either $\overline{AVEC}$, $\overline{DSACKX}$, or $\overline{BERR}$; otherwise, it will execute wait states until one of these input pins is activated externally.

If $\overline{AVEC}$ is asserted, the 68020 obtains the vector address internally (autovectored) automatically. If the 68020 $\overline{DSACKX}$ pins are asserted, the 68020 takes an 8-bit vector from the appropriate data lines ($D_7 - D_0$ pins for a 32-bit device, $D_{23}-D_{16}$ pins for a 16-bit device, $D_{31}-D_{24}$ pins for an 8-bit device). These are *nonautovectored interrupts*, and the 68020 obtains the interrupt vector address by adding VBR with 4 * (8-bit vector).

Figure 9.20 shows an example of autovectored and nonautovectored interrupt logic. Finally, if $\overline{BERR}$ is asserted, the interrupt is considered spurious and the 68020 assigns the appropriate vector number for handling this.

9.4   68020-based Voltmeter

A 68020-based voltmeter is designed in this section. A 68020/27C256/62256/68230-based microcomputer is used to implement the voltmeter to measure voltage in the range 0 to 5 V and display the result in two decimal digits: one integer part and one fractional part. The microcomputer will contain 16-bit I/O and will use two 68230 I/O chips; one containing even port addresses and the other containing odd port addresses. Three 8-bit I/O ports are used in the design. The two 8-bit ports (ports A and B) of the even 68230, and the 8-bit port (port A) of the odd 68230 will be used.

The 68230 port addresses are chosen arbitrarily and are given below.

- *Ports used from the even 68230:*   PGCR = $00002000, PACR = $0000200C, PBCR = $0000200E, PADDR = $00002004, PBDDR = $00002006, PADR = $00002010 = port A, and PBDR = $00002012 = port B.

TABLE 9.12   Exception Priorities and Recognition Times

Exception priorities			Time of recognition
Group 0	.0	Reset	End of clock cycle
Group 1	.0	Address error	
	.1	Bus error	
Group 2	.0	BKPT #N, CALLM, CHK, CHK2, cp TRAPcc	Within an instruction cycle
		cp mid-instruction	
		cp protocol violation, divide-by-zero, RTE,	
		RTM, TRAP #N, TRAPV	
Group 3	.0	Illegal instruction, unimplemented LINE F,	Before instruction cycle begins
		LINE A, privilege violation, cp preinstruction	
Group 4	.0	cp post-instruction	End of instruction cycle
	.1	Trace	
	.2	Interrupt	

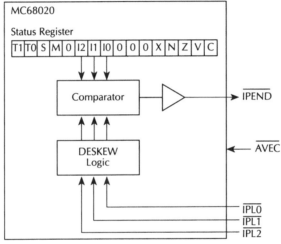

FIGURE 9.16   68020 interrupt control signals.

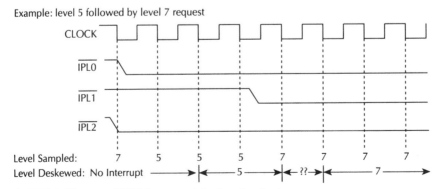

FIGURE 9.17   68020 interrupt deskewing logic.

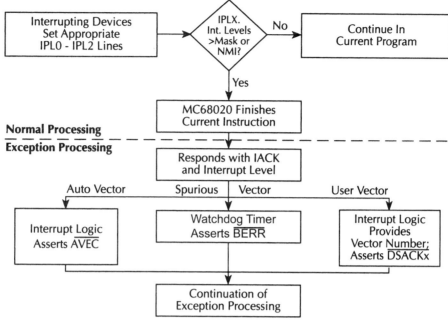

FIGURE 9.18   **68020 basic hardware interrupt sequence.**

•   *Ports used from the odd 68230:*   PGCR1 = $00002001, PACR1 = $0000200D, PADDR1= $00002005, and PADR1 = $00002011 = port AA.

     The 68020-based voltmeter will be designed using both programmed I/O, and interrupt I/O (nonmaskable and maskable).

9.4.1   Voltmeter Design Using Programmed I/O

Figure 9.21 shows the schematic of the voltmeter using the 68020-based microcomputer. The microcomputer is required to start the A/D converter at the falling edge of a pulse via bit

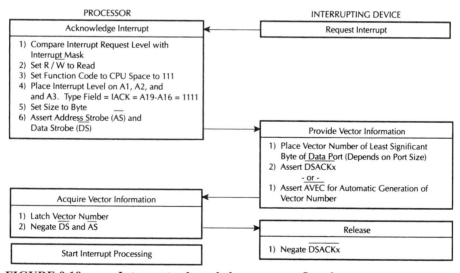

FIGURE 9.19   **Interrupt acknowledge sequence flowchart.**

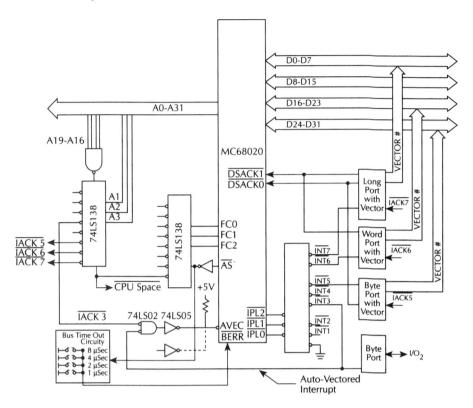

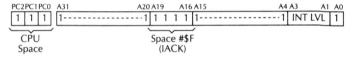

FIGURE 9.20   **68020 autovectored and nonautovectored interrupt logic.**

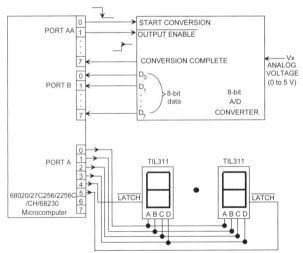

FIGURE 9.21   **68020-based voltmeter using programmed I/O.**

0 of port AA. When the conversion is completed, the A/D's CONVERSION COMPLETE signal will go to HIGH. During the conversion, the A/D's CONVERSION COMPLETE signal stays LOW.

Using programmed I/O, the microcomputer will poll the A/D's CONVERSION COMPLETE signal. When the conversion is completed, the microcomputer will send a LOW on the A/D converter's OUTPUT ENABLE line via bit 1 to port AA and then input the 8-bit output from A/D via port B and display the voltage (0 to 5 V) in two decimal digits (one integer and one fractional) via port A on two TIL 311 displays. Note that the TIL 311 has an on-chip BCD-to-seven-segment decoder. The microcomputer will output each decimal digit on the common lines (bits 0–3 of port A) connected to the ABCD inputs ('A' is the least significant bit and 'D' is the most significant bit) of the displays. Each display will be enabled by outputting LOW on each LATCH line in sequence (one after another) so that the input voltage V_x (0 to 5 V) will be displayed with one integer part and one fractional part. A 68020 assembly language program will accomplish this.

Because the maximum decimal value that can be accommodated in 8 bits is 255_{10} (FF_{16}), the maximum voltage of 5 V will be equivalent to 255_{10}. This means the display in decimal is given by

$$D = 5 \times (\text{input}/255)$$

$$= \text{input}/51$$

$$= \underbrace{\text{quotient}}_{\text{Integer part}} + \text{remainder}$$

This gives the integer part. The fractional part in decimal is

$$F = (\text{remainder}/51) \times 10$$

$$\simeq (\text{remainder})/5$$

For example, suppose that the decimal equivalent of the 8-bit output of A/D is 200.

$$D = 200/51 \Rightarrow quotient = 3, remainder = 47$$

$$\text{integer part } = 3$$

$$\text{fractional part}, F = 47/5 = 9$$

Therefore, the display will show 3.9 V. The 68020 assembly language program using programmed I/O can be written as follows:

PGCR	EQU	$00002000
PACR	EQU	$0000200C
PBCR	EQU	$0000200E
PADDR	EQU	$00002004
PBDDR	EQU	$00002006
PORTA	EQU	$00002010
PORTB	EQU	$00002012
PGCR1	EQU	$00002001
PACR1	EQU	$0000200D

PADDR1	EQU	$00002005		
PORTAA	EQU	$00002011		
	ANDI.B	#$3F,PGCR	;	Select mode 0
	BSET.B	#7,PACR	;	port A bit I/O
,	BSET.B	#7,PBCR	;	port B bit I/O
	MOVE.B	#$FF,PADDR	;	Configure port A as an output port
	MOVE.B	#0,PBDDR	;	Configure port B as an input port
	ANDI.B	#$3F,PGCR1	;	Select mode 0
	BSET.B	#7,PACR1	;	port AA bit I/O
	MOVE.B	#$03,PADDR1	;	Configure port AA
	MOVE.B	#3,D0	;	Send 1 to START pin of A/D
	MOVE.B	D0,PORTAA	;	and 1 to ($\overline{\text{OUTPUT ENABLE}}$)
	MOVE.B	#2,D0	;	Send 0 to start pin
	MOVE.B	D0,PORTAA	;	of A/D
BEGIN	MOVE.B	PORTAA,D0	;	Check conversion
	LSL.B	#1,D0	;	Complete bit for HIGH
	BCC	BEGIN		
	MOVE.B	#0,D0	;	Send LOW to ($\overline{\text{OUTPUT ENABLE}}$)
	MOVE.B	D0,PORTAA		
	MOVE.B	PORTB,D1	;	Input A/D data
	ANDI.L	#$000000FF,D1	;	Convert input data to 32-bit
			;	unsigned number in D1
	DIVU.W	#51,D1	;	Convert data to
			;	integer part
	MOVE.W	D1,D2	;	Save quotient (integer) in D2
	SWAP.W	D1	;	Move remainder to low word of D1
	ANDI.L	#$000000FF,D1	;	Convert remainder to unsigned
			;	32-bit number
	DIVU	#5,D1	;	Convert data to fractional part
			;	Quotient (fraction) is in D1.W
	ORI.W	#$20,D2	;	Disable fractional display
	ANDI.W	#$2F,D2	;	Enable integer display
	MOVE.B	D2,PORTA	;	Display integer part
	ORI.W	#$10,D1	;	Disable integer display
	ANDI.W	#$1F,D1	;	Enable fractional display
	MOVE.B	D1,PORTA	;	Display fractional part
FINISH	JMP	FINISH		

9.4.2 Voltmeter Design Using Interrupt I/O

In this section the 68020-based voltmeter is designed using interrupt I/O (both nonmaskable and maskable). The main program is written to initialize the 68230 control registers and then start the A/D. The service routine will input the A/D data, display the result, and stop. A 68020 assembly language program is written for both the main program and the service routine.

Using Autovector Level 7 (Nonmaskable Interrupt)   Figure 9.22 shows the pertinent connections for Autovector level 7 interrupt. The A/D CONVERSION COMPLETE signal is inverted, and then connected to 68020 $\overline{IPL2}$ $\overline{IPL1}$ $\overline{IPL0}$ pins and to the $\overline{AVEC}$ pin. Note that all addresses selectable by the user are chosen arbitrarily in the following.

The main programs and service routines are written at addresses $00005000 and $00016000, respectively. Also, the interrupt stack pointer A7' is initialized at $00006500. These addresses are chosen arbitrarily. The main program in 68020 assembly language is shown below.

PGCR	EQU	$00002000		
PACR	EQU	$0000200C		
PBCR	EQU	$0000200E		
PADDR	EQU	$00002004		
PBDDR	EQU	$00002006		
PORTA	EQU	$00002010		
PORTB	EQU	$00002012		
PGCR1	EQU	$00002001		
PACR1	EQU	$0000200D		
PADDR1	EQU	$00002005		
PORTAA	EQU	$00002011		
	ORG	$00005000	;	Main program starting address
	ANDI.B	#$3F,PGCR	;	Select mode 0

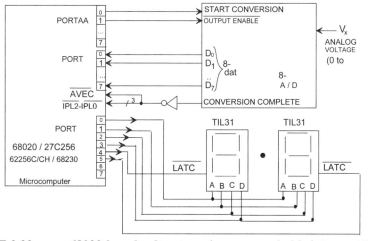

FIGURE 9.22   **68020-based voltmeter using nonmaskable interrupt I/O.**

```
            BSET.B    #7,PACR        ;   port A bit I/O
            BSET.B    #7,PBCR        ;   port B bit I/O
            MOVE.B    #$FF,PADDR     ;   Configure port A as an output port
            MOVE.B    #0,PBDDR       ;   Configure port B as an input port
            ANDI.B    #$3F,PGCR1     ;   Select mode 0
            BSET.B    #7,PACR1       ;   port AA bit I/O
            MOVE.B    #$03,PADDR1    ;   Configure port AA
            MOVE.B    #3,D0          ;   Send 1 to START pin of A/D
            MOVE.B    D0,PORTAA      ;   and 1 to (OUTPUT ENABLE)
            MOVE.B    #2,D0          ;   Send 0 to start pin
            MOVE.B    D0,PORTAA      ;   of A/D
WAIT        JMP       WAIT           ;   Wait for interrupt
```

The 68020 assembly language program for the interrupt service routine is provided below.

```
            ORG       $00016000      ;   Service routine starting address
            MOVE.B    #0,D0          ;   Send LOW to (OUTPUT ENABLE)
            MOVE.B    D0,PORTAA
            MOVE.B    PORTB,D1       ;   Input A/D data
            ANDI.L    #$000000FF,D1  ;   Convert input data to 32-bit
                                     ;   unsigned number in D1
            DIVU.W    #51,D1         ;   Convert data to
                                     ;   integer part
            MOVE.W    D1,D2          ;   Save quotient (integer) in D2
            SWAP.W    D1             ;   Move remainder to low word of D1
            ANDI.L    #$000000FF,D1  ;   Convert remainder to unsigned
                                     ;   32-bit number
            DIVU      #5,D1          ;   Convert data to fractional part
                                     ;   Quotient (fraction) is in D1.W
            ORI.W     #$20,D2        ;   Disable fractional display
            ANDI.W    #$2F,D2        ;   Enable integer display
            MOVE.B    D2,PORTA       ;   Display integer part
            ORI.W     #$10,D1        ;   Disable integer display
            ANDI.W    #$1F,D1        ;   Enable fractional display
            MOVE.B    D1,PORTA       ;   Display fractional part
FINISH      JMP       FINISH
```

Using 68020 assembler directive DC.L, the reset and service routine vectors can be written as follows:

Reset Vector

```
ORG    0
DC.L   $00006500        ;        Initialize  A7'
DC.L   $00005000        ;        Main program starting address
```

Service routine vector for nonmaskable interrupt (autovector level 7):

```
ORG    $0000007C        ; Vector address for autovector level 7
DC.L   $00016000
```

Note that in the above it is assumed that [VBR] = 0. Hence, the vector address for autovector level 7 is $0000007C.

Using Nonautovectoring (Maskable Interrupt, Vector $40)   Figure 9.23 shows the pertinent connections for the nonautovectoring interrupt. All connections for the A/D converter to ports AA and B and seven-segment displays to port A of the 68020-based microcomputer in Figure 9.23 will be the same as shown in Figure 9.21. The 68020 $\overline{\text{IPL2}}$, $\overline{\text{IPL1}}$, $\overline{\text{IPL0}}$ pins are connected in such a way that $\overline{\text{IPL2}}$, $\overline{\text{IPL1}}$, $\overline{\text{IPL0}}$ = 110 will interrupt the 68020 as 001 (level 1 interrupt) since the $\overline{\text{IPL2}}$, $\overline{\text{IPL1}}$, and $\overline{\text{IPL0}}$ pins are inverted internally. In response to the interrupt, the 68000 automatically pushes PC and SR onto the stack and generates FC2, FC1, FC0 = 111 (CPU space cycle) and A_{19}, A_{18}, A_{17}, A_{16} = 1111, indicating acknowledgment of the interrupt. These seven signals are NANDed in the figure to generate a LOW interrupt acknowledge signal, which is used to enable an octal buffer such as 74HC244.

Vector number 40_{16} can be placed at the input of the octal buffer as shown in the figure. A value of 10 is asserted at the 68020 $\overline{\text{DSACK1}}$ and $\overline{\text{DSACK0}}$ pins so that the 68020 will recognize the device as 8-bit and will input the vector number via the 68020's D_{31}- D_{24} pins. Hence, the output pins of the octal buffer are connected to the 68020,s D_{31}- D_{24} pins.

The main programs and service routines are written at addresses $00005000 and $00016000 respectively. Also, the interrupt stack pointer A7' is initialized at $00006500. These addresses are   chosen arbitrarily.The main program in 68020 assembly language is provided below.

PGCR	EQU	$00002000
PACR	EQU	$0000200C
PBCR	EQU	$0000200E
PADDR	EQU	$00002004
PBDDR	EQU	$00002006
PORTA	EQU	$00002010
PORTB	EQU	$00002012
PGCR1	EQU	$00002001

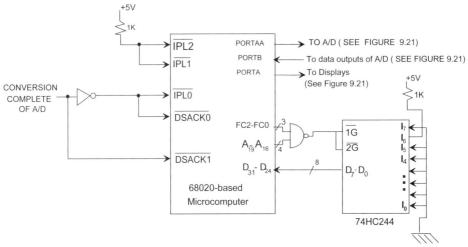

FIGURE 9.23   68020-based voltmeter using maskable interrupt I/O.

PACR1	EQU	$0000200D		
PADDR1	EQU	$00002005		
PORTAA	EQU	$00002011		
	ORG	$00005000	;	Main program starting address
	ANDI.B	#$3F,PGCR	;	Select mode 0
	BSET.B	#7,PACR	;	Port A bit I/O
	BSET.B	#7,PBCR	;	Port B bit I/O
	MOVE.B	#$FF,PADDR	;	Configure port A as an output port
	MOVE.B	#0,PBDDR	;	Configure port B as an input port
	ANDI.B	#$3F,PGCR1	;	Select mode 0
	BSET.B	#7,PACR1	;	Port AA bit I/O
	MOVE.B	#$03,PADDR1	;	Configure port AA
	ANDI.W	#F8FF,SR	;	Enable interrupts
	MOVE.B	#3,D0	;	Send 1 to $\overline{\text{START}}$ pin of A/D
	MOVE.B	D0,PORTAA	;	and 1 to ($\overline{\text{OUTPUT ENABLE}}$)
	MOVE.B	#2,D0	;	Send 0 to start pin
	MOVE.B	D0,PORTAA	;	of A/D
WAIT	JMP	WAIT	;	Wait for interrupt

The Service Routine is as follows:

	ORG	$00016000	;	Service routine starting address
	MOVE.B	#0,D0	;	Send LOW to (($\overline{\text{OUTPUT ENABLE}}$)
	MOVE.B	D0,PORTAA		

```
            MOVE.B     PORTB,D1        ;   Input A/D data
            ANDI.L     #$000000FF,D1   ;   Convert input data to 32-bit
                                       ;   unsigned number in D1
            DIVU.W     #51,D1          ;   Convert data to
                                       ;   integer part
            MOVE.W     D1,D2           ;   Save quotient (integer) in D2
            SWAP.W     D1              ;   Move remainder to low word of D1
            ANDI.L     #$000000FF,D1   ;   Convert remainder to unsigned
                                       ;   32-bit number
            DIVU       #5,D1           ;   Convert data to fractional part
                                       ;   Quotient (fraction) is in D1.W
            ORI.W      #$20,D2         ;   Disable fractional display
            ANDI.W     #$2F,D2         ;   Enable integer display
            MOVE.B     D2,PORTA        ;   Display integer part
            ORI.W      #$10,D1         ;   Disable integer display
            ANDI.W     #$1F,D1         ;   Enable fractional display
            MOVE.B     D1,PORTA        ;   Display fractional part
FINISH      JMP        FINISH
```

Using 68020 assembler directive DC.L, the reset and service routine vectors can be written as follows:

Reset Vector:

```
        ORG    0
        DC.L   $00006500      ;       Initialize A7'
        DC.L   $00005000      ;       Main program starting address
```

Starting address for the maskable interrupt (vector number $40):

```
        ORG    $00000100      ; Vector address for vector number $40
        DC.L   $00016000
```

Note above that it is assumed that [VBR] = 0. The vector address for vector # 40 = 4 * $40 = $100. Hence, the 32-bit address $00000100 is used as the starting address of the service routine.

9.5   Interfacing a 68020-Based Microcomputer to a Hexadecimal Keyboard and a Seven-Segment Display

In this section we describe the basics of interfacing a 68020-based microcomputer to a hexadecimal keyboard and a seven-segment display.

9.5.1   Basics of Keyboard and Display Interface to a Microcomputer

A common method of entering programs into a microcomputer is via a keyboard. A popular way of displaying microcomputer results is by using seven-segment displays. The main functions to be performed for interfacing a keyboard are:

* Sense a key actuation.

* Debounce the key.

* Decode the key.

Let us now elaborate on keyboard interfacing concepts. A keyboard is arranged in rows and columns. Figure 9.24 shows a 2 × 2 keyboard interfaced to a typical microcomputer. In Figure 9.24 the columns are normally at a HIGH level. A key actuation is sensed by sending a LOW (closing the diode switch) to each row one at a time via PA0 and PA1 of port A. The two columns can then be input via PB2 and PB3 of port B to see whether any of the normally HIGH columns are pulled LOW by a key actuation. If so, the rows can be checked individually to determine the row in which the key is down. The row and column code for the key pressed can thus be found.

The next step is to debounce the key. *Key bounce* occurs when a key is pressed or released—it bounces for a short time before making the contact. When bounce occurs, it may appear to the microcomputer that the same key has been actuated several times instead of just once. This problem can be eliminated by reading the keyboard after about 20 ms and then verifying to see if it is still down. If it is, the key actuation is valid. The next step is to translate the row and column code into a more popular code, such as hexadecimal or ASCII. This can easily be accomplished by a program. Certain characteristics associated with keyboard actuations must be considered while interfacing to a microcomputer. Typically, these are two-key lockout and *N*-key rollover. The two-key lockout ensures that only one key is pressed. An additional key depressed and released does not generate any codes. The system is simple to implement and most often used. However, it might slow down the typing because each key must be released fully before the next one is pressed down. On the other hand, the N-key rollover will ignore all keys pressed until only one remains down.

Now let us elaborate on the interfacing characteristics of typical displays. The following functions are typically performed for displays:

1. Output the appropriate display code.
2. Output the code via right entry or left entry into the displays if there is more than one display.

These functions can easily be realized by a microcomputer program. If there is more than one display, the displays are typically arranged in rows. A row of four displays is shown in Figure 9.25. In the figure, one has the option of outputting the display code via right entry or left entry. If the code is entered via right entry, the code for the least significant digit of the four-digit display should be output first, then the next-digit code, and so on. The program outputs to the displays are so fast that visually all four digits will appear on the display simultaneously. If the displays are entered via left entry, the most significant digit must be output first and the rest of the sequence is similar to that of right entry.

Two techniques are typically used to interface a hexadecimal display to the microcomputer: nonmultiplexed and multiplexed. In nonmultiplexed methods, each hexadecimal display digit is interfaced to the microcomputer via an I/O port. Figure 9.26 illustrates this method. BCD-to-seven-segment conversion is done in software.

The microcomputer can be programmed to output to the two display digits in sequence. However, the microcomputer executes the display instruction sequence so fast that the displays appear to the human eye at the same time. Figure 9. 27 illustrates the multiplexing method of interfacing the two hexadecimal displays to the microcomputer. In the multiplexing scheme, appropriate seven-segment code is sent to the desired displays on seven lines common to all displays. However, the display to be illuminated is grounded. Some displays, such as Texas Instrument's TIL 311, have an on-chip decoder. In this case, the microcomputer is required to output 4 bits (decimal) to a display.

The keyboard and display interfacing concepts described here can be realized by either software or hardware. To relieve the microprocessor of these functions, microprocessor manufacturers have developed a number of keyboard/display controller chips. These chips are typically initialized by the microprocessor. The keyboard/display functions are then performed by the chip independent of the microprocessor. The number of keyboard/display functions performed by the controller chip varies from one manufacturer to another. However, these functions are usually shared between the controller chip and the

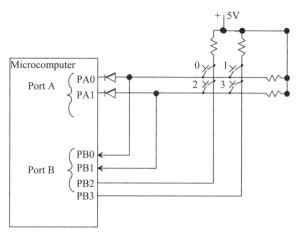

FIGURE 9.24   **Typical microcomputer-keyboard interface.**

FIGURE 9.25   **Row of four displays.**

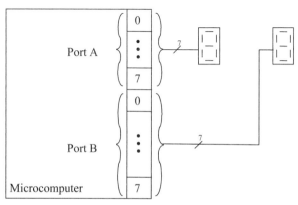

FIGURE 9.26   **Nonmultiplexed hexadecimal displays.**

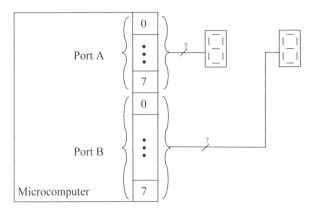

FIGURE 9. 27   Multiplexed displays

microprocessor.

9.5.2   68020 Interface to a Hexadecimal Keyboard and a Seven-Segment Display

In this section a 68020-based microcomputer is designed to display a hexadecimal digit entered via a keypad (16 keys). The microcomputer will contain 16-bit I/O and will use two 68230 I/O chips; one containing even port addresses and the other containing odd port addresses. Three 8-bit I/O ports are used in the design. The two 8-bit ports (ports A and B) of the even 68230 and the 8-bit port (port A) of the odd 68230 will be used.

Figure 9.27 shows the hardware schematic. Ports A, B, and AA are configured as follows:

- Port A is configured as an input port to receive the row–column code.

- Port B is configured as an output port to display the key(s) pressed.

- Port AA is configured as an output port to output zeros to the rows to detect a key actuation.

The 68230 port addresses are chosen arbitrarily, and are provided in the following:

Ports used from the even 68230:   PGCR = $00002000, PACR = $0000200C, PBCR = $0000200E, PADDR = $00002004, PBDDR = $00002006, PADR = $00002010= port A , and PBDR = $00002012 = port B.

Ports used from the odd 68230:   PGCR1= $00002001, PACR1 = $0000200D, PADDR1= $00002005, and PADR1 = $00002011 = port AA.

The 68020 is assumed to run at 8 MHz. Debouncing is provided to avoid unwanted oscillation caused by the opening and closing of key contacts. To ensure stability for the input signal, a delay of 20 ms is used for debouncing the input.

Typical 68020 software delay loops can be written using MOVE and DBF instructions. For example, the following instruction sequence can be used for a delay loop of 2 ms:

```
                MOVE.W        #count,D0
        DELAY   DBF.W         D0,DELAY
```

Note that DBF.W in the above decrements D0.W by 1, and if D0.W ≠ -1, branches to DELAY; if D0.W = -1, the 68020 executes the next instruction. Since DBF.W checks for

D0.W for -1, the value of "count" must be one less than the required loop count. The initial loop counter value of "count" can be calculated using the cycles (see the Motorola 68020 manual) required to execute the following 68000 instructions:

$$\begin{array}{lll} \text{MOVE.W} & \text{\#n,D0} & \text{(3 cycles)} \\ \text{DBF.W} & \text{D0,DELAY} & \text{(10 cycles)} \end{array}$$

Note that DBF.W requires 10 cycles when the 68020 branches if the content of D0.W is not equal to -1 after autodecrementing D0.W by 1. However, the 68020 goes to the next instruction and does not branch when [D0.W] = -1 after autodecrementing D0.W by 1, and this also requires 10 cycles. This means that the DELAY loop will require 10 cycles for "(count + 1)" times.

Assuming an 8-MHz 68020 clock, each cycle is 125 ns. For a 2-ms delay, total cycles = $\frac{2\,m\sec}{125\,n\sec}$ = 16,000. Hence, total cycles including the MOVE.W = 3 + 10 × (count +1) = 16,000. Hence, count ≅ 1599. Therefore, D0.W must be loaded with 1599_{10} for a 2-msec delay.

Now, to obtain a delay of 20 ms, the 2-ms DELAY loop above can be used with an external counter. Counter value = $\frac{20\,m\sec}{2\,m\sec}$ = 10. The following instruction sequence will provide an approximate delay of 2 seconds:

```
            MOVE.W    #10,D1      ;Initialize counter for 20-ms delay
BACK        MOVE.W    #1599,D0
DELAY       DBF.W     D0,DELAY    ;2-msec delay
            SUBQ.W    #1,D1
            BNE.B     BACK
```

Note that the 68020 instruction sequence above will provide a delay of 20 ms discarding the execution times of MOVE.W #10,D1, SUBQ.W, and BNE.B instructions.

The 68020 assembly language program for interfacing the 68020-based microcomputer to a hexadecimal keyboard and a seven-segment display follows. Note that to explain the program, line numbers are included with the comments.

```
PGCR     EQU    $00002000
PACR     EQU    $0000200C
PBCR     EQU    $0000200E
PADDR    EQU    $00002004
PBDDR    EQU    $00002006
PORTA    EQU    $00002010
PORTB    EQU    $00002012
PGCR1    EQU    $00002001
PACR1    EQU    $0000200D
PADDR1   EQU    $00002005
PORTAA   EQU    $00002011
OPEN     EQU    $F0              ;#1    Row/column codes if all
```

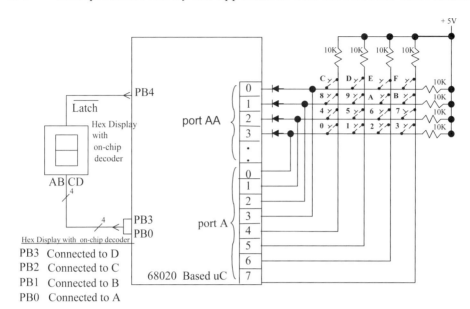

FIGURE 9.28   68020-based microcomputer interface to keyboard and display.

			;	keys are open
	ORG	$00005000	;#2	Starting address of the
			;	program
	ANDI.B	#$3F,PGCR	;#3	Select mode 0
	BSET.B	#7,PACR	;#4	Port A bit I/O
	BSET.B	#7,PBCR	;#5	Port B bit I/O
	MOVE.B	#0,PADDR	;#6	Configure port A as an
			;#7	input port for hex
			;	keyboard
	MOVE.B	#$FF,PBDDR	;#8	Configure port B as an
			;	output port
			;	or seven segment display
	ANDI.B	#$3F,PGCR1	;#9	Select mode 0
	BSET.B	#7,PACR1	;#10	port AA bit I/O
	MOVE.B	#$FF,PADDR1	;#11	Configure port AA for a hex
			;	keyboard row controls are
			;	opened
	MOVE.B	#0,D0	;#12	Send 0 to enable display
	MOVE.B	D0,PORTB	;#13	Initialize display with 0
SCAN_KEY	MOVE.B	D0,PORTAA	;#14	Output 0s to rows of the
			;	keyboard
KEY_OPEN	MOVE.B	PORTA,D1	;#15	Read PORTA

	CMP.B	#OPEN,D1	;#16	Are all keys opened?
	BNE.B	KEY_OPEN	;#17	Repeat if closed
	MOVE.W	#10,D1	;#18	Debounce for 20 ms
BACK	MOVE.W	#1599,D0	;#19	
DELAY	DBF.W	D0,DELAY	;#20	
	SUBQ.W	#1,D1	;#21	
	BNE.B	BACK	;#22	Delay loop
KEY_CLOSE	MOVE.B	PORTA,D0	;#23	Read port A
	CMPI.B	#OPEN,D0	;#24	Are all keys closed?
	BEQ.B	KEY_CLOSE	;#25	Repeat if opened
	MOVE.W	#10,D1	;#26	Debounce again for 20 ms
BACK	MOVE.W	#1599,D0	;#27	
DELAY1	DBF.W	D0,DELAY1	;#28	
	SUBQ.W	#1,D1	;#29	
	BNE.B	BACK	;#30	Delay loop
	MOVE.B	#$FF,D2	;#31	Set D2.B to all 1s
	ADDI.B	#0,D2	;#32	Clear X-bit to 0
NEXT_ROW	ROXL.B	#1,D2	;#33	Set up row mask
	MOVE.B	D2,D3	;#34	Save row mask in D3.B
	MOVE.B	D2,PORTAA	;#35	Set a row to zero
	MOVE.B	PORTA,D2	;#36	Read PORTA
	MOVE.B	D2,D4	;#37	Save row/column codes in
			;	D4.B
	ANDI.B	#$F0,D2	;#38	Mask row code
	CMPI.B	#$F0,D2	;#39	Is coln code affected?
	BNE.B	DECODE	;#40	If yes, decode column code
	MOVE.B	D3,D2	;#41	Restore row mask in D2.B
	MOVE.B	#$FF,D5	;#42	
	ADDQ.B	#1,D5	;#43	Set X-bit to 1
	JMP	NEXT_ROW	;#44	Check next row
DECODE	MOVE.B	#-1,D6	;#45	Initialize index register
	MOVE.W	#14,D7	;#46	Set up counter to 14
	MOVE.B	#$0F,D0	;#47	Initialize D0.B with F
SEARCH	ADDQ.B	#1,D6	;#48	Increment index
	CMP.B	(TABLE,D6.W),D4	;#49	Index thru table of codes
	DBNE.W	D7,SEARCH	;#50	Loop if not found
DONE	MOVE.B	D0,PORTB	;#51	Get character,enable display
			;	Display key pushed

	JMP	SCAN_KEY	;#52	Return to scan another key
	ORG	$00005300	;#53	Keyboard decode table
TABLE	DC.B	$77	;	Code for F
	DC.B	$B7	;	Code for E
	DC.B	$D7	;	Code for D
	DC.B	$E7	;	Code for C
	DC.B	$7B	;	Code for B
	DC.B	$BB	;	Code for A
	DC.B	$DB	;	Code for 9
	DC.B	$EB	;	Code for 8
	DC.B	$7D	;	Code for 7
	DC.B	$BD	;	Code for 6
	DC.B	$DD	;	Code for 5
	DC.B	$ED	;	Code for 4
	DC.B	$7E	;	Code for 3
	DC.B	$BE	;	Code for 2
	DC.B	$DE	;	Code for 1
	DC.B	$EE	;	Code for 0

In the program, a decode table for keys 0 through F are stored at address $00005300 (chosen arbitrarily). The codes for the hexadecimal numbers 0 through F are obtained by inspecting Figure 9.28. For example, consider key F. When key F is pressed and if a LOW is output by the program to bit 0 of port AA, the top row and rightmost column of the keyboard will be LOW. This will make the content of port A:

$$\text{Bit number}: \underset{7}{\underbrace{\begin{matrix} 7 & 6 & 5 & 4 \\ 0 & 1 & 1 & 1 \end{matrix}}} \quad \underset{7}{\underbrace{\begin{matrix} 3 & 2 & 1 & 0 \\ 0 & 1 & 1 & 1 \end{matrix}}} = 77_{16}$$

Thus, a code of 77_{16} is obtained at port A when key F is pressed. Diodes are connected at the 4 bits (bits 0-3) of port AA. This is done to make sure that when a 0 is output by the program to one of these bits (row of the keyboard), the diode switch will close and will generate a LOW on that row.

Now, if a key is pressed on a particular row that is LOW, the column connected to this key will also be LOW. This will enable the programmer to obtain the appropriate key code for each key.

Next, the assembly language program will be explained using the line numbers included in the comment field.

Line #1 equates label OPEN to data $F0. This is because when all keys are up (no keys are pushed) and 0's are output to the rows in Figure 9.28, data input at port A will be 11110000 ($F0). Note that bits 0 -3 are connected to rows and bits 4-7 are connected to columns of the keyboard. Line #2 includes the starting address of the program at $00005000. This address is chosen arbitrarily.

Lines 3 through 11 configure port A as input and ports B and AA as output ports. Lines 12 and 13 initialize the seven-segment display by outputting 0. Lines 14 through 17 check to see if any key is pushed. This is done by outputting 0's to all rows via port AA, and then inputting port A. If all keys are open, data at port A will be $F0. Hence, data at port A is compared with $F0. If Z = 0, the program waits in a loop with label KEY_OPEN until a key is pushed. When a key is closed, Z = 1, and the program comes out of the loop. Lines 18 through 22 debounce the keys by providing a delay of 20 ms.

Lines 23 through 25 detect a key closure. The program inputs port A and, compares input data with $F0. If Z = 1, the program waits in a loop with label KEY_CLOSE until a key is closed. If Z = 0, the program leaves the loop. Lines 26 through 30 provide debouncing if a key closure is detected. It is necessary to determine exactly which key is pressed. To do this, a sequence of row-control codes ($XE, $XD, $XB, and $X7, where X is don't care; the upper 4 bits are don't cares) are output via port AA . Lines 31 through 34 initialize D2.B to all 1's, clear the X-bit to 0, and rotate D2.B through X once to the left to contain the appropriate row control code. For example, after the first ROXL.B in line 33, D2.B will contain 11111110($FE). Note that the low 4 bits are the row-control code (the upper 4 bits are don't cares) for the first pass in the loop, labeled NEXT_ROW. Line 35 outputs this data to port AA to make the top row of the keyboard zero.

The row–column code is input via port A to determine if the column code changes corresponding to each different row code. Line 36 inputs port A into D2.B. The top row of the keyboard will be 0 if C or D or E or F is pushed. Line 37 saves this input data in D4.B.

Lines 38 through 40 make the low 4 bits 0's and retain the upper 4 bits. If the column code is not $F0 (changed), the input key is identified. The program then indexes through a look-up table to determine the row–column code saved in D0.B. If the code is found, the corresponding index value, which equals the input key's value (a single hexadecimal digit), is displayed.

Suppose that key F is pushed. Line 37 will store the code $77 in D4.B. The instruction CMPI.B at line 39 will make Z = 0. Hence, after execution of BNE.B at line 40, the program branches to DECODE (line 45). Lines 45 through 50 compare the key code saved in D4.B with $77 (data for F) stored at the address labeled TABLE ($00005300) in the decode table. Since there is a match, the Z-flag will be 1. The program comes out of the loop with the label SEARCH and outputs the character F to the seven-segment display at line 51.

However, if no key in the top row is pushed, a 0 is output to the second row, and the process continues. The program is written such that it will scan continuously for an input key and update the display for each new input. The memory and I/O maps are chosen arbitrarily.

Questions and Problems

9.1   Why is the 68020 provided with multiple Vcc and ground pins?

9.2   What is the purpose of each of the following 68020 pins?
       (a) $\overline{ECS}$ and $\overline{OCS}$ (b) $\overline{AS}$ and $\overline{DS}$

9.3   If there are no interrupts or DMA required in a 68020-based application, identify
       whether you would connect each of the following 68020 pins to HIGH or LOW
       or keep it floating: $\overline{IPL2}$, $\overline{IPL1}$, $\overline{IPL0}$, $\overline{BR}$, $\overline{BG}$, AND $\overline{DGACK}$.

9.4   Identify the function performed by the 68020 when FC2, FC1, FC0 = 111 and A_{19},
       A_{18}, A_{17}, A_{16} = 1111.

9.5   Assume a 25-MHz 68020 in Figure P9.5. Also, assume that data is ready at the
       output pins of the 32-bit device at 300 ns. For the timing diagram of Figure P9.5,
       determine the time at which data will be read by the 68020.

9.6   Assume the following data prior to execution of a 68020 hardware reset:
       [\$00000000] = \$00004000, [\$00000004] = \$10007000, [ISP] = \$23457180, [PC]
       = \$00405690, [VBR] = \$12345678, [D4.L] = \$45672368, and [SR] = \$4020. Find
       the contents of the memory locations and/or registers affected.

9.7   What is 68020 dynamic bus sizing?

9.8   Consider the 68020 instruction MOVE.B D1,\$00000016. Find the 68020 data
       pins over which data will be transferred if $\overline{DSACK1}$ $\overline{DSACK0}$ = 00. What are the
       68020 data pins if $\overline{DSACK1}$ $\overline{DSACK0}$ = 10?

9.9   If a 32-bit data is transferred using the 68020's MOVE.L D0,\$50607011 instruction
       to a 32-bit memory with [D0] = \$81F27561, how many bus cycles are needed
       to perform the transfer? What are A_1 and A_0 equal to during each cycle? What is
       the SIZ1,SIZ0 code during each cycle? What bytes of data are transferred during
       each bus cycle?

9.10   For a 16-bit device, use K-maps to express the memory enable lines $\overline{DBBE1}$
       (even) and $\overline{DBBE2}$ (odd) in terms of 68020 A_0, SIZ1, SIZE0, and $\overline{DS}$ signals
       in minimized form. Note that all 68020 signals mentioned above may not be
       necessary for each expression.

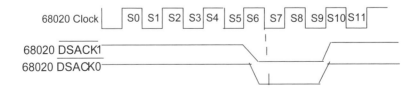

FIGURE P9.5

9.11 Assume a 16-bit memory system. Draw a schematic connecting the even 27C256 to the 68020. Determine the memory map. Also, assume that $A_{20} = 0$ will select the EPROMs and don't cares to be 1's. Use only the pins and signals shown in Figure P9.11. Use $\overline{DBBE1}$ of the enable logic from Problem 9.10 to select the even 27C256.

9.12 Assume a 16-bit memory system. Draw a schematic connecting the 68020 to an odd LH2256C/CH SRAM. Determine the memory map. Also, assume that $A_{30} = 1$ will select the SRAMs. Use only the pins and signals shown in Figure P9.12. Use $\overline{DBBE2}$ of the enable logic from Problem 9.10 to select the odd SRAM. Assume don't cares to be ones.

9.13 It is desired to connect the 68020 to an odd 68230 chip in a 16-bit system. Assuming that $A_{21} = 1$ is used to select I/O, draw a schematic showing the connections between the 68230 chip and the 68020, and obtain the I/O map for 68230 PGCR, PADDR, PACR, PADR, PBDDR, PBCR, and PBDR. Use the pins and signals shown in Figure P9.13. Assume don't cares to be 0's. Use $\overline{DBBE2}$ of the enable logic from Problem 9.10 to select the odd 68230.

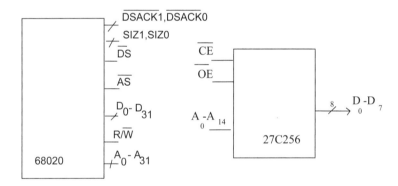

FIGURE P 9.11

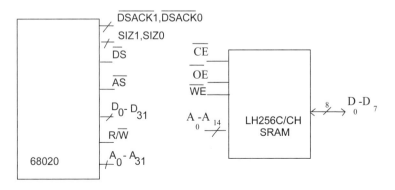

FIGURE P 9.12

9.14   Write a 68020 assembly language program that will convert a BCD number in D0.B to a seven-segment code using a look-up table containing the seven-segment codes of the 10 BCD numbers. The program will then output this code to a common-cathode display connected at 68230's port A as shown in Figure P9.14. Assume that the look-up table is stored in memory starting at address $00002000. Also, assume that A0 contains $00001000 and address $00001000 contains $000020000. Use A0 as the pointer in your program to access the table.

9.15   In Figure P9.15, if $V_M > 12$ V, turn an LED ON connected at bit 3 of port A. If $V_M < 11$ V, turn the LED OFF. Using ports, registers, and memory locations as needed and level 1 autovectored interrupt:

(a)   Draw a neat block diagram showing a 68020/68230 microcomputer and the connections in Figure P9.15 to 68230 ports.

(b)   Write the main program and the service routine in 68020 assembly language. The main program will initialize ports and wait for interrupt. The service routine will accomplish the task and stop.

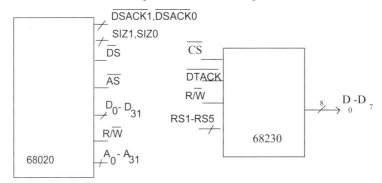

FIGURE P 9.13

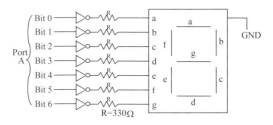

FIGURE P9.14

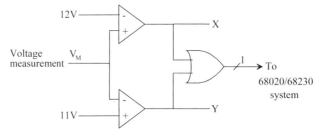

FIGURE P9.15

10

ASSEMBLY LANGUAGE PROGRAMMING WITH THE PENTIUM: PART 1

In this chapter we describe the fundamental concepts associated with assembly language programming with the Intel Pentium microprocessor. The first part of the Pentium's instruction set is introduced in this chapter. Topics include Pentium registers, addressing modes, and data transfer and arithmetic instructions. Several examples of assembly language programming using these instructions are provided.

Note that the Pentium contains 32 address pins and hence can directly address 2^{32} or 4 Gigabytes (GB) of memory. This large addressing space allows the Pentium to perform many operating system features, such as multitasking. The Pentium operates in two modes of operation: real mode and protected mode.

The real mode appears to programmers as a fast 8086 with a few new instructions. Like the 8086, the Pentium can directly address a maximum of one Megabyte (MB) of main memory. Since DOS is a real mode operating system, a Pentium-based PC that boots up into DOS operates in real mode. The real mode is the mode of operation of the Pentium upon hardware reset.

While in the real mode, the protected mode can be selected via execution of a single instruction. With a large directly addressable memory in protected mode, the Pentium provides support for multitasking, virtual memory addressing, memory management and protection, and control over instruction and data cache. Microsoft took advantage of these features and designed the Windows operating system to run in protected mode.

To write programs in the protected mode, a background in operating systems theory is required. Hence, real mode operation is emphasized in this book to present programming concepts with the Pentium in a very simplified manner. Note that real mode operation of the Pentium is widely used in many industrial applications.

The Pentium uses segmented memory in both real mode and, protected mode utilizing segmentation. This means that each address used by the programmer (also called "logical address") consists of two components. In real mode, these components are a 16-bit segment and a 16-bit offset. The Pentium translates these two 16-bit components for each logical address into a 20-bit physical address using on-chip hardware. In protected mode, the Pentium uses 32-bit physical addresses, and the technique of translating each logical address into a 32-bit physical address is quite different than real mode. Note that the Pentium provides a special mechanism to use 32-bit offsets in real mode. Hence, both 16- and 32-bit offsets can be used in real mode.

10.1   Introduction

The Intel Pentium is a 32-bit microprocessor based on their 80486. The 80486, on the other hand, is an enhanced 80386. Hence, before proceeding further, an overview of the basic features of the 80386 and 80486 will be helpful. The Intel 80386 was Intel's first 32-bit microprogrammed microprocessor. Its introduction in 1985 facilitated the introduction of Microsoft's Windows operating systems. The high-speed computer requirement of the graphical interface of Windows operating systems was supplied by the 80386. Also, the on-chip memory management of the 80386 allowed memory to be allocated and managed by the operating system. In the past, memory management was performed by software.

The 80386 is based on Intel's 16-bit microprocessor, the 8086. The 80386 is software compatible with the 8086 at the object code level. The 80386 includes eight 32-bit general-purpose registers. The processor can handle 8-, 16-, and 32-bit data types. It has separate 32-bit data and 32-bit address pins, and generates a 32-bit physical address. The 80386 can address directly up to 4 GB (2^{32}) of physical memory. The 80386 can be interfaced to external cache memory. The chip has 132 pins and is typically housed in a pin grid array (PGA) package. The 80386 is designed using high-speed HCMOS III technology.

The 80386 is pipelined and can perform instruction fetching, decoding, execution, and memory management functions in parallel. The on-chip memory management and protection hardware translates logical addresses to physical addresses and provides the protection rules required in a multitasking environment. The 80386 contains a total of 129 instructions. The 80386 protection mechanism, paging, and instructions to support them are not present in the 8086.

The main differences between the 8086 and the 80386 are that the 80386 contains 32-bit addresses and data types and paging and memory management. To provide these features and other applications, several new instructions are added in the 80386 instruction

TABLE 10.1   Basic Differences Between the 80486 and Original Pentium Microprocessors

Feature	80486 Microprocessor	Original Pentium Microprocessor
Address and data buses	32-bit address bus	32-bit address bus
	32-bit data bus	64-bit data bus
Clock	25 to 100 MHz	60MHz, 66 MHz, 75 MHz, 90 MHz, 100 MHz, 120 MHz, 133 MHz, 150 MHz, 166 MHz, 200 MHz
Pipeline model	Single	Dual
Type of Microprocessor	Scalar	Superscalar
Internal cache	8K for both data and instruction	8k for data and 8k for instruction
Number of transistors	1.2 million	3.2 million
Performance at 66 MHZ in MIPS (millions of instructions per second)	54 MIPS	112 MIPS
Number of pins	168	273

set beyond those of the 8086.

Like the 80386, the 80486, introduced in 1989, is a 32-bit microprocessor. It executes the complete instruction sets of the 80386 and the 80387DX floating-point coprocessor. Unlike the 80386, the 80486 on-chip floating-point hardware eliminates the need for an external floating-point coprocessor chip, and the on-chip cache minimizes the need for an external cache and associated control logic.

The 80486 is object code compatible with the 8086 and 80386 microprocessors. Like the 80386, the 80486 contains separate 32-bit address and 32-bit data pins.

The 80486 has an internal 8-kB cache memory. This provides fast access to recently used instructions and data. The internal write-through cache can hold 8 kB of data or instructions. The on-chip floating-point unit performs floating-point operations on the 32-, 64-, and 80- bit arithmetic formats specified in the IEEE standard. The fetching, decoding, execution, and address translation of instructions are overlapped within the 80486 processor using instruction pipelining. This allows a continuous execution rate of one clock cycle per instruction for most instructions. Hence, the 80486 is a scalar microprocessor.

The original Pentium was introduced in 1993. Intel could not name it the 80586 because of problems with trademarking the numbers. The Pentium is very similar to the 80486 except that it has a 64-bit data bus. The Pentium contains two independent pipelines and has the capability of executing two instructions per cycle. Hence, the Pentium is a superscalar microprocessor.

Table 10.1 summarizes the fundamental differences between the basic features of the 80486 and the original Pentium. Like its predecessor, the 80486, the Pentium is 100% object code compatible with 8086/80386 systems. BICMOS (Bipolar and CMOS) technology is used for the Pentium.

In December 1994, Intel detected a flaw in the Pentium chip while performing certain division calculations. The Pentium is not the first chip that Intel has had problems with. The first version of the Intel 80386 had a math flaw that Intel fixed before there were any complaints. Some experts feel that Intel should have acknowledged the math problem in the Pentium when it was first discovered and then offered to replace the chips. In that case, the problem with the Pentium probably would have been ignored by users. However, Intel was heavily criticized by computer magazines when the division flaw in the Pentium chip was detected.

The flaw in the division algorithm in the Pentium was caused by a problem with a look-up table used in the division. Errors occur in the fourth through the fifteenth significant decimal digits. This means that in a result such as 5.78346, the last three digits could be incorrect. For example, the correct answer for the operation 4,195,835 - (4,195,835 + 3,145,727) + (3,145,727) is zero. The Pentium provided the wrong answer: 256. IBM claimed that this problem can occur once every 24 days. Intel eventually fixed the division flaw in the Pentium.

The Pentium microprocessor contains the complete 80486 instruction set along with some new ones that are discussed later. Pentium's on-chip memory management unit is completely compatible with that of the 80486.

Pentium's on-chip floating-point hardware has been redesigned completely over the 80486. Faster algorithms provide up to ten fold speed-up for common operations such as add, multiply, and load. The two instruction pipelines and on-chip floating-point unit are capable of independent operations. Each pipeline issues frequently used instructions in a single clock cycle. The dual pipelines can jointly issue two integer instructions in one clock cycle or one floating-point instruction (under certain circumstances, two floating-point instructions) in one clock cycle.

Branch prediction is implemented in the Pentium by using two prefetch buffers, one to prefetch code in a linear fashion and one to prefetch code according to the contents of the branch target buffer (BTB), so the code required is almost always prefetched before it is needed for execution. Note that the branch addresses are stored in the BTB.

There are two instruction pipelines, the U-pipe and the V-pipe, which are not equivalent and interchangeable. The U-pipe can execute all integer and floating-point instructions, whereas the V-pipe can execute only simple integer instructions and floating-point exchange register contents (FXCH) instructions. The instruction decode unit decodes the prefetched instructions so that the Pentium can execute them. The control ROM includes the microcode for the Pentium processor and has direct control over both pipelines. A barrel shifter is included in the chip for fast shift operations.

10.2   Pentium Registers

Figures 10.1(a) and 10.1(b) show the Pentium registers. The Pentium contains 8-, 16-, and 32-bit registers classified into four groups: general-purpose registers, stack pointers and index registers, extended instruction pointer and flag register, and Segment registers. These are described next.

10.2.1   General-Purpose Registers
As shown in   Figure 10.1(a), the Pentium has four 32-bit general-purpose registers: EAX, EBX, ECX, and EDX. These registers can be used for arithmetic, logic, and other operations as follows:
* EAX, EBX, ECX, and EDX as four 32-bit registers

* AX (low 16 bits of EAX), BX (low 16 bits of EBX), CX (low 16 bits of ECX), and DX (low 16 bits of EDX) as four 16-bit registers

* AH, AL, BH, BL, CH, CL, DH, and DL as eight 8-bit registers
    Some general-purpose registers perform specific functions for certain instructions as follows:
* The uses of EAX, AX, and AL registers are assumed by some instructions. The I/O (IN or OUT) instructions always use the EAX, AX, or AL for inputting or outputting 32-, 16- or 8-bit data from or to an I/O port. Multiplication and division instructions also use the EAX, AX, or AL.

* The ECX or CX register is known as the *counter* register respectively in protected mode and real mode because some instructions use these registers for a loop count for iterative instructions.

* The EDX or DX register is used during multiplication and division instructions. EDX is used by 32 X 32 multiplication and 64 ÷ 32 instructions. DX, on the other hand, is used by 16×16 multiplication   and   32 ÷ 16 division instructions.
    Note that BX can be used as a 16-bit pointer to memory while EAX, EBX, ECX, and EDX can be used as 32-bit pointers to memory.

10.2.2   Stack Pointers and Index Registers
The Pentium stack pointer registers can be used as 32-bit or 16-bit registers as follows:

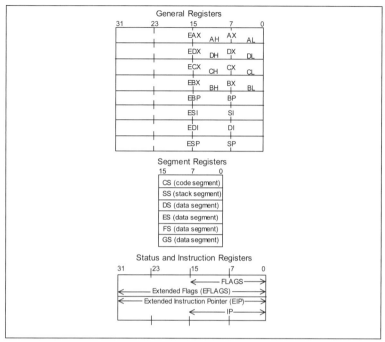

FIGURE 10.1(a): Pentium registers: Applications register set

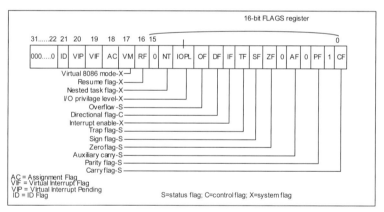

FIGURE 10.1(b): Pentium registers: EFLAGS register

FIGURE 10.1   Pentium Registers

- ESP and EBP as 32-bit system stack pointer and 32-bit user stack pointer respectively in protected mode

- SP and BP as 16-bit system stack pointer and 16-bit user stack pointer respectively in real mode (the stack pointer registers are typically used for stack operations)

The Pentium index registers can be used as 32- or 16-bit registers as follows:

- ESI and EDI as 32-bit registers

- SI and DI as 16-bit registers [the index registers (SI, DI, ESI, EDI) can also be used as general-purpose registers or memory pointers or by string instructions]

10.2.3   Extended Instruction Pointer and Flag Register

The extended instruction pointer (EIP) contains the offset address relative to the start of the current code segment of the next sequential instruction to be executed in protected mode. The low-order 16 bits of EIP is named IP and is useful when the Pentium executes instructions in real mode. The flag register is a 32-bit register, named EFLAGS is shown in Figure 10.1(b). The low-order 16 bits of EFLAGS is named FLAGS. The Pentium flags in the EFLAGS register are grouped into three types: status flags, control flags, and system flags. In the real mode, the status flags and control flags are used. The system flags along with status and control flags are used in the protected mode.

The status flags include CF, PF, AF, ZF, SF, and OF.

*   **AF** (the auxiliary carry flag) is set to 1 if there is a carry due to addition of the low 4 bits into the high 4 bits or a borrow due to the subtraction of the low 4 bits from the high 4 bits of a number; otherwise, AF = 0. This flag is used by BCD arithmetic instructions.

*   **CF** (the carry flag) is set to 1 if there is a carry from addition or a borrow from subtraction; otherwise, CF = 0.

*   **OF** (the overflow flag) is set to 1 if there is an arithmetic overflow (i.e., if the size of the result exceeds the capacity of the destination location) ; otherwise, OF = 0. Note that overflow, OF = $C_f \oplus C_p$ where C_f is the final carry and C_p is the previous carry. An interrupt on overflow instruction is available to generate an interrupt indicating the occurrence of an overflow.

*   **SF** (the sign flag) is set to 1 if the most significant bit of the result is 1 indicating a negative number; SF = 0 if the most significant bit of the result is 0 indicating a positive number.

*   **PF** (the parity flag) is set to 1 if the result has even parity; PF = 0 when the result has odd parity.

*   **ZF** (the zero flag) is set to 1 if the result is zero; ZF = 0 for a nonzero result.

    The Pentium has 3 control bits in the flag register that can be set or cleared by the programmer:

*   Setting **DF** (the direction flag) to 1 causes string instructions to autodecrement; clearing DF to 0 causes string instructions to autoincrement.

*   Setting **IF** (the interrupt flag) to 1 causes the Pentium to recognize external maskable interrupts; clearing IF to 0 disables these interrupts.

*   Setting **TF** (the trap flag) to 1 places the Pentium in the single-step mode. In this mode, the Pentium generates an internal interrupt after execution of each instruction. The user can write a service routine at the interrupt address vector to display the contents of desired registers and memory locations. The user can thus debug a program.

    The system flags control I/O, maskable interrupts, debugging, task switching, and enabling of virtual 8086 execution in a protected, multitasking environment.

*   **IOPL** (I/O privilege level) is a 2-bit field that supports the Pentium protection feature.

*   **NT** (nested task) controls the IRET operation. If NT = 0, a usual return from interrupt is taken by the Pentium by popping EFLAGS, CS, and EIP from the stack. If NT = 1, the Pentium returns from an interrupt via task switching.

*   **RF** (resume flag) is used during debugging.

- **VM** (virtual 8086 mode): when the VM bit is set to 1, the Pentium executes 8086 programs. When the VM bit is 0, the Pentium operates in protected mode.

- **AC** (alignment check): When the AC bit is set to 1, the Pentium operates in alignment check mode and generates exceptions when reference is made to an unaligned memory address.

- **VIF** (virtual interrupt flag) is a copy of the interrupt flag bit.

- **VIP** (virtual interrupt pending) is used in multitasking to provide the operating system with virtual interrupt flags and interrupt pending information.

- **ID** (identification) gives the ability to set and clear the ID flag. It indicates that the processor supports the CPUID instruction. The CPUID instruction provides information to the software about the Pentium microprocessor, such as its version number and manufacturer.

10.2.4　Segment Registers

The six 16-bit segment registers (CS, SS, DS, ES, FS, and GS) generate memory addresses when combined with certain registers in the Pentium. These registers support the segmented memory mechanism of the Pentium. In this mechanism, memory is divided into segments in which each segment is a small section of the memory. The Pentium, at any time, can point to six segments of the main memory.

    A program contains instructions and data. The Pentium uses segmented memory to store instructions in a code segment and the data portion of the program in a data segment. The CS register points to the code segment while the DS register points to the data segment. The SS register points to the stack segment. The three other data segment registers, ES, FS, and GS, are used in a similar manner as the DS register. These registers can be used if the program needs additional memory for storing data.

    A segment register works differently in the real and protected modes of operation. Let us discuss them in the following.

10.3　Modes of Operation

The Pentium has two primary processing modes: real and protected. In addition, the Pentium microprocessor is provided with a *system management mode* (SMM), which allows one to design for low power usage. SMM is entered through activation of an external interrupt pin (system management interrupt, SMI#). *Real mode* is the mode of operation of the processor upon hardware reset. This mode appears to programmers as a fast 8086 with a few new instructions. The architecture of the Pentium processor in the real mode is identical to that of the 8086 microprocessor. *Protected mode* is the normal 32-bit application of the Pentium. All instructions and features of the Pentium are available in this mode only. While in protected mode, the pentium can execute "real address" mode instructions directly in a protected, multitasking environment using a feature called the *Virtual 8086 mode* (also called *V86 mode*). Virtual 8086 is not really a Pentium mode, but an attribute that can be enabled for any task with appropriate software while in protected mode. This feature allows the Pentium to go back and forth repeatedly between the protected and V86 modes at a fast speed. When entering into V86 mode, the Pentium can execute an 8086 program. The processor can then leave V86 mode and enter the protected mode to execute a Pentium program.

As mentioned before, the Pentium enters the real mode upon hardware reset. The Pentium contains a control register called CR0 to facilitate mode switching. In the real mode, the protection enable (PE) bit at bit 0 in the 32-bit control register, CR0 is cleared to zero. Setting the bit 0 in control register, CR0 (PE bit) by executing a MOV instruction such as MOV CR0,reg32 will place the Pentium in protected mode. Note that reg32 can be one of the Pentium's 32-bit general-purpose registers, such as EAX. Also, data cannot be moved into CR0 using the immediate mode. When the Pentium is in protected mode, setting the VM (virtual mode) bit in the flag register (the EFLAGS register) places the Pentium in the V86 mode. The real and protected modes of the Pentium are described in more detail below.

10.3.1   Real Mode

The real mode is provided with the Pentium to run programs for the 8086. In real mode operation, the Pentium can address a maximum of 1 MB of the main memory directly using a 20-bit physical address. This means that the starting physical address is 00000H and the last addressable physical address is FFFFFH. In this mode, the Pentium uses a segmented memory. Two components, a segment value and an offset value, are required to specify a memory location (referred to as a logical address) in segmented memory organization. The programmer uses the logical addresses. The Pentium's on-chip hardware translates a logical address to its corresponding 20-bit physical address by shifting the contents of the segment register four times to the left, and then adding the 16-bit offset to it. There are some advantages to working with the segmented memory. First, after initializing the 16-bit segment registers, the Pentium has to deal only with offsets. That is, the Pentium has to manipulate and store 16- and 32-bit offsets. Second, because of memory segmentation, the Pentium can be used effectively in time-shared systems. For example, in a time-shared system, several users may share one Pentium. Suppose that the Pentium works with one user's program for, say, 5 ms. After spending 5 ms with one of the other users, the Pentium returns to execute the first user's program. Each time the Pentium switches from one user's program to the next, it must execute a new section of code and new sections of data. Segmentation makes it easy to switch from one user program to another.

In real mode, the Pentium's main memory can be divided into 16 segments of 64 kB each (16×64 kB = 1 MB). A segment may contain codes or data. The Pentium uses 16-bit registers to address segments. For example, to address codes, the code segment (CS) register must be initialized in some manner (to be discussed later). A 16-bit Pentium register called the *instruction pointer* (IP), which is similar to the program counter of a typical microprocessor, addresses each location in a code segment linearly. Because the size of the IP is 16 bits, the segment size is 64 kB (2^{16}). Similarly, a 16-bit data segment register (DS, ES, FS, or GS) must be initialized to hold the segment value of a data segment. The contents of certain 16-bit registers are designed to hold a 16-bit offset in a 64-kB data segment. One of these address registers can be used to address each location linearly once the data segment is initialized by an instruction.

To access the stack segment in real mode, the Pentium's 16-bit stack segment (SS) register must be initialized; the 64-kB stack is addressed linearly by a 16-bit stack pointer (SP) register. Note that the stack memory must be a read/write (RAM) memory. Whenever the programmer reads from or writes to the Pentium stack, two components of a memory address must be considered: a segment value and an offset value. The SS register points to the current stack. The 20-bit physical stack address is calculated from the SS and SP for stack instructions such as PUSH and POP. The programmer can

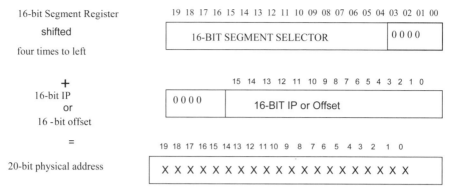

FIGURE 10.2   Pentium address translation in real mode.

create a programmer's stack with the BP (base pointer) instead of the SP for accessing the stack using the based addressing mode. In this case, the 20-bit physical stack address is calculated from BP and SS.

The Pentium assembly language program works with two components in real mode while accessing memory. These two 16-bit components (the contents of a 16-bit segment register and a 16-bit offset or IP) form a logical address. As mentioned before, the programmer writes programs using these logical addresses in assembly language programming. The Pentium logically shifts the contents of the 16-bit segment register four times to left, and then adds the 16-bit IP or 16-bit offset to obtain the 20-bit physical address in the real mode.This is depicted in Figure 10.2. Note that because of the possibility of a carry, the resulting linear address may have as many as 21 bits. However, the carry (bit 20) is discarded and 20 bits are used as the linear address.

As an example, consider a logical address with the 16-bit code segment (CS) register contents of 2050H and the 16-bit Pentium instruction pointer (IP) containing a value of 0004H. When the Pentium executes this program and encounters the logical address, it will generate the 20-bit physical address as follows: Since the 16-bit contents of IP = 0004H, the 16-bit contents of code segment = 2050H, and the 16-bit contents of code segment value after shifting logically four times to the left = 20500H, the 20-bit physical address generated by the Pentium on the address bus is 20504H.

The segments can be contiguous, partially overlapped, fully overlapped, or disjointed. An example of how five segments (0 through 4), may be stored in physical memory is shown in Figure 10.3. In this example, segments 0 and 1 are contiguous

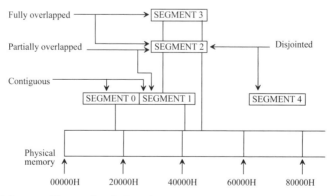

FIGURE 10.3   Example of Pentium memory segments.

(adjacent), 1 and 2 are partially overlapped, 2 and 3 are fully overlapped, and 2 and 4 are disjointed.

Every segment must start on 16-byte memory boundaries. Typical examples of values of segments should then be selected based on physical addresses starting at 00000_{16}, 00010_{16}, 00020_{16}, 00030_{16}, ..., $FFFF0_{16}$. A physical memory location may be mapped into (contained in) one or more logical segments. For example, consider a physical address 32040H. This address can be mapped as offset 2040H in segment 3000H or as offset 2000H in segment 3004H. Note that many applications can be written simply to initialize the segment registers and then forget them.

A segment can be pointed to by more than one segment register. For example, the DS and ES may point to the same segment in memory if a string located in that segment is used as a source segment in one string instruction and a destination segment in another string instruction. Note that for string instructions, a destination segment must be pointed to by the ES. One example of six currently addressable segments is shown in Figure 10.4.

In summary, the Pentium has six segment registers: CS, SS, DS, ES, FS, and GS. The four data segment registers (DS, ES, FS, and GS) can access four separate data segments. In the real mode, some examples of the default segment registers with the corresponding 16-bit offsets or values shown in Table 10.2 are shown.

In real mode, the Pentium obtains the 20-bit physical address as follows:

* For instructions: 16-bit segment register, CS and 16-bit offset in IP.

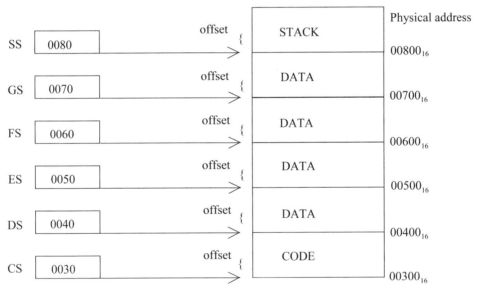

FIGURE 10.4   Six currently addressable Pentium segments.

TABLE 10.2   Some Examples of Registers and Offsets in Real Mode

Segment Register	16-bit Offset
CS	IP
DS	BX, SI, DI, 16-bit value
SS	SP or BP

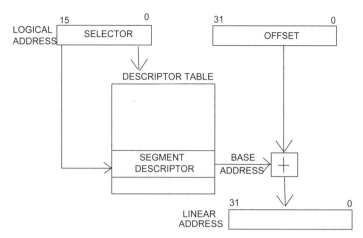

FIGURE 10.5 **Segment translation.**

- For data: 16-bit segment register, DS and 16-bit offset in BX, SI, DI, or an offset value.

- For system stack: 16-bit segment register, SS and 16-bit offset in SP.

- For user stack: 16-bit segment register, SS and 16-bit offset in BP.

10.3.2 Protected Mode

In the protected mode, the Pentium uses 32-bit addresses. In this mode the Pentium supports both segmentation and paging. Paging is useful for implementing virtual memory. Note that paging is transparent to the application program, whereas segmentation is not. Pentium's paging feature will not be described here. Rather, a brief overview of the protected mode segmented memory architecture is provided.

In the proteced mode, Pentium's on-chip segment translation hardware translates a logical address into a 32-bit linear address. The mechanism of generating physical addresses in the protected mode is quite different from that of the real mode. As mentioned before, in real mode, the Pentium generates 20-bit physical addresses by shifting 16-bit segment registers four times to the left, and then adding to a 16-bit offset.

Accessing a large memory of 4 GB in the protected mode requires a change of segment plus offset addressing technique used in the real mode. While accessing memory in the protected mode, the Pentium still uses offset to obtain information in a memory segment. However, it does not use the segment register directly. Instead, the contents of the segment register are used as an index (upper 13 bits of the selector) to a table. Hence, during the segment translation process, the contents of the segment register are used as an index into a segment descriptor table to obtain a descriptor. Segment descriptors contain the 32-bit segment base address, its size, and access rights. The Pentium adds a 16- or

TABLE 10.3 **Some Examples of Registers and Offsets in Protected Mode**

Segment Register	32-bit Offset
CS	EIP
DS	EAX, EBX, ECX, EDX, E`SI, EDI, an offset value
SS	ESP or EBP

32-bit offset to the 32-bit base address to translate a logical address to its corresponding linear address. This is depicted in Figure 10.5. The on-chip paging translation hardware then translates the linear address into a 32-bit physical address. If no paging is used, the linear address is the same as the physical address. In the protected mode, some examples of the default segment registers with the corresponding 32-bit offsets or values shown in Table 10.3 are shown.

10.4   Pentium data Organization

The Pentium microprocessor contains instructions that can operate on various types of data. These data types include bit, byte, 16-bit word, and 32-bit doubleword. Shift and rotate instructions typically operate on bits. Bytes are stored in Pentium's 8-bit registers such as AH, AL, BH, BL, CH, CL, DH, and DL. Word data types are stored in Pentium's 16-bit registers AX, BX, CX, DX, SI, DI, and BP. Also, each of the 16-bit registers AX, BX, CX, and DX can hold 2 bytes. For example, 8-bit registers AH and AL will contain 23H (the upper byte) and 45H (the lower byte) of the 16-bit data 2345H stored in the 16-bit register AX. Doubleword (32-bit) data types are normally stored in 32-bit registers such as EAX, EBX, ECX, EDX, ESI, EDI, and EBP.

The memory of a Pentium-based microcomputer is organized as bytes. In the real mode, each byte is addressed uniquely with 20-bit addresses of 00000_{16}, 00001_{16}, ... ,$FFFFF_{16}$. A Pentium word in memory consists of any two consecutive bytes; the low-addressed byte is the low byte of the word, and the high-addressed byte contains the high byte as follows:

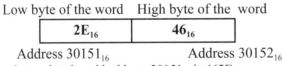

Low byte of the word   High byte of the word

02_{16} $A1_{16}$

Address 02000_{16} Address 02001_{16}

The 16-bit word at the even address 02000_{16} is $A102_{16}$. Next, consider a word stored at an address 30151_{16} as follows:

Low byte of the word   High byte of the word

$2E_{16}$ 46_{16}

Address 30151_{16} Address 30152_{16}

The 16-bit word stored at the odd address 30151_{16} is $462E_{16}$.

The Pentium assigns the low address to the low byte of a 16-bit register and the high address to the high byte of the 16-bit register for 16-bit transfers between the Pentium and main memory. This is called *little-endian byte ordering*. In contrast, Motorola microprocessors such as the 68020 use *big-endian byte ordering,*, in which the 68020 assigns the high address to the low byte of a 16-bit register and the low address to the high byte of the 16-bit register for 16-bit transfers between the 68020 and main memory.

10.5   Assembly Language Programming with the Pentium

The assembly language program is translated into binary via a program called an *assembler*. The assembler program reads each assembly instruction of a program as ASCII characters

TABLE 10.4   **Conversion of HLT into Its Binary Op-Code**

Assembly Code	Binary Form of ASCII Codes as Seen by the Assembler	Binary Op-Code Created by the Assembler
H	0100 1000	
L	0100 1100	1111 0100
T	0101 0100	

and translates them into the respective binary op-codes. For example, the Pentium assembler translates the HLT instruction into its binary op-code is 1111 0100 (F4 in hex) as depicted in Table 10.4.

An advantage of the assembler is address computation. Most programs use addresses within the program as data storage or as targets for jumps or calls. When programming in machine language, these addresses must be calculated by hand. The assembler solves this problem by allowing the programmer to assign a symbol to an address. The programmer may then reference that address elsewhere by using the symbol. The assembler computes the actual address for the programmer and fills it in automatically. One can obtain hands-on experience with a typical assembler for a microprocessor by downloading it from the Internet.

As mentioned in Chapter 5, each line in an assembly language program includes four fields:

1. Label field
2. mnemonic or op-code field
3. Operand field
4. Comment field

The assembler ignores the comment field but translates the other fields. The label field must start with an uppercase alphabetic character.

The assembler must know where one field starts and another ends. Most assemblers allow the programmer to use a special symbol or delimiter to indicate the beginning or end of each field. Typical delimiters used are spaces, commas, semicolons, and colons:

- Spaces are used between fields.

- Commas (,) are used between addresses in an operand field.

- A semicolon (;) is used before a comment.

- A colon (:) is used after a label.

To handle numbers, most assemblers including the Pentium assembler, consider all numbers as decimal numbers unless specified. Most assemblers will also allow binary, octal, or hexadecimal numbers. The user must define in some way the type of number system used. This is generally done by using a letter following the number. Typical letters used are B for binary, Q for octal, and H for hexadecimal. Typical assemblers, such as the MASM32, require hexadecimal numbers to start with a digit (0 through 9). A 0 is typically used if the first digit of the hexadecimal number is a letter. This is done to distinguish between numbers and labels. For example, typical assemblers will normally require the number F3H to be represented as 0F3H; otherwise, the assembler will generate an error. Assemblers use pseudoinstructions or directives to make the formatting of the edited text easier. These directives are not translated directly into machine language instructions. Typical assembler directives are discussed in the following.

ORIGIN (ORG)   The directive ORG lets the programmer place the programs anywhere in memory. Typical ORG statements are

> ORG 7000H
> CLC

Most assemblers assign a value of zero to starting address of a program if the programmer does not define this by means of an ORG.

Equate (EQU)   The EQU assigns a value in its operand field to an address in its label field. This allows the user to assign a numerical value to a symbolic name. The user can then use the symbolic name in the program instead of its numerical value. A typical example of EQU is START EQU 0200H, which assigns the value 0200H in hexadecimal to the label START.

Typical assemblers, such as the MASM32 (used to assemble Pentium programs in this book), require hexadecimal numbers to start with a digit. A 0 is used if the first digit of the hexadecimal number is a letter; otherwise, an error will be generated by the assembler. This is done to distinguish between numbers and labels. For example, TEST EQU 0A5H will assign A5 in hex to the label TEST.

Define Byte (DB)   The directive DB is generally used to set a memory location to a certain byte value. For example,

> START DB   45H

will store the data value 45 hex to the address START. The DB directive can be used to generate a table of data as follows:

> ORG   7000H
> TABLE DB   20H,30H,40H,50H

In this case, 20 hex is the first data of the memory location 7000; 30 hex, 40 hex, and 50 hex occupy the next three memory locations. Therefore, the data in memory will look like this:

> 7000   20
> 7001   30
> 7002   40
> 7003   50

Define Word (DW)   The directive DW is typically used to assign a 16-bit value to two memory locations. For example,

> ORG   7000H
> START   DW   4AC2H

will assign C2 to location 7000 and 4A to location 7001. It is assumed that the assembler will assign the low byte first (C2) and then the high byte (4A). The DW directive can be used to generate a table of 16-bit data as follows:

> ORG   8000H
> POINTER   DW   5000H,6000H,7000H

In this case, the three 16-bit values 5000H, 6000H, and 7000H are assigned to memory locations starting at the address 8000H. That is, the array would look like this:

8000	00
8001	50
8002	00
8003	60
8004	00
8005	70

Define Doubleword (DD)   Similar to DB and DW, the directive DD is typically used to assign a 32-bit value to four memory locations. The directive DD can be used to create a table in memory containing 32-bit data.

END   The directive END indicates the end of the assembly language source program.

.CODE   The .CODE directive is used to indicate the start of a code segment.

.DATA   The .DATA directive is used to indicate the start of a data segment.

.MODEL   The .MODEL directive tells the assembler the type of program being created. Two examples of model types are SMALL and FLAT. SMALL programs contain one code segment and one data segment with 16-bit addressing. FLAT programs, on the other hand, contains one code segment and one data segment with 32-bit addressing. All Pentium assembly language programs in this book are either SMALL or FLAT. Also, STDCALL must be included with a model for inclusion of assembler's standard library routines required to assemble the programs.

    To develop Pentium assembly language programs in this book, MASM32 assembler and OllyDebugger simulator are used. These programs are very user friendly, and can be downloaded from the Internet free of charge, using the following web sites.

- *MASM32*   http://www.assemblercode.com/masm32/m32v9r.zip

- *OllyDebugger*   http://www.ollybg.de/odbg110.zip
    The zip files for the MASM32 and OllyDebugger are provided in a CD. The CD also contains a tutorial showing a step-by-step procedure for installing, assembling, and debugging a typical Pentium assembly language program using the MASM32 and OllyDebugger. Most of the Pentium programming examples in this book are assembled using the MASM32 and debugged using OllyDebugger. Screen shots are provided on the CD verifying correct operation of all assembly language programs via simulations using test data.
    As an example, a typical program for adding two 16-bit numbers written in Pentium assembly language is shown below.

LABEL FIELD	MNEMONIC FIELD	OPERAND FIELD	COMMENT FIELD
	.486		; include 486 instruction set
	.MODEL	SMALL,STDCALL	; Model type and calling
	.CODE		; convention

START:	MOV	AX,1	; Move 1 into AX
	MOV	BX,2	; Move 2 into BX
	ADD	AX,BX	; Add contents of AX with ; BX
	HLT		
END	START		; End of program

The assembly language program above called a *source file* contains all instructions required to execute a program. The assembler converts the source file into an object file containing the binary codes or machine codes that the Pentium will understand. In typical assemblers, including the Pentium, the source file must be stored with a file extension called .ASM. Suppose that the programmer stores the source file above as SUM.ASM. To assemble the program, SUM.ASM is presented as input to the assembler. The assembler typically generates two files: SUM.OBJ and SUM.LST.

The SUM.OBJ is an *object file*, a binary file containing the machine code and data that correspond to the assembly language program in the source file (SUM.ASM). The object file includes additional information about relocation and external references. The object file is not normally ready for execution.

The SUM.LST, a *list file,* shows how the assembler interprets the source file. SUM.LST may be displayed on the screen. Suppose that the source file SUM.ASM is assembled at CS = 0040H, and IP = 1000H using the MASM32. The SUM.LST file is as follows:

00401000		START:	
00401000	66B80100	MOV	AX,1
00401004	66BB0200	MOV	BX,2
00401008	6603C3	ADD	AX,BX
0040100B	F4	HLT	

The first column gives the default CS and IP values where codes are stored. These values are generated automatically by the MASM32. For example, the machine code (66B80100H) for the first instruction, MOV AX,1 is stored in CS:IP = 0040H:1000H. Since this instruction takes 4 bytes, the machine code for the next instruction, MOV BX,2 starts at CS:IP = 0040H:1004H. Note that the comment fields in the SUM.ASM file are not translated by the MASM32.

To develop a large program by a group of programmers, each programmer may write a portion of the whole program. The individual programs must be tested and assembled to ensure their proper operation. When all portions of the program are verified for correct operation, their object files must be combined into a single object program using a *linker*, a program that checks each object file and finds certain characteristics, such as the size in bytes and its proper location in the single object program. The linker also resolves any issues in regard to cross-references to labels. Also, a library of object files is typically used to reduce the size of the source file. The library files may contain frequently used subroutines and/or sections of codes. Rather than writing these codes repeatedly in the source file, a special pseudoinstruction is used to tell the assembler that the code must be inserted at the linking time by the linker. When linking is completed, the final object file is called an *executable* (.EXE) *file*. Finally, a program called the *loader* can be used to load the .EXE file in memory for execution.

10.6   Pentium Addressing Modes

Assembly language programs in Pentium typically contain two logical parts: data and code. The ways of specifying the locations of the operands are called *addressing modes*. Note that an operand may typically be immediate data, or data stored in a Pentium's register or in a data segment.

Several instruction types along with a number of addressing modes and data types, make the Pentium a very powerful microprocessor. For simplicity, most of the examples of addressing modes described below use the Pentium instruction MOV destination,source. This instruction transfers the contents of a source (register or a memory location) into a destination (register or a memory location).

Also, when a physical address is generated by the Pentium in the real mode, a 20-bit value appears on Pentium's low 20 of the total 32 address pins. Note that Pentium address pins A2 A1 A0 are encoded from the byte enable pins, BE7# through BE0#. As mentioned earlier, this 20-bit physical address is generated by the Pentium using two components (logical address) provided by the programmer. These components are a 16-bit segment value and a 16-bit offset value. The Pentium shifts the segment four times to left and then adds the offset to generate a 20-bit physical address.

When accessing a memory location, the programmer must provide a segment value and an offset value. Data transfer instructions such as MOV use the data segment register (DS) as default; the offset is provided by the contents of certain registers (mentioned before) or an offset value. For instructions, the 20-bit physical address is computed from CS and IP. For stack operations, SS and SP are used automatically to compute the physical address for the system stack.

The programmer can initialize the data segment registers (DS, ES, FS, GS) and the stack segment register (SS) using AX, BX, CX, or DX. For example, to initialize DS to 5000H, the following instruction sequence can be used:

MOV   BX,5000H
MOV   DS,BX

These segment registers cannot be initialized with immediate data. Also, CS cannot be initialized via programming. CS is typically initialized upon hardware reset. Note that while accessing a memory location, initialization of a segment register is required for generation of the 20-bit physical address. This will ensure correct execution of a program.

10.6.1   Pentium's 32-Bit Addressing in Real Mode

Although the 32-bit offsets are designed for protected mode applications, 32-bit offsets can be used for real mode applications. In the real mode, these 32-bit offsets must fall within the 64-kB range (0000H-FFFFH) used within a segment. This means that the contents of a 32-bit register holding an offset must be between 00000000H and 0000FFFFH. The advantage is that an extended register may be used as a base register or an index register or both in the same instruction. However, the ESP register is the only one that may be used as a base register, and cannot be used as an index register.

Sixteen- and 32-bit addresses (offsets) and data can be mixed using two override prefixes:

66H   Oprand size override prefix
67H   Address size override prefix

In the real mode, the value of a 32-bit offset may not exceed 65,535 (64K). This means that the low 16-bit of a 32-bit register can be used to hold the 16-bit offset in real mode. Both 16- and 32-bit data and offsets can be used in real mode, as illustrated below by examples.

The Pentium assembler (MASM32) translates the following instruction with 32-bit data:

MOV   EAX,2000715AH

into machine code: B85A710020.

The Pentium assembler translates the following instruction with a 32-bit operand, ECX, and a 32-bit offset in EBX:

MOV   ECX,[EBX]

into machine code: 8B0B.

However, one can use 16-bit data and offsets for the Pentium assembler using the prefixes above as shown in the examples below.

The assembler translates the following instruction with a 16-bit operand, AX:

MOV   AX,2

into machine code: 66B80200.

The Pentium assembler automatically inserts 66H (Operand size override prefix).

The assembler translates the following instruction with 16-bit operand CX:

MOV   CX,[EBX]

into machine code: 668B0B.

The Pentium assembler automatically inserts 66H (operand size override prefix).

Next, Pentium assembler translates the instruction with 16-bit offset

MOV EAX, [BX]

into machine code: 678B07.

The Pentium assembler automatically inserts 67H (address size override prefix).

Note that both override prefixes can be mixed in an instruction as illustrated in the following. For example, the Pentium assembler translates the following instruction with a 16-bit offset and 16-bit operand:

MOV   DX,[BX]

into machine code: 67668B17

In this case, the Pentium assembler automatically inserts 6766 for address and operand override prefixes.

The Pentium provides various addressing modes to access instruction operands. Operands may be contained in registers, within the instruction op-code, in memory, or in I/O ports. The Pentium has 13 addressing modes, which can be classified into five groups:

1.   Register and immediate modes (two modes)
2.   Memory addressing modes (seven modes)
3.   Port addressing mode (two modes)
4.   Relative addressing mode (one mode)
5.   Implied addressing mode (one mode)

      The addressing modes are illustrated utilizing Pentium instructions with directives of a typical assembler. Note that in the following, parentheses, ( ) are used to indicate the contents of a Pentium register or a memory location.

10.6.2   Register and Immediate Modes

Register Mode.   In register mode, source operand, destination operand, or both may be contained in Pentium's 8-, 16-, or 32-bit registers. For example, MOV EAX,EBX

Table 10.5   **Memory Addressing Modes for 16-bit Offset**

Memory Addressing	Offset Value	Assembler Syntax
Direct	Contained in instruction	[offset]
Indirect		
Register Indirect	Contained in BX or BP or SI or DI	[BX] or [BP] or [SI] or [DI]
Based	BX (or BP) + d	[BX + d] or [BP + d]
Indexed	SI (or DI) + d	[SI + d] or [DI + d]
Based Indexed	BX + SI + d or BP + SI + d or	[BX + SI + d] or [BP + SI + d] or
	BX + DI + d or BP + DI + d	[BX + DI+ d] or [BP + DI+ d]
In the above 'd' is displacement		

Table 10.6   **Memory Addressing Modes for 32-Bit Offset**

Memory Addressing	Offset Value	Assembler Syntax
Direct	Contained in instruction	[offset]
Indirect		
Register Indirect	Contained in base	[Base]
Based	Contained in (base + d)	[Base + d]
Indexed	Contained in (index * s + d)	[Index*s + d]
Based Indexed (with no scaling)	Contained in (base + index + d)	[Base + index + d]
Based Indexed (with scaling)	Contained in (base + index * s + d)	[Base + index * s + d]

*In the above, 'd' is displacement, Scale factor, s = 1 or 2 or 4 or 8, base = EAX or EBX or ECX or EDX or ESI or EDI or EBP or ESP, and index = EAX or EBX or ECX or EDX or ESI or EDI or EBP. ESP cannot be used as index register. Effective address = segment register + base + (index * s) + d.*

moves the 32-bit contents of EBX into EAX, MOV AX,BX moves the 16-bit contents of BX into AX, and MOV AH,BL moves the 8-bit contents of BL into AH. In these examples, both operands are in register mode.

Immediate Mode.   In the immediate mode, 8-, 16-, or 32-bit data can be specified as part of the instruction. For example, MOV ECX,2A715062H moves the 32-bit data 2A715062H into register ECX. Similarly, MOV DX, 4C00H moves the 16-bit data 4C00H into register DX. On the other hand, MOV BH, 2DH moves 8-bit data 2DH into register BH.

10.6.3   Memory Addressing Mode

The Pentium provides several addressing modes while accessing data in memory. Note that the programmer must specify a logical address to identify a memory location. Recall that the logical address contains two components: a segment value and an offset value. Memory addressing modes vary in how they specify the offset.

The memory addressing modes available for 16-bit offsets are the same as for the 8086. Tables 10.5 and 10.6 list the memory addressing modes for 16-bit and 32-bit offsets, respectively. Note that for memory indirect addressing with 32-bit offset (Table 10.6), the offset within the segment selected is the sum of maximum four components: a displacement, a base register, an index register, and a scaling factor of 1, 2, 4, or 8. The offset that results from adding these components is called an *effective address*. Note that all general purpose registers can be used as index registers. ESP cannot be used as an index register.

The various memory addressing modes are described below. Note that the numerical valuesare chosen arbitrarily for illustrative purposes.

Memory Direct Addressing.   The direct addressing mode includes the offset directly in the instruction. A typical Pentium instruction such as the MOV transfers data between an 8-bit register such as AL ,or a 16-bit register such as BX, or a 32-bit register such as EDX, and an offset located in the data segment. Memory-to-memory transfers are not allowed.

For example, MOV [2000H],AL, in real mode, transfers 8-bit contents of AL into a 20-bit physical address computed from the segment register DS and offset 2000H. Typical assemblers use square brackets around the offset 2000H to indicate that the contents of the memory location are at an offset 2000H from the segment DS.

Next, consider MOV BX, [5000H] in real mode. This instruction moves the contents of a 20-bit physical address computed from the segment register DS and offset 5000H to BX.

Finally, consider MOV [3000H], ECX in real mode. If (DS) = 2000H, (ECX) = 12345678H, (23000H) = 01H, (23001H) = 02H, (23002H) = 03H, and (23003H) = 04H, then after execution of MOV [3000H],ECX, the byte contents of four 20-bit physical addresses will be [23000H] = 78H, [23001H] = 56H, [23002H] = 34H, and [23003H] = 12H.

Register Indirect Addressing.   In the register indirect mode, the offset is contained in one of the 16- or 32-bit general-purpose registers. The offset of a memory operand may be taken directly from one of the base or index 16-bit registers (BX, BP, SI, DI) or 32-bit registers (EAX, EBX, ECX, EDX,ESI, EDI, EBP). Note that 16-bit registers AX, CX, DX, and SP and the 32-bit register ESP cannot be used indirectly to hold 16-bit or 32-bit offset, respectively.

Next, consider MOV CX,[BX] in real mode. If prior to execution of the instruction, (DS) = 2000H, (BX) = 0004H, and (20004H) = 24H, (20005H) = 02H, then, after execution of MOV CX,[BX], the contents of CH and CL are 02H and 24H respectively. Note that the segment register used in MOV CX,[BX] can be overridden, such as MOV CX,ES:[BX]. Now, the MOV instruction will use ES instead of DS. If prior to execution of MOV CX,ES:[BX], (BX) = 0004H, (ES) = 1000H, and (10004H) = 02H, (10005H) = 00H, then after MOV CX,ES:[BX] , the register CX will contain 0002H.

Typical examples of indirect addressing using 32-bit registers for offset include MOV DX,[ECX] and MOV [EAX],EBX. Next, consider as an example MOV AX,[EDX] in real mode. Note that in real mode, the contents of EDX can have a value between 00000000H and 0000FFFFH. If prior to execution of this instruction, (AX) = F092H, (EDX) = 00002000H, (DS) = 3000H, (32000H) = 20H, and (32001H) = 30H, then after execution of MOV AX,[EDX], the 16-bit register AX will contain 16-bit data 3020H; (AH) = 30H, (AL) = 20H. Note that all numerical values in the above are chosen arbitrarily for illustrative purposes.

For register indirect addressing mode using BX, DI, or SI to contain the 16-bit offset, the DS register is used as the segment register by default. The SS register is used as a default segment register if BP is used indirectly to hold the 16-bit offset. For a 32-bit offset, the DS is used by default as the segment register if EAX, EBX, ECX, EDX, ESI, or EDI is used to hold the 32-bit offset; SS is used as a default segment register if EBP is used to hold the 32-bit offset.

Note that in the real address mode the contents of the 32-bit register holding the offset must be between 00000000H and 0000FFFFH.

The size of the data is typically specified by the register size when one of the operands is a register. For example, MOV BH, [SI] in the real mode transfers the 8-bit contents of a 20-bit physical address computed from 16-bit offset in SI and the segment register DS into BH. Note that in this case, the 8-bit register specifies the 8-bit data size. However, there are certain instances in which the size of the data needs to be specified by assembler directives BYTE PTR, WORD PTR, or DWORD PTR. For example, MOV BYTE PTR [BX], 50H defines the location addressed by offset in BX and the segment register, DS as a byte. The instruction, MOV WORD PTR [BX],5 in the real mode will treat the location addressed by the 20-bit physical address computed from BX and DS as 16-bit. This means that this instruction will convert decimal number 5 into 16-bit as 0000000000000101 in binary, and then transfer this data into 16-bit memory. Similarly, MOV DWORD PTR [SI],70 specifies the memory location as 32-bit.

Based Addressing.   For 16-bit offset, the effective address is the sum of a displacement value (0 or signed 8-bit or signed 16-bit) and the contents of register BX or BP. The signed 8-bit displacement gives a range of -128_{10} to $+127_{10}$, with 0 being positive. The signed 16-bit, on the other hand, provides a range of -32768_{10} to $+32767_{10}$, with 0 being positive. Note that if the displacement is 8-bit, and the register is 16-bit, the displacement is sign-extended to 16 bits before adding it to the 16-bit register. Typical example includes MOV [BX + 3], AL.

Assume real mode. If prior to execution of this instruction, (BX) = 0200H, (DS) = 5000H, (50203H) = A2H, and (AL) = 05H, then after execution of this instruction, the contents of 20-bit physical address 50203H will be 05H. Note that a typical assembler uses either MOV [BX+3], AL or MOV 3 [BX],AL.

For a 32-bit offset, the effective address is the sum of a displacement value (0 or signed 8-bit or signed 32-bit) and the contents of a base register. A typical example include MOV [ECX + 8], EDX. Assume the real mode. Note that ECX + 8 in real mode can have a maximum value of 0000FFFFH. If prior to execution of this instruction, (ECX) = 00000200H, (DS) = 3000H, (30208H) = A2H, (30209H) = 05H, (3020AH) = 06H, (3020BH) = 02H, and (EDX) = 0102F305H, then after execution of this instruction, the contents of the four affected 20-bit physical addresses will be as follows: (30208H) = 05H, (30209H) = F3H, (3020AH) = 02H, and (3020BH) = 01H. If the displacement is 8-bit, and the register is 32-bit, the displacement is sign-extended to 32 bits before adding it to the 32-bit register.

Next, consider MOV AX,[BX+4] in real mode. This instruction moves the contents of the 20-bit physical address computed from a segment register and BX + 4 into AX. The segment register is DS (when the content of BX is used as offset), or SS (when the content of BP is used as offset). The content of BX is unchanged. The displacement (4 in this case) can be unsigned 16-bit or signed 8-bit. This means that if the displacement is 8-bit, the Pentium sign-extends this to 16-bit. Segment register SS is used when the stack is accessed; otherwise, this mode uses segment register DS. When memory is accessed, the 20-bit physical address is computed from BX and DS. On the other hand, when the stack is accessed, the 20-bit physical address is computed from BP and SS. Note that BP may be considered as the user stack pointer while SP is the system stack pointer. This is because SP is used automatically by some Pentium instructions (such as the CALL subroutine).

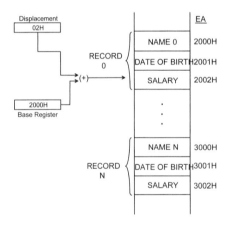

(a)   Accessing a fixed record stored in different places in memory using based mode

(b)   Using BP as the stack pointer using based mode

FIGURE 10.6   Uses of based addressing mode.

Based addressing mode is useful when one wants to access the same record type among several occurrences in a data structure which may be stored at different places in memory. For example, consider Figure 10.6(a). In the figure, personal records of *N* employees are stored starting at an offset 2000H. Assume that each record type is 8 bits wide. For example, the element "salary" of the employee with NAME 0 can be loaded into an 8-bit register such as AL of the Pentium using the instruction MOV AL, [ALPHA + BX], where ALPHA is the 8-bit displacement 02H and BX contains the starting address of RECORD 0. Now, to access the salary of RECORD N, the programmer simply changes the contents of BX to 3000H.

The based addressing mode with BP is also a very convenient way to access stack data in the real mode, as shown in Figure 10.6(b). BP can be used as a stack pointer in SS to access local variables. Consider the following instruction sequence (chosen arbitrarily to illustrate the use of BP for stack):

```
PUSH   BP          ;   Save BP
MOV    BP,SP        ;   Establish BP
PUSH   CX           ;   Save CX
SUB    SP, 6        ;   Allocate three words of stack for local
MOV    [BP-4], BX   ;   variables. Push BX onto stack.
MOV    [BP-6], AX   ;   using BP. Push AX onto stack using
MOV    [BP-8], DX   ;   BP. Push DX onto stack using BP
ADD    SP, 6        ;   Deallocate stack
POP    CX           ;   Restore CX
POP    BP           ;   Restore BP
```

This mode can also be used to access an element in an array. Assume the real mode. Assume that an array of 50 bytes is stored in memory at an offset 3000H in DS. Note that the first element in the array is element 0 and the last element is element 49. Now, to access, say, element 4 in the array, register BX can be initialized with offset 3000H and the instruction MOV CL,[BX + 4] can be executed to read element 4 from the array into CL.

Indexed Addressing.   In this mode, the 16-bit effective address is calculated from the sum of a displacement value and the contents of register SI or DI. For example, MOV AX,[SI + 6] in real mode moves the 16-bit contents of the 20-bit physical address computed from SI + 6 and the segment register into AX. The segment register is DS. The content of SI is unchanged. The displacement (6 in this case) can be signed 8- or 16-bit. This means that the displacement can be positive or negative. Note that if the displacement is 8-bit, and the register is 16-bit, the displacement is sign-extended to 16 bits before adding it to the 16-bit register. This mode can be used to access an array when the size of each element is a byte.

TABLE 10.7	Sample Array
Offset (Hex)	**Memory Contents (Hex)**
00002000H	0507H
00002002H	F214H
00002004H	5171H
00002006H	1234H

For 32-bit offset, the scaled indexed with displacement mode can be used. In this case, the effective Address = (index * scale factor) + displacement. Note that ESP cannot be used as index register. A typical example is MOV EBX, [ESI*2 + 10H]. Assume the real mode. If prior to execution of this instruction, (EBX) = 02030405H, (ESI) = 00000030H, (DS) = 1000H, (10070H) = 02H, (10071H) = B7H, (10072H) = 24H, and (10073H) = 07H, then after execution of this instruction, (EBX) = 0724B702H.

Based Indexed Addressing with No Scaling.   The 16-bit effective address is computed from the sum of a base register (BX or BP), an index register (SI or DI), and a displacement. For example, MOV AX,[4 + BX + SI] moves the 16-bit contents of the 20-bit physical address computed from the segment register and (BX) + (SI) + 4 into AX. The segment register is DS. In this mode, 32-bit effective address = base + index + displacement. A typical example is MOV AL,[EAX + ESI + 2]. This mode can also be used to access an array when each element size is a byte.

Based Indexed with scaling.   In this mode, 32-bit effective address = base + (index * scale)+ displacement. A typical example is MOV DX, [EAX + ESI*2 + 10]. This mode can be used to access two-dimensional arrays such as matrices. This mode can also be used to access an array when the element size is 2, 4, or 8 bytes. The base register can address the beginning of the array, the index register can hold the subscript (the element number in the array), and the Pentium automatically converts the element number into an index by applying the scaling factor. Note that scaling is only allowed for 32-bit offsets.

For example, consider the array shown in Table 10.7 at offset 00002000H in the real mode containing four 16-bit elements (0 through 3). Now, to read an element from this array, the based indexed with scaling addressing mode can be used. First, a base register such as EAX can be loaded with the starting offset 00002000H using the instruction, MOV EAX,00002000H. To load F214H (element 1), an index register such as EDX can be loaded with 1 (the element number) using the instruction MOV EDX,1. Since the size of the element is 16 bits (2 bytes), a scaling factor of 2 can be used to load element 1 into register BX using the instruction MOV BX, [EAX + 2*EDX]. Note that this instruction loads the 16-bit contents of offset 00002002H (00002000H + 2 * 1) which is F214H, into BX. The Pentium assembly language program to accomplish this is

```
00401000 B800200000        MOV    EAX,00002000H
00401005 BA01000000        MOV    EDX,1
0040100A 668B1C50          MOV    BX,[EAX+EDX*2]
0040100E F4                HLT
```

Similarly, element 3 (1234H) can be loaded into a 16-bit register such as CX using the following assembly language program:

```
00401000 B800200000        MOV    EAX,00002000H
00401005 BA03000000        MOV    EDX,3
0040100A 668B1C50          MOV    BX,[EAX + EDX*2]
0040100E F4                HLT
```

String Addressing.   This mode uses index registers. In real mode, SI is assumed to point to the first byte or word (16-bit) or doubleword (32-bit) of the source string, and DI is assumed to point to the first byte or word (16-bit) or doubleword (32-bit) of the destination when a string instruction is executed. The SI or DI is incremented (DF = 0) or decremented (DF = 1) automatically by 1 for byte, 2 for word, or 4 for doubleword to point to the next byte or word or doubleword, depending on DF. An example of string addressing mode is MOVSW. The default segment register for the source is DS with SI pointing to the source string, and it may be overridden; the segment register used for the destination must be ES with DI pointing to the destination string and ES cannot be overridden. An example is ES:MOVSW. In this case, both source and destination strings will use ES as the segment register. Next, consider a numerical example of string mode. Assume the real mode. If (DF) = 0, (DS) = 3000H, (SI) = 0020H, (ES) = 5000H, (DI) = 0040H, (30020H) = 30H, (30021H) = 05H, (50040H) = 06H, and (50041H) = 20H, then after this MOVSW, (50040H) = 30H,

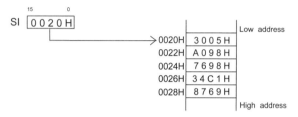

SOURCE STRING (DS=3000H,SI=0020H)

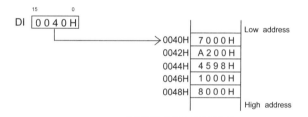

DESTINATION STRING (ES=5000H,DI=0040H)

FIGURE 10.7 (a)   Source and Destination strings Prior to execution of MOVSW.

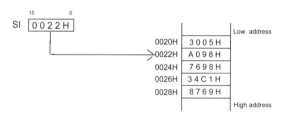

SOURCE STRING (DS=3000H,SI=0020H)

DESTINATION STRING (ES=5000H,DI=0040H)

FIGURE 10. 7 (b)   Source and Destination strings After execution of MOVSW.

(50041H) = 05H, (SI) = 0022H, and (DI) = 0042H.

Figures 10.7 (a) and 10.7 (b) respectively show data in the source and destination strings prior to and after execution of MOVSW. All numerical values in the figures are chosen arbitrarily. Note that for 16-bit offset, SI and DI contain offsets for both source and destination strings while for 32-bit offset, ESI and EDI contain offsets for both source and destination strings. Also, for 32-bit offset in real mode, the contents of ESI and EDI vary from 00000000H to 0000FFFFH.

10.6.4   Port Addressing Mode

Two I/O port addressing modes can be used: direct port and indirect port. In either case, 8- or 16- or 32-bit I/O transfers must take place via AL or AX or EAX, respectively. In *direct port mode,* the port number is an 8-bit immediate operand to access 256 ports. For example, IN AL,02H moves the contents of 8-bit port 02H to AL. OUT 04H,AX, on the other hand, outputs the 16-bit contents of AX into 16-bit port 0405H. Finally, IN EAX,02H will input the 32-bit contents of a 32-bit port 02030405H into EAX.

In *indirect port mode,* the port number is taken from DX, allowing 64 kB or 32K words of ports. For example, suppose that (DX) = 0020H, (port 0020H) = 02H, and (port 0021H) = 03H; then after IN AX,DX, register AX contains 0302H. On the other hand, after IN AL,DX, register AL contains 02H. Next, consider, IN EAX,DX. Prior to execution of this instruction, if (DX) = 0050H, (port 0050H) = 01H, (port 0051H) = 02H, (port 0052H) = 03H, (port 0053H) = 04H, then after execution of IN EAX, DX, register EAX will contain 04030201H.

10.6.5   Relative Addressing Mode

Instructions using the relative addressing mode specify the operand as a signed 8-bit displacement relative to IP. An example is JNC START. This instruction means that if carry = 0, IP is loaded with the current IP contents plus the 8-bit signed value of START; otherwise, the next instruction is executed.

An advantage of the relative mode is that the destination address is specified relative to the address of the instruction after the conditional jump instruction. Since the Pentium conditional Jump instructions do not contain an absolute address, the program can be placed anywhere in memory which can still be executed properly by the Pentium. A program that can be placed anywhere in memory and can still run correctly is called a *relocatable program.* It is a good practice to write relocatable programs.

The Pentium contains a 1-byte unconditional JMP instruction with a 1- or 2-byte displacement that adds to the instruction pointer (IP). A JMP with an 8-bit displacement called a *short jump* has a range of -128 to +127 bytes, with 0 being positive. A JMP with a 16-bit displacement, called a *near jump* has a range of -32768 to +32767 bytes, with 0 being positive. The Pentium assembler determines automatically whether the Jump is *short* or *near* based on the size of the displacement. Finally, a JMP with a 32-bit displacement has a range of +2 to -2 GB. Note that a 32-bit displacement can be used only in the protected mode. Conditional and Unconditional Jumps are covered in more detail in Chapter 11.

10.6.6   Implied Addressing Mode

Instructions using the implied addressing mode have no operands. An example is CLC, which clears the carry flag to zero.

10.7   Pentium Instructions

The Pentium instruction set contains no-operand, single-operand, two-operand, and three-operand instructions. Except for string instructions that involve array operations, the Pentium instructions do not permit memory-to-memory operations. The Pentium instructions can be classified into nine groups:

1. Data transfer instructions
2. Arithmetic instructions
3. Logic, bit manipulation, set on condition, shift, and rotate instructions
4. String instructions
5. Unconditional transfer instructions
6. Conditional branch instructions
7. Iteration control instructions
8. Interrupt instructions
9. Processor control instructions

Instruction groups 1 and 2 are covered in this chapter. Instruction groups 3 through 9 are included in Chapter 11. Appendix F provides Pentium instruction format and timing. Appendix H shows some of the Pentium's instruction set. Let us now explain some of the Pentium instructions (Groups 1 and 2) with numerical examples in real mode. Note that in the following examples, parentheses ( ) are used to indicate the contents of a register or a memory location. As mentioned in section 10.6.3 (memory addressing modes), segment override prefix can be used in any instruction with any memory addressing mode to override the default segment register. Most memory instructions use DS as the default segment register. The segment override prefix can be used to change DS to ES, FS, GS, or SS. Note that CS cannot be overridden. This means that JUMP and CALL instructions cannot be prefixed.

Consider MOV AX,[SI]. This instruction transfers the 16-bit contents of a memory location addressed by the offset in SI, and the segment register is DS. The segment register DS can be changed to ES using the instruction MOV AX,ES: [SI]. Next, consider MOV [BP], CH. This instruction transfers 8-bit data in CH into a memory location addressed by BP in SS. The default segment register is SS. The segment register SS can be changed to DS using the instruction MOV DS: [BP],CH.

10.7.1   Data Transfer Instructions
Table 10.8 lists most of Pentium's data transfer instructions.

In the table, the data transfer instructions move single bytes, 16-bit words, and 32-bit doublewords between a register, a memory location, or an I/O port. Let us explain some of the instructions in Table 10.8.

TABLE 10.8   Pentium Data Transfer Instructions

General Purpose	
MOV d, s	(d) ← (s) MOV byte or word
MOVSX dest, src	Move and sign-extend
MOVZX dest, src	Move and zero-extend
PUSH operand	PUSH operand into stack
PUSHA	PUSH all 16-bit registers
PUSHAD	PUSH all 32-bit registers
POP operand	POP operand off stack
POPA	POP all 16-bit registers
POPAD	POP all 32-bit registers
XCHG reg/mem, reg/mem	(reg/mem) ↔ (reg/mem); No mem to mem.
XLAT	AL ← (20 bit address computed from AL, BX, and DS) in real mode
Input / Output	
IN A, DX or Port	Input byte or word or doubleword
OUT DX or Port, A	Output byte or word or doubleword
Address Object	
LEA reg, mem	LOAD Effictive Address
LDS reg, mem	LOAD pointer using DS
LES reg, mem	LOAD pointer using ES
LFS reg, mem	LOAD pointer using FS

TABLE 10.8   Cont.

LGS reg, mem	LOAD pointer using GS
LSS reg, mem	LOAD pointer using SS

Flag Transfer

LAHF	LOAD AH register from flags
SAHF	STORE AH register in flags
PUSHF	PUSH lower 16 bits of Flag register
POPF	POP lower 16 bits of Flag register off the stack

dest = "reg16" or "reg32"   src = "reg8" or "mem8" or   A = EAX, AX, or AL
d = "mem", "reg" or "segreg"   "reg16" or "mem16"
                                s = "data" or "mem" or "reg"
                                        or "segreg"

- MOV CX,DX copies the 16-bit contents of DX into CX. MOV AX,2025H moves immediate data 2025H into the 16-bit register AX. MOV CH,[BX] moves the 8-bit contents of a memory location addressed by BX in segment register DS into CH. If prior to execution of this instruction, (BX) = 0050H, (DS) = 2000H, and (20050H) = 08H, then after execution of the MOV CH,[BX] instruction, the contents of CH will be 08H. MOV [BP + 6],CX moves the 16-bit contents of CX into two memory locations addressed by the sum of register BP and displacement 6 in segment register SS (CL to the first location and CH to the next location). For example, if (CX) = 5009H, (BP) = 0030H, (SS) = 3000H, then, after execution of the MOV [BP + 6],CX instruction, (30036H) = 09H and (30037H) = 50H. Next, consider MOV ECX,ESI. If prior to execution of this instruction, (ECX) = 50A00050H and (ESI) = 7C002000H, then after execution of the MOV ECX,ESI instruction, (ECX) = 7C002000H and the contents of ESI are 7C002000H (unchanged).

- Next, consider MOVSX and MOVZX instructions as follows:

MOVSX	dest,	src	Move and sign-extend
MOVZX	dest,	src	Move and zero-extend
	reg16,	reg8	
	reg16,	mem8	
	reg32,	reg8	
	reg32,	mem8	
	reg32,	reg16	
	reg32,	mem16	

MOVSX reads the contents of the effective address or register as a byte or a word from the source, sign-extends the value to the operand size of the destination (16 or 32 bits), and stores the result in the destination. No flags are affected. MOVZX, on the other hand, reads the contents of the effective address or register as a byte or a word, zero-extends the value to the operand size of the destination (16 or 32 bits), and stores the result in the destination. No flags are affected. For example, consider MOVSX BX,CL. If (CL) = 81H and (BX) = 21AFH, then, after execution of this MOVSX, register BX contains FF81H and the contents of CL do not change. Now, consider MOVZX CX,DH. If (CX) = F237H and (DH) = 85H, then after execution of this MOVZX, register CX contains 0085H and DH contents do not change.

- Pentium PUSH operand or POP operand instruction writes or reads register or data to or from the stack respectively. The data may be any 16- or 32-bit register, 8-, 16- or 32-bit immediate data, segment registers (except CS), or 16- or 32-bit contents of memory. In the real mode, for 16-bit operand, the SP is decremented by 2 for PUSH and incremented by 2 for POP ; for 32-bit operand, the SP is decremented by 4 for PUSH and incremented by 4 for POP. Note that SS:SP is used to address stack for real mode while SS:ESP is used to address stack for the protected mode.

  As an example, consider PUSH BX. If prior to execution of this instruction, (BX) = 0200H, (SP) = 3000H, (SS) = 4000H, (42FFFH) = 01H, and (42FFEH) = 78H then after execution of PUSH BX instruction, memory locations 42FFFH and 42FFEH will contain 02H and 00H, respectively, and the contents of SP will be 2FFEH. This is depicted in Figure 10.8. Next, consider POP AX. If prior to execution of this instruction, (SS) = 4000H, (SP) = 3000H, (AX) = 0050H, (43001H) = 01H, and (43002H) = 05H, then after execution of POP AX, (AX) = 0501H, and (SP) = 3002H. This is depicted in Figure 10.9.

- For 16-bit data, each Pentium stack segment is 64kB long and is organized as 32K 16-bit words. The lowest byte (valid data) of the stack is pointed to by the 20-bit physical address computed from current SP and SS. This is the lowest memory location in the stack (top of the stack) where data is pushed. The Pentium can have

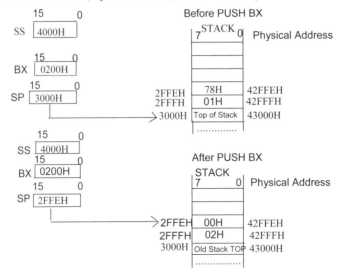

FIGURE 10.8   Pentium PUSH BX operation

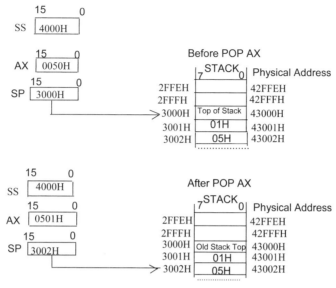

FIGURE 10.9   Pentium POP AX operation

several stack segments; however, only one stack segment is active at a time.

When the Pentium uses 16-bit data for PUSH and POP operations from the top of the stack, the Pentium PUSH instruction first decrements SP by 2 and then the 16-bit data is written onto the stack. Therefore, the Pentium stack grows from high to low memory addresses of the stack. On the other hand, when 16-bit data is popped from the top of the stack using the Pentium POP instruction, the Pentium reads 16-bit data from the stack into the specified register or memory, the Pentium increments the SP by 2. Note that the 20-bit physical address computed from SP and SS always points to the last data pushed onto the stack. Memory locations can also be saved and restored using PUSH and POP instructions without using any Pentium 16-bit registers. Finally, one must POP registers in the reverse order in which they are PUSHed. For example, if the registers BX, DX, and SI are PUSHed using

PUSH   BX
PUSH   DX
PUSH   SI

then the registers must be popped using

POP   SI
POP   DX
POP   BX

• The PUSHA instruction saves all the 16-bit register onto the stack in the following order AX, CX, DX, BX, SP, BP, SI, and DI. The SP is then decremented by 16. The PUSHAD instruction pushes all 32-bit registers onto the stack in the order EAX, ECX, EDX, EBX, ESP, EBP, ESI, and EDI. The POPA instruction pops all 16-bit registers from the stack in the order DI, SI, BP, SP, BX, DX, CX, and AX. The SP is then incremented by 16. Note that the value popped for SP is discarded. This is done to keep the SP unchanged. The POPAD instruction, on the other hand, pops all 32-bit registers from the stack in the order EDI, ESI, EBP, ESP, EBX, EDX, ECX, and EAX. The value popped for ESP is discarded.

- PUSH d8 instruction pushes 8-bit immediate data onto the stack. The SP is then decremented by 1. PUSH d16 instruction, on the other hand, pushes 16-bit immediate data onto the stack. The SP is then decremented by 2. PUSH d32 instruction, on the other hand, pushes 32-bit immediate data onto the stack. The SP is then decremented by 4.
  As an example, consider PUSH 3000H. If prior to execution of this instruction, (SS) = 4000H, (SP) = 3000H, (42FFFH) = 01H, and (42FFEH) = 05H, then after execution of PUSH 3000H, (42FFFH) = 30H, (42FFEH) = 00H, and (SP) = 2FFEH.

- XCHG has three variations: XCHG reg,reg, XCHG mem,reg, or XCHG reg, mem. Both operands cannot be memory locations. XCHG instruction is used to exchange the 8-, 16-, or 32-bit contents of two operands. Note that segment registers are not allowed in the XCHG instruction. Also, the segment for the memory location must be in DS. Consider XCHG AX,BX. This instruction exchanges the contents of 16-bit register BX with the contents of AX. If prior to execution of the XCHG AX,BX instruction, (AX) = 2050H and (BX) = 70A0H, then after execution of the XCHG AX, BX instruction, (AX) = 70A0H, and (BX) = 2050H. Next, consider XCHG [SI], CX. If prior to excecution of the XCHG [SI], CX instruction, (SI)= 0050H, (DS) = 2000H, (CX) = 5000H, (20050H) = 56H, and (20051H) = 78H, then after execution of the XCHG [SI],CX instruction, (CX) = 7856H, (20050H) = 00H, and (20051H) = 50H.

- XLAT can be used to employ an index in a table or for code conversion. This instruction utilizes DS:BX to hold the starting address of the table in memory consisting of 8-bit data elements. AL should be the unsigned index into a table addressed by DS:BX. No flags are affected. The index in the table is assumed to be in the AL register. Note that the XLAT instruction is the same as MOV AL,[AL + BX]. For example, if (BX) = 0200H, (AL) = 04H, and (DS) = 3000H, then after XLAT, the contents of location 30204H will be loaded into AL. The XLAT instruction can be used to convert from one code to another. This is illustrated in Example 10.3. The XLATB instruction should be used if BX is always resident in the DS segment. Note that DS cannot be overridden if XLATB is used while XLAT instruction allows for the possibility of segment override.

- The IN and OUT instructions of the Pentium use only the registers AL, AX, or EAX to transfer data between an I/O port (register) and the microprocessor. Two types of I/O addressing are used:

  1. Direct addressing

For 8-bit port:	IN AL, PORT
	OUT PORT, AL
For 16-bit port:	IN AX, PORT
	OUT PORT, AX
For 32-bit port:	IN EAX, PORT
	OUT PORT, EAX

  2. Indirect addressing

For 8-bit port: IN AL, DX
                    OUT DX, AL
For 16-bit port: IN AX, DX
                    OUT DX, AX
For 32-bit port: IN EAX, DX
                    OUT DX, EAX

Consider direct port addressing, in which the 8-, 16-, or 32-bit port address is specified directly as part of the instruction. For example, IN AL,38H inputs 8-bit data from port 38H into AL. On the other hand, the instruction IN AX,38H inputs 16-bit data from ports 38H and 39H into AX. The instruction OUT 38H,AL outputs the contents of AL to port 38H. The instruction OUT 38H,AX outputs the 16-bit contents of AX to ports 38H and 39H. For indirect port addressing, the port address is specified in the DX register. Assume that (DX) = 3124H in all the following examples.

IN AL,DX inputs 8-bit data from an 8-bit port addressed by 3124H into AL.

IN AX,DX inputs 16-bit data from two 8-bit ports addressed by 3124H and 3125H into AX.

IN EAX,DX inputs 32-bit data from four 8-bit ports addressed by 3124H, 3125H, 3126H, and 3127H into EAX.

OUT DX,AL outputs 8-bit data from AL into an 8-bit port addressed by 3124H.

OUT DX,AX outputs 16-bit data from AX into two 8-bit ports addressed by 3124H and 3125H.

OUT DX,EAX outputs 32-bit data from EAX into four 8-bit ports addressed by 3124H, 3125H, 3126H, and 3127H.

Indirect port addressing allows up to 65,536 ports with addresses from 0000H to FFFFH. The port addresses in indirect port addressing can be calculated dynamically in a program. For example, assume that an Pentium-based microcomputer is connected to three printers via three separate ports. Now, to output to each of the printers, separate programs are required if fixed port addressing is used. However, with indirect port addressing, one can write a general subroutine to output to the printers and then supply the address of the port for a particular printer in which data output is desired to register DX in the subroutine.

*   LEA is used to load 16-bit or 32-bit offset into a specified register. As an example, LEA BX, 3000H has the same meaning as MOV BX,3000H. On the other hand, if (SI) = 2000H, then LEA BX, [SI + 4] will load 2004H into BX while MOV BX, [SI+4] will initialize BX with the contents of offset 2004H in DS. LEA can be used when address computation is desirable in a program.
    LDS, LES, LFS, LGS, and LSS are similar to LEA except that they load a specified register as well as the segment register indicated. Next, consider LDS SI,[DI]. This instruction loads SI and DS from memory. For example, if (DS) = 2000H, (DI) = 0010H, (20010H) = 0200H, and (20012H) = 0100H, then, after LDS SI,[DI] , SI and DS will contain 0200H and 0100H, respectively. Note that LDS, LES, LFS, and LGS can be used with a 32-bit extended register. Typical examples are LDS EBX,[ESI], LFS EAX, [ECX], and LSS ESP, [EDI].
*   LAHF loads the lower byte of the FLAGS register into AH. This will enable the programmer to check the state of the flags. For example, if the contents of the lower byte of the FLAGS register is 43H, then after execution of the LAHF instruction,

(AH) = 43H.

- SAHF is used to store the contents of AH into the lower byte of the FLAGS register. This will load a new set of flags into the FLAGS register of Figure 10.1 (b).

- PUSHF pushes the lower 16 bits of the EFLAGS register onto the stack. Suppose, prior to execution of PUSHF, (SS) = 3000H, (SP) = 0000H, and (FLAGS register) = 0083H. This means that the 20-bit physical address pointing to the valid data in the stack is 30000H. After execution of the PUSHF instruction, the stack address will be decremented by 2 and (2FFFFH) = 00H, and (2FFFEH) = 83H. Note that the lower byte is pushed to the lower address and the upper byte is pushed to the higher address. This is because Pentium follows the little endian format.

- POPF pops 16 bits from the stack and places them in the FLAGS register.

EXAMPLE 10.1   Determine the effect of each of the following Pentium instructions:
(a) MOVSX   ECX,E7H
(b) MOVZX   ECX,E7H
(c) MOVSX   AX,DL if (AX) = 2000H, (DL) = 75H
(d) MOV   CL,ES:[BP] if (CL) = 32H, (SS) = 2000H, (DS) = 5000H, (ES) = 1000H, (GS) = 4000H, (BP) = 0030H, (10030H) = F2H, (20030H) = 07H, and (40030H) = 02H.

Solution

(a) (ECX) = FFFFFFE7H since the most significant bit of E7H is 1, bits 8 through 31 of ECX are 1's.
(b) (ECX) = 000000E7H since this instruction moves E7H to the lowest byte of ECX, and then zero extends (write 0's) from bits 8 to 31 of ECX.
(c) (AX) = 0075H since this instruction moves 75H to the lower byte of AX, and then zero-extends or write 0's from bits 8 through 15 of AX.
(d) (CL) = F2H since ES instead of SS is used as the segment register. Hence, the contents of physical address 10030H are moved to CL.

EXAMPLE 10.2   Determine the effect of each of the following Pentium instructions:
(a) PUSH [BX] if (DS) = 2000H, (BX) = 0200H, (SP) = 3000H, (SS) = 4000H, (20200H) = 20H, (20201H) = 01H, (42FFFH) = 01H, and (42FFEH) = 20H
(b) POPA if (SS) = 2000H, (SP) = 2FF0H, and (22FF0H) through (22FFFH) = 07H

Solution

(a) After execution of PUSH [BX], memory locations 42FFFH and 42FFEH will contain 01H and 20H, respectively, and the contents of SP will be 2FFEH.

(b) After POPA, a set of two consecutive bytes, 0707H from locations (22FF0H) through (22FFFH), will be loaded into Pentium's 16-bit registers in the order DI, SI, BP, SP (discarded), BX, DX, CX, and AX. The contents of SP are incremented by 16 (10H) to point to 3000H.

EXAMPLE 10.3   Assume a Pentium-based microcomputer with an ASCII keyboard is connected to port A and an EBCDIC printer is connected to port B. Suppose that it is desired to enter numerical data via the ASCII keyboard and then print them on the EBCDIC printer. Use addresses for Port A and Port B as 60H and 68H respectively. Write a Pentium assembly language program to accomplish this.

Solution

Note that numerical data entered into this microcomputer via the keyboard will be in ASCII code. Since the printer only understands EBCDIC code, an ASCII-to-EBCDIC code conversion program is required. As discussed in Section 1.2.2 in Chapter 1, the ASCII codes for numbers 0 through 9 are 30H through 39H, while the EBCDIC codes for numbers 0 to 9 are F0H to F9H. The EBCDIC codes for the numbers 0 to 9 can be stored in a table starting at an offset 2030H , data can be input from the keyboard using IN AL,PORTA, then the ASCII data converted to EBCDIC using an XLAT instruction, and output to port B using OUT PORTB,AL. The assembly language for the code conversion program is

```
                .486
                .MODEL   SMALL,STDCALL
                .DATA
                ORG      2030H
                DB       0F0H,0F1H,0F2H,0F3H,0F4H,0F5H,0F6H,0F7H,0F8H,0F9H
                .CODE
START:
PORTA    EQU     60H
PORTB    EQU     68H
                MOV      BX,2000H        ;INITIALIZE BX
                IN       AL,PORTA        ;INPUT ASCII DATA
                XLAT                     ;OBTAIN EBCDIC CODE FROM TABLE
                OUT      PORTB,AL        ;OUTPUT TO EBCDIC PRINTER
                HLT
END      START
```

Disassembly of the program above using the MASM32 is as follows:

```
00401000                START:
00401000 66BB0020        MOV         BX,2000H
00401004 E460            IN          AL,PORT
00401006 D7              XLAT
00401007 E668            OUT         PORTB,AL
00401009 F4              HLT
```

In the program, a table is created at offset 2030H in the data segment containing the EBCDIC codes for the BCD numbers 0 through 9. The assembler directive DB is used for the purpose. Note that assemblers generally require that hexadecimal numbers start with a digit. A 0 is typically used if the first digit of the hexadecimal number is a letter. This is done to distinguish between numbers and labels. For example, most assemblers will require the number F5H to be represented as 0F5H. This is the reason that each EBCDIC code in the table contains a leading 0.

Now, suppose that the number 4 is pushed on the ASCII keyboard connected to PORT A. The instruction IN AL,PORTA inputs 34H (ASCII for 4) into register AL. The instruction XLAT, which is equivalent to MOV AL,[BX + AL], transfers the contents of memory offset 2034H (BX + AL) into AL. This means that F4H (the contents of offset 2034H in the table) will be moved into AL. The instruction OUT PORT B,AL outputs F4H (EBCDIC for 4) into PORT B, where the EBCDIC printer is connected. Hence, the printer prints the number 4.

EXAMPLE 10.4   Write a Pentium assembly language program to clear 50_{10} consecutive bytes from LOW to HIGH addresses starting at offset 1000H. Assume that DS is already initialized.

Solution

```
            .486
            .MODEL      SMALL,STDCALL
            .CODE
START:
            MOV         BX,1000H        ;initialize BX to 1000H
            MOV         CX,50           ;initialize loop count to 50
AGAIN:      MOV         BYTE PTR[BX],0  ;clear memory byte to 0
            INC         BX              ;update pointer
            LOOP        AGAIN           ;decrement CX and loop until CX = 0
            HLT                         ;halt
END         START
```

The instructions INC and LOOP in the program above are described later. The instruction MOV BX,1000H initializes BX with offset 1000H (offset 1000H is chosen arbitrarily). The instruction MOV CX,50 initializes the loop counter CX with 50. MOV BYTE PTR[BX],0 clears a memory byte addressed by the contents of BX in DS to 0. INC BX increments BX by 1 to point to the next memory byte. LOOP AGAIN decrements CX by 1 and checks for CX = 0. If CX ≠ 0, the program returns to label AGAIN. The program stops when CX = 0.

10.7.2   Arithmetic Instructions

Table 10.9 shows the Pentium arithmetic instructions. These instructions basically include addition, subtraction, signed and unsigned multiplication and division operations.

Typical microprocessors utilize common hardware to perform addition and subtraction operations for both unsigned and signed numbers. The instruction set of microprocessors typically include the same ADD and SUBTRACT instructions for both unsigned and signed numbers. The interpretations of unsigned and signed ADD and SUBTRACT operations are performed by the programmer. More detailed coverage is provided in chapter 5.

Unsigned and Signed multiplication and division operations can be performed using various algorithms. Typical 32-bit microprocessors such as the Pentium contain

TABLE 10.9   **Pentium Arithmetic Instructions**

Addition		
ADD a, b	Add	$(a) \leftarrow (a) + (b)$
ADC a, b	Add with carry	$(a) \leftarrow (a) + (b) + CF$
XADD a, b	Exchange and Add	$(a) \leftarrow (a) + (b), (b) \leftarrow$ original (a)
INC reg/mem	Increment by one	$(reg/mem) \leftarrow (reg/mem) + 1$
AAA	ASCII adjust after addition	
DAA	Decimal adjust [AL], to be used after ADD or ADC	

Subtraction		
SUB a, b	Subtract	$(a) \leftarrow (a) - (b)$
SBB a, b	Subtract with borrow	$(a) \leftarrow (a) - (b) - CF$
DEC reg/mem	Decrement by one	$(reg/mem) \leftarrow (reg/mem) - 1$
NEG reg/mem	Negate	$(reg/mem) \leftarrow 0 - (reg/mem)$
CMP a, b	Compare	$(a) - (b) \rightarrow$ Flags are affected. No result.
CMPXCHG a, b	Compare and Exchange	
AAS	ASCII adjust after subtraction	
DAS	Decimal adjust (AL) after subtraction	

Multiplication		
MUL reg/mem (unsigned)	Multiply byte or word or double word (unsigned)	for 8 X 8
		$(AX) \leftarrow (AL) * (reg8/mem8)$
or		for 16 X 16
		$(DX:AX) \leftarrow (AX) * (reg16/mem16)$

TABLE 10.9   Cont.

IMUL reg/mem (signed)	Integer multiply byte or word or double word (signed)	for 32 X 32 (EDX:EAX)←(EAX)* (reg32/mem32)
AAM	ASCII adjust after multiplication	

Division		
DIV reg/mem (unsigned)	Divide byte or word or double word unsigned	16 ÷ 8 bit; (AX)←(AX)/(reg8/mem8)
		(AH)← remainder
		(AL) ← quotient
		32÷16bit;(DX:AX) ←(DX:AX)/(reg16 or mem16)
or		(DX) ← remainder, (AX) ← quotient
IDIV reg/mem (signed)	Integer divide byte or word (signed)	64÷32bit; (EDX:EAX) ← (EDX:EAX)/(reg32 or mem32) (EAX) = quotient, (EDX) = remainder.
AAD	ASCII adjust before division	

Sign-Extension	
CBW	Sign-extend byte in AL to word in AX
CWD	Sign-extend AX to 32 bits in DX:AX
CWDE	Sign extend 16-bit contents of AX to 32-bit double word in EAX
CDQ	Sign extend a 32-bit double word in EAX to a quadword (64 bits) in EDX:EAX

a= "reg" or "mem", b = "reg" or "mem" or "data".

separate instructions for performing these multiplication and division operations. These topics along with some multiplication and division algorithms are covered in Chapter 5.

Let us explain some of the instructions in Table 10.9.

- Consider ADD a,b. The destination operand 'a' can be memory or register, while the source operand 'b' can be memory, register, or immediate data. This instruction adds source and destination data and stores the result in destination. The operand sizes can be 8-, 16-, or 32-bit. There is no ADD mem,mem instruction. All flags in the low byte of the Flag register are affected. Typical examples include ADD CL,DL, ADD BL,[SI], ADD AX,BX, ADD CX,25A7H, ADD [BP],AX, ADD EAX,ECX, ADD BYTE PTR [SI],5 and ADD EDX,[EAX]. For example, consider ADD CL, DL. If prior to execution of this instruction, (CL) = 20H, (DL) = 03H, then, after ADD CL,DL, the contents of register CL = 20 + 03 = 23H; CF = 0, PF = 0 (result with odd parity), AF = 0 (intermediate carry from bit 3 to bit 4 is 0), ZF = 0 (nonzero result), SF = 0 (most significant bit of the result is zero), and OF = 0 since C_f (carry final) = 0 and C_p (carry previous) = 0. Note that as mentioned in chapter 1, overflow, V = $C_f \oplus C_p$.

- Consider ADC a,b. The destination operand 'a' can be memory or register while the source operand 'b' can be memory, register, or immediate data. This instruction adds source and destination data along with the carry flag and stores the result in destination. The operand size can be 8-, 16-, or 32-bit. There is no ADC mem,mem instruction. All flags in the low byte of the Flag register are affected. For example, if (AX) = 0020_{16}, (BX) = 0300_{16}, CF = 1, (DS) = 2020_{16}, and (20500) = 0100_{16}, then after execution of ADC AX,[BX], the contents of register AX = 0020 + 0100 + 1 = 0121_{16}; CF = 0, PF = 0 (result with odd parity), AF = 0, ZF = 0 (nonzero result), SF = 0 (most significant bit of the result is zero), and OF = 0 since C_f (carry final) = 0 and C_p (carry previous) = 0.

- Consider XADD a,b. The destination operand 'a' can be memory or register while the source operand 'b' can be memory, register, or immediate data. This instruction adds the source to the destination, stores the result in the destination, and copies the original value of the destination into the source. The operand sizes can be 8-, 16-, or 32-bit. There is no XADD mem,mem instruction. For example, if (AH) = 20H, and (BL) = 03H, then after execution of XADD AH, BL instruction, (AH) = 20H + 03H = 23H, and (BL) = 20H.

- Consider SUB a,b. The destination operand 'a' can be memory or register while the source operand 'b' can be memory, register, or immediate data. This instruction subtracts source data from destination data, and stores the result in destination. The operand sizes can be 8-, 16-, or 32-bit. There is no SUB mem, mem instruction. Typical examples include SUB BH, DL, SUB CX, DX, SUB AX, 2, SUB EAX, EBX and, SUB [EDX], ECX. All flags in the low byte of the Flag register are affected. For example, if (AH) = 03H, (BL) = 02H, then, after SUB AH,BL, the contents of register AH = 03H - 02H = 01H.

1111 110 ← intermediate carries

Using two's-complement subtraction, (AH) =   0000 0011 (+3)
Add twos complement of 2 (DL)   = + 1111 1110 (-2)
                             ----

final carry → 1   0000 0001

The final carry is one's-complemented after subtraction to reflect the correct borrow. Hence, CF = 0. Also, PF = 0 (odd parity; number of 1's in the result is 1), AF = 1 (intermediate carry from bit 3 to bit 4 is 1), ZF = 0 (nonzero result), SF = 0 (most significant bit of the result is zero), and OF = $C_f \oplus C_p$ = 1 $\oplus$ 1 = 0. Similarly, SUB EBX, 4 subtracts immediate data 4 from the 32-bit contents of EBX, and stores the result in EBX. All flags are affected.

- Consider SBB a,b. The destination operand 'a' can be memory or register while the source operand 'b' can be memory, register, or immediate data. This instruction subtracts source data and the carry flag from destination data, and stores the result in destination. The operand sizes can be 8-, 16-, or 32-bit. There is no SBB mem , mem instruction. All flags in the low byte of the flag register are affected. For example, if (CH) = 03H, (DL) = 02H, and CF = 1, then, after SBB CH,DL, the contents of register CH = 03H - 02H - 1 = 00H.

$$1111\ 111 \leftarrow \text{intermediate carries}$$

Using two's complement subtraction, (CH) =   0000 0011 (+3)
Add two's complement of 3 (DL plus CF)   = + 1111 1101 (-3)

----

final carry $\rightarrow$ 1   0000 0000

The final carry is one's-complemented after subtraction to reflect the correct borrow. Hence, CF = 0. Also, PF = 1 (Even parity; number of 1's in the result is 0 and 0 is an even number), AF = 1, ZF = 1 (Zero Result), SF = 0 (Most Significant bit of the result is zero), and OF = $C_f \oplus C_p = 1 \oplus 1 = 0$.

- NEG reg/mem subtracts the contents of a register or a memory location from 0. In other words, this instruction finds the two's-complement of the data contained in the operand field. The operand size can be 8-, 16-, or 32-bit. Typical examples include NEG CL, NEG DX, NEG BYTE PTR [SI], NEG EAX, and NEG DWORD PTR [ECX]. As an example, consider NEG ECX. If (ECX) = FFFFFFFFH, then after execution of NEG ECX, the contents of ECX are 00000001H. All flags are affected.

- Consider INC reg/mem. This instruction increments the contents of a register or a memory location by 1. The operand size can be 8-, 16-, or 32-bit. The INC reg/mem instruction affects SF, ZF, AF, OF, and PF. This instruction does not affect CF (carry flag). Typical examples include INC AH, INC BP, INC EDX, INC BYTE PTR[SI], and INC DWORD PTR[EAX].

- Consider DEC reg/mem. This instruction decrements the contents of a register or a memory location by 1. The operand size can be 8-, 16-, or 32-bit. DEC reg/mem instruction affects SF, ZF, AF, OF, and PF. Like INC mem/reg, this instruction does not affect CF (carry flag) . Typical examples include DEC AH, DEC BP, DEC EDX, DEC BYTE PTR[SI], and DEC DWORD PTR[EAX].

- Consider the CMP a,b instruction. The destination operand 'a' can be memory or register, while the source operand 'b' can be memory, register, or immediate data. This instruction subtracts source from destination, providing no result of subtraction; all status flags are affected based on the result. The operand sizes can be 8-, 16-, or 32-bit. There is no CMP mem,mem instruction. Note that the SUBTRACT instruction provides the result and also affects the status flags. Consider CMP DH,BL. If prior to execution of the instruction, (DH) = 40H and (BL) = 30H, then after execution of CMP DH,BL, the flags are CF = 0, PF = 0, AF = 0, ZF = 0, SF = 0, and OF = 0; the result 10H is not provided. Suppose that it is desired to find the number of matches for an 8-bit number in a Pentium register such as DL in a data array of 50 bytes in memory pointed to by BX in DS. The following instruction sequence with CMP DL,[BX] rather than SUB DL,[BX]can be used :

```
             MOV    AL,0      ; Clear AL to 0, AL to hold number of matches
             MOV    CX,50     ; Initialize array count
START:       CMP    DL,[BX]   ; Compare the number to be matched in DL
             JZ     MATCH     ; with a data byte in the array. If there is
                             ; a match, ZF=1. Branch to label MATCH.
             JMP    DOWN      ; Unconditional jump to label DOWN.
MATCH:       INC    AL        ; increment AL to hold number of matches.
DOWN:        INC    BX        ; Increment BX to point to next data byte.
             LOOP   START     ; Decrement CX by 1, go back to START if
                             ; CX ≠ 0. If CX = 0, go to the next instruction
                             ; AL contains the number of matches
```

In the above, if SUB DL,[BX] were used instead of CMP DL,[BX], the number to be matched needed to be loaded after each subtraction because the contents of DL would have been lost after each SUB. Since we are only interested in the match rather than the result, CMP DL,[BX] instead of SUB DL,[BX] should be used in the above.

- Consider CMPXCHG a,b. The destination operand 'a' can be memory or register, while the source operand 'b' can be memory, register, or immediate data. This instruction compares the destination with AL (for 8-bit), AX (for 16-bit) or EAX (for 32-bit). If they are equal, the contents of the source are transferred to the destination. If they are not equal, the contents of the destination are moved into AL (for 8-bit), AX (for 16-bit), or EAX (for 32-bit). The operand sizes can be 8-, 16-, or 32-bit. There is no CMPXCHG mem,mem instruction. As an example, consider CMPXCHG BL,DH. If prior to execution of this instruction, (AL) = F2H, (BL) = F2H, and (DH) = 05H, then after execution of the CMPXCHG BL,DH instruction, (BL) = 05H since (BL) = (AL) = F2H.

- DAA is used to adjust the result of adding two packed BCD numbers in AL using ADD or ADC to provide a correct packed BCD number. If, after the addition, the low 4 bits of the result in AL are greater than 9 (or if AF = 1), the DAA adds 6 to the low 4 bits of AL. On the other hand. if the high 4 bits of the result in AL are greater than 9 (or if CF = 1), DAA adds 6 to the high 4 bits in AL. Consider the following instruction sequence:

```
MOV AL,29H          ; Move 29H into AL
ADD AL,54H          ; Add 29H with 54H and store the result in AL
DAA                 ; Decimal adjust AL to provide the correct packed BCD result
```

The details of the result obtained by the instruction sequence above are provided in the following:

```
    (AL) = 29H  = 0010 1001 (Packed BCD 29, same as 29H)
    Add   54H  = 0101 0100  (Packed BCD 54, same as 54H)
                 --------------
         (AL) = 0111 1101
                     0110    Add 6 (BCD correction by DAA since low 4 bits
                 --------------  of the sum in AL are greater than 9)
                1000 0011 = 83H correct packed BCD result since 29 + 54 = 83
```

Note that packed BCD is covered in section 1.2.3 of Chapter 1.

- DAS may be used to adjust the result of subtraction in AL of two packed BCD numbers using SUB or SBB to provide the correct packed BCD. If, after the subtraction, the low 4 bits of the result in AL is greater than 9 (or if AF = 1), then the DAS subtracts 6 from the low 4 bits of AL. On the other hand. if the high 4 bits of the result in AL are greater than 9 (or if CF = 1), then DAS subtracts 6 from AL While performing these subtractions, any borrows from low and high 4 bits are ignored. For example, consider subtracting packed BCD 55 in DL from packed BCD 94 in AL: Packed BCD 55 = 55H = 0101 0101$_2$ and Packed BCD 94 = 94H = 1001 0100$_2$.

$$\text{Packed BCD 94 (94H)} = 1001\ 0100$$
$$\text{Add Two's complement of } 0101\ 0101\ (55H) = 1010\ 1011$$
$$\text{--------------}$$
$$\text{Ignore Carry} \rightarrow 1\ \ 0011\ 1111 = 3FH$$

The invalid BCD digit (F) in the low 4 bits of the result can be corrected by subtracting 6 from F:

$$\text{Low 4 bits} = \text{F} = 1111$$
$$-6 = 1010$$
$$\text{---------------}$$

ignore carry $\rightarrow 1 \quad 1001$ This will provide the correct packed BCD result of 39 (94 - 55 = 39).

The following Pentium instruction sequence will accomplish this:

```
MOV     AL,94H      ; Move 94H into AL
MOV     DL,55H      ; Move 55H into DL
SUB     AL,DL       ;(AL) = 3FH
DAS                 ;(AL) = 39H
```

- Consider CBW. This instruction extends the sign from the AL register to the AH register. For example, if AL = F1$_{16}$, then after execution of CBW, register AH will contain FF$_{16}$ because the most significant bit of F1H is 1. Note that the sign extension is very useful when one wants to perform an arithmetic operation on two signed numbers of different lengths. For example, the 16-bit signed number 0020$_{16}$ can be added with the 8-bit signed number E1H by sign-extending E1 as follows:

$$0020_{16} = 0000\ 0000\ 0010\ 0000\ (32_{10})$$
$$\text{Sign} \quad E1_{16} = \boxed{1111\ 1111}\ 1110\ 0001\ (-31_{10})$$
$$\text{extension} \quad 1\ 0000\ 0000\ 0000\ 0001\ (+1_{10})$$

Ignore carry   0   0   0   1

- Another example of sign extension is that to multiply a signed 8-bit number by a signed 16-bit number, one must first sign-extend the signed 8-bit into a signed 16-bit number and then the instruction IMUL can be used for 16 × 16 signed multiplication. For unsigned multiplication of a 16-bit number by an 8-bit number, the 8-bit number must be zero-extended to 16 bits using logical instruction such as AND before using the MUL instruction.

For example, suppose that IMUL BX will be used to multiply the 8-bit contents of AL by the 16-bit contents of BX. If prior to execution of this instruction, (AL) = FFH =

-1 and (BX) = 0002H = +2. To perform this signed multiplication, the 8-bit contents of AL must be sign-extended to 16 bits using the CBW instruction so that (AX) = FFFFH = -1. The multiplication instruction IMUL BX can then be executed so that the contents of DX:AX will be the 32-bit correct result, FFFFFFFEH (-2).

Now, to perform unsigned multiplication MUL BX with the same data, the 8-bit contents of AL must be zero-extended so that (AX) = 00FFH (+255). This can be accomplished by the instruction MOV AH,0. The instruction MUL BX can then be executed so that DX:AX will contain the correct 32-bit product, 000001FEH (+510) since (BX) = 0002H.

- CWD sign-extends the AX register into the DX register. For example, if (DX) = 08A0H and (AX) = A205H, then after execution of CWD, (DX) = FFFFH and (AX) = A205H since the most significant bit (sign bit) of AX is 1.

- CWDE sign-extends the AX register into the upper 16 bits of EAX. For example, if (EAX) = A5020277H, then after execution of CWDE, (EAX) = 00000277H since (AX) = 0277H with the sign bit (bit 15) = 0.

- CDQ sign-extends the EAX register into the EDX register. This provides a 64-bit result in EDX: EAX. For example, if (EDX) = 2F00 A7FFH and (EAX) = 0FFF FFFFH, then after execution of CDQ, (EDX) = 00000000H and (EAX) = 0FFF FFFFH.

- For 8-bit by 8-bit signed or unsigned multiplication between the contents of a memory location and AL, assembler directive BYTE PTR can be used. Example: IMUL BYTE PTR[BX]. On the other hand, for 16-bit by 16-bit signed or unsigned multiplication between the 16-bit contents of a memory location and register AX, assembler directive WORD PTR can be used. Example: MUL WORD PTR[SI].

- Consider 16 × 16 unsigned multiplication, MUL WORD PTR [BX]. If (BX) = 0050H, (DS) = 3000H, (30050H) = 0002H, and (AX) = 0006H, then after MUL WORD PTR [BX], (DX) = 0000H and (AX) = 000CH.

- MUL mem/reg provides unsigned 8 × 8 or unsigned 16 × 16 multiplication. Consider MUL BL. If (AL) = 20_{16} and (BL) = 02_{16}, then after MUL BL, register AX will contain 0040_{16}.

- IMUL mem/reg provides signed 8 × 8 or signed 16 × 16 multiplication. As an example, if (CL) = FDH = -3_{10} and (AL) = FEH = -2_{10}, then, after IMUL CL, register AX contains 0006H.

- Consider IMUL DH. If (AL) = FF_{16} = -1_{10} and (DH) = 02_{16}, then, after IMUL DH, register AX will contain $FFFE_{16}$ (-2_{10}).

- Consider IMUL reg16,reg16/mem16, imm8/imm16. This is an immediate signed multiplication. This is a three-operand instruction. The first operand is the 16-bit destination register, the second operand is a register or memory location containing the 16-bit multiplicand, and the third operand is either 8- or 16-bit immediate data as the multiplier. If the immediate data is 8 bits, this instruction automatically sign-extends to 16 bits before multiplication. Also, after multiplication, the low 16 bits of the product is provided. Typical example is IMUL BX, CX,2534H. Note that there is no unsigned multiplication instruction of this type.

- Consider MUL reg32/mem32. This instruction multiplies the 32-bit contents of EAX by the 32-bit contents of a 32-bit register or memory location. This is an unsigned multiplication. The 64-bit product is placed in EDX:EAX. IMUL reg32/mem32 works in the same way as the MUL reg32/mem32 except that the multiplication is signed. Typical examples include MUL EDX, IMUL EBX, and IMUL DWORD PTR [ECX].

• DIV mem/reg performs unsigned division and divides (AX) or (DX:AX) registers by reg or mem. For example, if (AX) = 0005H and (CL) = 02H, then after DIV CL, (AH) = 01H = remainder and (AL) = 02H = quotient.

• Consider DIV BL. If (AX) = 0009H and (BL) = 02H, then after DIV BL,

   (AH) = remainder = 01H
   (AL) = quotient = 04H

• IDIV mem/reg performs signed division and divides 16-bit contents of AX by an 8-bit number in a register or a memory location, or 32-bit contents of DX:AX registers by a 16-bit number in a register or a memory location. Consider IDIV CX. If (CX) = 2 and (DXAX) = -5_{10} = FFFFFFFBH, then, after this IDIV, registers DX and AX will contain

DX	AX
FFFF	FFFE

16-bit remainder = -1_{10} 16-bit quotient = -2_{10}

Note that in the Pentium, after IDIV, the sign of remainder is always the same as the dividend unless the remainder is equal to zero. Therefore, in this example, because the dividend is negative (-5_{10}), the remainder is negative (-1_{10}).

• For 16-bit by 8-bit signed or unsigned division of the 16-bit contents of AX by 8-bit contents of a memory location, assembler directive BYTE PTR can be used. Example: IDIV BYTE PTR[BX]. On the other hand, for 32-bit by 16-bit signed or unsigned division of the 32-bit contents of DXAX by the 16-bit contents of a memory location, assembler directive WORD PTR can be used. Example: MUL WORD PTR[SI].

• Consider IDIV WORD PTR [BX]. If (BX) = 0020H, (DS) = 2000H, (20020H) = 0004H, and (DX) (AX) = 00000011H, then, after IDIV WORD PTR [BX],

   (DX) = remainder = 0001H
   (AX) = quotient = 0004H

• Consider DIV reg32/mem32. This instruction divides the 64-bit contents of EDX:EAX by the 32-bit contents of a register or a memory location. The division is unsigned. After the division, the 32-bit remainder is in EDX, and the 32-bit quotient is in EAX. The instruction IDIV reg 32/mem32 works in the same way as the DIV reg32/mem32 except that the division is signed. Typical examples include IDIV EBX, DIV DWORD PTR [ESI], and DIV ECX.

• Consider the AAA instruction. The addition of two one-digit ASCII numbers will not provide meaningful information. For example, if 35H (ASCII for 5) is added with

39H (ASCII for 9), the sum will be 6EH. This is not a useful number. The result of adding 5 and 9 in ASCII should have been the ASCII equivalent of 14, which is 3134H. If the sum 6EH is saved in AL, and if the instruction AAA is executed, the contents of AL (6EH) will be converted to correct unpacked BCD (0104H) in AX. Note that the AAA instruction first checks the contents of AL, adjusts the lower four bits to provide the correct BCD result. Furthermore, the AAA instruction then clears the upper four bits of AL to 0. Finally, the AAA instruction clears AH to 0 (AH = 00H) if the result is less than or equal to 9, and adds 1 to AH (AH = 01H) if the result is greater than 9. Only CF and AF are affected.

The following example illustrates how the AAA instruction provides the correct BCD result:

(AL) = 6EH = 0110 1110

            0110 Add 6 for BCD correction

            0111 0100 = 74H in AL .

Since AAA clears upper 4 bits to 0, AL will contain 04H.
Also, because the low 4 bits of AL are greater than 9 (EH) prior to the execution of AAA, the contents of AH = 01H after execution of AAA. Hence, (AX) after execution of AAA = 0104H. Note that 0104H can be converted to 3134H (ASCII for 14H) by adding 3030H.

Next, consider adding 32H (ASCII for 2) and 35H (ASCII for 5). The result will be 67H. If the result is saved in AL and the AAA instruction is executed, AX will contain 0007H as follows: (AL) = 67H = 0110 0111 will be converted to 07H in AL by the AAA instruction. Also, since the low 4 bits of AL are 7 (less than 9), the AAA instruction clears AH to 0 so that (AH) = 00H. Hence, (AX) = 0007H.

Numerical data received by a Pentium-based microcomputer from an ASCII keyboard is in ASCII codes, which for numbers 0 to 9 is 30H through 39H. Two 8-bit data items can be entered into a Pentium-based microcomputer via the ASCII keyboard. The ASCII codes for these data items (with 3 as the upper 4 bits of each data byte) can be added. The AAA instruction can then be used to provide the correct unpacked BCD. Suppose that the ASCII codes for 6 (36H) and 5 (35H) are entered into a Pentium-based microcomputer via the keyboard. These ASCII codes can be added and then the result can be adjusted to provide the correct unpacked BCD using the AAA instruction. The unpacked BCD can then be converted to ASCII by adding 3030H. The following instruction sequence will accomplish this:

```
ADD     CL,DL     ;    (CL) = 36H = ACSII for 6
                  ;    (DL) = 35H = ASCII for 5
                  ;    Result (CL) = 6BH
MOV     AL,CL     ;    Move ASCII result
                  ;    into AL because AAA
                  ;    adjusts only (AL)
AAA               ;    (AX) = 0101H, unpacked for 11
ADD     AX,3030H  ;    Convert result to ASCII (3131H)
```

Note that in to print the result 11 on an ASCII printer, (AX) = 0101H is added with 3030H to provide 3131H, the ASCII code for 11. Note that unpacked BCD numbers are covered in Section 1.2.3 in Chapter 1.

- Consider the AAS instruction. This instruction is similar to AAA except that it is used to adjust AX after an ASCII subtraction using SUB or SBB. Suppose that (AX) = 0038H and (DH) = 32H = ASCII for 2. With this data, after execution of SUB AL,DH, the contents of AL will be 06H. After execution of AAS, the result is not changed since the the low 4 bits of AL (6) are less than 9. Hence, the final value of AX is 0006H. Adding 3030H to AX, the contents of AX will be 3036H (ASCII for the number 06).

  Now, suppose that (DH) = 39H and (AX) = 0035H. After execution of SUB AL,DH, register AL will contain FCH as follows:

$$(AL) = 35H = 0010\ 0011$$
$$\text{Add 2's complement of } (DH),\quad 39H = 1101\ 1001$$
$$------------$$
$$1111\ 1100 = FCH = (AL)$$

  After execution of AAS, the upper 4 bits of AL (F) are cleared to zero so that (AL) = 0CH, and the number in AH is decremented by 1 so that AH will contain FFH (-1). Also, after execution of the AAS instruction, 6 is subtracted from C (since C is greater than 9) as follows:

$$\text{Low 4 bits of AL} = C_{16} = 1100$$
$$\text{Add 2's complement of } 6 = 1010$$
$$-------$$
$$\text{Carry is 1's complemented to } 0 \leftarrow 1\ \ 0110$$

  Hence, AL will contain 06H, and FFH in AH indicates that a borrow has occurred. Note that 5 - 9 = -6 (after BCD correction). AL will contain 36H (ASCII for 6) after adding 30H to AL.

- Consider the AAM instruction. The AAM instruction adjusts the product of two unpacked BCD   digits in AX. If (AL) = 03H (unpacked BCD for 3) = 00000011_2 and (CH) = 08H (unpacked BCD for 8) = $0000\ 1000_2$, then, after MUL CH, the contents of AX are 0000000000011000_2 (0018H), and after using AAM, the contents of AX are 0000001000000100_2 = unpacked BCD 0204. The following instruction sequence accomplishes this:

      MUL CH
      AAM

  Note that the Pentium does not allow multiplication of two ASCII codes. Therefore, before multiplying two ASCII bytes received from an ASCII keyboard, one must make the upper 4 bits of each one of these bytes zero, multiply them as two unpacked BCD digits, and then use AAM to convert the binary product to unpacked BCD. The unpacked BCD product can be converted back to ASCII by adding the product with 3030H. For example, by adding 3030H with 0204H, the result 3234H (ASCII for 24) is obtained. The result 24 in decimal can then be printed on an ASCII printer.

- Consider the AAD instruction. The AAD instruction converts two unpacked BCD digits in AH and AL to an equivalent binary number in AL. AAD must be used before dividing two unpacked BCD digits in AX by an unpacked BCD byte. For example, consider dividing (AX) = unpacked BCD 0408H (48H packed BCD) by (DH) = 06H. (AX) must first be converted to binary by using AAD in order to use the binary division instruction DIV. The register AX will then contain 0030H = 48H Packed BCD. After

DIV DH, the contents of AL = quotient = 08H (unpacked BCD), and the contents of AH = remainder = 00H. The following instruction sequence will accomplish this:

```
MOV    DH,6         ;  Move divisor 6 into DH
MOV    AX, 0408H    ;  Move dividend 0408H into AX
AAD                 ;  Convert AX contents to binary (0030H)
DIV    DH           ;  (AL) = quotient = 08H. remainder = 00H
```

Note that packed and unpacked BCD are covered in Section 1.2.3 in Chapter 1.

- One-dimensional arrays (tables) can be be accessed using Pentium MOV instructions with the appropriate addressing mode. For example, consider a table of of five elements containing 5 bytes stored starting at an offset 2000H in DS. The table is stored in memory such that 2000H points to element 0, 2001H points to element 1, and 2004H points to element 4. This is depicted in Figure 10.10. An index register such as DI can be initialized with the element number to read an element from this array into an 8-bit register such as CL. For example, if (DI) = 2, then MOV CL,[2000H + DI] will load element 2 from offset 2002H into CL. On the other hand, if (DI) = 4, then MOV CL,[2000H + DI] transfers element 4 into CL.

  Suppose that an array of 10 elements containing 32-bit data words is stored starting at an offset 4000H. This means that 4 bytes are needed to store each element. That is, offset 4000H through 4003H will contain element 0 while offset 4024H through 4027H will store element 9. Hence, offset 4000H will contain element 0, offset 4004 will contain element 1, Offset 4008 will contain element 2, and so on. The based indexed addressing mode with a scaling of 4 can be used to access the array since the element size is 4 bytes (32 bits). Now, to move element 2 into EAX, the following instruction sequence can be used:

```
MOV    ECX,00004000H     ;  Load starting offset of the array into ECX
MOV    EDX,2             ;  Move element number 2 into EDX
MOV    EAX,[ECX +EDX*4]  ;  Load value of element 2 into EAX
```

In the instruction sequence above, the starting offset (4000H) of the table is first loaded into a 32-bit register such as ECX. The element number (2) is then transferred to EDX. Register EDX is scaled by 4 since each element is 4 bytes (32 bits). The value of element 2 is then loaded into a 32-bit register such as EAX using MOV EAX,[ECX + EDX*4]. Note that arithmetic operations can be performed on array elements in a table. This is

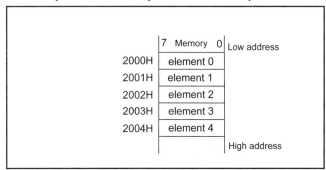

FIGURE 10.10   One dimensional array stored in memory

illustrated in Example 10.18.

Next, consider two-dimensional arrays or matrices. For example, assume a 2 x 3 matrix (two rows and three columns) as follows:

Column 0	Column 1	Column 2
a [0,0]	a[0,1]	a[0,2]
a[1,0]	a[1,1]	a[1,2]

Since memory is one-dimensional, this matrix is stored in memory using column-major or row-major ordering. In column-major ordering the elements are stored column by column, starting with the first column:

a[0,0]
a[1,0]
a[0,1]
a[1,1]
a[0,2]
a[1,2]

In row-major ordering the elements are stored in memory row by row, starting with the first row:

a[0,0] --column 0 (start of array)
a[0,1]-- column 1
a[0,2]-- column 2
a[1,0]-- column 0
a[1,1]-- column 1
a[1,2]-- column 2

Since row-major ordering and subscripts start with 0 in C language, the same convention will be used here.

Assume that an offset 2000H addresses the first element a[0,0] of the array. This means that offset 2000H points to the first element of the array, a[0,0]. In the C language, which uses row-major ordering and subscripts starting with zero, one can express displacement d of an element at row i and column j as $d = (i* t + j) * s$, where t is the total number of columns and s is the element size (1 for byte, 2 for 16-bit, and 4 for 32-bit).

Now, to find the displacement of element a[1,0] assuming that each element is 16-bit, the offset can be determined as follows. Note that $i = 1, j = 0$, $t = 3$ (since 2 x 3 matrix), and $s=2$ (16-bit element). Hence, $d = (1*3 + 0)*2 = 6$. Therefore, the offset where element a[1,0] is stored $= 2000H + 6 = 2006H$. Hence, the matrix above with row-major ordering can be stored with starting offset 2000H as follows:

2000H   a[0,0]
2002H   a[0,1]
2004H   a[0,2]
2006H   a[1,0]
2008H   a[1,1]
200AH   a[1,2]

Next to load element , a[1,0] into BX from the array, the following Pentium instruction sequence can be used:

```
MOV    ESI,00002000H    ; Low 16 bits of ESI to hold 16-bit offset
                        ; 2000H with upper 16 bits as zero
MOV    CX, 0            ; Load  j = 0, column number into CL
MOV    DL,1             ; Load i=1, row number into DL
MOV    AL,3             ; Load t = 3 into AL
MUL    DL               ;compute  i*t, result in AX
ADD    AX,CX            ;compute i*t+j, result in AX
CWDE                    ; sign-extend AX into EAX so that all upper
                        ; 16 bits are 0
MOV    BX,[ESI +  EAX*2]  ; Move 16-bit a[1,0] from offset 00002006H
                        ; into BX
```

Note that arithmetic operations can be performed on array elements of a two-dimensional matrix. This is illustrated in Example 10.19.

EXAMPLE 10.5   Determine the effect of each of the following   Pentium instructions:
(a) CBW (b) CDQ (c) IMUL BX, DX, 0FFH   (d) DIV CH   Assume the following data prior to execution of each of these instructions independently (assume that all numbers are in hexadecimal): (CX) = 0300H, (EAX) = A2130091H, and (EDX) = 52F10002H.

Solution

(a)   CBW sign-extends the AL register into the AH register. Because the content of AL is 91H, the sign bit is 1. Therefore, after CBW, (AX) = FF91H.
(b)   CDQ sign-extends EAX into EDX, providing a 64-bit result EDX:EAX. Since the sign bit (the most significant bit of EAX is 1, the content of EDX is FFFFFFFFH.
(c)   IMUL BX,DX,0FFH first sign-extends FFH to FFFFH (16-bit) and interprets this as a signed number (-1). It then performs signed multiplication between the contents of DX (0002H) and FFFFH and provides the low 16 bis of the answer as FFFEH (-2) in BX. The upper 16 bits of the product are discarded.
(d)   Before unsigned division, CH contains 03_{10} and AX contains 145_{10} (91H). Therefore, after DIV CH, (AH) = remainder = 01H and (AL) = quotient = 48_{10} = 30H.

EXAMPLE 10.6   Write a Pentium assembly language program for the following C language program structure:
    if   (x >= y)
            x = x + 10;
    else   y = y - 12;

Assume that x and y are addresses of two 16-bit signed integers.

Solution

Assume addresses x and y are initialized with the contents of the Pentium memory locations addressed by offsets BX and SI in segment register DS.

```
            .486
            .MODEL   SMALL,STDCALL
            .CODE
START:
            MOV      AX,[BX]            ; Move (x) into AX
            CMP      AX,[SI]            ; Compare (x) with (y)
            JGE      TEN                ; jump to TEN if (x) is greater than or equal
                                        ; to (y)
            SUB      WORD PTR[SI],12    ; Execute else part
            JMP      FINISH
TEN:        ADD      WORD PTR[BX],10    ;execute then part
FINISH:     HLT                         ; halt
END         START
```

EXAMPLE 10.7   Write a Pentium assembly language program for the following C language program structure:
        sum = 0;
        for (i = 0; i <= 9; i = i + 1)
        sum = sum + a[i];
Assume that sum is the address of the 16-bit result.

Solution

        Assume register SI holds the address of the first element of the array while BX contains the offset of the sum.

```
            .486
            .MODEL   SMALL,STDCALL
            .CODE
START:
            MOV      CX,10              ;initialize CX to loop count of 10
            MOV      WORD PTR [BX],0    ;sum = 0
AGAIN:      MOV      AX,[SI]            ; move a[i] into AX
            ADD      [BX],AX            ; sum = sum + a[i]
            ADD      SI,2               ; increment SI to point to address of next a[i]
            LOOP     AGAIN              ; decrement cx by 1, go back to AGAIN until
                                        ;CX=0
            HLT                         ; If CX = 0, stop
END         START
```

EXAMPLE 10.8   Write a Pentium assembly program to find $(X^2)/255$ where X is an 8-bit signed number stored in CH. Store the 16-bit result onto the stack. Initialize SS and SP to 1000H and 2000H, respectively.

Solution

```
        .486
        .MODEL  SMALL,STDCALL
        .CODE
START:
        MOV     AX,1000H        ; Initialize SS
        MOV     SS,AX           ; to 1000H
        MOV     SP,2000H        ; Initialize SP to 2000H
        MOV     AL,CH           ; Move X into AL
        IMUL    CH              ; Compute X**2 and store in AX
        MOV     CL,255          ; Since X**2 and 255 are both positive, use
        DIV     CL              ; unsigned division. Remainder in AH
        PUSH    AX              ; and quotient in AL. Push AX to stack
        HLT
END     START
```

EXAMPLE 10.9   What are the remainder, quotient, and registers containing them after execution of the following Pentium assembly language program?

```
        .486
        .MODEL  SMALL,STDCALL
        .CODE
START:
        MOV     AH,0FFH
        MOV     AL,0FFH
        MOV     CX,2
        IDIV    CL
        HLT
END     START
```

Solution

```
        MOV     AH,0FFH         ; AH = FFH
        MOV     AL,0FFH         ; AL = FFH, hence AX = FFFFH = -1
        MOV     CX,2
        IDIV    CL              ; AX / CL = -1/2
```

AH	AL
FFH	00H

8-bit remainder   8-bit quotient
$= -1_{10}$ $= 0$

EXAMPLE 10.10   Write a Pentium assembly language program to add two 16-bit numbers in CX and DX and store the result in offset 1000H addressed by DI.

Solution

```
        .486                        ;Includes 486 instruction set
        .MODEL  SMALL,STDCALL       ;Specifies memory model
        .CODE                       ; Start of code
START:
        MOV     DX,0012H            ; Move 0012H into DX
        MOV     CX,0094H            ; Move 0094H into CX
        MOV     DI,1000H            ; Initialize DI with 1000H
        ADD     DX,CX               ; Add Dx with CX, Store result in DX
        MOV     [DI],DX             ; Store result in memory
        HLT                         ; Stop
END     START                       ;End of code
```

EXAMPLE 10.11   Write a Pentium assembly language program to add four 16-bit numbers stored in consecutive locations starting at a 32-bit offset pointed to by EBX. Store the 16-bit result in AX. Use ADC instruction for addition. Initialize DS to 5000H, and EBX to 00001000H.

Solution

```
        .486
        .MODEL  FLAT,STDCALL
        .CODE
PROG:
        MOV     AX,5000H            ; Initialize AX
        MOV     DS,AX               ; Initialize DS
        MOV     EBX,00001000H       ; Initialize BX to 00001000H
        MOV     CX,4                ; Initialize loop count
        MOV     AX,0                ; Initialize AX to 0 to store 16-bit sum
        CLC                         ; clear carry
START:  ADC     AX,[EBX]            ; Add
        INC     EBX                 ; Update pointer. INC does not
                                    ; affect CF
        INC     EBX                 ; Update pointer
        LOOP    START               ; Decrement CX & loop
        HLT                         ; Stop
END     PROG
```
EXAMPLE 10.12   Write a Pentium assembly language program to add two 64-bit numbers. Assume that ESI and EDI contain the starting offsets of the numbers. Store the result in memory pointed to by EDI. Initialize DS to 3000H, ESI to 0, and EDI to 8.

Solution

```
        .486                        ;Includes 486 instruction set
        .MODEL  FLAT, STDCALL       ;Specifies memory model
        .DATA
DATA1   DW      0FFFFH              ;DATA1 low
```

```
            DW      0FFFFH
            DW      0FFFFH              ;DATA1 high
            DW      0FFFFH
DATA2       DW      0FFFFH              ;DATA2 low
            DW      0FFFFH
            DW      0FFFFH              ;DATA2 high
            DW      0FFFFH
            .CODE                       ; Start of code
BEGIN:
            MOV     AX, 3000H
            MOV     DS,AX               ;Initialize DS to 3000H
            MOV     DX,2                ;Load 2 into DX
            MOV     ESI,0               ;Initialize ESI to 0
            MOV     EDI,8               ;Initialize EDI to 8
            CLC                         ;Clear Carry to 0
START:      MOV     EAX,[ESI]           ;Load DATA1 into AX
            ADC     [EDI],EAX           ;Add both data with carry
            INC     ESI                 ;Update pointers
            INC     ESI                 ;by 4 for 32-bit
            INC     ESI
            INC     ESI
            INC     EDI                 ;Update pointers
            INC     EDI                 ;by 4 for 32-bit
            INC     EDI
            INC     EDI
            DEC     DX                  ;decrement DX by 1
            JNZ     START               ;Jump to start if ZF is 0
            HLT                         ;Stop if ZF = 1
END         BEGIN                       ;End of code
```

In the program above, ESI and EDI are added with 4 using the INC instruction four times rather than ADD SI,4 and ADD DI,4. This is because the INC instruction does not affect the carry flag, whereas the ADD instruction does. Note that the ADC [EDI], EAX instruction is used to add two 32-bit data with the carry flag. For adding high 32-bit numbers, the carry flag must not be altered. Hence, INC rather than ADD is used. Also, JNZ START checks whether ZF is 0 or 1. Note that ZF =1 when DEC DX decrements DX to 0. In that case, the program will execute HLT and stop. However, if ZF = 0 (i.e., DX is not decremented to 0 by DEC DX), the program loops back to START.

EXAMPLE 10.13   Write a Pentium assembly language program to multiply two 32-bit unsigned numbers to provide a 64-bit result. Assume that the two numbers are stored in ECX and EDX.

Solution

```
            .486
            .MODEL      SMALL, STDCALL
            .CODE
PROG:
```

```
          MOV       EAX,EDX              ;Move first data into EAX
          MUL       ECX                  ;(EDX:EAX)<--(EAX]*[ECX)
          HLT                            ; Stop
END       PROG
```

EXAMPLE 10.14   Write a Pentium assembly language program to multiply two 8-bit signed numbers stored in the same 16-bit register, AX; AH holds one number and AL holds the other number. Store the 16-bit result in DX.

Solution

```
          .486
          .MODEL    SMALL,STDCALL
          .CODE
PROG:
          IMUL      AH                   ;(AH)*(AL)-->(AX)
          MOV       DX,AX                ;Store result in DX
          HLT
END       PROG
```

EXAMPLE 10.15   Write a Pentium assembly program that converts a temperature (signed) from Fahrenheit degrees stored at an offset contained in SI to Celsius degrees. The program stores the 8-bit integer, which is part of the result at an offset contained in DI. Assume that the temperature can be represented by one byte and that DS is already initialized. The source byte is assumed to reside at offset 2000H in the data segment, and the destination byte at an offset of 3000H in the same data segment. Use the formula C = (F-32)/9 x 5

Solution

```
          .486
          .MODEL    SMALL, STDCALL
          .CODE
PROG:
          MOV       SI,2000H             ; Initialize source pointer
          MOV       DI,3000H             ; Initialize destination pointer
          MOV       AL,[SI]              ; Get degrees F
          CBW                            ; Sign extend
          SUB       AX,32                ; Subtract 32
          MOV       CX,5                 ; Get multiplier
          IMUL      CX                   ; Multiply by 5
          MOV       CX,9                 ; Get divisor
          IDIV      CX                   ; Divide by 9 to get Celsius
          MOV       [DI],AL              ; Put result in destination
          HLT                            ; Stop
END       PROG
```

EXAMPLE 10.16   Write a Pentium assembly   program to implement the following C language program loop:

sum = 0;
for (i = 0; i <=99; i = i + 1)
sum = sum + x[i] * y[i];

The assembly language program will compute $\sum_{i=1}^{100} X_i Y_i$ where the X_i's and Y_i's are signed 8-bit numbers stored at offsets 4000H and 5000H, respectively. Initialize DS at 2000H. Store the 16-bit result in DX. Assume no overflow.

Solution

```
          .486
          .MODEL    SMALL,STDCALL
          .CODE
PROG:
          MOV       AX,2000H            ;Initialize
          MOV       DS,AX              ;Data Segment to 2000H
          MOV       CX,100             ;Initialize loop count
          MOV       BX,4000H           ;Initialize pointer of Xi
          MOV       SI,5000H           ;Initialize pointer of Yi
          MOV       DX,0000H           ;Initialize sum to 0
START:    MOV       AL,[BX]            ;Load data into AL
          IMUL      BYTE PTR [SI]      ;Signed 8x8 multiplication
          ADD       DX,AX              ;Sum XiYi
          INC       BX                 ;Update pointer
          INC       SI                 ;Update pointer
          LOOP      START              ;Decrement CX & loop
          HLT
END       PROG
```

EXAMPLE 10.17   Write a Pentium assembly language program to add two words; each contains two ASCII digits. The first word is stored in two consecutive locations with the low byte pointed to by SI at offset 0300H, and the second word is stored in two consecutive locations with the low byte pointed to by DI at offset 0700H. Store the unpacked BCD result in memory location pointed to by DI.

Solution

```
          .486
          .MODEL    SMALL, STDCALL
          .CODE
PROG:
          MOV       AX,2000H           ;initialize ;data segment
          MOV       DS,AX              ;at 2000H
          MOV       CX,2               ;initialize loop count
          MOV       SI,0300H           ;initialize SI
```

```
              MOV      DI,0700H            ;initialize DI
START:        MOV      AL,[SI]             ;load data into AL
              ADD      AL,[DI]             ;perform addition
              AAA                          ;ASCII adjust
              MOV      [DI],AL             ;store result
              INC      SI                  ;update pointer
              INC      DI                  ;update pointer
              LOOP     START               ;decrement CX & loop
              HLT                          ;halt
END           PROG
```

EXAMPLE 10.18   Write a Pentium assembly language program to add   all the elements in a table containing eight 16-bit elements stored in memory addressed by offset 00005000H. Store the 16-bit result in DX.

Solution

```
              .486
              .MODEL   FLAT,STDCALL
              .DATA
              ORG      5000H
              DW       1,2,3,4
              DW       5,6,7,8
              .CODE
START:
              MOV      EAX,00005000H       ; Load starting address of table into
                                           ;  EAX
              MOV      EBX,0               ; Move element number 0 into EBX
              MOV      EDI,EBX             ; Copy element number 0 into EDI
              MOV      DX,0                ; Clear 16-bit sum to 0
              MOV      CX,8                ; Initialize CX with loop count
BACK:         ADD      DX,[EAX+EBX*2]      ; Add elements with sum in DX
              INC      EDI                 ; Increment element in EDI by 1
              MOV      EBX,EDI             ; Copy element number in EBX
              LOOP     BACK                ; Branch to BACK until CX=0
              HLT
END           START
```

EXAMPLE 10.19   Write a Pentium assembly language program to find the trace (sum of the elements in the diagonal) of a 3 x 3 matrix containing 16-bit words. Store the 16-bit result in DI. Assume that the matrix is stored in row-major ordering starting at an offset 1000H:

```
1000H   a[0,0]
1002H   a[0,1]
1004H   a[0,2]
1006H   a[1,0]
1008H   a[1,1]
```

100AH   a[1,2]
100CH   a[2,0]
100EH   a[2,1]
1010H   a[2,2]

Note that trace = a[0,0] + a[1,1] + a[2,2] and displacement, $d = (i *t +j) *s = i*t*s + j*s$ where i = row number, j = column number, t = total number of columns in the matrix, and s = element size. In this example, $t = 3$ for 3x3 matrix, and $s = 2$ since each element is 16-bit. Hence, $d = 3*(2*i) + 2*j = 6 * i + 2 *j$. Hence, the offset where each element, aij will be stored = A0 + 6*i +2*j where A0 = starting offset of the array, i = row number, and j = column number.

Solution

```
            .486
            .MODEL      FLAT,STDCALL
            .DATA
            ORG         1000H
            DW          1,2,3,4
            DW          5,6,7,8,9
            .CODE
START:
            MOV         EBX,0               ; Load column number 0 into EBX
            MOV         ESI,0               ; Load row number 0 into ESI
            MOV         CX,3                ; Initialize CX with loop count
            MOV         BP,0                ; Clear sum in BP to 0
            MOV         EDI,00001000H       ; Load starting address into EDI
BACK:       MOV         AX,6                ; EAX will contain 00000006H
                                            ; Perform 6*i
            MUL         SI                  ; Since DX is 0, result in AX,
                                            ; hence, in EAX
            ADD         EDI,EAX             ; Add EDI with 6*i
            ADD         BP,[EDI+EBX*2]      ; sum diagonal elements in BP
            INC         EBX                 ; Increment column number in EBX
                                            ;  by 1
            INC         ESI                 ; Increment row number in ESI by 1
            MOV         EDI,00001000H       ; Re-initialize EDI to 1000H since
                                            ;  (EDI) was  altered
            LOOP        BACK                ; Branch to BACK until CX = 0
            HLT
END         START
```

Questions and Problems

10.1   Assume the real mode. If (DS) = 1000H, (SS) = 2000H, (CS) = 3000H, (BP) = 000FH, and (BX) = 000AH before   execution of the following Pentium instructions:
    (a)   MOV   CX,[BX]
    (b)   MOV   DX,[BP]

Find the 20-bit physical address after execution of each of the instructions above.

10.2   If (DS) = 205FH and OFFSET = 0052H, what is the 20-bit physical address in real mode?

10.3   In a Pentium system in real the mode, segments 1and 2 both contain addresses 00100H–00200H. What are these segments called?

10.4   Determine the addressing modes for the following Pentium instructions:
    (a)   CLC
    (b)   CALL   WORDPTR [BX]
    (c)   MOV   AX,DX
    (d)   ADC   EBX,[EAX+4*ESI +2000H]

10.5   Assume the following Pentium register contents

    (EBX) = 00001000H
    (ECX) = 04000002H
    (EDX) = 20005000H

prior to execution of each of the following Pentium instructions. Determine the contents of the affected registers and/or memory locations after execution of each of the following instructions and identify the addressing modes:
    (a)   MOV [EBX * 4] [ECX],EDX
    (b)   MOV [EBX * 2] [ECX + 2020H],EDX

10.6   Determine the effect after execution of each of the following Pentium instructions:
    (a)   MOVZX EAX,CH
          Prior to execution of this MOVZX instruction, assume

          (EAX) = 80001234H
          (ECX) = 00008080H

    (b)   MOVSX EDX,BL
          Prior to execution of this MOVSX assume

          (EDX) = FFFFFFFFH
          (EBX) = 05218888H

10.7   Find the overflow, direction, interrupt, trap, sign, zero, parity, and carry flags after execution of the following Pentium instruction sequence:

```
MOV   AH, 0FH
SAHF
```

10.8   What is the content of AL after execution of the following Pentium instruction sequence?

```
MOV   BH,33H
MOV   AL,32H
ADD   AL,BH
AAA
```

10.9   What happens after execution of the following Pentium instruction sequence? Comment.

```
MOV   DX,001FH
XCHG  DL,DH
MOV   AX,DX
IDIV  DL
```

10.10   What are the remainder, quotient, and registers containing them after execution of the following Pentium instruction sequence?

```
MOV   AH,0
MOV   AL,0FFH
MOV   CX,2
IDIV  CL
```

10.11   Determine the effect after execution of each of the following Pentium instructions.
(a)   CDQ
(b)   MOVSX ECX,E7H
Assume (EAX) = FFFFFFFFH, (ECX) = F1257124H, and (EDX) = EEEEEEEEH prior to execution of each of these instructions.

10.12   Write the Pentium instruction sequence to clear the trap flag in the FLAGS register without affecting the other flags.

10.13   Write a Pentium assembly program to find the minimum value of a string of 10 signed 8-bit numbers using indexed addressing. Assume that offset 5000H contains the first number.

10.14   Write a Pentium assembly language program that will convert a BCD number in AL to a seven-segment code using a look-up table containing the seven-segment codes of the BCD numbers. Use a common-cathode display. Assume that the table is stored in memory starting at offset 2000H. Use the XLAT instruction. Initialize DS to 3000H.

10.15   Write a Pentium assembly program to add a 64-bit number in ECX: EDX with another 64-bit number in EAX: EBX. Store the result in EAX: EDX.

10.16   Write a Pentium assembly language program to subtract two 64-bit numbers. Assume that SI   and DI point to the low words of the numbers.

10.17   Write a   Pentium assembly program to add a 16-bit number stored in BX (bits 0 to 7 containing the high-order byte of the number and bits 8 to 15 containing the low-order byte) with another 16-bit number stored in CX (bits 0 to 7 containing the low-order 8 bits of the number and bits 8 thorough 15 containing the high-order 8 bits). Store the result in AX.

10.18   Write a Pentium assembly program to add twenty five 16-bit numbers stored in consecutive memory locations starting at displacement 0100H in DS = 0020H. Store the 16-bit result onto the stack. Initialize SS to 2000H, SP to 1000H, and DS to 0020H.

10.19   Write a Pentium assembly language program to subtract a 24-bit number (x) stored in low 24 bits of EAX from another 24-bit number (y) stored in consecutive memory locations starting at offset 6080H in BX (the highest byte at 6082H and the lowest byte at 6080H). Store the 24-bit result in the low 24 bits of EAX; ignore the highest byte of EAX.

10.20   If (EBX) = 0123A212H and (EDX) = 46B12310H, then what are the contents of EBX and EDX after execution of the Pentium instruction XADD EBX,EDX?

10.21   If (BX) = 271AH, (AX) = 712EH, and (CX) = 1234H, what are the contents of AX after execution of the Pentium instruction CMPXCHG CX,BX?

10.22   Write a Pentium assembly language program to perform $(X^2 + Y^2)$ where X is a signed 8-bit number stored in CL and Y is an unsigned 16-bit number stored in low 16 bits of SI. Save the 32-bit result onto the stack. Assume SP is already initialized.

10.23   Write a Pentium assembly language program to multiply a 16-bit signed number stored in AX by an 8-bit unsigned number stored in the low BL.Store the 32-bit result in BX:CX.

10.24   Assume that AL, CX,and DXBX contain a signed byte, a signed word, and a signed 32-bit number, respectively. Write a Pentium assembly language program that will compute the signed 32-bit result: AL – CX + DXBX → DXBX.

10.25   Write a Pentium assembly language program to multiply a signed 8-bit number in AL by a signed 32-bit number in ECX. Store 64-bit result in EDX:EAX.

10.26   Write a Pentium assembly program to multiply the top two 16-bit unsigned words of the stack. Store the 32-bit result onto the stack. Initialize SS to 5000H and SP to 0020H.

10.27   Write a Pentium assembly language program to convert 255 degrees in Celsius in BL to Fahrenheit degrees and store the value in AX. Use the equation

$$F = (C/5) * 9 + 32$$

10.28   Write a Pentium assembly program to divide an 8-bit signed number in CH by an 8-bit signed number in CL. Store the quotient in CH and the remainder in CL.

10.29   Write a Pentium assembly program to divide a signed 32-bit number in DX:AX by an 8-bit unsigned number in BH. Store the 16-bit quotient and 16-bit remainder in DX and AX respectively.

11

ASSEMBLY LANGUAGE PROGRAMMING WITH THE PENTIUM: PART 2

In this chapter we provide the second part of the Pentium's instruction set. Topics include logic, bit manipulation, set on conditions, shift and rotate, unconditional transfers including subroutine calls/returns, conditional branch, iteration control, interrupt, and processor control instructions. Several assembly language programming examples using most of these instructions are provided. Finally, delay routines using Pentium's instructions are covered.

11.1 Logic, Bit Manipulation, Set on condition, Shift, and Rotate Instructions

The logic, bit manipulation, set on condition, shift, and rotate instructions of the Pentium are listed in Table 11.1. Let us explain some of the instructions in the table.

- The NOT mem/reg instruction finds the one's complement of the operand. That is, this

TABLE 11.1 Pentium Logic, Bit Manipulation, Set on condition, Shift and Rotate Instructions

Logic Instructions	
NOT reg / mem	(reg / mem) ← NOT (reg / mem)
AND a, b	(a) ← (a) AND (b)
OR a, b	(a) ← (a) OR (b)
XOR a, b	(a) ← (a) XOR (b)
TEST a, b	(a) AND (b); no result, flags are affected.

Bit Manipulation Instructions	
Operands d and s are defined later in this chapter.	

BSF d,s	Bit Scan Forward
BSR d,s	Bit Scan reverse
BT d,s	Bit Test
BTC d,s	Bit test and complement
BTR d,s	Bit test and reset
BTS d,s	Bit test and set

TABLE 11.1   Cont.

Set on condition *Instructions*	
SETcc reg / mem8	If condition code, cc is true, then load operand byte with 01H; otherwise, clear operand byte to 00H
Shift Instructions	
SHL/SAL reg / mem, CNT	Shift logical/arithmetic left byte, word, or doubleword
SHR/SAR reg / mem, CNT	Shift logical/arithmetic right byte, word, or doubleword
Operands x, y and z for SHLD and SHRD are defined later in this chapter.	
SHLD x,y,z	Double precision Shift Left
SHRD x,y,z	Double precision Shift Right
Rotate Instructions	
ROL reg / mem, CNT	Rotate left byte, word, or doubleword
ROR reg / mem, CNT	Rotate right byte, word , or doubleword
RCL reg / mem, CNT	Rotate through carry left byte, word, or doubleword
RCR reg / mem, CNT	Rotate through carry right byte, word, or doubleword

a = "reg" or "mem," b = "reg" or "mem" or "data." mem/reg in shift and rotate instructions can be 8-, 16- or 32-bit register or memory location. CNT represents the number of times to be shifted. CNT = imm8, or contained in low 5 bits of CL. The value in CNT may varry from 1 to 31. Zero or negative shifts and rotates are illegal.

instruction converts all 0's to 1's, and vice versa. No flags are affected. The operand mem/reg can be 8-, 16-, or 32-bit. Typical examples include NOT BL, NOT AX, NOT EDX, and NOT DWORD PTR [EBX]. As an example, consider NOT BL. If prior to execution of this instruction, the contents of BL = 2AH = $0010\ 1010_2$, then after execution of NOT BL, the contents of BL = $1101\ 0101_2$ = D5H.

- AND a,b performs bit-by-bit logical AND operation between the two operands and stores the result in the destination operand. The destination operand 'a' can be memory or register while the source operand 'b' can be memory, register, or immediate data. The operand sizes can be 8-, 16-, or 32-bit. Typical examples include AND DL, AH, AND AX, BX, AND EAX, EDX, AND EDI, 2134A500H, and AND WORD PTR [SI],4. As an example, consider the AND BH,8FH instruction. If prior to execution of this instruction, (BH) = 72H, then after execution of AND BH,8FH, the following result is obtained:

$$(BH) = 72H = 01110010$$
$$AND\ 8FH = 10001111$$
$$-----------$$
$$(BH) = 00000010$$

ZF = 0 (result is nonzero), SF = 0 (most significant bit of the result is 0), and PF = 0 (result has odd parity). CF, AF, and OF are always cleared to 0 after a logic operation. The status flags are similarly affected after execution of other logic instructions, such as OR, XOR, NOT, and TEST.

The AND instruction can be used to perform a masking operation. If the bit value in a particular bit position is desired in a word, the word can be logically ANDed with appropriate data to accomplish this. For example, the bit value at bit 2 of an 8-bit number 01001Y10 (where an unknown bit value of Y is to be determined) can be obtained as follows:

```
            0 1 0 0 1 Y 1 0 -- 8-bit number
     AND    0 0 0 0 0 1 0 0 -- masking data
            ---------------------
            0 0 0 0 0 Y 0 0 -- result
```

If the bit value Y at bit 2 is 1, the result is nonzero (flag Z = 0); otherwise, the result is zero (flag Z = 1). The Z flag can be tested using typical conditional JUMP instructions such as JZ (jump if Z = 1) or JNZ (jump if Z = 0) to determine whether Y is 0 or 1. This is called a *masking operation*. The AND instruction can also be used to determine whether a binary number is ODD or EVEN by checking the least significant bit (LSB) of the number (LSB = 0 for even and LSB = 1 for odd).

- OR a,b   performs bit-by-bit logical OR operation between the two operands and stores the result in the destination operand. The destination operand 'a' can be memory or register, while the source operand 'b' can be memory, register, or immediate data. The operand sizes can be 8-, 16-, or 32-bit. All flags are affected. Typical examples include OR CL, AH, OR AX, DX, OR ESI, EDX, OR EAX, 2F34A500H, and OR WORD PTR [BX], 4. As an example, consider OR DL,AH. If prior to execution of this instruction, (DL) = A2H and (AH) = 5DH, then after exection of OR DL,AH, the content of DL is FFH. The flags are affected in the same manner as the AND instruction. The OR instruction can typically be used to insert a 1 in a particular bit position of a binary number without changing the values of the other bits. For example, a 1 can be inserted using the OR instruction at bit 3 of the 8-bit binary number 0 1 1 1 0 0 1 1 without changing the values of the other bits as follows:

```
            0 1 1 1 0 0 1 1 -- 8-bit number
     OR     0 0 0 0 1 0 0 0 -- data for inserting a 1 at bit 3
            -------------------
            0 1 1 1 1 0 1 1 -- Result
```

- XOR a,b performs bit-by-bit Exclusive-OR operation between the two operands and stores the result in the destination operand. Destination operand 'a' can be memory or register while the source operand 'b' can be memory, register, or immediate data. The operand sizes can be 8-, 16-, or 32-bit. All flags are affected. Typical examples include XOR CL,BL, XOR SI,BX, XOR ECX,EDX, XOR EBX,24C4A500H or XOR BYTE PTR [DI],2AH.

  As an example, consider XOR CX,2. If prior to execution of this instruction,(CX) = 2342H, then after execution of XOR CX,2, the 16-bit contents of CX will be 2340H.

All flags are affected in the same manner as the AND instruction. The Exclusive-OR instruction can be used to find the ones complement of a binary number by XORing the number with all 1's as follows:

```
          0 1 0 1 1 1 0 0 - - 8-bit number
  XOR     1 1 1 1 1 1 1 1 - - data
          --------------------------
          1 0 10 0 0 1 1 -- result ( one's complement of the 8-bit number 0 1 0 1 1 1 0 0 )
```

- TEST a,b performs a bit-by-bit logical AND operation between the two operands but does not store the result in the destination operand; the flags are affected in the same manner as the AND instruction. The destination operand 'a' can be memory or register while the source operand 'b' can be memory, register, or immediate data. The operand sizes can be 8-, 16-, or 32-bit. Typical examples include TEST DL,AH, TEST CX,BX, TEST EBX,EDX, TEST EDI,2C34A500H, and TEST WORD PTR [DI],4. As an example, consider TEST CL,05H. This instruction logically ANDs (CL) with 00000101_2 but does not store the result in CL. All flags are affected.

- BSF d,s takes the form:

```
        BSF      d      ,      s
                 reg16  ,      reg16/mem16
                 reg32  ,      reg32/mem32
```

The source operand (s) can be 16- or 32-bit register or memory location. The destination operand (d) can be a 16- or 32-bit register. This instruction scans the bits of the source operand (s) starting with the least significant bit (bit 0) in order to find the first bit that equals 1. The bit number of the first 1 found is stored in d, and the ZF flag is cleared to 0. The ZF is set to 1 if the whole 16- or 32-bit number is 0, and in that case, the contents of any register or memory location do not change. The other flags OF, SF, AF, PF, and CF are undefined. For example, consider BSF EBX,EDX. If (EDX) = 01241240H, then after execution of the BSF EBX,EDX instruction, (EBX) = 00000006H and ZF = 0 since (EDX) is nonzero. Bit 6 in EDX (contained in the lower byte of EDX) is the first 1 found when (EDX) is scanned from the right.

- Consider BSR d,s . Operands d and s for BSR are the same as BSF. The source operand (s) can be 16- or 32-bit register or memory location. The destination operand (d) can be a 16- or 32-bit register. This instruction scans the bits of the source operand, (s) starting with the most significant bit (bit 31 or bit 15) to find the first bit that equals 1. The bit number of the first one found is stored in 'd', and the ZF is set to 1 if the whole 16- or 32-bit number is 0; otherwise, the ZF flag is cleared to 0. The other flags OF, SF, AF, PF, and CF are undefined. For example, consider BSR AX,CX. If (CX) = 25F1H, then after execution of the BSF AX, CX instruction, (AX) = 13_{10} = 000DH since bit 13 is the first bit set to 1 when scanned from left. ZF = 0 since (CX) is nonzero.

- BT (bit test) takes the form :

	d,	s
BT		
	reg16,	reg16
	mem16,	reg16
	reg16,	imm8
	mem16,	imm8
	reg32,	reg32
	mem32,	reg32
	reg32,	imm8
	mem32,	imm8

BT assigns the bit value of the destination operand d, specified by the source operand s (bit offset) to the carry flag. Only CF is affected. CF contains the value of the bit selected. If operand 's' is immediate data, only 8 bits are allowed in the instruction. This operand is taken modulo 32; hence, the range of immediate bit offset is from 0 to 31. This permits any bit within a register to be selected. If d is a register, the bit value assigned to CF is defined by the value of the bit number defined by s taken modulo the register size. Note that BSF and BSR instructions do not provide modulo operands. For memory bit strings, immediate field gives only the bit offset within a word or doubleword. When accessing a bit in memory, the Pentium may access four bytes starting from the memory address given by: Effective Address + (4* (Bit offset DIV 32)) for a 32-bit operand size or two bytes starting from the memory address given by: Effective Address + (2 * (Bit offset DIV 16)) for a 16-bit operand size.

Next, as an example, consider BT EAX,2. If (EAX) = FFFF0080H, then after BT EAX,2, the CF will be cleared to 0 since bit 2 of EAX is 0. Next, consider BT ECX,33. If (ECX) = 1234081FH, then after BT ECX,33, because the immediate data (s) is 33_{10}, bit 1 (the remainder of 33/32 = bit 1 of ECX) is reflected in CF, and therefore CF = 1.

- BTC (bit test and complement) takes the form

$$BTC \quad d,s$$

where d and s have the same definitions as for the BT instruction. The bit of d defined by s is reflected in CF. After CF is assigned, the same bit of d defined by s is one's-complemented. The Pentium determines the bit number from s (whether s is immediate data or register) and d (whether d is register or memory) in the same way as for the BT instruction.

- BTR (bit test and reset) takes the form

$$BTR \quad d,s$$

where d and s have the same definitions as for the BT instruction. The bit of d defined by s is reflected in CF. After CF is assigned, the same bit of d defined by s is reset to 0. Everything else applicable to the BT instruction also applies to BTR.

- BTS (bit test and set) takes the form

  BTS   d,s

  BTS is the same as BTR except that the bit in d specified by s is set to 1 after the bit value of d defined by s is reflected in CF. Everything else applicable to the BT instruction also applies to BTS.

- Consider SETcc reg8 / mem8. This instruction checks the specified condition and sets a byte in mem/reg to 01H if true or reset the byte in mem/reg to 00H if false. Appendix F lists the various conditions used with the SETcc instruction. Typical examples of this include SETC mem/reg (set byte in operand if the carry flag is 1), SETZ mem/reg (set byte in operand if the zero flag is 1), and SETO mem/reg (set byte in operand if the overflow flag is 1). Note that mem/reg can be a byte located in memory or in the lowest byte of the general register. No flags are affected. As an example, consider SETZ BL. If (BL) = 52H and ZF = 1, then, after this instruction is executed, (BL) = 01H. On the other hand, if ZF = 0, then, after execution of this instruction, (BL) = 00H. The other SET*cc* instructions can be explained similarly.

- The basic concepts associated with shift and rotate operations are covered in Chapter 5. In this section, some of the Pentium shift and rotate instructions are illustrated by means of numerical examples. Consider SHR mem/reg,CNT which has the following operands:

SHR	reg/mem	,CNT
	reg8/mem8	,CL
	reg8/mem8	,imm8
	reg16/mem16	,CL
	reg16/mem16	,imm8
	reg32/mem32	,CL
	reg32/mem32	,imm8

  SHR mem/reg,CNT   instruction performs logical right shift on the contents of the destination operand (mem/reg) specified by the shift count in the source operand. The source operand can be 8-bit immediate data or contained in register CL. The shift count may vary from 1 to 31. If a shift count greater than 31 is attempted, only the bottom five bits of the shift count are used. When CL is the shift count, its contents do not change after execution of the shift instruction. Figure 11.1 shows the operation of SHR mem/reg,CNT. Note that the least significant bit shifted out goes to CF (the carry flag) and 0 is shifted into the most significant bit. Finally, the content of register or memory is shifted to right based on the shift count. As an example, consider the following instruction sequence:

  MOV   CL,2
  SHR   DL,CL

The above instruction sequence is equivalent to SHR DL, 2.

If prior to execution of the instruction sequence above, the contents of DL are 97H and CF = 0, then after execution of this instruction sequence , (DL) = 25H and CF = 1.

SHR can be used to divide an unsigned number by 2^n by shifting the number n times to the right as long as a 1 is not shifted out of the least significant bit. Since execution time of the unsigned division instruction (DIV) is longer, unsigned division by SHR may be more efficient.

- SHL mem/reg,CNT works in the same way as the SHR mem/reg,CNT except that the contents of mem/reg are logically shifted to the left. Operation of the instruction SHL mem/reg , CNT is shown in Figure 11.1. This instruction has the same operands as SHR mem/reg, CNT. As an example, consider SHL BL,1. This instruction logically shifts the contents of BL one bit to the left. Suppose that prior to execution of this instruction, if (BL) = A1H and CF = 0, then after SHL Bl,1, the contents of BL are 42H and CF = 1.

  SHL can be used to multiply an unsigned number by 2^n by shifting the number, n times to the left as long as a 1 is not shifted out of the most significant bit. Since the execution time of the unsigned multiplication instruction (MUL) is longer, unsigned multiplication by SHL may be more efficient.

- Figure 11.2 shows the operations of SAR mem/reg,CNT or SAL mem/reg,CNT. These instructions have the same operands as the SHR mem/reg, CNT. SAR can be used to divide a signed number by 2^n by shifting the number n times to right as long as a 1 is not shifted out of the least significant bit. Since execution time of the signed division instruction (IDIV) is longer, signed division by SAR may be more efficient.

  SAL and SHL perform the same operation except that SAL sets OF to 1 if the sign bit of the number being shifted changes during or after shifting. SAL can be used to multiply a signed number by 2^n by shifting the number n times to left; the result is correct if OF = 0 while the result is incorrect if OF = 1. Since the execution time of the signed multiplication instruction (IMUL) is longer, multiplication by SAL may be more efficient.

- Multiplication and division by shifting a binary number by 2^n is desirable in applications such as communication systems. Note that in communication systems,the number of samples is normally chosen by the designer as powers of 2. Hence, to multiply or divide other parameters by the number of samples, multiplication or division using shift instructions rather than Pentium's multiplication or division instructions (MUL, IMUL, DIV, IDIV) are desirable. This may be very useful in real-time systems.

- ROL mem/reg,CNT rotates (mem/reg) left by the specified number of bits (Figure 11.3). The operands are the same as the SHR mem/reg,CNT. The number of bits to be rotated is either 8-bit immediate data or contained in CL. For example, if CF = 0, (BX) = 0010H, and (CL) = 03H then, after ROL BX, CL, register BX will contain 0080H and CF = 0. On the other hand, ROL BL, 5 rotates the 8-bit contents of BL five times to the left. ROR mem/reg, CNT is similar to ROL except that the rotation is to the right (Figure 11.3).

- Figure 11.4 shows the operations of the instructions, RCL mem/reg,CNT and RCR mem/reg, CNT.

- Consider SHLD   x,y,z and   SHRD   x,y,z instructions. The operands for these instructions are as follows:

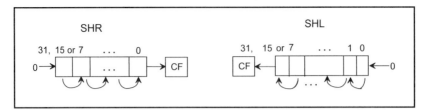

FIGURE 11.1   SHR and SHL instructions.

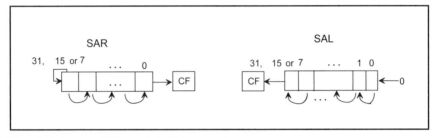

FIGURE 11.2   SAR and SAL instructions.

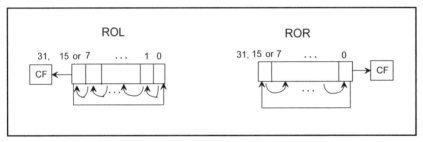

FIGURE 11.3   ROL and ROR instructions.

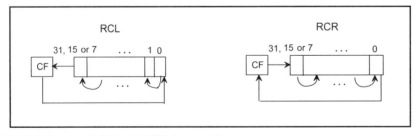

FIGURE 11.4   RCL and RCR instructions.

SHLD	x,	y,	z	Shift left double
SHRD	x,	y,	z	Shift right double
	reg16,	reg16,	imm8	
	mem16,	reg16,	imm8	
	reg16,	reg16,	CL	
	mem16,	reg16,	CL	
	reg32,	reg32,	CL	

```
            mem32,   reg32,   CL
            reg32,   reg32,   imm8
            mem32,   reg32,   imm8
```

For both SHLD and SHRD, the shift count is defined by an immediate byte or the contents of CL. These operands are taken modulo 32 to provide a number between 0 and 31 by which to shift. Note that modulo 32 means that a shift count of 34 will shift the data twice (34/32 = remainder of 2).

SHLD shifts the contents of *d:s* by the specified shift count, with the result stored back into *d*; *d* is shifted to the left by the shift count with the low-order bits of *d* filled from the high-order bits of *s*. The bits in *s* are not altered after shifting. The carry flag becomes the value of the bit shifted out of the most significant bit of *d*. If the shift count is zero, this instruction works as a NOP. For the specified shift count, the SF, ZF, and PF flags are set according to the result in *d*. CF is set to the value of the last bit shifted out. OF and AF are undefined.

SHRD shifts the contents of *d:s* by the specified shift count to the right with the result stored back into *d*. The bits in *d* are shifted right by the shift count, with the high-order bits filled from the low-order bits of *s*. The bits in *s* are not altered after shifting. If the shift count is zero, this instruction operates as a NOP. For the specified shift count, the SF, ZF, and PF flags are set according to the value of the result. CF is set to the value of the last bit shifted out. OF and AF are undefined.

As an example, consider SHLD BX, DX, 2. If (BX) = 183FH and (DX) = 01F1H, then after execution of this SHLD instruction, (BX) = 60FCH, (DX) = 01F1H (unchanged), CF = 0, SF = 0, ZF = 0, and PF = 1. Similarly, the SHRD instruction can be illustrated.

EXAMPLE 11.1 It is desired to multiply a 32-bit unsigned number in EBX by 4 to provide a 32-bit product and then perform the following operations on the contents of EBX:

* Set bits 0 and 3 to 1 without changing other bits in EBX.

* Clear bit 30 to zero without changing other bits in EBX.

* Ones-complement bit 5 without changing other bits in EBX.

Assume data is already stored in EBX.

(a) Write a Pentium assembly language program to accomplish the above using only logic and shift instructions. Do not use any multiplication or any other instructions.

(b) Write a Pentium assembly language program to accomplish the above using only bit manipulation and shift instructions. Do not use multiplication, logic, or any other instructions.

Solution

(a)
```
            .486
            .MODEL   FLAT,STDCALL
            .CODE
START:
            SHL      EBX,2              ; Unsigned multiply EBX by 4
```

	OR	EBX,00000009H	; set bits 0 and 3 in EBX to one
	AND	EBX,0BFFFFFFFH	; clear bit 30 in EBX to zero
	XOR	EBX,00000020H	; ones complement bit 5 in EBX
	HLT		; Stop
END	START		

(b)

```
          .486
          .MODEL   FLAT,STDCALL
          .CODE
START:
```

	SHL	EBX,2	; Unsigned multiply EBX by 4
	BTS	EBX,0	; set bit 0 in EBX to one
	BTS	EBX,3	; set bit 3 in EBX to one
	BTR	EBX,30	; clear bit 30 in EBX to zero
	BTC	EBX,5	; ones complement bit 5 in EBX
	HLT		; Stop
END	START		

EXAMPLE 11.2   Write a Pentium assembly language program that will perform :
$5 \times X + 6 \times Y + (Y/8) \to (BP)(BX)$ where X is an unsigned 8-bit number stored at offset
0100H and Y is a 16-bit signed number stored as two bytes at offsets 0200H and 0201H
respectively. Neglect the remainder of Y/8. Store the result in registers BX and BP. BX
holds the low 16 bits of the 32-bit result and BP holds the high 16 bits of the 32-bit result.
Initialize DS to 1000H.

Solution

```
          .486
          .MODEL   SMALL,STDCALL
          .CODE
START:
```

	MOV	AX,1000H	;Initialize DS
	MOV	DS,AX	
	MOV	SI,0100H	;Pointer to X
	MOV	DI,0200H	;Pointer to Y
	MOV	AL,[SI]	;Move X to AL
	MOV	BX,0	;Clear 16-bit sum to zero
	MOV	CL,5	
	MUL	CL	;Unsigned MUL, (AX) = 5*X
	ADD	BX,AX	;Sum 5*X with BX
	MOV	BP,0	;Convert 5*X to unsigned 32-bit
	MOV	AX,[DI]	;Move Y to AX
	MOV	CL,3	
	SAR	AX,CL	;Divide by 8
	CWD		;Convert Y/8 into 32-bit in (DX)(AX)
	ADD	BX,AX	;Sum 5*X and Y/8
	ADC	BP,DX	;in BP BX

```
        MOV    AX,[DI]           ;Move Y to AX
        MOV    CX,6
        IMUL   CX                ;(DX)(AX) <- 6*Y
        ADD    BX,AX             ;32-bit result
        ADC    BP,DX             ;in BP BX
        HLT                      ;Halt
END     START
```

11.2   String Instructions

Table 11.2 lists the Pentium string instructions. Note that *string* means that an array of data bytes, 16-bit words, or 32-bit doublewords is stored in consecutive memory locations. String instructions are available to MOVE, COMPARE, or SCAN for a value as well as to move string elements to and from AL, AX, or EAX. The instructions in Table 11.2, contain "repeat" prefixes that cause these instructions to be repeated in hardware, allowing long strings to be processed much faster than if done in a software loop.

Let us explain some of the instructions in Table 11.2.

- MOVSB, MOVSW, or MOVSD moves 8-, 16-, or 32-bit data from the memory location addressed by SI in DS to the memory location addressed by DI in ES. SI and DI are incremented automatically by 1 for byte, 2 for word, and 4 for doubleword if DF = 0; on the other hand, if DF = 1, then registers SI and DI are automatically decremented by 1 for byte, 2 for word, and 4 for doubleword. The instruction CLD can be used to clear the DF flag to 0 while the STD sets the DF flag to one. Automatic incrementing or decrementing of SI and DI will enable the programmer to move data between two strings from low to high addresses or from high to low addresses in memory. As mentioned in Chapter 10, the default segment register for source is DS, and it may be overridden; the segment register used for the destination must be ES, and cannot be overridden. An example is ES:MOVSW. In this case, both source and destination strings will use ES as the segment register.

  Note that for 16-bit offset, SI and DI contain offsets for both source and destination strings while for 32-bit offset, ESI and EDI contain offsets for both source and destination strings. Also, for 32-bit offset in real mode, the contents of ESI and EDI vary from 00000000H to 0000FFFFH; this means that SI and DI contain offsets for doubleword string instructions such as MOVSD in real mode since low 16 bits of ESI and EDI are the same as SI and DI.

TABLE 11.2   Pentium String Instructions

REP	Repeat MOVS or STOS until CX = 0
REPE / REPZ.	Repeat CMPS or SCAS until ZF = 1 or CX = 0
REPNE / REPNZ	Repeat CMPS or SCAS until ZF = 0 or CX = 0
MOVSB / MOVSW / MOVSD	Move byte or word or doubleword string
SCASB /SCASW / SCASD	Scan byte or word or doubleword string
LODSB /LODSW / LODSD	Load from memory into AL or AX or EAX
STOSB /STOSW/ STOSD	Store AL or AX or EAX into memory

As an example of MOVS instruction, consider MOVSW. If (DF) = 0, (DS) = 1000H, (ES) = 3000H, (SI) = 0002H, (DI) = 5000H. Assume that the contents of offset pointed to by SI =0002H in DS = 1000H are 1234H. That is, (physical address 10002H) = 1234H. This is depicted along with other data (chosen arbitrarily) in the Figure 11.5 (a).

Now, after execution of the MOVSW instruction along with the above data, the contents of offset pointed to by DI = 5000H in ES = 3000H are 1234H. That is (physical address 35000H) = 1234H. Also, The contents of SI and DI are incremented (since DF =0) by 2 for word. Hence, (SI) = 0004H, and (DI) = 5002H. This is depicted in Figure 11.5 (b).

Assuming (10002H) = 1234H, the following   Pentium   instruction sequence will accomplish the above:

```
CLD                         ;DF = 0
MOV    AX,1000H             ;DS = 1000H
MOV    DS,AX
MOV    BX,3000H             ;ES = 3000H
MOV    ES,BX
MOV    SI,0002H             ;Initialize SI to 0002H
MOV    DI,5000H             ;Initialize DI to 5000H
MOVSW
```

Note that DS (source segment) in MOVS instruction can be overridden while the destination   segment, ES is fixed, cannot be overridden. For example, the instruction ES: MOVSW will override the source segment, DS by ES while the destination segment remains at ES so that data will be moved in the same extra segment, ES.

- REP repeats the string instruction (such as MOVS) follows until the CX register is decremented to 0. As mentioned before, REP is implemented in hardware for faster operation. Next , consider moving (offset 1000H) to (offset 5000H), (offset 1001H) to (offset 5001H), and so on. Note that (offset 1000H) indicates the contents of offset 1000H in DS (source string) while (offset 5000H) means the contents of offset 5000H in ES (destination string). Assume (DS) = 2000H and (ES) = 4000H. The following Pentium assembly language program using LOOP instruction for moving 50 bytes from source to destination (from low to high addresses) will accomplish this:

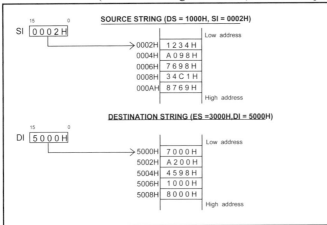

FIGURE 11.5 (a)   Source and destination strings prior to execution of MOVSW instruction

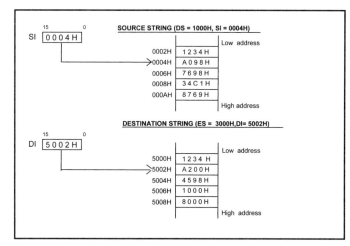

FIGURE 11.5(b)　　　**Source and destination strings after execution of MOVSW instruction**

```
        .486
        .MODEL  SMALL, STDCALL
        .CODE
START:
        CLD                     ; Clear DF to 0 for autoincrementing SI and DI by 1
                                ; for byte move
        MOV     AX,2000H        ;DS = 2000H
        MOV     DS,AX
        MOV     BX,4000H        ;ES = 4000H
        MOV     ES,BX
        MOV     SI,1000H        ;Initialize SI to 1000H
        MOV     DI,5000H        ;Initialize DI to 5000H
        MOV     CX,50           ;Initialize CX to 50
BACK:   MOVSB                   ;Move a byte from source to destination
        LOOP    BACK            ;decrements CX by 1
                                ;and goes to label BACK if CX ≠ 0. If CX = 0, goes
                                ;to the next instruction. Thus, 50 bytes are moved
        HLT                     ; Stop
END     START
```

The above assembly language program can be replaced using REP prefix as follows:

```
        .486
        .MODEL  SMALL, STDCALL
        .CODE
START:
        CLD                     ;Clear DF to 0 for autoincrementing SI and DI by 1
                                ; for byte move
        MOV     AX,2000H        ;DS = 2000H
        MOV     DS,AX
        MOV     BX,4000H        ;ES = 4000H
```

```
        MOV     ES,BX
        MOV     SI,1000H    ;Initialize SI to 1000H
        MOV     DI,5000H    ;Initialize DI to 5000H
        MOV     CX,50       ; Initialize CX to 50
        REP     MOVSB       ; Move a byte from source array to destination
                            ; array in the direction based on DF. REP  prefix
                            ; decrements CX by 1
                            ; and executes MOVSB 50 times.
                            ; Thus, 50 bytes are moved.
        HLT                 ; Stop
END     START
```

Next, consider moving string data from high to low addresses. For example, suppose it is desired to move 8-bit data from (offset 2006H) to (offset 5008H), (offset 2005H) to (offset 5007H), and so on. The following Pentium assembly language program using LOOP instruction for moving 50 bytes from source to destination (from high to low addresses) will accomplish this:

```
        .486
        .MODEL  SMALL, STDCALL
        .CODE
START:
        STD                 ;Set DF to 1 for autodecrementing  SI and DI by 1
                            ;for byte move
        MOV     AX,2000H    ;DS = 2000H
        MOV     DS,AX
        MOV     BX,4000H    ;ES = 4000H
        MOV     ES,BX
        MOV     SI,2006H    ;Initialize SI to 2006H
        MOV     DI,5008H    ;Initialize DI to 5008H
        MOV     CX,50       ; Initialize CX to 50
BACK:   MOVSB               ;Move a byte from source array to destination
        LOOP    BACK        ;array in the direction based on DF. LOOP
                            ;decrements CX by 1
                            ;and goes to label BACK if CX ≠ 0.If CX = 0,
                            ;goes to the next instruction. Thus, 50 bytes are moved
        HLT                 ;Stop
END     START
```

The above program can be replaced using REP prefix as follows:

```
        .486
        .MODEL SMALL, STDCALL
        .CODE
START:
        STD                 ;Set DF to 1 for autodecrementing  SI and DI by 1
                            ;for byte move
        MOV     AX,2000H    ;DS = 2000H
```

```
        MOV     DS,AX
        MOV     BX,4000H        ;ES = 4000H
        MOV     ES,BX
        MOV     SI,2006H        ;Initialize SI to 2006H
        MOV     DI,5008H        ;Initialize DI to 5008H
        MOV     CX,50           ;Initialize CX to 50
        REP     MOVSB           ;Move a byte from source array to destination
                                ; array in the direction based on DF. REP prefix
                                ; decrements CX by 1
                                ; and executes MOVSB 50 times.
                                ; Thus, 50 bytes are moved.
        HLT                     ; Stop
END     START
```

- CMPSB or CMPSW or CMPSD in real mode subtracts without any result (affects flags accordingly) 8- , 16-, or 32-bit data in the source memory location addressed by SI in DS from the destination memory location addressed by DI in ES. SI and DI are incremented or decremented depending on the DF flag. For example, if (DF) = 0, (DS) = 1000H, (ES) = 3000H, (SI) = 0002H, (DI) = 0004H, (10002H) = 1234H, and (30004H) = 1234H then, after CMPSW, CF = 0, PF = 1, AF = 1, ZF = 1, SF = 0, OF = 0, (10002H) = 1234H, and (30004H) = 1234H , (SI) = 0004H, and (DI) = 0006H. Note that SI and DI are used as source and destination pointers for 16-bit offsets while ESI and EDI are used as source and destination pointers for 32-bit offsets.

- Consider SCASB / SCASW / SCASD. This compares the memory addressed by (DI) in ES with AL or AX or EAX. If (DI) = 0000H, (ES) = 2000H, (DF) = 0, (20000H) = 05H, and (AL) = 03H, then, after SCASB, register DI will contain 0001H because (DF) = 0 and all flags are affected based on the operation (AL) - (20000H). Hence, OF = 0, SF = 1, ZF = 0, AF = 0, PF = 0, and CF = 1.

- REPE/REPZ or REPNE/REPNZ prefix can be used with CMPS or SCAS to cause one of these instructions to continue executing until ZF = 0 (for the REPNE/REPNZ prefix) or CX = 0. The prefixes REPE and REPZ also provide similar purpose. If CMPS is prefixed with REPE or REPZ, the operation is interpreted as "compare while not end-of-string (CX ≠ 0) or strings are equal (ZF = 1)." If CMPS is preceded by REPNE or REPNZ, the operation is interpreted as "compare while not end-of-string (CX ≠ 0) or strings not equal (ZF = 0)." Thus, repeated CMPS instructions can be used to find matching or differing string elements.

- If SCAS is prefixed with REPE or REPZ, the operation is interpreted as "scan while not end-of-string (CX ≠ 0) or string-element = scan-value (ZF = 1)" This form may be used to scan for departure from a given value. If SCAS is prefixed with REPNE or REPNZ, the operation is interpreted as "scan while not end-of-string (CX ≠ 0) or string-element is not equal to scan-value (ZF = 0)." This form may be used to locate a value in a string.

- LODSB or LODSW or LODSD loads a byte into AL or a word into AX or a doubleword into EAX respectively from a string in memory addressed by SI in DS ; SI is then automatically incremented or decremented by 1for byte, 2 for word, or 4 for doubleword based on DF. For example, prior to execution of LODSB, if (SI)=

0020H, (DS) = 3000H, (30020H) = 05H, DF = 0, then after execution of LODSB, data 05H is loaded into AL; SI is then automatically incremented to 0021H since DF = 0.

• STOSB or STOSW or STOSD stores a byte in AL or a word in AX, or a doubleword in EAX respectively into a string memory addressed by DI in ES. DI is then automatically incremented or decremented by 1 for byte, 2 for word, or 4 for doubleword based on DF.

EXAMPLE 11.3   Write a Pentium assembly language program to compare a source string of 50_{10} words from low to high addresses pointed to by an offset 1000H in the data segment at 2000H with a destination string pointed to by an offset 3000H in the extra segment at 4000H. The program should be halted as soon as a match is found or the end of string is reached.

Solution

```
        .486
        .MODEL  SMALL, STDCALL
        .CODE
START:
        MOV     AX,2000H      ;Initialize
        MOV     DS, AX        ;Data Segment at 2000H
        MOV     AX, 4000H     ;Initialize
        MOV     ES, AX        ;ES at 4000H
        MOV     SI, 1000H     ;Initialize SI at 1000H for DS
        MOV     DI, 3000H     ;Initialize DI AT 3000H for ES
        MOV     CX, 50        ;Initialize CX
        CLD                   ;Clear DF so that
                              ;SI and DI will
                              ;autoincrement
                              ;after compare
        REPNE   CMPSW         ;Repeat CMPSW until CX=0 or
                              ;until compared words are equal
        HLT                   ;Halt
END     START
```

Note: REPNE CMPSW instruction in the above program will automatically decrement CX by 1, and checks whether ZF = 1. The CMPSW instruction is executed CX times if CX is not equal to 0 or strings are not equal (ZF = 0). This means that as soon as a match is found (ZF=1), the program will go to the next instruction (HLT). However, if no match is found (ZF = 0), the instruction, CMPSW will be executed CX times, and the program will then go the next instruction (HLT).

11.3   Unconditional Transfer Instructions

Unconditional transfer instructions transfer control to a location either in the current executing memory segment (intrasegment) or in a different code segment (intersegment). Table 11.3 lists the unconditional transfer instructions.

The jump instruction in Table 11.3 can be either intrasegment or near JMP (Jump within the current code segment; only IP changes) or intersegment or far JMP (Jump from one code segment to another code segment; both CS and IP contents are modified). The programmer can use NEAR and FAR directives to indicate intrasegment and intersegment Jump instructions.

    Intrasegment Jump can have an operand with a short label (signed 8-bit displacement), near label (signed 16-bit displacement), reg16 or mem16. For example, the short label and near label operands use relative addressing mode. This means that the Jump is performed relative to the address of the JMP instruction. For jumps with short label, IP changes and CS is fixed. JMP disp8 adds the second object code byte (signed 8-bit displacement) to (IP + 2), and (CS) is unchanged. With an 8-bit signed displacement, jump with a short label operand is allowed in the range from -128 to +127 (0 being positive) from the address of the JMP instruction. Near label operand allows a JMP instruction to have a signed 16-bit displacement with a range -32K to +32K bytes from the address of the JMP instruction. An example of JMP short label or near label is JMP START.

    The Pentium assembler automatically computes the value of the displacement START at assembly time. The programmer does not have to worry about it. Based upon the displacement size of START (in this case), the assembler determines whether the JMP is to be performed with short or near label. Short or Near Jumps are used in real mode. In protected mode, the Pentium can use a range of -2 Gigabytes to +2 Gigabytes.

    The short jump and near jump are relocatable since they use relative addressing mode. This means that if the code segment moves to a new address in memory, the distance between the jump instruction, and the jump address stays the same. Thus, the code segment can easily be moved to anywhere in memory without modification. This is very convenient for the programmer.

    In order to illustrate the concept of short jump, consider the following Pentium instruction sequence along with machine code provided by the MASM32 assembler:

```
1000                START:
1000 6683C303                       ADD     BX, 3
1004 668BC1                         MOV     AX, CX
1007 660BCA       BACK:             OR      CX, DX
100A 6623D8                         AND     BX, AX
100D EB06                           JMP     DOWN
100F 8AC8                           MOV     CL, AL
1011 6683C105                       ADD     CX, 5
1015 6683EB05     DOWN:             SUB     BX, 5
1019 EBEC                           JMP     BACK
101B F4                             HLT
```

    Note that all instructions, addresses, and data are arbitrarily chosen. The first jump instruction (JMP DOWN) at offset 100DH (automatically generated by the assembler) has a machine code EB06H. This instruction unconditionally jumps to address DOWN. The machine code EB06H means that the opcode for JMP is EBH, and the relative displacement value is 06H (positive value meaning forward jump). This is a short jump since the range is between -128 and + 127. Note that the instruction pointer normally points to the next instruction. Hence, at offset 100DH, the IP will contain 100FH. The displacement 06H is added to 100FH to find the offset value where the program will unconditionally jump. The jump offset is calculated as follows:

TABLE 11.3   Pentium unconditional transfers

JMP disp/reg/mem	Unconditional jump
CALL disp/reg/mem	Call subroutine
RET or RET disp 16	Return from subroutine

```
     100FH = 0001 0000 0000 1111
  +    06H = 0000 0000 0000 0110 (sign-extendedd to 16 bits)
       --------------------------------------------------------------------
     1015H = 0001 0000 0001 0101
```

Hence, the instruction jumps to offset 1015H. This is verified in the above instruction sequence.

Next, consider the second jump instruction, JMP BACK. The machine code for this instruction at offset 1019H is EBECH where EBH is the opcode, and ECH is the signed displacement value. Since ECH is a negative number (-20), this is a backward jump. Note that the instruction pointer normally points to the next instruction. Hence, at offset 1019H, the IP will contain 101BH. The displacement 20 is subtracted from 101BH to find the offset value where the program will unconditionally jump. The jump offset is calculated as follows:

```
    101BH =    0001 0000   0001  1011
  +   ECH =    1111 1111   1110  1100 (sign-extendedd to 16 bits)
       -----------------------------------------------------------------
   1007H = ↗1   0001 0000   0000  0111
           Ignore final carry
```

The jump offset is 1007H which is verified in the above instruction sequence. In the case of the short jump, the relative displacement is signed 8-bit contained in a byte with a range of -128 to +127 (0 being positive). When the jump offset is outside this range, but in the same segment, a near jump is used, and the jump offset is two bytes long.

JMP reg specifies the jump offset by the 16- or 32-bit contents of of a register. This is an indirect jump. In the real mode, the contents of the specified register are transferred directly into the IP. The range for this JMP is from -32K to +32K bytes from the address of the JMP. An example of JMP reg is JMP SI which copies the contents of SI into IP. SI contains the 16-bit displacement. In the real mode, JMP EBX can also be used to hold the jump offset in the low 16 bits of EBX. However, in the protected mode, since 32-bit offset is needed, EBX will contain the 32-bit offset, and the code segment can be 4 Gigabytes long.

An example of JMP mem16 is JMP [DI] which uses the contents of DI as the address of the memory location containing the offset. This offset is placed into IP. The physical address is computed from this IP value and the current CS value.

Jump with FAR PTR directive uses a 32-bit immediate operand ; the first 16 bits are loaded into IP while the next 16 bits are loaded into CS. An example of far jump is JMP FAR PTR BEGIN which unconditionally branches to a label BEGIN in a different code segment. Finally, JMP mem32 indirectly specifies the offset and the code segment values. IP and CS are loaded from the 32-bit contents of four consecutive memory locations; each memory location contains a byte. As an example, JMP FAR PTR [SI] loads IP and CS with the contents of four consecutive bytes pointed to by SI in DS.

The Pentium CALL instructions provide the mechanism to call a subroutine into operation while the RETinstruction placed at the end of the subroutine transfers control back to the main program. There are two types of Pentium CALL instruction. These are near, or intrasegment CALL (IP changes, CS is fixed) ,and far, or intersegment CALL (both IP and CS are changed).

Near and Far CALLs are defined by the various operands of the CALL instruction. For example, the three operands NEAR PROC, mem16, and reg16 define intrasegment CALLs to a subroutine. Upon execution of the intrasegment CALL with any of the three operands, the Pentium pushes the current contents of IP onto the stack; the SP is then decremented by 2. The saved IP value is the offset that contains the next instruction to be executed in the main program. The Pentium then places a new 16-bit value (offset of the first instruction in the subroutine) into IP. The three types of operands for the intrasegment CALL will be discussed next.

These are near CALL, CALL mem16, and CALL reg16.

As an example of near CALL, consider the Pentium instruction sequence shown below:

```
            .486
            .MODEL    SMALL, STDCALL
            .CODE
BEGIN:
            MOVE      BX, 5       ; Start of the main program
            ------------
            CALL      MULTI       ; Call the subroutine in the same segment
            ------------
            ------------
            HLT
MULTI       PROC      NEAR        ; Start of the subroutine, MULTI
            ------
            ------
            RET
MULTI       ENDP
END         BEGIN
```

In the above, the main program, and the subroutine called MULTI are located in the same code segment. The assembler directive NEAR in the statement CALL NEAR PROC specifies the CALL instruction with relative addressing mode in the same code segment. This means that NEAR determines a 16-bit displacement, and the offset is computed relative to the address of the CALL instruction. With 16-bit displacement, the range of the CALL instruction is limited to -32766 to + 32765 (0 being positive). The Pentium uses 32-bit offset in protected mode with a range of -2Gigabytes to +2 Gigabytes. Since this subroutine is in the same code segment as the main program containing the CALL instruction, the contents of CS are not altered to access it. Note that use of the assembler directive NEAR in the statement MULTI PROC NEAR tells the Pentium assembler that the main program and the subroutine are located in the same code segment.

The instructions CALL mem16 and CALL reg16 specify a memory location or a 16-bit register such as BX to hold the offset to be loaded into IP. Thus, these two CALL instructions use indirect addressing mode. An example of CALL mem16 is CALL [BX] which loads the 16-bit value stored in the memory location pointed to by BX into IP. The physical address of the offset is calculated from the current DS and the contents of BX. The first instruction of the subroutine is contained in the address computed from new IP value and current CS. Next, typical examples of CALL reg16 are CALL BX and CALL BP; these instructions load the 16-bit contents of BX or BP into IP. The starting address (physical address) of the subroutine is computed from the new value of IP and the current CS contents. Note that intrasegment CALL instructions are used when the main program and the subroutine are located in the same code segment.

Intersegment CALL instructions are used when the main program and the subroutine are located in two different code segments. The two intersegment CALL instructions are CALL FAR PTR and CALL mem32. These instructions define a new offset for IP and a new value for CS. Upon execution of these two instructions, the Pentium pushes the current contents of IP and CS onto the stack, the new values of IP and CS are then loaded. For example consider CALL FAR PTR MULTI which loads the new value of IP from the next two bytes, and the new value of CS from the following two bytes. As an example, consider the following Pentium instruction sequence:

```
            .486
            .MODEL    SMALL, STDCALL
            .CODE
START:
            MOV       CX, 2              ; Start of the main program
            ------------

            ------------
            CALL      FAR PTR MULTI    ; Call the subroutine in a different code seg
            ------------

            ------------
            HLT
            .CODE
MULTI       PROC      FAR

            ------
            ------
            RET
MULTI       ENDP
END         START
```

Since this subroutine is in a different code segment from the CALL instruction, the contents of CS must be altered to access it. Use of the assembler directive FAR in the statement MULTI PROC FAR tells the Pentium assembler that the main program and the subroutine are located in different code segments.

CALL FAR PTR [SI] stores the pointer for the subroutine as four bytes in data memory. The location of the first byte of the four-byte pointer is specified indirectly by one of the Pentium registers (SI in this case). In this example, in real mode, the 20-bit physical address of the first byte of the four-byte pointer is computed from DS and SI. Finally, CALL FAR PTR [BX] pushes CS and IP onto the stack and loads IP and CS with the contents of four consecutive bytes pointed to by BX.

RET instruction is usually placed at the end of a subroutine which pops IP (pushed onto the stack by the intrasegment CALL instruction) or both IP and CS (pushed onto the stack by the intersegment CALL instruction), and returns control to the main program. RET disp 16, on the other hand, adds 16-bit value (disp 16) to SP after placing the return address into IP (for intrasegment CALL) or into IP and CS (for intersegment CALL). The main objective of inclusion of the 16-bit displacement operand with the RET instruction is to discard the parameters that were saved onto the stack before execution of the subroutine CALL instruction.

EXAMPLE 11.4   Write a subroutine in Pentium assembly language which can be called by a main program in the same code segment. The subroutine will multiply a signed 16-bit number in CX by a signed 8-bit number in AL. The main program will perform initializations (DS to 5000H, SS to 6000H, SP to 0020H, BX to 2000H, SI to 0000H, and DI to 0004H)), call this subroutine, store the result in two consecutive memory words, and stop. Assume SI and DI contain pointers to the signed 8-bit and 16-bit data respectively. Store 32-bit result in a memory location pointed to by BX.

Solution

```
            .486
            .MODEL    SMALL, STDCALL
            .CODE
BEGIN:
            MOV       AX, 5000H      ; Initialize Data Segment at
            MOV       DS, AX         ; 5000H
            MOV       AX, 6000H      ; Initialize SS at
            MOV       SS, AX         ; 6000H
            MOV       SP, 0020H      ; Initialize SP at 0020H
            MOV       BX, 2000H      ; Initialize BX at 2000H
            MOV       SI, 0000H      ; Initialize SI
            MOV       DI, 0004H      ; Initialize DI
            MOV       AL, [SI]       ; Load 8-bit data into AL
            MOV       CX, [DI]       ; Load 16-bit data into CX
            CALL      MULTI          ; Call MULTI subroutine
            MOV       [BX], DX       ; Store high word of result
            MOV       [BX+2], AX     ; Store low word of result
            HLT                      ; Halt
    MULTI   PROC      NEAR           ; Define MULTI as near subroutine
            CBW                      ; Sign extend AL
            IMUL      CX             ; [DX] [AX] < - - [AX]*[CX]
            RET                      ; Return
    MULTI   ENDP                     ; End of procedure
    END     BEGIN
```

EXAMPLE 11.5   Write a subroutine in Pentium assembly language in the same code segment as the main program to implement the C language assignment statement: $p = p + q$; where addresses p and q hold two 16-digit (64-bit) packed BCD numbers (N1 and N2). The main program will initialize addresses p and q to DS:2000H and DS:3000H respectively.

Address DS:2007H will hold the highest byte of N1 with the lowest byte at address DS:2000H while address DS:3007H will hold the highest byte of N2 with the lowest byte at address DS:3000H. Also, write the main program which will perform all initializations including DS to 2000H, SS to 6000H, SP to 0020H, SI to 2000H, DI to 3000H, loop count to 8 and, then call the subroutine.

Solution

```
        .486
        .MODEL   SMALL, STDCALL
        .CODE
BEGIN:
        MOV      AX,2000H        ;Initialize Data segment at 2000H
        MOV      DS,AX
        MOV      AX,6000H        ;Initialize Stack segment at 6000H
        MOV      SS,AX
        MOV      SP,0020H        ;Initialize SP at 0020H
        MOV      CX,8            ;Initialize Count
        MOV      SI,2000H        ;Initialize pointer to N1 -> q
        MOV      DI,3000H        ;Initialize pointer to N2 -> p
        MOV      AL,0            ;Clear SUM to 0
        CALL     PBCD            ;Call PBCD subroutine
        HLT
PBCD    PROC     NEAR
        CLC                      ;Clear Carry
START:  MOV      AL,[SI]         ;Move Data to AL
        MOV      BL,[DI]         ;Move Data to BL
        ADC      AL,BL           ;Add  into AL
        DAA                      ;BCD adjust (AL) and AL contains the result
        MOV      [DI],AL         ;Store result in [DI]
        INC      SI              ;Update pointers
        INC      DI              ;Update pointers
        LOOP     START
        RET                      ;Return
PBCD    ENDP
END     BEGIN
```

EXAMPLE 11.6   Write a subroutine in Pentium assembly language which can be called by a main program in a different code segment. The subroutine will compute ΣX_i^2 / N. Assume the X_i's are 16-bit signed integers , N = 100 and, ΣX_i^2 is 32-bit wide. The numbers are stored in consecutive locations. Assume SI points to the X_i's. The subroutine will initialize SI to 4000H, compute ΣX_i^2 / N, and store 32-bit result in DX:AX (16-bit remainder in DX and 16-bit quotient in AX). Also, write the main program which will initialize DS to 2000H, SS to 6000H, SP to 0040H, call the subroutine, and stop.

Solution

```
              .486
              .MODEL SMALL, STDCALL
              .CODE                   ; Main program code segment
BEGIN:
              MOV   AX,2000H          ;Initialize Data segment at 2000H
              MOV   DS,AX
              MOV   AX,6000H          ;Initialize Stack segment at 6000H
              MOV   SS, AX
              MOV   SP,0040H          ; Initialize SP to 0040H
              CALL  FAR PTR SQRDIV    ;Call SQRDIV subroutine
              HLT
              .CODE                   ; subroutine code segment
SQRDIV  PROC  FAR
              MOV   CX,100            ;Initialize CX to 100
              MOV   BX,0000H          ;Clear low 16-bit sum to zero
              MOV   SI,4000H          ;Initialize pointer of Xi
              MOV   DI,3000H          ;Initialize pointer DI of High 16-bit sum
                                      ;in memory
              MOV   WORD PTR[DI],0    ;Clear 16-bit location addressed by DI to zero
BACK:  MOV   AX,[SI]           ;Load Xi into AX
              IMUL  WORD PTR[SI]      ;Signed multiplication Xi*Xi, 32-bit result
                                      ;in DXAX
              ADD   BX,AX            ;Add low 16-bits of (Xi **2) in AX to low
                                      ;16-bit sum
              ADC   [DI],DX          ;Add with CF, high word of (Xi**2) in DX
                                      ;to high word of sum
              INC   SI               ;Update pointer
              INC   SI               ;twice for WORD
              LOOP  BACK             ;Jump and decrement CX. If CX not zero,
                                      ;go to START
              MOV   DX,[DI]          ;If CX = 0, store high 16-bits of sum in DX
              MOV   AX,BX            ;Store low 16-bits of sum in AX
              MOV   CX,100           ;Load 100 into CX
              DIV   CX               ;unsigned division since both (Xi**2) and
                                      ;100 are positive.  Perform DX:AX / CX.
              RET                    ;Return
SQRDIV  ENDP
END       BEGIN
```

11.4   Conditional Branch Instructions

All Pentium conditional branch instructions use 8- bit displacement with a branch range of -128 to +127, (0 being positive) or 16-bit displacement with a branch range of -32766 to + 32765 (0 being positive. The structure of a typical conditional branch instruction is as follows:

If condition is true,

then IP ← IP + displacement,

otherwise IP ← IP + 2 and execute next instruction.

There are two types of conditional branch instructions. In one type, the various relationships that exist between two numbers such as equal, above, below, less than, or greater than can be determined by the appropriate conditional branch instruction after a COMPARE instruction. These instructions can be used for both signed and unsigned numbers. When comparing signed numbers, terms such as "less than" and "greater than" are used. On the other hand, when comparing unsigned numbers, terms such as "below zero" or "above zero" are used.

Table 11.4 lists the Pentium signed and unsigned conditional branch instructions. Note that in Table 11.4, the instructions for checking which two numbers are "equal" or "not equal" are the same for both signed and unsigned numbers. This is because when two numbers are compared for equality, irrespective of whether they are signed or unsigned, they will provide a zero result (ZF = 1) if they are equal and a nonzero result (ZF = 0) if they are not equal. Therefore, the same instructions apply for both signed and unsigned numbers for "equal to" or "not equal to" conditions. The second type of conditional branch instructions is concerned with the setting of flags rather than the relationship between two numbers. Table 11.5 lists these instructions.

Now, in order to check whether the result of an arithmetic or logic operation is zero, nonzero, positive or negative, did or did not produce a carry, did or did not produce a parity, or did or did not cause overflow, the following instructions should be used: JZ, JNZ, JS, JNS, JC, JNC, JP, JNP, JO, JNO. However, in order to compare two signed or unsigned numbers (*a* in address A or *b* in address B) for various conditions, we use CMP A, B, which will form *a* - *b*. and then one of the instructions in Table 11.6.

Now let us illustrate the concept of using the preceding signed or unsigned instructions by an example. Consider clearing a section of memory word starting at B up to and including A, where (A) = 3000H and (B) = 2000H in DS = 1000H, using the following

TABLE 11.4   Pentium Signed and Unsigned Conditional Branch Instructions

Signed		*Unsigned*	
Name	*Alternate Name*	*Name*	*Alternate Name*
JE disp (JUMP if equal)	JZ disp (JUMP if result zero)	JE disp (JUMP if equal)	JZ disp (JUMP if zero)
JNE disp (JUMP if not equal)	JNZ disp (JUMP if not zero)	JNE disp (JUMP if not equal)	JNZ disp (JUMP if not zero)
JG disp (JUMP if greater)	JNLE disp (JUMP if not less or equal)	JA disp (JUMP if above)	JNBE disp (JUMP if not below or equal)
JGE disp (JUMP if greater or equal)	JNL disp (JUMP if not less)	JAE disp (JUMP if above or equal)	JNB disp (JUMP if not below)
JL disp (JUMP if less than)	JNGE disp (JUMP if not greater or equal)	JB disp (JUMP if below)	JNAE disp (JUMP if not above or equal)
JLE disp (JUMP if less or equal)	JNG disp (JUMP if not greater)	JBE disp (JUMP if below or equal)	JNA disp (JUMP if not above)

TABLE 11.5 **Pentium Conditional Branch Instructions Affecting Individual Flags**

JC disp8	JUMP if carry, i.e., CF = 1
JNC disp8	JUMP if no carry, i.e., CF = 0
JP disp8	JUMP if parity, i.e., PF = 1
JNP disp8	JUMP if no parity. i.e., PF = 0
JO disp8	JUMP if overflow, i.e., OF = 1
JNO disp8	JUMP if no overflow, i.e., OF = 0
JS disp8	JUMP if sign, i.e., SF = 1
JNS disp8	JUMP if no sign, i.e.. SF = 0
JZ disp8	JUMP if result zero, i.e.. ZF = 1
JNZ disp8	JUMP if result not zero, i.e., ZF = 0

TABLE 11.6 **Pentium Instructions to be used after CMP A, B; a and b are data.**

Signed "a" and "b"		Unsigned "a" and "b"	
JGE disp8	if a ≥ b	JAE disp8	if a ≥ b
JL disp8	if a < b	JB disp8	if a < b
JG disp8	if a > b	JA disp8	if a > b
JLE disp8	if a ≤ b	JBE disp8	if a ≤ b

instruction sequence:

```
            MOV     AX, 1000H
            MOV     DS, AX              ;Initialize DS
            MOV     BX, 2000H
            MOV     CX, 3000H
AGAIN:      MOV     WORD PTR[BX], 0000H
            INC     BX
            INC     BX
            CMP     CX, BX
            JGE     AGAIN
```

JGE treats CMP operands as twos complement numbers. The loop will terminate when BX = 3002H. Now, suppose that the contents of A and B are as follows: (A) = 8500H and (B) = 0500H.

In this case, after CMP CX,BX is first executed,

$$(CX) - (BX) = 8500H - 0500H$$
$$= 8000H$$
$$= 1000\ 0000\ 0000\ 0000$$
$$\uparrow$$

$$SF = 1 \text{ i.e., a negative number}$$

Because 8000_{16} is a negative number, the loop terminates.

The correct approach is to use a branch instruction that treats operands as unsigned numbers (positive numbers) and uses the following instruction sequence:

```
              MOV     AX,1000H
              MOV     DS,AX                    ;          initialize DS
              MOV     BX,0500H
              MOV     CX,8500H
AGAIN:        MOV     WORD PTR[BX],0000H
              INC     BX
              INC     BX
              CMP     CX,BX
              JAE     AGAIN
```

JAE will work regardless of the values of A and B.

   Also, note that addresses are always positive numbers (unsigned).   Hence, unsigned conditional jump instruction must be used to obtain the correct answer. The examples above are included for illustrative purposes.

11.5   Iteration Control Instructions

Table 11.7 lists iteration control instructions. All these instructions have relative addressing modes. Also, these instructions use CX register as a 16-bit counter in real mode, and ECX register as a 32-bit counter in protected mode. In this section, iteration control instructions in real mode will be discussed. LOOP disp8 decrements the CX register by 1 without affecting the flags and then acts in the same way as the JMP dsp8 instruction except that if CX ≠ 0, then the JMP is performed: otherwise, the next instruction is executed. The LOOP uses signed 8-bit displacement.

   LOOPE (loop while equal)/LOOPZ (loop while zero) decrements CX by 1 without affecting the flags. The contents of CX are then checked for zero, and the zero flag (ZF), which results from execution of previous instruction, is checked for 1. If CX ≠ 0 and ZF = 1, the loop continues. If either CX = 0 or ZF = 0, the next instruction after LOOPE or LOOPZ is executed. The following Pentium instruction sequence compares an array of 50 bytes with data byte 00H. As soon as a match is not found or the end of the array is reached, the loop exits. The LOOPE instruction can be used for this purpose. The following Pentium instruction sequence illustrates this.

```
        MOV     SI, START        ; Intitialize SI with the starting offset of
                                 ;the array

        DEC     SI

        MOV     CX,50            ; Initialize CX with array count
BACK:   INC     SI               ;Update pointer
        CMP     BYTE PTR[SI],00H  ; Compare array element with 00H
        LOOPE   BACK
```

LOOPNE (LOOP while not equal) / LOOPNZ (Loop while not zero) is similar to LOOPE/ LOOPZ except that the loop continues if CX ≠ 0 and ZF = 0. On the other hand, If CX = 0 or ZF = 1, the next instruction is executed. The following Pentium instruction sequence compares an array of 50 bytes with data byte 00H for a match. As soon as a match is found or the end of the array is reached, the loop exits. LOOPNE instruction can be used for this purpose. CX = 0 and ZF = 0 upon execution of the CMP instruction 50 times in the following would imply that data byte 00H was not found in the array. The following Pentium instruction sequence illustrates this.

```
          MOV      SI,START              ; Intitialize SI with the starting offset of
                                         ; the array
          DEC      SI
          MOV      CX,50                 ; Initialize CX with array count
BACK: INC          SI                    ; Update pointer
          CMP      BYTE PTR[SI],00H      ; Compare array element with 00H
          LOOPNE   BACK
```

JCXZ   START jumps to label START if CX = 0. This is normally used to skip a loop as follows:

```
                  ---------------------
                  ---------------------
          JCXZ    DOWN               ; If CX is already 0, skip the loop
BACK:     SUB     WORD PTR[SI], 4    ; Subtract 4 from the 16-bit  contents
                                     ; addressed by SI
          ADD     SI,2               ; Update SI to point to next value
          LOOP    BACK               ; Decrement CX by 1 and loop
DOWN:             --------------------   ; until CX = 0
                  --------------------
```

11.6   Interrupt Instructions

Table 11.8 shows the interrupt instructions. INT n is a software interrupt instruction. Execution of INT n causes the Pentium to push current CS, IP, and flags onto the stack, and loads CS and IP with new values based on interrupt type n; an interrupt service routine is written at this new address. IRET at the end of the service routine transfers control to the main program by popping old CS, IP, and flags from the stack.

The interrupt on overflow is a type 4 (n = 4) interrupt. This interrupt occurs if the overflow flag (OF) is set and the INTO instruction is executed. The overflow flag is affected, for example, after execution of a signed arithmetic (such as IMUL, signed multiplication) instruction. The user can execute an INTO instruction after the IMUL. If there is an overflow, an error service routine written by the user at the type 4 interrupt address vector is executed.

The IRET instruction is used in the real mode and is typically placed at the end of

TABLE 11.7   Pentium Iteration Control Instructions

LOOP disp8	Decrement CX by 1 without affecting the flags and branch to label if CX ≠ 0; otherwise, go to the next instruction.
LOOPE/LOOPZ disp8	Decrement CX by 1 without affecting the flags and branch to label if CX ≠ 0 and ZF = 1; otherwise (CX=0 or ZF=0), go to the next instruction.
LOOPNE/LOOPNZ disp8	Decrement CX by 1 without affecting the flags and branch to label if CX ≠ 0 and ZF = 0; otherwise (CX=0 or ZF=1), go to the next instruction.
JCXZ disp8	JMP if register CX = 0; else go the next instruction..
JECXZ disp8	Jump if ECX = 0; else go to the next instruction.

an interrupt service routine. The IRET pops IP, CS, and flags (lowest byte) from the stack. Interrupt instructions are discussed in detail in Chapter 12.

11.7   Processor Control Instructions

Table 11.9 shows some of the processor control instructions. Let us explain some of the instructions in the table.

* The LOCK prefix allows the Pentium to ensure that another processor does not take control of the system bus while it is executing an instruction that uses the system bus. The LOCK prefix is placed in front of an instruction so that when the instruction is executed, the Pentium outputs a LOW on the LOCK # pin for the duration of the next instruction. This lock signal is connected to an external bus controller which prevents any other processor from taking over the system bus. Thus the LOCK prefix is used in multiprocessing. A typical example of a locked instruction is LOCK:MOV CL, [BX].

* ENTER and LEAVE are used with stack frames used to pass parameters to a subroutine through the stack. The ENTER imm16,imm8 instruction creates a stack frame. The data imm8 defines the nesting depth of the subroutine and can be from 0 to 31. The value 0 specifies the first subroutine only. Data imm8 defines the number of stack frame pointers copied into the new stack frame from the preceding frame. After the instruction is executed, the Pentium uses EBP as the current frame pointer and ESP as

TABLE 11.8   Pentium Interrupt Instructions

INT n	Software interrupt instructions $\cdot$
(n can be 0-255$_{10}$)	(INT 32$_{10}$ – 255$_{10}$ available to the user.)
INTO	Interrupt on overflow
IRET	Interrupt return (Real mode)

TABLE 11..9   Pentium Processor Control Instructions

ENTER	
STC	Set carry CF $\leftarrow$ 1
CLC	Clear carry CF $\leftarrow$ 0
CMC	Complement carry, CF $\leftarrow \overline{\text{CF}}$
STD	Set direction flag
CLD	Clear direction flag
STI	Set interrupt enable flag
CLI	Clear interrupt enable flag
NOP	No operation
HLT	Halt
LOCK	Lock bus during next instruction
ENTER	Create stack frame
LEAVE	Reverses the action of ENTER; High level procedure exit
BOUND	Check array index against bounds

the current stack pointer. Data imm16 specifies the number of bytes of local variables for which stack space is to be allocated. If imm8 is zero, ENTER pushes the frame pointer EBP onto the stack; ENTER then subtracts the first operand, imm16, from the ESP and sets EBP to the current ESP.

For example, a procedure with 28 bytes of local variables would have an ENTER 28,0 instruction at its entry point and a LEAVE instruction before every RET. The 28 local bytes would be addressed as offset from EBP. Note that the LEAVE instruction sets ESP to EBP and then pops EBP. The Pentium uses BP (the low 16 bits of EBP) and SP (the low 16 bits of ESP) for 16-bit operands and uses EBP and ESP for 32-bit operands.

- The BOUND instruction ensures that a signed array index is within the limits specified by a block of memory containing an upper and a lower bound. The Pentium provides two forms of the BOUND instruction:

$$\text{BOUND} \qquad \text{reg16,mem32}$$
$$\text{BOUND} \qquad \text{reg32,mem64}$$

The first form is for 16-bit operands. The second form is for 32-bit operands and is included in the Pentium instruction set. For example, consider BOUND EDI,ADDR. Suppose that (ADDR) = 32-bit lower bound d_l and (ADDR + 4) = 32-bit upper bound d_u. If, after execution of this instruction, (EDI) < d_l or > d_u the Pentium traps to interrupt 5; otherwise, the array is accessed.

The BOUND instruction is usually placed following the computation of an index value to ensure that the limits of the index value are not violated. This permits a check to determine whether or not an address of an array being accessed is within the array boundaries when the register indirect with index mode is used to access an array element. For example, the following instruction sequence will allow accessing an array with base address in ESI, index value in EDI, and an array length of 50 bytes; assuming that the 32-bit contents of memory location, 20000100_{16} and 20000104_{16} are 0 and 49, respectively:

$$\vdots$$

$$\text{BOUND} \qquad \text{EDI, 20000100H}$$
$$\text{MOV} \qquad \text{EAX,[EDI][ESI]}$$

$$\vdots$$

11.8   Pentium Delay routine

Typical Pentium software delay loops can be written using MOV and LOOP instructions. For example, the following instruction sequence can be used for a delay loop:

$$\text{MOV} \quad \text{CX,count}$$
$$\text{DELAY:} \qquad \text{LOOP} \quad \text{DELAY}$$

The initial loop counter value of "count" can be calculated using the cycles required to execute the following Pentium instructions (Appendix F):

$$\text{MOV} \quad \text{reg/imm (1 cycle)}$$
$$\text{LOOP} \quad \text{label (5/6 cycles)}$$

Note that the Pentium LOOP instruction requires two different execution times. LOOP requires six cycles when the Pentium branches if the CX is not equal to zero after autodecrementing CX by 1. However, the Pentium goes to the next instruction and does not branch when CX = 0 after autodecrementing CX by 1, and this requires five cycles. This means that the DELAY loop will require six cycles for (count - 1) times, and the last iteration will take five cycles.

For a 100-MHz Pentium clock, each cycle is 10 ns. For 2 ms, total cycles = $\frac{2\,m\sec}{10\,n\sec}$ = 200,000. The loop will require six cycles for (count - 1) times when CX $\neq$ 0, and five cycles will be required when no branch is taken (CX = 0). Thus, total cycles including the MOV = 1 + 6 × (count - 1) + 5 = 200,000. Hence, count $\cong$ 33,333$_{10}$. Therefore, CX must be loaded with 33,333$_{10}$.

Now, in order to obtain delay of 2 seconds, the above DELAY loop of 2 ms can be used with an external counter. Counter value = (2 sec)/(2 msec) = 1000. The following instruction sequence will provide an approximate delay of 2 seconds:

```
              MOV     DX,1000      ; Initialize counter for 2 second delay
    BACK:     MOV     CX, 33333
    DELAY:    LOOP    DELAY        ; 2 msec delay
              DEC     DX
              JNE     BACK
```

Next, the delay time provided by the instruction sequence above can be calculated. From Appendix F, we obtain the number of cycles required to execute the following Pentium instructions:

```
        MOV reg / imm     (1 cycle)
        DEC reg16         (1 cycle)
        JNE               (1 cycle)
```

As before, assuming a 100-MHz Pentium clock, each cycle is 10ns. The total time from the above instruction sequence for 2-second delay = execution time for MOV + 1000 * (2 msec delay) + 1000 * (execution time for DEC) + 1000* (execution time for JNE) = 1 * 10 ns + 1000 * 2 msec + 1000 * 1 * 10ns + 1000 * 1 * 10ns $\cong$ 2 seconds discarding the execution times of MOV, DEC, and JNE.

Questions and Problems

11.1   It is desired to multiply a 32-bit unsigned number in ECX by 16 to provide
a 32-bit product and then perform the following operations on the contents of
ECX: Set bit 30 of ECX to 1 if the 32-bit unsigned number in register EBX
contains an odd number; one's-complement bit 30 of ECX if the 32-bit unsigned
number in register EBX contains an even number. Assume that data are already
stored in EBX and ECX.
(a)   Write a Pentium assembly language program to accomplish the above.
Do not use any multiplication or bit manipulation instructions.
(b)   Write a Pentium assembly language program to accomplish the above.
Do not use any multiplication, or logic instructions.

11.2   Find the contents of AX, DX, CF, SF, ZF, and PF after execution of the Pentium
instruction SHRD AX,DX,3. Assume the following data prior to execution of
SHRD AX,DX,3: (AX) = 2700H, (DX) = A271H, CF = 0, SF = 1, ZF = 1, and PF
= 0.

11.3   Write a   Pentium assembly program to divide a 28-bit unsigned number in the
high 28 bits of DX AX by 8_{10}. Do not use a divide instruction. Store the quotient
in the low 28 bits of DX AX. Discard the remainder.

11.4   Write a Pentium assembly language program that will check whether the 16-bit
signed number in AX is positive or negative. If the number is positive, the program
will multiply the 16-bit unsigned number in BX by 16 and provide a 16-bit result;
otherwise, the program will load 01H into BL. Use only shift, bit manipulation,
and program control instructions. Assume that the 16-bit numbers are already
loaded into AX and BX.

11.5   Write a Pentium assembly language program to insert a '1' at bit 2 of BX without
changing the other bits if BX contains a negative number. On the other hand,
insert a '0' at bit 2 of BX without changing the other bits if BX contains a positive
number.

11.6   Write a   Pentium assembly program to move 100 words from a source with offset
0010H in ES to a destination with offset 0100H in the same extra segment.

11.7   Write a Pentium assembly language program to compare two strings of 15 ASCII
characters from LOW to HIGH memory. The first character (string 1) is stored
starting at offset 5000H in DS= 0020H followed by the string. The first character
of the second string (string 2) is stored starting at 6000H in ES = 1000H. The
ASCII character in the first location of string 1 will be compared with the first
ASCII character of string 2, and so on. As soon as a match is found, store 00EEH
onto the stack; otherwise, store 0000H onto the stack.. Initialize SS to 0500H and
SP to 2000H.

11.8   Write a Pentium assembly language program to move two columns of 100 32-bit numbers from A (i) at offset 4000H in DS to B (i) at offset 5000H in ES from LOW to HIGH memory. In other words, move A (1) to B (1), A (2) to B (2), and so on.

11.9   Write a subroutine in Pentium assembly language that can be called by a main program in the same code segment. The subroutine will compute the 16-bit sum

$$\Sigma a_{kk}^2$$

where a_{kk} are diagonal elements of a 3 x 3 matrix and k = 0 to 2. Assume that each element in the matrix is signed 8-bit. The subroutine will store the 16-bit result in DX. The main program will initialize DS to 1000H, SS to 5000H, SP to 0800H, obtain the three diagonal elements from memory stored starting at offset 2000H in row-major order, obtain the diagonal elements, call the subroutine, perform all other necessary steps, and then stop.

11.10   Write a subroutine in Pentium assembly language that can be called by a main program in a different code segment. The subroutine will compute the 16-bit sum

$$\sum_{i=1}^{100} X_i$$

Assume the X_i's are unsigned 8-bit numbers and are stored in consecutive locations starting at offset 0050H. Also, write the main program that will initialize DS to 2020H, SS to 0020H and SP to 1000H, SI to 0050H, DI to 0400H, call this subroutine to compute

$$\sum_{i=1}^{100} \frac{Xi}{100}$$

and store the 16-bit result (8-bit remainder and 8-bit quotient) in two consecutive memory bytes starting at offset 0400H, and then stop.

11.11   Write a subroutine in Pentium assembly language that can be called by the main program in the same code segment to compute $Y = \sum_{i=1}^{256} X_i$.
Assume that the X_i's are unsigned 32-bit numbers and the array starts at 00005021H. The main program will initialize SUM in EDX to 0, pointer ESI to 00005021H, DS to 7000H, SS to 0300H, SP to 4000H, loop count to 256, call the subroutine, compute (Y /256), store 32-bit result in EDX, and then stop. Discard the remainder. Do not use any division instructions.

11.12   It is desired to convert a four-digit unpacked BCD number to binary using the following equation: binary value, V of the four-digit BCD number,
$$V = \quad D_3 * 1000 + D_2 * 100 + D_1 * 10 + D_0$$
where D_3 is the most significant digit and D_0 is the least significant digit.
Write a subroutine in Pentium assembly language that will compute 10* D where D is an unsigned 8-bit number in AL. The main program will be located in the same code segment as the subroutine. The most significant digit is stored in a memory location starting at offset 4000H, and the least significant is stored at offset 4003H. The main program will call the subroutine , and compute V via multiplications by 10 and additions as follows:

$V = (((D_3 * 10) * 10) * 10) + ((D_2 * 10) * 10) + (D_1 * 10) + D_0$.
The main program will first initialize DS to 6000H, SS to 1000H, SP to 0080H, SUM in DX to 0, obtain each digit from memory, call the subroutine as many times as needed, store the 16-bit result in DX, and then stop.

11.13 Assume a 100-MHz Pentium. Write a Pentium assembly language program to obtain a delay routine for 40 milliseconds. Using this 40-msec routine, write another Pentium assembly language program to provide a delay for 80 seconds.

12

PENTIUM HARDWARE AND INTERFACING

In this chapter we describe hardware aspects of the Intel Pentium. Topics include Pentium pins and signals, timing diagrams, and memory and I/O interfacing techniques. Finally, design concepts associated with a Pentium-based voltmeter and Pentium-based microcomputer interface to a hexadecimal keyboard and a seven-segment display are covered.

12.1 Pentium Pins and Signals

The Pentium contains 273 pins packaged in a ceramic pin grid array (PGA). The pins are arranged in a 21 x 21 matrix. Figure 12.1 shows a selected group Pentium pins. Note that the pin diagram of the figure contains a total of 212 pins. The other pins (not shown in Figure 12.1) provide functions such as parity check for address / data , and cache control. Appendix H provides the pin diagram and a description of all the pins.

To explain Pentium's interface to EPROMs, SRAMs, and I/O in a simplified manner, a selected group of relevant pins and signals are included in Figure 12.1. The '#' symbol at the end of the signal name or the '—' symbol above a signal name indicates the active or asserted state when it is LOW. When the symbol '#' is absent after the signal name or the symbol '—' is absent above a signal name, the signal is asserted when HIGH. Pins labeled NC (not connected) must remain unconnected.

For reliable operation, unused inputs should be connected to an appropriate signal level. Unused active LOW inputs should be connected to Vcc. Unused active HIGH inputs should be connected to GROUND. There are 50 Vcc and 49 GND pins. These multiple power and ground pins are used to distribute power in order to reduce noise. Preferably, the circuit board should contain Vcc and GND planes.

A brief description of the pins and signals depicted in Figure 12.1 is provided below.

CLK pin provides basic timing for the Pentium. Its frequency is the internal operating frequency of the Pentium and requires TTL levels. An external clock oscillator is required to generate the clock. A20M# input pin must be asserted when the Pentium is in the real mode. The address space of the Pentium may wrap around at one megabyte in the real mode. The A20M# pin forces wraparound if enabled. The Pentium can directly address 1 MB of main memory in real mode. However, with a segment value of FFFFH, and an offset value of FFFFH, the physical address would be FFFF0H + FFFFH = 10FFEFH (one megabyte + 65519 bytes). The Pentium which can form addresses up to 20 bits long in real mode, truncates the uppermost bit which wraps this address to 0FFEFH. Note that the Pentium does not truncate this bit if A20M# is not enabled. Upon assertion of the A20M# pin, the Pentium masks the address bit A20 before performing lookup to the internal cache

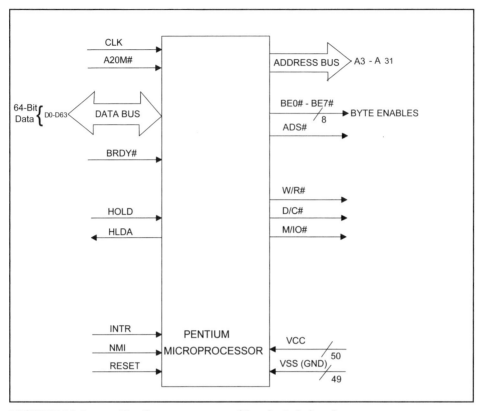

FIGURE 12.1   Pentium processor with selected signals.

or driving a memory cycle on the bus. The effect of asserting A20M# in the protected mode is undefined.

The bidirectional pins D63-D0 provides the 64-bit data bus. Pins D7-D0 specify the least significant byte of the data bus, while pins D63-D56 specify the most significant byte of the data bus. During read operation, the Pentium samples the data bus when BRDY# is returned. During a write operation, the Pentium drives the data lines during the T2 clock (second cycle) for that write cycle for nonpipelined operation.

The BRDY# (burst ready) input pin indicates that the external device has presented valid data on the data pins in response to a read or that the external device has accepted data from the Pentium in response to a write. Any number of wait states can be added to Pentium bus cycles by maintaining BRDY# inactive.

HOLD and HLDA pins are used for DMA transfers. Another bus master can take complete control of the Pentium bus after asserting the HOLD input pin. In response to HOLD, the Pentium will complete all outstanding bus cycles, float most of the input/output pins, and then assert HLDA.

The Pentium contains two interrupt pins: INTR (maskable) and NMI (nonmaskable) pins. NMI is leading-edge sensitive, whereas INTR is level sensitive. When INTR is asserted and if the IF bit in the EFLAGS is 1, the Pentium (when ready) responds to the INTR by performing two interrupt acknowledge cycles, and at the end of the second cycle latches an 8-bit vector on D0-D7 to identify the source of the nterrupt.

For power-up reset, the Pentium RESET pin must be HIGH for at least one millisecond after Vcc and the clock have reached their specified levels. The Pentium is reset manually by asserting the RESET pin HIGH by a pushbutton for at least 15 CLK periods. The RESET signal is level sensitive. Since the power-up reset is much higher than the manual reset, the reset circuit should be designed using the power-up reset time of 1 msec which will satisfy the minimum time for both power-up and manual reset.

After hardware RESET, the Pentium will start executing instructions at address FFFF FFF0H. When the first intersegment JUMP or CALL instruction is executed, address lines A20-A31 will be driven LOW for CS-relative memory cycles and the Pentium will only execute instructions in the lower one Megabyte of physical memory. This allows the system designer to use a ROM or EPROM at the top of physical memory to initialize the system.

The Pentium asserts the ADS# (address status) pin to indicate that a new valid bus cycle is currently being driven. ADS# is used by external bus circuitry as the indication that the Pentium has started a bus cycle. The Pentium outputs LOW on the ADS# pin to indicate a valid bus cycle. W/R#, D/C#, and M/IO# output pins specify the type of bus cycle being performed by the Pentium.

Note that the W/R# pin, when HIGH, identifies a write cycle and, when LOW, indicates a read cycle. The D/C# pin, when HIGH, identifies the data cycle, and when LOW, indicates the code cycle. The M/IO# pin differentiates between memory and I/O cycles. The Pentium outputs a HIGH on the M/IO# pin for a memory-oriented instruction, and outputs a LOW on this pin for IN or OUT instruction.

Address pins A3-A31 along with byte enable signals BE0# through BE7# are used to generate physical memory or I/O port addresses. Using the pins, the Pentium can directly address 4 gigabytes by physical memory (00000000H through FFFFFFFFH) in the protected mode.

The byte enable outputs are used in conjunction with the address lines to provide physical memory and I/O port addresses. The byte enable outputs, BE7# through BE0# of the Pentium, define which bytes of D63-D0 are utilized in the current data transfer. These definitions are given in Table 12.1. Address pins A31- A3 along with byte enable signals (BE7#-BE0#) form the address bus and define the physical addresses of memory or I/O ports.

12.2   Pentium READ and WRITE Timing Diagrams

The Pentium supports several different types of read and write (bus) cycles. The simplest type of bus cycle is a single-transfer noncacheable 64-bit cycle without wait states. Figure 12.2 shows the timing diagram for nonpipelined read and write cycles without wait states in Pentium's real mode.

In order to explain the timing diagram of Figure 12.2 in a simplified manner, suppose that a 64-bit SRAM system is interfaced to the Pentium. Assume that eight 32K

TABLE 12.1   Pentium Byte Enables and Associated Data Bytes
BE7# is low when data is transferred via D63-D56
BE6# is low when data is transferred via D55-D48
BE5# is low when data is transferred via D47-D40
BE4# is low when data is transferred via D39-D32
BE3# is low when data is transferred via D31- D24
BE2# is low when data is transferred via D23- D16
BE1# is low when data is transferred via D15-D8
BE0# is low when data is transferred via D7-D0

X 8 SRAM chips (SRAM 0 through SRAM 7) are connected as follows. SRAM 0 will be enabled by Pentium BE0# with eight output lines of the SRAM connected to Pentium D7-D0 pins, SRAM 1 will be enabled by Pentium BE1# with eight output lines of the SRAM connected to D15-D8 pins, and so on. The Pentium will assert BE0# when A2 A1 A0 bits of the address are 000. On the other hand, the Pentium will assert BE1# when A2 A1 A0 bits of the address are 001, and so on.

Next, consider a read operation such as the Pentium instruction MOV BL,[1001H] or a write operation such as the Pentium instruction MOV [1001H],AL. Assume (DS) = 3000H. The 20-bit physical address is 31001H. These values are arbitrarily chosen. The Pentium in real mode performs the following steps in Figure 12.2:

1.   The Pentium initiates the cycle by asserting the ADS# pin in T1 (the first clock in the bus cycle).

2.   Since A2 A1 A0 = 001 in 31001H, the Pentium outputs LOW on BE1# pin (not shown in the figure), and also outputs upper 17 bits of 31001H on A19-A3 pins.

3.   The Pentium outputs a LOW on the W/R# pin for read and outputs a HIGH on the W/R# pin for write.

4.   For a zero wait-state transfer, the Pentium checks the BRDY# input pin (returned by the external device) in the second clock cycle of the bus cycle. BRDY# indicates that the external device has presented valid data on the DATA pins (D15 -D8 pins in this case since BE1# is asserted) or the external device has accepted data in response to a write. If the system is not ready to drive or accept data, wait states can be added to these cycles by not returning BRDY# to the Pentium at the end of the second clock. Note that the Pentium will assert BE1# pin since the 20-bit address is 31001H (not shown in Figure 12.2) for the byte read or write operation to enable the appropriate memory chip.

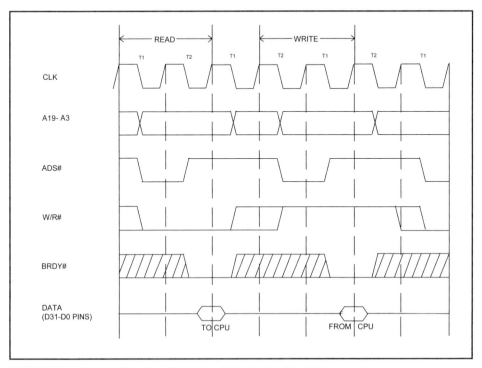

FIGURE 12.2   Pentium Read and Write Timing Diagrams.

TABLE 12.2   **Generating A2- A0 from BE7#- BE0# (X means don't care)**

A2	A1	A0	BE7#	BE6#	BE5#	BE4#	BE3#	BE2#	BE1#	BE0#
0	0	0	X	X	X	X	X	X	X	0
0	0	1	X	X	X	X	X	X	0	1
0	1	0	X	X	X	X	X	0	1	1
0	1	1	X	X	X	X	0	1	1	1
1	0	0	X	X	X	0	1	1	1	1
1	0	1	X	X	0	1	1	1	1	1
1	1	0	X	0	1	1	1	1	1	1
1	1	1	0	1	1	1	1	1	1	1

12.3   Pentium's interface to memory and I/O

The Pentium can be interfaced to 8-, 16-, 32-, and 64-bit memories. Pentium's I/O is accessible in 8-, 16-, or 32-bit quantities. This section contains Pentium's interface to 27C256 (32K x 8 EPROM), Sharp LH52256C/CH (32K x 8 SRAM), and Intel 82C55 I/O chips. Memory and I/O maps are also determined.

12.3.1   Memory Interface

As mentioned before, the Pentium contains 64 data pins (D63 -D0), 29 address pins (A31-A3), 8 byte enable pins (BE7#-BE0#). Address pins A2, A1 , and A0 are not provided with the Pentium. They are encoded from BE7#-BE0# pins. Table 12.2 shows generation of A2, A1 , and A0 from BE7#-BE0# pins. Note that decimal number, n in BEn# represents A2 A1 A0 in binary. For example, 7 in BE7# means that A2 A1 A0 = 111 ($7_{10} = 111_2$).

In order to illustrate how data is transferred via Pentium's data pins using BE7#-BE0# , consider the instruction such as MOV CL, [5007H] with (CS) = 1000H in real mode. The 20-bit physical address is 15007H. Note that all numerical values in this section are arbitrarily chosen. Since the address bits, A2 A1 A0 = $111_2 = 7_{10}$, the Pentium outputs a LOW on BE7# , 8-bit data will be transferred from address 15007H to CL via Pentium's D63 -D56 pins (Table 12.1). From Tables 12.1 and 12.2, it can be concluded that each byte enable pin, BE7# through BE0# is associated with a specific value of A2 A1 A0, and the value of A2 A1 A0 specifies how data should be routed to which data pins

As mentioned before, the Pentium can be interfaced to 64-, 32-, 16-, and 8-bit memories. Since the Pentium's data bus is 64-bit, external byte swap circuitry are needed to route data to appropriate data pins for memories smaller than 64 bits. For 64-bit memories, each 64-bit quadword begins at a byte address that is a multiple of 8. A31-A3 pins are used as an 8-byte quadword select, and BE7#-BE0# pins select individual bytes within a word. This means that for 64-bit memories, Pentium's A31-A3 pins are used to address eight 8-bit memory chips such as 27C256, and BE7# -BE0# pins select individual bytes at the appropriate section(s) of the 64-bit data bus. Figure 12.3 shows a block diagram of Pentium's interface to 64-bit memory.

Assume a Pentium/27C256 EPROM system in a 64-bit configuration in real mode. Note that in order to provide 64-bit memory, eight 27C256's will be connected to Pentium's 64-bit data bus. Let us call the 27C256 enabled by BE0# as EPROM0, the 27C256 enabled by BE1# as EPROM1, and so on. The data output pins of EPROM0 will be connected to Pentium D7 -D0 pins, the data output pins of EPROM1 will be connected

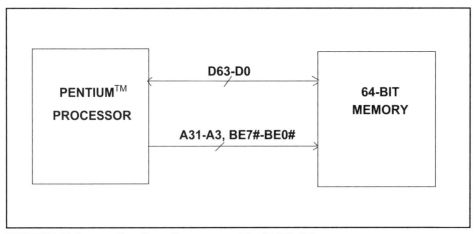

FIGURE 12.3   Pentium Processor with 64-Bit Memory.

to Pentium D15 -D8 pins, and so on.

Next, consider the Pentium instruction, MOV CL, [0003H] with (CS) = 0100H in real mode. The 20-bit physical address is 01003H. In order to execute this instruction, the Pentium generates the high 17 bits of the address on its A31- A3 pins while low three address bits are encoded from BE3#. This is because the Pentium does not have A2- A0 pins on the chip. Since bits 2 through 0 of the address 01003H are 011_2 (3H), BE3# pin of the Pentium must be used to enable the EPROM3 chip connected to D31 -D24 pins. No external routing circuit is required. This is because both memory and Pentium's data bus are 64-bit wide.

The concept of aligned and misaligned transfers for 64-bit memory will be covered in the following. Consider Pentium instruction, MOV EAX, [0004H] with (DS) = 0100H in real mode. The 20-bit physical address is 01004H. Assume Pentium/27C256 64-bit EPROM configuration. Since A2 A1 A0 = 100, EPROM4 through EPROM7 are enabled by BE4# through BE7# respectively. The contents of address 01004H are transferred via

TABLE 12. 3   When BE3'# is active (X means don't care) for 32-bit memory

BE7#	BE6#	BE5#	BE4#	BE3#	BE2#	BE1#	BE0#	BE3'#
0	X	X	X	0	X	X	X	0

TABLE 12. 4   When BE2'# is active (X means don't care) for 32-bit memory

BE7#	BE6#	BE5#	BE4#	BE3#	BE2#	BE1#	BE0#	BE2'#
X	0	X	X	X	0	X	X	0

TABLE 12. 5   When BE1'# is active (X means don't care) for 32-bit memory

BE7#	BE6#	BE5#	BE4#	BE3#	BE2#	BE1#	BE0#	BE1'#
X	X	0	X	X	X	0	X	0

TABLE 12. 6   When BE0'# is active (X means don't care) for 32-bit memory

BE7#	BE6#	BE5#	BE4#	BE3#	BE2#	BE1#	BE0#	BE0'#
X	X	X	0	X	X	X	0	0

D39 -D32 pins, the contents of 01005H are transferred via D47 -D40 pins, and so on. The 32-bit data will be transferred to EAX in one cycle. This is called aligned transfer.

Next, consider a misaligned transfer . Assume that the Pentium executes MOV BX, [0007H] with (DS) = 0200H in real mode. The 20-bit physical address is 02007H. This is a misaligned transfer, and will require two cycles. In the first cycle, the Pentium outputs LOW on BE7#, and BE7# will enable EPROM7. The byte contents of address 02007H will be transferred into BL. In the second cycle, BE0# will enable EPROM0, and the contents of 02008H will be transferred into BH.

Memories that are 32-bit wide require external logic for generating A2, and BE3'# - BE0'#. Pins BE3'#-BE0'# are decoded as shown in Tables 12.3 through 12.6. Note that four 8-bit memory chips such as four 27C256,s will provide a 32-bit EPROM system. For example, consider 32-bit memories, Pentium's A31- A3 pins are used to address four 8-bit memory chips and BE7#-BE0# pins are used to select individual bytes at the appropriate section(s) of the 64-bit data bus. Since Pentium data bus is 64-bit wide, a routing logic circuit must be designed for interfacing 32-bit memories. Address bit 2 along with the appropriate byte enable signals need to be generated by external hardware (Byte Select Logic circuit). The external circuit must be designed to generate A2 using Table 12.2, and to generate new byte enable signals BE3'# through BE0'# using Tables 12.3 through 12.6.

As an example of 32-bit memory, consider the Pentium instruction, MOV CL, [0002H] with (DS) = 0100H in real address mode. The 20-bit physical address is 01002H. In order to execute this instruction, the Pentium outputs the high 17 bits of the address on its A19- A3 pins, and low three bits of the address are generated by the byte select logic. Since bits 0, 1, 2 of the address are 010 (2H). This means A2= 0, and A1A0 =10. The external circuit is designed in such way that A2A1A0 = 010 will make BE2'# = 0. Since BE2# is used to obtain BE2'# (Table 12.4), the 8-bit contents of the address 01002H will be routed to the D23- D16 pins of the Pentium.

16-bit memories are organized as arrays of physical words (16 bits). Note that two 8-bit memory chips such as two 27C256,s will provide a 16-bit EPROM system. Address bits A2 and A1 can be decoded from the byte enables according to Tables 12.7 and 12.8. Note that BLE# will be LOW for even addresses while, BHE# will be LOW for odd addresses.

Address bits A2- A0 of the physical address can be decoded from the byte enables according to Table 12.2. The byte enables can be decoded to generate BLE# (byte low enable) and BHE# (byte high enable) to address 16-bit memory (Tables 12.7 and 12.8).

To address 8-bit memories, the lower three address lines (A2- A0) must be decoded from the byte enables as shown in Table 12.2. Suppose that it is desired to connect an 8-bit EPROM such as the 27C256 (32K X 8) to the Pentium. Note that the 27C256 will contain all addresses according to the EPROM map. Since the Pentium contains 64 data pins, external byte swapping logic must be designed for memories less than 64-bit for routing data to the appropriate data lines.

Figure 12.4 shows the Pentium address bus interface to 64-, 32-, 16-, and 8-bit memories. Figure 12.5 shows the Pentium data bus interface to 32-, 16-, and 8-bit wide memories. External byte swapping logic is needed on the data lines so that data is supplied to and received from the Pentium on the correct data pins (Table 12.1).

Pentium's interface to typical EPROM and SRAM chips in a 64-bit configuration in real mode are covered later in this section. Hence, basic concepts associated with Pentium's interface to 64-bit memory in the real mode will be discussed in more detail in

TABLE 12.7   When BLE# is active (X means don't care) for 16-bit memory

BE7#	BE6#	BE5#	BE4#	BE3#	BE2#	BE1#	BE0#	BLE#
X	X	X	X	X	X	X	0	0
X	X	X	X	X	0	1	1	0
X	X	X	0	1	1	1	1	0
X	0	1	1	1	1	1	1	0

TABLE 12.8   When BHE# is active (X means don't care) for 16-bit memory

BE7#	BE6#	BE5#	BE4#	BE3#	BE2#	BE1#	BE0#	BHE#
X	X	X	X	X	X	0	X	0
X	X	X	X	0	X	1	1	0
X	X	0	X	1	1	1	1	0
0	X	1	1	1	1	1	1	0

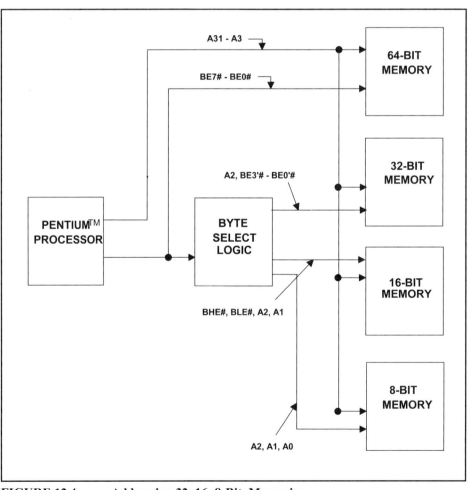

FIGURE 12.4   Addressing 32, 16, 8-Bit Memories.

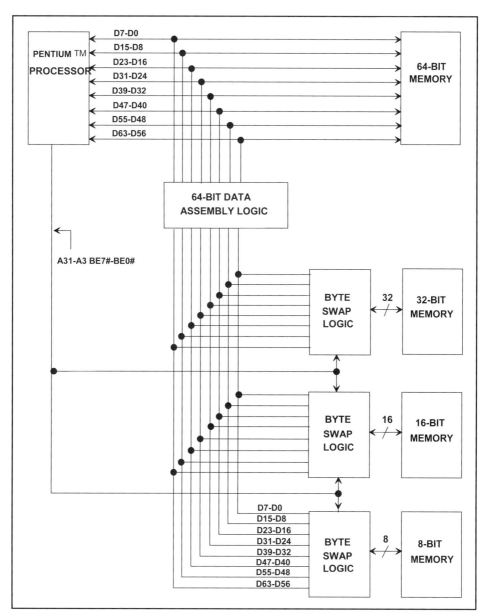

FIGURE 12.5   **Data Bus Interface to 32, 16, and 8-bit Memories.**

the following. As mentioned in the last section, the Pentium address and data lines are not multiplexed. There is a total of 29 address pins (A31-A3) on the chip. Note that A2, A1, A0 are decoded internally to generate eight byte enable outputs, BE7# through BE0#.

All data transfers occur as a result of one or more bus cycles. Data sizes of 8-bit (byte), 16-bit (word), 32-bit (doubleword), and 64-bit (quadword) may be transferred. Data may be accessed any byte boundary, but two cycles may be required for misaligned data transfers. The Pentium address pins A2, A1 and A0 specify the eight addresses of an 8-byte (64-bit) quadword on the data pins as shown in Figure 12.6. Note that for 64-bit memory, each bank can have a maximum of 128K byte of memory in real mode.

D_{63} D_{56}, D_{55} D_{48}, D_{47} D_{40}, D_{39} D_{32}, D_{31} D_{24}, D_{23} D_{16}, D_{15} D_8, D_7 D_0

BYTE 7	BYTE 6	BYTE 5	BYTE 4	BYTE 3	BYTE 2	BYTE 1	BYTE 0	Data Pins

FIGURE 12.6   **Definition of 64-bit quadword on Pentium's data pins**

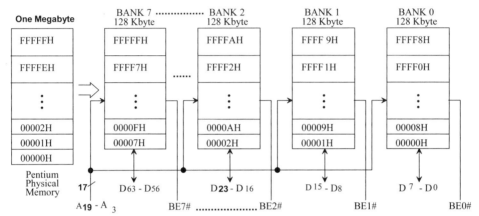

FIGURE 12.7   **Pentium's one Megabyte of main memory in real mode divided into 8 memory banks of 128K X 8 (20-bit physical addresses are shown inside the memory banks in the Figure).**

The contents of the memory addresses in increments of 8, which include 0, 8, 16 ... with A2A1A0 = 000_2 are transferred over D0-D7. Similarly, the contents of addresses which include 1,9,17, ..., with A2A1A0 = 001_2 are transferred over D8-D15. On the other hand, the contents of memory addresses 2, 10, 18, ... with A2A1A0 = 010_2 are transferred over D16-D23, and the contents of memory addresses 7, 15, 23, ... with A2A1A0 = 111_2 are transferred over D56-D63. Note that A2A1A0 pins are encoded from BE7# -BE0#.

In real mode, the maximum size of the main memory is one megabyte (20-bit physical address). This one megabyte of memory can be divided into eight memory banks of 128K X 8 memory in a 64-bit configuration as depicted in Figure 12.7. The concepts associated with aligned and misaligned transfers in a 64-bit memory are discussed in the following.

For example, consider the Pentium instruction, MOV BL,[0002H] with (DS) = 0300H in real mode. The 20-bit physical address is 03002H. The Pentium outputs LOW on BE2# and HIGH on BE0#, BE1# and BE3# through BE7#, and the content of location 03002H is read into BL in a single bus cycle. This is an aligned transfer for 8-bit data. On the other hand, when the Pentium executes a 16-bit MOVE instruction such as MOV AX,[0008H] with (DS) = 1000H in real mode. The 20-bit physical address is 10008H. The Pentium will drive BE0# and BE1# to low. The   locations 10008H and 10009H are read into AL and AH via D_0-D_7 and D_8-D_{15} respectively in a single cycle (aligned transfer). For 32-bit transfer, suppose the Pentium executes a MOVE instruction from an aligned address such as MOV EAX,[0050H] with (DS) = 2000H in real mode. The 20-bit physical address is 200050H. The Pentium will drive all bus enable pins (BE0# -BE3#) to low and reads four bytes of memory locations 20050H through 20053H into EAX. This is an aligned transfer, and is completed by the Pentium in a single bus cycle.

The Pentium performs misaligned transfers in two cycles. For example, consider the Pentium executing a misaligned word MOVE instruction such as MOV AX,[0007H] with (DS) = 1000H in real mode. The 20-bit physical address is 10007H. The Pentium will drive BE7# to low in the first bus cycle and reads the byte contents of location 10007H (bank 7) into AL in the first bus cycle. The Pentium will then drive BE0# to low in the second bus cycle and reads the byte contents of location 10008H (bank 0) into AH. This is a misaligned transfer, and is completed by the Pentium in two bus cycles.

A 32-bit misaligned transfer such as MOV EAX,[0006H] with (DS) = 2000H also takes two bus cycles. In the first bus cycle, the Pentium asserts BE6# and BE7#, and reads the byte contents of addresses 20006H and 20007H from banks 6 and 7 into lower 16 bits of EAX respectively. In the second cycle, the Pentium asserts BE0# and BE1# to LOW and then reads the contents addresses 20008H and 20009H into upper 16-bits of EAX. This is a misaligned transfer, and is completed by the Pentium in two bus cycles.

To manipulate memory configuration, 64-bit data bus control byte enable logic is incorporated to generate eight byte enable signals (BE7# - BE0#). These byte enables are generated internally by the Pentium by using A2, A1, and A0 pins as shown in Table 12.2.

For memory-mapped I/O, the concepts described above can be used to determine memory addresses for I/O ports. However, for standard I/O, the port addresses are determined using Pentium's M/IO# pin to distinguish between memory and I/O.

12.3.2   Pentium-EPROM Interface

The Pentium system is designed with 256K x 8 EPROM consisting of eight 27C256's (64-bit EPROM configuration), each connected to its associated portion of the Pentium's 64-bit data bus (D63–D56, D55–D48, D47–D40, D39–D32, D31–D24, D23–D16, D15–D8, and D7–D0). Pentium pins A3 through A17 are connected to A0 through A14 of each 27C256. For example, Pentium A3 is connected to A0 of the 27C256's, Pentium A4 to A1 of the 27C256's, and so on. A schematic of the Pentium–27C256 interface is shown in Figure 12.8. Note that the size of each 27C256 is 32K X 8.

Both A20M# and BRDY# input pins of the Pentium are asserted by the output of the OR gate. The inputs of the OR gate are M/IO# (inverted), R/W#, and A18 (inverted) pins. A18 = 1 will select EPROMs, and A18 = 0 is used to select SRAMs. Note that the A20M# pin must be asserted in Pentium's real mode in order to mask the A20 pin so that the Pentium emulates the address wraparound at 1 MB of main memory. Also, the BRDY# is asserted since this will indicate to the Pentium that one or more EPROM chips has presented valid data on the data pins in response to a read. Linear decoding is used for selecting memory banks to enable the appropriate memory chips.

The pertinent connections for EPROM #0 obtained from Figure 12.8 are shown in Figure 12.9. The memory map for EPROM #0 can be determined as follows:

EPROM #0

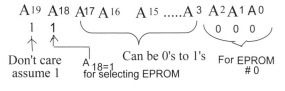

Note that theA0 pin of EPROM # 0 is connected to Pentium A3 pin, A1 pin of EPROM # 1 is connected to Pentium A4 pin, and so on: hence the address range for EPROM #0

C0000H, C0008H, … , FFFF8H and the 27C256 memory map:

EPROM #0	C0000H, C0008H, …, FFFF8H
EPROM #1	C0001H, C0009H, …, FFFF9H
EPROM #2	C0002H, C000AH,.....,FFFFAH
EPROM #3	C0003H, C000BH,.....,FFFFBH
EPROM #4	C0004H, C000CH,.....,FFFFCH
EPROM #5	C0005H, C000DH,.....,FFFFDH
EPROM #6	C0006H, C000EH,....., FFFFEH
EPROM #7	C0007H, C000FH,....., FFFFFH

     As far as the timing parameters are concerned, the access time of 27C256 is 90 ns. Since a LOW on BRDY# input tells the Pentium that an external memory such as 27C256 has presented valid data on the data pins in response to a READ. From the timing diagram in Figure 12.2, BRDY# is sampled in the T2 state (approximately 20 ns for a 100-MHz Pentium). Also, any number of wait states can be added to Pentium bus cycles by maintaining BRDY# inactive. Using typical propagation delay times of the OR gate and the inverter as 10 ns, data will be available at the output pins of each 27C256 after approximately 120 ns (two OR delays + one inverter delay + access time of 27C256). Hence, for 100-MHz Pentium, delaying BRDY# pin by at least 120 ns - 20 ns (since the Pentium checks BRDY# pin for LOW after 2 cycles) = 100 ns is necessary. With this delay, valid data will be available at the output pins of the 27C256 at the appropriate time. The delay circuit can be obtained using a ring counter (see Figure 7.20).

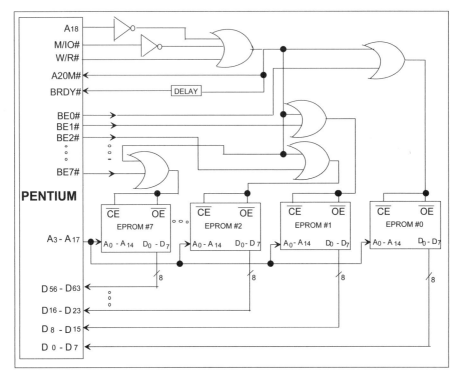

FIGURE 12.8   **Pentium / 27C256 Interface.**

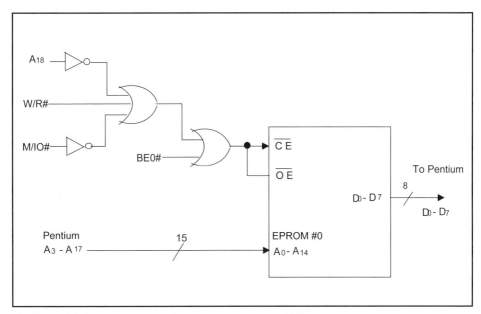

FIGURE 12.9   Pentium interface to EPROM #0.

12.3.3   Pentium-SRAM interface

The Pentium system is designed with 256K x 8 SRAM consisting of eight 52256C/CH's (64-bit SRAM configuration), each connected to its associated portion of the Pentium's 64-bit data bus (D63–D56 , D55–D48 , D47–D40 , D39–D32 , D31–D24 , D23–D16 , D15–D8 , and D7–D0). Pentium pins A_3 through A_{17} are connected to A_0

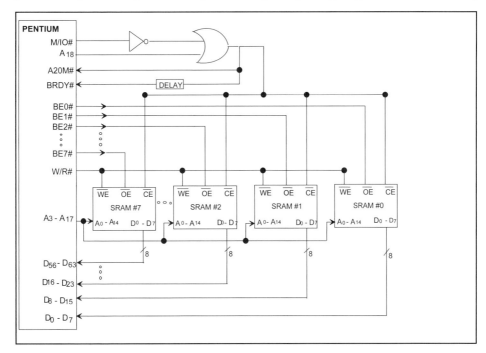

FIGURE 12.10   Pentium/SRAM   interface.

TABLE 12.9   **Decoding Guide**

CE	OE	WE	Operation performed
L	L	H	READ
L	X	L	WRITE
L	H	H	OUTPUT DISABLE

Note: X means don't care

through A_{14} of each of the 52256C/CH's. For example, Pentium A3 is connected to A0 of the 52256C/CH's, Pentium A4 to A1 of the 52256C/CH's, and so on. A schematic of the Pentium–52256C/CH interface is shown in Figure 12.10. Sharp LH52256C/CH is a 32K x 8 CMOS SRAM. The LH52256C/CH READ and WRITE operations are decoded as shown in Table 12.9.

The A20M# and BRDY# input pins of the Pentium are both asserted by the OR gate. The inputs of the OR gate are inverted M/IO# and A18 pins. A18 = 0 will select SRAMs. A18 = 1 is used to deselect SRAMs and to select EPROMs. Note that the A20M# pin must be asserted in Pentium's real mode in order to mask the A20 pin so that the Pentium emulates the address wraparound at 1 MB of main memory. Also, the BRDY# is asserted since this will indicate to the Pentium that one or more SRAM chips has presented valid data on the data pins in response to a read or that the SRAM has accepted the Pentium data in response to a write operation.

Linear decoding is used for selecting memory banks to enable the appropriate memory chips. The pertinent connections for SRAM #0 obtained from Figure 12.10 are shown in Figure 12.11. The 52256C/CH memory map can be determined as follows:

SRAM #0 memory map

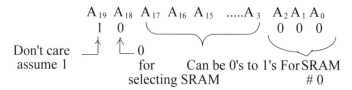

Note that the A0 pin of SRAM #0 is connected to the Pentium A3 pin, the A1 pin of SRAM #1 is connected to the Pentium A4 pin, and so on: hence, the address range for SRAM #0 80000H, 80008H, … , BFFF8H and the 52256C/CH memory map:

SRAM #0	80000H, 80008H, …, BFFF8H
SRAM #1	80001H, 80009H, … ,BFFF9H
SRAM #2	80002H, 8000AH,.....,BFFFAH
SRAM #3	80003H, 8000BH,..... ,BFFFBH
SRAM #4	80004H, 8000CH,..... ,BFFFCH
SRAM #5	80005H, 8000DH,.... ,BFFFDH
SRAM #6	80006H, 8000EH,.....,BFFFEH
SRAM #7	80007H, 8000FH,.....,BFFFFH

As far as the timing parameters are concerned, the read and write cycle times of the 52256C/CH are 70 ns. Note that a LOW on the BRDY# input tells the Pentium

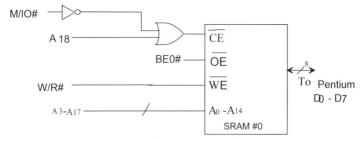

FIGURE 12.11   Pentium interface to SRAM #0.

that the SRAM 52256C/CH has presented valid data on the data pins in response to a READ or that the SRAM 52256C/CH has accepted the Pentium data in response to a write operation.

From the timing diagram of Figure 12.2, BRDY# is sampled in the T2 state (approximately 20 ns for a 100-MHz Pentium). Also, any number of wait states can be added to Pentium bus cycles by maintaining BRDY# inactive. Using typical propagation delay times of the OR gate and the inverter as 10 ns, data will be read or written by each of the 52256C/CH's after approximately 90 ns (one OR delay + one inverter delay + the 52256C/CH cycle time). Hence, for a 100-MHz Pentium, delaying BRDY# pin by at least 90 ns - 20 ns (since the Pentium checks BRDY# pin for LOW after 2 cycles) = 70 ns is necessary. With this delay, valid data will be available at the output pins of the 52256C/CH at the appropriate time. The delay circuit can be obtained using a ring counter (see Figure 7.21).

12.3.4   Pentium Programmed I/O

The Pentium uses either standard I/O or memory-mapped I/O. The standard I/O uses the instructions IN and OUT. The standard I/O can transfer either 8- or 16-bit data to or from a peripheral device. All I/O transfers using standard I/O between the Pentium and peripheral devices take place via AL for 8-bit ports, AX for 16-bit ports, and EAX for 32-bit ports. I/O port addressing can be done either directly or indirectly. Two I/O port addressing modes can be used: direct port and indirect port. In either case, 8-, or 16-, or 32-bit I/O transfers must take place via AL, AX, or EAX, respectively.

In *direct port mode,* the port number is an 8-bit immediate operand to access 256 ports. For example, IN AL,02H moves the contents of the 8-bit port 02H to AL. OUT 04H,AX outputs the 16-bit contents of AX into the 16-bit port 0405H; and IN EAX,02H will input the 32-bit contents of the 32-bit port 02030405H into EAX.

In *indirect port mode,* the port number is taken from DX, allowing 64K bytes or 32K words of ports. For example, suppose that (DX) = 0020H, (port 0020H) = 02H, and (port 0021H) = 03H. Then, after IN AX,DX, register AX contains 0302H. After IN AL,DX, register AL contains 02H. Next, consider, IN EAX,DX. Prior to execution of this instruction, if (DX) = 0050H, (port 0050H) = 01H, (port 0051H) = 02H, (port 0052H) = 03H, and (port 0053H) = 04H, then after execution of IN EAX, DX, register EAX will contain 04030201H.

In memory-mapped I/O, ports are mapped as memory locations. An unused address pin rather than M/IO# pin should be used to distinguish between memory and I/O. In other words, the M/IO# pin is not used in memory-mapped I/O. Also, in memory-mapped I/O, a memory read such as MOV reg8,mem and,a memory write such as MOV mem,reg8 instructions are used as input and output instructions respectively. IN and OUT instructions are not used in memory-mapped I/O. Note that any 8-, 16-, or 32-bit general-purpose register and memory modes can be used in memory-mapped I/O for 8-, 16-, or 32-bit ports. For example, MOV CL,[SI] will input an 8-bit port defined by SI and DS into CL. MOV [BX], AX, on the other hand, will output the 16-bit data in AX to a 16-bit port addressed by the 20-bit address computed from BX and DS. Finally, MOV ECX, [DI] will input a 32-bit port defined by DI and DS into ECX.

In standard I/O, the I/O address space consists of 2^{16} (64K) individually addressable 8-bit ports; any two consecutive 8-bit ports can be treated as a 16-bit port, and any four consecutive ports can be a 32-bit port. This means that using standard I/O, the program can specify the following:

- 256 8-bit ports numbered 0 through 255.

- 128 16-bit ports numbered 0, 2, 4, ...252, 254.

- 64 32-bit ports numbered 0, 4, 8, ...248, 252.

Note that I/O port addresses F8H through FFH are reserved by Intel. I/O ports to these addresses must not be assigned.

The Pentium programmed I/O capability will be explained in the following paragraphs using the 82C55 CMOS I/O chip. The 82C55 chip is a general-purpose programmable I/O chip. The 82C55 has three 8-bit I/O ports: ports A, B, and C. Ports A and B are latched 8-bit ports for both input and output. Port C is also an 8-bit port with latched output, but the inputs are not latched.

Port C can be used in two ways: It can be used either as a simple I/O port or as a control port for data transfer using handshaking via ports A and B.

The Pentium configures the three ports by outputting appropriate data to the 8-bit control register. The ports can be decoded by two 82C55 input pins A_0 and A_1, in Table 12.10. The definitions of the control register are shown in Figure 12.12.

Bit 7 (D_7) of the control register must be 1 to send the definitions for bits 0–6 (D_0–D_6) as shown in the diagram. In this format, bits D_0–D_6, are divided into two groups: A and B. Group A configures all 8 bits of port A and the upper 4 bits of port C; group B defines all 8 bits of port B and the lower 4 bits of port C. All bits in a port can be configured as a parallel input port by writing a 1 at the appropriate bit in the control register by the Pentium OUT instruction, and a 0 in a particular bit position will configure the appropriate port as a parallel output port. Group A has three modes of operation: modes 0, 1, and 2. Group B has two modes: modes 0 and 1. Mode 0 for both groups provides simple I/O operation for each of the three ports. No handshaking is required. Mode 1 for both groups is the strobed I/O mode used for transferring I/O data to or from a specified port in conjunction with strobes or handshaking signals. Ports A and B use the pins on port C to generate or accept these handshaking signals. Mode 2 of group A is the strobed bidirectional bus I/O and may be used for communicating with a peripheral device on a single 8-bit data bus for both transmitting and receiving data (bidirectional bus I/O). Handshaking signals are required.

TABLE 12.10   Decoding 82C55 I/O ports

A_1	A_0	Port Name
0	0	Port A
0	1	Port B
1	0	Port C
1	1	Control register

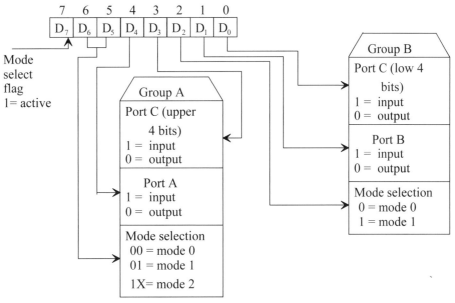

FIGURE 12.12   82C55 control register.

Interrupt generation and enable/disable functions are also available.

When D7 = 0, the bit set/reset control word format is used for the control register as follows:

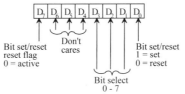

This format is used to set or reset the output on a pin of port C or when it is desired to enable the interrupt output signals for handshake data transfer. For example, the 8 bits (0XXX1100) will clear bit 6 of port C to zero. Note that the control word format can be output to the 82C55 control register by using the Pentium OUT instruction. Now, let us define the control word format for mode 0 more precisely by means of a numerical example. Assume that the control word format is 10000010_2. With this data in the control register, all 8 bits of port A are configured as outputs and the 8 bits of port C are also configured as outputs. All 8 bits of port B, however, are defined as inputs. On the other hand, outputting 10011011_2 into the control register will configure all three 8-bit ports (A, B, and C) as inputs.

Next, the I/O map for the 82C55 is determined. Figure 12.13 shows pertinent connections between the Pentium and the 82C55.

As mentioned before, I/O port addresses F8H through FFH are reserved by Intel. I/O ports to these addresses must not be assigned. Hence, A7= 0 is used to select the 82C55. In Figure 12.13, the Pentium outputs LOW on its M/$\overline{IO}$ pin (M/$\overline{IO}$ = 0) when it executes an IN or OUT instruction. M/$\overline{IO}$ = 0 and A7 = 0 will produce a LOW (output of the OR gate in Figure 12.13) on the $\overline{CS}$ pin of the 82C55. The 82C55 will thus be selected. Since the Pentium encodes A2A1A0 from BE0#, the address bits A2A1A0 will be 000.

Using Pentium A_4 and A_3 pins for port addresses, the I/O map for the 82C55 chip can be determined as shown in Table 12.11. Note that an unused address pin to distinguish between memory and I/O is not required in standard I/O. This is accomplished by the M/IO# pin of the Pentium.

EXAMPLE 12.1   Write a Pentium assembly language program to drive an LED connected to bit 7 of port A based on a switch input at bit 0 of port A. If the switch is HIGH, turn the LED ON; otherwise, turn the LED OFF. Assume a Pentium /82C55-based microcomputer.

Solution

```
            .486
            .MODEL    SMALL,STDCALL
            .CODE
PORTA   EQU       60H
CTLREG  EQU       78H
BEGIN:
BACK:   MOV       AL,90H
        OUT       CTLREG,AL       ; set PORTA as input
        IN        AL,PORTA        ; read switch
        MOV       BL,AL           ; save switch status
        MOV       AL,80H
        OUT       CTLREG,AL       ; set PORTA as output
        MOV       AL,BL           ; get switch status
        ROR       AL,1            ; rotate switch status
        OUT       PORTA,AL        ; output to LED
        JMP       BACK            ; repeat
END     BEGIN
```

EXAMPLE 12.2   A Pentium-82C55-based microcomputer is required to drive an

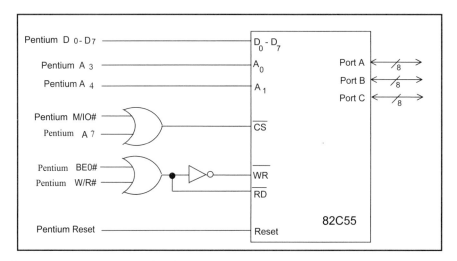

FIGURE 12.13   **82C55 interface to the Pentium.**

TABLE 12.11   82C55 I/O Map (X indicates don't cares, assume 1's)

Port Name	Address
Port A	A_7 A_6 A_5 A_4 A_3 A_2 A_1 A_0 = 60H 0 X X 0 0 0 0 0 Port A
Port B	0 X X 0 1 0 0 0 =68H Port B
Port C	0 X X 1 0 0 0 0 = 70H Port C
Control Register	0 X X 1 1 0 0 0 = 78H Control register

LED connected to bit 2 of port B based on two switch inputs connected to bits 6 and 7 of port A. If both switches are either HIGH or LOW, turn the LED ON; otherwise, turn it OFF. Assume a HIGH will turn the LED ON and a LOW will turn it OFF. Write a Pentium assembly language program to accomplish this.

Solution

```
        .486
        .MODEL SMALL,STDCALL
        .CODE
PORTA   EQU     60H
PORTB   EQU     68H
CNTRL   EQU     78H
BEGIN:
        MOV     AL,90H          ;   Configure port A as input
        OUT     CNTRL,AL        ;   and port B as output
BACK:   IN      AL,PORTA        ;   Input port A
        AND     AL,0C0H         ;   Retain bits 6 and 7
        JPE     LEDON           ;   If both switches are either
                                ;   HIGH or LOW, turn the LED ON
        MOV     AL,00H          ;   Otherwise turn the
        OUT     PORTB, AL       ;   LED OFF
        JMP     BEGIN           ;   Repeat
LEDON:  MOV     AL,04H          ;   Turn LED
        OUT     PORTB,AL        ;   ON
        JMP     BACK
END     BEGIN
```

12.3.5   Pentium Interrupts and Exceptions in Real Mode

Interrupts occur at random times during the execution of a program in response to external events. Exceptions occur when instructions are executed that provoke exceptions. Interrupts are used to handle events external to the Pentium. Exceptions handle conditions detected by the Pentium in the course of executing instructions such as division by zero.

There are two sources for interrupts and two sources for exceptions in the Pentium:
1.   Nonmaskable (NMI) and Maskable interrupt (INTR)
2.   Pentium-detected exceptions such as division by zero, and programmed exceptions such as the INTO (interrupt on overflow) instruction

In the real mode, the Pentium assigns every interrupt a type code so that the Pentium can identify it. Interrupts can be initiated by external devices or internally by software instructions or by exceptional conditions such as attempting to divide by zero. Interrupts and exceptions in the real mode work in the same way as the 8086. Interrupts and exceptions call interrupt procedures through an interrupt table. The Pentium multiplies the interrupt or exception identifier (type code) by 4 to obtain an address into an interrupt table. When an interrupt occurs, the Pentium pushes the current values of the flag, CS and IP registers onto the stack, disables interrupts, clears the TF flag, and transfers control to the location specified in the interrupt table. An IRET instruction at the end of the service routine pops IP, CS, and flag registers from the stack and returns control to the main program.

Upon hardware reset, the Pentium is in real mode, and the addresses for the interrupt pointer table are the same as the 8086 (addresses 00000H through 003FFH). In the real mode, if desired, addresses for the interrupt pointer table can be changed by an instruction such as LIDT. The LIDT instruction can be used to change the base and the limit values in the IDTR register. Note that the location and size of the interrupt pointer table depend on the contents of the Pentium IDTR register. Also, the Pentium reports some exceptions differently when executing in the real mode than when executing in protected mode.

In the following, interrupts and exceptions in the real mode are covered. Also, the addresses for the interrupt pointer table upon hardware reset are assumed.

Predefined Interrupts   The Pentium contains several predefined interrupts; the first five are:

Type 0:	INT0	Divide by zero
Type 1:	INT1	Single step
Type 2:	INT2	Nonmaskable interrupt (NMI pin)
Type 3:	INT3	Breakpoint
Type 4:	INT4	Interrupt on overflow

The interrupt vectors for these five interrupts are predefined by Intel. The user must provide the desired IP and CS values in the interrupt pointer table. The user may also initiate these interrupts through hardware or software. If a predefined interrupt is not used in a system, the user may assign some other function to the associated type.

The Pentium is interrupted automatically whenever a division by zero is attempted. This interrupt is nonmaskable and is implemented by Intel as part of the execution of the divide instruction.

Once TF is set to 1, the Pentium automatically generates a type 1 interrupt after execution of each instruction. The user can write a service routine at the interrupt address vector to display memory locations and/or register to debug a program. Single-step mode is nonmaskable and cannot be enabled by the STI (enable interrupt) or disabled by the CLI (disable interrupt) instruction. The TF can be set to 1 as follows:

PUSHF	;	Save flags
MOV BP, SP	;	Move [SP] to [BP]
OR [BP], 0100H	;	Set TF to one
POPF	;	Pop flags

The nonmaskable interrupt is initiated via the Pentium NMI pin. It is edge triggered (LOW to HIGH) and must be active for two clock cycles to guarantee recognition. It is normally used for catastrophic failures such as a power failure. The Pentium obtains the interrupt vector address by automatically executing the INT2 (type 2) instruction internally.

The type 3 interrupt is used for breakpoints and is nonmaskable. The user inserts the 1-byte instruction INT3 into a program by replacing an instruction. Breakpoints are useful for program debugging.

The interrupt on overflow is a type 4 interrupt. This interrupt occurs if the overflow flag (OF) is set and the INTO instruction is executed. The overflow flag is affected, for example, after execution of a signed arithmetic (such as IMUL, signed multiplication) instruction. The user can execute an INTO instruction after the IMUL. If there is an overflow, an error service routine written by the user at the type 4 interrupt address vector is executed.

Internal Interrupts   The user can generate an interrupt by executing the interrupt instruction **INT** *nn*. The **INT** *nn* instruction is not maskable by the interrupt enable flag (IF). The **INT** *nn* instruction can be used to test an interrupt service routine for external interrupts. Type codes 32–255 can be used.

External Maskable Interrupts   The Pentium maskable interrupts are initiated via the INTR pin. These interrupts can be enabled or disabled by STI (IF = 1) or CLI (IF = 0), respectively. If IF = 1 and INTR active (HIGH) without occurrence of any other interrupts, the Pentium, after completing the current instruction, generates interrupt acknowledge cycles twice, each time for about one cycle..

The state of address bit 2 (as decoded from byte enables) distinguishes the first and second interrupt acknowledge cycles. During the first interrupt acknowledge cycle, the Pentium drives BE4# (A2 A1 A0 = 100) to LOW, BE7# - BE5# to HIGH, BE3# - BE0# to HIGH, and A31 - A3 to LOW. During the second interrupt acknowledge cycle, the Pentium drives BE0# (A2 A1 A0 = 000) to LOW, BE7# - BE1# to HIGH, and A31 - A3 to LOW. This means that BE4# = 0 and BE0# = 1 during the first interrupt acknowledge cycle whereas BE4# = 1 and BE0# = 0 during the second interrupt acknowledge cycle.

Interrupt acknowledge cycles are terminated when the external system returns BRDY#. The first interrupt bus cycle indicates that an interrupt acknowledge cycle is in progress and allows the system to be ready to place the interrupt type code on the next interrupt acknowledge bus cycle. Data returned during the first cycle is ignored. The Pentium does not obtain information from the bus during the first cycle. The external hardware must place the type code on the D_0–D_7 pins of the Pentium's data bus during the second cycle.

Figure 12.14 shows a simplified interconnection between the Pentium and the 74HC244 for servicing the INTR. Inverted BE4# and BE0# are ORed to enable the 74HC244 to place type code *nn* (32 to 255) on the Pentium's D0 - D7 pins. A delay circuit may be required for BRDY#.

Interrupt Procedures   Once the Pentium has the interrupt type code (via the bus for hardware interrupts, from software interrupt instructions INT *nn*, or from the predefined interrupts), the type code is multiplied by 4 to obtain the corresponding interrupt vector in the interrupt vector table. The 4 bytes of the interrupt vector are the least significant byte of the instruction pointer, the most significant byte of the instruction pointer, the least significant byte of the code segment register, and the most significant byte of the code segment register. During the transfer of control, the Pentium pushes the flags and current code segment register and instruction pointer onto the stack. The new CS and IP values are loaded. Flags TF and IF are then cleared to zero. The CS and IP values are read by the Pentium from the interrupt vector table.

Interrupt Pointer Table   The interrupt pointer table provides interrupt address vectors (IP and CS contents) for all the interrupts. There may be up to 256 entries for the 256 type codes. Note that INT0 through INT4 are predefined interrupts, INT32 through INT255 can be used for internal and maskable interrupts, and INT5 through INT31 are reserved by Intel for system use. Each entry consists of two addresses, one for storing IP and the other for storing CS. Note that in the Pentium each interrupt address vector is a 20-bit address obtained from IP and CS.

To service an interrupt, the Pentium calculates the two addresses in the pointer table where IP and CS are stored for a particular interrupt type as follows:

$$\text{For INT } \underbrace{nn}_{\text{type code}}$$

The address for IP = 4 × *nn* and the address for CS = 4 × *nn* + 2. For example, consider INT2 (for NMI): Address for IP = 4 × 2 = 00008H, Address for CS = 00008 + 2 = 0000AH The values of IP and CS are loaded from locations 00008H and 0000AH in the pointer table. Similarly, the IP and CS addresses for other INT *nn* are calculated, and their values are obtained from the contents of these addresses in the pointer table in the real address mode (Table 12.12).
Interrupt service routines should be terminated with an IRET (interrupt return) instruction,

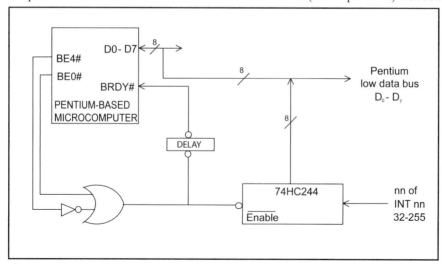

FIGURE 12.14   **Servicing the INTR in the real mode.**

which pops the top three stack words into the IP, CS, and flags registers, thus returning control to the right place in the main program.

12.4 Pentium-based voltmeter

In this section, a Pentium-based voltmeter is designed to measure voltage in the range 0 to 5 V and display the result in two decimal digits: one integer part and one fractional part. Both programmed I/O and interrupt I/O are used. Assume that the microcomputer contains EPROM and RAM. Note that the microcomputer must contain RAM for stack in order to service interrupt.

The following I/O port addresses are used in the assembly language programs: 82C55 control register = 78H, port A = 60H, port B = 68H, and port C = 70H. These port addresses are arbitrarily chosen.

Typical assembler directives such as ORG SEGREG:OFFSET or ORG CS:IP for the Hewlett-Packard HP 64XXX microcomputer development system are used in the assembly language programs for initializing DS and OFFSET or CS, and IP.

Because the maximum decimal value that can be accommodated in 8 bits is 255_{10} (FF_{16}), the maximum voltage of 5 V will be equivalent to 255_{10}. This means that the display in decimal is given by

$$D = 5 \times (\text{Input}/255)$$

$$= \text{Input}/51$$

$$= \underbrace{\text{Quotient}}_{\text{Integer part}} + \text{Remainder}$$

This gives the integer part. The fractional part in decimal is

TABLE 12.12 Pentium Interrupt Pointer Table

Interrupt Type Code		*20-Bit Memory Address*
0	IP	00000H
	CS	00002H
1	IP	00004H
	CS	00006H
2	IP	00008H
	CS	0000AH
.	.	.
	.	.
.	.	.
.	.	.
255	IP	003FCH
	CS	003FEH

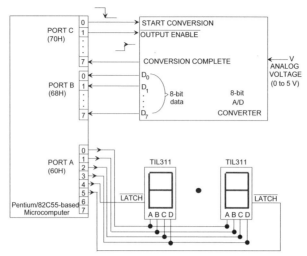

FIGURE 12.15   Pentium-based voltmeter using programmed I/O.

$$F = (\text{Remainder}/51)\times 10$$

$$\simeq (\text{Remainder})/5$$

For example, suppose that the decimal equivalent of the 8-bit output of A/D is 200.

$$D = 200/51 \Rightarrow Quotient = 3, Remainder = 47$$

Integer part = 3

Fractional part, $F = 47/5 = 9$

Therefore, the display will show 3.9 V.

12.4.1   Pentium-based voltmeter using programmed I/O

Figure 12.15 shows the block diagram for programmed I/O. The microcomputer is required to start the A/D converter at the falling edge of a pulse via bit 0 of port C. When the conversion is completed, the A/D's "conversion complete" signal will go to HIGH. During the conversion, the A/D's "CONVERSION COMPLETE" signal stays LOW.

Using programmed I/O, the microcomputer is required to poll the A/D's "conversion complete" signal. When the conversion is completed, the microcomputer will send a LOW on the A/D converter's "OUTPUT ENABLE" line via bit 1 to port C and then input the 8-bit output from A/D via port B and display the voltage (0 to 5 V) in two decimal digits (one integer and one fractional) via port A on two TIL 311 displays.

Note that the TIL 311 has an on-chip BCD to seven segment decoder. The microcomputer will output each decimal digit on the common lines (bits 0–3 of port A) connected to the ABCD inputs ('D' is the most significant bit and 'A' is the least significant bit) of the displays. Each display will be enabled by outputting LOW on each $\overline{\text{LATCH}}$ line in sequence (one after another) so that the input voltage V_x (0 to 5 V) will be displayed with an integer part and a fractional part. The Pentium assembly language program follows.

```
           .486
           .MODEL    SMALL,STDCALL
           .CODE
START:
           ORG       0FE00H:0100H      ;    CS=FE00H, IP=0100H
PORTA  EQU           60H
PORTB  EQU           68H
PORTC  EQU           70H
CNTRL  EQU           78H
           MOV       AL,8AH            ;    Configure PORTA, PORTB
           OUT       CNTRL,AL          ;    and PORTC
           MOV       AL,03H            ;    Send 1 to START pin of A/D
           OUT       PORTC,AL          ;    and 1 to (OUTPUT ENABLE)
           MOV       AL,02H            ;    Send 0 to start pin
           OUT       PORTC,A           ;    of A/D
BEGIN:  IN           AL,PORTC          ;    Check conversion
           ROL       AL,1              ;    Complete bit for HIGH
           JNC       BEGIN
           MOV       AL,00H            ;    Send  LOW   to   (OUTPUT
                                            ENABLE )
           OUT       PORTC,AL
           IN        AL,PORTB          ;    Input A/D data
           MOV       AH,0              ;    Convert input data to 16-bit
                                       ;    unsigned number in AX
           MOV       DL,51             ;    Convert data to
           DIV       DL                ;    integer part
           MOV       CL,AL             ;    Save quotient (integer) in CL
           XCHG      AH,AL             ;    Move remainder to AL
           MOV       AH,0              ;    Convert remainder to unsigned
                                       ;    16-bit number
           MOV       BL,5              ;    Convert data to
           DIV       BL                ;    fractional part
           MOV       DL,AL             ;    Save quotient (fraction) to DL
           MOV       AL,CL             ;    Move integer part
           OR        AL,20H            ;    Disable fractional display
           AND       AL,2FH            ;    Enable integer display
           OUT       PORTA,AL          ;    Display integer part
           MOV       AL,DL             ;    Move fractional part
```

```
OR       AL,10H        ;    Disable integer display
AND      AL,1FH        ;    Enable fractional display
OUT      PORTA,AL      ;    Display fractional part
HLT
END      START
```

12.4.2   Pentium-based voltmeter using NMI

In this section, the voltmeter is designed using NMI (Nonmaskable interrupt). The main program is written to initialize the 82C55 control register, and also, to start the A/D. The service routine will input the A/D data, display the result, and stop. A Pentium assembly language program is written for the main program and the service routine. The memory locations are arbitrarily chosen. The service routine for the NMI is written starting at IP=2000H, CS=1000H. In Figure 12.15, connect the "conversion complete" to Pentium NMI; all other connections in Figure 12.15 will remain unchanged. Note that all addresses selectable by the user are chosen arbitrarily in the following. The SS and SP are initialized arbitrarily to 3900H and 1000H respectively. The main program and service routine in Pentium assembly language for NMI are as follows:

```
         .486
         .MODEL    SMALL,STDCALL
         .DATA
         ORG       0000H:0008H    ;    DS = 0000H, Offset = 0008H
         DW        2000H          ;    Initialize IP = 2000H, CS = 1000H
         DW        1000H          ;    for Pointer Table
         .CODE
BEGIN:
PORTA    EQU       60H
PORTB    EQU       68H
PORTC    EQU       70H
CNTRL    EQU       78H
         ORG       0FE00H:0100H   ;    CS = FE00H, IP = 0100H
         MOV       AX,3900H       ;    Initialize
         MOV       SS,AX          ;    stack segment
         MOV       AX,0000H       ;    Initialize
         MOV       DS,AX          ;    data segment
         MOV       SP,1000H       ;    Initialize SP
         MOV       AL,8AH         ;    Configure PORTA, PORTB
         OUT       CNTRL,AL       ;    and PORTC
         MOV       AL,03H         ;    Send 1 to START pin of A/D
```

	OUT	PORTC,AL	; and 1 to ($\overline{\text{OUTPUT ENABLE}}$)
	MOV	AL,02H	; Send 0 to start pin
	OUT	PORTC,AL	; of A/D
DELAY:	JMP	DELAY	; Wait for interrupt
	.CODE		
	ORG	1000H:2000H	; CS = 1000H, IP = 2000H
			; Start Program at
			; CS = 1000H, IP = 2000H
	MOV	AL,00H	; Send LOW to ($\overline{\text{OUTPUT ENABLE}}$)
	OUT	PORTC,AL	
	IN	AL,PORTB	; Input A/D data
	MOV	AH,0	; Convert input to 16-bit unsig.num.
	MOV	DL,51	; Convert data to
	DIV	DL	; integer part
	MOV	CL,AL	; Save quotient (integer) in CL
	XCHG	AH,AL	; Move remainder to AL
	MOV	AH,0	; Conv. remainder to 16-bit unsigned
	MOV	BL,5	; Convert data to
	DIV	BL	; fractional part
	MOV	DL,AL	; Save quotient (fraction) to DL
	MOV	AL,CL	; Move integer part
	OR	AL,20H	; Disable fractional display
	AND	AL,2FH	; Enable integer display
	OUT	PORTA,AL	; Display integer part
	MOV	AL,DL	; Move fractional part
	OR	AL,10H	; Disable integer display
	AND	AL,1FH	; Enable fractional display
	OUT	PORTA,AL	; Display fractional part
	HLT		; Stop
END	BEGIN		

12.4.3   Pentium-based voltmeter using INTR

All connections in Figure 12.15 will be the same except A/D's "conversion complete" to Pentium INTR as shown in Figure 12.16. All other connections in Figure 12.15 will remain unchanged. INT FFH is used. In response to INTR, the Pentium pushes CS, IP and flags onto the stack, and generates two interrupt acknowledge cycles; BE4# is LOW during the first interrupt acknowledge cycle and HIGH during the second interrupt acknowledge cycle. Hence, inverted BE4# and BE0# are ORed to obtain the interrupt acknowledge output.

An octal buffer such as 74HC244 can be enabled by inverted BE4# to transfer FF_{16} in this case (can be entered via eight DIP switches connected to +5 V through a 1 KΩ resistor) to the input of the octal buffer. The output of the octal buffer is connected to the D0–D7 lines of the Pentium. A delay circuit may be required for BRDY# to terminate the interrupt acknowledge cycles.

The Pentium executes INT FFH and goes to the interrupt pointer table to load the contents of physical addresses 003FCH (logical address: CS = 0000H, IP = 03FCH) and 003FEH (logical address: CS = 0000H, IP = 03FEH) to obtain IP and CS for the service routine respectively. Since it is desired to write the service routine at IP = 2000H and CS = 1000H; these IP and CS values must be stored at addresses 003FCH and 003FEH, respectively. All user selectable addresses are chosen arbitrarily. The SS and SP are arbitrarily initialized to 3900H and 8500H, respectively.

The main program and service routine in Pentium assembly language for INTR are as follows:

```
                .486
                .MODEL    SMALL,STDCALL
                .DATA
                ORG       0000H:03FCH    ;  DS = 0000H, Offset = 03FCH
                DW        2000H          ;  Initialize IP = 2000H,
                DW        1000H          ;  CS = 1000H for Pointer Table
                .CODE
START:
PORTA   EQU     60H
PORTB   EQU     68H
PORTC   EQU     70H
CNTRL   EQU     78H
                ORG       0F300H:0100H   ;  CS = F300H, IP = 0100H
                MOV       AX,3900H       ;  Initialize
                MOV       SS,AX          ;  stack segment
                MOV       AX,0000H       ;  Initialize
                MOV       DS,AX          ;  data segment
                MOV       SP,8500H       ;  Initialize SP
                MOV       AL,8AH         ;  Configure port A, port B,
                OUT       CNTRL,AL       ;  and port C
                STI                      ;  Enable Interrupt
                MOV       AL,03H         ;  Send one to start pin of A/D
                OUT       PORTC,AL       ;  and one to (OUTPUT ENABLE)
                MOV       AL,02H         ;  Send zero to start pin of A/D
                OUT       PORTC,AL
```

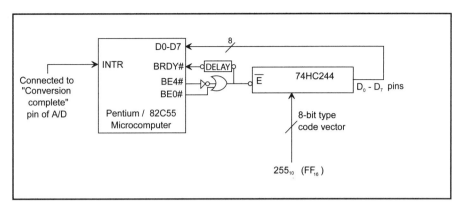

FIGURE 12.16   Hardware interface for the Pentium INTR

DELAY:	JMP	DELAY	;	Wait for interrupt
	.CODE			
	ORG	1000H:2000H	;	CS = 1000H, IP = 2000H
	MOV	AL,0	;	Send LOW to
	OUT	PORTC,AL	;	$\overline{\text{(OUTPUT ENABLE)}}$
	IN	AL,PORTB	;	Input A/D data
	MOV	AH,0	;	Convert input data to
			;	16-bit unsigned number in AX
	MOV	DL,51	;	Convert data
	DIV	DL	;	to integer part
	MOV	CL,AL	;	Save quotient (integer) in CL
	XCHG	AH,AL	;	Move remainder to AL
	MOV	AH,0	;	Convert remainder to unsigned
			;	16-bit
	MOV	BL,5	;	Convert data
	DIV	BL	;	to fractional part
	MOV	DL,AL	;	Save quotient (fraction) in DL
	MOV	AL,CL	;	Move integer part
	OR	AL,20H	;	Disable fractional display
	AND	AL,2FH	;	Enable integer display
	OUT	PORTA,AL	;	Display integer part
	MOV	AL,DL	;	Move fractional part
	OR	AL,10H	;	Disable integer display
	AND	AL,1FH	;	Enable fraction display
	OUT	PORTA,AL	;	Display fractional part
	HLT		;	Stop
END	START			

12.5   Interfacing a Pentium-based Microcomputer to a Hexadecimal Keyboard and a Seven Segment Display

In this section we describe the characteristics of the Pentium-based microcomputer used with a hexadecimal keyboard and a seven-segment display.

12.5.1   Basics of Keyboard and Display Interface to a Microcomputer

A common method of entering programs into a microcomputer is via a keyboard. A popular way of displaying results by the microcomputer is by using seven-segment displays. The main functions to be performed for interfacing a keyboard are:

- Sense a key actuation.

- Debounce the key.

- Decode the key.

Let us now elaborate on keyboard interfacing concepts. A keyboard is arranged in rows and columns. Figure 12.17 shows a 2 × 2 keyboard interfaced to a typical microcomputer. In Figure 12.17, the columns are normally at a HIGH level. A key actuation is sensed by sending a LOW (closing the diode switch) to each row one at a time via PA0 and PA1 of port A. The two columns can then be input via PB2 and PB3 of port B to see whether any of the normally HIGH columns are pulled LOW by a key actuation. If so, the rows can be checked individually to determine the row in which the key is down. The row and column code for the key pressed can thus be found.

The next step is to debounce the key. Key bounce occurs when a key is pressed or released—it bounces for a short time before making the contact. When this bounce occurs, it may appear to the microcomputer that the same key has been actuated several times instead of just once. This problem can be eliminated by reading the keyboard after about 20 ms and then verifying to see if it is still down. If it is, the key actuation is valid. The next step is to translate the row and column code into a more popular code such as hexadecimal or ASCII. This can be accomplished easily by a program. Certain characteristics associated with keyboard actuations must be considered while interfacing to a microcomputer. Typically, these are two-key lockout and N-key rollover. Two-key lockout ensures that only one key is pressed. An additional key depressed and released does not generate any codes. The system is simple to implement and most often used. However, it might slow down the typing because each key must be fully released before the next one is pressed down. On the other hand, the N-key rollover will ignore all keys pressed until only one remains down.

Now let us elaborate on the interfacing characteristics of typical displays. The following functions are typically performed for displays:

- Output the appropriate display code.
- Output the code via right entry or left entry into the displays if there is more than one display.

These functions can easily be realized by a microcomputer program. If there is more than one display, the displays are typically arranged in rows. A row of four displays is shown in Figure 12.18. In the figure, one has the option of outputting the display code via right or left entry. If the code is entered via right entry, the code for the least significant digit of the four-digit display should be output first, the next-digit code, and so on. The program outputs to the displays are so fast that visually all four digits will appear on the display simultaneously. If the displays are entered via left entry, then the most significant digit must be output first and the rest of the sequence is similar to the right entry.

Two techniques are typically used to interface a hexadecimal display to the microcomputer: nonmultiplexed and multiplexed. In nonmultiplexed methods, each hexadecimal display digit is interfaced to the microcomputer via an I/O port. Figure 12.19 illustrates this method. BCD-to- seven-segment conversion is done in software. The microcomputer can be programmed to output to the two display digits in sequence. However, the microcomputer executes the display instruction sequence so fast that the displays appear to the human eye at the same time. Figure 12.20 illustrates the multiplexing method of interfacing the two hexadecimal displays to the microcomputer. In the multiplexing scheme, appropriate seven-segment code is sent to the desired displays on seven lines common to all displays. However, the display to be illuminated is grounded. Some displays, such as Texas Instrument's TIL 311, have an on-chip decoder. In this case, the microcomputer is required to output 4 bits (decimal) to a display.

The keyboard and display interfacing concepts described here can be realized by either software or hardware. To relieve the microprocessor of these functions, microprocessor manufacturers have developed a number of keyboard/display controller chips. These chips are typically initialized by the microprocessor. The keyboard/display functions are then performed by the chip independent of the microprocessor. The amount of keyboard/display functions performed by the controller chip varies from one manufacturer to another. However, these functions are usually shared between the controller chip and the microprocessor.

12.5.2 Hexadecimal Keyboard and Seven-Segment Display Interface to a Pentium-Based Microcomputer

In this section, a Pentium-based microcomputer is designed to display a hexadecimal digit entered via a keypad (16 keys). The microcomputer will contain one 82C55 I/O chip along with EPROMs and SRAMs.

Figure 12.21 shows the hardware schematic. Port A, port B, and port C are configured as follows:

- port A is configured as an input port to receive the row–column code.

- port B is configured as an output port to display the key(s) pressed.

- port C is configured as an output port to output zeros to the rows to detect a key

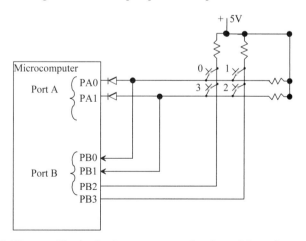

FIGURE 12.17   **Typical microcomputer-keyboard interface.**

FIGURE 12.18   Row of four displays.

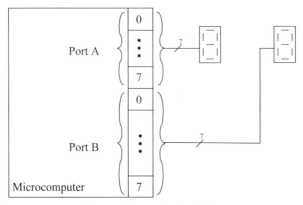

FIGURE 12.19   Nonmultiplexed hexadecimal displays.

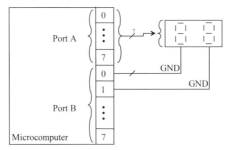

FIGURE 12.20   Multiplexed displays.

actuation.

The Pentium is assumed to run at 100 MHz. Debouncing is provided to avoid unwanted oscillation caused by the opening and closing of the key contacts. To ensure stability for the input signal, a delay of 20 ms is used for debouncing the input.

The program begins by performing all necessary initializations. Next, it makes sure that all the keys are opened (not pressed). A delay loop of 20 ms is included for debouncing, and the following instruction sequence is used (Section 11.8):

```
           MOV    DX,10
BACK:      MOV    CX,33333
DELAY:     LOOP   DELAY
           DEC    DX
           JNE    BACK
```

The Pentium assembly language program for interfacing the Pentium-based microcomputer to a hexadecimal keyboard and a seven-segment display follows:

Note that to explain the program , line numbers are included with the comments.

In the program, a decode table for the keys (0 through F) are stored in a table starting at an address $4000 (arbitrarily chosen) with a label named TABLE. The codes for the hexadecimal numbers 0 through F are obtained by inspecting Figure 12.21.

For example, consider key F. When key F is pressed and if a LOW is output by the program to bit 0 of port C, the top row and rightmost column of the keyboard will be LOW. This will make the content of port A

$$
\begin{array}{cccccccc}
\text{Bit number :} & 7 & 6 & 5 & 4 & 3 & 2 & 1 & 0 \\
\text{Data :} & 0 & 1 & 1 & 1 & 0 & 1 & 1 & 1 \\
\end{array}
= 77_{16}
$$

$$
\underbrace{\qquad}_{7} \qquad \underbrace{\qquad}_{7}
$$

Thus, a code of 77_{16} is obtained at Port A when the key F is pressed. Diodes are connected at the 4 bits (bits 0-3) of port C. This is done to make sure that when a 0 is output by the program to one of these bits (row of the keyboard), the diode switch will close and will generate a LOW on that row.

Now, if a key is pressed on a particular row that is LOW, the column connected to this key will also be LOW. This will enable the programmer to obtain the appropriate key code for each key.

Next, the assembly language program will be explained by using the line numbers included in the comment field.

Line #1 contains the code for key F, and the decode table is stored starting at address 4000H.

Line #2 equates the label OPEN to the data F0H. This is because when all keys are up (no keys are pushed) and 0's are output to the rows in Figure 12.24, data input at port A will be 11110000 (F0H). Note that bits 0 -3 are connected to rows and bits 4-7 are connected to columns of the keyboard.

Line 3 initializes DS to 0100H. This value is chosen arbitrarily.

Lines 4 through 6 configure port A as an input port, and ports B and C as output

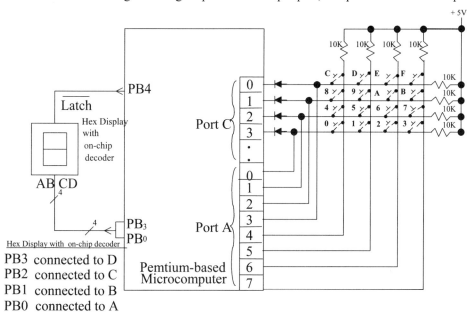

FIGURE 12.21   **Pentium-based microcomputer interface to keyboard and display.**

ports. Line 7 initializes the seven-segment display by outputting 0. Lines 8 through 10 check to see if any key is pushed. This is done by outputting 0's to all rows via port C, and then inputting port A. If all keys are open, the data at port A will be F0H. Hence, the data at port A is compared with F0H. If Z = 0, the program waits in a loop with label KEY_OPEN until all keys are up. When all keys are open, Z = 1, and the program comes out of the loop. Lines 11 and 12 debounce the keys by providing a delay of 20 ms.

Lines 13 through 15 detect a key closure. The program inputs port A, and compares input data with F0H. If Z = 1, the program waits in a loop with the label KEY_CLOSE until a key is closed. If Z = 0, the program leaves the loop. Lines 16 and 17 provide debouncing if a key closure is detected.

It is necessary to determine exactly which key is pressed. To do this, a sequence of row-control codes (XEH, XDH, XBH, and X7H, where X represents don't care; the upper 4 bits are don't cares) are output via port C. Lines 18 through 21 initialize AL to all 1's,

```
              .486
              .MODEL    SMALL,STDCALL
              .DATA
              ORG       4000H
TABLE         DB        77H        ;    #1 Code for F
              DB        0B7H       ;    Code for E
              DB        0D7H       ;    Code for D
              DB        0E7H       ;    Code for C
              DB        07BH       ;    Code for B
              DB        0BBH       ;    Code for A
              DB        0DBH       ;    Code for 9
              DB        0EBH       ;    Code for 8
              DB        7DH        ;    Code for 7
              DB        0BDH       ;    Code for 6
              DB        0DDH       ;    Code for 5
              DB        0EDH       ;    Code for 4
              DB        7EH        ;    Code for 3
              DB        0BEH       ;    Code for 2
              DB        0DEH       ;    Code for 1
              DB        0EEH       ;    Code for 0
              .CODE
BEGIN:
PORTA         EQU       60H        ;    Hex keyboard input (row/column)
PORTB         EQU       68H        ;    LED displays/controls
PORTC         EQU       70H        ;    Hex keyboard row controls
CNTRL         EQU       78H        ;    Control register
OPEN          EQU       0F0H       ;    #2 Row/column codes if all keys
```

```
                                         ;   are opened
                   MOV    BX,0100H       ;   #3 initialize DS
                   MOV    DS, BX
START:             MOV    AL,90H         ;   #4 Config ports A, B, C as i/o/o
                   OUT    CNTRL,AL
                   SUB    AL, AL         ;   #5 Clear AL
                   OUT    PORTB,AL       ;   #6 Enable/initialize display
SCAN_KEY:          SUB    AL,AL          ;   #7 Clear AL
                   OUT    PORTC,AL       ;   Set row controls to zero
KEY_OPEN:          IN     AL, PORTA      ;   #8 Read PORTA
                   CMP    AL, OPEN       ;   #9 Are all keys opened?
                   JNZ    KEY_OPEN       ;   #10 Repeat if closed
                   MOV    DX,10
BACK:              MOV    CX, 33333      ;   #11 Delay of 20 ms
DELAY1:            LOOP   DELAY1         ;   #12 key opened
                   DEC    DX
                   JNZ    BACK
KEY_CLOSE:         IN     AL, PORTA      ;   #13 read PORTA
                   CMP    AL, OPEN       ;   #14 Are all keys closed?
                   JZ     KEY_CLOSE      ;   #15 repeat if opened
                   MOV    DX, 10         ;   #16 delay of 20 ms
BACK:              MOV    CX, 33333
DELAY2:            LOOP   DELAY2         ;   #17 Debounce key closed
                   DEC    DX
                   JNZ    BACK
                   MOV    AL, 0FFH       ;   #18 Set AL to all 1's
                   CLC                   ;   #19 clear carry
NEXT_ROW:          RCL    AL,1           ;   #20 Set up row mask
                   MOV    CL, AL         ;   #21 Save row mask in CL
                   OUT    PORTC, AL      ;   #22 Set a row to zero
                   IN     AL,PORTA       ;   #23 Read PORTA
                   MOV    DL, AL         ;   #24 Save row/coln codes in DL
                   AND    AL, 0F0H       ;   #25 Mask row code
                   CMP    AL, 0F0H       ;   #26 Is coln code affected?
                   JNZ    DECODE         ;   #27 If yes, decode coln code
                   MOV    AL, CL         ;   #28 Restore row mask to AL
                   STC                   ;   #29 if no, set carry
                   JMP    NEXT_ROW       ;   #30 Check next row
DECODE:            MOV    SI, -1         ;   #31 Initialize index register
```

```
              MOV      CX, 000FH    ;   #32 Set up counter
SEARCH:       INC      SI           ;   #33 Increment index
              CMP      DL,[4000H+SI] ;  #34 Index thru table of
                                    ;   codes
              LOOPNE   SEARCH       ;   #35 Loop if not found
DONE:         MOV      AL,CL        ;   #36 get character and enable
                                    ;   display
              OUT      PORTB,AL     ;   #37 display key
              JMP      SCAN_KEY     ;   #38 Return to scan another key
                                    ;   input
END           BEGIN
```

clear the carry to 0, and then rotate AL through the carry bit once to the left to contain the appropriate row control code. For example, after the first RCL in line 20, AL will contain 1111 1110 (FEH). Note that the low 4 bits are the row-control code for the first pass in the loop labeled NEXT_ROW. Line 22 outputs this data to port C to make the top row of the keyboard 0.

The row–column code is input via port A to determine if the column code changes corresponding to each different row code. Line 23 inputs port A into AL. The top row of the keyboard will be 0 if C or D or E or F is pushed. Line 24 saves this input data in D4.B.

Lines 25 through 27 make the low 4 bits to 0's and retain the upper 4 bits. If the column code is not F0H (changed), the input key is identified. The program then indexes through a look-up table to determine the row–column code saved in DL. If the code is found, the corresponding index value, which equals the input key's value (a single hexadecimal digit), is displayed.

Suppose that key F is pushed. Line 24 will store the code 77H in DL. The instruction CMP AL,0F0 at line 26 will make Z = 0. Hence, after execution of JNZ DECODE at line 27, the program branches to DECODE (line 31). Lines 31 through 35 compare the key code saved in DL with $77 (data for F) stored at address 4000H (label TABLE) in the decode table. Since there is a match, the Z-flag will be 1. The program comes out of the loop with the label SEARCH and outputs the character F to the seven-segment display at line 37.

However, if no key is pushed in the top row, a 0 is output to the second row, and the process continues. The program is written such that it will scan continuously for an input key and update the display for each new input. The memory and I/O maps are chosen arbitrarily.

Questions and Problems

12.1   Why is the Pentium provided with multiple Vcc and ground pins?

12.2   What is the purpose of each of the following Pentium pins?
(a) BRDY# and A20M#   (b) BE0#-BE7#

12.3   If there are no interrupts or DMA required in a Pentium-based application, identify whether you would connect each of the following Pentium pins to HIGH or LOW or keep it floating: NMI, INTR, HOLD, and HLDA.

12.4   Identify the signals along with the levels for indicating Pentium's interrupt acknowledge cycles.

12.5   Identify each of the following instructions as aligned or misaligned transfer for 64-bit memory with (DS) = 0100H. Briefly explain for each case how data will be transferred via which data pins (D63- D0) by the Pentium using BE7# - BE0#.
(a) MOV   DH,[1001H]
(b) MOV   CX,[0052H]
(c) MOV   EDX, [0126H]

12.6   Assume that eight 27C256s are interfaced to a Pentium to obtain a 64-bit EPROM system. Connect one 27C256 to the Pentium in such a system to obtain the memory map for the real mode. Show only the connections for the pins shown in Figure P12.6. Assume all unused address lines to be zeros, and also that A19 = 0 will select EPROMs. Note: use only the bus enable pin, BE7# among BE7# - BE0# in the address decoding logic.

12.7   Assume that eight LH2256C/CHs are interfaced to a Pentium to obtain a 64-bit SRAM system. Connect one LH2256C/CH SRAM to the Pentium in such a system to obtain a memory map forthe real mode. Show only the connections for the pins shown in Figure P12.7. Assume that A19= 1 will select the SRAMs. Also, assume that all unused address lines to be 1's. Note: use only the bus enable pin, BE7# among BE7# - BE0# in the address decoding logic.

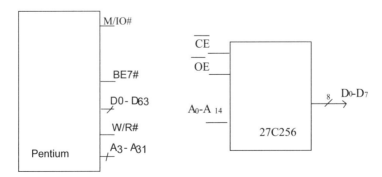

FIGURE P12.6

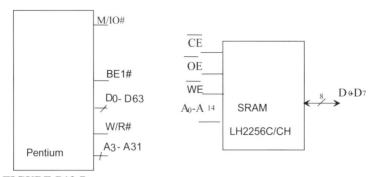

FIGURE P12.7

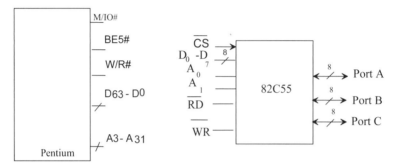

FIGURE P12.8

12.8   Interface one 82C55 to a Pentium to obtain the I/O map. Use Pentium A6 and A5 pins to select 82C55 I/O ports, and BE5# among BE7# - BE0# in the address decoding logic. Show only the connections for the pins shown in Figure P12.8. Assume all unused address lines to be zeros and that A7 = 1 will select the 82C55.

12.9   Assume a Pentium/82C55 microcomputer. Suppose that four switches are connected at bits 0 through 3 of port A and an LED is connected at bit 4 of port B. If the number of LOW switches is even, turn the port B LED ON; otherwise, turn the port B LED OFF. Write a Pentium assembly language program to accomplish this. Do not use any instructions involving the parity flag.

12.10   A Pentium/82C55-based microcomputer is required to drive the LEDs connected to bit 0 of ports A and B based on the input conditions set by switches connected to bit 1 of ports A and B. The I/O conditions are as follows:

  • If the input at bit 1 of port A is HIGH and the input at bit 1 of port B is low, the LED at port A will be ON and the LED at port B will be OFF.

  • If the input at bit 1 of port A is LOW and the input at bit 1 of port B is HIGH, the LED at port A will be OFF and the LED at port B will be ON.

  • If the inputs at both ports A and B are the same (either both HIGH or both LOW), both LEDs at ports A and B will be ON.

Write a Pentium assembly language program to accomplish this. Do not use any instructions involving the parity flag. Assume all segment register are initalized.

12.11 Write a Pentium assembly language program to turn an LED OFF connected to bit 2 of port A of a Pentium/82C55 microcomputer and then turn it ON after a delay of 20 seconds. Assume that the LED is ON initially. Assume 100-MHz Pentium.

12.12 A Pentium/82C55-based microcomputer is required to test a NAND gate. Figure P12.12 shows the I/O hardware needed to test the NAND gate. The microcomputer is to be programmed to generate the various logic conditions for the NAND inputs, input the NAND output, and turn the LED ON connected to bit 3 of port A if the NAND gate chip is found to be faulty. Otherwise, turn the LED ON connected to bit 4 of port A. Write a Pentium assembly language program to accomplish this.

12.13 A Pentium/82C55 microcomputer is required to add two 3-bit numbers in AL and BL and output the sum (not to exceed 9) to a common cathode seven-segment display connected to port A as shown in Figure P12.13. Write a Pentium assembly language program to accomplish this by using a look-up table. Do not use the XLAT instruction. Initialize DS to 3000H.

12.14 A Pentium/82C55-based microcomputer is required to input a number from 0 to 9 from an ASCII keyboard interfaced to it and output to an EBCDIC printer. Assume that the keyboard is connected to port A and the printer is connected to port B. Write a Pentium assembly language to accomplish this. Use the XLAT instruction. Use the Port addresses as follows: port A = 60H, port B = 68H, Control Register = 78H.

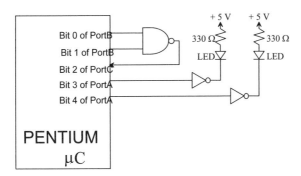

FIGURE P12.12 (**Assume that both LEDs are OFF initially.**)

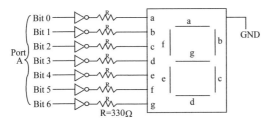

FIGURE P12.13

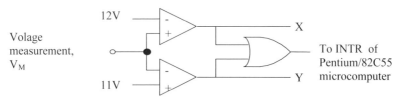

FIGURE P12.15

12.15   In Figure P12.15, if V_M > 12 V, turn the LED ON connected at bit 4 of port A. On the other hand, if V_M < 11 V, turn the LED OFF. Use ports, registers, and memory locations of your choice. Draw a hardware block diagram showing the microcomputer and the connections of the figure to its ports. Write a service routine in Pentium assembly language at CS = 1000H and, IP = 2000H. Assume that all segment registers are already initialized. Also, write the main program at CS = 3000H and IP = 0050H that will initialize SP to 2050H, initialize ports, and wait for interrupts. Use assembler directive ORG CS:IP to initialize CS and IP. Assume vector addresses after Pentium's hardware reset.

12.16   Repeat Problem 12.14 using the Pentium NMI interrupt.

12.17   What are the factors to be considered for interfacing a hex keyboard to a microcomputer?

12.18   Will the circuit shown in Figure P12.18 work? If so, determine the I/O map using memory-mapped I/O in hex. If not, justify briefly, modify the circuit, and determine the I/O map using memory-mapped I/O in hex. Use only the pins and signals provided. Assume all don't cares to be zeros. Note that the I/O map includes the addresses for port A, port B, port C, and the control register. Do not change any connection in Figure P12.18. You may connect unconnected signals to HIGH, GROUND, or to other signals as appropriate. You may use logic gates if necessary. Assume no interrupts or DMA. Use pins and signals as needed. Assume real mode.
Using the logical port addresses, write a Pentium assembly language to input a switch connected at bit 7 of Port A, and output to an LED connected bit 7 of Port B. Initialize DS to 0010H.

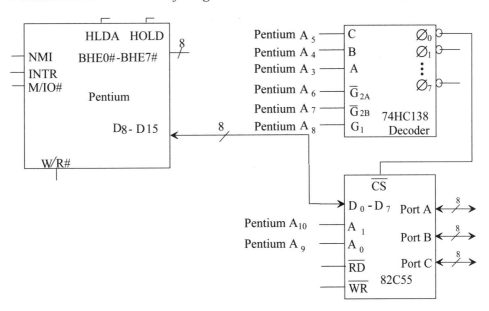

FIGURE P12.18

APPENDIX

ANSWERS TO SELECTED PROBLEMS

Chapter 2

2.1   Microprocessor: CPU in a single chip.

Single- chip Microcomputer : microprocessor, memory, and I/O in a single chip.

2.4 (a)   sign = 0, carry = 0, zero = 0, overflow = 0.
(d)   sign = 1, carry = 0, zero = 0, overflow = 1.

2.6 (a)   20BE
(b)   (20BE) = 05, (20BF) = 02.

2.11   Scalar microprocessor can execute one instruction per cycle. Intel 80486 is a scalar microprocessor.
Superscalar microprocessor can execute more than one instruction per cycle. Intel Pentium is a superscalar microprocessor.

Chapter 3

3.5 (a)   16,384
(b)   128 chips
(c)   4 bits

3.8 (a)   20
(b)   6 x 64 decoder

3.9   Maximum Directly Addressable Memory = 16 Megabytes;
14 unused address pins Available.

3.11   Memory Chip #1 EC00H - EDFFH
Memory Chip #2 F200H - F3FFH

3.12 (a)   ROM Map: 0000H - 07FFH
RAM Map: 2000H - 27FFH

3.21   Cache Tag Field = 1-bit
            Cache Index Field = 12-bits
            Cache Data Field = 32-bits

3.23   Cache word size = 36 bits.

Chapter 4

4.2   Using standard I/O, the microprocessor uses an output pin such as M/$\overline{\text{IO}}$ pin
            to distinguish between memory and I/O. Also, the microprocessor uses IN
            and OUT instructions to perform I/O operation in standard I/O.
            Using memory-mapped I/O, the microprocessor uses an unused address pin
            to distinguish between memory and I/O. The ports are mapped as memory
            locations. Memory-oriented instructions are used for performing I/O
            operation.

            Intel microprocessors can use either standard or memory-mapped I/O while
            Motorola microprocessors can use only memory-mapped I/O.

4.4   Memory-mapping provides the physical addresses for the microcomputer's
            main memory while memory-mapped I/O maps port addresses into memory
            locations.

4.7   Interrupt address vector is the starting address of the service routine.

4.10   Internal interrupt is generated by exceptional conditions such as division by
            zero where external interrupts are initiated via microprocessor's interrupt pins.

Chapter 5

5.2   Yes.

5.3   No.

5.7   Use the following identities:

            $a \oplus a = 0$ and $a \oplus 0 = a$ and $(a \oplus b) \oplus a = b$

5.8   Product = 0000 0000 0000 0100$_2$

5.9   Quotient = -8, Remainder = -1. The sign of the remainder is the same as the
            sign of the dividend unless remainder is zero.

Chapter 6

6.2   Supervisor mode.

6.7   TRAP occurs since odd address.

6.9(c)   Privileged

6.13 $0000 0000

6.14   MOVE.W   D1,D0
                 SWAP   D1
                 ADD   D0,D1
                 SWAP   D1
         FINISH JMP   FINISH

6.23   SWAP   D1
                 MOVE   D1,D0
                 EXT.L   D0
                 SWAP   D1
                 EXT.W   D1
                 DIVS   D1,D0
         FINISH JMP   FINISH

Chapter 7

7.2 $\overline{AS}$ = 0, FC2FC1FC0 = 101

          $\overline{LDS}$ = 1, $\overline{UDS}$ = 0

7.12   Memory map:
          even 2764 $000000,$000002,...,$003FFE
          odd 2764 $000001,$000003,...,$003FFF

          68230 I/O map: PGCR   = $004001,
          PADDR = $004005   PBDDR = $004007,
          PACR   = $00400D   PBCR   = $00400F,
          PADR   = $004011   PBDR   = $004013

Chapter 8

8.2   (D1.W) = $4567

8.4   CMP.L (0,A0,D5.L*2),D0

8.9

```
              ADD.L    D3,D0
              ADDX.L   D2,D1
   FINISH     JMP      FINISH
```

Chapter 9

9.8   *32-bit device: Byte data will be transferred via 68020 D_{15} - D_8 pins.
*8-bit device: Byte data will be transferred via D_{31} - D_{24} pins.

Chapter 10

10.2   20642H

10.4 (a)   Implied

10.6 (a)   (EAX) = 00000080H

10.8   (AL) = 05H, unpacked BCD for 5.

10.14

```
              .486
              .MODEL   FLAT,STDCALL
              .CODE
   PROG:
              ADD      EDX,EBX
              ADC      EAX,ECX
              HLT
   END        PROG
```

10.21   (AX) = 1234H

10.28

```
              .486
              .MODEL   SMALL,STDCALL
              .CODE
   PROG:
              MOV      AL,CH
              CBW
              IDIV     CL
              MOV      CL,AH
              MOV      CH,AL
              HLT
   END        PROG
```

10.29

```
                    .486
                    .MODEL     SMALL,STDCALL
                    .CODE
        PROG:
                    XCHG       BL,BH
                    MOV        BH,0
                    IDIV       BX
                    XCHG       DX,AX
                    HLT
        END         PROG
```

Chapter 11

11.3

```
                    .486
                    .MODEL     SMALL,STDCALL
                    .CODE
        PROG:
                    MOV        CX,4
        START:      CLC
                    RCR        DX,1
                    RCR        AX,1
                    LOOP       START
                    MOV        CX,3
        DIVIDE:     CLC
                    RCR        DX,1
                    RCR        AX,1
                    LOOP       DIVIDE
                    HLT
        END         PROG
```

11.6

Assuming segment registers are already initialized

```
                    .486
                    .MODEL     SMALL,STDCALL
                    .CODE
        PROG:
                    CLD
                    MOV        SI,  0010H
                    MOV        DI,  0100H
                    MOV        CX,100
                    ES: REPMOVSW
                    HLT
        END         PROG
```

11.7

```
                    .486
                    .MODEL     SMALL,STDCALL
                    .CODE
        PROG:
                    MOV        BX,0020H
                    MOV        DS,BX
                    MOV        BX,1000H
                    MOV        ES,BX
                    MOV        AX,0500H
                    MOV        SS,AX
                    MOV        SP,2000H
                    MOV        CX,15
                    MOV        SI,5000H
                    MOV        DI,6000H
                    CLD
                    REPNE CMPSB
                    JZ         START
                    MOV        AX,0000H
                    PUSH       AX
                    HLT
        START:      MOV        AX,00EEH
                    PUSH       AX
                    HLT
        END         PROG
```

11.8

```
                    .486
                    .MODEL  SMALL,STDCALL
                    .CODE
        PROG:
                    MOV        SI,4000H
                    MOV        DI,5000H
                    MOV        CX,100
                    CLD
                    REP        MOVSD
                    HLT
        END         PROG
```

Chapter 12

12.9

```
                        .486
                        .MODEL      SMALL,STDCALL
                        .CODE
            PROG:
                        MOV         CL,4
                        MOV         AL,90H
                        OUT         CNTRL,AL
                        MOV         BL,0
            BACK:       IN          AL,PORTA
                        RCR         AL,1
                        JC          START
                        INC         BL
            START:      DEC         CL
                        JNZ         BACK
                        RCR         BL,1
                        JNC         LEDON
                        MOV         AL,0
                        OUT         PORTB,AL
                        HLT
            LEDON:      MOV         AL,10H
                        OUT         PORTB,AL
                        HLT
            END         PROG
```

12.12

```
                        .486
                        .MODEL      SMALL,STDCALL
                        .CODE
            PROG:
                        MOV         AL,89H
                        OUT         CNTRL,AL
                        MOV         CL,3
                        MOV         AL,0FFH
                        OUT         PORTB,AL
                        NOP
                        IN          AL,PORTC
                        RCR         AL,CL
                        JC          LED
                        MOV         AL,0FEH
                        OUT         PORTB,AL
                        NOP
                        IN          AL,PORTC
                        RCR         AL,CL
                        JNC         LED
                        MOV         AL,0FDH
```

```
            OUT     PORTB,AL
            NOP
            IN      AL,PORTC
            RCR     AL,CL
            JNC     LED
            MOV     AL,0FCH
            OUT     PORTB,AL
            NOP
            IN      AL,PORTC
            RCR     AL,CL
            JNC     LED
            MOV     AL,10H
            OUT     PORTA,AL
            HLT
LED:        MOV     AL,08H
            OUT     PORTA,AL
            HLT
END         PROG
```

APPENDIX

B

GLOSSARY

Absolute Addressing: This addressing mode specifies the address of data with the instruction.

Accumulator: Register used for storing the result after most ALU operations; available with 8-bit microprocessors.

Address: A unique identification number (or locator) for source or destination of data. An address specifies the register or memory location of an operand involved in the instruction.

Addressing Mode: The manner in which a microprocessor determines the effective address of source and destination operands in an instruction.

Address Register: A register used to store the address (memory location) of data.

Address Space: The number of storage location in a microcomputer's memory that can be directly addressed by the microprocessor. The addressing range is determined by the number of address pins provided with the microprocessor chip.

American Standard Code for Information Interchange (ASCII): An 8-bit code commonly used with microprocessors for representing alphanumeric codes.

Analog-to-Digital (A/D) Converter: Transforms an analog voltage into its digital equivalent.

AND gate: The output is 1, if all inputs are 1; otherwise the output is 0.

Arithmetic and Logic Unit (ALU): A digital circuit which performs arithmetic and logic operations on two n-bit numbers.

ASIC: Application Specific IC. Chips designed for a specific, limited application. Normally reduces the total manufacturing cost of a product by reducing chip count.

Assembler: A program that translates an assembly language program into a machine language program.

Assembly Language: A type of microprocessor programming language that uses a semi-English-language statement.

Asynchronous Operation: The execution of a sequence of steps such that each step is initiated upon completion of the previous step.

Asynchronous Serial Data Transmission: The transmitting device does not need to be synchronized with the receiving device.

Autodecrement Addressing Mode: The contents of the specified microprocessor register are first decremented by n (1 for byte, 2 for 16-bit, and 4 for 32-bit) and then the resulting value is used as the address of the operand.

Autoincrement Addressing Mode: The contents of a specified microprocessor register are used as the address of the operand first and then the register contents are automatically incremented by n (1 for byte, 2 for 16-bit, and 4 for 32-bit).

Barrel Shifter: A specially configured shift register that is normally included in 32-bit microprocessors for cycle rotation. That is , the barrel shifter shifts data in one direction.

Base address: An address that is used to convert all relative addresses in a program to absolute (machine) addresses.

Baud Rate: Rate of data transmission in bits per second.

Binary-Coded Decimal (BCD):   The representation of 10 decimal digits, 0 through 9, by their corresponding 4-bit binary number.

Bit: An abbreviation for a binary digit. A unit of information equal to one of two possible states (one or zero, on or off, true or false).

Block Transfer DMA: A peripheral device requests the DMA transfer via the DMA request line, which is connected directly or through a DMA controller chip to the microprocessor. The DMA controller chip completes the DMA transfer and transfers the control of the bus to the microprocessor.

Branch: The branch instruction allows the computer to skip or jump out of program sequence to a designated instruction either unconditionally or conditionally (based on conditions such as carry or sign).

Breakpoint: Allows the user to execute the section of a program until one of the breakpoint conditions is met. It is then halted. The designer may then single step or examine memory and registers. Typically breakpoint conditions are program counter address or data references. Breakpoints are used in debugging assembly language programs.

Buffer: A temporary memory storage device deigned to compensate for the different data rates between a transmitting device and a receiving device (for example, between a CPU and a peripheral). Current amplifiers are also referred to as buffers.

Bus: A collection of wires that interconnects computer modules. The typical microcomputer interface includes separate buses for address, data, control, and power functions.

Bus Arbitration: Bus operation protocols (rules) that guarantee conflict-free access to a bus. Arbitration is the process of selecting one respondent from a collection of several candidates that concurrently request service.

Bus Cycle: The period of time in which a microprocessor carries out read or write operations.

Cache Memory: A high speed, directly accessible, relatively small, semiconductor read/write memory block used to store data/instructions that the microcomputer may need in the immediate future. Increases speed by reducing the number of external memory reads required by the processor. Typical 32 and 64-bit microprocessors are normally provided with on-chip cache memory.

CD (Compact Disc) Memory: Optical memory. Uses laser and stores audio information.

Central Processing Unit (CPU): The brains of a computer containing the ALU, register section, and control unit. CPU in a single chip is called microprocessor.

Chip: An Integrated Circuit (IC) package containing digital circuits.

CISC: Complex Instruction Set Computer. The Control unit is designed using microprogramming. Contains a large instruction set. Difficult to pipeline compared to RISC.

Clock: Timing signals providing synchronization among the various components in a microcomputer system. Analogous to heart beats of a human being.

CMOS: Complementary MOS. Dissipates low power, offers high density and speed compared to TTL.

Combinational Circuit: Output is provided upon application of inputs; contains no memory.

Compiler: A program which translates the source code written in a high-level programming language into machine language that is understandable to the processor.

Condition Code Register: Contains information such as carry, sign, zero, and overflow based on ALU operations.

Control Unit: Part of the CPU; its purpose is to translate or decode instructions read (fetched) from the main memory into the Instruction Register.

Coprocessor: A companion microprocessor that performs specific functions such as floating-point operations independently from the microprocessor to speed up overall operations.

Cycle Stealing DMA: The DMA controller transfers a byte of data between the microcomputer's memory and a peripheral device such as the disk by stealing a clock cycle of microprocessor.

Data: Basic elements of information represented in binary form (that is, digits consisting of bits) that can be processed or produced by a microcomputer. Data represents any group of operands made up of numbers, letters, or symbols denoting any condition, value, or state. Typical microcomputer operand sizes include: a word, which typically contains 2 bytes or 16-bits; a long word, which contains 4 bytes or 32 bits; a quad word, which contains 8 bytes or 64 bits.

Data Register: A register used to temporarily hold operational data being sent to and from a peripheral device.

Debugger: A program that executes and debugs the object program generated by the assembler or compiler. The debugger provides a single stepping, breakpoints, and program tracing.

Decoder: A chip, when enabled, selects one of 2^n output lines based on n inputs.

Digital to Analog (D/A) Converter: Converts binary number to analog signal.

Diode: Two terminal electronic switch.

Direct Memory Access (DMA):   A type of input/output technique in which data can be transferred between the microcomputer memory and external devices without the microprocessor's involvement.

Directly Addressable Memory: The memory address space in which the microprocessor can directly execute programs. The maximum directly addressable memory is determined by the number of the microprocessor's address pins.

DRAM: See Dynamic RAM.

Dynamic RAM: Stores data as charges in capacitors and therefore, must be refreshed since capacitors can hold charges for a few milliseconds. Hence, requires refresh circuitry.

EAROM (Electrically Alterable Read-Only Memory):   Same as EEPROM or E^2 PROM. Can be programmed one line at a time without removing the memory from its sockets. This memory is also called read-mostly memory since it has much slower write times than read times.

Editor: A program that produces an error-free source program, written in assembly or high-level languages.

EEPROM or E² PROM: Same as EAROM (see EAROM).

Effective Address: The final address used to carry out an instruction. Determined by the addressing mode.

Emulator: A hardware device that allows a microcomputer system to emulate (that is, mimic) another microcomputer system.

Encoder: Performs reverse operation of a decoder. Contains a maximum of 2^n inputs and n outputs.

EPROM (Erasable Programmable Read-Only Memory):   Can be programmed and erased all programs in an EPROM chip using ultraviolet light. The chip must be removed from the microcomputer system for programming.

Exception Processing: Includes the microprocessor's processing states associated with interrupts, trap instructions, tracing, and other exceptional conditions, whether they are initiated internally or externally.

Exclusive-OR: The output is 0, if inputs are same; otherwise; the output is 1.

Exclusive-NOR: The output is 1, if inputs are same; otherwise, the output is 0.

Extended Binary-Coded Decimal Interchange Code (EBCDIC):   An 8-bit code commonly used with microprocessors for representing alphanumeric codes. Normally used by IBM.

Firmware: Microprogram is sometimes referred to as firmware to distinguish it from hardwired control (purely hardware method).

Flag(s):   An indicator, often a single bit, to indicate some conditions such as trace, carry, zero, and overflow.

Flash Memory: Utilizes a combination of EPROM and EEPROM technologies. Used in cellular phones and digital cameras.

Flip-Flop: One-bit memory.

FPGA: Field Programmable Gate Arrays. This chip contains several smaller individual logic blocks along with all interconnections.

Gate: Digital circuits which perform logic operations.

Handshaking: Data transfer via exchange of control signals between the microprocessor and an external device.

Hardware: The physical electronic circuits (chips) that make up the microcomputer system.

Hardwired Control: Used for designing the control unit using all hardware.

HCMOS: High speed CMOS. Provides high density and consumes low power.

Hexadecimal Number System: Base-16 number system.

High-Level Language: A type of programming language that uses a more understandable human-oriented language such as C.

HMOS: High-density MOS reduces the channel length of the NMOS transistor and provides increased density and speed in VLSI circuits.

Immediate Address: An address that is used as an operand by the instruction itself.

Implied Address: An address is not specified, but is contained implicitly in the instruction.

In-Circuit Emulation: The most powerful hardware debugging technique; especially valuable when hardware and software are being debugged simultaneously.

Index: A number (typically 8-bit signed or 16-bit unsigned) is used to identify a particular element in an array (string). The index value typically contained in a register is utilized by the indexed addressing mode.

Indexed Addressing: The effective address of the instruction is determined by the sum of the address and the contents of the index register. Used to access arrays.

Index Register: A register used to hold a value used in indexing data, such as when a value is used in indexed addressing to increment a base address contained within an instruction.

Indirect Address: A register holding a memory address to be accessed.

Instruction: Causes the microprocessor to carry out an operation on data. A program contains instructions and data.

Instruction Cycle: The sequence of operations that a microprocessor has to carry out while executing an instruction.

Instruction Register (IR):   A register storing instructions; typically 32 bits long for a 32-bit microprocessor.

Instruction Set: Lists all the instructions that the microcomputer can execute.

Interleaved DMA: Using this technique, the DMA controller takes over the system bus when the microprocessor is not using it.

Internal Interrupt: Activated internally by exceptional conditions such as overflow and division by zero.

Interpreter: A program that executes a set of machine language instructions in response to each high-level statement in order to carry out the function.

Interrupt I/O: An external device can force the microcomputer system to stop executing the current program temporarily so that it can execute another program known as the interrupt service routine.

Interrupts: A temporary break in a sequence of a program, initiated externally or internally, causing control to jump to a routine, which performs some action while the program is stopped.

I/O (Input/Output): Describes that portion of a microcomputer system that exchanges data between the microcomputer system and an external device.

I/O Port: A register that contains control logic and data storage used to connect a microcomputer to external peripherals.

Inverting Buffer: Performs NOT operation. Current amplifier.

Keyboard: Has a number of push button-type switches configured in a matrix form (rows x columns).

Keybounce: When a mechanical switch opens or closes, it bounces (vibrates) for a small period of time (about 10-20 ms) before settling down.

Large-Scale Integration (LSI): An LSI chip contains 100 to 1000 gates.

LED: Light Emitting Diode. Typically, a current of 10 ma to 20 ma flows at 1.7v to 2.4v drop across it.

Logic Analyzer: A hardware development aid for microprocessor-based design; gathers data on the fly and displays it.

Logical Address Space: All storage locations with a programmer's addressing range.

Loops: A programming control structure where a sequence of microcomputer instructions are executed repeatedly (looped) until a terminating condition (result) is satisfied.

Machine Code: A binary code (composed of 1's and 0's) that a microcomputer understands.

Machine Language: A type of microprocessor programming language that uses binary or hexadecimal numbers.

Macroinstruction: Commonly known as an instruction; initiates execution of a complete microprogram. Example includes assembly language instructions.

Macroprogram: The assembly language program.

Mask: A pattern of bits used to specify (or mask) which bit parts of another bit pattern are to be operated on and which bits are to be ignored or "masked" out. Uses logical AND operation.

Mask ROM: Programmed by a masking operation performed on the chip during the manufacturing process; its contents cannot be changed by user.

Maskable Interrupt: Can be enabled or disabled by executing typically the interrupt instructions.

Memory: Any storage device which can accept, retain, and read back data.

Memory Access Time: Average time taken to read a unit of information from the memory.

Memory Address Register (MAR):   Stores the address of the data.

Memory Cycle Time: Average time lapse between two successive read operations.

Memory Management Unit (MMU):   Hardware that performs address translation and protection functions.

Memory Map: A representation of the physical locations within a microcomputer's addressable main memory.

Memory-Mapped I/O: I/O ports are mapped as memory locations, with every connected device treated as if it were a memory location with a specific address. Manipulation of I/O data occurs in "interface registers" (as opposed to memory locations); hence there are no input (read) or output (write) instructions used in memory-mapped I/O.

Microcode: A set of instructions called "microinstructions" usually stored in a ROM in the control unit of a microprocessor to translate instructions of a higher-level programming language such as assembly language programming.

Microcomputer: Consists of a microprocessor, a memory unit, and an input/output unit.

Microcontroller: Typically includes a microcomputer, timer, A/D (Analog to Digital) and D/A (Digital to Analog) converters in the same chip.

Microinstruction: Most microprocessors have an internal memory called control memory. This memory is used to store a number of codes called microinstructions. These microinstructions are combined to design the instruction set of the microprocessor.

Microprocessor: CPU on a single chip. The Central Processing Unit (CPU) of a microcomputer.

Microprocessor Development System: A tool for designing and debugging both hardware and software for microcomputer-based system.

Microprocessor-Halt DMA: Data transfer is performed between the microcomputer's memory and a peripheral device either by completely stopping the microprocessor or by a technique called cycle stealing.

Microprogramming: The microprocessor can use microprogramming to design the instruction set. Each instruction in the Instruction register initiates execution of a microprogram stored typically in ROM inside the control unit to perform the required operation.

Monitor: Consists of a number of subroutines grouped together to provide "intelligence" to a microcomputer system. This intelligence gives the microcomputer system the capabilities for debugging a user program, system design, and displays.

Multiplexer: A hardware device which selects one of n input lines and produces it on the output.

Multiprocessing: The process of executing two or more programs in parallel, handled by multiple processors all under common control. Typically each processor will be assigned specific processing tasks.

Multitasking: Operating system software that permits more than one program to run on a single microprocessor. Even though each program is given a small time slice in which to execute, the user has the impression that all tasks (different programs) are executing at the same time.

Multiuser: Describes a computer operating system that permits a number of users to access the system on a time-sharing basis.

Nanomemory: Two-level ROM used in designing the control unit.

Nested Subroutine: A commonly used programming technique in which one subroutine calls another subroutine.

Nibble: A 4-bit word.

Non-inverting Buffer: Input is same as output. Current amplifier.

Nonmaskable Interrupt: Occurrence of this type of interrupt cannot be ignored by microcomputer and even though interrupt capability of the microprocessor is disabled. Its effect cannot be disabled by instruction.

Non-Multiplexed: A non-multiplexed microprocessor pin that assigns a unique function as opposed to a multiplexed microprocessor pin defining two functions on time-shared basis.

Object Code: The binary (machine) code into which a source program is translated by a compiler, assembler, or interpreter.

Ones Complement: Obtained by changing 1's to ' 0's, and 0's to 1's of a binary number.

One-Pass Assembler: This assembler goes through the assembly language program once and translates the assembly language program into a machine language program. This assembler has the problem of defining forward references. See Two-Pass Assembler.

Op Code (Operation Code):   Part of an instruction defining the operation to be performed.

Operand: A datum or information item involved in an operation from which the result is obtained as a consequence of defined addressing modes. Various operand types contain information, such as source address, destination address, or immediate data.

Operating System: Consists of a number of program modules to provide resource management. Typical resources include microprocessors, disks, and printers.

Page: Some microprocessors, divide the memory locations into equal blocks. Each of these blocks is called a page and contains several addresses.

Parallel Operation: Any operation carried out simultaneously with a related operation.

Parallel Transmission: Each bit of binary data is transmitted over a separate wire.

Parity: The number of 1's in a word is odd for odd parity and even for even parity.

Peripheral: An I/O device capable of being operated under the control of a CPU through communication channels. Examples include disk drives, keyboards, CRT's, printers, and modems.

Personal Computer: Low-cost, affordable microcomputer normally used by an individual for word processing and Internet applications.

Physical Address Space: Address space is defined by the address pins of the microprocessor.

Pipeline: A technique that allows a microcomputer processing operation to be broken down into several steps (dictated by the number of pipeline levels or stages) so that the individual step outputs can be handled by the microcomputer in parallel. Often used to fetch the processor's next instruction while executing the current instruction, which considerably speeds up the overall operation of the microcomputer. Overlaps instruction fetch with execution.

Pointer: A storage location (usually a register within a microprocessor) that contains the address of (or points to) a required item of data or subroutine.

Polled Interrupt: A software approach for determining the source of interrupt in a multiple interrupt system.

POP Operation: Reading from the top or bottom of stack.

Port: A register through which the microcomputers communicate with peripheral devices.

Primary or Main Memory: Storage that is considered as part of the microcomputer. The microcomputer can directly execute all instructions in the main memory. The maximum size of the main memory is defined by the number of address pins in the microprocessor.

Privileged Instructions: An instruction which can only be executed by the microprocessor in the supervisor (operating system) mode.

Processor Memory: A set of microprocessor registers for holding temporary results when a computation is in progress.

Program: A self-contained sequence of computer software instructions (source code) that, when converted into machine code, directs the computer to perform specific operations for the purpose of accomplishing some processing task. Contains instructions and data.

Program Counter (PC):   A register that normally contains the address of the next instruction to be executed in a program.

Programmed I/O: The microprocessor executes a program to perform all data transfers between the microcomputer system and external devices.

PROM (Programmable Read-Only Memory):   Can be programmed by the user by using proper equipment. Once programmed, its contents cannot be altered.

Protocol: A list of data transmission rules or procedures that encompass the timing, control, formatting, and data representations by which two devices are to communicate. Also known as hardware "handshaking", which is used to permit asynchronous communication.

PUSH Operation: Writing to the top or bottom of stack.

Random Access Memory (RAM):   A read/write memory. RAMs (static or dynamic) are volatile in nature (in other words, information is lost when power is removed).

Read-Only-Memory (ROM):   A memory in which any addressable operand can be read from, but not written to, after initial programming. ROM storage is nonvolatile (information is not lost after removal of power).

Reduced Instruction Set Computer (RISC):   A simple instruction set is included. The RISC architecture maximizes speed by reducing clock cycles per instruction. The control unit is designed using hardwired control. Easier to implement pipelining.

Register: A high-speed memory usually constructed from flip-flops that are directly accessible to the microprocessor. It can contain either data or a specific location in memory that stores word(s) used during arithmetic, logic, and transfer operations.

Register Indirect: Uses a register which contains the address of data.

Relative Address: An address used to designate the position of a memory location in a routine or program.

RISC: See Reduced Instruction Set Computer.

Routine: A group of instructions for carrying out a specific processing operation. Usually refers to part of a larger program. A routine and subroutine have essentially the same meaning, but a subroutine could be interpreted as a self-contained routine nested within a routine or program.

Scalar Microprocessor: Provided with one pipeline. Allows execution rate of one clock cycle per instruction for most instructions. The 80486 is a scalar microprocessor.

Scaling: Multiplying an index register by 1,2,4 or 8. Used by the addressing modes of typical 32- and 64-bit microprocessors.

Schmitt Trigger: An analog circuit that provides high noise immunity.

SDRAM: Synchronous DRAM. This chip contains several DRAMs internally. The control signals and address inputs are sampled by the SDRAM by a common clock.

Secondary Memory Storage: An auxiliary data storage device that supplements the main (primary) memory of a microcomputer. It is used to hold programs and data that would otherwise exceed the capacity of the main memory. Although it has a much slower access time, secondary storage is less expensive. Examples include floppy and hard disks.

Sequential Circuit: Combinational circuit with memory.

Serial Transmission: Only one line is used to transmit the complete binary data bit by bit.

Server: Large computer performing actual work on the Internet.

Seven-Segment LED: Contains an LED in each of the seven segments. Can display numbers.

Single-Chip Microcomputer: Microcomputer (CPU, memory, and input/output) on a chip.

Single-chip Microprocessor: Microcomputer CPU (microprocessor) on a chip.

Single Step: Allows the user to execute a program one instruction at a time and examine contents of memory locations and registers.

Software: Programs in a microcomputer.

Source Code: The assembly language program written by a programmer using assembly language instructions. This code must be translated to the object (machine) code by the assembler before it can be executed by the microcomputer.

SRAM: See Static RAM.

Stack: An area of read/write memory typically used by a microcomputer during subroutine calls or occurrence of an interrupt. The microcomputer saves in the stack the contents of the program counter before executing the subroutine or program counter contents and other status information before executing the interrupt service routine. Thus, the microcomputer can return to the main program after execution of the subroutine or the interrupt service routine. The stack is a last in/first out (LIFO) read/write memory (RAM) that can also be manipulated by the programmer using PUSH and POP instructions.

Stack Pointer: A register used to address the stack.

Standard I/O: Utilizes a control pin on the microprocessor chip typically called the M/$\overline{\text{IO}}$ pin, in order to distinguish between input/output and memory; IN and OUT instructions are used for input/output operations.

Static RAM: Also known as **SRAM**. Stores data in flip-flops; does not need to be refreshed. Information is lost upon power failure unless backed up by battery.

Status Register: A register which contains information concerning the flags in a processor.

Subroutine: A program carrying out a particular function and which can be called by another program known as the main program. A subroutine needs to be placed only once in memory and can be called by the main program as many times as the programmer wants.

Superscalar Microprocessor: Provided with more than one pipeline and executes more than one instruction per clock cycle. The Pentium is a superscalar microprocessor.

Supervisor State: When the microprocessor processing operations are conducted at a higher privilege level, it is usually in the supervisor state. An operating system typically executes in the supervisor state to protect the integrity of "basic" system operations from user influences.

Synchronous Operation: Operations that occur at intervals directly related to a clock period.

Synchronous Sequential Circuit: The present outputs depend on the present inputs and the previous states stored in flip-flops.

Synchronous Serial Data Transmission: Data is transmitted or received based on a clock signal.

Tracing: Allows single stepping. A dynamic diagnostic technique permits analysis (debugging) of the program's execution.

Transistor: Electronic switch; performs NOT; current amplifier.

Tristate Buffer: Has three output states: logic 0, 1, and a high-impedance state. This chip is typically enabled by a control signal to provide logic 0 or 1 outputs. This type of buffer can also be disabled by the control signal to place it in a high-impedance state.

Two's Complement: The two's complement of a binary number is obtained by replacing each 0 with a 1 and each 1 with a 0 and adding one to the resulting number.

Two-Pass Assembler: This assembler goes through the assembly language program twice. In the first pass, the assembler assigns binary addresses to labels. In the second pass, the assembly program is translated to the machine language. No problem with forward branching.

User State: Typical microprocessor operations processing conducted at the user level. The user state is usually at lower privilege level than the supervisor state. In the user mode, the microprocessor can execute a subset of its instruction set, and allows protection of basic system resources by providing use of the operating system in the supervisor state. This is very useful in multiuser/multitasking systems.

Vectored Interrupts: A device identification technique in which the highest priority device with a pending interrupt request forces program execution to branch to an interrupt routine to handle exception processing for the device.

Very Large Scale Integration (VLSI):   a VLSI chip contains more than 1000 gates. More commonly, a VLSI chip is identified by the number of transistors rather than the gate count.

Virtual Memory: An operating system technique that allows programs or data to exceed the physical size of the main, internal, directly accessible memory of the microcomputer. Program or data segments/pages are swapped from external disk storage as needed. The swapping is invisible (transparent) to the programmer. Therefore, the programmer does need not to be concerned with the actual physical size of internal memory while writing the code.

Word: The bit size of a microprocessor refers to the number of bits that can be processed simultaneously by the basic arithmetic and logic circuits of the microprocessor. A number of bits taken as a group in this manner is called a word.

APPENDIX

C

MOTOROLA 68000 AND SUPPORT CHIPS

 MOTOROLA

Advance Information

16-BIT MICROPROCESSING UNIT

Advances in semiconductor technology have provided the capability to place on a single silicon chip a microprocessor at least an order of magnitude higher in performance and circuit complexity than has been previously available. The MC68000 is the first of a family of such VLSI microprocessors from Motorola. It combines state-of-the-art technology and advanced circuit design techniques with computer sciences to achieve an architecturally advanced 16-bit microprocessor.

The resources available to the MC68000 user consist of the following:

- 32-Bit Data and Address Registers
- 16 Megabyte Direct Addressing Range
- 56 Powerful Instruction Types
- Operations on Five Main Data Types
- Memory Mapped I/O
- 14 Addressing Modes

As shown in the programming model, the MC68000 offers seventeen 32-bit registers in addition to the 32-bit program counter and a 16-bit status register. The first eight registers (D0-D7) are used as data registers for byte (8-bit), word (16-bit), and long word (32-bit) data operations. The second set of seven registers (A0-A6) and the system stack pointer may be used as software stack pointers and base address registers. In addition, these registers may be used for word and long word address operations. All seventeen registers may be used as index registers.

MC68000L4
(4 MHz)
MC68000L6
(6 MHz)
MC68000L8
(8 MHz)
MC68000L10
(10 MHz)

HMOS
(HIGH-DENSITY, N-CHANNEL, SILICON-GATE DEPLETION LOAD)

16-BIT MICROPROCESSOR

L SUFFIX
CERAMIC PACKAGE
CASE 746

64-pin dual in-line package

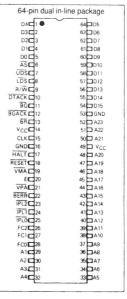

D4 ⨽1	64⨼ D5
D3 ⨽2	63⨼ D6
D2 ⨽3	62⨼ D7
D1 ⨽4	61⨼ D8
D0 ⨽5	60⨼ D9
$\overline{AS}$ ⨽6	59⨼ D10
$\overline{UDS}$ ⨽7	58⨼ D11
$\overline{LDS}$ ⨽8	57⨼ D12
R/$\overline{W}$ ⨽9	56⨼ D13
$\overline{DTACK}$ ⨽10	55⨼ D14
$\overline{BG}$ ⨽11	54⨼ D15
$\overline{BGACK}$ ⨽12	53⨼ GND
$\overline{BR}$ ⨽13	52⨼ A23
V$_{CC}$ ⨽14	51⨼ A22
CLK ⨽15	50⨼ A21
GND ⨽16	49⨼ V$_{CC}$
$\overline{HALT}$ ⨽17	48⨼ A20
$\overline{RESET}$ ⨽18	47⨼ A19
$\overline{VMA}$ ⨽19	46⨼ A18
E ⨽20	45⨼ A17
$\overline{VPA}$ ⨽21	44⨼ A16
$\overline{BERR}$ ⨽22	43⨼ A15
$\overline{IPL2}$ ⨽23	42⨼ A14
$\overline{IPL1}$ ⨽24	41⨼ A13
$\overline{IPL0}$ ⨽25	40⨼ A12
FC2 ⨽26	39⨼ A11
FC1 ⨽27	38⨼ A10
FC0 ⨽28	37⨼ A9
A1 ⨽29	36⨼ A8
A2 ⨽30	35⨼ A7
A3 ⨽31	34⨼ A6
A4 ⨽32	33⨼ A5

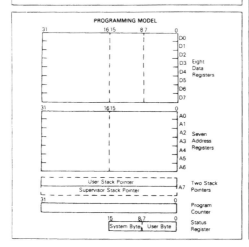

PROGRAMMING MODEL

Eight Data Registers (D0–D7)

Seven Address Registers (A0–A6)

User Stack Pointer / Supervisor Stack Pointer — A7, Two Stack Pointers

Program Counter

Status Register — System Byte, User Byte

68-Terminal Chip Carrier

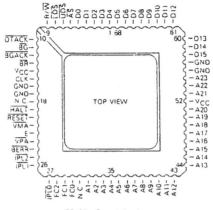

68-Pin Quad Pack

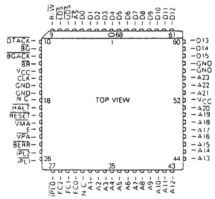

68-pin grid array.

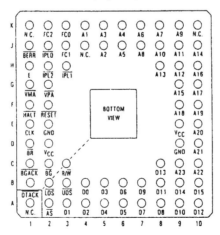

 **MOTOROLA**

| MC68230L8 |
| MC68230L10 |

Advance Information

HMOS
(HIGH-DENSITY N-CHANNEL
SILICON-GATE)

PARALLEL INTERFACE/TIMER

MC68230 PARALLEL INTERFACE/TIMER

The MC68230 Parallel Interface/Timer provides versatile double-buffered parallel interfaces and an operating system oriented timer to MC68000 systems. The parallel interfaces operate in unidirectional or bidirectional modes, either 8 or 16 bits wide. In the unidirectional modes, an associated data direction register determines whether the port pins are inputs or outputs. In the bidirectional modes the data direction registers are ignored and the direction is determined dynamically by the state of four handshake pins. These programmable handshake pins provide an interface flexible enough for connection to a wide variety of low, medium, or high speed peripherals or other computer systems. The PI/T ports allow use of vectored or autovectored interrupts, and also provide a DMA Request pin for connection to the MC68450 Direct Memory Access Controller or a similar circuit. The PI/T timer contains a 24-bit wide counter and a 5-bit prescaler. The timer may be clocked by the system clock (PI/T CLK pin) or by an external clock (TIN pin), and a 5-bit prescaler can be used. It can generate periodic interrupts, a square wave, or a single interrupt after a programmed time period. Also it can be used for elapsed time measurement or as a device watchdog.

- MC68000 Bus Compatible
- Port Modes Include:
  Bit I/O
  Unidirectional 8-Bit and 16-Bit
  Bidirectional 8-Bit and 16-Bit
- Selectable Handshaking Options
- 24-Bit Programmable Timer
- Software Programmable Timer Modes
- Contains Interrupt Vector Generation Logic
- Separate Port and Timer Interrupt Service Requests
- Registers are Read/Write and Directly Addressable
- Registers are Addressed for MOVEP (Move Peripheral) and DMAC Compatibility

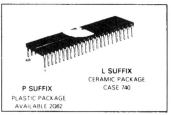

L SUFFIX
CERAMIC PACKAGE
CASE 740

P SUFFIX
PLASTIC PACKAGE
AVAILABLE 2Q82

PIN ASSIGNMENT

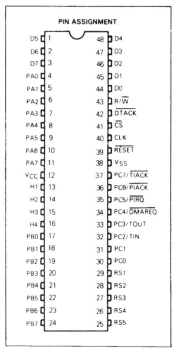

D5	1	48	D4
D6	2	47	D3
D7	3	46	D2
PA0	4	45	D1
PA1	5	44	D0
PA2	6	43	R/W̄
PA3	7	42	DTACK
PA4	8	41	C̄S̄
PA5	9	40	CLK
PA6	10	39	RESET
PA7	11	38	VSS
VCC	12	37	PC7/TIACK
H1	13	36	PC6/PIACK
H2	14	35	PC5/PIRQ
H3	15	34	PC4/DMAREQ
H4	16	33	PC3/TOUT
PB0	17	32	PC2/TIN
PB1	18	31	PC1
PB2	19	30	PC0
PB3	20	29	RS1
PB4	21	28	RS2
PB5	22	27	RS3
PB6	23	26	RS4
PB7	24	25	RS5

 **MOTOROLA**

MC6821 **(1.0 MHz)**	
MC68A21 **(1.5 MHz)**	
MC68B21 **(2.0 MHz)**	

PERIPHERAL INTERFACE ADAPTER (PIA)

The MC6821 Peripheral Interface Adapter provides the universal means of interfacing peripheral equipment to the M6800 family of microprocessors. This device is capable of interfacing the MPU to peripherals through two 8-bit bidirectional peripheral data buses and four control lines. No external logic is required for interfacing to most peripheral devices.

The functional configuration of the PIA is programmed by the MPU during system initialization. Each of the peripheral data lines can be programmed to act as an input or output, and each of the four control/interrupt lines may be programmed for one of several control modes. This allows a high degree of flexibility in the overall operation of the interface.

- 8-Bit Bidirectional Data Bus for Communication with the MPU
- Two Bidirectional 8-Bit Buses for Interface to Peripherals
- Two Programmable Control Registers
- Two Programmable Data Direction Registers
- Four Individually-Controlled Interrupt Input Lines; Two Usable as Peripheral Control Outputs
- Handshake Control Logic for Input and Output Peripheral Operation
- High-Impedance Three-State and Direct Transistor Drive Peripheral Lines
- Program Controlled Interrupt and Interrupt Disable Capability
- CMOS Drive Capability on Side A Peripheral Lines
- Two TTL Drive Capability on All A and B Side Buffers
- TTL-Compatible
- Static Operation

MOS
(N-CHANNEL, SILICON-GATE, DEPLETION LOAD)

PERIPHERAL INTERFACE ADAPTER

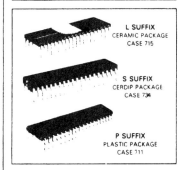

L SUFFIX
CERAMIC PACKAGE
CASE 715

S SUFFIX
CERDIP PACKAGE
CASE 734

P SUFFIX
PLASTIC PACKAGE
CASE 711

PIN ASSIGNMENT

V$_{SS}$	1	40	CA1
PA0	2	39	CA2
PA1	3	38	$\overline{\text{IRQA}}$
PA2	4	37	$\overline{\text{IRQB}}$
PA3	5	36	RS0
PA4	6	35	RS1
PA5	7	34	$\overline{\text{RESET}}$
PA6	8	33	D0
PA7	9	32	D1
PB0	10	31	D2
PB1	11	30	D3
PB2	12	29	D4
PB3	13	28	D5
PB4	14	27	D6
PB5	15	26	D7
PB6	16	25	E
PB7	17	24	CS1
CB1	18	23	$\overline{\text{CS2}}$
CB2	19	22	CS0
VCC	20	21	R/$\overline{\text{W}}$

MAXIMUM RATINGS

Characteristics	Symbol	Value	Unit
Supply Voltage	V$_{CC}$	− 0.3 to + 7.0	V
Input Voltage	V$_{in}$	− 0.3 to + 7.0	V
Operating Temperature Range MC6821, MC68A21, MC68B21 MC6821C, MC68A21C, MC68B21C	T$_A$	T$_L$ to T$_H$ 0 to 70 − 40 to + 85	°C
Storage Temperature Range	T$_{stg}$	− 55 to + 150	°C

THERMAL CHARACTERISTICS

Characteristic	Symbol	Value	Unit
Thermal Resistance Ceramic Plastic Cerdip	θ$_{JA}$	50 100 60	°C/W

This device contains circuitry to protect the inputs against damage due to high static voltages or electric fields; however, it is advised that normal precautions be taken to avoid application of any voltage higher than maximum-rated voltages to this high-impedance circuit. Reliability of operation is enhanced if unused inputs are tied to an appropriate logic voltage (i.e., either V$_{SS}$ or V$_{CC}$)

Expanded block diagram of the MC6821

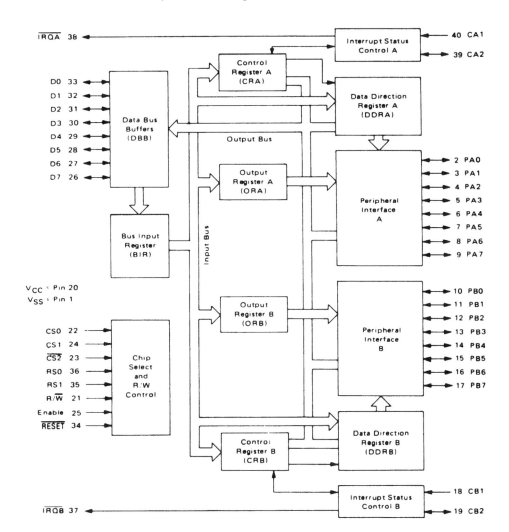

PIA INTERFACE SIGNALS FOR MPU

The PIA interfaces to the M6800 bus with an 8-bit bidirectional data bus, three chip select lines, two register select lines, two interrupt request lines, a read/write line, an enable line and a reset line. To ensure proper operation with the MC6800, MC6802, or MC6808 microprocessors, VMA should be used as an active part of the address decoding.

Bidirectional Data (D0-D7) — The bidirectional data lines (D0-D7) allow the transfer of data between the MPU and the PIA. The data bus output drivers are three-state devices that remain in the high-impedance (off) state except when the MPU performs a PIA read operation. The read/write line is in the read (high) state when the PIA is selected for a read operation.

Enable (E) — The enable pulse, E, is the only timing signal that is supplied to the PIA. Timing of all other signals is referenced to the leading and trailing edges of the E pulse.

Read/Write (R/$\overline{W}$) — This signal is generated by the MPU to control the direction of data transfers on the data bus. A low state on the PIA read/write line enables the input buffers and data is transferred from the MPU to the PIA on the E signal if the device has been selected. A high on the read/write line sets up the PIA for a transfer of data to the bus. The PIA output buffers are enabled when the proper address and the enable pulse E are present.

$\overline{RESET}$ — The active low $\overline{RESET}$ line is used to reset all register bits in the PIA to a logical zero (low). This line can be used as a power-on reset and as a master reset during system operation.

Chip Selects (CS0, CS1, and $\overline{CS2}$) — These three input signals are used to select the PIA. CS0 and CS1 must be high and $\overline{CS2}$ must be low for selection of the device. Data transfers are then performed under the control of the enable and read/write signals. The chip select lines must be stable

for the duration of the E pulse. The device is deselected when any of the chip selects are in the inactive state.

Register Selects (RS0 and RS1) — The two register select lines are used to select the various registers inside the PIA. These two lines are used in conjunction with internal Control Registers to select a particular register that is to be written or read.

The register and chip select lines should be stable for the duration of the E pulse while in the read or write cycle.

Interrupt Request ($\overline{IRQA}$ and $\overline{IRQB}$) — The active low Interrupt Request lines ($\overline{IRQA}$ and $\overline{IRQB}$) act to interrupt the MPU either directly or through interrupt priority circuitry. These lines are "open drain" (no load device on the chip). This permits all interrupt request lines to be tied together in a wire-OR configuration.

Each Interrupt Request line has two internal interrupt flag bits that can cause the Interrupt Request line to go low. Each flag bit is associated with a particular peripheral interrupt line. Also, four interrupt enable bits are provided in the PIA which may be used to inhibit a particular interrupt from a peripheral device.

Servicing an interrupt by the MPU may be accomplished by a software routine that, on a prioritized basis, sequentially reads and tests the two control registers in each PIA for interrupt flag bits that are set.

The interrupt flags are cleared (zeroed) as a result of an MPU Read Peripheral Data Operation of the corresponding data register. After being cleared, the interrupt flag bit cannot be enabled to be set until the PIA is deselected during an E pulse. The E pulse is used to condition the interrupt control lines (CA1, CA2, CB1, CB2). When these lines are used as interrupt inputs, at least one E pulse must occur from the inactive edge to the active edge of the interrupt input signal to condition the edge sense network. If the interrupt flag has been enabled and the edge sense circuit has been properly conditioned, the interrupt flag will be set on the next active transition of the interrupt input pin.

PIA PERIPHERAL INTERFACE LINES

The PIA provides two 8-bit bidirectional data buses and four interrupt/control lines for interfacing to peripheral devices.

Section A Peripheral Data (PA0-PA7) — Each of the peripheral data lines can be programmed to act as an input or output. This is accomplished by setting a "1" in the corresponding Data Direction Register bit for those lines which are to be outputs. A "0" in a bit of the Data Direction Register causes the corresponding peripheral data line to act as an input. During an MPU Read Peripheral Data Operation, the data on peripheral lines programmed to act as inputs appears directly on the corresponding MPU Data Bus lines. In the input mode, the internal pullup resistor on these lines represents a maximum of 1.5 standard TTL loads.

The data in Output Register A will appear on the data lines that are programmed to be outputs. A logical "1" written into the register will cause a "high" on the corresponding data

line while a "0" results in a "low." Data in Output Register A may be read by an MPU "Read Peripheral Data A" operation when the corresponding lines are programmed as outputs. This data will be read property if the voltage on the peripheral data lines is greater than 2.0 volts for a logic "1" output and less than 0.8 volt for a logic "0" output. Loading the output lines such that the voltage on these lines does not reach full voltage causes the data transferred into the MPU on a Read operation to differ from that contained in the respective bit of Output Register A.

Section B Peripheral Data (PB0-PB7) — The peripheral data lines in the B Section of the PIA can be programmed to act as either inputs or outputs in a similar manner to PA0-PA7. They have three-state capabiity, allowing them to enter a high-impedance state when the peripheral data line is used as an input. In addition, data on the peripheral data lines

PB0-PB7 will be read properly from those lines programmed as outputs even if the voltages are below 2.0 volts for a "high" or above 0.8 V for a "low". As outputs, these lines are compatible with standard TTL and may also be used as a source of up to 1 milliampere at 1.5 volts to directly drive the base of a transistor switch.

Interrupt Input (CA1 and CB1) — Peripheral input lines CA1 and CB1 are input only lines that set the interrupt flags of the control registers. The active transition for these signals is also programmed by the two control registers.

Peripheral Control (CA2) — The peripheral control line CA2 can be programmed to act as an interrupt input or as a peripheral control output. As an output, this line is compatible with standard TTL; as an input the internal pullup resistor on this line represents 1.5 standard TTL loads. The function of this signal line is programmed with Control Register A.

Peripheral Control (CB2) — Peripheral Control line CB2 may also be programmed to act as an interrupt input or peripheral control output. As an input, this line has high input impedance and is compatible with standard TTL. As an output it is compatible with standard TTL and may also be used as a source of up to 1 milliampere at 1.5 volts to directly drive the base of a transistor switch. This line is programmed by Control Register B.

INTERNAL CONTROLS

INITIALIZATION

A $\overline{\text{RESET}}$ has the effect of zeroing all PIA registers. This will set PA0-PA7, PB0-PB7, CA2 and CB2 as inputs, and all interrupts disabled. The PIA must be configured during the restart program which follows the reset.

There are six locations within the PIA accessible to the MPU data bus: two Peripheral Registers, two Data Direction Registers, and two Control Registers. Selection of these locations is controlled by the RS0 and RS1 inputs together with bit 2 in the Control Register, as shown in Table B.1.

Details of possible configurations of the Data Direction and Control Register are as follows:

TABLE B.1 INTERNAL ADDRESSING

RS1	RS0	Control Register Bit		Location Selected
		CRA-2	CRB-2	
0	0	1	X	Peripheral Register A
0	0	0	X	Data Direction Register A
0	1	X	X	Control Register A
1	0	X	1	Peripheral Register B
1	0	X	0	Data Direction Register B
1	1	X	X	Control Register B

X = Don't Care

PORT A-B HARDWARE CHARACTERISTICS

As shown in Figure 17, the MC6821 has a pair of I/O ports whose characteristics differ greatly. The A side is designed to drive CMOS logic to normal 30% to 70% levels, and incorporates an internal pullup device that remains connected even in the input mode. Because of this, the A side requires more drive current in the input mode than Port B. In contrast, the B side uses a normal three-state NMOS buffer which cannot pullup to CMOS levels without external resistors. The B side can drive extra loads such as Darlingtons without problem. When the PIA comes out of reset, the A port represents inputs with pullup resistors, whereas the B side (input mode also) will float high or low, depending upon the load connected to it.

Notice the differences between a Port A and Port B read operation when in the output mode. When reading Port A, the actual pin is read, whereas the B side read comes from an output latch, ahead of the actual pin.

CONTROL REGISTERS (CRA and CRB)

The two Control Registers (CRA and CRB) allow the MPU to control the operation of the four peripheral control lines CA1, CA2, CB1, and CB2. In addition they allow the MPU to enable the interrupt lines and monitor the status of the interrupt flags. Bits 0 through 5 of the two registers may be written or read by the MPU when the proper chip select and register select signals are applied. Bits 6 and 7 of the two registers are read only and are modified by external interrupts occurring on control lines CA1, CA2, CB1, or CB2. The format of the control words is shown in Figure B.3

DATA DIRECTION ACCESS CONTROL BIT (CRA-2 and CRB-2)

Bit 2, in each Control Register (CRA and CRB), determines selection of either a Peripheral Output Register or the corresponding Data Direction E Register when the proper register select signals are applied to RS0 and RS1. A "1" in bit 2 allows access of the Peripheral Interface Register, while a "0" causes the Data Direction Register to be addressed.

Interrupt Flags (CRA-6, CRA-7, CRB-6, and CRB-7) — The four interrupt flag bits are set by active transitions of signals on the four Interrupt and Peripheral Control lines when those lines are programmed to be inputs. These bits cannot be set directly from the MPU Data Bus and are reset indirectly by a Read Peripheral Data Operation on the appropriate section.

Control of CA2 and CB2 Peripheral Control Lines (CRA-3, CRA-4, CRA-5, CRB-3, CRB-4, and CRB-5) — Bits 3, 4, and 5 of the two control registers are used to control the CA2 and CB2 Peripheral Control lines. These bits determine if the control lines will be an interrupt input or an output control signal. If bit CRA-5 (CRB-5) is low, CA2 (CB2) is an interrupt input line similar to CA1 (CB1). When CRA-5 (CRB-5) is high, CA2 (CB2) becomes an output signal that may be used to control peripheral data transfers. When in the output mode, CA2 and CB2 have slightly different loading characteristics.

Control of CA1 and CB1 Interrupt Input Lines (CRA-0, CRB-1, CRA-1, and CRB-1) — The two lowest-order bits of the control registers are used to control the interrupt input lines CA1 and CB1. Bits CRA-0 and CRB-0 are used to enable the MPU interrupt signals $\overline{IRQA}$ and $\overline{IRQB}$, respectively. Bits CRA-1 and CRB-1 determine the active transition of the interrupt input signals CA1 and CB1.

FIGURE B.2 PORT A AND PORT B EQUIVALENT CIRCUITS

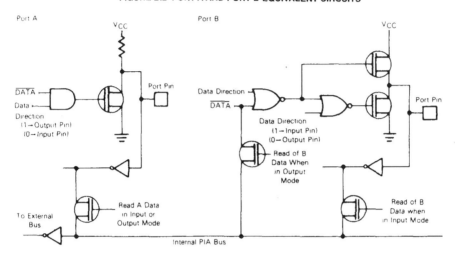

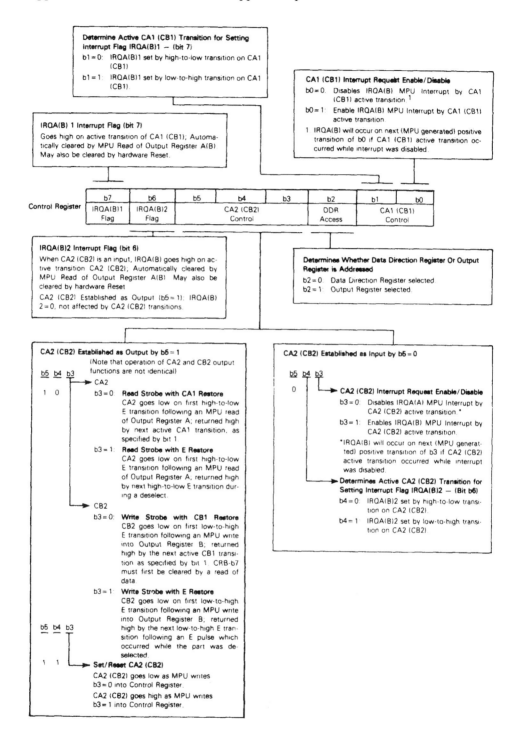

 **MOTOROLA**

MCM6116

16K BIT STATIC RANDOM ACCESS MEMORY

The MCM6116 is a 16,384-bit Static Random Access Memory organized as 2048 words by 8 bits, fabricated using Motorola's high-performance silicon-gate CMOS (HCMOS) technology. It uses a design approach which provides the simple timing features associated with fully static memories and the reduced power associated with CMOS memories. This means low standby power without the need for clocks, nor reduced data rates due to cycle times that exceed access time.

Chip Enable ($\overline{E}$) controls the power-down feature. It is not a clock but rather a chip control that affects power consumption. In less than a cycle time after Chip Enable ($\overline{E}$) goes high, the part automatically reduces its power requirements and remains in this low-power standby as long as the Chip Enable ($\overline{E}$) remains high. The automatic power-down feature causes no performance degradation.

The MCM6116 is in a 24-pin dual-in-line package with the industry standard JEDEC approved pinout and is pinout compatible with the industry standard 16K EPROM/ROM.

- Single +5 V Supply
- 2048 Words by 8-Bit Operation
- HCMOS Technology
- Fully Static: No Clock or Timing Strobe Required
- Maximum Access Time: MCM6116-12 — 120 ns
  MCM6116-15 — 150 ns
  MCM6116-20 — 200 ns
- Power Dissipation: 70 mA Maximum (Active)
  15 mA Maximum (Standby-TTL Levels)
  2 mA Maximum (Standby)
- Low Power Version Also Available — MCM61L16
- Low Voltage Data Retention (MCM61L16 Only):
  50 µA Maximum

HCMOS
(COMPLEMENTARY MOS)

2,048 × 8 BIT
STATIC RANDOM
ACCESS MEMORY

P SUFFIX
PLASTIC PACKAGE
CASE 709

PIN ASSIGNMENTS

A7	1	24	V_{CC}
A6	2	23	A8
A5	3	22	A9
A4	4	21	$\overline{W}$
A3	5	20	$\overline{G}$
A2	6	19	A10
A1	7	18	$\overline{E}$
A0	8	17	DQ7
DQ0	9	16	DQ6
DQ1	10	15	DQ5
DQ2	11	14	DQ4
V_{SS}	12	13	DQ3

PIN NAMES

A0-A10	Address Input
DQ0-DQ7	Data Input/Output
$\overline{W}$	Write Enable
$\overline{G}$	Output Enable
$\overline{E}$	Chip Enable
V_{CC}	Power (+5 V)
V_{SS}	Ground

BLOCK DIAGRAM

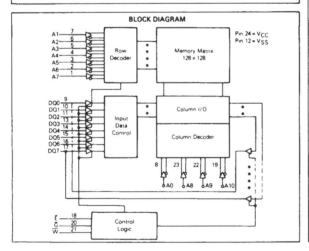

ABSOLUTE MAXIMUM RATINGS (See Note)

Rating	Value	Unit
Temperature Under Bias	-10 to $+80$	°C
Voltage on Any Pin With Respect to V_{SS}	-1.0 to $+7.0$	V
DC Output Current	20	mA
Power Dissipation	1.2	Watt
Operating Temperature Range	0 to $+70$	°C
Storage Temperature Range	-65 to $+150$	°C

This device contains circuitry to protect the inputs against damage due to high static voltages or electric fields, however, it is advised that normal precautions be taken to avoid application of any voltage higher than maximum rated voltages to this high-impedance circuit.

NOTE: Permanent device damage may occur if ABSOLUTE MAXIMUM RATINGS are exceeded. Functional operation should be restricted to RECOMMENDED OPERATING CONDITIONS. Exposure to higher than recommended voltages for extended periods of time could affect device reliability.

DC OPERATING CONDITIONS AND CHARACTERISTICS
(Full operating voltage and temperature ranges unless otherwise noted.)

RECOMMENDED OPERATING CONDITIONS

Parameter	Symbol	Min	Typ	Max	Unit
Supply Voltage	V_{CC}	4.5	5.0	5.5	V
	V_{SS}	0	0	0	V
Input Voltage	V_{IH}	2.2	3.5	6.0	V
	V_{IL}	-1.0^*	—	0.8	V

*The device will withstand undershoots to the -1.0 volt level with a maximum pulse width of 50 ns at the -0.3 volt level. This is periodically sampled rather than 100% tested.

RECOMMENDED OPERATING CHARACTERISTICS

Parameter	Symbol	MCM6116 Min	MCM6116 Typ*	MCM6116 Max	MCM61L16 Min	MCM61L16 Typ*	MCM61L16 Max	Unit
Input Leakage Current ($V_{CC} = 5.5$ V, $V_{in} = $ GND to V_{CC})	$|I_{LI}|$	—	—	1	—	—	1	μA
Output Leakage Current ($\overline{E} = V_{IH}$ or $\overline{G} = V_{IH}$ $V_{I/O} = $ GND to V_{CC})	$|I_{LO}|$	—	—	1	—	—	1	μA
Operating Power Supply Current ($\overline{E} = V_{IL}$, $I_{I/O} = 0$ mA)	I_{CC}	—	35	70	—	35	55	mA
Average Operating Current Minimum cycle, duty = 100%	I_{CC2}	—	35	70	—	35	55	mA
Standby Power ($\overline{E} = V_{IH}$)	I_{SB}	—	5	15	—	5	12	mA
Supply Current ($\overline{E} \geq V_{CC} - 0.2$ V, $V_{in} \geq V_{CC} - 0.2$ V or $V_{in} \leq 0.2$ V)	I_{SB1}	—	20	2000	—	4	100	μA
Output Low Voltage ($I_{OL} = 2.1$ mA)	V_{OL}	—	—	0.4	—	—	0.4	V
Output High Voltage ($I_{OH} = -1.0$ mA)**	V_{OH}	2.4	—	—	2.4	—	—	V

*$V_{CC} = 5$ V, $T_A = 25$°C
**Also, output voltages are compatible with Motorola's new high-speed CMOS logic family if the same power supply voltage is used.

CAPACITANCE ($f = 1.0$ MHz, $T_A = 25$°C, periodically sampled rather than 100% tested.)

Characteristic	Symbol	Typ	Max	Unit
Input Capacitance except $\overline{E}$	C_{in}	3	5	pF
Input/Output Capacitance and $\overline{E}$ Input Capacitance	$C_{I/O}$	5	7	pF

MODE SELECTION

Mode	$\overline{E}$	$\overline{G}$	$\overline{W}$	V_{CC} Current	DQ
Standby	H	X	X	I_{SB}, I_{SB1}	High Z
Read	L	L	H	I_{CC}	Q
Write Cycle (1)	L	H	L	I_{CC}	D
Write Cycle (2)	L	L	L	I_{CC}	D

AC OPERATING CONDITIONS AND CHARACTERISTICS

(Full operating voltage and temperature unless otherwise noted.)

Input Pulse Levels	0 Volt to 3.5 Volts	Input and Output Timing Reference Levels .... 1.5 Volts
Input Rise and Fall Times	10 ns	Output Load .... 1 TTL Gate and C_L = 100 pF

READ CYCLE

Parameter	Symbol	MCM6116-12 MCM61L16-12		MCM6116-15 MCM61L16-15		MCM6116-20 MCM61L16-20		Unit
		Min	Max	Min	Max	Min	Max	
Address Valid to Address Don't Care (Cycle Time when Chip Enable is Held Active)	t_{AVAX}	120	--	150	--	200	--	ns
Chip Enable Low to Chip Enable High	t_{ELEH}	120	--	150	--	200	--	ns
Address Valid to Output Valid (Access)	t_{AVQV}	--	120	--	150	--	200	ns
Chip Enable Low to Output Valid (Access)	t_{ELQV}	--	120	--	150	--	200	ns
Address Valid to Output Invalid	t_{AVQX}	10	-	15	--	15	--	ns
Chip Enable Low to Output Invalid	t_{ELQX}	10	--	15	--	15	--	ns
Chip Enable High to Output High Z	t_{EHQZ}	0	40	0	50	0	60	ns
Output Enable to Output Valid	t_{GLQV}	--	80	-	100	--	120	ns
Output Enable to Output Invalid	t_{GLQX}	10	--	15	-	15	--	ns
Output Enable to Output High Z	t_{GLQZ}	0	40	0	50	0	60	ns
Address Invalid to Output Invalid	t_{AXQX}	10	--	15	--	15	--	ns
Address Valid to Chip Enable Low (Address Setup)	t_{AVEL}	0	--	0	--	0	--	ns
Chip Enable to Power-Up Time	t_{PU}	0	-	0	--	0	--	ns
Chip Disable to Power-Down Time	t_{PD}	--	30	--	30	--	30	ns

WRITE CYCLE

Parameter	Symbol	MCM6116-12 MCM61L16-12		MCM6116-15 MCM61L16-15		MCM6116-20 MCM61L16-20		Unit
		Min	Max	Min	Max	Min	Max	
Chip Enable Low to Write High	t_{ELWH}	70	--	90	--	120	--	ns
Address Valid to Write High	t_{AVWH}	105	--	120	--	140	--	ns
Address Valid to Write Low (Address Setup)	t_{AVWL}	20	--	20	--	20	--	ns
Write Low to Write High (Write Pulse Width)	t_{WLWH}	70	--	90	--	120	--	ns
Write High to Address Don't Care	t_{WHAX}	5	--	10	--	10	--	ns
Data Valid to Write High	t_{DVWH}	35	--	40	--	60	-	ns
Write High to Data Don't Care (Data Hold)	t_{WHDX}	5	--	10	--	10	--	ns
Write Low to Output High Z	t_{WLQZ}	0	50	0	60	0	60	ns
Write High to Output Valid	t_{WHQV}	5	--	10	--	10	--	ns
Output Disable to Output High Z	t_{GHQZ}	0	40	0	50	0	60	ns

TIMING PARAMETER ABBREVIATIONS

```
                                    t  X  X  X  X
        signal name from which interval is defined ─┘  |  |  |
            transition direction for first signal ─────┘  |  |
         signal name to which interval is defined ────────┘  |
        transition direction for second signal ─────────────┘
```

The transition definitions used in this data sheet are

H = transition to high
L = transition to low
V = transition to valid
X = transition to invalid or don't care
Z = transition to off (high impedance)

TIMING LIMITS

The table of timing values shows either a minimum or a maximum limit for each parameter. Input requirements are specified from the external system point of view. Thus, address setup time is shown as a minimum since the system must supply at least that much time (even though most devices do not require it). On the other hand, responses from the memory are specified from the device point of view. Thus, the access time is shown as a maximum since the device never provides data later than that time.

APPENDIX

D

68000 EXECUTION TIMES

D.1 INTRODUCTION

This Appendix contains listings of the instruction execution times in terms of external clock (CLK) periods. In this data, it is assumed that both memory read and write cycle times are four clock periods. A longer memory cycle will cause the generation of wait states which must be added to the total instruction time.

The number of bus read and write cycles for each instruction is also included with the timing data. This data is enclosed in parenthesis following the number of clock periods and is shown as: (r/w) where r is the number of read cycles and w is the number of write cycles included in the clock period number. Recalling that either a read or write cycle requires four clock periods, a timing number given as 18(3/1) relates to 12 clock periods for the three read cycles, plus 4 clock periods for the one write cycle, plus 2 cycles required for some internal function of the processor.

NOTE

The number of periods includes instruction fetch and all applicable operand fetches and stores.

D.2 OPERAND EFFECTIVE ADDRESS CALCULATION TIMING

Table D-1 lists the number of clock periods required to compute an instruction's effective address. It includes fetching of any extension words, the address computation, and fetching of the memory operand. The number of bus read and write cycles is shown in parenthesis as (r/w). Note there are no write cycles involved in processing the effective address.

Table D-1. Effective Address Calculation Times

Addressing Mode		Byte, Word	Long
Register			
Dn	Data Register Direct	0(0/0)	0(0/0)
An	Address Register Direct	0(0/0)	0(0/0)
Memory			
(An)	Address Register Indirect	4(1/0)	8(2/0)
(An) +	Address Register Indirect with Postincrement	4(1/0)	8(2/0)
– (An)	Address Register Indirect with Predecrement	6(1/0)	10(2/0)
d(An)	Address Register Indirect with Displacement	8(2/0)	12(3/0)
d(An, ix)*	Address Register Indirect with Index	10(2/0)	14(3/0)
xxx.W	Absolute Short	8(2/0)	12(3/0)
xxx.L	Absolute Long	12(3/0)	16(4/0)
d(PC)	Program Counter with Displacement	8(2/0)	12(3/0)
d(PC, ix)*	Program Counter with Index	10(2/0)	14(3/0)
#xxx	Immediate	4(1/0)	8(2/0)

*The size of the index register (ix) does not affect execution time.

479

D.3 MOVE INSTRUCTION EXECUTION TIMES

Tables D-2 and D-3 indicate the number of clock periods for the move instruction. This data includes instruction fetch, operand reads, and operand writes. The number of bus read and write cycles is shown in parenthesis as (r/w).

Table D-2. Move Byte and Word Instruction Execution Times

Source	Destination								
	Dn	An	(An)	(An) +	– (An)	d(An)	d(An, ix)*	xxx.W	xxx.L
Dn	4(1/0)	4(1/0)	8(1/1)	8(1/1)	8(1/1)	12(2/1)	14(2/1)	12(2/1)	16(3/1)
An	4(1/0)	4(1/0)	8(1/1)	8(1/1)	8(1/1)	12(2/1)	14(2/1)	12(2/1)	16(3/1)
(An)	8(2/0)	8(2/0)	12(2/1)	12(2/1)	12(2/1)	16(3/1)	18(3/1)	16(3/1)	20(4/1)
(An) +	8(2/0)	8(2/0)	12(2/1)	12(2/1)	12(2/1)	16(3/1)	18(3/1)	16(3/1)	20(4/1)
– (An)	10(2/0)	10(2/0)	14(2/1)	14(2/1)	14(2/1)	18(3/1)	20(3/1)	18(3/1)	22(4/1)
d(An)	12(3/0)	12(3/0)	16(3/1)	16(3/1)	16(3/1)	20(4/1)	22(4/1)	20(4/1)	24(5/1)
d(An, ix)*	14(3/0)	14(3/0)	18(3/1)	18(3/1)	18(3/1)	22(4/1)	24(4/1)	22(4/1)	26(5/1)
xxx.W	12(3/0)	12(3/0)	16(3/1)	16(3/1)	16(3/1)	20(4/1)	22(4/1)	20(4/1)	24(5/1)
xxx.L	16(4/0)	16(4/0)	20(4/1)	20(4/1)	20(4/1)	24(5/1)	26(5/1)	24(5/1)	28(6/1)
d(PC)	12(3/0)	12(3/0)	16(3/1)	16(3/1)	16(3/1)	20(4/1)	22(4/1)	20(4/1)	24(5/1)
d(PC, ix)*	14(3/0)	14(3/0)	18(3/1)	18(3/1)	18(3/1)	22(4/1)	24(4/1)	22(4/1)	26(5/1)
#xxx	8(2/0)	8(2/0)	12(2/1)	12(2/1)	12(2/1)	16(3/1)	18(3/1)	16(3/1)	20(4/1)

* The size of the index register (ix) does not affect execution time.

Table D-3. Move Long Instruction Execution Times

Source	Destination								
	Dn	An	(An)	(An) +	– (An)	d(An)	d(An, ix)*	xxx.W	xxx.L
Dn	4(1/0)	4(1/0)	12(1/2)	12(1/2)	12(1/2)	16(2/2)	18(2/2)	16(2/2)	20(3/2)
An	4(1/0)	4(1/0)	12(1/2)	12(1/2)	12(1/2)	16(2/2)	18(2/2)	16(2/2)	20(3/2)
(An)	12(3/0)	12(3/0)	20(3/2)	20(3/2)	20(3/2)	24(4/2)	26(4/2)	24(4/2)	28(5/2)
(An) +	12(3/0)	12(3/0)	20(3/2)	20(3/2)	20(3/2)	24(4/2)	26(4/2)	24(4/2)	28(5/2)
– (An)	14(3/0)	14(3/0)	22(3/2)	22(3/2)	22(3/2)	26(4/2)	28(4/2)	26(4/2)	30(5/2)
d(An)	16(4/0)	16(4/0)	24(4/2)	24(4/2)	24(4/2)	28(5/2)	30(5/2)	28(5/2)	32(6/2)
d(An, ix)*	18(4/0)	18(4/0)	26(4/2)	26(4/2)	26(4/2)	30(5/2)	32(5/2)	30(5/2)	34(6/2)
xxx.W	16(4/0)	16(4/0)	24(4/2)	24(4/2)	24(4/2)	28(5/2)	30(5/2)	28(5/2)	32(6/2)
xxx.L	20(5/0)	20(5/0)	28(5/2)	28(5/2)	28(5/2)	32(6/2)	34(6/2)	32(6/2)	36(7/2)
d(PC)	16(4/0)	16(4/0)	24(4/2)	24(4/2)	24(4/2)	28(5/2)	30(5/2)	28(5/2)	32(5/2)
d(PC, ix)*	18(4/0)	18(4/0)	26(4/2)	26(4/2)	26(4/2)	30(5/2)	32(5/2)	30(5/2)	34(6/2)
#xxx	12(3/0)	12(3/0)	20(3/2)	20(3/2)	20(3/2)	24(4/2)	26(4/2)	24(4/2)	28(5/2)

* The size of the index register (ix) does not affect execution time.

D.4 STANDARD INSTRUCTION EXECUTION TIMES

The number of clock periods shown in Table D-4 indicates the time required to perform the operations, store the results, and read the next instruction. The number of bus read and write cycles is shown in parenthesis as (r/w). The number of clock periods and the number of read and write cycles must be added respectively to those of the effective address calculation where indicated.

In Table D-4 the headings have the following meanings: An = address register operand, Dn = data register operand, ea = an operand specified by an effective address, and M = memory effective address operand.

Table D-4. Standard Instruction Execution Times

Instruction	Size	op<ea>, An†	op<ea>, Dn	op Dn, <M>
ADD	Byte, Word	8(1/0) +	4(1/0) +	8(1/1) +
	Long	6(1/0) + * *	6(1/0) + * *	12(1/2) +
AND	Byte, Word	–	4(1/0) +	8(1/1) +
	Long	–	6(1/0) + * *	12(1/2) +
CMP	Byte, Word	6(1/0) +	4(1/0) +	–
	Long	6(1/0) +	6(1/0) +	–
DIVS	–	–	158(1/0) + *	–
DIVU	–	–	140(1/0) + *	–
EOR	Byte, Word	–	4(1/0) * * *	8(1/1) +
	Long	–	8(1/0) * * *	12(1/2) +
MULS	–	–	70(1/0) + *	–
MULU	–	–	70(1/0) + *	–
OR	Byte, Word	–	4(1/0) +	8(1/1) +
	Long	–	6(1/0) + * *	12(1/2) +
SUB	Byte, Word	8(1/0) +	4(1/0) +	8(1/1) +
	Long	6(1/0) + * *	6(1/0) + * *	12(1/2) +

NOTES:

+ add effective address calculation time
† word or long only
* indicates maximum value
* * The base time of six clock periods is increased to eight if the effective address mode is register direct or immediate (effective address time should also be added).
* * * Only available effective address mode is data register direct.
DIVS, DIVU — The divide algorithm used by the MC68000 provides less than 10% difference between the best and worst case timings.
MULS, MULU — The multiply algorithm requires 38 + 2n clocks where n is defined as:
    MULU: n = the number of ones in the <ea>
    MULS: n = concatanate the <ea> with a zero as the LSB; n is the resultant number of 10 or 01 patterns in the 17-bit source; i.e., worst case happens when the source is $5555.

D.5 IMMEDIATE INSTRUCTION EXECUTION TIMES

The number of clock periods shown in Table D-5 includes the time to fetch immediate operands, perform the operations, store the results, and read the next operation. The number of bus read and write cycles is shown in parenthesis as (r/w). The number of clock periods and the number of read and write cycles must be added respectively to those of the effective address calculation where indicated.

In Table D-5, the headings have the following meanings: # = immediate operand, Dn = data register operand, An = address register operand, and M = memory operand. SR = status register.

Table D-5. Immediate Instruction Execution Times

Instruction	Size	op #, Dn	op #, An	op #, M
ADDI	Byte, Word	8(2/0)	–	12(2/1) +
	Long	16(3/0)	–	20(3/2) +
ADDQ	Byte, Word	4(1/0)	8(1/0) *	8(1/1) +
	Long	8(1/0)	8(1/0)	12(1/2) +
ANDI	Byte, Word	8(2/0)	–	12(2/1) +
	Long	16(3/0)	–	20(3/1) +
CMPI	Byte, Word	8(2/0)	–	8(2/0) +
	Long	14(3/0)	–	12(3/0) +
EORI	Byte, Word	8(2/0)	–	12(2/1) +
	Long	16(3/0)	–	20(3/2) +
MOVEQ	Long	4(1/0)	–	–
ORI	Byte, Word	8(2/0)	–	12(2/1) +
	Long	16(3/0)	–	20(3/2) +
SUBI	Byte, Word	8(2/0)	–	12(2/1) +
	Long	16(3/0)	–	20(3/2) +
SUBQ	Byte, Word	4(1/0)	8(1/0) *	8(1/1) +
	Long	8(1/0)	8(1/0)	12(1/2) +

+ add effective address calculation time
* word only

D.6 SINGLE OPERAND INSTRUCTION EXECUTION TIMES

Table D-6 indicates the number of clock periods for the single operand instructions. The number of bus read and write cycles is shown in parenthesis as (r/w). The number of clock periods and the number of read and write cycles must be added respectively to those of the effective address calculation where indicated.

Table D-6. Single Operand Instruction Execution Times

Instruction	Size	Register	Memory
CLR	Byte, Word	4(1/0)	8(1/1) +
	Long	6(1/0)	12(1/2) +
NBCD	Byte	6(1/0)	8(1/1) +
NEG	Byte, Word	4(1/0)	8(1/1) +
	Long	6(1/0)	12(1/2) +
NEGX	Byte, Word	4(1/0)	8(1/1) +
	Long	6(1/0)	12(1/2) +
NOT	Byte, Word	4(1/0)	8(1/1) +
	Long	6(1/0)	12(1/2) +
S_{CC}	Byte, False	4(1/0)	8(1/1) +
	Byte, True	6(1/0)	8(1/1) +
TAS	Byte	4(1/0)	10(1/1) +
TST	Byte, Word	4(1/0)	4(1/0) +
	Long	4(1/0)	4(1/0) +

+ add effective address calculation time

D.7 SHIFT/ROTATE INSTRUCTION EXECUTION TIMES

Table D-7 indicates the number of clock periods for the shift and rotate instructions. The number of bus read and write cycles is shown in parenthesis as (r/w). The number of clock periods and the number of read and write cycles must be added respectively to those of the effective address calculation where indicated.

Table D-7. Shift/Rotate Instruction Execution Times

Instruction	Size	Register	Memory
ASR, ASL	Byte, Word	6 + 2n(1/0)	8(1/1) +
	Long	8 + 2n(1/0)	—
LSR, LSL	Byte, Word	6 + 2n(1/0)	8(1/1) +
	Long	8 + 2n(1/0)	—
ROR, ROL	Byte, Word	6 + 2n(1/0)	8(1/1) +
	Long	8 + 2n(1/0)	—
ROXR, ROXL	Byte, Word	6 + 2n(1/0)	8(1/1) +
	Long	8 + 2n(1/0)	—

+ add effective address calculation time
n is the shift count

D.12 MISCELLANEOUS INSTRUCTION EXECUTION TIMES

Tables D-12 and D-13 indicate the number of clock periods for the following miscellaneous instructions. The number of bus read and write cycles is shown in parenthesis as (r/w). The number of clock periods plus the number of read and write cycles must be added to those of the effective address calculation where indicated.

Table D-12. Miscellaneous Instruction Execution Times

Instruction	Size	Register	Memory
ANDI to CCR	Byte	20(3/0)	–
ANDI to SR	Word	20(3/0)	–
CHK	–	10(1/0) +	–
EORI to CCR	Byte	20(3/0)	–
EORI to SR	Word	20(3/0)	–
ORI to CCR	Byte	20(3/0)	–
ORI to SR	Word	20(3/0)	–
MOVE from SR	–	6(1/0)	8(1/1) +
MOVE to CCR	–	12(2/0)	12(2/0) +
MOVE to SR	–	12(2/0)	12(2/0) +
EXG	–	6(1/0)	–
EXT	Word	4(1/0)	–
EXT	Long	4(1/0)	–
LINK	–	16(2/2)	–
MOVE from USP	–	4(1/0)	–
MOVE to USP	–	4(1/0)	–
NOP	–	4(1/0)	–
RESET	–	132(1/0)	–
RTE	–	20(5/0)	–
RTR	–	20(5/0)	–
RTS	–	16(4/0)	–
STOP	–	4(0/0)	–
SWAP	–	4(1/0)	–
TRAPV	–	4(1/0)	–
UNLK	–	12(3/0)	–

+ add effective address calculation time

Table D-13. Move Peripheral Instruction Execution Times

Instruction	Size	Register → Memory	Memory → Register
MOVEP	Word	16(2/2)	16(4/0)
MOVEP	Long	24(2/4)	24(6/0)

D.13 EXCEPTION PROCESSING EXECUTION TIMES

Table D-14 indicates the number of clock periods for exception processing. The number of clock periods includes the time for all stacking, the vector fetch, and the fetch of the first two instruction words of the handler routine. The number of bus read and write cycles is shown in parenthesis as (r/w).

Table D-14. Exception Processing Execution Times

Exception	Periods
Address Error	**50**(4/7)
Bus Error	**50**(4/7)
CHK Instruction	**44**(5/4) +
Divide by Zero	**42**(5/4)
Illegal Instruction	**34**(4/3)
Interrupt	**44**(5/3) *
Privilege Violation	**34**(4/3)
RESET**	**40**(6/0)
Trace	**34**(4/3)
TRAP Instruction	**38**(4/4)
TRAPV Instruction	**34**(4/3)

+ add effective address calculation time

* The interrupt acknowledge cycle is assumed to take four clock periods.

** Indicates the time from when $\overline{RESET}$ and $\overline{HALT}$ are first sampled as negated to when instruction execution starts.

E

68000 / SELECTED 68020 INSTRUCTION SET

Instruction	Size	Length (words)	Operation
ABCD – (Ay), – (Ax)	B	1	– [Ay] 10 + – [Ax] 10 + X → [Ax]
ABCD Dy, Dx	B	1	[Dy]10 + [Dx]10 +X → Dx
ADD (EA), (EA)	B, W, L	1	[EA] + [EA] → EA
ADDA (EA), An	W, L	1	[EA] + An → An
ADDI #data, (EA)	B, W, L	2 for B, W 3 for L	data + [EA] → EA
ADDQ #data, (EA)	B, W, L	1	data + [EA] → EA
ADDX – (Ay), – (Ax)	B, W, L	1	– [Ay] + – [Ax] + X → [Ax]
ADDX Dy, Dx	B, W, L	1	Dy + Dx + X → Dx
AND (EA), (EA)	B, W, L	1	[EA] AND [EA] → EA
ANDI #data, (EA)	B, W, L	2 for B, W 3 for L	data AND [EA] → EA
ANDI #data8, CCR	B	2	data8 AND [CCR] → CCR
ANDI #data16, SR	W	2	data16 AND [SR] → SR if s = 1; else trap
ASL Dx, Dy	B, W, L	1	
ASL #data, Dy	B, W, L	1	
ASL (EA)	B, W, L	1	
ASR Dx, Dy	B, W, L	1	

Instruction	Size	Length (words)	Operation
ASR #data, Dy	B, W, L	1	Dy — number of shifts determined by immediate data → C, X
ASR (EA)	B,W, L	1	[EA] — shift once → C, X
BCC d	B, W (68000 and 68020) L (68020)	1 for B, 2 for W, 3 for L	Branch to PC + d if carry = 0; else next instruction
BCHG Dn, (EA)	B, L	1	[bit of [EA], specified by Dn]' → Z [bit of [EA] specified by Dn]' → bit of [EA]
BCHG #data. (EA)	B, L	2	Same as BCHG Dn, [EA] except bit number is specified by immediate data
BCLR Dn (EA)	B, L	1	[bit of [EA]]' → Z 0 → bit of [EA] specified by Dn
BCLR #data, (EA)	B, L	2	Same as BCLR Dn, [EA] except the bit is specified by immediate data
BCS d	B, W (68000 and 68020) L (68020)	1 for B, 2 for W, 3 for L	Branch to PC + d if carry = 1; else next instruction
BEQ d	B, W (68000 and 68020) L (68020)	1 for B, 2 for W, 3 for L	Branch to PC + d if Z = 1; else next instruction
BFCHG (EA), {offset : width} (68020)	unsized	2	NOT (Field) → Field
BFCLR (EA), {offset : width} (68020)	unsized	2	0's → Bit Field of destination
BFEXTS (EA) {offset : width}, Dn (68020)	unsized	2	Sign-extend Bit Field of Source→ Dn
BFEXTU (EA) {offset : width}, Dn (68020)	unsized	2	Zero-extend Bit Field of Source→ Dn
BFFFO (EA) {offset : width}, Dn (68020)	unsized	2	Bit Field of Source Bit Scan→ Dn
BFINS Dn, (EA) {offset : width} (68020)	unsized	2	Dn→ Bit Field of destination
BFSET (EA), {offset : width} (68020)	unsized	2	1's → Bit Field of destination

Instruction	Size	Length (words)	Operation
BFTST (EA) {offset : width} (68020)	unsized	2	Obtain the specified bit field and set condition codes.
BGE d	B, W (68000 and 68020) L (68020)	1 for B, 2 for W, 3 for L	Branch to PC + d if greater than or equal; else next instruction
BGT d	B, W (68000 and 68020) L (68020)	1 for B, 2 for W, 3 for L	Branch to PC + d if greater than; else next instruction
BHI d	B, W (68000 and 68020) L (68020)	1 for B, 2 for W, 2 for L	Branch to PC + d if higher; else next instruction
BLE d	B, W (68000 and 68020) L (68020)	1 for B, 2 for W, 3 for L	Branch to PC + d if less or equal; else next instruction
BLS d	B, W (68000 and 68020) L (68020)	1 for B, 2 for W, 3 for L	Branch to PC + d if low or same; else next instruction
BLT d	B, W (68000 and 68020) L (68020)	1 for B, 2 for W, 3 for L	Branch to PC + d if less than; else next instruction
BMI d	B,W (68000 and 68020) L (68020)	1 for B, 2 for W, 3 for L	Branch to PC +d if N = 1; else next instruction
BNE d	B, W (68000 and 68020) L (68020)	1 for B, 2 for W, 3 for L	Branch to PC +d if Z = 0; else next instruction
BPL d	B, W (68000 and 68020) L (68020)	1 for B, 2 for W, 3 for L	Branch to PC + d if N = 0; else next instruction
BRA d	B, W (68000 and 68020) L (68020)	1 for B, 2 for W, 3 for L	Branch always to PC + d
BSET Dn, (EA)	B, L	1	[bit of [EA]]' → Z 1 → bit of [EA] specified by Dn
BSET #data, (EA)	B, L	2	Same as BSET Dn, [EA] except the bit is specified by immediate data
BSR d	B, W (68000 and 68020) L (68020)	1 for B, 2 for W, 3 for L	PC → – [SP] PC + d → PC
BTST Dn, (EA)	B, L	1	[bit of [EA] specified by Dn]' → Z
BTST #data, (EA)	B, L	2	Same as BTST Dn, [EA] except the bit is specified by data
BVC d	B,W (68000 and 68020) L (68020)	1 for B, 2 for W, 3 for L	Branch to PC + d if V = 0; else next instruction
BVS d	B, W (68000 and 68020) L (68020)	1 for B, 2 for W, 3 for L	Branch to PC + d if V = 1; else next instruction

Instruction	Size	Length (words)	Operation
CHK (EA), Dn	W for 68000, 68020 W and L for 68020	1 for both 68000 and 68020	If Dn < 0 or Dn > [EA], then trap
CHK2 (EA), An (68020)	W, L	2	If An < source - Lower bound or An > Source - Upper bound then TRAP
CHK2 (EA), Dn (68020)	B, W, L	2	If Dn < source - Lower bound or Dn > Source - Upper bound then TRAP
CLR(EA)	B, W, L	1	0 → EA
CMP (EA), Dn	B, W, L	1	Dn − [EA] → Affect all condition codes except X
CMP (EA), An	W, L	1	An − [EA] → Attect all condition codes except X
CMPI #data, (EA)	B, W, L	2 for B, W 3 for L	[EA] − data → Affect all flags except X-bit
CMPM (Ay) +, (Ax) +	B, W, L	1	[Ax]+ - [Ay]+ → Affect all flags except X; update Ax and Ay
CMP2 (EA), An (68020)	W, L	2	Compare An < Source - Lower bound or An > Source - Upper bound and Set Condition Codes.
CMP2 (EA), Dn (68020)	B, W, L	2	Compare Dn < Source - Lower bound or Dn > Source - Upper bound and Set Condition Codes.
DBCS Dn, d	W	2	Same as DBCC except condition is C = 1
DBEQ Dn, d	W	2	Same as DBCC except condition is Z = 1
DBF Dn, d	W	2	Same as DBCC except condition is always false
DBGE Dn, d	W	2	Same as DBCC except condition is greater or equal
DBGT Gn, d	W	2	Same as DBCC except condition is greater than
DBHIDn, d	\V	2	Same as DBCC except condition is high
DBLE Dn, d	W	2	Same as DBCC except condition is less than or equal
DBLS Dn, d	W	2	Same as DBCC except condition is low or same
DBLT Dn, d	W	2	Same as DBCC except condition is less than
DBM1 Dn, d	W	2	Same as DBCC except condition is N = 1
DBNE Dn, d	W	2	Same as DBCC except condition Z = 0

Instruction	Size	Length (words)	Operation
DBPL Dn, d	W	2	Same as DBCC except condition $N = 0$
DBT Dn, d	W	2	Same as DBCC except condition is always true
DBVC Dn, d	W	2	Same as DBCC except condition is $V = 0$
DBVS Dn, d	W	2	Same as DBCC except condition is $V = 1$
DIVS (EA), Dn (Both 68000 and 68020)	W	1	Signed division $[Dn]_{32}/[EA]_{16} \rightarrow$ [Dn] 0-15 = quotient [Dn] 16-31 = remainder
DIVS (EA), Dq (68020)	L	2	$32/32 \rightarrow 32q$
DIVS (EA), Dr :Dq (68020)	L	2	$64/32 \rightarrow 32r : 32q$
DIVSL (EA), Dr :Dq (68020)	L	2	$32/32 \rightarrow 32r : 32q$
DIVU (EA), Dn (Both 68000 and 68020)	W	1	Signed division $[Dn]_{32}/[EA]_{16} \rightarrow$ [Dn] 0-15 = quotient [Dn] 16-31 = remainder
DIVU (EA), Dq (68020)	L	2	$32/32 \rightarrow 32q$
DIVU (EA), Dr :Dq (68020)	L	2	$64/32 \rightarrow 32r : 32q$
DIVUL (EA), Dr :Dq (68020)	L	2	$32/32 \rightarrow 32r : 32q$
EORI #d8, CCR	B	2	$d8 \oplus CCR \rightarrow CCR$
EORI #dl6, SR	W	2	$dl6 \oplus SR \rightarrow SR$ if $S = 1$; else trap
EXG Rx, Ry	L	1	$Rx \leftrightarrow Ry$
EXTDn (68000 and 68020)	W, L	1	Extend sign bit of Dn from 8-bit to 16-bit or from 16-bit to 32-bit depending on whether the operand size is B or W
EXTB Dn (68020)	L	1	Extend sign bit of Dn from 8-bit to 32-bit
JMP (EA)	Unsized	1	$[EA] \rightarrow PC$ Unconditional jump using address in operand
JSR (EA)	Unsized	1	$PC \rightarrow -[SP]$; $[EA] \rightarrow PC$ Jump to subroutine using address in operand
LEA (EA), An	L	1	$[EA] \rightarrow An$
LINK An, # -d d = 16-bit for 68000 d = 16-bit or 32-bit for 68020	Unsized	2	$An \leftarrow -[SP]$; $SP \rightarrow An$; $SP - d \rightarrow SP$

Instruction	Size	Length (words)	Operation
LSL Dx, Dy	B,W, L	1	
LSL #data, Dy	B,W, L	1	Same as LSL Dx, Dy except immediate data specify the number of shifts from 0 to 7
LSL (EA)	B,W, L	1	Same as LSL Dx, Dy except left shift is performed only once
LSR Dx, Dy	B,W, L	1	
LSR #data, Dy	B,W, L	1	Same as LSR except immediate data specifies the number of shifts from 0 to 7
LSR (EA)	B,W,L	1	Same as LSR, Dx, Dy except the right shift is performed only once
MOVE An, A7	L	1	If S = l, then An $\rightarrow$ A7; else TRAP
MOVE A7, An	W, L	1	[A7] $\rightarrow$ An if S=1; else TRAP
MOVE (EA), CCR	W	1	[EA] $\rightarrow$ CCR
MOVE CCR, (EA)	W	1	CCR $\rightarrow$ [EA]
MOVE (EA), SR	W	1	If S = l, then [EA] $\rightarrow$ SR; else TRAP
MOVE SR, (EA)	W	1	If S = l, then SR $\rightarrow$ [EA]; else TRAP
MOVEC Rc, Rn (68020) Note: Rn = An or Dn, Rc = Control reg such as VBR	L	2	If S = 1, Rc $\rightarrow$Rn; else TRAP
MOVEC Rn, Rc (68020) Note: Rn = An or Dn, Rc = Control reg such as VBR	L	2	If S = 1, Rn $\rightarrow$Rc; else TRAP
MOVEM register list, (EA)	W, L	2	Register list $\rightarrow$ [EA]
MOVEM (EA), register list	W, L	2	[EA] $\rightarrow$ register list
MOVEP Dx, d (Ay)	W, L	2	Dx $\rightarrow$ d[Ay]
MOVEP d (Ay), Dx	W, L	2	d[Ay] $\rightarrow$ Dx
MOVEQ #d8, Dn	L	1	d8 sign extended to 32-bit $\rightarrow$ Dn
MOVES (EA), Rn (68020) Note: Rn = An or Dn	B, W, L	2	If S=1, Source [SFC]$\rightarrow$Rn ; else TRAP
MOVES Rn, (EA) (68020) Note: Rn = An or Dn	B, W, L	2	If S=1, Rn$\rightarrow$Destination [DFC]; else TRAP
MULS(EA),(Dn) (Both 68000 and 68020)	W	1	Signed 16×16 multiplication $[EA]_{16} * [Dn]_{16} \rightarrow [Dn]_{32}$

Instruction	Size	Length (words)	Operation
MULS(EA),Dn (68020)	L	2	Signed 32 × 32 multiplication $[EA]_{32}$ * $[Dn]_{32} \rightarrow [Dn]_{32}$; Upper 32 bits of the result are ignored.
MULU(EA),(Dn) (Both 68000 and 68020)	W	1	Unsigned 16 × 16 multiplication $[EA]_{16}$ * $[Dn]_{16} \rightarrow [Dn]_{32}$
MULU(EA),Dn (68020)	L	2	Unsigned 32 × 32 multiplication $[EA]_{32}$ * $[Dn]_{32} \rightarrow [Dn]_{32}$; Upper 32 bits of the result are ignored.
MULU (EA),Dh:Dn (68020)	L	2	Unsigned multiplication, 32 X 32 $\rightarrow$ 64 (EA) * Dn $\rightarrow$ Dh:Dn
NEC (EA)	B,W, L	1	$0 - [EA] \rightarrow EA$
NEGX (EA)	B,W, L	1	$0 - [EA] - X \rightarrow EA$
NOP	Unsized	1	No operation
NOT (EA)	B,W, L	1	$[EA]' \rightarrow EA$
OR (EA), (EA)	B,W, L	1	$[EA]OR[EA] \rightarrow EA$
ORI #data, (EA)	B,W, L	2 for B, W 3 for L	data OR$[EA] \rightarrow EA$
ORI #d8, CCR	B	2	d8 OR CCR $\rightarrow$ CCR
ORI #dl6, SR	W	2	If S = 1, then dl6VSR -> SR; else TRAP
PACK -(Ax), -(Ay), #data (68020)	Unsized	2	Source (Unpacked BCD) + data $\rightarrow$ Destination (Packed BCD)
PACK Dx, Dy, #data (68020)	Unsized	2	Source (Unpacked BCD) + data $\rightarrow$ Destination (Packed BCD)
PEA (EA)	L	1	[EA] 16 sign extend to 32 bits $\rightarrow - [SP]$
RESET	Unsized	1	If S = l, then assert RESET line; else TRAP
ROL Dx, Dy	B, W, L	1	
ROL #data, Dy	B, W, L	1	Same as ROL Dx, Dy except immediate data specifies number of times to be rotated from 0 to 7
ROL (EA)	B, W, L	1	Same as ROL Dx, Dy except [EA] is rotated once
ROR Dx, Dy	B, W, L	1	
ROR #data, Dy	B, W, L	1	Same as ROR Dx, Dy except the number of rotates is specified by immediate data from 0 to 7
ROR (EA)	B, W, L	1	Same as ROR Dx, Dy except [EA] is rotated once

Instruction	Size	Length (words)	Operation
ROXL Dx, Dy	B, W, L	1	(diagram: X, C, Dy)
ROXL #data, Dy	B, W, L	1	Same as ROXL Dx, Dy except immediate data specifies number of rotates from 0 to 7
ROXL (EA)	B, W, L	1	Same as ROXL Dx, Dy except [EA] is rotated once
ROXR Dx, Dy	B, W, L	1	(diagram: X, Dy, C)
ROXR #data, Dy	B,W, L	1	Same as ROXR Dx, Dy except immediate data specifies number of rotates from 0 to 7
ROXR (EA)	B,W, L	1	Same as ROXR Dx, Dy except [EA] is rotated once
RTE	Unsized	1	If S = 1, then [SP] + $\to$ SR; [SP] + $\to$ PC, else TRAP
RTR	Unsized	1	[SP] + $\to$ CC; [SP] + $\to$ PC
RTS	Unsized	1	[SP] + $\to$ PC
SBCD -(Ay), -(Ax)	B	1	$-$ (Ax)10 $-$ (Ay)10 $-$ X $\to$ (Ax)
SBCD Dy, Dx	B	1	[Dx]10 $-$ [Dy]10 $-$ X $\to$ Dx
SCC (EA)	B	1	If C = 0, then 1s $\to$ [EA] else 0s $\to$ [EA]
SCS (EA)	B	1	Same as SCC except the condition is C = 1
SEQ (EA)	B	1	Same as SCC except if Z = 1
SF (EA)	B	1	Same as SCC except condition is always false
SGE (EA)	B	1	Same as SCC except if greater or equal
SGT (EA)	B	1	Same as SCC except if greater than
SHI (EA)	B	1	Same as SCC except if high
SLE (EA)	B	1	Same as SCC except if less or equal
SLS(EA)	B	1	Same as SCC except if low or same
SLT (EA)	B	1	Same as SCC except if less than
SMI (EA)	B	1	Same as SCC except if N = 1
SNE (EA)	B	1	Same as SCC except if Z = 0
SPL(EA)	B	1	Same as SCC except if N = 0

Instruction	Size	Length (words)	Operation
ST (EA)	B	1	Same as SCC except condition always true
STOP #data	Unsized	2	If S= 1, then data → SR and stop; TRAP if executed in user mode
SUB (EA), (EA)	B, W, L	1	[EA] − [EA] → EA
SUBA (EA), An	W,L	1	An − [EA] → An
SUBI #data, (EA)	B, W, L	2 for B, W 3 for L	[EA] − data → EA
SUBQ #data, (EA)	B, W, L	1	[EA] − data → EA
SUBX − (Ay), − (Ax)	B, W, L	1	− [Ax] − [Ay] − X → [Ax]
SUBX Dy, Dx	B, W, L	1	Dx − Dy − X → Dx
SVC (EA)	B	1	Same as SCC except if V = 0
SVS (EA)	B	1	Same as SCC except if V = 1
SWAP Dn	W	1	Dn [31:16] ↔ Dn [15:0]
TAS (EA)	B	1	[EA] tested; N and Z are affected accordingly; 1 → bit 7 of [EA]
TRAP #vector	Unsized	1	PC → − [SSP], SR → − [SSP], (vector) → PC; 16 TRAP
TRAPV	Unsized	1	If V = 1, then TRAP; else next instruction
TST (EA)	B,W, L	1	[EA] − 0 → condition codes affected; no result provided
UNLK An	Unsized	1	An → SP; [SP]+ → An
UNPK -(Ax), -(Ay), #data (68020)	Unsized	2	Source (Packed BCD) + data → Destination (Unpacked BCD)
UNPK Dx,Dy, #data (68020)	Unsized	2	Source (Packed BCD) + data → Destination (Unpacked BCD)

F

PENTIUM INSTRUCTION FORMAT AND TIMING

Table F-2, Table F-3, and Table F-5 list all instructions along with instruction encoding diagrams and clock counts.

F.1. INTEGER INSTRUCTION FORMAT AND TIMING

The following sections explain how to use each of the columns of Table F-2.

Format

All instruction encodings are subsets of the general instruction format shown in Figure F-1. Instructions consist of one or two primary opcode bytes, possibly an address specifier consisting of the **mod r/m** byte and scale-index-base byte, a displacement if required, and an immediate data field if required.

Within the primary opcode or opcodes, smaller encoding fields may be defined. These fields vary according to the class of operation. The fields define such information as direction of the operation, size of displacements, register encoding, or sign extension.

Almost all instructions referring to an operand in memory have an addressing mode byte following the primary opcode byte(s). This byte, the **mod r/m** byte, specifies the address mode to be used. Certain encodings of the **mod r/m** byte indicate that a second addressing

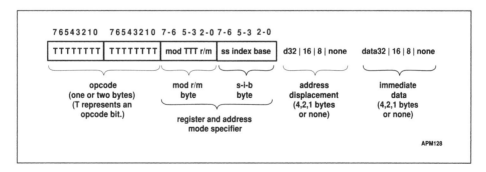

Figure F-1. **General Instruction Format**

byte, the scale-index-base byte, follows the **mod r/m** byte to fully specify the addressing mode.

Addressing modes can include a displacement immediately following the mod r/m byte or scale-index-base byte. If a displacement is present, the possible sizes are 8, 16, or 32 bits. If the instruction specifies an immediate operand, the immediate operand follows any displacement bytes. The immediate operand, if specified, is always the last field of the instruction.

Figure F-1 illustrates several of the fields that can appear in an instruction, such as the **mod** field and the **r/m** field, but the figure does not show all fields. Several smaller fields also appear in certain instructions, sometimes within the opcode bytes themselves. Table F-0 is a complete list of all fields appearing in the instruction set. Subsequent tables list the values for each of the fields.

Table F-1.   Fields within Instructions

Field Name	Description	Number of Bits
d	Specifies direction of data operation	1
eee	Specifies a special-purpose (test, debug, or control) register	
reg	General register specifier	3
s	Specifies if an immediate data field must be sign-extended	1
sreg2	Segment register specifier for CS, SS, DS, ES	2
sreg3	Segment register specifier for CS, SS, DS, ES, FS, GS	3
tttn	For conditional instructions, specifies a condition asserted or a condition negated	4
w	Specifies if data is byte of full-sized (full-sized is either 16 or 32 bits)	1

In many two-operand instructions, the **d** field indicates which operand is considered the source and which is the destination.

Encoding of Operation Direction (d) Field

d	Source	Destination
0	**reg** field	**mod r/m** or **mod ss index base** field
1	mod r/m or mod ss index base field	reg field

Encoding of Special-Purpose Register (eee) Field

eee	Control Register	Debug Register
000	CRO	DRO
001	reserved	DR1
010	CR2	DR2

eee	Control Register	Debug Register
011	CR3	DR3
100	CR4	reserved
101	reserved	reserved
110	reserved	DR6
111	reserved	DR7

NOTE:Do not use reserved encodings.

Encoding of reg Field When w Field is Not Present in Instruction

reg Field	Register Selected During 16-Bit Data Operations	Register Selected During 32-Bit Data Operations
000	AX	EAX
001	CX	ECX
010	DX	EDX
011	BX	EBX
100	SP	ESP
101	BP	EBP
110	SI	ESI
111	DI	EDI

Encoding of reg Field When w Field is Present in Instruction

The **s** field occurs primarily in instructions with immediate data fields. The **s** field has an effect only if the size of the immediate data is 8 bits and is being placed in a 16-bit or 32-bit destination.

Encoding of Sign-Extend (s) Field

s	Effect on Immediate Data8	Effect on Immediate Data16 or Data32
0	None	None
1	Sign-extend data8 to fill 16-bit or 32-bit destination	None

Encoding of the Segment Register (sreg) Field

For the conditional instructions (conditional jumps and set on condition), **tttn** is encoded such that **ttt** gives the condition to test and **n** indicates whether to use the condition (**n** = 0) or its negation (**n** = 1).

Encoding of Conditional Test (tttn) Field

tttn	Mnemonic	Condition
0000	0	Overflow
0001	NO	No overflow
0010	B, NAE	Below, Not above or equal
0011	NB, AE	Not below, Above or equal

tttn	Mnemonic	Condition
0100	E, Z	Equal, Zero
0101	NE, NZ	Not equal, Not zero
0110	BE, NA	Below or equal, Not above
0111	NBE, A	Not below or equal, Above
1000	S	Sign
1001	NS	Not sign
1010	P, PE	Parity, Parity Even
1011	NP, PO	Not parity, Parity Odd
1100	L, NGE	Less than, Not greater than or equal to
1101	NL, GE	Not less than, Greater than or equal to
1110	LE, NG	Less than or equal to, Not greater than
1111	NLE, G	Not less than or equal to, Greater than

For any given instruction performing a data operation, the instruction is executing as a 32-bit operation or a 16-bit operation. Within the constraints of the operation size, the **w** field encodes the operand size as either one byte or the full operation size, as shown in the following table.

Encoding of Operand Length (w) Field

w Field	Operand Size During 16-Blt Data Operations	Operand Size During 32-Blt Data Operations
0	8 bits	8 bits
1	16 bits	32 bits

Clock Counts

To calculate elapsed time for an instruction, multiply the instruction clock count as listed in the tables by the processor clock period (for example, 15 ns for a 66-MHz processor).
The clock count tables assume that data and instruction access hit their respective caches. A cache miss forces the processor to run an external bus cycle. The 64-bit burst bus of the Pentium processor is defined as r-b-w, where:

r= The number of clocks in the first cycle of a burst read or the number of clocks per data cycle in a nonburst read.

b= The number of clocks for the second and subsequent cycles in a burst read.

w= The number of clocks for a write.

The fastest bus the Pentium processor can support is 2-1-2, assuming zero wait states. The clock counts in the cache miss penalty column assume a 2-1-2 bus. For slower busses, add r — 2 clocks to the cache miss penalty for the first quadword accessed. Other factors also affect instruction clock counts.

To simplify the tables, the following assumptions are made:

1.   The external bus is available for reads or writes at all times. Otherwise, add clocks to reads until the bus is available. The processor stalls if the write buffers become full and the external bus is busy. In that case, add clocks to writes until the bus becomes available.

2.   If the write buffers become full, subsequent writes are delayed until the write buffers become empty. For the worst case, add w clocks.

3.   Accesses are aligned. Add three clocks to each misaligned access.

4.   Operands are in the data cache. Add 3 + (number of wait states) for each cache miss.

5.   The target of a jump is in the code cache. If not, add r clocks for accessing the destination instruction of a jump. If the destination instruction is not completely contained in the first qword read, add a maximum of 3b clocks. If the destination instruction is not completely contained in the first 32-byte burst, add a maximum of another r + 3b clocks. The penalty for branch misprediction is three clocks.

6.   Cache fills complete before subsequent accesses to the same line. If a read misses the cache during a cache fill due to a previous read or prefetch, the read must wait for the cache fill to complete. If a read or write accesses a cache line still being filled, it must wait for the fill to complete.

7. Page translation hits in TLB. A TLB miss typically adds from 13 to 28 clocks to the instruction depending on whether the Accessed or Dirty bit of the page entries needs to be set in memory. This assumes that neither page entry is in the data cache and that a page fault does not occur during address translation.

8.   No exceptions are detected during instruction execution. Refer to the Interrupt Clock Counts Table for extra clocks if an interrupt is detected.

9.   Instructions that read multiple consecutive data items (for example, task switch, POPA, etc.) and miss the cache are assumed to start the first access on a 32-byte boundary. If not, an extra cache line fill may be necessary, which may add up to r + 3b clocks to the cache miss penalty.

10. No address generation interlocks (AGI). AGIs occur when a register being used as part of an address calculation is the destination register of a previous instruction in either the pipelines. AGIs cause a one clock delay.

The following abbreviations are used in the clock count columns:

TS   The time for a task switch, which depends on the target TSS type as shown in the TaskSwitch Clock Counts Table.

INT The time for an interrupt, which depends on processor mode and type of gate used, as shown in the Interrupt Clock Counts Table.

Task Switch Clock Counts Table

Method		Value of TS
From	To	
32-Bit, 16-Bit, or V86 TSS	32-Bit TSS	85
32-Bit, 16-Bit, or V86 TSS	16-Bit TSS	85
32-Bit, 16-Bit, or V86 TSS	V86 TSS	71

Interrupt Clock Counts Table

Method	Value of INT		
	Cache Hit	Miss Penalty	Notes
Real Mode	11	3	
Protected Mode			
Interrupt/Trap gate, same level	25	6	9
Interrupt/Trap gate, different level	42	12	9
Task gate	17 + TS	3	9,10
Virtual 8086 Mode			
Interrupt/Trap, same level	13	3	
Interrupt/Trap gate, different level	54	12	
Task gate	17 + TS	3	10

Notes

The following abbreviations in the Notes column help to interpret the other columns:

16/32   Clocks apply to 16- and 32-bit modes respectively

L/NL   Clocks apply to loop and no loop cases respectively
MN/MX   Clocks shown define a range from minimum to maximum
P   Clocks apply to protected mode
R   Clocks apply to real-address mode
RV/P   First clock applies to real and V86 mode; second applies to protected mode
T/NT   Clocks apply to taken and not taken cases respectively
U/L   Clocks apply to unlocked and locked cases respectively
1.   Assuming that the operand address and stack address fall in different cache interleaves.
2.   Always locked. Always forced to miss cache.
4.   Clocks = { quotient(count/operand length) } *7 + 9 = 8 if count 5, operand length (8/16/32).
5.   Clocks = { quotient(count/operand length)}*7 + 9 = 9 if count operand length (8/16/32).

8.   Penalty for cache miss: add 2 clocks for every stack value copied to the new stack frame.

9.   Add 8 clocks for each load of an unaccessed descriptor.

10.   Refer to Task Switch Clock Counts Table for value of TS.

For notes 12 — 13:b = 0 — 3, nonzero byte number;

$i = 0 — 1$, nonzero nibble number; $n = 0 — 3$, nonzero bit number in nibble.

12.   Clocks= $8 + 4(b + 1) + 3(i + 1) + 3(n + 1) = 6$ if second operand = 0.

13.   Clocks= $9 + 4(b + 1) + 3(i + 1) + 3(n + 1) = 7$ if second operand = 0.

For notes 14 — 15: n = bit position (0 — 31).

14.   Clocks= $7 + 2(32 — n) = 6$ if second operand = 0.

15.   Clocks= $8 + 2(32 — n) = 7$ if second operand = 0.

16.   Assuming that the two string addresses fall in different cache interleaves.

21.   Refer to the Interrupt Clock Counts Table for value of INT.

23.   Add r + 3b for instruction cache miss. Add 3 for branch misprediction.

24.   Clocks shown define a range from minimum to maximum.

25.   Add r + 3b for instruction cache miss.

Pairing

The following abbreviations are used in the Pairing column:

PV   Pairable if issued to V-pipe

NP   Not pairable, executes in U-pipe

UV   Pairable in either pipe

PU   Pairable if issued to U-pipe

Table F-2.   **Integer Clock Count Summary**

Instruction	Format	Clocks	Notes
AAA — ASCII Adjust after Addition	0011 0111	3	
AAD — ASCII Adjust AX before Division	1101 0101 : 0000 1010	10	
AAM — ASCII Adjust AX after Multiply	1101 0100 : 0000 1010	18	
AAS — ASCII Adjust AL after Subtraction	0011 1111	3	
ADC — ADD with Carry			
reg1 to reg2	0001 000w : 11 reg1 reg2	1	
reg2 to reg1	0001 001w : 11 reg1 reg2	1	
memory to register	0001 001w : mod reg r/m	2	
register to memory	0001 000w : mod reg r/m	3	U/L
immediate to register	1000 00sw : 11 010 reg : immediate data	1	
immediate to accumulator	0001 010w : immediate data	1	

Table F-2. Cont.

Instruction	Format	Clocks	Notes
immediate to memory	1000 00sw : mod 010 r/m : immediate data	3	U/L
ADD — Add			
reg1 to reg2	0000 000w : 11 reg1 reg2	1	
reg2 to reg1	0000 001w : 11 reg1 reg2	1	
memory to register	0000 001w : mod reg r/m	2	
register to memory	0000 000w : mod reg r/m	3	U/L
immediate to register	1000 00sw : 11 000 reg : immediate data	1	
immediate to accumulator	0000 010w : immediate data	1	
immediate to memory	1000 00sw : mod 000 r/m : immediate data	3	U/L
AND — Logical AND			
reg1 to reg2	0010 000w 11 reg1 reg2	1	
reg2 to reg1	0010 001w 11 reg1 reg2	1	
memory to register	0010 001w mod reg r/m	2	
register to memory	0010 000w : mod reg r/m	3	U/L
immediate to register	1000 00sw : 11 100 reg : immediate data	1	
immediate to accumulator	0010 010w : immediate data	1	
immediate to memory	1000 00sw : mod 100 r/m : immediate data	3	U/L
ARPL — Adjust RPL Field of Selector			
from register	0110 0011 : 11 reg1 reg2	7	
from memory	0110 0011: mod reg r/m	7	
BOUND — Check Array Against Bounds	0110 0010: mod reg r/m		
if within bounds		8	
if out of bounds		INT + 32	21
BSF - Bit Scan Forward			
reg1, reg2	0000 1111 : 1011 1100 11 reg2 reg1		
word		6-34	MN/MX, 12
doubleword		6-42	MN/MX, 12

Table F-2.   Cont.

Instruction	Format	Clocks	Notes
memory, reg	0000 1111 : 1011 1100 mod reg r/m		
word		6-35	MN/MX, 13
doubleword		6-43	MN/MX, 13
doubleword		7-71	MN/MX,14
memory, reg	0000 1111 : 1011 1101: mod reg r/m		
word		7-40	MN/MX,15
doubleword		7-72	MN/MX,15
BSWAP — Byte Swap BT — Bit Test	0000 1111 : 1100 1 reg	1	
register, immediate data	0000 1111 1011 1010:11 100 reg: imm8	4	
memory, immediate imm8 data	0000 1111 1011 1010: mod 100 r/m :	4	
reg1, reg2	0000 1111 : 1010 0011 : 11 reg2 reg1	4	
memory, reg	0000 1111 : 1010 0011: mod reg r/m	9	
BTC — Bit Test and Complement			
register, immediate data	0000 1111 : 1011 1010 11 111 reg: imm8	7	
memory, immediate imm8 data	0000 1111: 1011 1010 : mod 111 r/m :	8	U/L
reg1, reg2	0000 1111 : 1011 1011 : 11 reg2 reg1	7	
memory, reg	0000 1111 : 1011 1011: mod reg r/m	13	U/L
BTR — Bit Test and Reset			
register, immediate data	0000 1111: 1011 1010: 11 110 reg: imm8	7	
memory, immediate imm8 data	0000 1111: 1011 1010: mod 110 r/m :	8	U/L

Table F-2.   Cont.

Instruction	Format	Clocks	Notes
reg1, reg2	0000 1111 : 1011 0011 : 11 reg2 reg1	7	
memory, reg	0000 1111: 1011 0011: mod reg r/m	13	U/L
BTS — Bit Test and Set			
register, immediate data	0000 1111 : 1011 1010: 11 101 reg: imm8	7	
memory, immediate imm8 data	0000 1111: 1011 1010 : mod 101 r/m :	8	U/L
reg1, reg2	0000 1111: 1010 1011: 11 reg2 reg1	7	
memory, reg	0000 1111 : 1010 1011 : mod reg r/m	13	U/L
CALL — Call Procedure (in same segment)			
direct	1110 1000 : full displacement	1	23
register indirect	1111 1111 : 11 010 reg	2	23
memory indirect	11111111:mod 010 r/m	2	23
CALL — Call Procedure (in other segment)			
direct	1001 1010 : unsigned full offset, selector	4	R,23
to same level		4-13	P,9,23,24
thru gate to same level		22	P,9,25
to inner level, no parameters		44	P,9,25
to inner level, x parameters (d)words		45+2x	P,9,25
to TSS		21+TS	P,10,9,25
thru task gate		22+TS	P,10,9,25
indirect	1111 1111 : mod 011 r/m	5	R,23
to same level		5-14	P,9,23,24
thru gate to same level		22	P,9,25
to inner level, no parameters		44	P,9,25
to inner level, x parameters (d)words		45+2x	P,9,25
to TSS		21+TS	P,10,9,25
thru task gate		22+TS	P,10,9,25

Table F-2. Cont.

Instruction	Format	Clocks	Notes
CBW - Convert Byte to Word CWDE — Convert Word to Doubleword	1001 1000	3	
CLC — Clear Carry Flag	1111 1000	2	
CLD — Clear Direction Flag	1111 1000	2	
CLI — Clear Interrupt Flag	1111 1010	7	
CLTS — Clear Task-Switched Flag in CRO	0000 1111 : 0000 0110	10	
CMC — Complement Carry Flag	1111 0101	2	
CMP — Compare Two Operands			
reg1 with reg2	0011 100w : 11 reg1 reg2	1	
reg2 with reg1	0011 101w : 11 reg1 reg2	1	
memory with register	0011 100w : mod reg r/m	2	
register with memory	0011 101w : mod reg r/m	2	
immediate with register	1000 00sw : 11 111 reg : immediate data	1	
immediate with accumulator	0011 110w : immediate data	1	
immediate with memory	1000 00sw : mod 111 r/m	2	
CMPS/CMPSB/CMPSW/ CMPSD — Compare String Operands	1010011w	5	16
CMPXCHG — Compare and Exchange			
reg1 , reg2	0000 1111 : 1011 000w : 11 reg2 reg1	5	
memory, reg	0000 1111 : 1011 000w : mod reg r/m	6	U/L
CMPXCHG8B — Compare and Exchange 8 Bytes			
memory, reg	0000 1111 : 1100 0111 : mod reg r/m	10	U/L
CWD — Convert Word to Dword COQ — Convert Dword to Qword	1001 1001	2	

Table F-2.   Cont.

Instruction	Format		Clocks	Notes
DAA — Decimal Adjust AL after Addition	0010 0111		3	
DAS – Decimal Adjust AL after Subtraction	0010 1111		3	
DEC – Decrement by 1				
reg	1111111w:11001 reg		1	
Or	0100 1 reg		1	
memory	1111 111w : mod 001 r/m		3	U/L
DIV – Unsigned Divide				
accumulator by register	1111 011w : 11 110 reg			
divisor —	byte		17	
	word		25	
	doubleword			
accumulator by memory	1111 011w : mod 110 r/m			
divisor —	byte		17	
	word		25	
	doubleword		41	
ENTER – Make Stack Frame	1100 1000 : 16-bit displace-ment : 8-bit			
level (L)				
for Procedure Parameters				
L = 0			11	
L = 1			15	
L> 1			15 + 2L	8
HLT – Halt	1111 0100			
IDIV – Signed Divide				
accumulator by register	1111 011w : 11 111 reg			
divisor —	byte		22	
	word		30	
	doubleword		46	
accumulator by memory	1111 011w : mod 111 r/m			
divisor —	byte		22	
	word		30	
	doubleword		46	
IMUL – Signed Multiply				
accumulator with register	1111 011w : 11 101 reg			
multiplier —	byte		11	

Table F-2.   Cont.

Instruction	Format	Clocks	Notes
	word	11	
	doubleword	10	
accumulator with memory	1111 011w : mod 101 reg		
multiplier —	byte	11	
	word	11	
	doubleword	10	
reg1 with reg2	0000 1111 : 1010 1111 : 11 : reg1 reg2		
multiplier —	byte	10	
	word	10	
	doubleword	10	
register with memory	0000 1111 : 1010 1111: mod reg r/m		
multiplier —	byte	10	
	word	10	
	doubleword	10	
reg1 with imm. to reg2	0110 10s1 : 11 reg1 reg2 : immediate data		
multiplier —	byte	10	
	word	10	
	doubleword	10	
mem. with imm. to reg	0110 10s1 : mod reg r/m : immediate data		
multiplier —	byte	10	
	word	10	
	doubleword	10	
INC – Increment by 1			
reg	1111111w : 11 000 reg	1	
Or	01 00 0 reg	1	
memory	1111 111w : mod 000 r/m	3	U/L
INT n - Interrupt Type n	1100 1101 : type	INT + 6	21,25
INT - Single-Step Interrupt 3	1100 1100	INT + 5	21,25
INTO - Interrupt 4 on Overflow	1100 1110		
not taken		4	21,25
INVD – Invalidate Cache	0000 1111: 0000 1000	15	

Table F-2.   Cont.

Instruction	Format	Clocks	Notes
INVLPG – Invalidate TLB Entry	0000 1111: 0000 0001 : mod 111 r/m	29	
IRET/IRETD – Interrupt Return	1100 1111		
real mode or virtual 8086 mode		7	R,23
protected mode			
to same level		10-19	P,9,23,24
to outer level		27	P,9,25
to nested task		10 + TS	P,9,10,25
Jcc – Jump if Condition is Met			
8-bit displacement	0111 tttn : 8-bit displacement	1	23
full displacement	0000 1111: 1000 tttn : full displacement	1	23
JCXZ/JECXZ – Jump on CX/ECX Zero	1110 0011 : 8-bit displace-ment	6/5	T/NT,23
address size prefix differentiates JCXZ from JECXZ			
JMP - Unconditional Jump (to same segment)			
short	1110 1011 : 8-bit displace-ment	1	23
direct	1110 1001: full displacement	1	23
register indirect	1111 1111 : 11 100 reg	2	23
memory indirect	1111 1111 : mod 100 r/m	2	23
JMP — Unconditional Jump (to other segment)			
direct intersegment	1110 1010 : unsigned full offset, selector	3	R,23
to same level		3-12	P,9,23,24
thru call gate ro same level		18	P,9,25
thru TSS		19 + TS	P,10,9,25
thru task gate		20 + TS	P,10,9,25
indirect intersegment	1111 1111: mod 101 r/m	4	R,23
to same level		4-13	P,9,23,24
thru call gate ro same level		18	P,9,25
thru TSS		19 + TS	P,10,9,25
thru task gate		20 + TS	P,10,9,25

Table F-2. **Cont.**

Instruction	Format	Clocks	Notes
LAHF - Load Flags into AH Register	1001 1111	2	
LAR - Load Access Rights Byte			
from register	0000 1111: 0000 0010 : 11 reg1 reg2	8	
from memory	0000 1111 : 0000 0010: mod reg r/m	8	
LDS — Load Pointer to DS	1100 0101: mod reg r/m	4-13	9,24
LEA - Load Effective Address	1000 1101: mod reg r/m	1	
LEAVE - High Level Procedure Exit	1100 1001	3	
LES — Load Pointer to ES	1100 0100 : mod reg r/m	4-13	9,24
LFS — Load Pointer to FS	0000 1111 : 1011 0100: mod reg r/m	4-13	9,24
LGDT — Load Global Descriptor Table Register	0000 1111 : 0000 0001 : mod 010 r/m	6	
LGS -- Load Pointer to GS	0000 1111 : 1011 0101 : mod reg r/m	4-13	9,24
LIDT — Load Interrupt Descriptor Table Register	0000 1111: 0000 0000 : 11 010 reg	6	
LLDT - Load Local Descriptor Table Register			
LDTR from register	0000 1111: 0000 0000 : 11 010 reg	9	
LDTR from memory	0000 0000 : mod 010 r/m	9	
LMSW — Load Machine Status Word			
from register	0000 1111 : 0000 0001 : 11 110 reg	8	
from memory	0000 1111 : 0000 0001 : mod 110 r/m	8	
LOCK - Assert LOCK# Signal Prefix	1111 0000	1	
LODS/LODSB/LODSW/ LODSD- Load String Operand	1010 110w	2	
LOOP — Loop Count	1110 0010 : 8-bit displacement	5/6	L/NL,23

Table F-2.   Cont.

Instruction	Format	Clocks	Notes
LOOPZ/LOOPE - Loop Count while Zero/Equal	1110 0001 : 8-bit displacement	7/8	L/NL,23
LOOPNZ/LOOPNE - Loop Count while not Zero/Equal	1110 0000 8-bit displacement	7/8	
LSL - Load Segment Limit			
from register	0000 1111 : 0000 0011 : 11 reg1 reg2	8	
from memory	0000 1111 : 0000 0011 : mod reg r/m	8	
LSS - Load Pointer to SS	0000 1111 : 1011 0010: mod reg r/m	4-13/8-17	L/NL,23
LTR - Load Task Register			
from register	0000 1111 : 0000 0000 : 11 011 reg	10	
from memory	0000 1111 : 0000 0000: mod 011 r/m	10	
MOV - Move Data			
reg1 to reg2	1000 100w : 11 reg1 reg2	1	
reg2 to reg1	1000 101w : 11 reg1 reg2	1	
memory to reg	1000 101w : mod reg r/m	1	
reg to memory	1000 100w : mod reg r/m	1	
immediate to reg	1100 011w : 11 000 reg : immediate data	1	
Or	1011 w reg : immediate data	1	
immediate to memory	1100 011w : mod 000 r/m : immediate data	1	
memory to accumulator	1010 000w : full displacement	1	
accumulator to memory	1010 001w : full displacement	1	
MOV - Move to/from Control Registers			
CRO from register	0000 1111 : 0010 0010: 11 000 reg	11	
CR2 from register	0000 1111 : 0010 0010 : 11 010reg	12	
CR3 from register	0000 1111 : 0010 0010 : 11 011 reg	21	

Table F-2.   Cont.

Instruction	Format	Clocks	Notes
CR4 from register	0000 1111 : 0010 0010 : 11 100 reg	14	
register from CR0-4	0000 1111 : 0010 0000 : 11 eee reg	4	
MOV - Move to/from De-bug Registers			
DR0-3 from register	0000 1111 : 0010 0011 : 11 eee reg	11	
DR4-5 from register	0000 1111 : 0010 0011 : 11 eee reg	12	
DR6-7 from register	0000 1111 : 0010 0011 : 11 eee reg	11	
register from DR6-7	0000 1111 : 0010 0001: 11 eee reg	11	
register from DR4-5	0000 1111 : 0010 0001: 11 eee reg	12	
register from DRO-3	0000 1111: 0010 0001: 11 eee reg	2	
MOV - Move to/from Seg-ment Registers			
reg to segment reg	1000 1110 : 11 sreg3 reg	2-11	9,24
reg to SS	1000 1110 : 11 sreg3 reg	2-11/ 8-17	RV/P,9,24
memory to segment reg	1000 1110: mod sreg3 r/m	3	9,24
memory to SS	1000 1110 : mod sreg3 r/m	3-12/ 8-17	RV/P,9,24
segment reg to reg	1000 1100 : 11 sreg3 reg	1	
segment reg to memory	1000 1100 : mod sreg3 r/m	1	
MOVS/MOVSB/MOVSW/	1010 010w	4	16
MOVSD - Move Data from String to String			
MOVSX - Move with Sign-Extend			
reg2 to reg1	0000 1111 : 1011 111w : 11 reg1 reg2	3	
memory to reg	0000 1111 : 1011 111w : mod reg r/m	3	
MOVZX - Move with Zero-Extend			
reg2 to reg1	0000 1111 : 1011 011w : 11 reg1 reg2	3	

Table F-2.   Cont.

Instruction	Format	Clocks	Notes
memory to reg	0000 1111 : 1011 011w : mod reg r/m	3	
MUL - Unsigned Multipli-cation of AL or AX			
accumulator with register	1111 011w : 11 100 reg		
multiplier —	byte	11	
	word	11	
	doubleword	10	
accumulator with memory	1111 011w : mod 100 reg		
multiplier —	byte	11	
	word	11	
	doubleword	10	
NEG - Two's Complement Negation			
reg	1111011w:11011 reg	1	
memory	1111 011w : mod 011 r/m	3	U/L
NOP - No Operation	1001 0000	1	
NOT - One's Complement Negation			
reg	1111 011w : 11 010 reg	1	
memory	1111 011w : mod 010 r/m	3	U/L
OR - Logical Inclusive OR			
reg1 to reg2	0000 100w : 11 reg1 reg2	1	
reg2 to reg1	0000 101w : 11 reg1 reg2	1	
memory to register	0000 101w : mod reg r/m	2	
register to memory	0000 100w : mod reg r/m	3	U/L
immediate to register	1000 00sw : 11 001 reg : im-mediate data	1	
immediate to accumulator	0000 110w : immediate data	1	
immediate to memory	1000 OOsw : mod 001 r/m : immediate data	3	U/L
POP — Pop a Word from the Stack			
reg	1000 1111:11 000 reg	1	
or	0101 1 reg	1	
memory	1000 1111: mod 000 r/m	3	1

Table F-2.   Cont.

Instruction	Format	Clocks	Notes
POP — Pop a Segment Register from the Stack			
segment reg CS, DS, ES	000 sreg2 111	3-12	9,24
segment reg SS	000 sreg2 111	3-12/ 8-17	RV/P,9,24
segment reg FS, GS	0000 1111: 10 sreg3 001	3-12	9,24
POPA/POPAD — Pop All	0110 0001	5	
General Registers			
POPF/POPFD — Pop Stack into	1001 1101	4/14	RV/P
FLAGS or EFLAGS Register			
PUSH — Push Operand onto the Stack			
reg	1111 1111 :11110 reg	1	
or	0101 0 reg	1	
memory	1111 1111 :mod 110 r/m	2	1
immediate	0110 10s0 : immediate data	1	
PUSH — Push Segment Register onto the Stack			
segment reg CS,DS,ES,SS	000 sreg2 110	1	
segment reg FS,GS	0000 1111: 10 sreg3 000	1	
PUSHA/PUSHAD — Push All	0110 0000	5	
General Registers			
PUSHF/PUSHFD — Push Flags	1001 1100	3/9	RV/P
Register onto the Stack			
RCL — Rotate thru Carry Left			
reg by 1	1101 000w : 11 010 reg	1	
memory by 1	1101 000w : mod 010 r/m	3	
reg by CL	1101 001w : 11 010 reg	7-24	MN/MX,4
memory by CL	1101 001w : mod 010 r/m	9-26	MN/MX,5
reg by immediate count	1100 000w : 11 010 reg : imm8 data	8-25	MN/MX,4
memory by immediate count	1100 000w : mod 010 r/m : imm8 data	10-27	MN/MX,5

Table F-2.   Cont.

Instruction	Format	Clocks	Notes
RCR — Rotate thru Carry Right			
reg by 1	1101 000w : 11 011 reg	1	
memory by 1	1101 000w : mod 011 r/m	3	
reg by CL	1101 001w : 11 011 reg	7-24	MN/MX,4
memory by CL	1101 001w : mod 011 r/m	9-26	MN/MX,5
reg by immediate count	1100 000w : 11 011 reg : imm8 data	8-25	MN/MX,4
memory by immediate count	1100 000w : mod 011 r/m : imm8 data	10-27	MN/MX,5
RDMSR — Read from Model-	0000 1111: 0011 0010	20-24	MN/MX
Specific Register			
REP LODS - Load String	1111 0011 : 010 110w		
C = 0		7	
C > 0		7 + 3c	16
REP MOVS - Move String	1111 0011 : 1010 010w		
C = 0		6	
C = 1		13	16
C > 1		13 + c	16
REP STOS - Store String	1111 0011 : 1010 101w		
C = 0		6	
C > 0		9 + c	
REPE CMPS - Compare String	1111 0011: 1010 011w		
(Find Non-Match)			
C = 0		7	
C > 0		8 + 4c	16
REPE SCAS - Scan String	1111 0011 : 1010 111w		
(Find Non-AL/AX/EAX)			
C = 0		7	
C > 0		8 + 4c	16
REPNE CMPS - Compare	1111 0010 : 1010 011w		
String (Find Match)			
C = 0		7	
C > 0		9 + 4c	16
REPNE SCAS - Scan String	1111 0010 : 1010 111w		

Table F-2. **Cont.**

Instruction	Format	Clocks	Notes
(Find AL/AX/EAX)			
C = 0		7	
C > 0		8 + 4c	16
RET - Return from Procedure (to same segment)			
	1100 0011	2	
adding immediate to SP	1100 0010 : 16-bit displacement	3	
RET - Return from Procedure (to other segment)			
intersegment	1100 1011	4	R,23
to same level		4-13	P,9,23,24
to outer level		23	P,9,25
adding immediate to SP	1100 1010 : 16-bit displacement	4	R,23
to same level	4-13	P,9,23,24	
to outer level	23	P,9,25	
ROL - Rotate (not thru Carry) Left			
reg by 1	1101 000w : 11 000 reg	1	
memory by 1	1101 000w : mod 000 r/m	3	
reg by CL	1101 001w : 11 000 reg	4	
memory by CL	1101 001w : mod 000 r/m	4	
reg by immediate count	1100 000w : 11 000 reg : imm8 data	1	
memory by immediate count	1100 000w : mod 000 dm : imm8 data	3	
ROR — Rotate (not thru Carry) Right			
reg by 1	1101 000w : 11 001 reg	1	
memory by 1	1101 000w : mod 001 r/m	3	
reg by CL	1101 001w : 11 001 reg	4	
memory by CL	1101 001w : mod 001 r/m	4	
reg by immediate count	1100 000w : 11 001 reg : imm8 data	1	
memory by immediate count	1100 000w : mod 001 r/m : imm8 data	3	

Table F-2.   Cont.

Instruction	Format	Clocks	Notes
RSM — Resume from System	0000 1111 : 1010 1010		
Management Mode			
SAHF — Store AH into Flags	1001 1110	2	
SAL — Shift Arithmetic Left	same instruction as SHL		
SAR — Shift Arithmetic Right			
reg by 1	1101 000w : 11 111 reg	1	
memory by 1	1101 000w : mod 111 r/m	3	
reg by CL	1101 001w : 11 111 reg	4	
memory by CL	1101 001w : mod 111 r/m	4	
reg by immediate count	1100 000w : 11 111 reg : imm8 data	1	
memory by immediate count	1100 000w : mod 111 r/m : imm8 data	3	
SBB — Integer Subtraction with Borrow			
reg1 to reg2	0001 100w : 11 reg1 reg2	1	
reg2 to reg1	0001 101w : 11 reg1 reg2	1	
memory to register	0001 101w : mod reg r/m	2	
register to memory	0001 100w : mod reg r/m	3	U/L
immediate to register	1000 00sw : 11 011 reg : immediate data	1	
immediate to accumulator	0001 110w : immediate data	1	
immediate to memory	1000 00sw : mod 011 r/m : immediate data	3	U/L
SCAS/SCASB/SCASW/ SCASD	1101 111w	4	
— Scan String			
SETcc — Byte Set on Condition			
reg	0000 1111 : 1001 tttn : 11 000 reg	1	
memory	0000 1111 : 1001 tttn : mod 000 r/m	2	
SGDT — Store Global	0000 1111 : 0000 0001 : mod 000 r/m	4	

Table F-2.   Cont.

Instruction	Format	Clocks	Notes
Descriptor Table Register			
SHL — Shift Left			
reg by 1	1101 000w : 11 100 reg	1	
memory by 1	1101 000w : mod 100 r/m	3	
reg by CL	1101 001w : 11 100 reg	4	
memory by CL	1101 001w : mod 100 r/m	4	
reg by immediate count	1100 000w : 11 100 reg : imm8 data	1	
memory by immediate count	1100 000w : mod 100 r/m : imm8 data	3	
SHLD — Double Precision Shift Left			
register by immediate count	0000 1111: 1010 0100: 11 reg2 reg1 :	4	
imm8			
memory by immediate count	0000 1111: 1010 0100 mod reg r/m	4	
imm8			
register by CL	0000 1111 1010 0101:11 reg2 reg1	4	
memory by CL	0000 1111 : 1010 0101: mod reg r/m	5	
SHR — Shift Right			
reg by 1	1101 000w : 11 101 reg	1	
memory by 1	1101 000w : mod 101 r/m	3	
reg by CL	1101 001w : 11 101 reg	4	
memory by CL	1101 001w : mod 101 r/m	4	
reg by immediate count	1100 000w : 11 101 reg : imm8 data	1	
memory by immediate count	1100 000w : mod 101 r/m : imm8 data	3	
SHRD — Double Precision Shift Right			
register by immediate count	0000 1111: 1010 1100 : 11 reg2 reg1 :	4	
imm8			
memory by immediate count	0000 1111: 1010 1100 mod reg r/m :	4	

Table F-2.   Cont.

Instruction	Format	Clocks	Notes
imm8			
register by CL	0000 1111 : 1010 1101 : 11 reg2 reg1	4	
memory by CL	0000 1111 : 1010 1101 : mod reg r/m	5	
SIDT — Store Interrupt	0000 1111 : 0000 0001 : mod 001 r/m	4	
Descriptor Table Register			
SLDT — Store Local Descriptor Table Register			
to register	0000 1111: 0000 0000 : 11 000 reg	2	
to memory	0000 1111: 0000 0000 : mod 000 r/m	2	
SMSW — Store Machine Status Word			
to register	0000 1111 : 0000 0001:11 100 reg	4	
to memory	0000 1111 : 0000 0001: mod 100 r/m	4	
STC — Set Carry Flag	1111 1001	2	
STD — Set Direction Flag	1111 1101	2	
STI — Set Interrupt Flag	1111 1011	7	
STOS/STOSB/STOSW/ STOSD	1010 101w	3	
— Store String Data			
STR — Store Task Register			
to register	0000 1111 : 0000 0000 : 11 001 reg	2	
to memory	0000 1111 : 0000 0000 : mod 001 r/m	2	
SUB — Integer Subtraction			
reg1 to reg2	0010 100w : 11 reg1 reg2	1	
reg2 to reg1	0010 101w : 11 reg1 reg2	1	
memory to register	0010 101w : mod reg r/m	2	
register to memory	0010 100w : mod reg r/m	3	U/L
immediate to register	1000 00sw : 11 101 reg : immediate data	1	
immediate to accumulator	0010 110w : immediate data	1	

Table F-2. **Cont.**

Instruction	Format	Clocks	Notes
immediate to memory	1000 00sw : mod 101 r/m : immediate data	3	U/L
TEST — Logical Compare			
reg1 and reg2	1000 010w : 11 reg1 reg2	2	
memory and register	1000 010w : mod reg r/m	1	
immediate and register	1111 011w : 11 000 reg : immediate data	1	
immediate and accumulator	1010 100w : immediate data	1	
immediate and memory	1111 011w : mod 000 r/m : immediate data	2	
VERR — Verify a Segment for Reading			
register	0000 1111 : 0000 0000 : 11 100 reg	7	
memory	0000 1111 : 0000 0000: mod 100 r/m	7	
VERW — Verify a Segment for Writing			
register	0000 1111 : 0000 0000 : 11 101 reg	7	
memory	0000 1111 : 0000 0000 mod 101 r/m	7	
WAIT — Wait	1001 1011	1/1	
WBINVD — Write-Back and	0000 1111: 0000 1001	2000+	
Invalidate Data Cache			
WRMSR — Write to Model-	0000 1111 : 0011 0000	30-45	MN/MX
Specific Register			
XADD — Exchange and Add			
reg1, reg2	0000 1111 : 1100 000w : 11 reg2 reg1	3	
memory, reg	0000 1111 : 1100 000w : mod reg r/m	4	U/L
XCHG — Exchange Register/Memory with Register			
reg1 with reg2	1000 011w : 11 reg1 reg2	3	2
accumulator with reg	1001 0 reg	2	2

Table F-2.   Cont.

Instruction	Format	Clocks	Notes
memory with reg	1000 011w : mod reg r/m	3	2
XLAT/XLATB — Table Look-up Translation	1101 0111	4	
XOR — Logical Exclusive OR			
reg1 to reg2	0011 000w : 11 reg1 reg2	1	
reg2 to reg1	0011 001w : 11 reg1 reg2	1	
memory to register	0011 001w : mod reg r/m	2	
register to memory	0011 000w : mod reg r/m	3	U/L
immediate to register	1000 00sw : 11 110 reg : im-mediate data	1	
immediate to accumulator	0011 010w : immediate data	1	
immediate to memory	1000 00sw : mod 110 r/m : immediate data	3	U/L
Prefix Bytes			
address size	0110 0111	1	
LOCK	1111 0000	1	
operand size	0110 0110	1	
CS segment override	0010 1110	1	
DS segment override	0011 1110	1	
ES segment override	0010 0110	1	
FS segment override	0110 0100	1	
GS segment override	0110 0101	1	
SS segment override	0011 0110	1	
External Interrupt		INT + 14	21
NMI — Non-Maskable Inter-rupt		INT + 6	21
Page Fault		INT + 40	21
Virtual 8086 Mode Excep-tions			
CLI		INT + 9	21
STI		INT + 9	21
INT n		INT + 9	21
PUSHF		INT + 9	
POPF		INT + 9	21
IRET		INT + 9	
IN			

Table F-2. **Cont.**

Instruction	Format	Clocks	Notes
fixed port		INT + 34	21
variable port		INT + 34	21
OUT			
fixed port		INT + 34	21
variable port		INT + 34	21
INS		INT + 34	21
OUTS		INT + 34	21
REP INS		INT + 34	21
REP INS		INT + 34	21
REP OUTS		INT + 34	21

Instruction	Format	Real Mode	Protected Mode CPL IOPL	Protected Mode CPL> OPL	Virtual 8086 Mode	Notes
IN - Input from:						
fixed pod number	1110 010w : pod	7	4	21	19	
variable port	1110 110w	7	4	21	19	
OUT — Output to:						
fixed port number	1110011w :port	12	9	26	24	
variable port	1110 111w	12	9	26	24	
INS — Input from DX Port	0110 110w	9	6	24	22	
OUTS — Output to DX Port	0110 111w	13	10	27	25	1
REP INS — Input String	1111 0011 :0110	11 +3c	8+3c	25+3c	23+3c	2
110w						
REP OUTS — Output String	1111 0011 :0110	13 + 4c	10 + 4c	27 + 4c	25 + 4c	3
111w						

NOTES:

1.   Two clock cache miss penalty in all cases.

2.   c = count in CX or ECX

3.   Cache miss penalty in all modes: Add 2 clocks for every 16 bytes. Entire penalty on second operation.

PENTIUM INSTRUCTION SET IN REAL MODE (SELECTED)

Instructions	Interpretation	Comments
AAA	ASCII adjust AL after addition	This instruction has implied addressing mode; this instruction is used to adjust the content of AL after addition of two ASCII characters.
AAD	ASCII adjust for division	This instruction has implied addressing mode; converts two unpacked BCD digits in AX into equivalent binary numbers in AL; AAD must be used before dividing two unpacked BCD digits by an unpacked BCD byte.
AAM	ASCII adjust after multiplication	This instruction has implied addressing mode; after multiplying two unpacked BCD numbers, adjust the product in AX to become an unpacked BCD result; ZF, SF, and PF are affected.
AAS	ASCII adjust AL after subtraction	This instruction has implied addressing mode used to adjust AL after subtraction of two ASCII characters.
ADC mem, data	mem ← mem + data + CF	Data can be 8-, 16- or 32-bit; mem uses DS as the segment register; all flags are affected.

Instructions	Interpretation	Comments
ADC reg, data	reg ←reg + data + CF	Data can be 8-, 16- or 32-bit; register cannot be segment register; all flags are affected.
ADD mem/reg 1, mem/reg 2	mem/reg 1 ← mem/reg 2 + mem/reg 1	Memory or register can be 8-, 16, or 32-bit; all flags are affected; no segment registers are allowed as source or destination; mem uses DS as segment register; all flags are affected; no memory-to-memory ADD is permitted.
ADD mem, data	mem ← mem + data	Mem uses DS as the segment register; data can be 8-, 16-, or 32-bit; all flags are affected.
ADD reg, data	reg ← reg + data	Data can be 8-, 16, or 32-bit; no segment registers are allowed; all flags are affected.
AND mem/reg 1, mem/reg 2	mem/reg 1 ← mem/reg 1 AND mem/reg 2	This instruction logically ANDs 8-, 16- or 32-bit data in mem/reg 1 with 8- or 16- or 32-bit data in mem/reg 2; all flags are affected; OF and CF are cleared to zero; no segment registers are allowed; no memory-to-memory operation is allowed; mem uses DS as the segment register.
AND mem, data	mem ←mem AND data	Data can be 8-, 16-or 32-bit; mem uses DS as the segment register; all flags are affected with OF and CF always cleared to zero.
AND reg, data	reg ← reg AND data	Data can be 8-, 16-, or 32-bit; reg cannot be segment register; all flags are affected with OF and CF cleared to zero.
BSF reg/mem, reg/imm8		Bit Scan Forward.

Instructions	Interpretation	Comments
BSR reg/mem, reg/imm8		Bit Scan Reverse.
BT reg/mem, reg/imm8		Bit Test.
BTC reg/mem, reg/imm8		Bit Test and Complement.
BTR reg/mem, reg/imm8		Bit Test and Reset.
BTS reg/mem, reg/imm8		Bit Test and Set.
CALL LABEL		Call a subroutine called "LABEL"in the same segment with signed 16-bit displacement (intrasegment CALL).
CALL reg 16	CALL a subroutine in the same segment addressed by the contents of a 16-bit general register	The Pentium decrements SP by 2 and then pushes IP onto the stack, then specified 16-bit register contents (such as BX, SI, and DI) provide the new value for IP; CS is unchanged (intrasegment CALL).
CALL mem 16	CALL a subroutine addressed by the content of a memory location pointed to by Pentium's 16-bit register such as BX, SI, and DI	The Pentium decrements SP by 2 and pushes IP onto the stack; the Pentium then loads the contents of a memory location addressed by the content of a 16-bit register such as BX, SI, and DI into IP; CS is unchanged (intrasegment CALL).
CALL FAR PTR LABEL		CALL a subroutine in another segment. FAR PTR indicates that the subroutine called 'LABEL' is in another segment, and both CS and IP change. (intersegment CALL).

Instructions	Interpretation	Comments
CBW	Convert a byte to a word	Extend the sign bit (bit 7) of AL register into AH.
CDQ	Convert a doubleword to a quadword	Extend the sign bit (bit 31) of EAX register into EDX:EAX.
CLC	$CF \leftarrow 0$	Clear carry to zero.
CLD	$DF \leftarrow 0$	Clear direction flag to zero.
CLI	$IF \leftarrow 0$	Clear interrupt enable flag to zero to disable maskable interrupts.
CMC	$CF \leftarrow NOT\ CF$	One's complement carry.
CMP mem/reg 1, mem/reg 2	mem/reg 1 – mem/reg 2, flags are affected	reg can be 8- or 16- or 32-bit; no memory-to-memory comparison allowed; result of subtraction is not provided; all flags are affected.
CMP mem/reg, data	[mem/reg] – data, flags are affected	Subtracts 8- , 16-, or 32-bit data from mem or reg and affects flags; no result is provided.
CMPSB	FOR BYTE (SI) – (DI), flags are affected $SI \leftarrow SI \pm 1$ $DI \leftarrow DI \pm 1$	8- , 16, or 32-bit data addressed by DI in ES is subtracted from 8- , 16- , or 32-bit data addressed by SI in DS and flags are affected without providing any result; if DF = 0, then SI and DI are incremented by one for byte, two for word, four for doubleword; if DF = 1, then SI and DI aredecremented by one for byte, two for word, four for doubleword; the segment register ES in destination cannot be overridden.

Instructions	Interpretation	Comments
CMPSD	FOR DOUBLE WORD $(SI) - (DI)$, flags are affected $SI \leftarrow SI \pm 4$ $DI \leftarrow DI \pm 4$	
CMPSW	FOR WORD $(SI) - (DI)$, flags are affected $SI \leftarrow SI \pm 2$ $DI \leftarrow DI \pm 2$	
CWDE	Convert a word to 32 bits in EAX	Extend the sign bit of AX (bit 15) into EAX.
DAA	Decimal adjust AL after addition	This instruction uses implied addressing mode; this instruction converts contents of AL into BCD; DAA should be used after addition of two packed BCD bytes.
DAS	Decimal adjust AL after subtraction	This instruction uses implied addressing mode; converts the contents of AL into BCD; DAS should be used after subtraction of two packed BCD bytes.
DEC mem / reg	mem/reg $\leftarrow$ mem/reg $- 1$	used to decrement an 8-, 16-, or 32-bit register (except segment registers) by 1. Can also decrement 8- or 16-, or 32-bit contents of memory by 1; does not affect the carry flag.
DIV mem/reg ((unsigned division)	16/8 bit divide: $\dfrac{AX}{mem8 / reg8}$ AH$\leftarrow$ Remainder AL $\leftarrow$ Quotient 32/16 bit divide: $\dfrac{DX\ AX}{mem16 / reg16}$ DX $\leftarrow$ Remainder, AX$\leftarrow$ Quotient	Mem/reg is 8-bit for 16-bit by 8-bit divide and 16-bit for 32-bit by 16-bit divide; this is an unsigned division; no flags are affected; division by zero automatically generates an internal interrupt.

Instructions	Interpretation	Comments
	(continued)	
	64/32 bit divide: $\dfrac{\text{EDXEAX}}{\text{mem32 / reg32}}$	
	EDX ← Remainder,	
	EAX ← Quotient	
HLT	HALT	Halt
IDIV mem/reg	Same as DIV mem/reg	Signed division.
IMUL mem/reg	Same as MUL mem/reg	Signed multiplication.
IN AL, DX	AL ← PORT (DX)	Input AL with the 8-bit content of a port addressed by DX; this is a one-byte instruction.
IN AX, DX	AX ← PORT (DX)	Input AX with the 16-bit content of a port addressed by DX and DX + 1; this is a one-byte instruction.
IN AL, PORT	AL ← PORT	Input AL with the 8-bit content of a port.
IN AX, PORT	AX ← PORT	Input AX with the 16-bit content of a port.
INC mem/reg	mem ← mem + 1 or reg ← reg + 1	Can be used to increment a byte, word or doubleword in memory or an 8-, 16-, or 32-bit register content by 1; segment registers cannot be incremented by this instruction; does not affect the carry flag.
INT n (n can be zero thru 255)	SP ← SP − 2 ,(SP) ← Flags IF ← 0, TF ← 0 SP ← SP − 2, (SP) ← CS CS ← 4*n + 2 SP ← SP − 2 (SP) ← IP IP ← 4 * n	Software interrupts can be used as supervisor calls; that is, request for service from an operating system; a different interrupt type can be used for each type of service that the operating system could supply for an application or program; software interrupt instructions can also be usedfor checking interrupt service

Instructions	Interpretation	Comments
		(continued) routines written for hardware-initiated interrupts.
INTO	Interrupt on Overflow	Generates an internal interrupt if OF = 1; executes INT 4; can be used after an arithmetic operation to activate a service routine if OF = 1; when INTO is executed and if OF = 1, operations similar to INT n take place.
IRET	Interrupt Return	POPS IP, CS and Flags from stack; IRET is used as return instruction at the end of a service routine for both hardware and software interrupts.
JA/JNBE disp 8	Jump if above/jump if not below or equal	Jump if above/jump if not below or equal with 8-bit signed displacement; that is, the displacement can be from -128_{10} to $+127_{10}$, zero being positive; JA and JNBE are the mnemonic which represent the same instruction; Jump if both CF and ZF are zero.
JAE/JNB/JNC disp 8	Jump if above or equal/jump if not below/jump if no carry	Same as JA/JNBE except that the Jump is taken if CF = 0.
JB/JC/JNAE disp 8	Jump if below/jump if carry/ jump if not above or equal	Same as JA/JNBE except that the jump is taken CF = 1.
JBE/JNA disp 8	Jump if below or equal/jump if not above	Same as JA/JNBE except that the jump is taken if CF = 1 or ZF = 0.
JCXZ disp 8	Jump if CX = 0	Jump if CX = 0; this instruction is useful at the beginning of a l oop to bypass the loop if CX = 0.
JE/JZ disp 8	Jump if equal/jump if zero	Jump if equal or if zero. Same as JA/JNBE except that the jump is taken if ZF = 1.

Instructions	Interpretation	Comments
JG/JNLE disp 8	Jump if greater/jump if not less or equal	Jump if greater than or not less than or equal. Same as JA/JNBE except that the jump is taken if $((SF \oplus OF)$ or $ZF) = 0$.
JGE/JNL disp 8	Jump if greater or equal/ jump if not less	Same as JA/JNBE except that the jump is taken if $(SF \oplus OF) = 0$.
JL/JNGE disp 8	Jump if less/Jump if not greater nor equal	Same as JA/JNBE except that the jump is taken if $(SF \oplus OF) = 1$.
JLE/JNG disp 8	Jump if less or equal/ jump if not greater	Same as JA/JNBE except that the jump is taken if $((SF \oplus OF)$ or $ZF) = 1$.
JMP Label	Unconditional Jump with a signed 8-bit (SHORT) or signed 16-bit (NEAR) displacement in the same segment	The label START can be signed 8-bit (called SHORT jump) or signed 16-bit (called NEAR jump) displacement; the assembler usually determines the displacement value. The assembler adds the signed displacement to IP; CS is unchanged; therefore, this JMP provides a jump in the same segment (intrasegment jump).
JMP regl6	IP ←reg 16; CS is unchanged	Jump to an address specified by the contents of a 16-bit register such as BX, Sl, and DI in the same code segment; in the example JMP BX, register BX is loaded into IP and CS is unchanged (intrasegment jump).
JMP mem 16	IP ← mem; CS is unchanged	Jump to an address specified by the contents of a 16-bit memory location addressed by 16-bit register such as BX, SI, and DI; in the example, JMP [BX] copies the content of a memory location addressed by BX in DS into IP; CS is unchanged (intrasegment jump).

Instructions	Interpretation	Comments
JMP FAR PTR Label		Unconditionally jump to another segment. Both IP and CS change(intersegment Jump).
JNE/JNZ disp 8	Jump if not equal/jump if not zero	Same as JA/JNBE except that the jump is taken if ZF = 0.
JNO disp 8	Jump if not overflow	Same as JA/JNBE except that the jump is taken if OF = 0.
JNP/JPO disp 8	Jump if no parity/jump if parity odd	Same as JA/JNBE except that the jump is taken if PF = 0.
JNS disp 8	Jump if not sign	Same as JA/JNBE except that the jump is taken if SF = 0.
JO disp 8	Jump if overflow	Same as JA/JNBE except that the jump is taken if OF = 1.
JP/JPE disp 8	Jump if parity/jump if parity even	Same as JA/JNBE except that the jump is taken if PF = 1.
JS disp 8	Jump if sign	Same as JA/JNBE except that the jump is taken if SF = 1.
LAHF	[AH] ← Flag low-byte	This instruction has implied addressing mode; it l oads AH with the low byte of the flag register; no flags are affected.
LDS reg, mem	reg ← (mem) DS ← (mem + 2)	Load a 16-bit register (AX, BX, CX, DX, SP, BP, SI, DI) with the content of specified memory and load DS with the content of the location that follows; no flags are affected; DS is used as the segment register for mem.

Instructions	Interpretation	Comments
LEA reg, mem	reg ← offset portion of address	LEA (load effective address) loads the value of the source operand rather than its content to register (such as SI, DI, BX) which are allowed to contain offset for accessing memory; no flags are affected.
LES reg, mem	reg← (mem) ES ← (mem+ 2)	DS is used as the segment register for mem; in the example LES DX, [BX], DX is loaded with 16-bit value from a memory location addressed by 20-bit physical address computed from DS and BX; the 16-bit content of the next memory is loaded into ES; no flags are affected.
LFS reg, mem	reg ← (mem) FS ← (mem+ 2)	DS is used as the segment register for mem; in the example LFS DX, [BX], DX is loaded with 16-bit value from a memory location addressed by 20-bit physical address computed from DS and BX; the 16-bit content of the next memory is loaded into FS; no flags are affected.
LGS reg, mem	reg]← (mem) GS ← (mem+ 2)	DS is used as the segment register for mem; in the example LGS DX, [BX], DX is loaded with 16-bit value from a memory location addressed by 20-bit physical address computed from DS and BX; the 16-bit content of the next memory is loaded into GS; no flags are affected.
LSS reg, mrm	reg ← (mem), SS ← (mem+ 2)	DS is used as the segment register for mem; in the example LSS DX, [BX], DX is loaded with 16-bit value from a memory location addressed by 20-bit physical address computed from DS and BX; the 16-bit content of the next memory is loaded into SS; no flags are affected.

Instructions	Interpretation	Comments
LOCK	LOCK bus during next instruction	Lock is a prefix that causes the Pentium to assert its bus LOCK signal while following instruction is executed; this signal is used in multiprocessing; the LOCK pin of the Pentium can be used to LOCK other processors off the system bus during execution of an instruction; in this way, the Pentium can be assured of uninterrupted access to common system resources such as shared RAM.
LODSB	FOR BYTE AL ← (SI) SI ← SI ± 1	Load 8-bit data into AL or 16-bit data into AX or 32-bit data into EAX from a memory location addressed by SI in segment DS; if DF = 0, then SI is incremented by 1 for byte , 2 for word, or 4 for doubleword after the load; if DF = 1, then SI is decremented by 1 for byte, 2 for word, or 4 for doubleword ; LODS affects no flags.
LODSW	FOR WORD AX ← (SI), SI ← SI ± 2	
LODSD	FOR DWORD EAX ← (SI), SI ← SI ± 4	
LOOP disp 8	Loop if CX not equal to zero	Decrement CX by one, without affecting flags and loop with signed 8-bit displacement (from −128 to +127, zero being positive) if CX is not equal to zero.
LOOPE/I.OOPZ disp 8	Loop while equal/loop while zero	Decrement CX by one without affecting flags and loop with signed 8-bit displacement if CX is equal to zero, and if ZF = 1 which results from execution of the previous instruction.

Instructions	Interpretation	Comments
LOOPNE/ LOOPNZ disp 8	Loop while not equal/loop while not zero	Decrement CX by one without affecting flags and loop with signed 8-bit displacement if CX is not equal to zero and ZF = 0 which results from execution of previous instruction.
MOV mem/reg 2, mem/reg 1	mem/reg 2 ← mem/reg 1	mem uses DS as the segment register; no memory-to-memory operation allowed; that is, MOV mem, mem is not permitted; segment register cannot be specified as source or destination; no flags are affected.
MOV mem, data	mem ← data	mem uses DS as the segment register; 8- or 16-, or 32-bit data specifies whether memory location is 8- or 16-, or 32-bit; no flags are affected.
MOV reg, data	reg ← data	Segment register cannot be specified as reg; data can be 8- 16-, or 32-bit; no flags are affected.
MOV segreg, mem/reg	segreg ← mem/reg	mem uses DS as segment register; used for initializing DS, ES, FS, GS, and SS; no flags are affected.
MOV mem/reg, segreg	mem/reg ← segreg	mem uses DS as segment register; no flags are affected.
MOVSB	FOR BYTE (DI)← (SI]) SI ← SI ± 1	Move 8-bit or 16- or 32-bit data from the memory location addressed by SI in segment DS location addressed by DI in ES; segment DS can be overridden by a prefix but destination segment must be ES and cannot be overridden; if DF = 0, then SI is incremented by one for byte or incremented by two for word, or incremented by four for

Instructions	Interpretation	Comments
		(Continued) doubleword; if DF = 1, then SI is decremented by one for byte or two for word, or four for doubleword.
MOVSW	FOR WORD (DI)← (SI) SI ← SI ± 2	
MOVSD	FOR DOUBLEWORD (DI)← (SI) SI ← SI ± 4	
MUL mem/reg (unsigned multiplication)	FOR 8 × 8 AX ← AL * mem8/reg8 FOR 16 × 16 DX:AX ← AX * mem16/reg16 FOR 32 × 32 EDX:EAX ← EAX * mem32/reg32	mem/reg can be 8- , 16-, or 32-bit; only CF and OF are affected; unsigned multiplication.
NEG mem/reg		mem/reg can be 8- , 16 or 32-bit; performs two's complement subtraction of the specified operand from zero, that is, two's complement of a number is formed; all flags are affected except CF = 0 if (mem/reg) is zero; otherwise CF = 1.
NOP	No Operation	Pentium does nothing
NOT reg	reg ← NOT reg	mem and reg can be 8- or 16-bit; segment registers are not allowed; no flags are affected; ones complement reg.
NOT mem	mem ← NOT mem	mem uses DS as the segment register; no flags are affected; ones complement mem.

Instructions	Interpretation	Comments
OR mem/reg 1, mem/reg 2	mem/reg 1 ← mem/reg 1 OR mem/reg 2	No memory-to-memory operation is allowed; mem or reg1 or reg2 can be 8- , 16 -, or 32-bit; all flags are affected with OF and CF cleared to zero; no segment registers are allowed; mem uses DS as segment register.
OR mem, data	mem ← mem OR data	mem and data can be 8- , 16-, or 32-bit; mem uses DS as segment register; all flags are affected with CF and OF cleared to zero.
OR reg, data	reg ← reg OR data	reg and data can be 8- , 16-, or 32-bit; no segment registers are allowed; all flags are affected with CF and OF cleared to zero.
OUT DX, AL	PORT(DX) ← AL	Output the 8-bit contents of AL into an I/O Port addressed by the 16-bit content of DX.
OUT DX, AX	PORT (DX) ← AX	Output the 16-bit contents of AX into an I/O Port addressed by the 16-bit content of DX.
OUT PORT, AL	PORT ← AL	Output the 8-bit contents of AL into the Port.
OUT PORT, AX	PORT ← AX	Output the 16-bit contents of AX into the Port.
POP d		POP word off stack.
POP mem	mem ← (SP),SP ←SP + 2	mem uses DS as the segment register; no flags are affected.
POP reg	reg← (SP) ,SP ← SP+ 2	Cannot be used to POP segment registers or flag register.
POP segreg	segreg ← (SP) SP ←SP + 2	POP CS is illegal.

Instructions	Interpretation	Comments
POPF	Flags ← (SP) SP ← SP + 2	This instruction pops the top two stack bytes in the16-bit flag register.
POPA		POP all 16-bit registers.
POPAD		POP all 32-bit registers.
POPF		POP lower 16 bits of Flag register off the stack.
POPFD		POP 32 bits of EFLAG register off the stack.
PUSH mem/reg/ segreg		PUSH word into stack.
PUSH mem	SP ← SP − 2 (SP) ← mem	mem uses DS as segment register; no flags are affected; pushes 16-bit memory contents.
PUSH reg	SP ← SP − 2 (SP) ← reg	reg must be a 16-bit register; cannot be used to PUSH segment register or Flag register.
PUSH segreg	SP ← SP − 2 (SP) ←segreg	PUSH CS is illegal.
PUSHF	SP ← SP − 2 (SP) ←Flags	This instruction pushes the 16-bit Flag register onto the stack.
PUSHFD		PUSH 32 bits of EFLAG register.
PUSHW data16		PUSH immediate 16-bit data.
PUSHD		PUSH immediate 32-bit data.

Instructions	**Interpretation**	**Comments**
RCL mem/reg, CL or imm8	ROTATE through carry left byte or word or doubleword in mem/reg by shift count specified by low five bits of CL or imm8.	FOR BYTE 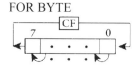 FOR WORD 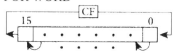 For doubleword, rotate operation is performed on 32-bit mem or reg.
RCR mem/reg, CL or imm8	ROTATE through carry right byte or word or doubleword in mem/reg by shift count specified by low five bits of CL or imm8.	FOR BYTE  FOR WORD 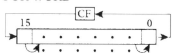 For doubleword, rotate operation is performed on 32-bit mem or reg.
RET	POPS IP for intrasegment CALLS POPS IP and CS for intersegment CALLS	The assembler generates an intrasegment return if the programmer has defined the subroutine as NEAR; for intrasegment return, the following operations take place: IP ← (SP), SP ← SP + 2; on the other hand, the assembler generates an intersegment return if the subroutine has been defined as FAR; in this case, the following operations take place: [IP] ← (SP), SP ← SP + 2, CS ← (SP), SP ← SP + 2; an optional 16-bit displacement 'START' can be specified with the intersegment

Instructions	Interpretation	Comments

(Continued)
return such as RET START; in
this case, the 16-bit displacement
is added to the SP value; this
feature may be used to discard
parameter pushed onto the stack
before the execution of the CALL
instruction.

ROL mem/reg,
CL or imm8

ROTATE through carry left
byte or word or doubleword
in mem/reg by shift count
specified by low five bits of
CL or imm8.

FOR BYTE
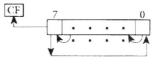

FOR WORD

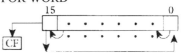

For doubleword, rotate operation
is performed on 32-bit mem or
reg.

ROR mem/reg,
CL or imm8

ROTATE through carry right
byte or word or doubleword
in mem/reg by shift count
specified by low five bits of
CL or imm8.

FOR BYTE
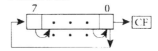

FOR WORD

For doubleword, rotate operation
is performed on 32-bit mem or
reg.

SAHF

Flags ← AH

This instruction stores the
contents of the AH register in
the l ow-byte of the flag register;
OF, DF, IF, and TF flags are not
affected.

Instructions	**Interpretation**	**Comments**
SAL mem/reg, CL or imm8	SHIFT arithmetic left byte or word or doubleword in mem/reg by the shift count specified by low 5 bits of CL or imm8.	FOR BYTE FOR WORD For doubleword, SAL operation is performed on 32-bit mem or reg.
SAR mem/reg, CL or imm8	SHIFT arithmetic right byte or word or doubleword in mem/reg by the shift count specified by low 5 bits of CL or imm8.	FOR BYTE FOR WORD For doubleword, SAR operation is performed on 32-bit mem or reg.
SBB mem/reg 1, mem/reg 2	mem/reg 1 ← mem/reg 1 - [mem/reg 2 – CF	Same as SUB mem/reg 1, mem/reg 2 except this is a subtraction with borrow.
SBB mem, data	mem ← mem - data - CF	Same as SUB mem, data except this is a subtraction with borrow.
SBB reg, data	[reg] ←[reg] – data – CF	Same as SUB reg, data except this is a subtraction with borrow.
SCASB	FOR BYTE, AL – (DI), flags are affected,DI ← DI ± 1	8- or 16- or 32-bit data addressed by DI in ES is subtracted from 8- , 16- or 32-bit data in AL or AX or EAX. Flags are affected without affecting AL or AX or EAX or string data; ES cannot be overridden; if DF = 0, then DI is incremented by one for byte, two for word, or four for doubleword; if DF = 1, then DI is decremented

Instructions	Interpretation	Comments
		(Continued) by one for byte , two for word, or four for doubleword.
SCASW	FOR WORD,AX - (DI), flags are affected,DI ← DI ± 2	
SCASD	FOR DWORD EAX - (DI), flags are affected, DI ← DI ± 4	
SETcc mem/reg		If condition code cc is true , then load operand byte.
SHL mem/reg, CL or imm8	SHIFT logical left byte or word or doubleword in mem/reg by the shift count in CL or imm8.	Same as SAL mem/reg, CL except overflow is cleared to zero.
SHLD reg/mem, reg, imm8 or CL		Double Precision shift left.
SHRD reg/mem, reg, imm8 or CL		Double Precision shift right.
SHR mem/reg, CL or imm8	SHIFT logical right byte or word or doubleword in mem/reg by the shift count specified by low 5 bits of CL or imm8.	FOR BYTE FOR WORD For doubleword, SHR operation is performed on 32-bit mem or reg.
STC	CF ← 1	Set carry to one.
STD	DF ← 1	Set direction flag to one.
STI	IF ← 1	Set interrupt enable flag to one to enable maskable interrupts.

Instructions	Interpretation	Comments
STOSB	FOR BYTE (DI) ← AL DI ← DI ± 1	Store 8-bit data from AL , 16-bit data from AX, or 32-bit data from EAX into a memory location addressed by DI in segment ES; segment register ES cannot be overridden; if DF = 0, then DI is incremented by one for byte, two for word or four for doubleword after the store; if DF = 1, then DI is decremented by one for byte , two for word, or four for doubleword after the store.
STOSW	FOR WORD (DI) ← AX,DI ← DI ± 2	
STOSD	FOR DWORD (DI) ← EAX, DI ← DI ± 4	
SUB mem/reg 1, mem/reg 2	mem/reg 1 ←mem/reg 1 - mem/reg 2]	No memory-to-memory SUB permitted; all flags are affected; mem uses DS as the segment register.
SUB mem, data	mem ← mem – data	Data can be 8- , 16-, or 32-bit; mem uses DS as the segment register; all flags are affected.
SUB reg, data	reg ← reg – data	Data can be 8-, 16,or 32-bit; all flags are affected.
TEST mem/reg 1, mem/reg 2	mem/reg 1- mem/reg 2, no result; flags are affected	No memory-to-memory TEST is allowed; no result is provided; all flags are affected with CF and OF cleared to zero; mem, reg 1 (Continued) or reg 2 can be 8-, 16-, or 32-bit; no segment registers are allowed; mem uses DS as the segment register.

Instructions	Interpretation	Comments
TEST mem, data	mem - data, no result; flags are affected	Mem and data can be 8-, 16-, or 32-bit; no result is provided;flagsareaffected with CF and OF cleared to zero; mem uses DS as the segment register.
TEST reg, data	reg AND data; no result; flags are affected	reg and data can be 8-, 16-, or 32-bit; no result is provided; all flags are affected with CF and OF cleared to zero; reg cannot be segment register.
WAIT	Pentium enters wait state	Causes CPU to enter wait state if the Pentium TEST pin is high; while in wait state, the Pentium continues to check TEST pin for low; if TEST pin goes back to zero, the Pentium executes the next instruction; this feature can be used to synchronize the operation of the Pentium to an event in external hardware.
XADD mem/ reg,mem/reg	dest ← dest + source, source ← original dest	Exchange and Add.
XCHG mem/reg, mem/reg	reg ↔ reg, reg ↔ mem, mem ↔ reg	reg and mem can be both 8-, 16-, or 32-bit; mem uses DS as the segment register; reg cannot be segment register; no flags are affected; no mem to mem.
XCHG reg,reg	reg ↔ reg	reg can be 8-, 16-, or 32-bit; reg cannot be segment register; no flags are affected.
XLAT	AL ←(AL + BX)	This instruction is useful for translating characters from one code such as ASCII to another such as EBCDIC; this is a no-operand instruction and is called an instruction with implied addressing mode; the instruction

Instructions	Interpretation	Comments
		(Continued) loads AL with the contents of a 20-bit physical address computed from DS, BX, and AL; this instruction can be used to read the elements in a table where BX can be loaded with a 16-bit value to point to the starting address (offset from DS) and AL can be loaded with the element number (0 being the first element number); no flags are affected; the XLAT instruction is equivalent to MOV AL, [AL] [BX].
XOR mem/reg 1, mem/reg 2	mem/reg 1 ← mem/reg 1 ⊕ mem/reg 2	No memory-to-memory operation is allowed; mem or reg 1 or reg 2 can be 8- , 16-, or 32-bit; all flags are affected with CF and OF cleared to zero; mem uses DS as the segment register.
XOR mem, data	reg← mem ⊕ data	Data and mem can be 8-, 16-, or 32-bit; mem uses DS as the segment register; mem cannot be segment register; all flags are affected with CF and OF cleared to zero.
XOR reg, data	reg ← reg ⊕ data	Same as XOR mem, data.

APPENDIX

PENTIUM PINOUT AND PIN DESCRIPTIONS

H.1. Pentium™ Processor Pinout

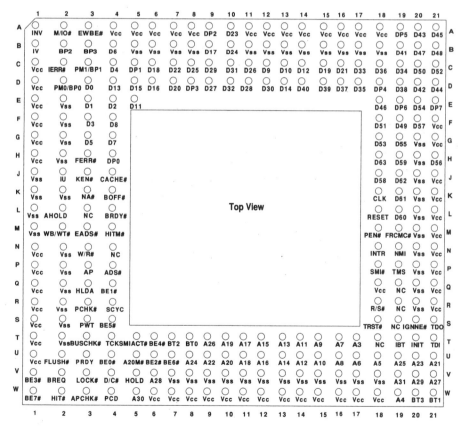

Figure H-1. **Pentium™ Processor Pinout (Top View)**

547

Pinout

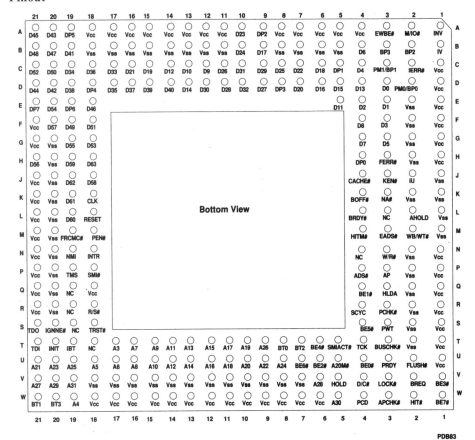

Figure H-2.   **Pentium™ Processor Pinout (Bottom View)**

Table H-1.   **Pentium™ Processor Pin Cross Reference Table by Pin Name**

Signal	Location
A3	T17
A4	W19
A5	U18
A6	U17
A7	T16
A8	U16
A9	T15
A10	U15
A11	T14
Al2	U14
A13	T13
A14	U13
A15	T12

Signal	Location
A20M#	U05
ADS#	P04
AHOLD	L02
AP	P03
APCHK#	W03
BE0#	U04
BE1#	004
BE2#	U06
BE3#	V01
BE4#	T06
BE5#	S04
BE6#	U07
BE7#	W01

Table H-1. **Cont.**

Signal	Location
A16	U12
A17	T11
A18	U11
A19	T10
A20	U10
A21	U21
A22	U09
A23	U20
A24	U08
A25	U19
A26	T09
A27	V21
A28	V06
A29	V20
A30	W05
A31	V19
D4	C04
D5	G03
D6	B04
D7	G04
D8	F04
D9	C12
D10	C13
D11	E05
D12	C14
D13	D04
D14	D13
D15	D05
D16	D06
D17	B09
D18	C06
D19	C15
D20	D07
D21	C16

Signal	Location
BOFF#	K04
BP2	B02
BP3	B03
BRDY#	L04
BREQ	V02
BT0	T08
BT1	W21
BT2	T07
BT3	W20
BUSCHK#	T03
CACHE#	J04
CLK	K18
D0	D03
D1	E03
D2	E04
D3	F03
D33	C17
D34	C19
D35	D17
D36	C18
D37	D16
D38	D19
D39	D15
D40	D14
D41	B19
D42	D20
D43	A20
D44	D21
D45	A21
D46	E18
D47	B20
D48	B21
D49	F19
D50	C20

Table H-1.   Cont.

Signal	Location
D22	C07
D23	A10
D24	B10
D25	C08
D26	C11
D27	D09
D28	D11
D29	C09
D30	D12
D31	C10
D32	D10
D62	J19
D63	H18
D/C#	V04
DP0	H04
DP1	C05
DP2	DP3
DP3	D08
DP4	D18
DP5	A19
DP6	E19
DP7	E21
EADS#	M03
EWBE#	A03
FERR#	H03
FLUSH#	U02
FRCMC#	M19
HIT#	W02
H ITM#	M04
HLDA	003
HOLD	V05
IBT	T19
IERR#	C02

Signal	Location
D51	F18
D52	C21
D53	G18
D54	E20
D55	G19
D56	H21
D57	F20
D58	J18
D59	H19
D60	L19
D61	K19
IV	B01
KEN#	J03
LOCK#	V03
M/IO#	A02
NA#	K03
NMI	N19
PCD	W04
PCHK#	R03
PEN#	M18
PM0/BP0	D02
PM1/BP1	C03
PRDY	U03
PWT	S03
RESET	L18
R/S#	R18
SCYC	R04
SMI#	P18
SMIACT#	T05
TCK	T04
TDI	T21
TDO	S21
TMS	P19

Table H-1. **Cont.**

Signal	Location
IGNNE#	S20
INIT	T20
INTR	N18
INV	A01
IU	J02

Signal	Location
TRST#	S18
WB/WT#	M02
W/R#	N03
NC	L03, N04, Q19, R19, S19, T18

Signal	Location
VCC	A04, A05, F21, G01, R21, S01, W17, W18 A06, A07, A08, Al 1 , Al2, A13, A14, A15, A16, A17, A18, 001, D01, E01, G21, H01, J21, K21, L21, M21, N01, N21, P01, P21, 001, 018, 021, R01, T01,U01, W06, W07, W08, W09, W10, W11, W12, W13, W14, W15, W16,W17,W18
VSS	B05, B06, B07, B08, B11, B12, B13, B14, B15, B16, B17, B18, E02,F02, G02, G20, H02,H20, J01, J20, K01, K02, K20, L01, L20, M01, M20, N02, N20, P02, P20, Q02, Q20, R02, R20, S02, T02, V07, V08, V09, V10, V11, V12, V13, V14, V15, V16, V17, V18

H.2. Design Notes

For reliable operation, always connect unused inputs to an appropriate signal level. Unused active low inputs should be connected to VCC. Unused active HIGH inputs should be connected to GND.

No Connect (NC) pins must remain unconnected. Connection of NC pins may result in component failure or incompatibility with processor steppings.

Note: The No Connect pin located at L03 (BRDYC#) along with BUSCHK# are sampled by the Pentium processor at RESET to configure the I/O buffers of the processor for use with the 82496 Cache Controller/82491 Cache SRAM secondary cache as a chip set (refer to the 82496 Cache Controller/82491 Cache SRAM Data Book for Use with the PentiumTM Processor for further information).

H.3. Quick Pin Reference

This section gives a brief functional description of each of the pins. For a detailed description, see the Hardware Interface chapter in this manual. **Note that all input pins must meet their AC/DC specifications to guarantee proper functional behavior.** In this section, the pins are arranged in alphabetical order. The functional grouping of each pin is listed at the end of this chapter.

The # symbol at the end of a signal name indicates that the active, or asserted state occurs when the signal is at a low voltage. When a # symbol is not present after the signal name, the signal is active, or asserted at the high voltage level.

Table H-2.   Quick Pin Reference

Symbol	Type*	Name and Function
A20M#	I	When the address bit 20 mask pin is asserted, the PentiumTM Processor emulates the address wraparound at one Mbyte which occurs on the 8086. When A20M# is asserted, the Pentium processor masks physical address bit 20 (A20) before performing a lookup to the internal caches or driving a memory cycle on the bus. The effect of A20M# is undefined in protected mode. A20M# must be asserted only when the processor is in real mode.
A31-A3	I/O	As outputs, the address lines of the processor along with the byte enables define the physical area of memory or I/O accessed. The external system drives the inquire address to the processor on A31-A5.
ADS#	0	The address status indicates that a new valid bus cycle is currently being driven by the Pentium processor.
AHOLD	I	In response to the assertion of address hold, the Pentium processor will stop driving the address lines (A31-A3), and AP in the next clock. The rest of the bus will remain active so data can be returned or driven for previously issued bus cycles.
AP	I/O	Address parity is driven by the Pentium processor with even parity information on all Pentium processor generated cycles in the same clock that the address is driven. Even parity must be driven back to the Pentium processor during inquire cycles on this pin in the same clock as EADS# to ensure that the correct parity check status is indicated by the Pentium processor.
APCHK#	0	The address parity check status pin is asserted two clocks after EADS# is sampled active if the Pentium processor has detected a parity error on the address bus during inquire cycles. APCHK# will remain active for one clock each time a parity error is detected.
BE7#-BE0#	0	The byte enable pins are used to determine which bytes must be written to external memory, or which bytes were requested by the CPU for the current cycle. The byte enables are driven in the same clock as the address lines (A31-3).
BOFF#	I	The backoff input is used to abort all outstanding bus cycles that have not yet completed. In response to BOFF#, the Pentium processor will float all pins normally floated during bus hold in the next clock. The processor remains in bus hold until BOFF# is negated at which time the Pentium processor restarts the aborted bus cycle(s) in their entirety.

Table H-2.   Cont.

Symbol	Type*	Name and Function
DP7-DP0	I/O	These are the data parity pins for the processor. There is one for each byte of the data bus. They are driven by the Pentium processor with even parity information on writes in the same clock as write data. Even parity information must be driven back to the Pentium processor on these pins in the same clock as the data to ensure that the correct parity check status is indicated by the Pentium processor. DP7 applies to D63-D56, DP0 applies to D7-D0.
EADS#	I	This signal indicates that a valid external address has been driven onto the Pentium processor address pins to be used for an inquire cycle.
EWBE#	I	The external write buffer empty input, when inactive (high), indicates that a write cycle is pending in the external system. When the Pentium processor generates a write, and EWBE# is sampled inactive, the Pentium processor will hold off all subsequent writes to all E or M-state lines in the data cache until all write cycles have completed, as indicated by EWBE# being active.
FERR#	0	The floating point error pin is driven active when an unmasked floating point error occurs. FERR# is similar to the ERROR# pin on the Intel387 math coprocessor. FERR# is included for compatibility with systems using DOS type floating point error reporting.
FLUSH#	I	When asserted, the cache flush input forces the Pentium processor to writeback all modified lines in the data cache and invalidate its internal caches. A Flush Acknowledge special cycle will be generated by the Pentium processor indicating completion of the writeback and invalidation. If FLUSH# is sampled low when RESET transitions from high to low, tristate test mode is entered.
FRCMC#	I	The Functional Redundancy Checking Master/Checker mode input is used to determine whether the Pentium processor is configured in master mode or checker mode. When configured as a master, the Pentium processor drives its output pins as required by the bus protocol. When configured as a checker, the Pentium processor tristates all outputs (except IERR# and TDO) and samples the output pins. The configuration as a master/checker is set after RESET and may not be changed other than by a subsequent RESET.
HIT#	0	The hit indication is driven to reflect the outcome of an inquire cycle. If an inquire cycle hits a valid line in either the Pentium processor data or instruction cache, this pin is asserted two clocks after EADS# is sampled asserted. If the inquire cycle misses Pentium processor cache, this pin is negated two clocks after EADS#. This pin changes its value only as a result of an inquire cycle and retains its value between the cycles.

Table H-2.   Cont.

Symbol	Type*	Name and Function
HITM#	0	The hit to a modified line output is driven to reflect the outcome of an inquire cycle. It is asserted after inquire cycles which resulted in a hit to a modified line in the data cache. It is used to inhibit another bus master from accessing the data until the line is completely written back.
HLDA	0	The bus hold acknowledge pin goes active in response to a hold request driven to the processor on the HOLD pin. It indicates that the Pentium processor has floated most of the output pins and relinquished the bus to another local bus master. When leaving bus hold, HLDA will be driven inactive and the Pentium processor will resume driving the bus. If the Pentium processor has bus cycle pending, it will be driven in the same clock that HLDA is deasserted.
HOLD	I	In response to the bus hold request, the Pentium processor will float most of its output and input/output pins and assert HLDA after completing all outstanding bus cycles. The Pentium processor will maintain its bus in this state until HOLD is deasserted. HOLD is not recognized during LOCK cycles. The Pentium processor will recognize HOLD during reset.
IBT	0	The instruction branch taken pin is driven active (high) for one clock to indicate that a branch was taken. This output is always driven by the Pentium processor.
IERR#	0	The internal error pin is used to indicate two types of errors, internal parity errors and functional redundancy errors. If a parity error occurs on a read from an internal array, the Pentium processor will assert the IERR# pin for one clock and then shutdown. If the Pentium processor is configured as a checker and a mismatch occurs between the value sampled on the pins and the corresponding value computed internally, the Pentium processor will assert IERR# two clocks after the mismatched value is returned.

Table H-2.   Cont.

Symbol	Type*	Name and Function
IGNNE#	I	This is the ignore numeric error input. This pin has no effect when the NE bit in CR0 is set to 1. When the CRONE bit is 0, and the IGNNE# pin is asserted, the Pentium processor will ignore any pending unmasked numeric exception and continue executing floating point instructions for the entire duration that this pin is asserted. When the CRONE bit is 0, IGNNE# is not asserted, a pending unmasked numeric exception exists (SW.ES = 1), and the floating point instruction is one of FINIT, FCLEX, FSTENV, FSAVE, FSTSW, FSTCW, FENI, FDISI, or FSETPM, the Pentium processor will execute the instruction in spite of the pending exception. When the CRONE bit is 0, IGNNE# is not asserted, a pending unmasked numeric exception exists (SW.ES = 1), and the floating point instruction is one other than FINIT, FCLEX, FSTENV, FSAVE, FSTSW, FSTCW, FENI, FDISI, or FSETPM, the Pentium processor will stop execution and wait for an external interrupt.
INIT	I	The Pentium processor initialization input pin forces the Pentium processor to begin execution in a known state. The processor state after INIT is the same as the state after RESET except that the internal caches, write buffers, and floating point registers retain the values they had prior to INIT. INIT may NOT be used in lieu of RESET after power-up. If INIT is sampled high when RESET transitions from high to low the Pentium processor will perform built-in self test prior to the start of program execution.
INTR	I	An active maskable interrupt input indicates that an external interrupt has been generated. If the IF bit in the EFLAGS register is set, the Pentium processor will generate two locked interrupt acknowledge bus cycles and vector to an interrupt handler after the current instruction execution is completed. INTR must remain active until the first interrupt acknowledge cycle is generated to assure that the interrupt is recognized.
INV	I	The invalidation input determines the final cache line state (S or I) in case of an inquire cycle hit. It is sampled together with the address for the inquire cycle in the clock EADS# is sampled active.
IU	0	The u-pipe instruction complete output is driven active (high) for 1 clock to indicate that an instruction in the u-pipeline has completed execution. This pin is always driven by the Pentium processor.
IV	0	The v-pipe instruction complete output is driven active (high) for one clock to indicate that an instruction in the v-pipeline has completed execution. This pin is always driven by the Pentium processor.

Table H-2.   Cont.

Symbol	Type*	Name and Function
KEN#	I	The cache enable pin is used to determine whether the current cycle is cacheable or not and is consequently used to determine cycle length. When the Pentium processor generates a cycle that can be cached (CACHE# asserted) and KEN# is active, the cycle will be transformed into a burst line fill cycle.
LOCK#	0	The bus lock pin indicates that the current bus cycle is locked. The Pentium processor will not allow a bus hold when LOCK# is asserted (but AHOLD and BOFF# are allowed). LOCK# goes active in the first clock of the first locked bus cycle and goes inactive after the BRDY# is returned for the last locked bus cycle. LOCK# is guaranteed to be deasserted for at least one clock between back to back locked cycles.
M/I0#	0	The Memory/Input-Output is one of the primary bus cycle definition pins. It is driven valid in the same clock as the ADS# signal is asserted. M/I0# distinguishes between memory and I/O cycles.
NA#	I	An active next address input indicates that the external memory system is ready to accept a new bus cycle although all data transfers for the current cycle have not yet completed. The Pentium processor will drive out a pending cycle two clocks after NA# is asserted. The Pentium processor supports up to 2 outstanding bus cycles.
NMI	I	The non-maskable interrupt request signal indicates that an external non-maskable interrupt has been generated.
PCD	0	The page cache disable pin reflects the state of the PCD bit in CR3, the Page Directory Entry, or the Page Table Entry. The purpose of PCD is to provide an external cacheability indication on a page by page basis.
PCHK#	0	The parity check output indicates the result of a parity check on a data read. It is driven with parity status two clocks after BRDY# is returned. PCHK# remains low one clock for each clock in which a parity error was detected. Parity is checked only for the bytes on which valid data is returned.
PEN#	I	The parity enable input (along with CR4.MCE) determines whether a machine check exception will be taken as a result of a data parity error on a read cycle. If this pin is sampled active in the clock a data parity error is detected, the Pentium processor will latch the address and control signals of the cycle with the parity error in the machine check registers. If in addition the machine check enable bit in CR4 is set to "1", the Pentium processor will vector to the machine check exception before the beginning of the next instruction.

Table H-2. **Cont.**

Symbol	Type*	Name and Function
PM/BP[1:01B P[3:2]	0	For more information on the performance monitoring pins, see Appendix A. The breakpoint pins BP[1:0] are multiplexed with the Performance Monitoring pins PM[1:0]. The PB1 and PB0 bits in the Debug Mode Control Register determine if the pins are configured as breakpoint or performance monitoring pins. The pins come out of reset configured for performance monitoring (for more information see Appendix A).
PRDY	0	The PRDY output pin indicates that the processor has stopped normal execution in response to the R/S# pin going active, or Probe Mode being entered (see Appendix A for more information regarding Probe Mode). This pin is provided for use with the Intel debug port described in the "Debugging" chapter.
PWT	0	The page write through pin reflects the state of the PWT bit in CR3, the Page Directory Entry, or the Page Table Entry. The PWT pin is used to provide an external writeback indication on a page by page basis.
RIS#	I	The R/S# input is an asynchronous, edge sensitive interrupt used to stop the normal execution of the processor and place it into an idle state. A high to low transition on the R/S# pin will interrupt the processor and cause it to stop execution at the next instruction boundary. This pin is provided for use with the Intel debug port described in the "Debugging" chapter.
RESET	I	Reset forces the Pentium processor to begin execution at a known state. All the Pentium processor internal caches will be invalidated upon the RESET. Modified lines in the data cache are not written back. FLUSH#, FRCMC# and INIT are sampled when RESET transitions from high to low to determine if tristate test mode or checker mode will be entered, or if BIST will be run.
SCYC	0	The split cycle output is asserted during misaligned LOCKed transfers to indicate that more than two cycles will be locked together. This signal is defined for locked cycles only. It is undefined for cycles which are not locked.
SMI#	I	The system Management Interrupt causes a system management interrupt request to be latched internally. When the latched SMI# is recognized on an instruction boundary, the processor enters System Management Mode.
SMI-ACT#	0	An active system management interrupt active output indicates that the processor is operating in System Management Mode (SMM).

Table H-2.   Cont.

Symbol	Type*	Name and Function
TCK	I	The testability clock input provides the clocking function for the Pentium processor boundary scan in accordance with the IEEE Boundary Scan interface (Standard 1149.1). It is used to clock state information and data into and out of the Pentium processor during boundary scan.
TDI	I	The test data input is a serial input for the test logic. TAP instructions and data are shifted into the Pentium processor on the TDI pin on the rising edge of TCK when the TAP controller is in an appropriate state.
TDO	0	The test data output is a serial output of the test logic. TAP instructions and data are shifted out of the Pentium processor on the TDO pin on the falling edge of TCK when the TAP controller is in an appropriate state.
TMS	I	The value of the test mode select input signal sampled at the rising edge of TCK controls the sequence of TAP controller state changes.
TRST#	I	When asserted, the test reset input allows the TAP controller to be asynchronously initialized.
W/R#	0	Write/Read is one of the primary bus cycle definition pins. It is driven valid in the same clock as the ADS# signal is asserted. W/R# distinguishes between write and read cycles.
WB/WT#	I	The writeback/writethrough input allows a data cache line to be defined as write back or write through on a line by line basis. As a result, it determines whether a cache line is initially in the S or E state in the data cache.

NOTE: the pins are classified as Input or Output based on their function in Master Mode. See the Functional Redundancy Checking section in the 'Error Detection' Chapter for further information.

H.4.   PIN REFERENCE TABLES

Table H-3.   Output Pins

Name	Active Level	When Floated
ADS#	LOW	Bus Hold, BOFF#
APCHK#	LOW	
BE7#-BE0#	LOW	Bus Hold, BOFF#
BREQ	HIGH	
BT3-BT0	n/a	
CACHE#	LOW	Bus Hold, BOFF#

Table H-3.   **Cont.**

FERR#	LOW	
HIT#	LOW	
HITM#	LOW	
HLDA	HIGH	
I BT	HIGH	
IERR#	LOW	
IU	HIGH	
IV	HIGH	
LOCK#	LOW	Bus Hold, BOFF#
M/IO#, D/C#, W/R#	n/a	Bus Hold, BOFF#
PCHK#	LOW	
BP3-2, PM1/BP1, PM0/BP0	HIGH	
PRDY	HIGH	
PWT, PCD	HIGH	Bus Hold, BOFF#
SCYC	HIGH	Bus Hold, BOFF#
SMIACT#	LOW	
TDO	n/a	All states except Shift-DR and Shift-IR

NOTE: All output and input/output pins are floated during tristate test mode and checker mode (except IERR#).

Table H-4.   **Input Pins**

Name	Active Level	Synchronous/ Asynchronous	Internal resistor	Qualified
A20M#	LOW	Asynchronous		
AHOLD	HIGH	Synchronous		
BOFF#	LOW	Synchronous		
BRDY#	LOW	Synchronous		Bus State T2,T12,T2P
BUSCHK#	LOW	Synchronous	Pullup	BRDY#
CLK	n/a			
EADS#	LOW	Synchronous		
EWBE#	LOW	Synchronous		BRDY#
FLUSH#	LOW	Asynchronous		
FRCMC#	LOW	Asynchronous		
HOLD	HIGH	Synchronous		
IGNNE#	LOW	Asynchronous		
INIT	HIGH	Asynchronous		

Table H-4.   Cont.

INTR	HIGH	Asynchronous		
INV	HIGH	Synchronous		EADS#
KEN#	LOW	Synchronous		First BRDY#/NA#
NA#	LOW	Synchronous		Bus State T2,TD,T2P
NMI	HIGH	Asynchronous		
PEN#	LOW	Synchronous		BRDY#
R/S#	n/a	Asynchronous	Pullup	
RESET	HIGH	Asynchronous		
SMI#	LOW	Asynchronous	Pullup	
TCK	n/a		Pullup	
TDI	n/a	Synchronous/ TCK	Pullup	TCK
TMS	n/a	Synchronous/ TCK	Pullup	TCK
TRST#	LOW	Asynchronous	Pullup	
WB/WT#	n/a	Synchronous		First BRDY#/NA#

Table H-5.   Input/Output Pins

Name	Active Level	When Floated	Qualified (when an input)
A31-A3	n/a	Address hold, Bus Hold, BOFF#	EADS#
AP	n/a	Address hold, Bus Hold, BOFF#	EADS#
D63-D0	n/a	Bus Hold, BOFF#	BRDY#
DP7-DP0	n/a	Bus Hold, BOFF#	BRDY#

NOTE: All output and input/output pins are floated during tristate test mode (except TDO) and checker mode (except IERR# and TDO).

H.5.   Pin Grouping According To Function

Table H-6 organizes the pins with respect to their function.

Table H-6.   Pin Functional Grouping

Function	Pins
Clock	CLK
Initialization	RESET, INIT
Address Bus	A31-A3, BE7# - BE0#

Table H-6.   Cont.

Address Mask	A20M#
Data Bus	D63-D0
Address Parity	AP, APCHK#
Data Parity	DP7-DP0, PCHK#, PEN#
Internal Parity Error	IERR#
System Error	BUSCHK#
Bus Cycle Definition	M/IO#, D/C#, W/R#, CACHE#, SCYC, LOCK#
Bus Control	ADS#, BRDY#, NA#
Page Cacheability	PCD, PWT
Cache Control	KEN#, WB/WT#
Cache Snooping/Consistency	AHOLD, EADS#, HIT#, HITM#, INV
Cache Flush	FLUSH#
Write Ordering	EWBE#
Bus Arbitration	BOFF#, BREQ, HOLD, HLDA
Interrupts	INTR, NMI
Floating Point Error Reporting	FERR#, IGNNE#
System Management Mode	SMI#, SMIACT#
Functional Redundancy Checking	FRCMC# (IERR#)
TAP Port	TCK, TMS, TDI, TDO, TRST#
Breakpoint/Performance Monitoring	PM0/BP0, PM1/BP1, BP3-2
Execution Tracing	BT3-BT0, IU, IV, IBT
Probe Mode	R/S#, PRDY

H.6.   Output Pin Grouping According To When Driven

This section groups the output pins according to when they are driven.

Group 1

The following output pins are driven active at the beginning of a bus cycle with ADS#. A31- A3 and AP are guaranteed to remain valid until AHOLD is asserted or until the earlier of the clock after NA# or the last BRDY#. The remaining pins are guaranteed to remain valid until the earlier of the clock after NA# or the last BRDY#:
A31-A3, AP, BE7#-0#, CACHE#, M/IO#, W/R#, D/C#, SCYC, PWT, PCD.

Group 2

As outputs, the following pins are driven in T2, T12, and T2P. As inputs, these pins are sampled with BRDY#:

D63-0, DP7-0.

Group 3

These are the status output pins. They are always driven:
BREQ, HIT#, HITM#, IU, IV, IBT, BT3-BTO, PMO/BPO, PM1/BP1, BP3, BP2, PRDY,
SMIACT#.

Group 4

These are the glitch free status output pins.
APCHK#, FERR#, HLDA, IERR#, LOCK#, PCHK#.

BIBLIOGRAPHY

Antonakos, James, The Pentium Microprocessor, *Prentice-Hall*, 1997.

Brey, Barry, The Intel Microprocessors , *Prentice-Hall,* 2006.

Burns, J., "Within the 68020," *Electronics and Wireless World*, pp 209-212, February 1985; pp 103-106, March 1985.

Dandamudi, Sivarama, Introduction to Assembly Language Programming, *Springer, Second Edition,* 2005.

Feibus, M. and Slater, M., "Pentium Power," *PC Magazine*, April 27, 1993.

Hall, Douglas, *Microprocessors and Interfacing*, *McGraw-Hill*, 1986.

Intel, *Microprocessors and Peripheral Handbook, Vol.1, Microprocessors*, Intel Corporation, 1988.

Intel, *Microprocessors and Peripheral Handbook, Vol.2, Peripheral*, Intel Corporation, 1988.

Intel, *80386 Programmer's Reference Manual*, Intel Corporation, 1986.

Intel, *80386 Hardware Reference Manual*, Intel Corporation, 1986.

Intel, *80386 Advance Information*, Intel Corporation, 1985.

Intel, *Intel 486 Microprocessor Family Programmer's Reference Manual*, Intel Corporation, 1992.

Intel, *Intel 486 Microprocessor Hardware Reference Manual*, Intel Corporation, 1992.

Intel, *Pentium Processor User's Manual, Volume 1: Pentium Processor Data Book,*1993.

Intel, *Pentium Processor User's Manual, Volume 3: Architecture and Programming Manual,*1993.

Intel, *The 8086 Family User's Family*, Intel Corporation, 1979.

Intel, *Intel Component Data Catalog*, Intel Corporation, 1979.

Intel, *MCS-86 User's Manual*, Intel Corporation, 1982.

Intel, *Memory Components Handbook*, Intel Corporation, 1982.

Intel, "Marketing Communications," *The Semiconductor Memory Book*, John Wiley &   Sons, 1978.

Miller, M., Raskin, R., and Rupley, S., "The Pentium That Stole Christmas," *PC Magazine*, February 27, 1995.

Motorola, *MC68000 User's Manual*, Motorola Corporation, 1979.

Motorola, *16-Bit Microprocessor - MC68000 User's Manual*, 4th ed., Prentice-Hall, 1984.

Motorola, *MC68000 16-Bit Microprocessor User's Manual*, Motorola Corporation, 1982.

Motorola, *MC68000 Supplement Material (Technical Training),* Motorola Corporation, 1982.

Motorola, *Microprocessor Data Material*, Motorola Corporation, 1981.

Motorola, *MC68020 User's Manual*, Motorola Corporation, 1985.

Motorola, "MC68020 Course Notes,"MTTA20 REV 2, July 1987.

Motorola, "MC68020/68030 Audio Course Notes," 1988.

Motorola, *68020 User's Manual*, 2nd ed., MC68020 UM/AD Rev. 1, Prentice-Hall, 1984.

Motorola, *MC68040 User's Manual*, 1989.

Motorola, *Power PC 601, RISC Microprocessor User's Manual*, 1993.

Motorola, *Technical Summary, 32-bit Virtual Memory Microprocessor*, MC68020 BR243/D. Rev. 2, Motorola Corporation, 1987.

Rafiquzzaman, M., *Fundamentals of Digital Logic and Microcomputer Design, Wiley, 5th Edition,* 2005.

Rafiquzzaman, M., *Microprocessors and Microcomputer Development Systems - Designing Microprocessor-Based Systems, Harper and Row,* 1984.

Rafiquzzaman, M., *Microcomputer Theory and Applications with the INTEL SDK-85,* 2nd ed., *John Wiley & Sons,* 1987.

Rafiquzzaman, M., *Microprocessors - Theory and Applications - Intel and Motorola, Prentice-Hall,* 1992.

Rafiquzzaman, M., and Chandra, R., *Modern Computer Architecture, West / PWS,* 1988.

Rafiquzzaman, M., *Microprocessors and Microcomputer-Based System Design,* 1st ed., *CRC Press,* 1990.

Rafiquzzaman, M., *Microprocessors and Microcomputer-Based System Design,* 2nd ed. *CRC Press,* 1995.

Shen, John and Lipasti, Mikko, *Modern Processor Design, McGraw-Hill, 2005.*

Stokes, Jon, *Inside the Machine, Jon Stokes, 2007.*

Zorpette, G., "Microprocessors - The Beauty of 32-Bits," *IEEE Spectrum,* Vol. 22, No.9, pp 65-71, September 1994.

INDEX